Public Relations Today

Managing Competition and Conflict

Glen T. Cameron
School of Journalism
University of Missouri

Dennis L. Wilcox
School of Journalism & Mass Communications
San Jose State University

Bryan H. Reber
Grady College of Journalism & Mass Communication
University of Georgia

Jae-Hwa Shin
School of Mass Communication & Journalism
University of Southerm Mississippi

PEARSON

Boston   New York   San Francisco
Mexico City   Montreal   Toronto   London   Madrid   Munich   Paris
Hong Kong   Singapore   Tokyo   Cape Town   Sydney

Series Editor: *Jeanne Zalesky*

Series Editorial Assistant: *Brian Mickelson*

Marketing Manager: *Susan Czajkowski*

Editorial Production Service: *TexTech International*

Composition Buyer: *Linda Cox*

Manufacturing Buyer: *Megan Cochran*

Electronic Composition: *TexTech International*

Interior Design: *Gina Hagen*

Photo Researcher: *Kate Cebik*

Cover Administrator: *Joel Gendron*

For related titles and support materials, visit our online catalog at www.ablongman.com.

Between the time website information is gathered and then published, it is not unusual for some sites to have closed. Also, the transcription of URLs can result in typographical errors. The publisher would appreciate notification where these errors occur so that they may be corrected in subsequent editions.

ISBN-13: 978-0-205-49210-7
ISBN-10:   0-205-49210-X

Library of Congress Cataloging-in-Publication Data

Public relations today : managing competition and conflict / Glen
T. Cameron . . . [et al.].
     p.   cm.
   Includes bibliographical references and index.
   ISBN-13: 978-0-205-49210-7
   ISBN-10:   0-205-49210-X
     1. Public relations—Management. I. Cameron, Glen T.
HD59.P827 2008
659.2—dc22   2007033848

Printed in the United States of America

10 9 8 7 6 5 4 3 2 1 VHP 11 10 09 08 07

Brief Contents

Contents

Chapter 3   Public Relations: A Historical Perspective   61

Chapter 4   Today's Practice: Departments and Firms   89

Chapter 5 The Public Relations Process 114

Chapter 6 Public Opinion and Persuasion 171

Chapter 7 Ethics and the Law 202

Chapter 8 Reaching the Audience 242

Chapter 9   Tech Tools and Trends   267

Chapter 10   Public Relations Tactics   290

Chapter 11   Global Public Relations   341

Chapter 12   Business, Sports, Tourism, and Entertainment   365

Chapter 13   Nonprofit, Education, and Government   405

Preface

*P*ublic Relations Today: Managing Competition and Conflict is a comprehensive book that successfully blends theory and practice in a clear and easy-to-read format. Its writing style and real-world applications will engage undergraduates and appeal to instructors who want their students to have an in-depth understanding of public relations as a strategic, problem-solving process involving the application of key principles.

However, it is not simply another standard textbook in an already cluttered field. *Public Relations Today: Managing Competition and Conflict* defines public relations as the management of competition and conflict on behalf of one's organization, and when possible, also in the interests of the publics that impact the organization. This assertive approach is reflected throughout the book with vigorous examples that lend excitement to the profession for undergraduates.

Competition and conflict have long been essential news pegs because reporters and editors know that readers are drawn to the tension created by market forces, contention, crisis, and the like. In the same way, examples and boxes throughout the book cover interesting topics that also give students a sense of the increasingly crucial role of public relations in modern life. Above all, we intend for the book to embrace the complexity and variety of public relations as it makes itself felt in our everyday lives.

The definition of public relations used in this text builds upon the ideas of relationship management and two-way symmetrical communication developed over the past several decades. While public relations traditions are incorporated, the book challenges prevailing thought to extend the definition and character of the field as no other text has done. Indeed, readers will find new material in this book that updates and elaborates on recent research in public relations theory and practice, all the while retaining the extensive and clear exposition of the public relations profession that has made two of the book's authors, Wilcox and Cameron, trusted and widely adopted public relations authors.

Public Relations Today: Managing Competition and Conflict offers a truly novel entry to the introductory textbook choices in public relations by focusing on competition and conflict. But at the same time, the textbook draws on the highly successful content and the track record of Wilcox and Cameron's *Public Relations Strategies and Tactics*, Eighth Edition. Definitive and time-tested material that has evolved through eight editions is recast and fully updated to reflect the research and current debate that has surrounded the decade-long development of the contingency theory of public relations.

Essentially, the book brings together one of the deans of textbook writing (Wilcox), an experienced researcher and author (Cameron), and two of the fastest-rising young writers in the public relations academy (Reber and Shin) to provide students and faculty with the latest thinking about the field. All four authors bring extensive and ongoing professional work experience to this task that complements their academic credentials.

Public Relations Today: Managing Competition and Conflict provides a briefer, less expensive, and more specific introduction to public relations than any other text on the market. This new book's approach will appeal to adopters who are concerned about cost and readability of existing texts. It will also resonate with those who know from their experience in the practice of public relations that the field requires a level of conviction and advocacy that is often glossed over by existing texts.

Public Relations Today: Managing Competition and Conflict provides a clear overview and exposition of the contingency theory of conflict management and also reflects that work through coverage of all aspects of public relations. The book puts a face on an approach to public relations that emphasizes how practitioners deal with conflict and competition in the marketplace of public opinion and what winning strategies need to be developed for success on behalf of clients and employers.

Strengths of the Book

In addition to offering a vigorous, dynamic, and assertive approach to public relations practice, this new book also:

- Melds existing theories and definitions with new conflict management approach.

- Emphasizes importance of public relations to modern organizations.

- Offers new boxes and cases that bring public relations to life as an increasingly influential function in all aspects of 21st-century communication environments.

- Focuses on ethical questions and global practice in boxes in every chapter.

- Provides a summary of key points at the end of every chapter, including a classroom case activity.

- Provides a less expensive, highly readable text while also bringing the latest research insights of the field to bear on actual practice of public relations.

- Brings the thorough and authoritative voice of Wilcox and Cameron's other texts to this conflict management perspective.

Up-to-Date Coverage

This new textbook provides cases and discussion about lively topics showing how public relations earns its important management role today, covering such issues and events as:

- Current entry-level salaries in the field and those of more experienced professionals by practice area and geographical regions.

- Latest research about feminization of the field and the trend line for the future.

- The challenges facing the Dixie Chicks for speaking their minds—repeatedly.

- Wal-Mart, one of the world's largest corporations, and its efforts to become a better corporate citizen.

- The Bush administration and Hurricane Katrina.

- Using meet-ups and flash mobs as a communications strategy.

- The campaign by the People for Ethical Treatment of Animals (PETA) to change the policies of such corporations as KFC and Safeway.

- Duke University's response to charges of rape lodged against members of the lacrosse team.

- McDonald's response to the critical film *Super Size Me*.

- The controversy over the film *The DaVinci Code* and the organization of various protests.

- Product placements and sponsorships on the popular television show *American Idol.*

- The rapid development of blogs, podcasts, and Wikis in public relations practice.

- The Pentagon's public relations efforts to deal with the Abu Ghraib prison scandal in Iraq and other issues.

- American "public diplomacy" efforts around the globe to gain support for U.S. policies in areas of tension.

- The development of public relations campaigns to serve major audiences such as Hispanics, seniors, and the gay community.

- The expansion of Starbucks worldwide and the conflict with cultural norms in China.

Organization of the Book

The book has 13 chapters and is organized in such a way that the essential principles and concepts of public relations are covered in the first eight chapters. Students learn about public relations as a field and possible career opportunities in the first chapter, but this is followed by a second chapter that thoroughly explains the concepts of competition and conflict as essential aspects of today's public relations practice. This chapter also introduces students to the concepts of crisis communication and management.

Succeeding chapters give students a historical perspective regarding the development of public relations practice and principles, a description of departments and firms, and the public relations process of research, planning, communication, and evaluation.

There also are comprehensive chapters on public opinion and persuasion, ethics and public relations law, reaching different audiences and publics, new technologies and tools used in public relations, and the full explanation of such tactics as news release writing, production of broadcast materials, and even speechwriting and presentations.

The book ends with applications of practice. Global public relations is covered, as well as such specialized fields as business, sports, entertainment, tourism, nonprofits, education, and government.

Students will find the chapters highly informative and will particularly enjoy the numerous examples and case studies from recent headlines. The authors' intention is to make the book as relevant as possible to today's students instead of engaging in esoteric or dated discussions.

Student Learning Aids

Every chapter includes several learning tools to (l) help students better understand and remember the principles of public relations, and (2) give students the practice they need to apply those principles in real-life situations.

- *Chapter Opening Previews.* The preview, in outline format, gives students the major sections and structure of each chapter so they have a learning framework.

- *Boxed Inserts.* Each chapter includes "On the Job" boxes that highlight additional insights, global programs, and ethical considerations. They supplement information in the regular text and also challenge students to formulate their own solutions and opinions.

- *Casebook.* A real-life case study of a public relations program is provided that encapsulates and elaborates on the chapter topic. The objective is to show students how the concepts and principles covered in the text are used in actual practice.

- *End-of-Chapter Summaries.* The major themes and issues are summarized for the student at the end of each chapter.

- *"What Would You Do?" Case Studies.* A public relations situation or dilemma, based on actual cases, is posed and students are asked to apply what they have just read to a real-life situation.

- *Questions for Review and Discussion.* There is a list of questions to help students prepare for tests and to also stimulate classroom discussion.

- *Suggested Readings.* A bibliography gives students additional references for exploring topics brought up in the chapter.

Supplements

Instructors and students have a variety of ancillary tools available to them that help make teaching and learning with *Public Relations Today: Managing Competition and Conflict* easier.

- *Instructor's Resource Manual and Test Bank.* This manual includes chapter outlines, lecture topics, sample syllabi, chapter summaries, suggested projects and discussion questions, case activities, and answers to the questions from the review and discussion boxes in the text.

- *TestGen EQ: Computerized Test Bank.* The user-friendly interface enables instructors to view, edit, and add questions, transfer questions into tests, and print tests in a variety of fonts. Search and sort features allow instructors to locate questions quickly and arrange them in preferred order. Available on CD-ROM or downloadable through our Instructor's Resource Center at www.ablongman.com/irc.

- *PowerPoint Presentation Package,* prepared by the authors. This text-specific package consists of a collection of lecture outlines and graphic images keyed to every chapter in the text. Available on the Web at www.ablongman.com/irc.

- *Public Relations Study Site,* by Holly Pieper, Mansfield University. This Web site features public relations study materials for students, including flashcards and a complete set of practice tests for all major topics. Students will also find web links to valuable sites for further exploration of major topics. The site can be accessed from its own URL or by going through www.ablongman.com/irc.

- ***ResearchNavigator.com Guide: Mass Communication.*** This updated booklet, by Ronald Roat of Southern Indiana University, includes tips, resources, and URLs to help students. The first part introduces students to the basics of the Internet and the World Wide Web. Part Two includes over 30 Net activities that tie into the content of the text. Part Three lists hundreds of web resources for mass communication. The guide also includes information on how to correctly cite research and a guide to building an online glossary. In addition, the guide contains a student access code for the Research Navigator database, offering students free, unlimited access to a collection of more than 25,000 discipline specific articles from top-tier academic publications and peer-reviewed journals, as well as the *New York Times* and popular news publications. The guide is available packaged with new copies of the text.

Acknowledgments

We express or deep appreciation to many of our academic colleagues who reviewed this new textbook and made many suggestions that we have incorporated into the final product. Thank you: Lloyd Chiasson Jr., Nicholls State University; Karen A. Evans, Herkimer County Community College; Keith M. Hearit, Western Michigan University, Lee Honors College; Wanda Mouton, Stephen F. Austin St. University, Dept. of Communication; Kristine Parkes, La Salle University; David Ritchey, University of Akron; Michael Smilowitz, James Madison University, School of Communication Studies; Robin Street, University of Mississippi, Dept. of Journalism; Amy Thurlow, Mount Saint Vincent University.

Glen T. Cameron

Dennis L. Wilcox

Bryan H. Reber

Jae-Hwa Shin

Chapter One

What Is Public Relations?

The Challenge of Public Relations

It is 9 A.M. and Anne-Marie, an account executive in a St. Louis public relations firm, is at her computer working on a news release about a client's new software product. She receives an alert on her e-mail from the firm's student intern who has been collecting news clips pertaining to one of Anne-Marie's other clients so that the firm can take rapid, proactive responses to any emerging issues. She finishes edits on the software product news release as quickly as possible, gives it a once-over, and e-mails it to the client for approval. She also attaches a note that an electronic news service can deliver the release to newspapers across the country later in the day. Two minutes later she is managing the potentially serious issue noted by her intern. After several high-priority e-mails and a phone call to set up a meeting with her client to discuss next steps, she returns to tasks at hand.

Her next activity is a brainstorming session with other staff members to generate creative ideas about a campaign to raise funds for the local AIDS foundation. Anne-Marie finds this client to be one of her most challenging, not because of any possible controversy surrounding AIDS, but simply because the nonprofit sector is so incredibly competitive. She began her career at a nonprofit, working to recruit volunteers and generate donations. There she learned to compete without animosity toward the other good causes vying for the same resources. Nevertheless, she did learn to compete!

When she gets back to her office, she finds a number of telephone messages. A reporter for a trade publication needs background information on a story he is writing; a graphic designer has finished a rough draft of a client's brochure; a catering manager has called about making final arrangements for a reception at an art gallery; and a video producer asks if she can attend the taping of a video news release next week.

Anne-Marie has lunch with a client who wants her counsel on how to announce the closing of a plant in another state, a conflict positioning and crisis communication challenge that also is fraught with ethical quandaries. After lunch, Anne-Marie heads back to the office. She asks her assistant to check arrangements for a news conference next week in New York. She telephones a key editor to pitch a story about a client's new product. Anne-Marie also touches base with other members of her team, who are working on a 12-city media tour by an Olympic champion representing an athletic shoe manufacturer.

At 4 P.M., Anne-Marie checks several computer databases to gather information about the industry of a new client. She also checks online news updates to determine if anything is occurring that involves or affects her firm's clients. At 5 P.M., as she winds down from the day's hectic activities, she reviews news stories from a clipping service about one of her accounts, an association of strawberry producers. She is pleased to find that her feature story, which included recipes and color photos, appeared in 150 dailies.

As this scenario illustrates, the challenge of public relations is multifaceted. A public relations professional must have skills in written and interpersonal communication, research, negotiation, creativity, logistics, facilitation, and problem solving.

Indeed, those who seek a challenging career at the center of what's happening in modern organizations will find public relations to their liking. With plenty of variety in tasks ranging from layout of brochures to analysis of focus groups and polling data, working for clients and companies across the gamut of profit, nonprofit, and government sectors, more and more people like Anne-Marie choose the field of public relations every year. The U.S. Bureau of Labor Statistics estimates that the field already employs well over 200,000 nationwide and predicts a 39.8 percent increase in employment through 2014 for public relations specialists, contrasted with a 0 to 9 percent increase in journalism jobs. CNNMoney.com lists public relations specialist as one of the top 50 professions for job opportunity and potential salary, coming in at 20th on the list. The 10-year job growth projection is a very healthy 22.61 percent.

Global Scope

It's difficult to estimate worldwide figures, but the Global Alliance for Public Relations and Communications Management (www.globalpr.org), with 40 associations representing some 100,000 members, estimates that some 3 million people worldwide practice public relations as their main professional activity. Conservatively, about one-twelfth (360,000) probably belong to some professional organization.

Included in such groups are the Public Relations Institute of Southern Africa (PRISA), the Public Relations Association of Mauritius (PRAM), the Public Relations Institute of Australia (PRIA), the Italian Federation of Public Relations (FERPI), the Canadian Public Relations Society (CPRS), the Public Relations Society of Tanzania (PRAT), the Institute of Public Relations (United Kingdom), the Association of Public Relations Practitioners in Thailand, the Public Relations Association of Romania, and the Agencies Association of Mexico (PRAA).

Public relations is a well-established academic subject that is taught throughout the world. Large numbers of students around the world are studying public relations as a career field. In the United States, almost 200 universities have sequences or majors in public relations, and about 100 European universities offer studies in the subject. Many Asian universities, particularly those in Thailand, Singapore, and Malaysia, also offer major programs. China claims that more than 500,000 students are studying aspects of public relations in colleges and training institutions.

In terms of economics, the public relations field is most extensively developed in the United States, where organizations spend almost $4 billion annually on public relations, according to estimates by Veronis Suhler Stevenson, a specialty banker in the

A Variety of Definitions

People often define public relations by some of its most visible techniques and tactics, such as coverage in a newspaper, a television interview with an organization's spokesperson, or the appearance of a celebrity at a special event. Knowing what professionals do every day can provide an important grounding about public relations, but does not suffice as a definition.

Many people fail to understand that public relations is a process involving numerous subtle and far-reaching aspects beyond media coverage. It includes research and analysis, policy formation, programming, communication, and feedback from numerous publics. Its practitioners operate on two distinct levels—as advisers to their clients or to an organization's top management and as technicians who produce and disseminate messages in multiple media channels.

A number of definitions have been formulated over the years, culminating in our particular focus in Chapter 2 on competition and conflict management. One of the early definitions that gained wide acceptance was formulated by the newsletter *PR News:* "Public relations is the management function which evaluates public attitudes, identifies the policies and procedures of an individual or an organization with the public interest, and plans and executes a program of action to earn public understanding and patience."

More succinct definitions are provided by theorists and textbook authors. In *Effective Public Relations*, Scott M. Cutlip, Allen H. Center, and Glen M. Broom state that "public relations is the management function that identifies, establishes, and maintains mutually beneficial relationships between an organization and the various publics on whom its success or failure depends." This approach represents the current belief that public relations is more than persuasion. Public relations should foster open, two-way communication and mutual understanding with the principle that an organization changes its attitudes and behaviors in the process. Change and accommodation occur for the organization—not just the target audience.

Although current definitions of public relations have long emphasized the building of mutually beneficial relationships between the organization and its various publics, a more assertive definition has emerged over the past decade that forms the basis of this book.

Glen T. Cameron, of the Missouri School of Journalism, defines public relations as the "strategic management of competition and conflict for the benefit of one's own organization—and when possible—also for the mutual benefit of the organization and its stakeholders or publics." This definition places the public relations professional first and foremost as advocate for the employer or client, but acknowledges the importance of mutual benefit when circumstances allow. This definition should not imply that the public relations professional acts only in the self-interest of the employer without due regard to honesty, integrity, and organizational transparency. Indeed, there is an ethical framework that guides the professional in all his or her work. The definition of public relations as strategic conflict management is further explained in Chapter 2.

It isn't necessary, however, to memorize any particular definition of public relations because, as pioneer public relations educator Rex Harlow once found, there are about 500 definitions of varying lengths and quality. It's more important to remember the key words that are used in most definitions that frame today's modern public relations. The key words are:

> *Deliberate.* Public relations activity is intentional. It is designed to influence, gain understanding, provide information, and obtain feedback (reaction from those affected by the activity).

> *Planned.* Public relations activity is organized. Solutions to problems are discovered and logistics are thought out, with the activity taking place over a period of time. It is systematic, requiring research and analysis.

> *Performance.* Effective public relations is based on actual policies and performance. No amount of public relations will generate good will and support if an organization is unresponsive to community concerns. A Pacific Northwest timber company, despite a campaign with the theme "For Us, Every Day Is Earth Day," became known as the villain of Washington State because of its insistence on logging old-growth forests and bulldozing a logging road into a prime elk habitat.

> *Public Interest.* Public relations activity should be mutually beneficial to the organization and the public; it is the alignment of the organization's self-interests with the public's concerns and interests. For example, Exxon/Mobil Corporation sponsors

quality programming on public television because it enhances the company's image; by the same token, the public benefits from the availability of such programming.

> *Two-way Communication.* Public relations is more than one-way dissemination of informational materials. It is equally important to solicit feedback. As Jim Osborne, former vice president of public affairs at Bell Canada, says, "The primary responsibility of the public relations counselor is to provide (management) a thorough grasp of public sentiment."

> *Strategic Management of Competition and Conflict.* Public relations is most effective when it is an integral part of decision making by top management. Public relations involves counseling and problem solving at high levels, not just the dissemination of information after a decision has been made by other leaders. Managing competition and conflict in the interests of the organization, but with integrity and high standards, brings a new vigor and increased relevance to public relations.

To summarize, a person can grasp the essential elements of effective public relations by remembering the following words and phrases: *deliberate . . . planned . . . performance . . . public interest . . . two-way communication . . . strategic management function.* These elements are part of an interactive process that comprise public relations activity. The following section discusses public relations as a process.

Public Relations as a Process

Public relations is a process—that is, a series of actions, changes, or functions that bring about a result. Any number of attempts have been made to capture the public relations process, several of which are offered here to provide a sense of how work in public relations unfolds. One popular way to describe the process, and to remember its components, is to use the RACE acronym, first articulated by John Marston in his book *The Nature of Public Relations.* Essentially, RACE means that public relations activity consists of four key elements:

1. *Research*—What is the problem or situation?
2. *Action* (program planning)—What is going to be done about it?
3. *Communication* (execution)—How will the public be told?
4. *Evaluation*—Was the audience reached and what was the effect?

Chapter 5 discusses this key four-step process.

Another approach is to think of the process as a never-ending cycle in which six components are links in a chain. Figure 1.1 shows the process.

In keeping with the model shown in Figure 1.1, the public relations process also may be conceptualized in several steps:

Level I

A. Public relations personnel use research and analysis to obtain insights into a problem from numerous sources.

B. Public relations personnel analyze these inputs and make recommendations to management as part of policy formation.

C. Based on policy, a public relations program is developed and approved by management.

FIGURE 1.1

In the conceptual-
ization of public
relations as a
cyclical process,
feed-back—or
audience response—
leads to assessment
of the program,
which becomes an
essential element
in the development
of another public
relations project.

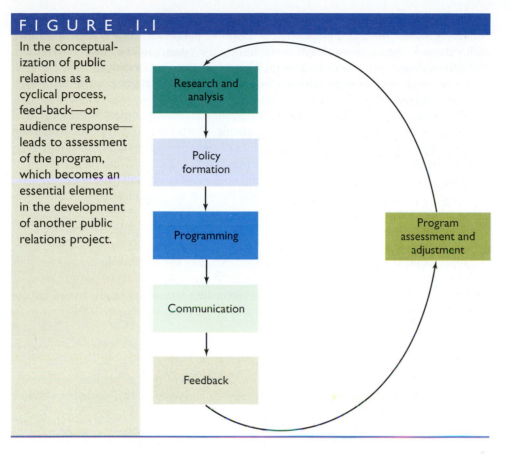

Level 2

D. Public relations personnel execute a program of action called the communication step.

E. Public relations personnel devote significant attention to capturing informal and often formal feedback about the communication process and its impact.

F. Public relations personnel evaluate the effectiveness of the communication program and make adjustments as the process begins over again.

Step A consists of inputs that determine the nature and extent of the public relations problem. These may include feedback from the public, media reporting and editorial comment, analysis of trend data, other forms of research, personal experience, and government pressures and regulations.

In Step B, public relations personnel assess these inputs, establish objectives and an agenda of activity, and convey their recommendations to management. As previously noted, this is the adviser role of public relations.

After management makes its decisions, in Step C public relations personnel fully develop a public relations program with measurable objectives, strategies, and tactics; a time line; budget; and evaluation guidelines. Personnel execute the action program in Step D through such means as news releases, publications, speeches, and community relations efforts. In Step E, the effect of these actions is measured by feedback from the same components that made up Step A. Step F involves postanalysis and adjustment of the public relations program. The cycle is then repeated to solve related aspects of the problem that may require additional decision making and action.

Note that public relations plays two distinct roles in this process, thus serving as a "middle ground" or "linking agent." On Level 1, public relations interacts directly with external sources of information, including the public, media, and government, and relays these inputs to management along with recommendations. On Level 2, public relations becomes the vehicle through which management reaches the public with assorted messages.

Diffusion-of-knowledge theorists call public relations people "linking agents." Sociologists refer to them as "boundary spanners" who act to transfer information between two systems. As the concluding lines of the official statement on public relations by the Public Relations Society of America (PRSA) note: "The public relations practitioner utilizes a variety of professional communication skills and plays an integrative role both within the organization and between the organization and the external environment."

The Components of Public Relations

The basic components of public relations, according to a monograph issued by the PRSA Foundation, include:

> *Counseling*—Providing advice to management concerning policies, relationships, and communications.

> *Research*—Determining the attitudes and behaviors of publics to plan public relations strategies. Such research can be used to generate mutual understanding or influence and persuade publics.

> *Media Relations*—Working with mass media in seeking publicity or responding to their interests in the organization.

> *Publicity*—Disseminating planned messages through selected media to further an organization's interests.

> *Employee/Member Relations*—Responding to concerns, informing, and motivating an organization's employees or members.

> *Community Relations*—Undertaking activities with a community to maintain an environment that benefits both an organization and the community.

> *Public Affairs*—Developing effective involvement in public policy and helping an organization adapt to public expectations. The term is also used by government agencies to describe their public relations activities and by many corporations as an umbrella term to describe multiple public relations activities.

> *Government Affairs*—Relating directly with legislatures and regulatory agencies on behalf of an organization. Lobbying can be part of a government affairs program.

> *Issues Management*—Identifying and addressing issues of public concern that affect an organization.

> *Financial Relations*—Creating and maintaining investor confidence and building good relationships with the financial community. Also known as investor relations or shareholder relations.

> *Industry Relations*—Relating with other firms in the industry of an organization and with trade associations.

— ON THE JOB >> ————————————

Public Relations Society of America
Official Statement on Public Relations

Insights

Public relations helps our complex, pluralistic society to reach decisions and function more effectively by contributing to mutual understanding among groups and institutions. It serves to bring private and public policies into harmony.

Public relations serves a variety of institutions in society such as businesses, trade unions, government agencies, voluntary associations, foundations, hospitals, and educational and religious institutions. To achieve their goals, these institutions must develop effective relationships with many different audiences or publics such as employees, members, customers, local communities, shareholders, and other institutions, and with society at large.

The managements of institutions need to understand the attitudes and values of their publics in order to achieve institutional goals. The goals themselves are shaped by the external environment. The public relations practitioner acts as a counselor to management, and as a mediator, helping to translate private aims into reasonable, publicly acceptable policy and action.

As a management function, public relations encompasses the following:

> Anticipating, analyzing, and interpreting public opinion, attitudes, and issues which might impact, for good or ill, the operations and plans of the organization.
> Counseling management at all levels in the organization with regard to policy decisions, courses of action and communication, and taking into account their public ramifications and the organization's social or citizenship responsibilities.
> Researching, conducting, and evaluating, on a continuing basis, programs of action and communication to achieve informed public understanding necessary to the success of an organization's aims. These may include marketing, financial, fund-raising, employee, community or government relations, and other programs.
> Planning and implementing the organization's efforts to influence or change public policy.

> Setting objectives, planning, budgeting, recruiting and training staff, and developing facilities—in short, managing the resources needed to perform all of the above.
> Examples of the knowledge that may be required in the professional practice of public relations include communication arts, psychology, social psychology, sociology, political science, economics, and the principles of management and ethics. Technical knowledge and skills are required for opinion research, public issues analysis, media relations, direct mail, institutional advertising, publications, film/video productions, special events, speeches, and presentations.

In helping to define and implement policy, the public relations practitioner utilizes a variety of professional communication skills and plays an integrative role both within the organization and between the organization and the external environment.

> *Development/Fund-Raising*—Demonstrating the need for and encouraging the public to support an organization, primarily through financial contributions.

> *Multicultural Relations/Workplace Diversity*—Relating with individuals and groups in various cultural groups.

> *Special Events*—Stimulating an interest in a person, product, or organization by means of a focused "happening" as well as activities designed to interact with publics and listen to them.

> *Marketing Communications*—Employing a combination of activities designed to sell a product, service, or idea, including advertising, collateral materials, publicity, promotion, direct mail, trade shows, and special events.

These components, and how they function, constitute the substance of this textbook.

How Public Relations Differs from Journalism

Writing is a common activity of both public relations professionals and journalists. Both also do their jobs in many of the same ways: They interview people, gather and synthesize large amounts of information, write in a journalistic style, and are trained to produce good copy on deadline. In fact, many reporters eventually change careers and become public relations practitioners.

This has led many people, including journalists, to the incorrect conclusion that little difference exists between public relations and journalism. For many, public relations is simply being a "journalist-in-residence" for a nonmedia organization. However, despite sharing techniques, the two fields are fundamentally different in scope, objectives, audiences, and channels.

Scope

Public relations, as stated earlier, has many components, ranging from counseling to issues management and special events. Journalistic writing and media relations, although important, are only two of these elements. In addition, effective practice of public relations requires strategic thinking, problem-solving capability, and other management skills carried out for the employer.

Objectives

Journalists gather and select information for the primary purpose of providing the public with news and information. Professors David Dozier and William Ehling state that in journalism, "communication activities are an end in themselves." Public relations personnel also gather facts and information for the purpose of informing the public, but their objective is different. Communication activity is simply a means to the end—managing competition and conflict in the best interests of one's employer. In other words, the objective is not only to inform but also to change people's attitudes and behaviors in order to further an organization's goals and objectives.

Whereas journalists are objective observers, public relations personnel are advocates. Harold Burson, chairman of Burson-Marsteller, makes the point:

> To be effective and credible, public relations messages must be based on facts. Nevertheless, we are advocates, and we need to remember that. We are advocates of a particular point of view—our client's or our employer's point of view. And while we recognize that serving the public interest best serves our client's interest, we are not journalists. That's not our job.

Sometimes that advocacy is turned toward one's own management as the public relations professional argues for accommodation of the needs or interests of a key public. Making judgments about what stance to adopt is taken up in Chapter 2.

Audiences

Journalists write primarily for a mass audience—readers, listeners, or viewers of the medium for which they work. By definition, mass audiences are not well defined, and a journalist on a daily newspaper, for example, writes for the general public. A public relations professional, in contrast, carefully segments audiences into various demographic and psychological characteristics. Such research allows messages to be tailored to audience needs, concerns, and interests for maximum effect.

Channels

Most journalists, by nature of their employment, reach audiences through one channel—the medium that publishes or broadcasts their work. Public relations professionals use a variety of channels to reach their target audiences. The channels they employ may combine mass media outlets—newspapers, magazines, radio, and television. Or they may include direct mail, pamphlets, posters, newsletters, trade journals, special events, and messages on the Internet.

Special event planning, promotion, and publicity are important activities in public relations work. Here, national teams march into the stadium during the opening ceremonies of the 2006 Winter Olympic Games in Torino, Italy.

How Public Relations Differs from Advertising

Just as many people mistakenly equate publicity with public relations, there is also some confusion about the distinction between publicity (one area of public relations) and advertising.

Although publicity and advertising both utilize mass media for dissemination of messages, the format and context are different. Publicity—information about an event, an individual or group, or a product—appears as a news item or feature story in the mass media. Material is prepared by public relations personnel and submitted to news departments for consideration. Reporters and editors, in their crucial role as gatekeepers, determine whether the material will be used or simply thrown away.

Advertising, in contrast, involves paid space and broadcast time. For example, organizations and individuals contract with the advertising department of a mass media outlet for a full-page ad or a 60-second commercial. An organization writes the advertisement, decides the type and graphics, and controls where and when the advertisement will run. In other words, advertising is simply renting space in a medium with considerable control over the final message. The lion's share of revenue for all mass media comes from the sale of advertising space.

Other differences between public relations activities and advertising include:

> Advertising works almost exclusively through mass media outlets; public relations relies on a number of communication tools—brochures, slide presentations, special events, speeches, news releases, feature stories, and so forth.

> Advertising is addressed to external audiences—primarily consumers of goods and services; public relations presents its message to specialized external audi-

ences (stockholders, vendors, community leaders, environmental groups, and so on) and internal audiences (employees).

> Advertising is readily identified as a specialized communication function; public relations is broader in scope, dealing with the policies and performance of the entire organization, from the morale of employees to the way telephone operators respond to calls.

> Advertising is often used as a communication tool in public relations, and public relations activity often supports advertising campaigns. Advertising's function is primarily to sell goods and services; the public relations function is to create an environment in which an organization can thrive in complex, competitive environments. The latter calls for dealing with economic, social, and political factors that can affect the organization.

The major disadvantage of advertising, of course, is the cost. Typically, a full-page ad in *Parade* magazine, distributed weekly in almost 350 dailies, costs $421,000. Advertising campaigns on network television can run into the millions of dollars. For example, advertisers paid an average of $2.6 million for a 30-second Super Bowl ad in 2007. Because of this, companies are increasingly using a tool of public relations— product publicity—that is more cost-effective and often more credible because the message appears in a news context. One national study, for example, found that almost 70 percent of consumers place more weight on media coverage than advertising when determining their trust of companies and buying a product or service.

How Public Relations Differs from Marketing

Public relations is distinct from marketing in several ways, although their boundaries often overlap. The functions overlap, for example, because both deal with an organization's relationships and employ similar communication tools to reach the public. Both have the ultimate purpose of ensuring an organization's success and economic survival. Public relations and marketing, however, approach this task from somewhat different perspectives or worldviews. This difference is illustrated by the descriptions of each field that a distinguished panel of educators and practitioners in public relations and marketing developed during a colloquium at San Diego State University. After a day of debate, they formed this definition of public relations:

Public relations is the management process whose goal is to attain and maintain accord and positive behaviors among social groupings on which an organization depends in order to achieve its mission. Its fundamental responsibility is to build and maintain a hospitable environment for an organization.

The group defined market in different terms:

Marketing is the management process whose goal is to attract and satisfy customers (or clients) on a long-term basis in order to achieve an organization's economic objectives. Its fundamental responsibility is to build and maintain markets for an organization's products or services.

In other words, public relations is concerned with building relationships and generating goodwill for the organization; marketing is concerned with customers and selling products and services. Public relations does support sales, but additionally deals with a broad array of publics beyond customers.

James E. Grunig, editor of *Excellence in Public Relations and Communication Management*, put the differences between public relations and marketing in sharp contrast:

> [T]he marketing function should communicate with the markets for an organization's goods and services. Public relations should be concerned with all the publics of the organization. The major purpose of marketing is to make money for the organization by increasing the slope of the demand curve. The major purpose of public relations is to save money for the organization by building relationships with publics that constrain or enhance the ability of the organization to meet its mission.

In this passage, Grunig points out a fundamental difference between marketing and public relations in terms of how the public is described. Marketing and advertising professionals tend to speak of "target markets," "consumers," and "customers." Public relations professionals tend to talk of "publics," "audiences," and "stakeholders," that is, groups that are affected by or can affect an organization. According to Grunig, "Publics can arise within stakeholder categories—such as employees, communities, stockholders, governments, members, students, suppliers, and donors, as well as consumers."

Some public relations theorists point out another fundamental difference between public relations and marketing. In their view, "excellent" public relations avoids persuasion; its ideal purpose is to create mutual understanding and cooperation through two-way dialogue. Marketing, by definition, is persuasive in intent and purpose—to sell products and services. The four models of public relations are discussed in Chapter 3. This text allows a larger role for persuasion than do other theorists, while more progressive marketers strive to build relationships, causing further merging of the fields.

How Public Relations Supports Marketing

Philip Kotler, professor of marketing at Northwestern University and the author of a leading marketing textbook, calls public relations the fifth "P" of marketing strategy, which also includes product, price, place, and promotion. As he wrote in the *Harvard Business Review*, "Public relations takes longer to cultivate, but when energized, it can help pull the company into the market."

When public relations is used to support directly an organization's marketing objectives, it is called marketing communications. This was identified as a component of public relations earlier in the chapter. Another term, coined by Thomas Harris in his book *The Marketer's Guide to Public Relations*, is *marketing public relations*. He says:

> I make a clear distinction between those public relations functions which support marketing, which I call Marketing Public Relations (MPR) and the other public relations activities that define the corporation's relationships with its non-customer publics, which I label Corporate Public Relations (CPR).

Dennis L. Wilcox, in *Public Relations Writing and Media Techniques* (5th ed.), lists eight ways in which public relations activities contribute to fulfilling marketing objectives:

1. Developing new prospects for new markets, such as people who inquire after seeing or hearing a product release in the news media
2. Providing third-party endorsements—via newspapers, magazines, radio, and television—through news releases about a company's products or services, community involvement, inventions, and new plans

3. Generating sales leads, usually through articles in the trade press about new products and services

4. Paving the way for sales calls

5. Stretching an organization's advertising and promotional dollars through timely and supportive releases about it and its products

6. Providing inexpensive sales literature, because articles about a company and its products can be reprinted as informative pieces for prospective customers

7. Establishing a corporation as an authoritative source of information on a given product

8. Helping to sell minor products that don't have large advertising budgets

Thomas Harris summarizes:

In its market-support function, public relations is used to achieve a number of objectives. The most important of these are to raise awareness, to inform and educate, to gain understanding, to build trust, to make friends, to give people reasons to buy and finally to create a climate of consumer acceptance.

Toward an Integrated Perspective: Strategic Communication

Although well-defined differences exist among the fields of advertising, marketing, and public relations, there is an increasing realization that an organization's goals and objectives can be best accomplished through an integrated approach, not just through marketing but through all communication functions. Integration of communication tools is now widely adopted for accomplishing the organization's objectives (see the Insight box on the GRRIT model of integration).

This understanding gave rise in the 1990s to such terms as *integrated marketing communications*, *convergent communications*, and *integrated communications*. Don Schulz, Stanley Tannenbaum, and Robert Lauterborn, authors of *Integrated Marketing Communications*, explain the title of their book as follows:

A concept of marketing communication planning that recognizes the added value of a comprehensive plan that evaluates the strategic roles of a variety of communication disciplines—e.g., General Advertising, Direct Response, Sales Promotion, and Public Relations—and combines these disciplines to provide clarity, consistency, and maximum communication impact.

Several factors have fueled the trend toward integration. First is the downsizing and reengineering of organizations. Many of them have consolidated departments and have also reduced staff dedicated to various communication disciplines. As a result, one department, with fewer employees, is expected to do a greater variety of communication tasks.

Second, organizational marketing and communication departments are making do with tighter budgets. To avoid the high cost of advertising, many organizations look for alternative ways to deliver messages. These may include building buzz by word of mouth, targeting influentials, Web marketing, grassroots marketing, media relations and product publicity, and event sponsorship.

Third is the growing realization that advertising, with its high costs, isn't the silver bullet that it used to be. Part of the problem is the increasing clutter of advertising (one estimate is that the American consumer is exposed to 237 ads a day, or about 86,000 annually) and its general lack of credibility among consumers.

Al and Laura Ries, authors of the popular book (at least among public relations people) *The Fall of Advertising and The Rise of PR*, write, "We're beginning to see research that supports the superiority of PR over advertising to launch a brand. A recent study of 91 new product launches shows highly successful products are more likely to use PR-related activities than less successful ones." They go on to say that "PR creates the brand. Advertising defends the brand."

Fourth, it is now widely recognized that the marketing of products and services can be affected by public and social policy issues. Environmental legislation influences packaging and the content of products, a proposed luxury tax on expensive autos affects sales of those cars, and a company's support of Planned Parenthood or health benefits for same-sex partners may spur a product boycott.

The impact of such factors, not traditionally considered by marketing managers, has led many professionals to believe that organizations should do a better job of integrating public relations and public affairs into their overall marketing considerations. In fact, David Corona, writing in the *Public Relations Journal* some years ago, was the first to advance the idea that marketing's sixth "P" should be public policy.

Jack Bergen, senior vice president of corporate affairs and marketing for Siemens Corporation, agrees. He told *PRWeek* that public relations is the best place for leading strategy in marketing. He continued, "In developing strategy, you have multiple stakeholders. PR people understand the richness of the audience that have an interest in the company; advertising just focuses on customers. Strategy is the development of options to accomplish an objective. PR people can develop these as they have the multiplicity of audiences and channels to use to reach them."

The concept of integration, therefore, reflects the increasing sophistication of organizations to use a variety of strategies and tactics to convey a consistent message in many different forms. The metaphor might be the golfer with a variety of clubs in her bag. She may use one club (public relations) to launch a product, another club (advertising) to reinforce the message, and yet another club (Web marketing) to actually sell the product or service to a well-defined audience. The On-the-Job Insights box on page 16. Looks at the value of public relations to marketing.

The concept of integration is less controversial than its implementation. It makes

ON THE JOB >>

Integration Requires GRRIT

Insights

Strategic communication requires grit and determination, but more accurately GRRIT, to successfully integrate advertising, marketing and public relations. Strategic communication strives to use all available tools in the communication toolbox to solve problems. GRRIT enables professionals to battle for success on behalf of an organization across a broad range of goals—from increased sales or better community relations to brand loyalty or long-term donations for worthwhile causes. The following mnemonic device can help you keep in mind a versatile attitude that rises above traditional distinctions about communication in organizations.

Global/multicultural
Research-based
Relationship-focused
Internet/new media-oriented
Toolbox-driven tactics

Surveys conducted by the Center for Advanced Social Research in the Missouri School of Journalism found that alumni spanning fifty years of experience as well as current students at the University share a great deal of enthusiasm for the GRRIT model. Alumni particularly liked the idea of integrated communication not integrated marketing communication. The former is more comprehensive and affords a larger role for public relations in the mix of strategies and techniques employed.

The Value of Public Relations in the Marketing Mix

Insights

In its annual survey of marketing executives, PRWeek asked them to rate the effectiveness of advertising, direct marketing, and public relations in terms of accomplishing certain marketing objectives. The respondents rated public relations as the "most effective" in the following categories:

> Premarket conditioning
> Strategy development
> Generating word of mouth
> Message development
> Building a brand's reputation
> Building corporate reputation
> Cultivating industry thought leaders
> Overcoming a crisis

Direct marketing was rated most effective in (1) launching a new product/service, (2) promoting a new product/service, (3) acquiring customers, (4) retaining customers, and (5) targeting niche audiences. Advertising was rated most effective in only one category: building awareness.

Source: "Marketing Professionals Reveal the Role PR Plays in the Marketing Mix: Marketing Management Survey 2004." *PRWeek*, May 17, 2004, 1, 13–21.

sense for an organization to coordinate its messages and communication strategies, but considerable discord arises on exactly how to accomplish this.

According to the consulting firm Osgood O'Donnell & Walsh, "The single biggest obstacle is company structure." In an article for the *Strategist*, the firm's principals wrote, "The communications functions—corporate communications, advertising, investor relations, and governmental affairs—are usually in different silos within companies, and interaction between their leaders is, for the most part voluntary (i.e., not required by senior management) and informal."

In other organizations, the marketing department is the dominant voice. Public relations is relegated to a support function in terms of techniques instead of playing a role in overall strategy development. This often means that public relations is responsible only for tactical work, such as creating product publicity, planning event promotions, and arranging media interviews at a trade show. Problems also arise when advertising agencies attempt to do integrated programs. In many cases, 90 percent of the communication budget is spent on advertising and 10 percent or less is spent on public relations. Patrick Sherwood, formerly CEO of D'Arcy Masius Benton & Bowles, once summarized the ad agency approach to integration as follows: "The ad people take off and make a 30-second ad, and then invite other organizations in to see what they can do with the remaining budget."

Fortunately, such stories are becoming rarer as an increasing number of organizations emphasize the team approach to integrated communications. Experts in the various disciplines (advertising, public relations, direct promotion, marketing) now work as a team from the very beginning of a project. The role of public relations in the marketing mix is essentially defined by competition in the marketplace—competition between brands, competition for market share, and even competition for the loyalty of consumers. Chapter 2 looks at the role of public relations in managing conflict between organizations and groups—and even various publics—as a key component of the influence of public relations on the viability of companies and nonprofits alike.

It is often said that public relations is a management process, not an event. Patrick Jackson, active in the top leadership of the PRSA for many years and one of the best-known public relations counselors in the United States, formulated the chart in the Insights box on page 17 to show how public relations can contribute to the success of any organization.

— ON THE JOB >> ——

Nine Ways Public Relations Contributes to the Bottom Line

Insights

PROCESS	PRINCIPAL ACTIVITIES	OUTCOMES
1. Awareness and information	Publicity, promotion, audience targeting, publications	Pave the way for sales, fund-raising, stock offerings, and so on
2. Organizational motivation	Internal relations and communications	Build morale, teamwork, productivity, corporate culture
3. Issue anticipation	Research, liaison with all publics, issue anticipation teams	Early warning of issues, social/political change, constituency unrest
4. Opportunity identification	Interaction with internal and external audiences, "knowing the business"	Discover new markets, products, methods, allies, positive issues
5. Crisis management	Respond to or blanket issues, disasters, attacks; coalition building	Protect position, retain allies and constituents, keep normal operations going despite battles
6. Overcoming executive isolation	Counseling senior managers about what's really happening	Realistic, competitive, enlightened decisions
7. Change agentry	Corporate culture, similar techniques, research	Ease resistance to change, promote smooth transition, reassure affected constituencies
8. Social responsibility	Social accountancy, research, mount public interest projects and tie-ins, volunteerism, philanthropy	Create reputation, enhance economic success through "double bottom line," earn trust
9. Influencing public policy	Constituency relations, coalition building, lobbying, grassroots campaigns	Public consent to activities, products, policies; political barriers removed

Careers in Public Relations

A person entering public relations may develop a career that encompasses numerous areas of this increasingly diverse field. Similarly, the variety of personal traits and skills that lead to success is wide. Although certain abilities, such as writing well, are basic for all areas, experienced public relations practitioners may go on to develop specialized skills in a particular practice area, such as investor relations, governmental affairs, or brand management.

A Changing Focus in Public Relations

As already noted, competition and conflict management are more essential than ever to organizations in a complex world where public acceptance and support are crucial for a company or a nonprofit group to succeed. Now more than ever, this competition takes place on the global stage. Certainly, the daily news coverage of conflicts arising from heated competition or from clashing ideologies and worldviews showcases the importance of public relations skills.

Traditionally, it was widely believed that public relations practitioners should begin their careers as newspaper reporters or wire service correspondents to polish their writing skills and to learn firsthand how the media function. In an earlier era (see Chapter 3), a large percentage of public relations people did indeed have newspaper or broadcast experience. In fact, many of the leading pioneers in public relations were originally journalists.

This, however, is no longer true for several reasons. First, the field of public relations has broadened far beyond the concept of "media relations" and placing publicity in the mass media. Today, much writing in public relations is done for controlled media such as company publications, direct mail campaigns to key audiences, speech writing, brochures, and material posted on an organization's Web site. No media savvy or contacts are necessary. Writing skill and knowledge of the media are still vital, but so is training in management, logistics, event management, coalition building, budgeting, and supervision of personnel. Consequently, a *PRWeek* survey found that less than a third of current practitioners are former journalists.

Journalists still go into public relations, primarily for increased salaries and the opportunity to have a greater variety of job duties, but the ones who make a successful transition have the ability to adapt and are quick learners. Peter Himler, executive vice president of Burson-Marsteller, told *PRWeek* that many journalists fail to make the switch to public relations. He said, "They may not come into the PR field knowing how to create consensus among clients and PR teams and, while they may know how to write, they may lack an understanding of how to use PR tools appropriately—when to use a press release, when to have a press conference, or when to use a video news release, for example."

The growth of public relations as a career field distinctly separate from journalism has spawned any number of public relations courses, sequences, and majors. The Commission on Public Relations Education, which includes public relations educators and representatives from all of the major professional organizations, has set the standard for an ideal curriculum. In its updated 2006 report, the commission recommended seven basic courses: (1) introduction to public relations; (2) case studies in public relations; (3) public relations research, measurement, and evaluation; (4) public relations law and ethics; (5) public relations writing and production; (6) public relations planning and management; and (7) a supervised public relations internship.

Increasingly, many universities are offering joint public relations/advertising programs, in part because of the growing trend in integrated marketing communications, which was discussed earlier in this chapter.

In 2004, the 40th annual survey of programs, "Where Shall I Go to Study Advertising and Public Relations?" (www.whereshalligo.com) by Billy I. Ross of Louisiana State University and Keith F. Johnson of the University of Southern Mississippi, found that there were more than 43,000 advertising and public relations majors in the country at almost 200 colleges and universities. These schools represented 279 programs: 95 in advertising, 136 in public relations, and 48 with joint advertising–public relations programs. About 18,000 undergraduates were majoring in public relations, which was a 7 percent increase from the previous year. At the graduate level, there were approximately 650 master's degree candidates and 70 doctoral students.

Fortunately, the number of public relations jobs continues to increase as the field

ON THE JOB >>

The Wonderful World of Public Relations

Insights

Public relations is an exciting field that offers variety, creativity, and the opportunity to work on any number of projects. Here's a sampling of projects and campaigns that required the expertise of public relations specialists.

Society for the Prevention of Cruelty to Animals (SPCA), Richmond, Virginia

The organization, through a public relations firm, organized the Fur Ball, a gala dinner/auction fund-raiser, to obtain financial support for its new 64,000-square-foot facility. Through effective media publicity and the event itself, almost $400,000 was raised to support the care of homeless animals.

Cold Stone Creamery

The popular ice cream company, through its public relations firm, generated extensive media publicity for the opening of its flagship store in New York's Times Square. On the first day, lines ran out the doors and sales were 10 times that of the average operating store.

Statue of Liberty

After several years of being closed to the public, the Statue of Liberty in New York Harbor was opened to the public. The National Park Service hired a public relations firm to handle media previews and press coverage of the event.

Ford Mustang's 40th Anniversary

The Ford Motor Company planned a series of events across the country to celebrate the 40th anniversary of the classic car.

9/11 Commission

A major public relations firm was retained to generate public and political support for the recommendations of the 9/11 Commission, such as the creation of a Cabinet-level intelligence czar and increasing U.S. defenses against terrorism. The commission report, unlike most government documents, became a best seller.

Gillette Company

The new M3Power razor was launched with the help of a public relations firm that came up with the idea of having a popular Red Sox baseball player, with a real need for a shave, get rid of his beard at a public shaving. A thousand fans attended, and all the local media covered the event, creating local, and even national, coverage of the new product.

State of California

The California Department of Transportation enlisted the services of a public relations firm to conduct a 22-month campaign aimed at reducing litter on the state's highways and freeways. The theme: "Don't Trash California."

expands. The Bureau of Labor Statistics, as already noted on page 3, predicts a 31 to 39 percent increase in employment through 2014. See the Insights box on this page for examples of public relations campaigns.

According to the experts, some specialty areas of public relations will be particularly "job-rich" over the next five years. The industry group most often cited is the pharmaceutical/biotechnology industry. The spotlight also is on financial services, media companies, health care, and security segments of the technology industry.

Writing in *Tactics*, Belinda Hulin notes, "Knowing government protocols and procedures can provide an edge to both biotech and financial PR practitioners as Enron era scrutiny of public companies and their accounting practices has created a demand for such expertise."

Another expanding area of public relations practice is crisis communication counseling, a key role that strengthens the influence of public relations in organizations, but this is an area that requires considerable professional experience. Crisis management, taken in the larger context of strategic management of conflict, is where many practitioners find their greatest satisfaction as professionals who have an impact on their organization and add enormous value to the viability of their department.

The Range of Public Relations Work

Women and men entering public relations find employment in a variety of settings, including public relations firms; corporations; nonprofit organizations; entertainment, sports, and travel; government and politics; education; and international public relations. The largest single employer group is public relations firms, which handle a variety of tasks for any number of clients. Here are the major areas and the percentage of practitioners who work in each area, according to a 2006 survey of practitioners by *PRWeek*:

Public relations firms/Agencies: 42.0 percent

Corporations: 22.6 percent

Nonprofits/Charities: 11.7 percent

Self-employed/Freelance: 6.9 percent

Education: 4.3 percent

Trade associations: 3.1 percent

Government: 3 percent

Personal Qualifications and Attitudes

Any attempt to define a single public relations type of personality is pointless, because the field is so diverse that it needs people of differing personalities. Some practitioners deal with clients and the public in person on a frequent basis; others work primarily at desks, planning, writing, and researching. Many do both. Whether in a creative position, or a resident journalist slot pitching stories to the media, or a job requiring lots of people skills and socializing, or a top executive post shaping policy and direction for your employer in the external communication environment, the focus should be on helping meet the organization's goals and objectives, that is, managing competition and conflict.

Five Essential Abilities

Those who plan careers in public relations should develop knowledge and ability in five basic areas, no matter what type of work they enter. These are (1) writing skill, (2) research ability, (3) planning expertise, (4) problem-solving ability, and (5) business/economics competence.

Writing Skill

The ability to put information and ideas onto paper clearly and concisely is essential. Good grammar and good spelling are vital. Misspelled words and sloppy sentence structure look amateurish. The importance of writing skill is emphasized in a career advice column in *Working Woman:* "I changed careers, choosing public relations as having the best potential, but found it difficult to persuade employers that my writing and interpersonal skills were sufficient for an entry-level job in the profession."

Research Ability

Arguments for causes must be supported by facts rather than generalities. A person must have the persistence and ability to gather information from a variety of sources, as well as be able to conduct original research by designing and implementing opinion polls or audits. Too many public relations programs fail because the organization does not assess audience needs and perceptions. Skillful use of the Internet and computer databases is an important element of research work. Reading newspapers and magazines also is important. Social scientific research skills are taking on greater value as well, accounting for significantly higher salaries for masters-trained professionals who know the theory and research skills underlying campaign strategies.

Planning Expertise

A public relations program involves a number of communication tools and activities that must be carefully developed and coordinated. A person needs to be a good planner to make certain that materials are distributed in a timely manner, events occur without problems, and budgets are not exceeded. Public relations people must be highly organized, detail-oriented, and yet also able to see the big picture.

Problem-Solving Ability

Innovative ideas and fresh approaches are needed to solve complex problems and to make a public relations program unique and memorable. Increased salaries and promotions go to people who show top management how to solve problems creatively.

Business/Economics Competence

The increasing emphasis on public relations as a management function calls for public relations students to learn the "nuts and bolts" of business and economics. According to Joel Curren, senior vice president of CKPR in Chicago, "The greatest need PR people have is understanding how a business and, more importantly, how a public company operates." Elizabeth Allen, vice president of corporate communications for Dell Inc., agrees. She says, "You really have to be a business person first and a communicator second. If you don't understand the business, you can't make a direct link between business goals and what you're doing. Then you're just a fluffy publicist." In sum, students preparing for careers in public relations should obtain a solid grounding by taking elective courses in economics, marketing, and especially management.

It should be noted, of course, that all jobs in public relations don't require all five essential abilities in equal proportion. It often depends on your specific job responsibilities and assignments. See the Insight box What Employers Want on page 22 for more tips from employment specialists.

Systematic research has shown that there is a hierarchy of roles in public relations practice. Professors Glen Broom and David Dozier of San Diego State University were among the first researchers to identify organizational roles ranging from the communication technician to the communication manager.

Practitioners in the technician role, for example, are primarily responsible for producing communication products and implementing decisions made by others. They take photographs, write brochures, prepare news releases, and organize events. They function primarily at the "tactical" level of public relations work; they do not participate in policy decision making, nor are they responsible for outcomes. Many entry-level positions in public relations are at the technician level, but there are also many experienced practitioners whose specialty is tactical duties such as writing and

ON THE JOB >>

What Employers Want: 10 Qualities

Insights

PR Tactics, the monthly publication of the PRSA, asked job-placement experts what set of skills and experience was needed in today's employment market. Here are the top suggestions.

Good Writing
Excellent writing skills are more necessary now than ever before.

Intelligence
Although the descriptions vary from "bright," "clever," and "quick-witted," all placement executives agree that modern public relations isn't a refuge for those with a mediocre mind and only a good personality.

Cultural Literacy
Employers want individuals who are well rounded and well educated about the arts, humanities, and current events. According to *PR Tactics,* "You can't expect management to take your advice if you have no shared frame of reference."

Know a Good Story When You See One
The ability to manage your organization's image—in both large and small ways—starts with the identification and management of good stories that give the organization visibility, build brand recognition, and enhance the organization's reputation.

Media Savvy
Media convergence means that there are now multiple platforms—print media, Webcasts, Internet news sites, radio and television, and so on. Each platform has different deadlines, formats, and needs. Understanding this and being able to work with editors in each area is essential.

Contacts
"Cordial relationships with people in media, government, industry groups, and nonprofits, as well as colleagues in other companies will serve you well. The ability to pick up the phone and get crucial information or make things happen is essential."

Good Business Sense
The best companies weave public relations into their overall business strategy. To work at that level, however, public relations practitioners need to have a firm understanding of how the business operates in general and an employer's industry in particular.

Broad Communications Experience
All midlevel and senior positions require the individual to have familiarity with all aspects of communications, from the in-house newsletter to media relations and investor relations.

Specialized Experience
After getting some general experience, the individual should consider developing a specialty. Health care, finance, and technology are some of the promising areas.

Avoid Career Clichés
If the only reason for getting into the business is because you "like people" and enjoy organizing events, you should think about another field. Employers are looking for broad-based individuals with multiple communication and problem-solving skills.

Source: Hulin, Belinda. "10 Things You Need to Succeed in 2004—and Beyond." *Tactics,* April 2004, 11.

editing newsletters, maintaining information on the company's intranet or Web site, or even working primarily with the media in the placement of publicity.

At the other end of the scale is the communication manager. Practitioners playing this role are perceived by others as the organization's public relations experts. They make communication policy decisions and are held accountable by others and themselves for the success or failure of communication programs. Managers counsel senior management, oversee multiple communication strategies, and supervise a number of employees who are responsible for tactical implementation.

Other research conducted since Broom and Dozier's study indicates that the differences between managers and technicians aren't that clear-cut. In smaller opera-

FIGURE 1.2

This is a typical advertisement for a public relations manager and the qualifications that are sought in a candidate.

tions, a public relations professional may perform daily activities at both the manager and the technician level.

Another way of looking at jobs in public relations is given in the Job Levels Insights box on page 24. In addition, see the Florida Power & Light Company job ad (Figure 1.2) to see the kinds of skills and experience that employers are seeking.

The Value of Internships

Internships are extremely popular in the communications industry, and a student whose résumé includes practical work experience along with a good academic record has an important advantage. The Commission on Public Relations Education believes the internship is so important that it is one of the seven basic courses it recommends for any quality college or university public relations curriculum.

An internship is a win-win situation for both the student and the organization. The student, in most cases, not only receives academic credit but also gets firsthand knowledge of work in the professional world. This gives the student an advantage in getting that all-important first job after graduation. In many cases, recent graduates often are hired by their former internship employers because they have already proven themselves.

Indeed, *PRWeek* reporter Sara Calabro says:

Agencies and corporate communications departments are beginning to see interns as the future of their companies, not merely as gophers that they can pass the grunt work off to. While a few years ago, it was typical for an intern to work for nothing, it is almost unheard of for an internship to be unpaid these days. Examples of the essential work now entrusted to interns include tasks such as media monitoring, writing press releases, financial estimating, and compiling status reports. In many cases, interns are being included in all team and client meetings, as well as brainstorming sessions.

Many major public relations firms have formal internship programs. At Edelman Worldwide, for example, students enroll in "Edel-U," an internal training program that exposes them to all aspects of agency work. The summer internship program at Weber Shandwick in Boston is called "Weber University." Calabro cites Jane Dolan, a senior account executive, who says that upper management is always incredibly impressed with the work that interns do for their final projects. "It is amazing to see them go from zero to 100 in a matter of months," says Dolan.

Hill & Knowlton also has an extensive internship training program in its New York office, taking about 40 interns a year from an applicant pool of about 600 to 700 students. In its view, the internship program is "the cheapest and most effective recruiting tool available." Ketchum also places great emphasis on finding outstanding interns and making sure they are actively involved in account work rather than spending most of their time running the photocopier or stuffing media kits.

It's not always possible, of course, for a student to do an internship in Chicago or New York. However, many opportunities are available at local public relations firms, businesses, and nonprofit agencies. It is important, however, that the organization have at least one experienced public relations professional who can mentor a student and ensure that he or she gets an opportunity to do a variety of tasks to maximize the learning experience.

Although national and international firms routinely pay interns, this is often not the case at the local level. Many smaller companies claim that they cannot afford to pay an intern or that the opportunity to gain training and experience should be more than adequate compensation. Dave DeVries, a senior PR manager for the PCS Division of Sprint, disagrees. He wrote in PRSA's *Tactics*, "Unpaid internships severely limit the field of potential candidates" because, as he points out, the best and brightest students will always gravitate to employers who pay. Former Fortune 500 executive Tom Hagley also argued in *Tactics* that paying interns enables the students to focus effort and maintain high performance standards, resulting in an excellent return on any salary investment by the company.

Indeed, there seems to be a strong correlation between paid internships and starting salaries in the field. Most public relations firms and departments provide some level of paid internships, and entry-level salaries are comparatively high. On the other hand, television stations are notorious for not paying interns, and entry-level salaries ($22,000) are the lowest in the communications field. Salaries are discussed in the next section.

In sum, students should make a concentrated effort to negotiate paid internships. In general, these internships provide more meaningful experience and the employers have higher expectations.

Salaries in Public Relations

Public relations work pays relatively well compared to other communication professions. Many practitioners say they like the income and opportunities for steady advancement, and they also enjoy the variety and fast pace that the field provides.

Entry-Level Salaries

Several surveys have attempted to pinpoint the national average salary for recent graduates in their first full-time job in the public relations field. Probably the most definitive survey is the one conducted by Lee Becker and his associates at the University of Georgia. They work with journalism and mass communications programs throughout the nation to compile a list of recent graduates who are then surveyed (www.grady.uga .edu/annualsurveys/).

The latest data available, published in 2005 based on previous year data, show that the median annual salary for recent graduates working in public relations was $28,500. This is higher than the median national average for all communication fields, which is $26,000. The median yearly salaries reported by recent graduates for other communication fields are as follows:

Daily newspapers	$25,000
Weeklies	$24,000
Radio	$24,000
Television	$22,000
Cable television	$28,000
Advertising	$27,000
Consumer magazines	$25,000
Newsletters/Trades	$27,000
World Wide Web	$32,000

Another survey, conducted by *PRWeek*, places a more optimistic figure on starting salaries in public relations. Its 2006 survey of salaries, for example, found that the median salary for entry-level professionals with less than two years of experience was $43,860. The median salary for professionals with three to four years of experience was $51,340. Again, however, the data is based on a limited sample of about 100 respondents each who self-selected to fill out the *PRWeek* survey. The results certainly suggest that strong performers in the first for years of work enjoy very good pay prospects.

Salaries for Experienced Professionals

Key components of *PRWeek*'s 2006 salary survey are listed in the Insights box on page 26, but the national median for all practitioners is about $92,000. The median for practitioners with more than 20 years of experience is considerably higher—$158,930.

— ON THE JOB >> —

An Overview of Salaries in the Public Relations Field

Insights

PRWeek conducts an annual survey of salaries. The following tables are excerpted from its 2006 survey, which polled 1,401 practitioners in the field.

Practitioners by Gender

Female	60 percent
Male	40 percent

Chief Corporate Communication Officers by Gender

Female	28 percent
Male	72 percent

Median Overall Salaries

All professionals	$ 92,150
Men	$123,310
Females	$ 80,940

Median Salary by Years of Experience

1–2 years	$ 43,860
3–4 years	$ 51,340
5–6 years	$ 66,200
7–10 years	$ 78,070
11–15 years	$102,500
16–20 years	$132,690
21+ years	$158,930

Median Salary by Discipline

Financial/Investor Rel.	$165,620
Crisis Mgt.	$150,000
Reputation Mgt.	$143,000
Public Affairs	$ 98,500
Brand Mgt.	$ 91,430
Market Comm.	$ 90,690
Internal Comm.	$ 85,420
Community Relations	$ 59,910

Median Salary by Sector

Telecommunications	$131,250
Technology/Internet	$117,710
Financial Services	$116,410
Food/Beverage	$112,500
Sports	$100,000
Health care	$ 98,470
Industry/Manufacturing	$ 90,000
Arts/Entertainment	$ 82,500
Travel/Tourism	$ 82,140
Education	$ 69,140
Nonprofit/Charity	$ 68,530

Median Salary by Job Title

Executive vice president	$186,250
Senior vice president	$180,360
Vice president	$148,880
Managing director	$ 99,810
Freelance/Consultant	$ 92,500
Public relations manager	$ 69,440
Account supervisor	$ 64,000
Senior account executive	$ 59,240
Account executive	$ 41.390
Account coordinator	$ 27,040

Source: "Salary Survey 2006." *PRWeek*, Special Report, February 20, 2006, 16–22.

Salaries, of course, depend on a number of factors, including geographic location, job title, the industry, and even the type of public relations specialty. Major metropolitan areas, for example, generally have higher salaries, but there are some regional differences. Professionals get a median salary of $118,600 in the Northeast, but only $81,300 in the Plains states, and $92.400 in the Western states, including California. The median salary in the Southeastern states, including Florida, is $88,600.

Job title also means a lot. A senior vice president (SVP) receives a median of $180,360, whereas an account executive at a public relations firm gets $41,390. In terms of sector, individuals who work for a telecommunications company make a median salary of $131,250, but working for a nonprofit nets only $68,530. Some glamour areas, such as sports, report median salaries in the $100,000 range. In terms of specialty, financial/investor relations pays the most, with a median salary of $165,620, but crisis management is close behind at $150,000. Community relations work pays the least, with an average salary of $59,910.

In terms of the senior ranks, *PRWeek* notes a survey by Korn/Kerry consultants that profiled the chief communication officers of Fortune 200 companies. The average base salary was $335,000, and the total cash package (with bonuses and stock) was almost $600,000.

You should be aware, however, that the *PRWeek* salary figures are based on a poll of 1,401 respondents, and the salaries reported may or may not be indicative of the entire field. For example, the median salary for financial/investor relations was based on only 24 responses. The median salary for a senior vice president was based on 79 responses. In the absence of more complete salary data, however, surveys by publications such as *PRWeek* have become the standard reference in the industry.

A good source for checking current salaries for public relations in major cities throughout the United States and around the world is www.workinpr.com. It posts current openings and also provides the salary ranges for various job classifications. In Minneapolis/St. Paul, for example, the median salary for a vice president of public relations is $165,000. The median for a public relations specialist, on the other hand, is $42,000.

Salaries for Women: The Gender Gap

The *PRWeek* survey clearly shows an across-the-board gender gap in salaries. The median salary for men with 1 to 5 years of experience is $65,620, whereas women with the same level of experience made $45,280. Males with 5 or more years of experience earned median salaries of $133,160, while their female counterparts earned $90,670.

The salary advantage for men over women is not unique to public relations. It is widespread in most of American business and throughout the world. The American Federation of Labor Congress of Industrial Organizations (AFL-CIO) reports that women continue to be paid about 75 cents for every dollar men receive, a figure that hasn't changed much over the past 10 years.

A number of studies have probed the pay differential between men and women in public relations. The first studies, starting in the 1980s, simply noted the gap without taking into consideration the multiple factors that could lead to discrepancies. Some of these factors included (1) the number of years in the field, (2) technician duties versus managerial responsibilities, (3) the nature of the industry, (4) the size of the organization, and (5) women's attempts to balance work and family.

Some studies, for example, concluded that women were relatively new to the field and didn't have the experience yet to compete with men who had been in the field for some years. Inherent in this finding was that women traditionally are assigned low-paying "technician" roles. Julie O'Neil, a professor at Texas Christian University, summarizes the conclusion of several studies in the *Journal of Public Relations Research*: "Women are segregated into the lower-level technician role, spending time on routine activities such as writing, editing, and handling media relations. Conversely, more men are promoted into the more powerful managerial role, engaging in such activities as counseling senior management, and making key policy decisions."

Others have tried to explain the salary differential in other ways. *PRWeek* points out that male respondents to its survey have been in the business an average of 15 years, while the women respondents averaged only 11.7 years in the business. Others have pointed out that women have a tendency to work in areas of public relations that traditionally have low salaries, such as community relations, employee communications, or nonprofits. In contrast, a large percentage of practitioners in finance and investor relations—which pay well—are men.

Professors Linda Aldoory (University of Maryland) and Elizabeth Toth (formerly of Syracuse University and now at the University of Maryland) also explored discrepancies in salaries in an article for the *Journal of Public Relations Research* (2002). They presented a number of factors, but essentially concluded:

> The difference in the average salary of male respondents compared to female respondents was statistically significant. Regression analysis revealed that years of public relations experience accounted for much of the variance, but that gender and job interruptions also accounted for the salary difference. Age and education level were not found to be a significant influence on salary.

The role of women in public relations, and the increased feminization of the field (70 percent of the practitioners in the United States are women), will be discussed as a major trend line in Chapter 3.

The Value of Public Relations

This chapter has outlined the size and global scope of public relations, provided an overview of definitions including the new one that will be developed in Chapter 2 as the basis of this book, discussed the various activities of public relations, and explored how it differs from and is similar to journalism, advertising, and marketing. The case for an organization integrating all of its communications for maximum effectiveness has been made.

Today more than ever, the world needs not more information but also savvy communicators and facilitators who can explain the goals and aspirations of individuals, organizations, and governments to others in a socially responsive manner. Tom Glover, writing in *Profile*, the magazine of the Institute of Public Relations in the United Kingdom, stated, "Clear and consistent communication helps organizations achieve their goals, employees to work to their potential, customers to make informed choices, investors to make an accurate assessment of an organization, and society to form fair judgments of industries, organizations, and issues."

Public relations provides businesses and society with a vital service. On a practical level, Laurence Moskowitz, chairman and CEO of Medialink, says that public relations is "informative. It's part of the news, the program, the article, the stuff readers and viewers want. It's relevant. Positive messaging through the news lifts other forms of marketing, too. Good PR increases the effectiveness of ads, direct mail, sponsorship, and all other forms of 'permission' marketing."

But the latest developments in public relations push the field beyond information dissemination. Today's practitioner must understand what effect information and communication efforts will have on the competitive position of the employer, whether that employer operates in the for-profit or nonprofit sector of the economy. By helping the modern organization manage competition and conflict, public relations professionals in the new century bring added value to their employers, earning greater influence over the destiny of the organizations where they practice public relations. That earned influence leads to greater respect and better rewards in everything from salary to personal satisfaction.

PRCASEBOOK

Dixie Chicks Are Not Ready to Make Nice

Just when country music fans thought the Dixie Chicks had put their 2003 political flap behind them, the flamboyant group brewed new controversy and financial stress as their 2006 concert tour floundered. It all began with what many communication experts considered a public relations blunder. The following item ran on *PRNewswire*.

EXAMPLE: Ninth Annual PR Blunders List Unveiled

SAN FRANCISCO, Dec. 16 /PRNewswire/ — Arrogance, corporate greed, and communications casualties of the war in Iraq highlight this year's list of public relations blunders compiled annually by San Francisco's Fineman PR. The list is a collection of some of the year's worst public relations gaffes. The "winners" for 2003: . . .

5. Dixie Chicks Forget their Audience

Anti–Iraq war politics and country music don't mix well, but that didn't stop Dixie Chicks lead singer Natalie Maines from saying, "we're ashamed the president of the United States is from Texas." The remark in London last March immediately put the Texas group in country music's doghouse. Atlanta's Kicks radio station polled its listeners and 76 percent said, "If I could, I'd take my (Dixie Chicks) CDs back," according to CNN. Listener fury led radio stations to boycott the group's songs, and the Chicks got booed at the Country Music Awards, the Associated Press reported. With sales of Dixie Chicks' music suffering, Maines apologized.

But is the story of the Dixie Chicks' crisis and financial scrape, including the 2006 launch of a new CD and the subsequent collapse of the Chicks tour in the United States, really all that simple? Like most aspects of life, probably not. The "incident" as the Chicks have come to call it actually showcases a number of principles and practices of public relations, as well as quandaries in setting a strategy to manage conflict with key publics.

A Brief Time Line

At a concert in 2003 in London, Maines commented, "Just so you know, we're ashamed that the president of the United States is from Texas." Maines added that she felt George W. Bush's foreign policy was alienating the world. After an uproar in the United States, She apologized for the statement. However, she then withdrew her apology, perhaps stirring even more hostile feelings than if she had taken one or the other position and stayed with it.

After major fallout and outrage from the country music fan base, fast-forward to 2006, with the Dixie Chicks' release of a new album. Promotion of the new album, *Taking the Long Way,* was led by release of a single from the album titled, "Not Ready to Make Nice." Sales of this crossover disc, intended to appeal beyond the country market to adult contemporary audiences, were extremely strong, taking the album platinum in only four weeks.

According to the *Wall Street Journal*, however, music sales priced as low as $10 per disc pale by comparison with concert tour revenue with merchandise sales and $85 tickets. "Tours used to be promotional tools for albums; now, the reverse is often true." The backlash against inflammatory statements meant that as many as half of the 42 U.S. dates for the "Accidents and

Local country radio personalities Clariessa Kennedy and K. C. Daniels have been tossing darts at a poster of the Dixie Chicks, taped to the studio door at radio station KRMD-FM in Shreveport, Louisiana. The two morning radio partners organized what they call the first "Pro-America, Anti-Dixie Chicks Bash" in 2003 in response to comments made in London, England by Natalie Maines, the lead singer, who said she was ashamed that President George W. Bush hails from Texas.

(continued)

Accusations" concert tour had to be postponed and the Dixie Chicks gave up $500,000 guarantees as part of negotiations with concert promoters.

Years after "the incident," their organization made the argument that the Dixie Chicks stood firm for the sake of their kids. A release quoted firebrand Natalie Maines: "When all this was happening, I had a two-year-old, and Emily had a baby. I know a lot of people who would have just said 'sorry,' but I had to think about when my son gets old enough to ask me what they were talking about. I could never say, 'Oh, I said this thing about the president because I didn't agree with us [America] going to war, but then I took it back. I want him to know that I stood up for what I know to be right." This fairly astute position, falling back on principle, was counterbalanced by further inflammatory statements by Maines. As the program director of WXBM in Pensacola put it, "The Bush thing may have died down, but then she went and said that stuff about 'Country listeners are a bunch of rednecks, we don't need 'em.' Every time things seem to die down, she opens her mouth again." Having a frank, flamboyant client such as Maines is not exactly a dream come true for public relations specialists. While the band's media relations efforts garnered a *Time* magazine cover and a large inside story, Maines was quoted in the article regarding country music fans: "We don't want those kinds of fans. They limit what you can do."

Artistic freedom and principles, or a compulsion to rebel? *Time*'s profile of the Chicks' fiery vocalist highlights the complexity of Natalie Maines, describing her this way: "Natalie Maines is one of those people born middle finger first." But the article also makes the following observation about clinging to principles over knee-jerk crisis management strategy: "The celebrity playbook for navigating a scandal is one word

Technique

Several public relations techniques are exemplified by the Chicks.

> Outstanding Web site. Check out the Dixie Chicks Web site at www.dixiechicks.com to see a full-featured and polished Web site, but one with a dark and almost "goth" tone to it. Not by coincidence, the makeup and wardrobe of the Chicks on the site sets the same tone. This design is likely intended to make a statement about the group's decision to appeal to a noncountry or less-traditional country audience. On the Web site, the "Incident" and the remark about the redneck audience are notably absent. A statement on the site alludes to the turmoil: "We will go where the fans are with great anticipation and no regrets."

> Polarizing of audience does create buzz for the band. Here is just one of thousands of posting to blogs (short for "Web logs" which are online journals or diaries that are updated frequently and allow guests to comment) regarding the Dixie Chicks.

Joho the Blog at www.hyperorg.com/blogger/mtarchive/001342.html

Whoa there, pardner! If the Dixie Chicks want to bad-mouth Bush while touring Europe, they certainly have that right. They should also realize that words, as do actions, have consequences. They are entitled to speak their minds, but that doesn't mean they should be given a free pass. You wouldn't be running out to buy a CD by a pro Bush artist of his or her comments cause stations to pull the artist from their playlists would you? I don't think you're defending absolute "free speech," but only defending those whose utterances you agree with. Am I correct?

> Message framing. The spokesperson for the Chicks is deft at framing the challenges of the Chicks as opportunities. Regarding the cancellation of concerts, the *Wall Street Journal* quoted Cindy Berger on behalf of the band: "They're not canceling dates. They are moving dates to accommodate a demand in Canada and Australia." The political martyrdom of the group has increased popularity of the act outside the United States.

> Blogger embedded on the Dixie Chicks Web site. Keith O'Brien, editor of *PRWeek* was ambivalent at the news that the Dixie Chicks have an "embedded blogger." If bloggers are defined as journalists, then perhaps embedding co-opts the independent role of a journalist. But entertainment journalists are often close to their industry—think about television's *Entertainment Tonight* with behind-the-award-show coverage and intimate, insider interviews galore. What is your opinion of this strategy?

> Globalization. The Dixie Chicks recognized long ago that the marketplace for their music and concerts spanned the globe, helping to make them the best-selling country group of all time. It is no coincidence that the public relations professionals working for the Chicks garner mass media coverage coinciding with album releases throughout the world. For example, the *Time* cover and the long story dated May 23, 2006, fell on the launch date of the new album.

long: repent. But apologies are for lapses of character, not revelations of it, and sensing that they were being asked to apologize for their beliefs as much as their timing, the Chicks decided not to back down." Their stance didn't seem to hurt them at the 2007 Grammy Awards. They completed a major comeback by winning five awards, including the trio's defiant anthem, "Not Ready to Make Nice," and the album, *Taking the Long Way*. It is somewhat ironic, however, that the album won as the best "country" album although the group members don't consider themselves country artists anymore.

Several questions to consider: Is all the uproar over the group's criticism of President Bush and denigrating the country audience poor public relations, or part of a brilliant marketing strategy that capitalizes on the inclination of the Dixie Chicks to speak their minds and, at the same time, move to a broader audience base? Given the experience of the Dixie

Chicks, should entertainers refrain from making political statements or be more outspoken? Draw some tentative conclusions now, but keep this case in mind as you explore throughout the text how public relations plays a key role in the management of competition and conflict.

Some questions to consider: Are the Dixie Chicks acting on principle or committing spectacular public relations blunders (especially shaming President Bush and denigrating the "redneck" audience)? Or both—principled statements that then make life difficult for their media spokesperson? Or is all the to-do and turmoil, ultimately leading to a new creative direction, part of a brilliant marketing strategy that capitalizes on the inclination of the Dixie Chicks to speak their minds? Draw tentative conclusions now, but keep this case in mind as you explore throughout the text how public relations plays a key role in the management of competition and conflict.

Summary

Global Scope
Public relations is well established in the United States and throughout the world. Growth is strong in Europe and Asia, particularly China.

A Variety of Definitions
Common terms in most definitions of public relations include *deliberate*, *planned*, *performance*, *public interest*, *two-way communication*, and *strategic management of competition and conflict management function*.

Public Relations as a Process
The public relations process can be described with the RACE acronym: research, action, communication, evaluation. The process is a constant cycle; feedback and program adjustment are integral components of the overall process.

The Components of Public Relations
Public relations work includes the following components: counseling, media relations, publicity, community relations, governmental affairs, employee relations, investor relations, development/fund-raising, special events, and marketing communications.

How Public Relations Differs from Journalism
Although writing is an important activity in both public relations and journalism, the scope, objectives, and channels are different for each field.

How Public Relations Differs from Advertising
Publicity, one area of public relations, uses mass media to disseminate messages, as does advertising. The format and context, however, differ. Publicity goes through media gatekeepers who make the ultimate decision whether to use the material as part of a news story. Advertising involves paid space and time and is easily identified as being separate from news/editorial content.

How Public Relations Differs from Marketing
The functions of public relations often overlap with marketing, but the primary purpose of public relations is to build relationships and generate goodwill with a variety of publics. Marketing focuses on customers and the sale of products/services. Public relations can be part of a marketing strategy; in such cases, it is often called marketing communications.

Toward an Integrated Perspective
An organization's goals and objectives are best achieved by integrating the activities of advertising, marketing, and public relations to create a consistent message. Integration requires teamwork and the recognition that each field has strengths that complement and reinforce one another.

A Changing Focus in Public Relations

In the past, those entering public relations were often former journalists, but that is no longer the case because public relations has evolved beyond publicity and media relations. In addition, public relations is now widely recognized as its own distinct academic discipline in colleges and universities throughout the world.

The Range of Work

Public relations professionals are employed in a variety of fields: corporations, nonprofits, entertainment and sports, politics and government, education, and international organizations and businesses.

Five Essential Abilities

Those who plan careers in public relations should have the following abilities: writing skill, research ability, planning expertise, problem-solving ability, and business/economic competence.

The Value of Internships

Students should participate in internships throughout college as part of their preprofessional training in public relations.

Salaries in Public Relations

Entry-level salaries are higher in public relations than in many other communications fields. A person with one or two years of experience can earn a salary in the mid-30s, whereas a more experienced professional can earn in the six figures. Although the gender gap has somewhat narrowed, in general women earn less than men.

The Value of Public Relations

The world today doesn't need more information; it needs savvy, well-educated individuals who can interpret the information and determine why and how it is relevant to people's lives. Public relations people must explain the goals and objectives of their clients and employers to the public and, at the same time, provide them with guidance about their responsibility to the public interest.

CASE ACTIVITY >>

What Would You Do?

Managing Competition

Cold Stone Creamery is a relatively new ice cream company that faces stiff competition in the marketplace from such established brands as Ben & Jerry's, Baskin-Robbins, and Häagen-Dazs.

The first store was established in Tempe, Arizona, in 1998. Since then, the company has expanded to more than 500 stores (franchises) nationwide. Its market niche is that customers can personalize their servings by choosing a base flavor and then mixing it with a number of toppings. Employees do the mixing by hand on a frozen granite stone (hence the company name).

The challenge, of course, is to maximize more store revenue and to increase market share. Research shows that the typical Cold Stone customer is a woman between the ages of 24 and 35, who brings her friends and other family members with her.

The company has decided to do an integrated communications program for the next year that would involve public relations, advertising, and in-store marketing promotions for some new products, such as ice cream cakes and nonfat flavors. The focus would be on enhancing the visibility of its stores at the local level and making Cold Stone a distinct brand among the clutter of other ice cream franchises in the community. Do some brainstorming. What ideas and activities would you suggest? You have to be creative because you don't have a big budget.

Questions for Review and Discussion

1. How many people are estimated to work in public relations around the world? Is public relations growing as a field in terms of employees and revenues?

2. There are many definitions of public relations. Of those listed, which one do you prefer? Why?

3. What key words and phrases are found in most definitions of public relations?
4. What does the acronym RACE stand for?
5. What are the components of basic public relations practice? Which one sounds the most interesting to you as a possible career specialty?
6. How does public relations differ from the fields of journalism, advertising, and marketing?
7. How does public relations support marketing? Some experts say that public relations can launch a new product or service better than advertising. Do you agree or disagree? It's also asserted that public relations creates brands, and that advertising can only reinforce and defend a brand. What are your thoughts?
8. What is the concept of integrated communications (IC), which some people also call integrated marketing communications (IMC)? What four factors have led to the growth of integrated campaigns?
9. The text says that former journalists often don't always make a good transition to public relations work. What reasons were given as to why this is so?

10. Public relations people work for a variety of organizations. What type of organization would you prefer if you wanted to work in public relations?
11. The text mentions five essential qualities for working in public relations. On a scale of 1 to 10, how would you rate yourself on each ability?
12. Why is it important for a student to complete an internship in college? Do you think interns should be paid?
13. Job placement directors say that employers are looking for 10 qualities in applicants. Can you name at least 5 of the 10 qualities?
14. Discuss entry-level salaries in public relations. Do you think they are too low, or are they about what you expected? What about the salaries for experienced professionals?
15. Is there still a gender gap in salaries? If so, do you think that it is caused by overt discrimination or do other factors explain the salary gap?

Suggested Readings

Bowen, Shannon A. "I Thought It Would Be More Glamorous; Perceptions and Misconceptions Among Students in the Public Relations Principles Course." *Public Relations Review* 29, no. 2 (2003): 199–214.

Bureau of Labor Statistics. "Occupational Outlook Handbook: Public Relations Specialists." www.bls.gov/oco/ocos086.htm. Excellent overview with facts and figures.

Bush, Michael. "The PR Industry from the Outside: PR Pros Rightfully Tout the Discipline's Role in the Marketing Mix." *PRWeek,* September 11, 2006, 15.

Grunig, James E. "Furnishing the Edifice: Ongoing Research on Public Relations as a Strategic Management Function." *Journal of Public Relations Research* 18.2 (2006): 151–176.

Hallahan, Kirk. "The Dynamics of Issues Activation and Response: An Issues Process Model." *Journal of Public Relations Research* 13 no. 1 (2002): 27–59.

Ihlen, Oyvind. "The Power of Social Capital: Adapting Bourdieu to the Study of Public Relations." *Public Relations Review* 31 (2005): 492–496.

Lordan, Edward J. "Defining Public Relations and Press Roles in the Twenty-First Century." *Public Relations Quarterly* (Summer 2005): 41–43.

O'Brien, Keith. "Proactivity Is Crucial When Discussing Bad News." *PRWeek,* August 14, 2006, 9.

Ruler, Betteke van, Dejan Vercic, Gerhard Butschi, and Bertil Flodin. "A First Look for Parameters of Public Relations in Europe." *Journal of Public Relations Research* 16, no. 1 (2004): 35–63.

Trickett, Eleanor. Great Moments in Consumer PR. *PRWeek,* August, 14, 2006, 15.

Trickett, Eleanor. Outside Look Shows PR's Role in Marketing Gaining Respect. *PRWeek,* September 11, 2006, 9.

Ward, David. When a Stunt's Only a Starting Point. *PRWeek,* July 31, 2006, 18.

Chapter Two

Managing Competition and Conflict

A New Way of Thinking

Chapter 1 offered a general overview of public relations and working in the field. Building on that orientation, this chapter provides a more focused description of public relations as the management of competition and conflict.

Within this framework, public relations is best defined as the *strategic management of competition in the best interests of one's own organization and, when possible, also in the interests of key publics*. A breakdown of this definition is as follows:

> *Strategic*—For the purpose of achieving particular objectives
> *Management*—Planned, deliberate actions
> *Competition*—Striving for the same object, position, prize, and so on, as others
> *Conflict*—Sharp disagreement or opposition resulting in direct, overt threat of attack from another entity.

The definition implies that practitioners believe in their employers and work first and foremost in the interests of the employer to compete against others and to handle any conflict that might arise. In sum, provided the objectives are worthy and ethical, the paramount concern of professionals should be managing communication in the interests of employers and clients to enhance competitive position and handle conflict effectively.

This new definition is more assertive than most definitions that emphasize building mutually beneficial relationships between an organization and its various stakeholders. Indeed, building relationships is a key objective, but it is part of the larger role for public relations in helping an organization succeed.

Professor Glen T. Cameron, of the University of Missouri, says the newer definition emphasizing the strategic management of competition and conflict is a more "muscular PR" and uses the image of Olympic swimmer Natalie Coughlin to make his point. The swimmer embodies preparation, strength, and fair play required to compete against others. This image of public relations embraces competition and conflict as a sometimes necessary and usually healthy element of public relations practice.

The point here is that public relations plays a key role in enabling both profit and nonprofit organizations to compete for limited resources (customers, volunteers, employees, donations, grants, etc.) and to engage in healthy, honest conflict with others who hold different

Olympic swimmer Natalie Coughlin embodies the view of public relations as strong and competitive in spirit, yet not macho or underhanded.

views of what is best and right for society. Achieving these sorts of objectives increases the value of public relations to an organization. It is also how public relations professionals earn the influence that leads to greater recognition by top management, increased respect in the field, and ultimately, a better-paying, more secure position for public relations professionals.

Although competition and conflict are closely related to each other, this book makes a distinction between the two terms. *Competition*, a pervasive condition in life, occurs when two or more groups or organizations vie for the same resources. In business, these "resources" may be sales, market share, contracts, employees, and ultimately profits. In the nonprofit sector, the competition may be for donations, grants, clients, volunteers, and even political influence.

Conflict, on the other hand, occurs when two groups direct their efforts against each other, devising communication and actions that directly or verbally attack the other group. Conflict arises, for example, when labor unions pressure Wal-Mart to unionize or when an environmental group lobbies Home Depot to stop selling lumber from endangered hardwood forests. It also occurs when government regulators investigate Steve Jobs, CEO of Apple, for backdating stock options.

Experienced public relations experts, however, are quick to point out that many practitioners will spend most of their professional lives dealing with fairly moderate levels of competition (such as marketing communications) and perhaps have few, if any, situations that involve conflict. For example, the development director for the Audubon Society may compete for donations for a new program from the same donors who are being approached for donations by the Sierra Club. The two professionals may be friends; perhaps one even mentored the other. On the other hand, a more heightened level of competition might exist between public relations professionals at Wal-Mart, Target, and Costco, companies that compete with each other to increase consumer recognition and retail sales.

Most public relations activity and programs, as already noted, deal with competition between organizations for sales and customers. Conflict, in contrast, involves confrontations and attacks between organizations and various stakeholders or publics. An example of a conflict was when Target decided to ban the Salvation Army from collecting donations at its store entrances during the holiday season. The store immediately found itself in conflict with various community groups that charged the store with being a "grinch" and not supporting the needs of the poor and homeless. Target then had to manage the attacks on the company's charitable reputation, as well as a possible consumer boycott and threats to its revenues.

Admittedly, the distinction between competition and conflict is partly a matter of degree, but it is also a matter of focus. In competition, the eye is on the prize—such as sales or political support, for example. With conflict, the eye is on the opposition, on dealing with or initiating threats of some sort or another. In either case, professional practice by this definition is vitally important to organizations. It requires a sense of mission and conviction that

> Your organization's behavior is honorable and defensible

> Your organization is ethical

> Your organization's mission is worthy

> Your advocacy of the organization has integrity

> Your organization works at creating mutual benefit whenever possible.

The last point, striving for mutual benefit, is extremely important. It involves balancing the interests of an employer or client with those of a number of stakeholders. Often, professionals are able to accommodate both the interests of the organization and its various publics. By the same token, organizations may not be able to please all of their publics because there are differences in worldviews. Wal-Mart may please labor unions by paying more employee benefits, but consumers who like low prices may object. Environmentalists may want to close a steel plant, but the company's employees and the local community may be avid supporters of keeping the plant open despite its pollution problems. Given competing agendas and issues, the public relations professional will need to look first to the needs of the organization, and then manage the inevitable conflicts that arise.

The Role of Public Relations in Managing Conflict

Conflict takes many forms, from warfare between nations to spats between kids on a playground. Any sharp disagreement or collision of interests and ideas can be defined as a conflict, with many such conflicts falling under the purview of public relations. This means that public relations professionals must develop communication strategies and processes to influence the course of conflicts to the benefit of their organizations and, when possible, to the benefit of the organizations' many constituents This deliberate influence applied to publics is called *strategic conflict management* (see the Insights box on real-world strategic conflict management).

ON THE JOB >>

Strategic Conflict Management in the Real World

Insights

The following scenarios provide just a few examples of the conflict-related challenges public relations professionals tackle every day around the world.

> A public relations pro takes charge of the temporary press briefing room that was built near the site of a plant explosion, funneling all press and family inquires through her makeshift operation and offering fax, phone, and Internet access for a flock of reporters.
> Recognizing the need for domestic fuel sources in an uncertain world, a D.C. lobbyist works with his PR firm to bolster arguments for federal subsidies to ethanol producers in the U.S. corn belt.
> As American waistlines bulge, the National Institutes of Health calls for the creation of centers to prevent obesity and related diseases.
> Anticipating a strike by Teamster truckers delivering products to a nonunion plant, the plant's public relations team launches a philanthropic campaign to aid widows of the Iraqi war in plant communities.
> Having allowed yet another instance of sexual harassment in the workplace, a spokesperson expresses mortification about the performance of her company and pledges to change the company culture.

These scenarios share a common theme: the strategic management of conflict. Conflict management is one of the most interesting, vibrant, and essential functions of public relations.

Strategic efforts also run a wide gamut, corresponding to the four phases of the conflict management life cycle:

1. Monitoring media for emerging issues (proactive phase)
2. Taking preventive actions that forestall conflict (strategic phase)
3. Dealing with crisis or disaster, whether caused by the organization or by nature (reactive phase)
4. Repairing relations and public image in the aftermath of a conflict (recovery phase)

The influence of public relations on the course of a conflict can involve reducing conflict, as is often the case in crisis management. At other times conflict is escalated for activist purposes, such as when antiabortion advocates not only picket health clinics but also assault clients, doctors, and nurses. Other strategies are less dramatic, such as oil industry advocates lobbying to open parts of the Alaskan wilderness to exploration, striving to win approval over time from the public—and ultimately, Congress.

Indeed, conflict management often occurs when a business or industry contends with government regulators or activist groups that seem determined to curtail operations through what the industry considers excessive safety or environmental standards. At the same time, both the regulatory body and the activists engage in their own public relations efforts to make their case against the company. For example, the deep-shaft coal mining industry in the Appalachian area of the United States has simultaneously worked to improve mine safety while also lobbying to ensure that regulations do not excessively curtail profits. On the other side, unions and environmental groups lobby government regulatory agencies for further reforms, especially as tragic deaths continue to occur in the mining industry.

Professor Jae-Hwa Shin, now a professor at the University of Southern Mississippi, describes this dialogue between multiple parties as the "wrangle in the marketplace of ideas." And much like Olympic swimmers in the pool striving to represent their own interests (to win), this wrangle is inevitable and perfectly acceptable, according to Shin. In fairness, sometimes the event resembles an aggressive water polo match more than a 100-meter butterfly race.

Sometimes, an organization is able to catch a conflict at an early stage and reduce damage to the organization. However, in other cases, an issue may smolder before turning into a major fire. The prison abuse scandal at Abu Ghraib prison in Iraq is a good example. The Pentagon ignored reports about humiliation of prisoners until the problem became front-page news. Dealing with problems early on is not only more efficient, it is usually the right thing to do. The basic concepts of issue and risk management will be discussed shortly.

Unfortunately, most conflict situations are not clear-cut in terms of an ideal solution. In many cases, public relations professionals will not be able to accommodate the concerns of an activist group or a particular public because of many other factors, including the survivability of the organization. KFC, for example, is not going out of the fried chicken business just because People for the Ethical Treatment of Animals (PETA) is picketing stores about the inhumane slaughter of chickens. In such cases, public relations professionals have to make tough calls and advocate strictly on behalf of their organizations. How they decide what position to take is the subject of the next section.

It Depends: A System for Managing Conflict

Working with management, a public relations professional or team must determine the stance its organization will take toward each public or stakeholder involved in a conflict situation. Stance then determines strategy—what will be done and why. The stance-driven approach to public relations began with the discovery that virtually all practitioners share an unstated, informal approach to managing conflict and competition: "It depends."

In other words, the stance taken toward publics "depends" on many factors, which cause the stance to change in response to changing circumstances. Simply put, the outstanding practitioner monitors for threats, assesses them, arrives at a stance for the organization, and then begins communication efforts from that stance.

Practitioners face a complex set of forces that must be monitored and considered. One approach is the *threat appraisal model*. Essentially, a threat to an organization requires an assessment of the demands that the threat makes on the organization as well as consideration of the resources available to deal with the threat. An identified threat, for example, forces the public relations professional to consider a variety of factors. One is organizational. Do you have the knowledge, time, finances, and management commitment to combat the threat? On another level, how do you assess the severity of the danger to the organization? What effort is required by you? Is it a difficult situation with potential for long duration, or is it a relatively simple matter that can be resolved fairly quickly?

An example of how the threat appraisal model is used in the real world, is the 1996 Summer Olympic Games that took place in Atlanta. The communication department of the Atlanta Organizing Committee needed to select a radio station to serve as the clearinghouse and distributor of audio news releases related to the games. A radio station was chosen primarily because of its large staff and state-of-the-art equipment. It just so happened that the station was an AM news/talk station with a fairly conservative talk show host who was occasionally accused of racial stereotyping. Through word of mouth it came to light that a protest movement was being mounted against the selection of the conservative radio station.

The protest group posed a potential threat to the Olympic Committee, first as a source of immediate criticism and then in terms of the subtle message they could give to the world that Atlanta was not a modern progressive city, but remained a "typical" Southern facist bastion. C. Richard Yarbrough, director of communication, had the protest group checked out by a staffer who found that only a handful of local people were involved. Given that they were neither well organized nor very well connected to the media or powerbrokers in Atlanta and

given that the Olympic Committee was not endorsing station programming, but simply using it as a clearinghouse, the decision was made not to dignify the criticism of the station with any response whatsoever. The threat was appraised and a stance of nonaccommodation was taken. As it turned out, the issue never did emerge as a public problem for the committee.

In making his decision, Yarbrough considered a number of factors—which are part of the threat appraisal model. First, what was the danger to the image and reputation of Atlanta? Could this movement gain coverage and support, resulting in embarrassment? Once under way, would a protest on racial grounds take a great deal of time and money to address? The emerging activist group certainly posed an issue and a possible public conflict. In this case, uncertainty was reduced by learning that the

ON THE JOB >>

Moral Conflicts Pose Special Challenges

Ethics

When organizations clash over a heated issue or a moral conflict such as embryonic stem cell research or capital punishment, charges leveled at the opposition often include impugning the ethics of the opponent. Oftentimes, such charges can be paraphrased as "We are just trying to tell the truth, but they are lying and twisting facts." Sometimes this "truth telling" is contrasted with the "spin" practiced by the other side—even though both sides often use the same tactics and a full range of persuasive public relations strategies. When proponents embrace absolute moral values, they fail to reach out and understand the other side.

Do you find it ironic or perfectly appropriate for activists to garner publicity by accusing the opposition of using "PR ploys" when such publicity is a standard component of public relations? Watch for examples of this double bind in the media to share with your instructor and the class.

Most news conferences begin with an opening statement by the organization holding the news conference. Write an opening statement for a press conference on a current moral conflict somewhere in the world. You might write the opening script for the Department of Defense or for a peace advocacy group. Write your statement for the side that you support most strongly. Then try to understand the worldview of the other side and sketch an opening statement for that group as well.

Having written both opening statements, consider how it is that both sides claim to be right. Discuss in class whether this exercise illustrates moral relativism or whether it shows that moral absolutes do exist, but that diametric values can be held by different groups.

group was not likely to get well organized or reach a critical mass. Consequently, the threat appraisal resulted in a stance-based strategy to ignore the group, allowing the "movement" to quietly pass away.

It Depends: Two Basic Principles

The threat appraisal model—assessing the seriousness of the threat and the resources needed to combat the threat—is common in the practice of strategic public relations. The model illustrates the "it depends" approach, but there are two other principles that are important.

The first principle is that many factors determine the stance or position of an organization when it comes to dealing with conflict and perceived threats against one's organization. The second principle is that the public relations stance for dealing with a particular audience or public is dynamic; that is, it changes as events unfold. This is represented by a continuum of stances from pure advocacy to pure accommodation. These two principles, which form the basis of what is called *contingency theory*, are further elaborated upon in the next sections.

A Matrix of Contingency Factors

The public relations approach that is used is "contingent" on many factors that professionals must take into account. Glen Cameron and his colleagues identified at least 86 contingency variables divided into 11 groups that on two levels caused organizations to adopt a particular stance on a conflict. Five groups comprised external variables identified as (l) external threats, (2) industry-specific environment, (3) general political/social environment, (4) external public characteristics, and (5) the issue under consideration. The six groups of internal variables were (l) general corporate/organizational characteristics, (2) characteristics of the public relations department, (3) top management characteristics, (4) internal threats, (5) personality characteristics of involved organization members, and (6) relationship characteristics.

Glen Cameron, Jae-Hwa Shin, and Fritz Cropp at the University of Missouri then conducted a survey of 1,000 members of the Public Relations Society of America (PRSA) to explore what variables affect the stance that public relations professionals take, ranging from more advocacy to more accommodation with a public regarding an issue, in order to accomplish organizational goals. The survey found that most practitioners reported the primary influence of individual-level variables on public relations practice and adopting an organizational stance. This included such contingency variables as individual communication competency, personal ethical values, ability to handle complex problems, ability to recognize potential or existing problems, and familiarity with external publics or its representatives. In other words, the expertise and experience of the public relations professional play a major role in formulating the proper strategy for dealing with a conflict or issue.

Organizational-level variables, however, are also important. Factors affecting the stance of an organization included top management support of public relations, public relations department communication competency, public relations representation in top management, top management's frequency of external contact, the public relations department's perception of the external environment, department funding, and the organization's experience with the public. In other words, the values and attitudes of top management (known as the dominant coalition) also has a great influence on how an organization responds to conflict and threats.

In fact, in a *Public Relations Review* article, Astrid Kersten, of LaRoche College in Pittsburgh, noted that an organization's everyday culture and operations highly influence how the organization responds to conflict. She writes, "What appears to us as rational and real is determined by the organizational culture we exist within and the economic and political reality that structures that culture." Conflict and crisis often reinforce organizational dysfunction. "In times of uncertainty and danger, the organization reverts to denial, ritual, and rigidity and invokes its own version of reality as a basic defense against external evidence or attack," says Kersten.

The Contingency Continuum

The matrix, or list of possible variables, that influence an organization's response are helpful in understanding inputs into the complex decision-making process. Depending on circumstances, the attitudes of top management, and the judgment of public relations professionals, such factors may move the organization toward or away from accommodation of a public.

The range of response can be shown on a continuum from pure advocacy to pure accommodation (see Figure 2.1). Pure advocacy might be described as a hard-nosed stance of completely disagreeing or refuting the arguments, claims, or threats of a competitor or a group concerned about an issue. Later in the chapter, for example, the conflict management of Pepsi is examined when it was claimed that used syringes were

FIGURE 2.1

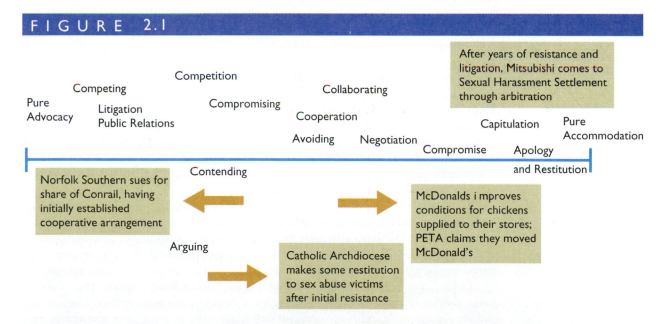

Note: PR professionals will change stance as events and factors emerge as is indicated in the real life examples.

Contingency Continuum This continuum from pure advocacy to pure accommodation forms the foundation for identifying the stance of an organization toward a given public at a given time. The diagram also illustrates how fast-moving public relations can be by showing how some organizations shift positions along the continuum as a conflict evolves.

found in cans of its product. In this case, Pepsi took the stance that such claims were a hoax and stood 100 percent behind its product, resisting suggestions that a product recall was needed.

The other extreme of the continuum is pure accommodation. In this case, the organization agrees with its critics, changes its policies, makes restitution, and even makes a full public apology for its actions. The example given in the chart is Mitsubishi Motors. After years of resistance and litigation, it capitulated and settled a class action suit regarding sexual harassment. Another good example of pure accommodation is Odwalla. After the company found that a problem in production caused food poisoning of customers, it immediately issued a product recall. Odwalla also offered to pay all medical expenses of the victims, and made a full apology to the public.

There are other stances along the continuum that an organization can take. Norfolk Southern railroad, for example, used litigation public relations to shift stockholder opinion concerning an offer to take over Conrail. The Catholic Church can be placed in the middle of the continuum, as various archdioceses finally moved from pure advocacy (denial of a problem) to cooperation and negotiation by making restitution to sex abuse victims. Another part of the continuum is compromise; KFC improved condition for chickens supplied to their stores as a result of complaints by the animal rights group PETA.

The key point about the continuum is that it identifies the stance of an organization toward a given public at a given time. It also shows the dynamism of strategic conflict management. In many cases, an organization will initially adopt a pure advocacy stance, but as the situation changes, new information comes to light, and public opinion shifts, the stance will change toward more accommodation. A variation of this continuum is also used to portray how organizations respond to a crisis situation, which is discussed on pages 44–53.

The Conflict Management Life Cycle

Much of what has been presented so far involves functions and processes for managing competition and conflict for one's organization. The concept of assessing the degree of threat, and its potential harm to the organization, has been discussed. Threat appraisal requires extensive knowledge, experience, and expertise on the part of a public relations professional in order to make correct assessments that will help the organization correctly manage the situation.

The competence of the public relations professional and staff, for example, are significant factors in the matrix of variables that influence an organization's stance on a particular issue. We have also seen that the values and attitudes of top management play a significant role. And finally, a chart was presented showing how an organization's stance can be placed on a continuum from pure advocacy to pure accommodation.

Indeed, the true value and the highest professionalism requires that students today also embrace their roles as managers of competition and conflict. Outstanding and successful public relations professionals must serve as more than communication technicians carrying out the tactics of organizing events, writing news releases, handling news conferences, and pitching stories to journalists. They must also take on the responsibility within the organization for managing conflict and weathering inevitable crisis situations faced by all organizations at one time or another.

This conflict management process can be depicted as a life cycle for a problem or an issue that professionals must track. Figure 2.2 shows the conflict management life

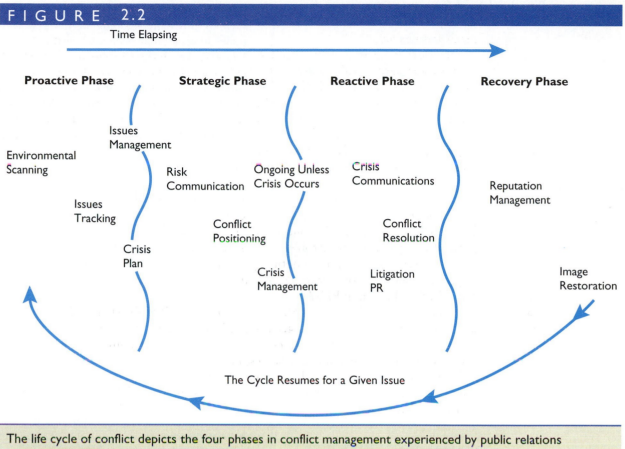

FIGURE 2.2

The life cycle of conflict depicts the four phases in conflict management experienced by public relations professionals. The cycle also includes a few of the numerous public relations strategies that professionals employ to deal with conflict.

cycle and includes numerous techniques that public relations people use to deal with conflict. Typically, events move through time from left to right along the life cycle. At the end of the cycle, persistent issues will require that the process begins all over again on the left side of the cycle.

The conflict management life cycle shows the "big picture" of how to manage a conflict. Strategic conflict management can be divided into four general phases, but bear in mind that the lines between the phases are not absolute and that some techniques overlap in actual practice. Furthermore, in the exciting world of public relations, busy practitioners may be actively managing different competitive situations as well as conflicts in each of the four phases simultaneously. To better understand the conflict management life cycle, each phase will be briefly explained.

Proactive Phase

The proactive phase includes activities and thought processes that can prevent a conflict from arising or from getting out of hand. The first step in the phase is environmental scanning—the constant reading, listening, and watching of current affairs with an eye toward the organization's interests. As issues emerge, issues tracking becomes more

— ON THE JOB >> —

Wal-Mart Makes Bold Move in Conflict Positioning

Insights

Both nonprofit and corporate strategists occasionally get out ahead of an issue or respond deftly to an issue that has recently emerged. For example, Wal-Mart Stores announced in September of 2006 that a test program was under way in Tampa, Florida, to offer some generic drugs at a flat rate of $4 per prescription. Plans included a statewide rollout of the program, with the intention of eventually offering the savings nationwide. In making the announcement, Wal-Mart emphasized that the drugs would not be sold below cost as a "loss leader" just to get customers in the store.

Given the expense of prescriptions, particularly for older Americans, this was a welcome development. It came at a time when activist groups such as WakeUp Walmart (WakeUpWalmart.com) were attacking Wal-Mart health coverage for employees; the generic prescription move provided a high-profile response. It positioned Wal-Mart to appear concerned about health care costs and access to reasonable treatment solutions.

Devon Herrick, an economist at the National Center for Policy Analysis stated. "That's a great price for a 30-day supply of drugs and will be a tremendous boon for seniors." Nevertheless, the move did not placate activists: "Providing low-cost drugs is a good thing. But not providing affordable health care to workers is not a good thing," stated Chris Kofinis of WakeUp Walmart.

It remains to be seen how key publics such as employees or county planning boards who approve Wal-Mart locations will respond. Conceivably, Wal-Mart has earned some good will that may serve the company well in future negotiations required for the company to maintain employee morale and customer loyalty.

focused and systematic through processes such as the daily clipping of news stories. Issues management occurs when the organization makes behavioral changes or creates strategic plans for ways to address emerging issues. In the proactive phase, well-run organizations also develop a general crisis plan as a first step in preparing for the worst—an issue or an event that escalates to crisis proportions.

Strategic Phase

In the strategic phase, an issue that has become an emerging conflict is identified as needing concerted action by the public relations professional.

Three broad strategies are undertaken in this phase. Through risk communication, dangers or threats to people or organizations are conveyed to forestall personal injury, health problems, and environmental damage. This risk communication continues so long as the risk exists or until the risk escalates into a crisis. Conflict-positioning strategies enable the organization to position itself favorably in anticipation of actions such as litigation, boycott, adverse legislation, elections, or similar events that will play out in "the court of public opinion" (see the Insights box on Wal-Mart). To be prepared for the worst outcome—that is, an issue that resists risk communication efforts and becomes a conflict of crisis proportions—a specific crisis management plan is developed for that particular issue.

Reactive Phase

Once the issue or imminent conflict reaches a critical level of impact on the organization, the public relations professional must react to events as they unfold in the external communication environment.

Crisis communications includes the implementation of the crisis management plan as well as the hectic 24/7 efforts to meet the needs of publics such as disaster victims, employees, government officials, and the media. When conflict has emerged but is not careening out of control, conflict resolution techniques are used to bring a heated conflict, such as collapsed salary negotiations, to a favorable resolution. The public relations practitioner may employ strategies to assist negotiation or arbitration efforts to resolve conflict.

Often, the most intractable conflicts end up in the courts. Litigation public relations employs communication strategies and publicity efforts in support of legal actions or trials

— ON THE JOB >>

Litigation Public Relations Impacts Long-Term Reputation

Insights

Litigation public relations involves managing communication during the course of any legal dispute so as to affect the outcome of litigation or the impact of the trial process on the overall reputation of a client. Because litigation is a serious matter, it is fair to say that litigation public relations—strategic communication advice to top management and its legal counsel—is actually a crisis management specialty. However, the stakes in litigation public relations go far beyond winning the case and minimizing financial costs because cases not only play out in courtrooms but also, in high-profile instances, play out as "trial by media" with significant consequences in the "court of public opinion."

Clearly, litigation public relations has as much to do with reputation as with how the court case unfolds. Effectively managing the crisis that surrounds litigation will not only contain a crisis but also save a company's good name.

According to Richard S. Levick, an expert in litigation public relations, the following 10 rules of litigation communication are essential guidelines for public relations professionals to safe-guard the long-term corporate reputation, market positioning, and share price of clients in the midst of litigation-driven crisis:

1. *Safe Harbor*—"No comment" may be a fine legal strategy but it is usually a horrific media strategy, which concedes the entire public came to the opposing side.
2. *Protect the Brand*—You're not in the legal defense business; you're in the brand protection business. There's no greater time to propel the value of the brand and no more vulnerable time.
3. *Recognize the Problems*—In 90 percent of high-profile cases the reporters call the lawyers first—before the lawyer informs the client that this may be a media issue. When reporters call, the story is already written.
4. *The "Rule of Jobs"*—Everyone has got a job to do. The reporters job is to write an interesting story. Your job is to help them tell an interesting story. If you think that they are unfair, it may be because you are "no comment"-ing and you are not available. If you think reporters have a bias, they do. It's not anticorporate—it's anti-boring.
5. *The Rule of ST*—Lawyers confront big issues all the time. How do they know to anticipated something is newsworthy? If it ends in "ST"—firST; biggeST; worST; beST.
6. *The Rule of Audiences*—If you want to communicate, target your audiences. Think like your customer, not like a lawyer.
7. *Perception Rules*—Perception trumps reality 100 percent of the time. Lawyers think it's all about facts—it's about the perception.
8. *Anticipate trends*—If you track the media, you can anticipate what the media's interest is going to be. To the media something occurring once is a fact; something occurring twice is a trend. Journalists are addicted to trends.
9. *Total, Headline, Story*—It's the pictures, not the words that prevail. What is your picture, both literally and figuratively? People don't read—they scan. What we see is far more powerful than what we hear.
10. *The Rule of Thinking Differently*—To take away for a lawyer is stare-decisis—"what's come before, precedent." For a journalist, "truth" is what they know by 4 P.M. You've got to play by their rules.

Source: "Courting Public Opinion: Litigation and Communication." *Corporate Public Issues* 28, no. 6 (2006) 43–45.

(see Chapter 7 for details on legal issues in public relations). The Insights box above examines the impact of litigation public relations on an organization's reputation.

Recovery Phase

In the aftermath of a crisis or a high-profile, heated conflict with a public, an organization should employ strategies either to bolster or repair its reputation in the eyes of key publics.

Reputation management includes systematic research to learn the state of the organization's reputation and then taking steps to improve it. As events and conflicts occur, the organization responds with actions and communication about those actions.

Poorly managed issues, imposing excessive risk to others, and callous responses to a crisis damage an organization's reputation. When this damage is extreme, image restoration strategies can help, provided they include genuine change by the organization.

Managing the Life Cycle

Not only do public relations practitioners face the challenge of addressing different conflicts in different phases of the life cycle, no sooner do they deal with a conflict, then the process starts over again for that very same issue. Environmental scanning is resumed to ensure that the conflict does not reemerge as an issue. Although challenging, conflict management is not impossible. Systematic processes described in the next sections of this chapter provide guidance and structure for this highly rewarding role played by public relations professionals in managing competition and conflict. These four processes are (1) issues management, (2) risk communications, (3) crisis management, (4) and reputation management.

Issues Management

Identifying and dealing with issues early on is one of the more important functions during the proactive phase of the conflict management life cycle. The interaction of organizations with various elements of society has led to the emergence of issues management as an important part of effective public relations and strategic planning. Essentially, issues management is a proactive and systematic approach to (1) predicting problems, (2) anticipating threats, (3) minimizing surprises, (4) resolving issues, and (5) preventing crises. Martha Lauzen, a professor at San Diego State University, says that effective issues management requires two-way communications, formal environmental scanning, and active sense-making strategies.

Another definition of issues management has been formulated by Joseph Coates, and his collegues in their book *Issues Management: How You Can Plan, Organize, and Manage for the Future*. They say, "Issues management is the organized activity of identifying emerging trends, concerns, or issues likely to affect an organization in the next few years and developing a wider and more positive range of organizational responses toward the future."

The basic idea behind issues management is proactive planning. Writing in *Public Relations Review* Philip Gaunt and Jeff Ollenburger say, "Issues management is proactive in that it tries to identify issues and influence decisions regarding them before they have a detrimental effect on a corporation." Issues management involves assessment of an issue to determine its importance to an organization.

Gaunt and Ollenburger contrast the issues management approach with crisis management, which is essentially reactive in nature. They note, "Crisis management tends to be more reactive, dealing with an issue after it becomes public knowledge and affects the company." In other words, active planning and prevention through issues management can often mean the difference between a noncrisis and a crisis, or, as one practitioner put it, the difference between little or no news coverage and a front page headline. This point is particularly relevant because studies have shown that the majority of organizational crises are self-inflicted, in that management ignored early warning signs. The issue of the exploitation of women and children in Third World factories by American companies, for example, simmered for several years before it finally broke into the headlines after a worker activist group publicly accused Nike of using "sweatshop" labor to make its expensive and profitable athletic shoes and apparel.

Such revelations put the entire U.S. garment industry on the defensive. David Birenbaum, a consultant to the garment industry, wrote in the *Wall Street Journal* that the issue of using cheap Third World labor was not really new, but the public reaction to such practices was different. He wrote in an op-ed article, "What's changed is that for the first time human rights concerns could become a major marketing issue. . . . More and more importers are now considering safety and other conditions in Asian factories. Few can afford not to, because all it takes is one disaster to damage a label's reputation." All of the publicity and public outrage, however, might have been avoided if the various clothing and athletic shoe manufacturers had paid attention to the concept of issues management.

Public relations counselors W. Howard Chase and Barrie L. Jones were among the first practitioners to specialize in issues management. They defined the process as consisting of five basic steps: (1) issue identification, (2) issue analysis, (3) strategy options, (4) an action plan, and (5) the evaluation of results. The following is an illustration of how these steps could have been implemented by the garment industry.

Issue Identification.
Organizations should track the alternative press, mainstream media, online chat groups, and the newsletters of activist groups to learn what issues and concerns are being discussed. Of particular importance is establishing a trend line of coverage. Concern about the working conditions of women and children in the garment industry began showing up as an emerging issue several years before it became a major public issue.

Issue Analysis.
Once an emerging issue has been identified, the next step is to assess its potential impact on and threat to the organization. Another consideration is to determine whether the organization is vulnerable on the issue. Are its policies exploitative? Is the company being ethical and socially responsible by turning a blind eye to violations of human rights in the interest of high profit margins? Can revelations about sweatshop conditions affect sales or damage a label's reputation?

Strategy Options.
If the company decides that the emerging issue is potentially damaging, the next step is to consider what to do about it. One option might be to set higher standards for foreign contractors seeking the company's business. Another option: Work with human rights groups to monitor possible violations in foreign factories that produce the company's products. A third option might be to establish a new policy that would ensure that Third World workers receive decent pay and health benefits. The pros and cons of each option are weighed against what is most practical and economical for the company.

Action Plan.
Once a specific policy (stance) has been decided on, the fourth step is to communicate it to all interested publics. In the garment industry example, such publics could include consumers, the U.S. Department of Labor, labor unions and worker activist groups, company employees, and the financial community. This step could involve using the new policy as a marketing tool among consumers who make buying decisions based on a company's level of social responsibility.

Evaluation.
With the new policy in place and communicated, the final step is to evaluate the results. Has news coverage been positive? Have activist groups called off product boycotts? Have the working conditions for women and children in the factories improved? Is the company being positioned as an industry leader? Have public perceptions of the company and the industry improved? If the company has acted soon enough, perhaps the greatest measurement of success is avoiding the media coverage that occurs when a problem becomes a crisis.

Issues and situations can be managed or even forestalled by public relations professionals before they become crises, or before their conflictual nature leads to significant losses for the organization, such as a diminished reputation, alienation of key stakeholders, and financial damage to the organization.

Strategic Positioning and Risk Communication

Following upon issues management is strategic positioning Any verbal or written exchange that attempts to communicate information that positions the organization favorably regarding competition or an anticipated conflict is called strategic positioning. Ideally, the public relations professional communicates in a way that not only positions the organization favorably in the face of competition and imminent conflict but also favorably influences the actual behavior of the organization. For example, facing enormous financial losses and the need to lay off thousands of employees, General Motors announced that it was freezing executive salaries. Doing so reduced the level of criticism of employee layoffs that followed.

Often, public relations professionals can engage in communication that reduce risks for affected publics and for their employers. Communicating risks to public health and safety and the environment is a particularly important role for public relations professionals. (See Chapter 13 for more on health communication as an important risk communication field in public relations.) Such risks may occur naturally, such as beach undertows and riptides that require warning signs and flyers in hotel rooms. Or, the risk may be associated with a product, such as an air bag or a lawn mower.

Organizations, including large corporations, increasingly engage in risk communication to inform the public of risks, such as those associated with food products, chemical spills, radioactive waste disposal, or the placement of drug abuse treatment centers or halfway houses in neighborhoods. These issues deserve public notice in fairness to the general populace. In addition, expensive lawsuits, restrictive legislation, consumer boycotts, and public debate may also result if organizations fail to disclose potential hazards. As is often the case, doing the right thing in conflict management is also the least disruptive in the long run.

An example of somewhat unsuccessful risk communication was the 2003 "mad cow scare" in Canada. Despite assurances by Canadian health officials and the beef industry that the fatal disease posed an "extremely small" risk to consumers, many countries stopped buying Canadian beef, severely damaging the Canadian cattle industry and driving up beef prices worldwide. In contrast, Jeff Zucker of Burson-Marsteller points out that U.S. cattlemen have worked for years to get the message out that U.S. beef is the safest in the world. Thus, the discovery of a possibly infected cow in Washington State did not result in dire consequences for U.S. producers. Effective risk communication can minimize adverse effects on publics, and it can also reduce risks to the organization itself such as lawsuits, of damaged employee morale, and diminished reputation. When risk communication fails, however, an organization often faces a crisis.

Variables Affecting Risk Perceptions.

Risk communication researchers have identified several variables that affect public perceptions:

> Risks voluntarily taken tend to be accepted. Smokers have more control over their health situation, for example, than airline passengers do over their safety.

> The more complex a situation, the higher the perception of risk. Dangers associated with disposal of radioactive waste is more difficult to understand than the dangers of cigarette smoking.

> Familiarity breeds confidence. If the public understands a problem and its factors, it perceives less risk.

> Perception of risk increases when the messages of experts conflict.

> The severity of consequences affects risk perceptions. There is a difference between having a stomachache and getting cancer.

Suzanne Zoda, writing on risk communication in *Communication World*, gives the following suggestions to communicators:

> Begin early and initiate a dialogue with publics that might be affected. Do not wait until the opposition marshals its forces. Early contact with anyone who may be concerned or affected is vital to establishing trust.

> Actively solicit and identify people's concerns. Informal discussions, surveys, interviews, and focus groups are effective in evaluating issues and identifying outrage factors.

> Recognize the public as a legitimate partner in the process. Engage interested groups in two-way communication and involve key opinion leaders.

> Address issues of concern, even if they do not directly pertain to the situation.

> Anticipate and prepare for hostility. To defuse a situation, use a conflict resolution approach. Identify areas of agreement and work toward common ground.

> Understand the needs of the news media. Provide accurate, timely information and respond promptly to requests.

> Always be honest, even when it hurts.

Crisis Management

In public relations, high-profile events such as accidents, terrorist attacks, disease pandemics, and natural disasters can dwarf even the best strategic positioning and risk management strategies. This is when crisis management takes over. The conflict management process, which includes ongoing issues management and risk communication efforts, is severely tested during crisis situations in which a high degree of uncertainty exists. Unfortunately, even the most thoughtfully designed conflict management process cannot prepare an organization to deal with certain crises, such as planes flying into the World Trade Center. And sometimes, in spite of risk communication to prevent an issue from becoming a major problem, that issue will grow into a crisis right before a professional's eyes. At such times, verifiable information about what is happening or has happened may be lacking.

Uncertainty causes people to become more active seekers of information and, as research suggests, more dependent on the media for information to satisfy the human desire for closure. A crisis situation, in other words, puts a great deal of pressure on organizations to respond with complete and accurate information as quickly as possible. How an organization responds in the first 24 hours, experts say, often determines whether the situation remains an "incident" or becomes a full-blown crisis.

What Is a Crisis? Kathleen Fearn-Banks, in her book *Crisis Communications: A Casebook Approach*, defines a crisis as a "major occurrence with a potentially negative outcome affecting the organization, company, or industry, as well as its publics, products, services, or good name." In other words, an organizational crisis can constitute any number of situations. A *PRWeek* article includes "a product recall; a plane crash; a very public sexual harassment suit; a gunman holding hostages in your office; an E. coli bacteria contamination scare; a market crash, along with the worth of your company stock; a labor union strike; [and] a hospital malpractice suit" in a list of crisis scenarios.

Nor are crises always unexpected. One study by the Institute for Crisis Management found that only 14 percent of business crises were unexpected. The remaining 86 percent were what the institute called "smoldering crises," in which an organization was aware of a potential business disruption long before the public found out about it. The study also found that management—or in some cases, mismanagement—caused 78 percent of the crises.

"Most organizations have a crisis plan to deal with sudden crises, like accidents," says Robert B. Irvine, president of the institute, "However, our data indicates many businesses are denying or ducking serious problems that eventually will ignite and cost them millions of dollars and lost management time." With proper issues management and conflict planning, perhaps many smoldering crises could be prevented from bursting into flames.

A Lack of Crisis Planning. Echoing Irvine's thought, another study by Steven Fink found that 89 percent of the chief executive officers of Fortune 500 companies reported that a business crisis was almost inevitable; however, 50 percent admitted that they did not have a crisis management plan. This situation has prompted crisis consultant Kenneth Myers to write, "If economics is the dismal science, then contingency planning is the abysmal science." As academics Donald Chisholm and Martin Landry have noted, "When people believe that because nothing has gone wrong, nothing will go wrong, they court disaster. There is noise in every system and every design. If this fact is ignored, nature soon reminds us of our folly."

Many smoldering crises could be prevented if professionals had used more environmental scanning and issues management, leading to the development of a strategic management plan. Instead, issues are left to fester and ultimately ignite in national headlines. This nearsighted performance can be reduced by public relations professors adopting the conflict life cycle in training the next generation of students. Professionals who are keenly aware of the progression that an issue can take will do a better job of forestalling catastrophe for their organization.

How to Communicate During a Crisis.

Many professionals offer advice on what to do during a crisis. Here's a compilation of good suggestions:

> Put the public first.
> Take responsibility. An organization should take responsibility for solving the problem.
> Be honest. Don't obscure facts and try to mislead the public.
> Never say, "No comment." A Porter Novelli survey found that nearly two-thirds of the public feel that "no comment" almost always means that the organization is guilty of wrongdoing.
> Designate a single spokesperson.
> Set up a central information center.
> Provide a constant flow of information. When information is withheld, the cover-up becomes the story.
> Be familiar with media needs and deadlines.

> Be accessible.
> Monitor news coverage and telephone inquiries.
> Communicate with key publics.

How Various Organizations Respond to Crises.

The list just presented offers sound, practical advice, but recent research has shown that organizations don't all respond to crises in the same way. Indeed, W. Timothy Coombs postulates that an organization's response may vary on a continuum from defensive to accommodative. Here is a list of crisis communication strategies that an organization may use:

> *Attack the Accuser*—The party that claims a crisis exists is confronted and its logic and facts are faulted; sometimes the organization threatens a lawsuit.
> *Denial*—The organization explains that there is no crisis.
> *Excuse*—The organization minimizes its responsibility for the crisis by denying any intention to do harm and saying that it had no control over the events that led to the crisis. This strategy is often used when there is a natural disaster or product tampering.
> *Justification*—The crisis is minimized with a statement that no serious damage or injuries resulted. Sometimes, the blame is shifted to the victims, as was the case in the Firestone recall. This is often done when a consumer misuses a product or when there is an industrial accident.
> *Ingratiation*—The organization acts to appease the publics involved. Consumers who complain are given coupons or the organization makes a donation to a charitable organization. Burlington Industries, for example, gave a large donation to the Humane Society after the discovery that it had imported coats from China with fur collars containing dog fur instead of "coyote" fur.
> *Corrective Action*—The organization takes steps to repair the damage from the crisis and to prevent it from happening again.
> *Full Apology*—The organization takes responsibility and asks forgiveness. Some compensation of money or aid is often included.

The Coombs typology gives options for crisis communication management depending on the situation and the stance taken by the organization. He notes that organizations do have to consider more accommodative strategies (ingratiation, corrective action, full apology) if defensive strategies (attack accuser, denial, excuse) are not effective. The more accomodative strategies not only meet immediate crisis communication demands but also can help to subsequently repair an organization's reputation and or restore previous sales levels. He says, "Accommodative strategies emphasize image repair, which is what is needed as image damage worsens. Defensive strategies, such as denial or minimizing, logically become less effective as organizations are viewed as more responsible for the crisis."

Often, however, an organization doesn't adopt an accommodative strategy because of corporate culture and other constraints included in the contingency theory of conflict management matrix. Organizations do not, and sometimes cannot, engage in two-way communication and accommodative strategies when confronted with a crisis or conflict with a given public. Six variables proscribing accommodation, according to Cameron, include: (1) management's moral conviction that the public is wrong; (2) moral neutrality when two contending publics want the organization to take sides on a policy issue; (3) legal constraints; (4) regulatory constraints such as the Federal Trade Commission or the Securities and Exchange Commission; (5) prohibition by senior management against an accommodative stance; and (6) possible conflict between departments of the organization over what strategies to adopt.

In some cases, the contingency theory contends that the ideal of mutual understanding and accommodation doesn't occur because both sides have staked out highly rigid positions and are not willing to compromise their strong moral positions. For example, it is unlikely that the pro-life and pro-choice forces will ever achieve mutual understanding and accommodation. Taking an inflexible stance, however, can be a foolish strategy and a sign of unprofessionalism. At other times, conflict is a natural state between competing interests, such as oil interests seeking to open Alaskan wildlife refuges to oil exploration and environmental groups seeking to block that exploration. Frequently, one's stance and strategies for conflict management entail assessment and balancing of many factors.

How Some Organizations Have Handled Crises.

The crisis communication strategies outlined by Coombs are useful in evaluating how an organization handles a crisis. Intel, for example, first denied in 1994 that there was a problem with its new Pentium chip. As the crisis deepened and was covered in the mainstream press, Intel tried the strategy of justification by saying that the problem wasn't serious enough to warrant replacing the chips. It minimized the concerns of end users such as engineers and computer programmers. Only after considerable damage had been done to Intel's reputation and IBM had suspended orders for the chip did Intel take corrective action to replace the chips, and Andy Grove, Intel's president, issue a full apology.

Exxon is still highly identified with the major oil spill that occurred in Prince William Sound, Alaska, in 1989. The company chose a defensive strategy when one of its ships, the *Exxon Valdez*, hit a reef in 1989 and spilled nearly 240,000 barrels of oil into a pristine environment. The disaster, one of history's worst environmental accidents, was badly mismanaged from the beginning.

Exxon management started its crisis communication strategy by making excuses. Management claimed that Exxon, as a corporation, wasn't at fault because (1) the weather wasn't ideal, (2) the charts provided by the U.S. Coast Guard were out-of-date, and (3) the captain of the ship was derelict in his duties by drinking while on duty. As cleanup efforts began, Exxon also tried to shift the blame by maintaining that government bureaucracy and prohibitions against the use of certain chemicals hampered the company's efforts.

Exxon also used the strategy of justification to minimize the damage, saying that environmentalists in the government were exaggerating the ill effects of the spill on bird and animal life. Meanwhile, negative press coverage was intense, and public outrage continued to rise. William J. Small of Fordham University, who researched the press coverage, wrote, "Probably no other company ever got a more damaging portrayal in the mass media." More than 18,000 customers tore up their Exxon credit cards, late-night talk show hosts ridiculed the company, and congressional committees started hearings. Exxon dropped from 8th to 110th on Fortune's list of most-admired companies.

Exxon's response to all of these developments was somewhat ineffective. It did try the strategy of ingratiation by running full-page advertisements stating that the company was sorry for the oil spill—but did not take responsibility for it. Instead of calming the storm, that approach only further enraged the public. Exxon also took corrective action and cleaned up the oil spill, spending about $3 billion on its efforts. The company received little credit for this action, however, because most of the public believed it was done only under government pressure. And by the time the cleanup was finished, public attitudes about Exxon had already been formed.

It is important to note, however, that not all successful crisis communication strategies need to be accommodative. Pepsi-Cola was able to mount an effective defensive crisis communication strategy and avoid a recall when a hoax of nationwide proportions created an intense but short-lived crisis for the soft-drink company.

The crisis began when the media reported that a man in Tacoma, Washington, claimed that he had found a syringe inside a can of Diet Pepsi. As the news spread, men and women across the country made similar claims of finding a broken sewing needle, a screw, a bullet, and even a narcotics vial in their Pepsi cans. As a consequence, demands for a recall of all Pepsi products arose, an action that would have had major economic consequences for the company.

Company officials were confident that insertion of foreign objects into cans on high-speed, closely controlled bottling lines was virtually impossible, so they chose to defend their product. The urgent problem, then, was to convince the public that the product was safe, and that any foreign objects found had been inserted after the cans had been opened.

Pepsi officials and their public relations staff employed several strategies. One approach was to attack the accuser. Company officials said the foreign objects probably got into the cans after they were opened, and even explained that many people make such claims just to collect compensation from the company. The company also announced that it would pursue legal action against anyone making false claims about the integrity of the company's products.

Pepsi also adopted the strategy of denial, saying that there was no crisis. Pepsi president Craig E. Weatherup immediately made appearances on national television programs and gave newspaper interviews to state the company's case that its bottling lines were secure. Helping to convince the public was U.S. Food and Drug Administration Commissioner David Kessler, who said that a recall was not necessary.

These quick actions deflated the public's concern, and polls showed considerable acceptance of Pepsi's contention that the problem was a hoax. A week after the scare began, Pepsi ran full-page advertisements with the headline, "Pepsi is pleased to announce. . . Nothing." It stated, "As America now knows, those stories about Diet Pepsi were a hoax. . . ."

These varied cases illustrate one emphasis of contingency theory: No single crisis communication strategy is appropriate for all situations. Therefore, as Coombs indicates, "It is only by understanding the crisis situation that the crisis manager can select the appropriate response for the crisis."

The PR Casebook for this chapter discusses how two corporations faced a major public relations crisis in 2000.

Reputation Management

Reputation is defined as the collective representation of an organization's past performance that describes the firm's ability to deliver valued outcomes to multiple stakeholders. Put in plain terms, reputation is the track record of an organization in the public's mind.

Public relations scholar Lisa Lyon makes the point that reputation, unlike corporate image, is owned by the public. Reputation isn't formed by packaging or slogans. A good reputation is created and destroyed by everything an organization does, from the way it manages employees to the way it handles conflicts with outside constituents.

The Three Foundations of Reputation. Reputation scholars offer three foundations of reputation: (1) economic performance, (2) social responsiveness, and (3) the ability to deliver valuable outcomes to stakeholders. Public relations plays a role

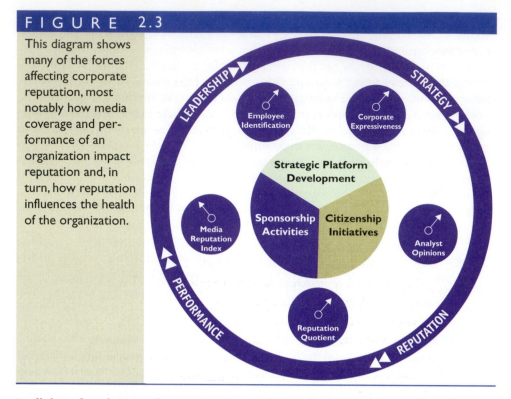

FIGURE 2.3

This diagram shows many of the forces affecting corporate reputation, most notably how media coverage and performance of an organization impact reputation and, in turn, how reputation influences the health of the organization.

in all three foundations of reputation, but professionals who manage conflict effectively will especially enhance the latter two. The social responsiveness of an organization results from careful issue tracking and effective positioning of the organization. It is further enhanced when risk communication is compelling and persuasive. The ability to make valuable contributions to stakeholders who depend on the organization results in part from fending off threats to the organization that would impair its mission.

Research techniques called *reputation audits* can be used to assess and monitor an organization's reputation. These can be as basic as *Fortune* magazine's list of "Most Admired Companies" (www.cnn.com/magazines/fortune/mostadmired/2007/index.html) to rigorous global reputation measures, such as the Reputation Quotient offered by the Reputation Institute (www.reputationinstitute.com) in conjunction with Harris Interactive. Of particular interest to public relations professionals is the Media Reputation Index (MRi), which measures the effects of media coverage on corporate reputations. Working with Delahaye Medialink, the project documents the important role of media in reputation management. This relationship is depicted in Figure 2.3.

In addition to tracking and dealing proactively with issues, conveying risks to publics, and managing crises as they arise, public relations practitioners also will be faced with the need to apologize at those times when all efforts to manage conflict have fallen short. The future trust and credibility of the organization are at stake in how well this recovery phase of conflict management is handled.

The frequent platitude in postcrisis communication is that practitioners should acknowledge failings, apologize, and then put the events in the past as quickly as possible. However, Lyon has found that apology is not always effective because of the hypocrisy factor. When an organization has a questionable track record (i.e., a bad reputation), the apology may be viewed as insincere and hypocritical. Coombs suggests a relational approach, which assumes that crises are episodes within a larger stakeholder–organizational relationship. Applying the contingency theory, considering how stakeholders perceive the situation can help communicators determine which strategy is best to rebuild the stakeholder–organization relationship and restore the organization's reputation.

Image Restoration. Reputation repair and maintenance is a long-term process, but one of the first steps in the process is the final one in the conflict management life cycle discussed earlier in this chapter. Professor William Benoit of the University of Missouri offers five general strategies for image restoration and a number of sub-strategies, adding to the options available to the public relations professional that can be used when the worst of a crisis has passed:

1. Denial
   > *Simple Denial*—Your organization did not do what it is accused of.
   > *Shift the Blame*—Someone else did it.
2. Evade Responsibility
   > *Provocation*—Your organization was provoked.
   > *Defeasibility*—Your organization was unable to avoid its actions.
   > *Accident*—The bad events were an accident.
   > *Good intentions*—Good intentions went awry.
3. Reduce Offensiveness
   > *Bolstering*—Refer to the organization's clean record and good reputation.
   > *Minimization*—Reduce the magnitude of negative feelings.
   > *Differentiation*—Distinguish the act from other similar, but more offensive, acts
   > *Transcendence*—Justify the act by placing it in a more favorable context.
   > *Attack the Accuser*—Reduce the credibility of the accusations.
   > *Compensation*—Reduce the perceived severity of the injury.
4. Corrective Action—Ensure the prevention or correction of the action.
5. Mortification—Offer a profuse apology.

Benoit's typology for image restoration is somewhat similar to the Coombs list on page 51 about how organizations should respond to a crisis. Both scholars outline a response continuum from defensive (denial and evasion) to accommodative (corrective action and apology).

The image restoration strategy that an organization chooses depends a great deal on the situation, or what has already been described as the "it depends" concept. If an organization is truly innocent, a simple denial is a good strategy. However, not many situations are that clean-cut. Consequently, a more common strategy is acknowledging the issue, but making it clear that the situation was an accident or the result of a decision with unintentional consequences. Benoit calls this the strategy of "evading" responsibility.

Another way of restoring an organization's reputation is reducing offensiveness. Benoit lists six response strategies – all the way from "bolstering" by telling the public about the organization's good record to "compensation" for the victims. Ultimately, the most accommodative response is a profuse apology by the organization to the public and its various stakeholders.

The Benoit and Coombs continuums give a tool chest of possible strategies for dealing with a crisis or beginning image restoration, but it should be noted that a strategy or combination of strategies may not necessarily restore reputation. A great deal depends on the perceptions of the public and other stakeholders. Do they find the explanation credible? Do they believe the organization is telling the truth? Do they

ON THE JOB >>

Managing Reputation Through Crises: A Tale of Two Crashes

Global

How does an organization, with an excellent record of global service and safety, but beset by two high-profile crises, rebuild its image and bounce back into public acceptance, approval, and favor?

The organization in question was Singapore Airlines, one of the top airlines in the world and what *Fortune* magazine described as Asia's most admired organization. Singapore Airlines' unblemished 27-year track record was shattered one afternoon on December 19, 1997, when a Boeing 737 jet belonging to its subsidiary, SilkAir, mysteriously crashed in Palembang, Indonesia. All 104 passengers and crew on MI 185 perished. While the cause of the crash remains unsolved, what became evident was the airline's apparent busi-

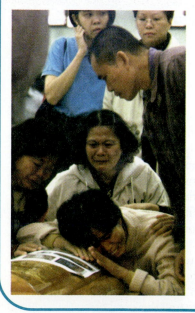

Relatives grieve over the loss of loved ones after the crash of a Singapore Airlines jet in Taipei.

nesslike and emotionally cold crisis communication efforts to its different publics, particularly the families of the deceased. A negative impression was conveyed to anyone with an interest in the first-ever disaster involving a Singapore aircraft. The accusations included:

> The airline's less accommodative stance in addressing speculations involving the cause of the crash
> The possibility of pilot suicide
> Its legalistic approach to awarding compensation to families
> Its failure to keep the families informed of the progress of the investigations

Though Singapore Airlines became increasingly more generous in meeting the practical needs of the families, in trying to repair its image by being more accommodative through corrective action to revise compensation figures, and in releasing up-to-date investigation findings, the damage had already been done.

By a cruel twist of fate, even before the airline could recover fully from this tragedy, a second disaster followed. On October 30, 2000, at Chiang Kai-shek International Airport in Taipei, Taiwan, one of its Boeing 747 aircraft crashed into a crane on the runway, killing 83 passengers and crew. The plane was later found to have taxied into a closed runway. Consequently, the airline's solid reputation, riddled by another round of negative publicity, sufered another crushing blow.

This time, however, the airline rose to the occasion.

More than just providing generously for the families and catering to their varied needs, when evidence showed that the plane had, indeed, taxied onto the wrong runway, the CEO immediately took responsibility. The airline did not attempt to deny or shift blame to Taiwanese authorities even though questions were being asked about the responsibility of the air traffic controllers in guiding the plane to the wrong runway. Instead, it promised corrective action that such accidents did not happen again. When an enraged relative barged into the middle of a televised press conference demanding answers, the Company's vice president for public affairs, who was chairing the conference, allowed him to vent his frustrations instead of asking the guards to remove him. After the emotionally exhausted man had calmed down, the PR chief went up to him, gave him a hug, and said, "I'm very sorry."

The decisiveness, compassion, and expeditiousness with which the second crisis was handled attracted widespread accolades. The Geneva-based International Air Transport Association (IATA) lauded the airlines' management of the crisis as "nothing short of outstanding." Members of the public wrote to the press singing its praises, particularly the humility and humanity its CEO and public affairs chief displayed. At least three newspaper editorials lauded the airline's crisis communications. In a commentary, *China Press* hailed Singapore Airlines' efforts as "very important and yet quite rare for an airline to display this quality."

Source: Augustine Pang, Doctoral Dissertation, University of Missouri, 2006.

think the organization is acting in the public interest? In many cases, an organization may start out with a defensive strategy only to find that the situation ultimately demands corrective action or an apology in order to restore its reputation.

Déjà Vu—All Over Again

Empirical evidence from Benoit's work is ongoing, but it appears that image restoration can be an effective final stage in the conflict management process. But, to paraphrase Yogi Berra, conflict management is like déjà vu all over again. The best organizations, led by the best public relations professionals, will strive to improve performance by starting once again along the left side of the conflict management life cycle (Figure 2.2) with tasks such as environmental scanning and issues tracking. Issues that are deemed important receive attention for crisis planning and risk communication. When preventive measures fail, the crisis must be handled with the best interests of all parties held in a delicate balance. Then reputation must be given due attention. At all times, the goal is to change organizational behavior in ways that minimize damaging conflict, not only for the sake of the organization, but also for its many stakeholders.

PRCASEBOOK

Firestone versus Ford: An Epic Public Relations Battle

The reputation and credibility of a major corporation can be seriously damaged if it doesn't take the proper corrective action and public relations steps to solve a conflict with its customers, the public and even government regulators. Firestone/Bridgestone and Ford Motor Company learned this lesson the hard way.

Firestone had to recall 6.5 million of its tires after the National Highway Traffic Safety Administration (NHTSA) began investigating reports that 46 deaths and more than 300 accidents were linked to its tires. Later, it was determined that the number of deaths was actually 148, with an additional 525 individuals injured. Of the tires recalled, more than 60 percent were used on Ford vehicles, primarily the Explorer.

Firestone's announcement followed basic public relations concepts. The company said that it was working closely with regulatory agencies, apologized for the lack of information in previous weeks before the recall, and made assurances that "nothing is more important to us than the safety of our customers." Ford, in the meantime, announced a separate public relations and advertising campaign notifying customers about possible tire problems with the Ford Explorer, but assuring them that the vehicles were completely safe.

Critics, including congressional investigators, challenged both Firestone's and Ford's assertions that they were doing everything possible to ensure the safety of their customers. Ford, for example, continued to use Firestone tires on their vehicles, even though evidence suggested that Ford knew the tires were subject to blowouts on vehicles that already had a reputation for instability and rolling over.

Firestone was also criticized for the way it handled the public relations element of the recall. Paul Hicks, head of corporate practice at Ogilvy Public Relations, said, "I have yet to see a senior officer from the parent company quoted in any fashion. It's a grievous error in strategy that will cost them millions, if not hundreds of millions in the long run."

In addition, Firestone committed another public relations blunder before the voluntary recall because it tried to blame the consumer. Company spokespersons said the tires shredded or peeled because consumers didn't maintain proper inflation and drove on poor roads. As Paul Holmes of *Inside PR* pointed out, "By blaming the consumers, the company appeared to be shirking its own responsibility for the problem."

Although Firestone seemed to come across as highly defensive, Ford decided on a more proactive public relations strategy. In addition to using Ford's CEO as a major spokesperson on the crisis, about 30 members of the company's internal public relations staff worked on the automaker's crisis team. Ford PR chief Jason Vines was widely quoted, and Ford

(continued)

announced that new purchasers of Ford Explorers could choose any brand of tire they wanted.

The stakes for both Firestone and Ford were extremely high. Both companies saw a decline in sales of its products, and stock prices plunged as a result of both companies spending almost $1.3 billion on the recall. Bridgestone shareholders saw two-thirds of their stock value vanish practically overnight, whereas Ford experienced a $4 billion loss in shareholder value. Both companies were highly vulnerable to multiple lawsuits, requiring assertive litigation public relations. It was important to wage defense in the court of public opinion, which did have some impact on the number of lawsuits filed and the predisposition of juries to award large damages.

Ford's public relations strategy was relatively simple with a stance definitely based in advocacy rather than accommodation. The company understood that it was necessary to allay customer's concerns as well as those of congressional investigators, so the legal department's intent to paint Firestone as the responsible party was highly supported. Firestone took major exception to Ford projecting itself as the "good guy." The stage was set for an epic public relations battle for the hearts and minds of the American consumer.

Firestone used reports, surveys, and statistics to make the case that Ford had known for several years that the Explorer was unstable and subject to rollover in the case of a tire blowout, failing to recognize the issue and to minimize risk to customers. Ford countered by trotting out internal memos from Firestone about the failure rate of its tires and noting that the company had opposed Ford's recall of Explorers with Firestone tires in other nations. Firestone raised the ante by announcing at a news conference that it would no longer do business with the automaker.

Ford then announced that it would spend about $3 billion of its own money to replace Firestone tires on its Explorer model. It again blamed Firestone for any problems, but it had its own public relations problems in trying to explain new design changes in the Explorer without admitting that the older models were unsafe.

Public relations experts thought the "finger-pointing" and the "blame game" were not effective strategies for either company. Unfortunately, adversarial stances predictably escalate conflict, often hardening the position of each side. One public relations veteran said, "This is a no-win for both sides. The more they fight, the more uncertain the public becomes." Indeed, one opinion poll indicated that Firestone had made some headway in eroding consumer confidence in Ford, but its own corporate reputation and consumer confidence continued to be at an all-time low.

Both Firestone and Ford, several years after the tire recall, have yet to regain the level of consumer confidence they had before what one newspaper called "one of the biggest and deadliest auto safety problems in U.S. history."

The expression of public opinion affects the corporate reputation of a company. Here a woman lets everyone know that she is unhappy with the Firestone tires on her vehicle after it was announced that the tires had a high rate of failure on Ford Explorers.

Summary

A New Way of Thinking

By defining public relations as strategic management of competition and conflict, a fresh and vigorous approach to public relations is envisioned. Public relations is positioned to earn influence within organizations by focusing on achieving objectives.

Contingency Theory of Conflict Management

Some of the most crucial roles played by public relations professionals involve the strategic management of conflict. The contingency theory argues for a dynamic and multifaceted approach to dealing with conflict in the field.

Life Cycle of Conflict Management

Strategic conflict management can be broadly divided into four phases with specific techniques and functions falling into each phase. The life cycle emphasizes that conflict management is ongoing and cyclical in nature.

Issues Management

Issues management is a proactive and systematic approach to predicting problems, anticipating threats, minimizing surprises, resolving issues, and preventing crises. The five steps in the issues management process are issue identification, issue analysis, strategy options, an action plan, and the evaluation of results.

Risk Communication

Risk communication attempts to convey information regarding risks to public health and safety and the environment. It involves more than the dissemination of accurate information. The communicator must begin early, identify and address the public's concerns, recognize the public as a legitimate partner, anticipate hostility, respond to the needs of the news media, and always be honest.

Crisis Communication

The communications process is severely tested in crisis situations, which can take many forms. A common problem is the lack of crisis management plans even when a smoldering crisis is building. Organizations' responses vary from defensive to accommodative. Corporate culture and other constraints prevent adoption of an appropriate strategy.

Reputation Management

One of an organization's most valuable assets is its reputation. This asset is impacted by how the organization deals with conflict, particularly those crises that generate significant media attention. Using research to monitor reputation and making realistic responses after crises have passed can minimize damage to an organization's reputation. More importantly, returning to the proactive phase of conflict management to improve organizational performance will ultimately improve reputation.

CASE ACTIVITY >>

What Would You Do?

Managing Conflict

Many businesses never recovered from the wrath of Hurricane Katrina, but Oreck Corporation was an exception. It gained the gratitude of its employees and townspeople in Long Beach, Mississippi, by reopening its storm-damaged plant 10 days after the storm. Sixteen months later, however, the manufacturer of vacuum cleaners stunned the community and state officials by announcing that it was closing the plant and moving its operations to Tennessee.

In making the announcement, company executives said they could no longer get enough insurance to cover the plant and could not hire enough skilled workers to replace those who never returned after the storm, primarily because they had nowhere to live. The decision was criticized by the local newspaper and government officials, including Senator Trent Lott, also blasted the company for abandoning the city. In addition, the employees expressed anger at the company and expressed concern about finding new employment. Obviously, the affected publics want Oreck to reconsider its decision.

The decision to relocate has definitely created a conflict situation for the company and its public relations department. The company, at present, is taking a stance of advocacy (see the contingency continuum on page 41). As you review the continuum, how would you evaluate the company's stance? Should the company move to a more accommodative stance or not? From the standpoint of reputation management (see the conflict management life cycle on page 43), is there anything the company could do to restore its image or appease the affected publics?

Questions for Review and Discussion

1. Do you accept the proposition that conflict management is one of the most important functions of public relations? Why or why not?
2. What are the five steps in the issues management process?
3. How can effective issues management prevent organizational crises?
4. Do you think Wal-Mart's offer of $4 generic drugs was an effective conflict positioning strategy? Why or why not? In general, do you think these "olive branches" have any real impact in the "court of public opinion."
5. Both Exxon and Pepsi used defensive crisis communication strategies. However, one succeeded and the other failed. What factors do you think made the difference?
6. What is risk communication?
7. How would you use the contingency theory of conflict management (the continuum from accommodation to advocacy) in advising management on a rising conflict situation?
8. Do you think that image restoration is merely a superficial fix or a substantive solution to adverse events? Support your view with some examples from current news stories.
9. Why would lawyers benefit from working closely with public relations counsel? For litigation? For dispute resolution through effective negotiation?
10. Do you think it is ethical for legal counsel to be assisted by public relations expertise?

Suggested Readings

Cancel, Amanda E., Glen T. Cameron, Lynne M. Sallot, and Michael Mitrook. "It Depends: A Contingency Theory of Accommodation in Public Relations." *Journal of Public Relations Research* 9, no. 1 (1997): 31–64.

Christen, Cindy T. The Utility of Coorientational Variables as Predictors of Willingness to Negotiate. *Journalism and Mass Communication Quarterly* 82, no. 1 (Spring 2005): 7–24.

Frank, John N. "All Hands on Deck: When Crisis Hits, a Whole Host of People Are Needed to Pitch in and Help Out." *PRWeek*, February 16, 2004, 15.

Fombrun, Charles J., and Cees van Riel. *Fame and Fortune: How Successful Companies Build Winning Reputations.* Upper Saddle River, NJ: Financial Times Prentice Hall, 2003.

Hallahan, Kirk. "The Dynamics of Issues Activation and Response: An Issues Process Model." *Journal of Public Relations Research* 13, no. 1 (2001): 27–59.

Hazley, Greg. "Beef Industry Passes Its First Run-in with Mad Cow." *O'Dwyer's PR Services Report*, February 2004, 1, 15, 17.

Kersten, Astrid Sidky, Mohammed. Realigning Rationality: Crisis Management and Prisoner Abuses in Iraq. *Public Relations Review*, Vol. 31, 2005, pp. 471–478.

Lyon, Lisa, and Cameron, Glen T. "Fess Up or Stonewall? An Experimental Test of Prior Reputation and Response Style in the Face of Negative News Coverage." *Web Journal of Mass Communication Research* 1, no. 4 (September 1998): 1–24, www.scripps .ohiou.edu/wjmcr.

Martin, Ryan M., and Lois A. Boynton. "From Liftoff to Landing: NASA's Crisis Communications and Resulting Media Coverage Following the Challenger and Columbia Tragedies." *Public Relations Review* 31 (2005): 253–261.

McCauley, Kevin. "U.S. Needs to Adopt Private Sector PR Tactics for Diplomacy." *O'Dwyer's PRReport* 20, no. 6 (June 2006): 1, 15, 38.

McGuire, Craig. "Assembling a Crisis Management Toolkit." *PRWeek*, July 25, 2005, 18

O'Brien, Keith. "Nothing 'Neutral' about Internet Dispute." *PRWeek*, July 10, 2006, 6.

Pang, A., Y. Jin, & G. T. Cameron. Do We Stand on Common Ground? A Threat Appraisal Model for Terror Alerts Issued by the Department of Homeland Security. *Journal of Contingencies and Crisis Management* 14, no. 2 (2006): 82–96.

Reber, Bryan H, and Bruce K. Berger. "Finding Influence: Examining the Role of Influence in Public Relations Practice," *Journal of Communication Management* 10 no. 3 (2006): 235–249.

Chapter Three

Public Relations:
A Historical Perspective

A Brief History of Public Relations

The practice of public relations is not new. It has a long tradition. Even ancient practitioners used public relations tactics to manage conflict and sometimes to gain a competitive advantage over rival individuals or points of view.

Ancient Beginnings

Ancient civilizations used persuasion to promote the authority of governments and religions. Of course, these efforts were not known as "public relations," but the techniques would certainly be familiar to public relations practitioners today: interpersonal communication with opinion leaders, public speeches, written and visual communication, staged events, publicity, and other tactics. The roots of public relations reach back to the civilizations of Babylonia, Greece, and Rome.

It has often been said that the Rosetta Stone, which provided a key for modern understanding of ancient Egyptian hieroglyphics, was basically a publicity release touting the pharaoh's accomplishments. Similarly, the ancient Olympic Games used promotional techniques to enhance the perception of athletes as heroes in much the same way as today's Olympic Games. Not only do athletes compete on the field, they compete for the hearts and minds of sports fans through public relations tactics such as public appearances, media interviews, and the like. Even speech writing in Plato's time was similar to speech writing today. The speechwriter had to know the composition of the audience, never talk down to it, and impart credible and persuasive information.

Roman politician Julius Caesar had ambitions to become emperor of the Roman Empire. He organized elaborate parades whenever he returned from winning a battle to burnish his image as an outstanding commander and leader. After Caesar became a consul of Rome in 59 BCE, he had clerks make a record of senatorial and other public proceedings and post them on walls throughout the city. These *Acta diurna*, or "daily doings," were among the world's first newspapers.

Saint Paul, the New Testament's most prolific author, also qualifies as an early public relations practitioner. R. E. Brown of Salem State College says, "Historians of early Christianity actually regard Paul, author and organizer, rather than Jesus himself, as the founder of Christianity."

The concept of conflict, discussed in Chapter 2, is also not a new theme in the practice of public relations. Pope Urban II persuaded thousands of followers to serve God and gain forgiveness of their sins by engaging in the Holy Crusades against the Muslims. Six centuries later, the church was among the first to use the word *propaganda*, with the establishment by Pope Gregory XV of the College of Propaganda to supervise foreign missions and train priests to propagate the faith.

Meanwhile, Venetian bankers in the 15th and 16th centuries practiced the fine art of investor relations. They were probably the first, along with local Catholic bishops, to adopt the concept of corporate philanthropy by sponsoring such artists as Michelangelo.

Public Relations in Colonial America

The United States was first settled by immigrants, primarily those from England, and various Crown-sanctioned land companies. The Virginia Company in 1620, for example, distributed fliers and brochures throughout Europe offering 50 acres of free land to anyone willing to migrate. In 1584, Sir Walter Raleigh sent back to England glowing accounts of what was actually a swamp-filled Roanoke Island. Eric the Red did the same thing back in c. 985 CE when he discovered a land of ice and rock and named it Greenland. The Spanish explorers publicized the never-discovered Seven Cities of Gold and even the fabled Fountain of Youth to attract prospective adventurers and colonists.

During the American colonial period, publicity and public relations techniques were also used to promote institutions. In 1641, Harvard College published a fund-raising brochure. King's College (now Columbia University) issued its first news release in 1758, announcing its commencement exercises.

Public relations played an active role in building support for the conflict—now termed *conflict positioning* on the conflict management life cycle (pp. 43)—that led to American independence. The Boston Tea Party, which *PRWeek* has called the "the greatest and best-known publicity stunt of all time," was the inspiration of Samuel Adams, a man who understood that symbolism can sway public opinion, and that American colonists would have to advocate for only one acceptable solution—the rejection of British rule. The colonists threw crates of tea leaves from a British trade ship into Boston harbor to protest excessive British taxation, and the rest is history. Adams and his colleagues (known as the Sons of Liberty) also labeled the killing of several colonists by British troops at a demonstration as the "Boston Massacre," furthering the revolt fervor among colonists.

Thomas Paine's persuasive writing was also instrumental in bringing lukewarm citizens into the Revolutionary movement. His pamphlet titled "Common Sense" sold

The Rosetta Stone was found by Napoleon's army and dates to 196 BCE. It contains a decree acknowledging the first anniversary of the coronation of Ptolemy V.

more than 120,000 copies in three months. Influencing the makeup of the new political system were the *Federalist Papers*, which comprised 85 letters written by Alexander Hamilton, James Madison, and John Jay.

The Age of the Press Agent

The 1800s was a period of growth and expansion in the United States. It was an era when competition for consumers' attention and loyalty was growing. It also was the golden age of the press agent—a publicist who works for recognition of an organization or individual. The period was also the age of hype, which uses the media and various tactics to promote an individual, a cause, or even a product or service.

Press agents succeeded in glorifying Davy Crockett as a frontier hero to draw political support from Andrew Jackson and made a legend of frontiersman Daniel Boone. John Burke attracted thousands to the touring shows of Buffalo Bill and sharpshooter Annie Oakley. These old-time press agents and the people they represented played on the gullibility of the public in its longing to be entertained. Advertisements and press releases were exaggerated to the point of being outright lies. Doing advance work for an attraction, press agents dropped tickets on the desk of a newspaper editor, along with the announcements. Voluminous publicity generally followed, and the journalists and their families flocked to the free entertainment with little regard for the ethical considerations that largely prohibits such practices today.

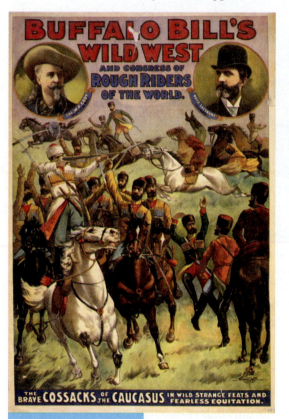

The 1800s was the golden age of the press agent. John Burke was the press agent that made Buffalo Bill's Wild West Show a household name throughout the United States. Buffalo Bill and Annie Oakley were the rock stars of their age.

It is no surprise, then, that today's public relations practitioner, exercising the highly sophisticated skills of evaluation, counseling, communications, and influencing management policies, shudders at the suggestion that public relations grew out of press agentry. And yet some aspects of modern public relations have their roots in the practice.

King of the Press Agents. Phineas T. Barnum, the great American showman of the 19th century, was the master of what historian Daniel Boorstin calls the *pseudoevent*—a planned happening that occurs primarily for the purpose of being reported. Barnum used flowery language and exaggeration to promote his various attractions in an age when the public was hungry for any form of entertainment.

Through Barnum's press agentry, Tom Thumb became one of the sensations of the century. He was a little person, standing just over two feet and weighing 15 pounds, but he was exceptional at singing, dancing, and performing comedy monologues. Barnum even made Thumb a European phenomenon by introducing him first to society leaders in London. An invitation to Buckingham Palace followed, and from then on Thumb played to packed houses every night. Barnum knew the value of opinion leaders and third-party endorsement.

Another Barnum success was the promotion of Jenny Lind, the "Swedish Nightingale." Barnum promoted her and her beautiful singing on a national tour, making her a pop icon even before the Civil War. Barnum filled auditoriums on opening nights by donating part of the proceeds to charity. As a civic activity, the event attracted many of the town's opinion leaders, whereupon the general public flocked to attend succeeding performances—a device still employed today by entertainment publicists.

Settling the American West

Just as they were used to bring colonists to 17th-century America, publicity and promotion were used in the 19th century to populate the western United States. Land speculators distributed pamphlets and publicity that described almost every community as "the garden spot of the West," which one critic of the time called "downright puffery, full of exaggerated statements, and high-wrought and false-colored descriptions." One brochure about Nebraska, for example, described the territory as the "Gulf stream of migration. . . bounded on the north by the 'Aurora Borealis' and on the south by the Day of Judgment." Other brochures were more down-to-earth, describing the fertile land and abundant water, and touting the opportunity to build a fortune.

American railroads, in particular, used extensive public relations and press agentry to attract settlers and expand operations. People and communities were necessary throughout the western United States to provide a business opportunity for rail companies. Consequently, such companies as the Burlington and Missouri Railroad took it upon themselves to promote western settlement from England and other places. The Burlington and Missouri Railroad set up an information office in Liverpool that distributed fact sheets and maps and placed stories in the local press. In addition, the railroad promoted lectures about migrating to the American West. According to Andy Piasecki, lecturer at Queen Margaret University College in Edinburgh, "The pièce de resistance for the Burlington was a kind of early road show. . . an elaborately illustrated lecture with 85 painted views, each covering 250 square feet."

P.T. Barnum, through savvy promotion and publicity, helped Tom Thumb become a major show business personality.

The railroad companies' publicity and promotion paid off. Piasecki wrote, "During the 1870s and the 1880s, the railroads attracted something like 4.5 million people to the Midwestern states, and they were responsible for the establishment there of almost 2 million farms. None of this could have been achieved without complex communication strategies closely linked to business objectives."

In addition, the railroads solicited the services of "independent" observers who wrote and spoke about the glories of the American West as the land of opportunity. Bernhard Warkentin was one such spokesperson. He "traveled widely with railroad officials," according to historian David A. Haury. Warkentin arrived from Russia in 1872 to survey the U.S. political and economic situation on behalf of the members of his Mennonite religious sect. His task was embraced by the rail companies and he was taken by train to several locales. He wrote home about what he saw. Haury notes: "Railroad representatives met the Mennonite delegates, financed tours, promised freedom of conscience, and offered land at bargain prices." Between 1874 and 1884, 15,000 Mennonites settled in the plains states.

Near the end of the 19th century, the Atchison, Topeka and Santa Fe Railway launched a campaign to lure tourists to the Southwest. It commissioned dozens of painters and photographers to depict the dramatic landscape and show romanticized American Indians weaving, grinding corn, and dancing.

The Rise of Politics and Activism

The 19th century also saw the development and use of public relations tactics on the political and activist front. Amos Kendall, a former Kentucky newspaper editor, became an intimate member of President Andrew Jackson's "Kitchen Cabinet" and could be considered the first presidential press secretary.

Kendall sampled public opinion on issues, advised Jackson, and skillfully interpreted his rough ideas, molding them into speeches and news releases. He also served as Jackson's advance agent on trips, wrote glowing articles that he sent to supportive newspapers, and likely was the first to use newspaper reprints in public relations; almost every complimentary story or editorial about Jackson was reprinted and widely circulated. Article reprints are still a standard tactic in today's practice.

Supporters and leaders of such causes as abolition, suffrage, and prohibition employed publicity to maximum effect throughout the century. One of the most influential publicity ventures for the abolition movement was the publication of Harriet Beecher Stowe's *Uncle Tom's Cabin*. Sarah J. Hale, editor of *Godey's Lady's Book*, a best-selling magazine, ardently promoted women's rights. Amelia Bloomer, a women's rights advocate, garnered plenty of media publicity by wearing loose-fitting trousers in protest of the corset. Noted temperance crusader Carrie Nation became nationally known by invading saloons and destroying the liquor bottles and bars with an axe.

Professor Carolyn M. Byerly of Ithaca College says that these campaigns for social reform qualify as public relations operations and deserve a place in the history of the field. She cites Genevieve Gardner McBride, who points out that in Wisconsin support for a constitutional amendment giving women the right to vote was carried out through a carefully managed information campaign that included "publicity, press agentry, publications, petition drives, advertising, merchandising, lobbying, membership recruitment and training, special events, fund-raising, issues management, and crisis PR."

Professors Michael Smith of La Salle University and Denise Ferguson of the University of Indianapolis note that the primary purpose of activist organizations "is to influence public policy, organizational action, or social norms and values." They also note that activist organizations face the same challenges as other organizations and, therefore, use the same strategic communication tactics to achieve their goals. For example, activists often embrace conflict as a means of gaining news coverage and stirring up support from their grassroots base.

Activists have been using public relations tactics throughout history. In the 1860s, naturalist John Muir wrote in the *New York Times* and other publications about the importance of protecting the Yosemite Valley in California. In 1889, he worked with the editor of *Century Magazine*, Robert Underwood Johnson, to promote a campaign requesting congressional support for Yosemite National Park. The activist public relations campaign succeeded and generations have enjoyed the benefits of a protected Yosemite.

The Beginnings of Corporate Public Relations

A wave of industrialization and urbanization swept the nation after the Civil War. Concentrations of wealth developed through manufacturing and trade. Amid the questioning of business practices, which intensified in the early 20th century, in 1888 the Mutual Life Insurance Company hired a journalist to write news releases designed to stave off criticism and improve its image. In 1889, Westinghouse Corporation established what is thought to be the first in-house publicity department. In 1897, the term *public relations* was first used by the Association of American Railroads in a company listing.

Modern Public Relations Comes of Age

As the use of publicity gained acceptance, the first publicity agency, known as the Publicity Bureau, was established in Boston in 1900 with Harvard College as its most prestigious client. George F. Parker and Ivy Ledbetter Lee opened a publicity office in New York City in 1904.

At the corporate level, the Chicago Edison Company broke new ground in public relations techniques under the skillful leadership of its president, Samuel Insull. Well aware of the special need for a public utility to maintain a sound relationship with its customers, Insull created a monthly customer magazine, issued a constant stream of news releases, and even used films for public relations purposes. In 1912, he started the "bill stuffer" by inserting company information into customer bills—a technique used by many utilities today. Meanwhile, Theodore N. Vail, president of AT&T, greatly expanded that company's press and customer operations.

Twentieth-Century Public Relations Luminaries. Public relations practice continued to evolve in the 1900s. Business leaders and politicians increasingly employed public relations tactics. This growth also provided an opportunity for the rise of the independent counselor.

Henry Ford. Henry Ford was America's first major industrialist, and he was among the first to use two basic public relations concepts. The first was the notion of positioning, the idea that credit and publicity always go to those who do something first. The second idea was being accessible to the press.

In 1900, Ford obtained coverage of the prototype Model T by demonstrating it to a reporter from the *Detroit Tribune*. By 1903, Ford was achieving widespread publicity by racing his cars—a practice still used by today's automakers. Ford hired Barney Oldfield, a champion bicycle racer and a popular personality, to drive a Model T at a record speed of about 60 miles per hour. The publicity from these speed runs gave Ford financial backing and a ready market.

Ford became a household name because he was willing to be interviewed by the press on almost any subject, including the gold standard, evolution, alcohol, foreign affairs, and even capital punishment.

Theodore Roosevelt. President Theodore Roosevelt was a master at generating publicity. He was the first president to make extensive use of news conferences and interviews to build support for projects. He knew the publicity value of a presidential tour. On a trip to Yosemite National Park, Roosevelt was accompanied by a large group of reporters and photographers who wrote glowing articles about Roosevelt's pet project—the need to preserve areas for public recreational use.

The toy teddy bear had its origins on a hunting trip during which Roosevelt also was accompanied by reporters. During the trip he spared the life of a small bear, an incident that impressed the journalists who, in turn, wrote about it. A toymaker saw the story and began to make and market "Teddy" bears in recognition of the president's humane gesture.

Ivy Ledbetter Lee. Though public relations practitioners through the ages have been thoughtful about their communication approaches, the idea of public relations as a strategic endeavor really took hold in the early 20th century. Ivy Ledbetter Lee was the first public relations counselor. The Georgia-born and Princeton-educated Lee began as a journalist, became a publicist, and soon expanded that role to become the first public relations counsel.

Public relations counselor Ivy Lee convinced John D. Rockefeller that he should visit miners at the family's Colorado Fuel & Iron Company, the site of considerable labor unrest and union organizing activity that led to the "Ludlow Massacre." Here, Rockefeller watches children of miners marching into school.

When Lee opened his public relations firm, he issued a declaration of principles that signaled a new practice model: public information. Lee's emphasis was on the dissemination of truthful, accurate information rather than the distortions, hype, and exaggerations of press agentry. Lee's declaration, which stemmed from his journalistic orientation, said, in part, "This is not a secret press bureau. All our work is done in the open. We aim to supply news. . . . In brief, our plan is, frankly and openly, in behalf of business concerns and public institutions, to supply to the press and the public of the United States prompt and accurate information concerning subjects which is of value and interest to the public."

Lee began handling media relations for the Pennyslvania Railroad, but is best known for his work for John D. Rockefeller, Jr. Lee was hired to provide strategic counsel in the wake of the vicious strikebreaking activities known as the Ludlow Massacre at the Rockefeller family's Colorado Fuel and Iron (CF&I) company plant.

Lee employed strategies central to the conflict management life cycle (see p. 43). In the proactive phase, he did environmental scanning by going to Colorado to do some fact-finding (research) and talking to both sides. He found that labor leaders were effectively getting their views out by freely talking to the media, but that the company's executives were tight-lipped and inaccessible. The result, of course, was a barrage of negative publicity and public criticism directed at CF&I and the Rockefeller family. He did research to understand the miners' grievances and their conflict methods.

In the strategic phase, he proposed a series of informational bulletins to get the Rockefeller side of the story out to opinion leaders in Colorado and beyond. Lee recognized the value of directly reaching opinion leaders who, in turn, were highly influential in shaping public discussion and opinion.

In the reactive phase, Lee convinced the governor of Colorado to write an article supporting the position taken by CF&I. He also convinced Rockefeller to visit the plant and talk with miners and their families. Lee made sure the press was there to record Rockefeller eating in the worker's hall, swinging a pickax in the mine, and having a beer with the workers after hours. The press loved it, which led to the recovery phase of the conflict management life cycle. Rockefeller was portrayed as being seriously concerned about the plight of the workers, and the visit led to policy changes and more worker benefits.

Through a *muscular approach* to public relations—that is, by employing careful strategy and a broad array of tactics—Lee prevented the United Mine Workers from gaining a foothold in the Rockefeller mines. Through strategic counsel, Lee provided both his client and the miners with some level of success and satisfaction and put their conflict to rest.

Lee continued as a counselor to the Rockefeller family and its various companies, but he also counseled a number of other clients, too. He advised the American Tobacco Company to initiate a profit-sharing plan, the Pennsylvania Railroad to beautify its stations, and the movie industry to stop inflated advertising and form a voluntary code of censorship. See the PR Casebook box on page 69 for his work with New York's first subway.

He is remembered today for four important contributions to public relations:

1. Advancing the concept that business and industry should align themselves with the public interest

PRCASEBOOK

Constructive Public Relations for the New York Subway

Ivy Lee, known as the first public relations counselor, was retained by the New York subway system in 1916 to foster public understanding and support.

The Interborough Rapid Transit Company (IRT) faced many new challenges as it began its second decade of service. It was completing construction and expanding service, but it also faced competition from a rival system, the Brooklyn Rapid Transit Company (later known as BMT).

Under Lee's direction, the IRT took an innovative approach, communicating directly with its passengers through pamphlets, brochures, and posters "to establish a close understanding of its work and policies." The most famous and influential products of Lee's campaign were two concurrently appearing poster series: *The Subway Sun* and the *Elevated Express*.

Between 1918, when the first posters appeared, and 1932, when the series ended, these posters became New York institutions. They entertained and informed millions of subway commuters during the First World War and through the Great Depression.

Posters, for example, were used to announce the introduction of coin-operated turnstiles, which Lee called "a change which revolutionized the daily habits of millions of people." They were also used to explain the need for fare increases in the 1920s and to extol fast and direct train service to baseball games at Yankee Stadium and the Polo Grounds. Posters also offered riders information on how to get to other city institutions. The poster shown promotes the Museum of Natural History and provides directions.

Designed to resemble the front page of a newspaper, *The Subway Sun* and *The Elevated Express* announced the opening of the 42nd Street shuttle between Grand Central Station and Times Square; asked riders to not block the doors; and urged them to visit the city's free swimming pools. As the subways became more crowded, the IRT used these posters to promote its "open air" elevated lines as a more comfortable alternative.

Today, more than 90 years later, Lee's idea of communicating directly to passengers through posters, pamphlets, and brochures is still being used by public transit systems around the world. And many of the themes are the same as in Lee's day—public safety, system improvements, travel advisories, subway etiquette, and public service announcements.

2. Dealing with top executives and carrying out no program unless it has the active support of management

3. Maintaining open communication with the news media

4. Emphasizing the necessity of humanizing business and bringing its public relations down to the community level of employees, customers, and neighbors.

George Creel. George Creel, also a former newspaper reporter, was asked by President Woodrow Wilson to organize a massive public relations effort to unite the nation and to influence world opinion during World War I. President Wilson accepted Creel's advice that hatred of the Germans should be downplayed and that loyalty and confidence in the government should be emphasized. The Committee on

Public Information also publicized the war aims and ideals of Woodrow Wilson—to make the world safe for democracy and to make World War I the war to end all wars.

This massive publicity effort had a profound effect on the development of public relations by demonstrating the success of these techniques. It also awakened an awareness in Americans of the power of mediated information in changing public attitudes and behavior. This, coupled with postwar analysis of British propaganda devices, resulted in a number of scholarly books and college courses on the subject. Among these books was Walter Lippmann's classic *Public Opinion* (1922), in which he pointed out how people are moved to action by "the pictures in our heads."

Edward B. Bernays. Edward B. Bernays was one of several individuals who served on the Creel Committee and went on to become a successful and widely known public relations counselor. Bernays, through brilliant campaigns and extensive self-promotion, became known as the "father of modern public relations" by the time of his death in 1995 at the age of 103.

Bernays, who was the nephew of Sigmud Freud, conceptualized a third model of public relations that emphasized the application of social science research and behavioral psychology to formulate campaigns and messages that could change people's perceptions and encourage certain behaviors. Unlike Lee's public information model that emphasized the distribution of accurate news, Bernays' model was essentially one of advocacy and scientific persuasion. It included listening to the audience, but the purpose of feedback was to formulate a better persuasive message.

Bernays became a major spokesperson for the "new" public relations through his 1923 book, *Crystallizing Public Opinion*. His first sentence announced: "In writing this book I have tried to set down the broad principles that govern the new profession of public relations counsel." In the pages that followed, Bernays outlined the scope, function, methods, techniques, and social responsibilities of a *public relations counsel*—a term that was to become the core of public relations practice.

The editor of the *New York Herald Tribune* was unimpressed and wrote, "Bernays has taken the sideshow barker and given him a philosophy and a new and awesome language. He is no primitive drum-beater. . . . He is devoid of swank and does not visit newspaper offices (as did the circus press agents); and yet, the more thoughtful newspaper editors. . . should regard Bernays as a menace, and warn their colleagues of his machinations."

Clients, however, did not seem to share such concerns and Bernays, over the course of his long career, had many successful campaigns that have become classics. For example:

> *Procter & Gamble's Ivory Soap.* Procter & Gamble sold its Ivory Soap by the millions after Bernays came up with the idea of sponsoring soap sculpture contests for school-age children. In the first year alone, 22 million schoolchildren participated in the contest, which eventually ran for 35 years. Bernays' brochure with soap sculpture tips, which millions of children received at their schools, advised them to "use discarded models for face, hands, and bath," adding, "You will love the feeling of cleanliness that comes from Ivory soap bath once a day."

> *Light's Golden Jubilee.* To celebrate the 50th anniversary of Thomas Edison's invention of the electric light bulb, Bernays arranged the worldwide attention-getting Light's Golden Jubilee in 1929. It was his idea, for example, that the world's utilities would all shut off their power at one time, for one minute, to honor Edison. President Herbert Hoover and many dignitaries were on hand, and the U.S. Post Office issued a commemorative two-cent postage stamp.

Journalist Larry Tye has outlined a number of campaigns conducted by Bernays in his book *The Father of Spin: Edward B. Bernays and the Birth of Public Relations.* Tye credits Bernays with having a unique approach to solving problems. Instead of thinking first about tactics, Bernays would always think about the "big idea" on how to motivate people. The bacon industry, for example, wanted to promote its product, so Bernays came up with the idea of having doctors across the land endorse a hearty breakfast. No mention was made of bacon, but sales soared anyway as people took the advice and started eating the traditional breakfast of bacon and eggs.

Bernays, as previously mentioned, is widely acknowledged as the founder of modern public relations. One historian even described him as "the first and doubtless the leading ideologist of public relations." Bernays constantly wrote about the profession of public relations and its ethical responsibilities—even to the point of advocating the licensing of public relations counselors. He also eventually advocated that public relations should be a two-way street of mutual understanding and interaction with the public rather than just scientific persuasion.

Although he was named by *Life* magazine in 1990 as one of the 100 most important Americans of the 20th century, it should be noted that he had a powerful partner in his wife, Doris E. Fleischman, who was a talented writer, ardent feminist, and former Sunday editor of the *New York Tribune*. Fleischman was an equal partner in the work of Bernays' firm, interviewing clients, writing news releases, editing the company's newsletter, and writing and editing books and magazine articles.

Edward L. Bernays, a legendary figure in public relations with a career spanning about three-quarters of a century, died at the age of 103 in 1995. He outlived all his contemporaries and became known as the "father of modern public relations."

Public Relations Expands in Postwar America

During the second half of the 20th century, the practice of public relations became firmly established as an indispensable part of America's economic, political, and social development.

The booming economy after World War II produced rapid growth in all areas of public relations. Companies opened public relations departments or expanded existing ones. Government staffs increased in size, as did those of nonprofits such as educational institutions and health and welfare agencies. Television emerged in the early 1950s as a national medium and as a new challenge for public relations professionals. New counseling firms sprang up nationwide.

The growth of the economy was one reason for the expansion of public relations, but there were other factors, too. They included:

> Major increases in urban and suburban populations

> The growth of a more impersonal society represented by big business, big labor, and big government

> Scientific and technological advances, including automation and computerization

> The communications revolution and proliferation of mass media

> Replacement by bottom-line financial considerations of the more personalized decision making of a previous, more genteel, society.

Many people felt bewildered by such rapid change, cut off from the sense of community that characterized previous generations. They sought power through innumerable pressure groups, focusing on causes such as environmentalism, working conditions, and civil rights. Public opinion, registered through new, more sophisticated methods of polling, became increasingly powerful in both opposing and effecting change.

Physically and psychologically separated from their publics, American business and industry turned increasingly to public relations specialists for audience analysis, strategic planning, issues management, and even the creation of supportive environments for the selling of products and services. Mass media also became more complex and sophisticated, so specialists in media relations were also in demand.

By 1950, an estimated 17,000 men and 2,000 women were employed as practitioners in public relations and publicity. Typical of the public relations programs of large corporations at midcentury was that of the Aluminum Company of America (ALCOA). Heading the operation was a vice president for public relations-advertising, who was aided by an assistant public relations director and advertising manager. Departments included community relations, product publicity, motion pictures and exhibits, employee publications, the news bureau, and speech writing. The *Alcoa News* magazine was published for all employees, and separate publications were published for each of the 20 plants throughout the United States. The company's main broadcast effort was sponsorship of Edward R. Murrow's *See It Now* television program.

By 1960, the U.S. Census counted 23,870 men and 7,271 women in public relations, although some observers put the figure at approximately 35,000. Since 1960, the number of public relations practitioners has increased dramatically to about 200,000 nationwide. The latest estimate from the U.S. Department of Labor predicts that public relations jobs will grow faster than most fields, with a projected increase of 39.8 percent for public relations specialists and 36.6 percent for public relations managers from 2004 to 2014.

Evolving Practice and Philosophy

The period from 1950 to 2000 marked distinct changes in the practice and philosophy of public relations. To place these changes in context, it's worthwhile to review some of what has been presented so far. First, the 1800s were marked by the press agentry model, which was best represented by the hype and exaggeration of P. T. Barnum and the railroad companies. By the early 20th century, however, public relations began to reinvent itself along journalistic lines, mainly because former newspaper reporters such as Ivy Lee started to do public relations work and counseling. James Grunig, in his interpretation of the evolutionary models of public relations, called this the public information model of public relations (see the Insights box on page 73).

In the 1920s, thanks to breakthroughs in social science research, the focus of public relations shifted to the psychological and sociological effects of persuasive communication on target audiences. Edward Bernays, among others, believed that any campaign should be based on feedback and an analysis of an audience's dispositions and value system so messages could be structured for maximum effect. Grunig labeled this the two-way asymmetric model because it involved scientific persuasion based on the research of the target audience. Practitioners such as Arthur W. Page, vice president of the American Telephone & Telegraph Company beginning in the 1920s, also contributed to the maturing of the public relations profession. See the Insights box on page 74 for Page's principles.

The 1960s saw Vietnam War protests, the civil rights movement, the environmental movement, interest in women's rights, and a host of other issues. Antibusiness sentiment was high, and corporations adjusted their policies to generate public good-

ON THE JOB >>

Four Classic Models of Public Relations

Insights

A four-model typology of public relations practice was presented by Professors James Grunig of the University of Maryland and Todd Hunt of Rutgers State University in their 1984 book *Managing Public Relations*. The models, which have been used widely in public relations theory, help to explain how public relations has evolved over the years. Although all four models are practiced today in varying degrees, the "ideal" one is the two-way symmetric model.

Press Agentry/Publicity

This is one-way communication, primarily through the mass media, to distribute information that may be exaggerated, distorted, or even incomplete to "hype" a cause, product, or service. Its purpose is advocacy, and little or no research is required. P. T. Barnum was the leading historical figure during this model's heyday from 1850 to 1900. Sports, theater, music, film, and the classic Hollywood publicist are the main fields of this practice model today.

Public Information

One-way distribution of information, not necessarily with a persuasive intent, is the purpose. It is based on the journalistic ideal of accuracy and completeness, and the mass media is the primary channel. There is fact-finding for content, but little audience research regarding attitudes and dispositions. Ivy Lee, a former journalist, is the leading historical figure during this model's development from about 1910 into the 1920s. Government, nonprofit groups, and other public institutions are the primary fields of this practice model today.

Two-Way Asymmetric

Scientific persuasion is the purpose, and communication is two-way, with imbalanced effects. The model has a feedback loop, but the primary purpose of the model is to help the communicator better understand the audience and how to persuade it. Research is used to plan activities and establish objectives as well as to learn whether objectives have been met. Edward Bernays was the leading historical figure during the model's beginning in the 1920s. Marketing and advertising departments in competitive businesses and public relations firms are the primary places of this practice model today.

Two-Way Symmetric

Gaining mutual understanding is the purpose, and communication is two-way with balanced effects. Formative research is used mainly to learn how the public perceives an organization and to determine what consequences organizational actions/policy might have on the public. The result may be counseling management to take certain actions or change policies. Evaluative research is used to measure whether public relations efforts have improved public understanding. This idea, also expressed as "relationship building" is to have policies and actions that are mutually beneficial to both parties. Edward B. Bernays, later in his life, supported this model and is considered a leading advocate of this approach. Educators and professional leaders are the main proponents of this model, which has been used by many professionals since the 1980s. Today this model is practiced in organizations that engage in issue identification, crisis and risk management, and long-range strategic planning.

will and understanding. Thus, the idea of issues management was added to the job description of the public relations manager. This was the first expression of the idea that public relations should do more than persuade people that corporate policy was correct. During this period, the idea emerged that perhaps it would be beneficial to have a dialogue with various publics and adapt corporate policy to their particular concerns. Grunig labeled this approach two-way symmetric communication because there's balance between the organization and its various publics; that is, the organization and the public can influence each other.

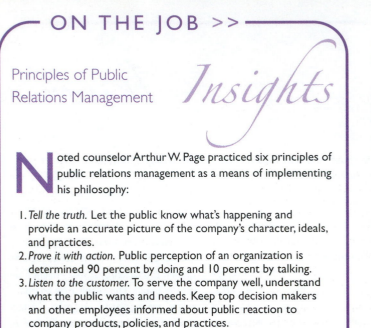

Principles of Public
Relations Management

Insights

Noted counselor Arthur W. Page practiced six principles of public relations management as a means of implementing his philosophy:

1. *Tell the truth.* Let the public know what's happening and provide an accurate picture of the company's character, ideals, and practices.
2. *Prove it with action.* Public perception of an organization is determined 90 percent by doing and 10 percent by talking.
3. *Listen to the customer.* To serve the company well, understand what the public wants and needs. Keep top decision makers and other employees informed about public reaction to company products, policies, and practices.
4. *Manage for tomorrow.* Anticipate public reaction and eliminate practices that create difficulties. Generate goodwill.
5. *Conduct public relations as if the whole company depends on it.* Corporate relations is a management function. No corporate strategy should be implemented without considering its impact on the public. The public relations professional is a policy maker capable of handling a wide range of corporate communications activities.
6. *Remain calm, patient, and good-humored.* Lay the groundwork for public relations miracles with consistent, calm, and reasoned attention to information and contacts. When a crisis arises, remember that cool heads communicate best.

Page recognized an additional truth: A company's true character is expressed by its people. This makes every active and retired employee a part of the public relations organization. So it is the responsibility of the public relations function to support each employee's capacity to be an honest, knowledgeable ambassador to customers, friends, and public officials.

Source: *Membership Directory,* Arthur W. Page Society, New York.

The 1970s was an era of reform in the stock market. The field of investor relations boomed.

By the 1980s, the concept that public relations was a management function was in full bloom. The practice was actively moving toward the strategic approach. The concept of management by objective (MBO) was heavily endorsed by public relations practitioners as they sought to convince higher management that public relations did indeed contribute to the bottom line. Many definitions from this time emphasized public relations as a management function. As Derina Holtzhausen of the University of South Florida notes, "Public relations management highlights organizational effectiveness, the strategic management of the function through strategic identification of publics, and issues management to prevent crisis."

An awareness of reputation, or perception, management began to dominate in the 1990s. Burson-Marsteller, one of the largest public relations firms, decided that its business was not public relations, but rather "perception management." Other firms declared that their business was "reputation management." Public relations as conflict management is directly linked to the notion of reputation management. When organizations are engaged in conflict the outcome can have a dramatically positive, or negative, effect on stakeholders' perceptions of the organization (see the section on life cycle in Chapter 2.)

The basic idea was that public relations people worked to maintain credibility, to build solid internal and external relationships, and to manage issues. Inherent in this conceptualization was the idea that public relations personnel should use research to do (1) environmental monitoring, (2) public relations audits, (3) communication audits, and (4) social audits. By doing these four things, it would be possible to enhance corporate social responsibility (CSR).

By 2000, a number of scholars and practitioners began to conceptualize the practice of public relations as "relationship management," the basic idea being that public relations practitioners are in the business of building and fostering relationships with an organization's various publics. Relationship management builds on Grunig's idea of two-way symmetric communication, but goes beyond it by recognizing that an organization's publics are, as Stephen Bruning of Capital University notes, "active, interactive, and equal participants of an ongoing communication process."

ON THE JOB >>

Classic Campaigns Show the Power of Public Relations

Insights

During the last half of the 20th century, a number of organizations and causes used effective public relations to accomplish highly visible results. *PRWeek* convened a panel of public relations experts and came up with some of the "greatest campaigns ever" during this time period.

> *The Civil Rights Campaign.* Martin Luther King, Jr. was an outstanding civil rights advocate and a great communicator. He organized the 1963 civil rights campaign and used such techniques as well-written, well-delivered speeches; letter writing; lobbying; and staged events (nonviolent protests) to turn a powerful idea into reality.

The power of public relations was used in the civil rights movement to create public awareness and support. Here, Martin Luther King, Jr. addresses a massive rally in Washington, D.C., and delivers his "I have a dream" speech.

> *NASA.* From the very beginning NASA fostered media accessibility at Houston's Johnson Space Center. For example, NASA director Chris Kraft insisted that television cameras be placed on the lunar lander in 1969, and in later years reporters were invited inside mission control during the Apollo 13 mission. According to *PRWeek,* "Those historic moments have helped the public overlook the huge taxpayer expense and numerous technical debacles that could otherwise have jeopardized the future of the organization."

> *Cabbage Patch Kids.* Public relations launched the craze for the adoptable dolls and created a "must have" toy. The campaign set the standard for the introduction of a new product and showed what a strong media relations program can do for a product.

> *Seat Belt Campaign.* In the 1980s, the U.S. automotive industry got the nation to "buckle up" through a public relations campaign. Tactics included winning the support of news media across the country, interactive displays, celebrity endorsements, letter-writing campaigns, and several publicity events, such as buckling a 600-foot-wide safety belt around a Hollywood sign. Notes *PRWeek,* "The results of one of the biggest public relations campaigns of all time were phenomenal, with the number of people 'buckling up' rising from 12 to 50 percent—it is now even higher."

> *Hands Across America.* The largest human gathering in history was a public relations stunt in 1986 that saw 7 million people across 16 states join hands to form a human chain to raise money for the hungry and the homeless. Even President Ronald Reagan participated.

> *StarKist Tuna.* When negative media coverage threatened the tuna industry because dolphins were getting caught in fishermen's nets, StarKist led the industry in changing fishing practices with conferences, videos, and an Earth Day coalition. About 90 percent of the public heard about the company's efforts, and StarKist was praised as an environmental leader.

> *Tylenol Crisis.* This has become the classic model for a product recall. When Johnson & Johnson found out that several people had died from cyanide-laced Tylenol capsules, a national panic erupted. Many thought the company would never recover from the damage caused by the tampering. However, the company issued a complete recall, redesigned the packaging so that it was tamperproof, and launched a media campaign to keep the public fully informed. The result was that Tylenol survived the crisis and again became a best seller.

> *Windows 95 Launch.* This campaign is easily in the product launch hall of fame. Microsoft, through media relations and publicity, achieved a unprecedented 99 percent awareness level among consumers even before the product hit the shelves.

> *Understanding AIDS.* This successful health education campaign changed the way that AIDS was perceived by Americans. In addition to a national mailing of a brochure titled *Understanding AIDS,* there were grassroots activities that specifically targeted African Americans and Hispanics.

Source: "The Greatest Campaigns Ever." *PRWeek,* July 15, 2002, 14–15.

An extension of relationship management is the dialogic (dialogue) model of public relations that has emerged since 2000. Michael Kent and Maureen Taylor of Western Michigan University wrote in a *Public Relations Review* article that a "theoretical shift, from public relations reflecting an emphasis on managing communication, to an emphasis on communication as a tool of negotiating relationships, has been taking place for some time."

Although this textbook values healthy long-term relationships with various publics, moral obligations and other forces within an organization require professionals to make difficult decisions on occasion. For example, Yahoo! came under fire for censoring search results in China in order to gain entrée to that country's enormous Internet market. The decision made some Yahoo! supporters angry, but the company determined that cooperating with the Chinese government was a good and ethical business decision. According to *PRWeek*, "Yahoo! cofounder Jerry Yang. . . addressed the company's China policies, arguing that Yahoo! could have a greater impact on the Chinese government by being in the market, as opposed to not being there at all."

The concept of dialogue places less emphasis on mass media distribution of messages and more on interpersonal channels. Kent and Taylor, for example, say that the Internet and World Wide Web are excellent vehicles for dialogue if web sites are interactive.

Although there has been a somewhat linear progression in public relations practice and philosophy as the field has expanded, today's practice represents a mixture of public relations models. The Hollywood publicist/press agent and the public information officer for the government agency are still with us. We also still have marketing communications, which almost exclusively uses the concept of scientific persuasion and two-way asymmetric communication. However, when it comes to issues management and relationship building, the two-way symmetric and dialogue models seem to be the most appropriate.

Trends in Today's Practice of Public Relations

Technological and social changes continue to transform aspects of public relations practice during the first decade of the 21st century. The following sections discuss the feminization of the field, the search for more ethnic and cultural diversity, and other trends that will shape the practice in the years to come.

Feminization of the Field

In terms of personnel, the most dramatic change has been the transformation of public relations from a male-dominated field to one in which women now constitute 70 percent of practitioners. The shift has been going on for several decades. In 1979, women made up 41 percent of the public relations workforce; by 1983, they became the majority (50.1 percent). A decade later, the figure stood at 66.3 percent. By 2000, the percentage had leveled off at about 70 percent, where it remains today. In contrast, the total number of women in the U.S. workforce was about 59 percent in 2004, according to the U.S. Bureau of Labor Statistics. The national organizations also reflect the trend. About 75 percent of the membership in the International Association of Business Communicators (IABC) are now women, and the PRSA says that more than 50 percent of its members are women. However, the Arthur W. Page Society, which is composed of senior-level communication executives, still has a majority of males (70 percent). Data from *PRWeek* in February 2006 affirmed this senior disparity by gender: 72 percent of the chief communications officers of Fortune 200 companies are men, 28 percent are women.

About 65 percent of all majors in journalism and mass communications programs are now women, and 70 to 75 percent of public relations majors are female. It's worth noting that women also constitute the majority of students in law school, veterinary programs, and a number of other academic disciplines.

A number of reasons are given for the major influx of women into the field of public relations. Some of these reasons include the following:

> Women find a more welcoming environment in public relations and see more opportunities for advancement than in other communications fields, such as newspaper work.

> Women still make more money in public relations than comparable female-dominated fields, such as teaching and social work.

> A woman can start a public relations firm without a lot of capital.

> Women tend to have better listening and communication skills than men.

> Women are more sensitive than men in facilitating two-way communication.

Salary and job description disparities between men and women remain in public relations. A number of studies show that the majority of women in public relations earn less money than their male counterparts and are usually found at the tactical level of public relations practice rather than the management/counseling role. The optimists say that women are still relatively new to the field and, with time, will eventually rise to their fair share of top posts. Feminist scholars refer to this assimilation model as liberal feminism. Those labeled by scholars as "radical feminists," however, disagree with this reasoning. They say that increasing the number of women in management is not enough, and that nothing less than a complete restructuring of society and its institutions will end gender discrimination and bias.

Writing in the *Journal of Public Relations Research*, University of Maryland professors Linda Aldoory and Elizabeth Toth say "Surveys and focus groups continue to [show]. . . that, although the public relations profession is almost 70 percent women today, men are often favored for hiring, higher salaries, and promotions to management positions." Indeed, women in higher levels of management are still unusual in business and industry. A study by D. Meyerson and J. Fletcher that was published in the *Harvard Business Review* found that women only constituted 10 percent of the senior managers in Fortune 500 companies and less than 4 percent of the uppermost ranks of CEOs, presidents, and executive vice presidents. Another interesting statistic is that women earn about 76 cents for every dollar earned by a man. In fact, the actual figure actually dropped to 75 cents in 2004.

Some women in public relations have become the top communications officers of their corporations. However, Professor Larissa Grunig of the University of Maryland is concerned about highlighting women who have made it to the top, calling it compensatory feminism. According to Grunig, it gives women the false idea that progress is being made. A number of feminist scholars have explored the dimensions and impact of women in public relations, and some of their works are listed in the Suggested Readings at the end of the chapter.

As early as the 1970s, there was passionate debate about the large influx of women into the field. Many public relations leaders (men, of course) expressed a deep concern that feminization of the field would lower the status of public relations as a management function and that salaries in the field would drop given the history of other female-dominated fields, such as nursing, education, and social work.

Some alleged that business and industry were simply hiring women in public relations to show a commitment to affirmative action. Indeed, the Velvet Ghetto study of 1978 by the International Association of Business Communicators (IABC) found that companies did tend to load up their public relations departments with women to compensate for their scarcity in other professional and managerial capacities that led to top management. The idea was that a company could have a woman vice president of public relations as "window dressing" without giving her any real management authority.

These arguments and fears have somewhat dissipated over the years. That public relations is a high-status profession may still be debated, but the power and influence of women in the management suite is stronger today than it has ever been. Also, salaries remain fairly high compared to other female-dominated fields. As for the Velvet Ghetto, most women who now occupy top positions reject the idea that they were hired as "window dressing." Aedhmar Hynes, CEO of Text 100, told *PRWeek*, "I have worked damned hard to get to where I am, but so have all the men who are in senior management positions."

Statistics and surveys still show, however, that there is a gender gap in salaries and that there continue to be fewer women than men in senior management. A number of reasons have been offered, but the most recent research seems to indicate that the biggest factor is years of experience in the field. Youjin Choi and Linda Childers Hon of the University of Florida found that "[t]he number of years of respondents' professional experience was the single significant predictor of income." Aldoory and Toth also found years of experience to be a significant factor in income inequity, but they cited evidence that gender and interrupting a career also had an effect on salaries and job advancement.

Organizational environment may affect a woman's rise to top management. This theory is called the *structionalist perspective*. Toth argues that more women than men fulfill the technician role—a less powerful role than the managerial role—because of different on-the-job experiences. Choi and Hon also say organizational structure is a problem because women in many organizations are excluded from influential networks, have a paucity of role models, and must work in male-dominated environments.

Choi and Hon, however, did find that organizations (such as many public relations firms) where women occupied 40 to 60 percent of the managerial positions were "gender integrated" and more friendly environments for the advancement of women than male-dominated organizational structures. In other words, organizations committed to gender equity were those organizations that practiced the most excellent public relations.

The Search for Diversity

According to the U.S. Census Bureau, minorities now constitute 33 percent of the 300 million people in the United States. The fastest-growing, and now largest group, is Hispanics. Hispanics account for 14 percent of the population, compared with

12.8 percent for Blacks/African Americans—a statistical difference of about 500,000 people. Asian/Pacific Islanders make up 4 percent, and Native Americans comprise 1 percent of the population.

The number of minorities in public relations falls considerably short of equaling the population at large, and one major goal is to somehow make the field of public relations more representative of the population as a whole. In 1997, the membership profile for the PRSA showed that 93 percent of the members were white, 3 percent black, 2 percent Hispanic, and 1 percent Asian. Since that time, there has been some improvement. In 2003, a *PRWeek* survey found that professionals in public relations firms were 81 percent Caucasian, 7 percent African American, 7 percent Hispanic, and 4 percent Asian or Pacific Islander. Company public relations departments reported about the same statistics for ethnic groups but, for some reason, registered a large percentage of Native Americans (20 percent).

Many public relations employers express the desire to hire more minority candidates, but they have difficulty doing so because they receive so few applications. One problem is the education pipeline. About 200,000 undergraduates are studying journalism and mass communications (including public relations) across the country. Of that number, about 30 percent are minorities. Hispanics, the largest minority in the general population at 14 percent, constitute 10 percent of journalism enrollments. African Americans also make up about 10 percent of journalism enrollments, Asian Americans are 3 percent, and Native Americans comprise 2 percent.

Admittedly, the percentage of ethnic groups in public relations has improved over the past decade, but there is now a concerted effort to attract more minorities. Hispanics, in particular, constitute a major audience for marketers and public relations specialists because of their spending power. It's estimated that the Hispanic market is now worth about $400 billion to $500 billion annually, and will climb to more than $900 billion by 2010. Reaching this audience, and other major ethnic audiences, will require specialized knowledge and messages tailored to their particular cultures and values.

The PRSA (www.diversity.prsa.org) and other major public relations organizations are increasing minority scholarships, organizing career fairs, and giving awards to local chapters that institute diversity programs. PRSA informs members of diversity issues by including news from the Hispanic PR wire and Black PR wire on its Web site home page (www.prsa.org).

In addition, groups such as the National Black Public Relations Society (BPRS), the Hispanic Public Relations Association (HPRA), and the Asian American Advertising and Public Relations Association (AAAPRA) are being asked to help public relations firms and companies identify qualified job applicants. Leaders of these minority associations, however, say that employers must make a greater effort to recruit minorities to public relations by going to traditionally black colleges, participating in more college career fairs, enlisting the aid of college professors to identify good candidates, and even placing job ads in publications that reach a variety of ethnic groups.

The globalization of public relations has also created a strong need for diverse ethnic staffs (see the Global box on page 80). Firms need staff who possess language skills, personal knowledge of other nations, and sensitivity to the customs and attitudes of others. Knowledge of Spanish and Asian languages, such as Chinese, will be especially valuable.

ON THE JOB >>

Public Relations Is a Growing Presence in Singapore

Global

In an increasingly globalized world, the Asian Pacific is growing in importance to public relations practitioners. While other Asian locales, such as Japan, have had a historically strong public relations presence, over the past decade Singapore has arisen as a country whose appetite for PR is growing, according to *PRWeek*.

Burson-Marsteller, Edelman, Hill & Knowlton, Ogilvy Public Relations, Text 100, and Weber Shandwick all have offices in Singapore. Tarun Deo of Text 100 told *PRWeek*, "If there's a budget issue in North America, what they're doing is taking the [PR] budget completely out of the U.S. and still continuing to spend in Asia."

Growth categories in Singaporean public relations are corporate, sports, government, hospitality, energy, and technology. "With the new integrated resorts and casinos being built in Singapore, I predict the hospitality and service industry sectors to increase," said Louise Harris, president and managing director of Ruder-Finn in Asia.

Source: "Singapore: Gateway to the Far East." *PRWeek*, May 22, 2006, p. 29.

Other Major Trends

Feminization of the field and the recruitment of a more diverse workforce are major trends, but a number of other issues also will impact the practice of public relations in the coming years.

The Advent of Transparency.
Instant global communications, corporate finance scandals, government regulation, and the increased public demand for accountability have made it necessary for all society's institutions, including business and industry, to be more transparent in their operations.

The Expanding Role of Public Relations.
Professionals have already repositioned public relations as being more than media relations and publicity, but those hard-fought gains will need to be reinforced in the coming years as marketing and management consultants enter the field offering the ability to also build relationships with various publics.

Increased Emphasis on Evaluation.
Public relations professionals will continue to improve measurement techniques for showing management how their activities actually contribute to the bottom line.

One dimension is the return on investment (ROI). According to Kathy Cripps, chair of the Council of Public Relations Firms, two other important dimensions of measurement are (1) measuring outcomes—the long-term effectiveness of a public relations program, and (2) measuring outputs—how well a program was executed and how effective its tactics were.

PR consultant Katie Paine, on her PR measurement blog (www.kdpaine.blogs.com), has addressed the importance of emphasizing evaluation. She blogged on Dec. 29, 2005, "It is clear. . . that PR is starting to truly gain the respect and ear of the C-suite. The problem is that when we get to that table, if we're armed with 'gut instinct'. . . and the marketing folks show up with charts, graphs, and hard data about what has worked in the past, we're going to look like idiots. Can you imagine if the CFO walked in and said, 'I know we're making money because my gut says so and I see checks coming in'? He'd be out the door. . . . And we should be too if we can't come up with some good numbers given all the measurement tools that are out there. It's simply fiscally irresponsible not to measure your PR results."

Managing the 24/7 News Cycle.
The flow of news and information is now a global activity that occurs 24 hours day, 7 days a week. This means that public relations personnel must constantly update information, answer journalists' inquiries at all hours of the day, and be aware that any and all information is readily available to a worldwide audience.

New media and technology make it possible to disseminate news and information all day long, but the effect is often information overload. In addition to the proliferation of traditional media outlets, there are virtually millions of Web sites. A major challenge to today's practitioners is how to cope with the cascade of information and how to give it shape and purpose so that it's relevant to multiple audiences.

New Directions in Mass Media. Traditional media isn't what it used to be. U.S. circulation of English-language dailies has dropped 11 percent since 1990. Network evening news ratings have fallen 34 percent since 1993. Local news share is down 16 percent since 1997. Even cable news ratings have been flat since late 2001. Public relations personnel are expanding their communication tools to account for the fact that no single mass medium will be a good vehicle for reaching key publics.

One new avenue is the ethnic press. For example, over the past 13 years, Spanish-language newspaper circulation has nearly quadrupled to 1.7 million. Another avenue is the Internet. More than 55 percent of Internet users from 18 to 34 years old obtain news online in a typical week, according to a UCLA Internet study.

Another trend is the electronic preparation of media materials. The printed news release and media kit are quickly becoming historic artifacts. An IABC study found that electronic newsletters, e-mail notices, Web sites, and CDs or DVDs are rapidly replacing print materials.

Outsourcing to Public Relations Firms. The outsourcing trend developed some years ago, but now it's almost universal. A survey by Ian Mitroff, Gerald Swerling, and Jennifer Floto published in the *Strategist* notes, "The use of agencies is now the norm in American business across all revenue categories and industries in this study: 85 percent of respondents (corporate executives) work with outside PR firms." This is not to say that corporate public relations departments are disappearing, but increasingly such tasks as media relations, annual reports, and sponsored events are being outsourced to public relations firms.

The Need for Lifelong Learning. Given the rapid additions to knowledge in today's society, public relations personnel will need to continually update their knowledge base just to stay current. New findings in a variety of fields are emerging that can be applied to public relations practice. Some of these fields are behavioral genetics, evolutionary social psychology, economics, the physics of information, social network analysis, semiotic game theory, and the use of technology to create relationships and dialogue with various publics.

In addition, the need to specialize in a particular field or area of public relations will increase because it's becoming almost impossible for a generalist to master the detailed knowledge required for such areas as health care and financial relations. One growing specialty area is environmental communication.

Professional organizations such as the Public Relations Society of America and consulting companies provide learning opportunities through workshops and "webinars," which are seminars conducted on the Web.

Increased Emphasis on Financial Relations. The corporate scandals involving Enron, WorldCom, and Tyco have prompted a whole new series of government regulations. One new regulation is the Sarbanes-Oxley Act of 2002, which dictates how companies must disclose information (see Chapter 7).

A Growing Professional Practice

Public relations as a profession faces several criticisms — practitioners are often accused of being unethical, spinmeisters, and more. One way that the profession has chosen to address such criticism is through the education of practitioners about issues related to professional practice. By "professional" practice we mean that public relations practitioners should have a common set of ideals and expectations for what is acceptable in practice. Like lawyers, doctors, teachers, nurses, accountants, and other professions, for public relations to be considered a respected and admired profession, many practitioners argue, there must be guiding standards. The following sections address some of the issues related to what it means to be a professional public relations practitioner.

The Public Relations Society of America (PRSA)

The largest national public relations organization in the world is the Public Relations Society of America (PRSA); the group's Web site can be found at www.prsa.org. PRSA is headquartered in New York City. It has more than 20,000 members organized into 112 chapters nationwide. It also has 19 professional interest sections that represent such areas as business and industry, counseling firms, independent practitioners, the military, government agencies, associations, hospitals, schools, nonprofit organizations, and even educators.

PRSA has an extensive professional development program that offers short courses, seminars, teleconferences, and Webcasts throughout the year. In addition to workshops and seminars, PRSA holds an annual meeting and publishes *Tactics*, a monthly tabloid of current news and professional tips, and the *Strategist*, a quarterly magazine with in-depth articles about the profession and issues related to practice. The organization also sponsors the Silver Anvil and Bronze Anvil awards to recognize outstanding public relations campaigns.

PRSA is also the parent organization of the Public Relations Student Society of America (PRSSA), whose Web site can be found at www.prssa.org. This group is the world's largest preprofessional public relations organization, having 286 campus chapters and 9,600 student members.

The student groups offer career-related programs at the local chapter level and provide mentoring and networking with the local professional PRSA chapter. It has a national publication, *Forum*, and sponsors a national case study competition to encourage students to exercise the analytical skills and mature judgment required for public relations problem solving. After graduation, PRSSA members are eligible to become associate members of PRSA.

The International Association of Business Communicators (IABC)

The second-largest organization of communication and public relations professionals is the International Association of Business Communicators (IABC). The group's Web site can be accessed at www.iabc.com. It has more than 13,000 members in 60 nations. Most members live in the United States, but it has many members in Canada, the United Kingdom, and Hong Kong. The Toronto chapter, for example, has about 1,300 members, or about 10 percent of the entire IABC membership.

IABC, headquartered in San Francisco, has similar objectives as the PRSA. Its mission is to "provide lifelong learning opportunities that give IABC members the tools and information to be the best in their chosen disciplines." It does this through year-round seminars and workshops and an annual meeting. The organization also has an awards program, the Gold Quill, that honors excellence in business communication.

The IABC's publication is *Communication World*, which features professional tips and articles on current issues. IABC also sponsors campus student chapters, but it is not comparable to PRSSA in size or organizational structure.

The International Public Relations Association (IPRA)

A third organization, thoroughly global in scope, is the International Public Relations Association (IPRA), which is based in London. The group's Web site is available at www.ipra.org. IPRA has 1,000 members in 96 nations. Its membership is primarily senior international public relations executives, and its mission is "to provide intellectual leadership in the practice of international public relations by making available to our members the services and information that will help them to meet their professional responsibilities and to succeed in their careers."

IPRA organizes regional and international conferences to discuss issues in global public relations, but it also reaches its widespread membership through its Web site and *Frontline*, its premier publication, which is available online. It also issues Gold Papers on public relations practice and conducts an annual awards competition (Golden World Awards).

Other Groups

The PRSA, IABC, and IPRA are the largest broad-based organizations for communicators and public relations professionals. In addition, there are smaller, more specialized organizations. Three of the better known ones in the United States include the Council for the Advancement and Support of Education (CASE), the National Investor Relations Institute (NIRI), and the National School Public Relations Association (NSPRA). There also are a number of statewide groups, such as the Florida Public Relations Association, the Maine Public Relations Council, the Texas Public Relations Association, and the Puerto Rico Public Relations Association (Asociacion de Relacionistas Profesionales de Puerto Rico).

Professionalism, Licensing, and Accreditation

Is public relations a profession? Should its practitioners be licensed? Does the accreditation of practitioners constitute a sufficient guarantee of their talents and integrity? These and related questions face the public relations profession.

Professionalism

Among public relations practitioners, there are considerable differences of opinion about whether public relations is a craft, a skill, or a developing profession. Certainly, at its present level, public relations does not qualify as a profession in the same sense that medicine and law do. Public relations does not have prescribed standards of educational preparation, a mandatory period of apprenticeship, or state laws that govern admission to the profession.

Adding to the confusion about professionalism is the difficulty of ascertaining what constitutes public relations practice. John F. Budd, Jr., a veteran counselor, wrote in *Public Relations Quarterly:* "We act as publicists, yet we talk of counseling. We perform as technologists in communication, but we aspire to be decision-makers dealing in policy."

On the other hand, there is a rapidly expanding body of literature about public relations—including this text and many others in the field. The two major scholarly publications serving the field are *Public Relations Review* and the *Journal of Public Relations Research*. Substantial progress also is being made in developing theories of public relations, conducting research, and publishing scholarly journals.

There is also the idea, advanced by many professionals and PRSA itself, that the most important thing is for the individual to act like a professional in the field. This means that a practitioner should have:

> A sense of independence
> A sense of responsibility to society and the public interest
> Manifest concern for the competence and honor of the profession as a whole
> A higher loyalty to the standards of the profession and fellow professionals than to the employer of the moment

Unfortunately, a major barrier to professionalism is the attitude that many practitioners themselves have toward their work. As James Grunig and Todd Hunt note in their book *Managing Public Relations*, practitioners tend to hold more "careerist" values than professional values. In other words, they place higher importance on job security, prestige in the organization, salary level, and recognition from superiors than on the values just listed. For example, 47 percent of the respondents in a survey of IABC members gave a neutral or highly negative answer when asked if they would quit their jobs rather than act against their ethical values. And 55 percent considered it "somewhat ethical" to present oneself misleadingly as the only means of achieving an objective. Almost all agreed, however, that ethics is an important matter, worthy of further study.

On another level, many practitioners are limited in their professionalism by what might be termed a "technician mentality." These people narrowly define professionalism as the ability to do a competent job of executing the mechanics of communicating (preparing news releases, brochures, newsletters, and so on) even if the information provided by management or a client is in bad taste, is misleading, lacks documentation, or is just plain wrong.

In other words, readers may get the impression that the public relations expertise of a firm is available to the highest bidder, regardless of professional values, fair play, and ultimately, the public interest. When public relations firms and departments take no responsibility for what is communicated—only how it is communicated in terms of techniques—they reinforce the perception that public relations is more flackery than profession.

Some practitioners defend the technician mentality, however, arguing that public relations people are like lawyers in the court of public opinion. Everyone is entitled to his or her viewpoint, these practitioners argue, and whether the public relations person agrees or not, the client or employer has a right to be heard. Thus, they say, a public relations representative is a paid advocate, just as a lawyer is. The only flaw in this argument is that public relations people are not lawyers, who operate in a court of law where judicial standards are applied. In addition, lawyers have been known to turn down clients or resign from a case because they doubted the client's story.

Finally, courts are increasingly holding public relations firms accountable for information disseminated on behalf of a client. Thus, it is no longer acceptable to say, "The client told me to do it."

Licensing

Proposals that public relations practitioners be licensed were discussed even before PRSA was founded 60 years ago. One proponent, Edward B. Bernays, believed that licensing would protect the profession and the public from incompetent, shoddy opportunists who do not have the knowledge, talent, or ethics required of public relations professionals. He argued unsuccessfully for legislation requiring licensing in his home state of Massachusetts.

Under the licensing approach, only those individuals who pass rigid examinations and tests of personal integrity could call themselves "public relations" counselors. Those not licensed would have to call themselves "publicists" or adopt some other designation.

Advocates say licensing would help define public relations, establish uniform educational criteria, set uniform professional standards, protect clients and employers from imposters, protect qualified practitioners from unethical or unqualified competition, and raise practitioners' overall credibility. Opponents of licensing say that it won't work because: any licensing in the communications field would violate the First Amendment; civil and criminal laws exist to deal with malpractice; licensing is a function of state governments, but public relations people often work on a national and international level; licensing ensures only minimum competence and professional standards, not high ethical behavior; the credibility and status of an occupation are not necessarily ensured through licensing; and setting up the machinery for licensing and policing would be very expensive to taxpayers.

The opponents seem to have won the day. Today, there is no particular interest on the part of the public relations industry, the consumer movement, or even state governments to initiate any form of legislated licensing. An alternative to licensing is accreditation.

Accreditation

The major effort to improve standards and professionalism in public relations around the world has been the establishment of accreditation programs. This means that practitioners voluntarily go through a process by which they are "certified" by a national organization that they are competent, qualified professionals.

PRSA, for example, began its accreditation program more than 40 years ago. A testing process for members provides the opportunity to earn Accredited in Public Relations (APR) status. Other national groups, including the IABC, the Canadian Public Relations Society (CPRS), the British Institute of Public Relations (BIPR), the Public Relations Institute of Australia (PRIA), and the Public Relations Institute of Southern Africa (PRISA), to name just a few, also have established accreditation programs.

The approach used by most national groups is to administer written and oral exams and require candidates to submit a portfolio of work samples to a committee of professional peers. IABC, for example, places a major emphasis on the individual's portfolio of accomplishments as part of its Accredited Business Communicator (ABC) certification. The candidate also must outline the objectives of a campaign, present the overall communications strategy, and provide evaluation of the results. About 10 percent of IABC's 13,000 members have the ABC designation.

Most groups also have guidelines as to how many years of experience are required before a person can apply for accredited or membership status. Some groups are beginning to require continuing education as a prerequisite for professional certification.

The PRSA Approach. When it developed a program for its members in 1965, PRSA was one of the first public relations organizations to offer accreditation. Candidates are required to take a preview course (available online), complete a "readiness" questionnaire, and show a portfolio of work to a panel of professional peers before taking the written exam, which is available at test centers throughout the United States. In addition, the member must have five years of professional experience.

The 2.5-hour exam tests knowledge of the field and gives proportional weight to various core topics: research, planning, execution, and evaluation of programs (30 percent); ethics and law (15 percent); communication models and theories (15 percent); business literacy (10 percent); management skills (10 percent); crisis communication management (10 percent); media relations (5 percent); information technology (2 percent); history and current issues in public relations (2 percent); and advanced communication skills (1 percent). Candidates who pass earn the APR credential. To date, about 5,000 practitioners have earned APR status, or about 18 percent of the PRSA's membership.

A Changing Profession

As you can see, public relations ideas and tactics have been around a long time. A historic view of this dynamic profession provides an understanding of how public relations is continuing to grow and evolve through the help of public relations professional organizations, scholars and innovative practitioners.

Summary

A Brief History of Public Relations

Although *public relations* is a 20th-century term, the roots of the practice go back to ancient Egyptian, Greek, and Roman times. The American Revolution, in part, was the result of such staged events as the Boston Tea Party, and the publication of the *Federalist Papers* help cement the federal system of the new government. The 1800s were the golden age of the press agent. P.T. Barnum used many techniques that are still employed today. In addition, the settlement of the West was due in large part to promotions by land developers and American railroads. Toward the end of the 19th century, corporations began to use public relations as a response to public criticism of their policies and actions. From 1900 to 1950, the practice of public relations was transformed by individuals such as Henry Ford, Ivy Lee, George Creel, and Edward B. Bernays. The concept moved from press agentry to the more journalistic approach of distributing accurate public information. The period from 1950 to 2000 saw the consolidation of public relations as a major established force in American society. As the U.S. population grew, the economy expanded, and big business became the norm, organizations found it necessary to employ public relations specialists to effectively communicate with the mass media and a variety of publics. This was the age of scientific persuasion, management by objective, and strategic thinking.

Trends in Today's Practice of Public Relations

A major trend in public relations has been the influx of women into the field. Women now comprise 70 percent of public relations practitioners in the United States. This has raised questions about gender discrimination, why women hold more tactical than managerial positions, and whether there is still a "glass ceiling." The public relations workforce is still overwhelmingly white. Efforts are being made to diversify the workforce to better represent ethnic/minority groups. Hispanics now constitute the largest minority in the United States, but are poorly represented in public relations practice.

A Growing Professional Practice

Professional organizations such as PRSA, IABC, and IPRA play an important role in setting standards and providing education and networking opportunities for public relations professionals.

Professionalism, Licensing, and Accreditation

Freedom of speech concerns severely limit the concept of licensing in the communication fields, including public relations. Accreditation programs for practitioners, with continuing education, is an attractive alternative.

CASE ACTIVITY >>

What Would You Do?

Analyzing Trends and Historic Figures

The latter part of this chapter identified a number of trends in public relations, including the feminization of the field and the drive for a more diversified workforce. Other trends include the decline of the mass media, the need for lifelong learning, and the public's demand for organizational transparency.

Select one of these issues and do some additional research. Write a short paper or make a presentation from the standpoint of what a public relations person should know about this issue and how it may affect working in public relations.

An alternative is to do more research on one of the pioneers in public relations and give a short report.

Questions for Review and Discussion

1. Which concepts of publicity and public relations practiced by P. T. Barnum should modern practitioners use? Which should they reject?

2. What are the four important contributions Ivy Lee made to public relations?

3. The Boston Tea Party has been described as the "greatest and best-known publicity stunt of all time." Would you agree? Do you feel that staged events are a legitimate way to publicize a cause and motivate people?

4. Describe briefly the publicity strategies employed by Henry Ford.

5. What's your assessment of Ivy Lee's work for the Rockefeller family in the Colorado Fuel & Iron Company labor strife? Do you think his approach was sound? What would you have done differently?

6. Arthur W. Page enunciated six principles of public relations management. Do you think these principles are as relevant today as they were in the 1930s?

7. Summarize the major developments in the philosophy and practice of public relations from the 1920s to 2000.

8. James Grunig outlined four models of public relations practice. Name and describe each one? Do the models help explain the evolution of public relations theory?

9. Public relations is now described as "relationship management." How would you describe this concept to a friend? A newer concept is the idea that the purpose of public relations is to establish a "dialogue" with individuals and various publics. Is this a worthy concept?

10. Females now constitute the majority of public relations personnel. How do you personally feel about

this? Does it make the field of public relations more attractive or less attractive to you?

11. Should public relations practitioners be licensed? What are the pros and cons of licensing?

12. Why do "careerism" and the "technician mentality" undermine efforts to establish professional standards in public relations?

Suggested Readings

Aldoory, Linda, and Elizabeth Toth. "Leadership and Gender in Public Relations: Perceived Effectiveness of Transformational and Transactional Leadership Styles." *Journal of Public Relations Research* 16, no. 2 (2004): 157–183.

Brody, E. W. "Have You Made the Transition? Are You Practicing Public Relations in the 21st Century Rather Than the 20th?" *Public Relations Quarterly* (Spring 2004): 7–8.

Choi, Youjin, and Linda Childers Hon. "The Influence of Gender Composition in Powerful Positions on Public Relations Practitioners' Gender-Related Perceptions." *Journal of Public Relations Research* 14, no. 3 (2002): 229–263.

Cutlip, Scott M. *The Unseen Power: A History of Public Relations.* Mahwah, NJ: Erlbaum, 1994.

David, Prabu. "Extending Symmetry: Toward a Convergence of Professionalism, Practice, and Pragmatics in Public Relations." *Journal of Public Relations Research* 16, no. 2 (2004): 185–211.

Grunig, Larissa A., Elizabeth L. Toth, and Linda C. Hon. *Women in Public Relations: How Gender Influences Practice.* New York: Guilford, 2001.

Hallahan, Kirk. "Ivy Lee and the Rocefellers' Response to the 1913–1914 Colorado Coal Strike." *Journal of Public Relations Research* 14, no. 4 (2002): 265–315.

Kent, Michael L., and Maureen Taylor. "Toward a Dialogic Theory of Public Relations." *Public Relations Review* 28, no. 1 (2002): 21–37.

Lukaszewski, James E. "Five Crucial Questions to Ask: Making Managers Better Communicators (or Even Leaders)." *Public Relations Tactics,* October 2006, 10.

Mercer, Laura. "For Those Entering Public Relations: How to Be Recognized as a True Professional." *Public Relations Tactics,* April 2004, 24.

Piasecki, Andy. "Blowing the Railroad Trumpet: Public Relations on the American Frontier." *Public Relations Review* 26, no. 1 (2000): 53–65.

Pompper, Donnalyn. "Linking Ethnic Diversity and Two-Way Symmetry: Modeling Female African American Practitioner Roles." *Journal of Public Relations Research* 16, no. 3 (2004): 269–299.

Van Ruler, Betteke.: The communication grid: an introduction of a model of four communication strategies." *Public Relations Review* 30, no. 2 (2004): 123–143.

Chapter Four

Today's Practice:
Departments and Firms

Public Relations Departments

Public relations departments serve various roles and functions within companies and organizations. The following sections discuss the public relations function in various organizational structures and the pros and cons of working in a public relations department.

Role in Various Organizational Structures

For more than a century, public relations departments have served companies and organizations. George Westinghouse reportedly created the first corporate public relations department in 1889 when he hired two men to publicize his pet project, alternating current (AC) electricity. Their work was relatively simple compared to the mélange of physical, sociological, and psychological elements that contemporary departments employ. Eventually Westinghouse won out over Thomas A. Edison's direct current (DC) system, and his method became the standard in the United States. Westinghouse's public relations department concept has also grown into a fundamental part of today's electronic world.

Importance in Today's World.
Today, public relations is expanding from its traditional functions to exercise influence in the highest levels of management. In a changing environment, and faced with the variety of pressures previously described, executives increasingly see public relations not as simply publicity and one-way communication, but as a complex and dynamic process of negotiation and compromise with a number of key publics. James Grunig, professor of public relations at the University of Maryland, calls the new approach "building good relationships with strategic publics," which require public relations executives to be "strategic communication managers rather than communication technicians."

Grunig, head of a six-year IABC Foundation research study on Excellence in Public Relations and Communications Management, continues:

> When public relations helps that organization build relationships, it saves the organization money by reducing the costs of litigation, regulation, legislation, pressure campaign boycotts, or lost revenue that result from bad relationships with publics—publics that become activist groups when relationships are bad. It also helps the organization make money by cultivating relationships with donors, customers, shareholders and legislators.

The results of the IABC study seem to indicate that chief executive officers (CEOs) consider public relations to be a good investment. A survey of 200 organizations showed that CEOs gave public relations operations a 184 percent return on investment (ROI), a figure just below that of customer service and sales/marketing.

Ideally, professional public relations people assist top management in developing policy and communicating with various groups. Indeed, the IABC study emphasizes that CEOs want communication that is strategic, based on research, and involves two-way communication with key publics.

Dudley H. Hafner, executive vice president of the American Heart Association (AHA), echoed these thoughts:

> In the non-profit business sector, as well as in the for-profit business of America, leadership needs to pay close attention to what our audiences (supporters or customers as well as the general public) want, what they need, what their attitudes are, and what is happening in organizations similar to ours. Seeking, interpreting, and communicating this type of critical information is the role of the communications professional.

Importance of Organizational Structure. Research indicates, however, that the role of public relations in an organization often depends on the type of organization, the perceptions of top management, and even the capabilities of the public relations executive. Research studies by Professor Larissa Grunig at the University of Maryland and Mark McElreath at Towson State University, among others, show that large, complex organizations have a greater tendency than do smaller firms to include public relations in the policy-making process.

Companies such as IBM and General Motors, which operate in a highly competitive environment, are more sensitive than many others to policy issues and public attitudes and to establishing a solid corporate identity. Consequently, they place more emphasis on news conferences, formal contact with the media, writing executive speeches, and counseling management about issues that could potentially affect the corporate bottom line. In such organizations, which are classified as mixed organic/mechanical by management theorists, the authority and power of the public relations department are quite high. Public relations is part of what is called the "dominant coalition" and has a great deal of autonomy.

In contrast, a small-scale organization of low complexity that offers a standardized product or service feels few public pressures and face little governmental regulatory interest. It has scant public relations activity, and staff members are relegated to such technician roles as producing the company newsletter and issuing routine news releases. Public relations in such traditional organizations has little or no input into management decisions and policy formation.

Research also indicates that the type of organization involved may be less significant in predicting the role of its public relations department than are the perceptions and expectations of its top management. In many organizations, top-level management perceives public relations as primarily a journalistic and technical function—media relations and publicity. In large-scale mechanical organizations of low complexity, there is also a tendency to think of public relations as merely a support function of the marketing department.

Such perceptions by top management severely limit the role of the public relations department as well as its power to take part in management decision making. Instead, public relations is relegated to a tactical function—simply preparing messages without input on what should be communicated. In many cases, however, public relations personnel self-select technician roles because they lack a knowledge base in research, environmental scanning, problem solving, and managing total communications strategies. Research by Professors Elizabeth Toth, Linda Hon, Linda Aldoory, and Larissa Grunig also suggests that many practitioners prefer and choose the technician roles because they are more personally fulfilled by working tactically rather than strategically.

The most admired Fortune 500 corporations, in terms of reputation, tend to think of public relations as more of a strategic management tool. A study by the University of Southern California (USC) Annenberg Strategic Public Relations Center and the Council of Public Relations Firms found that these companies dedicated a larger percentage of their gross revenues to public relations activities, extensively used outside public relations firms to supplement their own large staffs, and didn't have public relations staff report to the marketing department. Summarizing the survey, *PRWeek* said, "PR Departments that closely align their own goals with their companies' strategic business goals receive greater executive support, have larger budgets, and have a higher perceived contribution to their organizations' success."

The primary indicator of a department's influence and power, however, is whether the top communications officer has a seat at the management table. To gain and maintain a seat at the management table should be an ongoing goal of public relations practitioners. Experts indicate that it is increasingly common for the top public relations practitioner in an organization to report to the CEO. But these PR pros must know how to behave to maintain their place at the table, according to Tom Martin, SVP of corporate relations for ITT Industries. In its 2006 survey of 500 senior-level practitioners, the Annenberg Strategic Public Relations Center found that almost two-thirds of all respondents and 77 percent of Fortune 500 respondents reported to the "C-Suite" (CEO, COO, or chairperson). The report adds, "They were much more likely to indicate that their CEOs believe PR contributes to market share, financial success, and sales, than those reporting to other parts of the organization."

Jerry Swerling, director of the Annenberg survey, summarizes:

C-Suite reporting leads to many other pluses for PR. Statistical correlations revealed that respondents reporting to the C-Suite were significantly more likely to report that PR is taken seriously within the organization, gets a higher level of support from senior management, and participates in organizational strategic planning; that their CEOs believe reputation contributes to organizational success; that the various communications functions within the organization are bettter integrated and coordinated; and that their organizations are flexible, people first, and proactive.

Julie O'Neil of Texas Christian University researched the sources of influence for corporate public relations practitioners. She reported in a *Public Relations Review* article that having influence in the company was based on four factors: (1) perception of value by top management, (2) practitioners taking on the managerial role, (3) reporting to the CEO, and (4) years of professional experience. In another study, Bruce Berger of the University of Alabama and Bryan Reber of the University of Georgia interviewed 162 public relations professionals and found that the top sources of influence among those practitioners were (1) relationships with others, (2) professional experience, (3) performance record, (4) persuasive skills with top executives, and (5) professional expertise.

Names of Departments

A public relations department in an organization goes by many names. And most often it is not "public relations." In the largest corporations (the Fortune 500), the terms *corporate communications* or *communications* outnumber public relations by almost four to one.

O'Dwyer's PR Services Report, in a survey of the Fortune 500 companies, found 200 such communications departments and only 48 public relations departments. Among those switching from public relations to corporate communications in recent years are Procter & Gamble and Hershey Candies. In both cases, the companies say that the switch occurred because the department had expanded beyond "public relations" to include such activities as employee communications, shareholder communications, annual reports, consumer relations, and corporate philanthropy.

Such activities, however, are considered subcategories of modern public relations, so consultant Alfred Geduldig has offered another reason. He told *O'Dwyer's PR Services Report* that the term *public relations* had suffered from repeated derogatory usage, causing companies to move away from the term. He also thought that the term *corporate communications* was a sign that public relations people were doing many more things in a company than in the past, reflecting an integration of communications services.

Echoing this thought is Linda Ambrose, director of corporate affairs for Tenneco. She says that the company changed the department name from public relations to "elevate the function of the department." The unit now handles internal relations, speech writing, and community affairs. It is headed by a vice president who reports to the chairman of the company. "So corporate affairs is precisely what it is," Ambrose told *O'Dwyer's PR Services Report.*

Other names used for public relations departments in the corporate world include corporate relations, investor relations, public affairs, marketing communications, public and community relations, and external affairs. Government agencies, educational institutions, and charitable organizations use such terms as public affairs, community relations, public information, and even market services.

Organization of Departments

The head executive of a public relations or similarly named department usually has one of three titles: manager, director, or vice president. A vice president of corporate communications may have direct responsibility for the additional activities of advertising and marketing communications.

A department usually is divided into specialized sections that have a coordinator or manager. Common sections found in a large corporation are media relations, investor relations, consumer affairs, governmental relations, community relations, marketing communications, and employee communications. The organizational chart of IBM's corporate communications department is shown in Figure 4.1.

One of the world's largest corporations, General Motors, has more than 300 public relations personnel with a wide range of job titles based on geography and operating divisions. Each division, such as Buick or the Saginaw Steering Gear Division, has its own director of public relations. General Electric, another corporate giant, has several hundred persons in various public relations functions.

These examples should not mislead you about the size and budget of public relations departments. The USC study found that Fortune 500 companies typically have 24 professionals in the corporate communications/public relations department and an average annual budget of $8.5 million. Another study by the Conference Board of other large U.S. corporations found that the typical public relations department had nine professionals. The USC study found that the average annual budget for Fortune 501 to 1,000 companies was $2.2 million. Of course, thousands of even smaller companies employ only one or two public relations practitioners.

Public relations personnel may also be dispersed throughout an organization in such a manner that an observer can have difficulty ascertaining the extent of public relations activity. Some staff may be housed under marketing communications in the

FIGURE 4.1

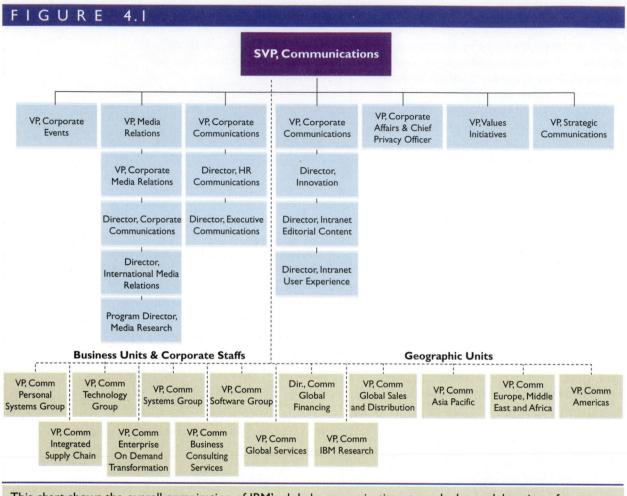

This chart shows the overall organization of IBM's global communications team. It shows delegation of responsibilities by function, business unit, and geography under a senior vice president of communications. Courtesy of Jon Iwata, IBM Corporation.

marketing department. Others may be assigned to the personnel department as communication specialists producing newsletters and brochures. Still others may be in marketing, working exclusively on product publicity. Decentralization of the public relations function, and the frictions it causes, will be discussed later in this chapter.

Line and Staff Functions

Traditional management theory divides an organization into line and staff functions. A line manager, such as a vice president of manufacturing, can delegate authority, set production goals, hire employees, and directly influence the work of others. Staff people, in contrast, have little or no direct authority. Instead, they indirectly influence the work of others through suggestions, recommendations, and advice.

According to accepted management theory, public relations is a staff function. Public relations professionals are experts in communication (see the Insights box on this page); line managers, including the chief executive officer, rely on them to use their skills in preparing and processing data, making recommendations, and executing communication programs to meet organizational objectives.

Public relations staff members, for example, may find through a community survey that people have only a vague understanding of what their company manufactures. To improve community comprehension and create greater rapport, the public relations department may recommend to top management that a community open house be held at which product demonstrations, tours, and entertainment would be featured.

Notice that the department recommends this action. It would have no direct authority to decide on its own to hold an open house or to order various departments within the company to cooperate. If top management approves the proposal, the department may take responsibility for organizing the event. Top management, as line managers, has the authority to direct all departments to cooperate in the activity.

Although public relations departments can function only with the approval of top management, there are varying levels of influence that departments may exert. These levels will be discussed shortly.

ON THE JOB >>

The Functions of a Corporate PR/Communications Department

Insights

A 2006 survey of corporations by *PRWeek* asked respondents what activities their departments performed. Listed below is the percent of in-house departments responsible for the following public relations functions:

Media relations	79.5%
Crisis management	62.6%
Employee communications	59.4%
Online communications	58.0%
Special events	56.6%
Community relations	55.7%
Reputation management	54.8%
Product/Brand communication	51.1%
Marketing	45.7%
Public affairs/Governmental relations	35.2%
Annual/Quarterly reports	34.7%
Product/Brand advertising	34.2%
Issues advertising	31.1%
Cause-related marketing	27.9%
Financial/Investor relations	21.5%
Monitoring blogs	20.5%
Writing blogs	12.3%
Blog relations	11.9%

Source: "Corporate Survey 2006." *PRWeek*, October 9, 2006, 21.

Access to Management. The power and influence of a public relations department usually result from access to top management, which uses advice and recommendations to formulate policy. That is why public relations, as well as other staff functions, is located high in the organizational chart and is called on by top management to make reports and recommendations on issues affecting the entire company. In today's environment, public acceptance or nonacceptance of a proposed policy is an important factor in decision making—as important as costing and technological ability. This is why the former president of RJR Nabisco, F. Ross Johnson, told the *Wall Street Journal* in an interview that his senior public relations aide was "Numero Uno" and quipped, "He is the only one who has an unlimited budget and exceeds it every year."

Levels of Influence. Management experts state that staff functions in an organization operate at various levels of influence and authority. On the lowest level, the staff function may be simply advisory: Line management has no obligation to take recommendations or even request them.

When public relations is purely advisory, it often is not effective. A good example is the Enron scandal. The energy company generated a great deal of public, legislative, and media criticism because public relations was relegated to such a low level, it was, for all practical purposes, nonexistent.

Johnson & Johnson, on the other hand, gives its public relations staff function higher status. The Tylenol crisis, in which seven persons died after taking capsules containing cyanide, clearly showed that the company based much of its reaction and quick recall of the product on the advice of public relations staff. In this case, public relations occupied a compulsory-advisory position.

Under a compulsory-advisory setup, organization policy requires that line managers (top management) at least listen to the appropriate staff experts before deciding on a strategy. Don Hellriegel and John Slocum, authors of the textbook *Management*, state: "Although such a procedure does not limit the manager's decision-making discretion, it ensures that the manager has made use of the specialized talents of the appropriate staff agency."

Another level of the advisory relationship within an organization is concurring authority. For instance, an operating division wishing to publish a brochure cannot do so unless the public relations department approves the copy and layout. If differences arise, the parties must agree before work can proceed. Many firms use this mode to prevent departments and divisions from disseminating materials that do not conform with company standards. In addition, the company must ascertain that its trademarks are used correctly to ensure continued protection.

Concurring authority, however, may also limit the freedom of the public relations department. Some companies have a policy that all employee magazine articles and external news releases must be reviewed by the legal staff before publication. The material cannot be disseminated until legal and public relations personnel have agreed on what will be said. The situation is even more limiting on public relations when the legal department has command authority to change a news release with or without the consent of public relations. This is one reason that newspaper editors find some news releases so filled with "legalese" as to be almost unreadable.

There are times when legal counsel and public relations practitioners work collaboratively. When Norfolk Southern railroad embarked on a bid to buy Conrail, Norfolk Southern's public relations executive Robert Fort recalled that in-house representatives of public relations and law met daily. "We had to be very careful what we said and how we said it and also to get it reported to the Securities and Exchange Commission on a daily basis," said one of Norfolk Southern's in-house lawyers. Fort said that legal and public relations personnel were on equal footing. "In the past. . . eventually, if there is a point of contention between PR and law, law usually wins," he explained. "In this case, the law department was actually asking us, and not only asking us for our advice, but then used it when we gave it to them. I think they recognized that this was historic event about to take place here and that as it unfolded it was going to have to be won on the basis of public opinion."

Sources of Friction

Ideally, public relations is part of the managerial subsystem and contributing to organizational strategy. Public relations is, say professors James and Larissa Grunig, "the management of communication between an organization and its publics." However, other staff functions also are involved in the communication process with internal and external publics. And, almost invariably, friction occurs. The four areas of possible friction are legal, human resources, advertising, and marketing.

Legal. The legal staff is concerned about the possible effect of any public statement on current or potential litigation. Consequently, lawyers often frustrate public relations personnel by taking the attitude that any public statement can potentially be used against the organization in a lawsuit. Conflicts over what to release and when often have a paralyzing effect on decision making, causing the organization to seem unresponsive to public concerns. This is particularly true in a crisis, when the public demands immediate information. Public relations practitioners who are members of the management team often combat this situation, when appropriate, by taking a tough stance and aggressively making a case to the CEO that public opinion and erosion of brand or market share may be more expensive than the outcome of potential litigation.

Human Resources. The traditional personnel department has now evolved into handling the expanded role of "human resources," and there are often turf battles over who is responsible for employee communications. Human resources personnel believe they should control the flow of information. Public relations administrators counter that satisfactory external communications cannot be achieved unless effective employee relations are conducted simultaneously. Layoffs, for example, affect not only employees but also the community and investors.

Advertising. Advertising and public relations departments often collide because they compete for funds to communicate with external audiences. Philosophical differences also arise. Advertising's approach to communications is, "Will it increase sales?" Public relations asks, "Will it make friends?" These different orientations frequently cause breakdowns in coordination of overall strategy.

Marketing. Marketing, like advertising, tends to think only of customers or potential buyers as key publics. Public relations, on the other hand, defines *publics* in a broader sense—any group that can have an impact on the operations of the organization. These publics include governmental agencies, environmental groups, neighborhood groups, and a host of other publics that marketing would not consider customers.

This led James Grunig, editor of the IABC study, to conclude, "We believe, then, that public relations must emerge as a discipline distinct from marketing and that it must be practiced separately from marketing in the organization." Logic dictates, however, that an organization needs a coordinated and integrated approach to communications strategy. Indeed, one survey found that 65 percent of corporate managers were now spending more time on developing integrated communications programs. The following suggestions may help achieve this goal:

> Representatives of departments should serve together on key committees to exchange information on how various programs can complement each other to achieve overall organizational objectives. If representatives from human resources, public relations, legal, and investor relations would present a united front to senior managers, their influence would likely be increased exponentially.

> Collaboration or coalition building among departments with shared interests in communication issues can also help achieve organization-wide business goals.

This chart depicts three examples of corporate management organization, showing the important position of public relations.

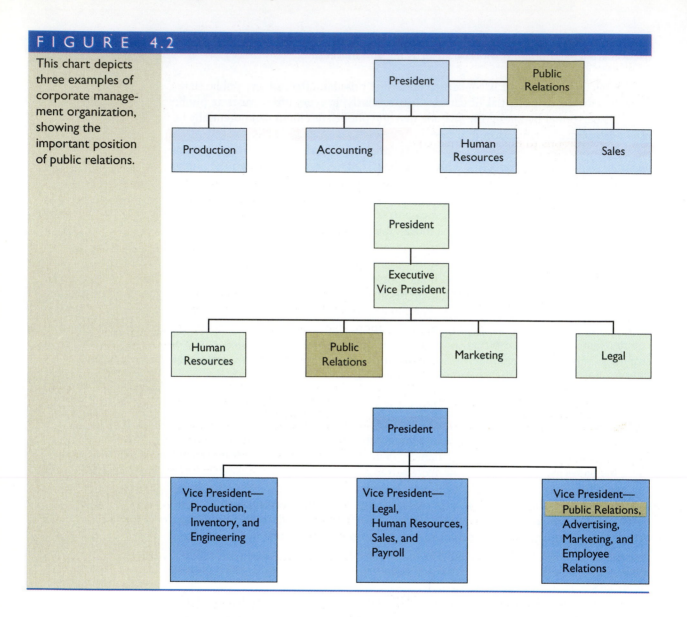

> Heads of departments should be equals in job title. In this way, the autonomy of one department is not subverted by another.

> All department heads should report to the same superior, so that all viewpoints can be considered before an appropriate strategy is formulated.

> Informal, regular contacts with representatives of other departments help dispel mind-sets and create understanding and respect for each other's viewpoints.

> Written policies should be established to spell out the responsibilities of each department. Such policies are helpful in settling disputes over which department has authority to communicate with employees or alter a news release.

Some organizational charts for public relations and other departments are shown in Figure 4.2.

The Trend Toward Outsourcing

A major trend for American corporations has been the outsourcing of services, whether telecommunications, accounting, customer service, software engineering, or even legal services. The trend line is for more organizations to outsource their communication activities to public relations firms and outside contractors. Indeed, the USC and Council of Public Relations Firms study found that Fortune 500 companies now spend 25 percent of their public relations budgets on outside firms. Almost 90 percent of the companies use outside public relations counsel to varying degrees.

A national survey by *PRWeek* found that companies of all sizes spent an average of more than 40 percent of their public relations budget on the services of outside firms. In high technology, the percentage was even higher—a whopping 66 percent of the corporate budget. In contrast, nonprofits allocated an average of 38 percent of their budgets for external public relations services. The most frequent reason given for outsourcing is to obtain expertise and resources to the organization that can't be found internally. A second reason is the need to supplement internal staffs during peak periods of activity. The most frequently outsourced activities, according to a study by Bisbee & Co. and Leone Marketing Research were, in descending order, (1) writing and communications, (2) media relations, (3) publicity, (4) strategy and planning, and (5) event planning.

Every year since 2002, the University of Southern California Annenberg Strategic Public Relations Center has conducted a survey of senior-level public relations practitioners. The survey, named the GAP (Generally Accepted Practices) Study, examines everything from percentage of gross revenue spent on public relations to the profession's reporting structure. In 2005, the GAP IV results showed:

> PR budgets increased 4 percent.
> The average PR budget was only 1.28 percent of the average advertising budget.
> CEOs believe PR contributes to positive corporate reputation, market share, financial success, and sales.
> Only 4 percent of the average PR budget is allocated to evaluation or measuring success.
> The PR function reports to the CEO, COO, or chairperson in 64 percent of organizations; it reports to marketing in 25 percent of organizations.
> Some 79 percent of Fortune 500 companies used outside agencies in 2005; 9 percent fewer than in 2004.
> Fortune 500 companies worked with three to four agencies; Fortune 501–5000 companies worked with two to three agencies.

Source: USC Annenberg Strategic Public Relations Center, *Public Relations Generally Accepted Practices (GAP) Study,* http://annenberg.usc.edu/images/PDFs/spre/section2.pdf.

The trend toward outsourcing, say many experts, follows what has occurred in advertising. Today, about 90 percent of corporate and institutional advertising is handled by agencies rather than by in-house departments. It currently appears that public relations firms will be the major beneficiaries of this trend.

The traditional "agency of record" concept, however, seems to be in decline. Today's major corporations, instead of using just one firm, now use multiple firms for various projects. The 2006 Annenberg study, for example, found that Fortune 500 companies now work with three or four different agencies in order to "cherry-pick" the best agency for a particular situation (see the Insights box above for more information from the Annenberg study).

Public Relations Firms

Public relations firms are found in every industrialized nation and most of the developing world.

A public relations firm was retained to publicize and organize the grand opening of the Smithsonian's National Museum of the American Indian. The ceremonies, which generated extensive media coverage, featured representatives from various tribes in full regalia.

With regard to size, public relations firms range from one- or two-person operations to global giants such as Weber Shandwick, which employs almost 3,000 professionals in 81 offices around the world (www.webershandwick.com). The scope of services provided to clients varies, but there are common denominators. Large or small, each firm gives counsel and performs technical services required to carry out an agreed-upon program. The firm may operate as an adjunct to an organization's public relations department or, if no department exists, conduct the entire effort.

The United States, because of its large population and economic base, is home to most of the world's public relations firms (about 9,000, according to one count) and generates the most fee income. In fact, the international committee of the Public Relations Consultancies Association reported in a worldwide study that the fee income of U.S. firms "plainly dwarfs those in all other regions."

A survey by the Council of Public Relations Firms in 2000, for example, found that U.S. industry revenues grew 33 percent over 1999 to $3 billion. Worldwide revenues were $4.6 billion. About 50 percent of the U.S. revenues were generated by the 10 largest firms. The major sectors of growth in 2000, according to the survey, were technology, 46 percent; financial products and services, 37 percent; industry, 36 percent; government and non-profit, 36 percent; health care, 30 percent; and consumer and retail, 22 percent. Fueling all this growth, as already mentioned, was the increased outsourcing of work by corporations.

American public relations firms have proliferated in proportion to the growth of the global economy. As American companies expanded after World War II into booming domestic and worldwide markets, many corporations felt a need for public relations firms that could provide them with professional expertise in communications. Also stimulating the growth of public relations firms were increased urbanization, expansion of government bureaucracy and regulation, more sophisticated mass media systems, the rise of consumerism, international trade, and the demand for more information. Executives of public relations firms predict future growth as more countries adopt free-market economies and more international media outlets such as CNN are established. In addition, the skyrocketing use of the Internet has fueled the global reach of public relations firms.

Services They Provide

Today, public relations firms provide a variety of services:

> *Marketing Communications.* This involves promotion of products and services through such tools as news releases, feature stories, special events, brochures, and media tours.
> *Executive Speech Training.* Top executives are coached on public affairs activities, including personal appearances.
> *Research and Evaluation.* Scientific surveys are conducted to measure public attitudes and perceptions.

> *Crisis Communication.* Management is counseled on what to say and do in an emergency such as an oil spill or a product recall.

> *Media Analysis.* Appropriate media are examined for targeting specific messages to key audiences.

> *Community Relations.* Management is counseled on ways to achieve official and public support for such projects as building or expanding a factory.

> *Events Management.* News conferences, anniversary celebrations, rallies, symposiums, and national conferences are planned and conducted.

> *Public Affairs.* Materials and testimony are prepared for government hearings and regulatory bodies, and background briefings are prepared.

> *Branding and Corporate Reputation.* Advice is given on programs that establish a company brand and its reputation for quality.

> *Financial Relations.* Management is counseled on ways to avoid takeover by another firm and effectively communicate with stockholders, security analysts, and institutional investors.

Public relations firms also offer specialty services as trend lines are identified. Burson-Marsteller now has a practice specialty in labor to help corporations deal with unions. Earlier, the firm set up a specialty area in environmental communications. After September 11, 2001, Fleishman-Hillard set up a practice in homeland security. Other firms offer specialty services in such areas as litigation public relations to help organizations give their side of the story when a major lawsuit is filed.

Public relations firms are also beginning to discard the term *public relations* from their official names. Thus, it's "Burson-Marsteller," and not "Burson-Marsteller Public Relations." Other firms use the term *communications.* For example, Fenton Communications describes itself as a "public interest communications firm."

Increasingly, public relations firms emphasize the counseling aspect of their services, although most of their revenues come from implementing tactical aspects, such as writing news releases and organizing special events or media tours. The transition to counseling is best expressed by Harold Burson, chairman of Burson-Marsteller, who once told an audience, "In the beginning, top management used to say to us, 'Here's the message, deliver it.' Then it became, 'What should we say?' Now, in smart organizations, it's 'What should we do?'"

Because of the counseling function, we use the phrase *public relations firm* instead of agency throughout this book. Advertising firms, in contrast, are properly called agencies because they serve as agents, buying time or space on behalf of a client.

A good source of information about public relations counseling is the Council of Public

Public relations firms with global reach offer prospective clients a variety of services. This advertisement for Fleishman-Hillard emphasizes the number of staff and offices around the world.

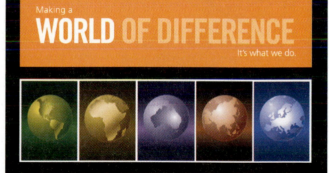

ON THE JOB >>

Firms Win Golden World Awards

Global

Public relations firms around the world handle a variety of assignments. Here are some that have received a Golden World award from the International Public Relations Association (IPRA):

> *Sigma International* (Poland). Conducted a heart disease prevention campaign to encourage high-risk individuals to get screened by medical personnel. Over 300,000 Poles underwent examination and received counseling.

> *Ruder Finn Asia* (Singapore). Organized a series of events celebrating Citigroup's 100 years of business in Asia. One event was sponsorship of 21 concerts by the New York Philharmonic in 14 Asian cities. As a result, Citigroup gained new business.

> *Strategic Objectives* (Canada). Developed a campaign to increase brand awareness of Guinness beer and increase sales. One initiative was to create grassroots support for declaring St. Patrick's Day a national holiday in Canada.

> *Weber-Shandwick* (Germany). Coordinated a campaign by McDonald's in Germany to celebrate World Children's Day by having children use tray liners to pen their wishes for the future. The top two wishes: peace/no war and better schools and playgrounds.

> *United Partners Ltd.* (Bulgaria). The firm, on behalf of Procter & Gamble, organized and publicized a "Teen Information Center" Web site. Experts in psychology, sex education, drug abuse, and personal relationships were trained to answer inquiries from teenagers via the Web site. Procter & Gamble's objective was corporate citizenship.

> *Kaizo* (United Kingdom). Developed a campaign to increase printer manufacturer Epson's market share by showing small businesses how the use of a color printer could enhance their sales materials and improve sales.

Relations Firms, which has about 100 member firms. The group provides information on its Web site (www.prfirms.org) about trends in the industry and how to select a public relations firm, as well as a variety of other materials. It also offers the popular publication *Careers in Public Relations: Opportunities in a Dynamic Industry*. The group also operates a career center and posts résumés on its Web site of individuals looking for employment with a public relations firm.

Global Reach

Public relations firms, large and small, usually are found in metropolitan areas. On an international level, firms and their offices or affiliates are situated in most of the world's major cities and capitals. Fleishman-Hillard, for example, has more than 2,000 employees in 83 offices across six continents. Edelman Worldwide, the world's largest independently owned firm, has almost 2,000 employees in 27 offices abroad. For examples of international award-winning work see the Global box on this page.

The importance of international operations is reflected in the fact that most of the major public relations firms generate substantial revenues from international operations. Edelman, for example, had $324 million in revenues in 2006, but more than a third of this revenue came from its international offices. Burson-Marsteller, with 42 offices abroad, generates about 40 percent of its revenues from international operations. London-based Incepta/Citigate generates almost 70 percent of its income from international operations.

International work isn't only for large firms. Small- and medium-sized firms around the world have formed working partnerships with each other to serve client needs. The largest such group is Worldcom, with 100 firms in 35 nations. Other major groups include Pinnacle, with 60 firms in 31 nations, and Iprex, with 52 firms in 20 nations.

Essentially, in an affiliation firms cooperate with each other to service clients with international needs. A firm in India may call its affiliate in Los Angeles to handle the details of news coverage for a visiting trade delegation from India. One of Worldcom's accounts is Bausch & Lomb, which involves 17 affiliates in 20 separate markets. Bob Oltmanns, head of Iprex, told *PRWeek*, "One of the reasons we started in the first place was to provide clients with a need for reach beyond their own markets with a viable

— ON THE JOB >> —

Major Public Relations Firms Are Owned by Conglomerates

Insights

An estimated 60 percent of the global business in public relations is conducted by firms that are owned by communication conglomerates that also own advertising agencies, marketing firms, billboard companies, direct mail firms, and special event specialty shops. The following is a list of the major holding companies by 2005 total revenues, including the percentage that came from nonadvertising sources.

Omnicom
Total revenue: $11.38 billion
Percent of revenue not from
  advertising: 56 percent
Public relations firms owned:
  Brodeur, Porter Novelli,
  Fleishman-Hillard, Cone,

Ketchum, Gavin Anderson, and
Clark & Weinstock

WPP
Total revenue: $10.9 billion
Percent of revenue not from
  advertising: 52 percent
Public relations firms owned: Hill &
  Knowlton; Cohn & Wolfe;
  Burson-Marsteller; Ogilvy Public
  Relations; Robinson Lerer &
  Montgomery; and the GCI
  Group

Interpublic Group
Total revenue: $6.2 billion
Percent of revenue not from
  advertising: Not given
Public relations firms owned:
  MWW Group, Weber
  Shandwick, GolinHarris, DeVries

Public Relations, Carmichael
Lynch Spong, BNC, Slay PR,
Rogers & Cowan, Tierney
Communications, and PMK/HBH

Publicis Groupe
Total revenue: $5.84 billion
Percent of revenue not from
  advertising: 45 percent
Public relations firms owned:
  Publicis Dialog, Publicis
  Consultants, Winner &
  Associates, and MS&L

Havas
Total revenue: $1.96 billion
Percent of revenue not from
  advertising: Not given
Public relations firms owned: Euro
  RSCG Magnet and Abernathy
  MacGregor

Source: "Agency Business Report 2007." *PRWeek*, April 23, 2007, 45–51.

alternative to the large multinational agencies." International public relations is an area of growth that is discussed in detail in Chapter 11.

The Rise of Communication Conglomerates

Until the 1970s, the largest public relations firms were independently owned by their founders or, in some cases, by employee stockholders. A significant change began in 1973 when Carl Byoir & Associates, then the largest U.S. public relations firm, was purchased by the advertising firm of Foote, Cone & Belding. In short order, other large public relations firms were purchased by major advertising agencies.

Today, both public relations firms and advertising agencies have become part of large, diversified holding companies with global reach (see the Insights box above). Interpublic Group (IPG) not only owns Foote, Cone & Belding (now called Draftfcb) and other advertising agencies but also six major public relations firms. They include the world's largest, Weber Shandwick, as well as Golin Harris, Carmichael Lynch Spong, DeVries Public Relations, MWW Group, and Tierney Communications.

IPG, despite total 2006 revenues of $6.2 billion, is only the third-largest holding company. Omnicom, the largest with $11.38 billion in revenues, generates almost 60 percent of its revenues outside of advertising. It owns, like the other communication conglomerates, a host of companies specializing in such areas as advertising, marketing, billboards, direct mail, special event promotion, graphic design studios, survey research firms, and public relations firms. For example, it owns seven major firms, including Brodeur Worldwide, Porter Novelli, Fleishman-Hillard, Cone, Ketchum, Gavin Anderson, and Clark & Weinstock.

London-based WPP is the second-largest holding company, with revenues of $10.9 billion. Among its holdings are three advertising agencies, JWT (J. Walter Thompson), Ogilvy & Mather Worldwide, and Y&R, and six leading public relations firms, including Burson-Marsteller, Hill & Knowlton, and Cohn & Wolfe.

Large conglomerates acquire public relations firms for several reasons. One is the natural evolutionary step of integrating various communication disciplines into "total communication networks." Supporters of integration say that no single-function agency or firm is equipped with the personnel or resources to handle complex, often global, integrated marketing functions efficiently for a client. In addition, joint efforts by public relations and advertising professionals can offer prospective clients greater communications impact, generate more business, and expand the number of geographical locations around the world.

A second reason is pure business. Holding companies find public relations firms to be attractive investments. According to *PRWeek*, revenues from advertising clients have remained somewhat static over the years, whereas public relations firms have experienced double-digit growth during the same time period.

Toward More Integration. Although earlier efforts to create total communication networks for clients often met with limited success, there is now increasing evidence that the strategy may be working. Considerable new business is also generated when units of the same conglomerate refer customers to each other. As communication campaigns become more integrated, even more synergy will become commonplace.

Holding companies originally started out primarily as a stable of advertising agencies under one umbrella, but they have evolved considerably beyond that with the acquisition of public relations firms and other specialty communication companies. London-based WPP, for example, now employs 69,000 people in more than 100 nations. Sir Martin Sorrell, chairman of WPP (London), told a *Wall Street Journal* interviewer:

> If you want to upset me, call me an advertising agency. The strategic objective is for two-thirds of our revenue to come from nontraditional advertising in 5 to 10 years. Because of fragmentation, TiVo, and Sky Plus, clients and ourselves have to look at everything. Instead of focusing on network television, we have to look at public relations and radio and outdoor and mobile messaging and satellite. Media planning becomes more important.

Sir Martin also makes the point that one size doesn't fit all when it comes to global communications strategies and campaigns. Campaigns still have to be tailored to local customs, ethnic groups, and religious preferences. Muslims now constitute 26 percent of the world's population, and by 2014 they will be 30 percent. By the same year, two-thirds of the world's population will be Asian.

Structure of a Counseling Firm

A small public relations firm may consist only of the owner (president) and an assistant (vice president) who are supported by an administrative assistant. Larger firms generally have a more extended hierarchy.

The organization of Ketchum in San Francisco is fairly typical. The president is based in Ketchum's New York office, so the executive vice president is the on-site director in San Francisco. A senior vice president is associate director of operations. Next in line are several vice presidents who primarily do account supervision or special projects.

An account supervisor is in charge of one major account or several smaller ones. An account executive, who reports to the supervisor, is in direct contact with the client and handles most of the day-to-day activity. At the bottom of the list is the assistant account executive, who does routine maintenance work compiling media lists, gathering information, and writing rough drafts of news releases.

Recent college graduates usually start as assistant account executives. Once they learn the firm's procedures and show ability, promotion to account executive may occur within 6 to 18 months. After two or three years, it is not uncommon for an account executive to become an account supervisor.

Executives at or above the vice presidential level usually are heavily involved in selling their firm's services. In order to prosper, a firm must continually seek new business and sell additional services to current clients. Consequently, the upper management of the firm calls on prospective clients, prepares proposals, and makes new business presentations. In this very competitive field, a firm that is not adept at selling itself frequently fails.

Firms frequently organize account teams, especially to serve a client whose program is multifaceted. One member of the team, for example, may set up a nationwide media tour in which an organization representative is booked on television talk shows. Another may supervise all materials going to the print media, including news stories, feature articles, background kits, and artwork. A third may concentrate on the trade press or perhaps arrange special events.

Pros and Cons of Using a Public Relations Firm

Because public relations is a service industry, a firm's major asset is the quality of its people. Potential clients thinking about hiring a public relations firm usually base their decisions on that fact, according to a survey of Fortune 500 corporate vice presidents.

Thomas L. Harris, a consultant who conducted a survey of corporate communication directors, found that clients believe that meeting deadlines and keeping promises are the most important criteria for evaluating firms. Other important considerations were, in descending order: (1) client services; (2) honest, accurate billing; (3) creativity; and (4) knowledge of the client's industry. Firms that represent so many clients, oftentimes within the same industry, sometimes face ethical concerns.

Advantages

Public relations firms offer several advantages:

> *Objectivity.* The firm can analyze a client's needs or problems from a new perspective and offer fresh insights.

> *A Variety of Skills and Expertise.* The firm has specialists, whether in speech writing, trade magazine placement, or helping with investor relations.

Senior positions in agencies require a diversity of skills as this advertisement for Edelman indicates.

Edelman, the world's largest independent public relations firm, is seeking a senior account supervisor/vice president to join one of the fastest growing corporate practices in NY. This is a career-making opportunity to impact the most difficult challenges in health care today, on behalf of one of our largest clients.

Ideal candidates will have experience in campaign management, public affairs or issues management; general knowledge of state and federal public policy experience in proactive and reactive media relations; agility to execute a crisis preparedness plan ability to apply critical thinking to complex issue areas; and a strategic approach to influence public policy. Health care/pharmaceutical experience is highly desirable but not required. Agency experience a plus.

Responsibilities:
- Build relationships and provide strategic counsel among multiple stakeholders within the client's organization.
- Create and manage campaigns to seed public debate around key issue areas
- Drive toward measurable results, glean key learnings, and reassess strategies as necessary
- Develop and align messages and talking points around campaigns/key issue areas across the organization
- Provide strategic media relations counsel at national and local levels

If you are an ideal candidate, please visit www.edelman.com and complete an online application for job #002484 (SAS) or 002547 (VP).

> *Extensive Resources.* The firm has abundant media contacts and works regularly with numerous suppliers of products and services. It has research materials, including data information banks, and experience in similar fields. International jobs, like handling the corporate sponsorship issues with the Olympics, benefits from the extensive resources of a firm (see the PR Casebook on page 110).

> *Offices Throughout the Country.* A national public relations program requires coordination in major cities. Large firms have on-site staffs or affiliate firms in many cities and even around the world.

> *Special Problem-Solving Skills.* A firm may have extensive experience and a solid reputation in desired areas. For example, Burson-Marsteller is well known for expertise in crisis communications, health and medical issues, and international coordination of special projects. Hill & Knowlton is known for expertise in public affairs, and Ketchum is the expert in consumer marketing.

> *Credibility.* A successful public relations firm has a solid reputation for professional, ethical work. If represented by such a firm, a client is likely to get more attention among opinion leaders in mass media, government, and the financial community.

Disadvantages

There are also drawbacks to using public relations firms:

> *Superficial Grasp of a Client's Unique Problems.* Although objectivity is gained from an outsider's perspective, there is often a disadvantage in the public relations firm's not thoroughly understanding the client's business or needs.

> *Lack of Full-Time Commitment.* A public relations firm has many clients. Therefore, no single client can monopolize its personnel and other resources.

> *Need for Prolonged Briefing Period.* Some companies become frustrated because time and money are needed for a public relations firm to research the organization and make recommendations. Consequently, the actual start of a public relations program may take weeks or months.

> *Resentment by Internal Staff.* The public relations staff members of a client organization may resent the use of outside counsel because they think it implies that they lack the ability to do the job.

— ON THE JOB >> —

When It's Time to Resign an Account

Ethics

Credibility and a reputation for integrity are important assets to a public relations firm in terms of keeping clients and adding new ones. Because of this, a firm will sometimes resign an account for ethical reasons.

Patrice Tanaka, CEO of PT& Company, resigned her agency's biggest account after the client adopted an antigay position. She told *PRWeek,* "We tried to explain that it wasn't smart business practice, and we didn't think it was ethical to not welcome any segment of the population."

Fleishman-Hillard resigned from the Firestone tire account after deciding the firm could not ethically defend Firestone's position regarding the safety of its tires during a tire-recall controversy and allegations that Firestone failed to act on information that defective tires were causing a number of injuries and deaths.

In Washington, D.C., three executives of Qorvis Communications left

the firm because, according to press reports, they felt uneasy defending the government of Saudi Arabia against accusations that Saudi leaders had turned a blind eye to terrorism. Following 9/11, the firm had a $200,000 monthly retainer with Saudi Arabia to help to improve that country's image with the American public. According to the *New York Times,* friends said that the three executives were concerned that the firm's reputation was being tarnished by its work for the Saudi government.

On occasion, a public relations firm finds it necessary to resign an account because of client behavior. A Michigan firm, for example, decided to terminate a contract with a resort client because the point of contact was rude and abusive to agency staff and even to their own employees. In such a situation, the firm didn't feel it could service the client in an effective manner.

Many public relations firms, before taking on a possibly controversial client, will discuss the situation with their employees to determine if any staff would feel uncomfortable working with the client. Some years ago, Hill & Knowlton made the mistake of signing on the Catholic Bishops for an antiabortion campaign. Several employees quit, and others said they would refuse to work on the account.

Public relations firms may also resign from accounts if the client asks them to distribute misleading or incorrect information. The code of ethics for the Council of Public Relations Firms notes, "In communicating with the public and media, member firms will maintain total accuracy and truthfulness. To preserve both the reality and perception of professional integrity, information that is found to be misleading or erroneous will be promptly corrected."

> *Need for Strong Direction by Top Management.* High-level executives must take the time to brief outside counsel on specific objectives sought.

> *Need for Full Information and Confidence.* A client must be willing to share its information, including the skeletons in the closet, with outside counsel. See the Ethics box above for an illustration of why cooperation between the firm and client is essential.

> *Costs.* Outside counsel is expensive. In many situations, routine public relations work can be handled at lower cost by internal staff.

Fees and Charges

A public relations firm charges for its services in several ways. The three most common methods, also used by law firms and management consultants, are

1. *Basic Hourly Fee, Plus Out-of-Pocket Expenses.* The number of hours spent on a client's account is tabulated each month and billed to the client. Work by personnel in the counseling firm is billed at various hourly rates. Out-of-pocket expenses, such as cab fares, car rentals, airline tickets, and meals, are also billed

to the client. In a typical $100,000 campaign, about 70 percent of the budget is spent on staff salaries.

2. *Retainer Fee.* A basic monthly charge billed to the client covers ordinary administrative and overhead expenses for maintaining the account and being "on call" for advice and strategic counseling. Many clients have in-house capabilities for executing communication campaigns but often need the advice of experts during the planning phase. Many retainer fees also specify the number of hours the firm will spend on an account each month. Any additional work is billed at normal hourly rates. Out-of-pocket expenses are usually billed separately.

3. *Fixed Project Fee.* The public relations firm agrees to do a specific project, such as an annual report, a newsletter, or a special event, for a fixed fee. For example, a counseling firm may write and produce a quarterly newsletter for $30,000 annually. The fixed fee is the least popular among public relations firms because it is difficult to predict all work and expenses in advance. Many clients, however, like fixed fees for a specific project because it is easier to budget and there are no "surprises."

A fourth method, not widely used, is the concept of pay-for-placement. Clients don't pay for hours worked but for actual placements of articles in the print media and broadcast mentions. Fees for a major story can range anywhere from $1,500 to $15,000 depending on the prestige, circulation, or audience size of the media outlet that uses a story proposed by a pay-for-placement firm.

The vast majority of public relations firms don't use this business model for several reasons. First, it reduces public relations to media relations and media placement, when it is in reality a much broader field. Second, it presents cash-flow problems because payment isn't made until a placement is made. Third, media gatekeepers ultimately decide what to use and what not to use; placement is never guaranteed despite countless hours spent by a staff person "pitching" the story.

The primary basis of the most common methods—the basic hourly fee, the retainer fee, and the fixed project fee—is to estimate the number of hours that a particular project will take to plan, execute, and evaluate. The first method—the basic hourly fee—is the most flexible and most widely used among large firms. It is preferred by public relations people because they are paid for the exact number of hours spent on a project and because it is the only sound way that a fee can be determined intelligently. The retainer fee and the fixed project fee are based on an estimate of how many hours it will take to service a client.

A number of variables are considered when a public relations firm estimates the cost of a program. These include the size and duration of the project, geographical locations involved, the number of personnel assigned to the project, and the type of client. A major variable, of course, is billing the use of the firm's personnel to a client at the proper hourly rate.

An account supervisor, for example, may earn $60,000 annually and receive benefits (health insurance, pension plan, and so on) that cost the firm an additional $13,000. Thus, the annual cost of the employee to the firm totals $73,000. Using 1,600 billable hours in a year (after deducting vacation time and holidays), the account executive makes $45.63 per hour.

The standard industry practice, however, is to bill clients at least three times a person's salary. This multiple allows the firm to pay for office space, equipment, insurance, supplies, and try to operate at a profit level of about 10 to 20 percent before taxes. Thus, the billing rate of the account supervisor (3 × $45.63) rounds off at $137 per hour. The principals of a counseling firm, because of their much higher salaries,

— ON THE JOB >> —

A Job at a Corporation or a PR Firm?

Insights

Recent college graduates often ponder the pros and cons of joining a corporate department or going to work for a public relations firm. The following summarizes some of the pluses and minuses:

PR FIRM: BREADTH OF EXPERIENCE	CORPORATE PR: DEPTH OF EXPERIENCE
Experience gained quickly; tip—find a mentor you can learn from.	Jobs more difficult to find without experience; duties more narrowly focused.
Variety. Usually work on several clients and projects at same time. Opportunity for rapid advancement.	Sometimes little variety at entry level.
Fast-paced, exciting.	Growth sometimes limited unless you are willing to switch employers.
Seldom see the impact of your work for a client; removed from "action."	Can be slower paced.
Abilities get honed and polished. (This is where a mentor really helps.)	Heavy involvement with executive staff; see impact almost instantly. You are an important component in the "big picture."
Networking with other professionals leads to better job opportunities.	Strength in all areas expected. Not a lot of time for coaching by peers.
Learn other skills, such as how to do presentations and budgets and establish deadlines.	Sometimes so involved in your work, you don't have time for networking.
Intense daily pressure on billable hours, high productivity. Some firms are real "sweatshops."	Same "client" all the time. Advantage: Get to know organization really well. Disadvantage: Can become boring.
Somewhat high employment turnover.	Less intense daily pressure; more emphasis on accomplishing longer-term results.
Budgets and resources can be limited.	Less turnover.
Salary traditionally low at entry level.	More resources usually available.
Insurance, medical benefits can be minimal.	Salaries tend to be higher.
Little opportunity for profit-sharing, stock options.	Benefits usually good, sometimes excellent.
High emphasis on tactical skills, production of materials	More opportunities available.
	Can be more managerial and involved in strategic planning.

often command $175 to $500 per hour, depending on the size and capabilities of the firm. On the other hand, an assistant account executive may be billed out at only $85 per hour. One nationwide survey conducted by an executive search firm found that the average hourly rate, across all public relations firm sizes and billable titles, was $213.

The primary income of a public relations firm comes from the sale of staff time, but some additional income results from markups on photocopying, telephone, fax, and artwork the firm supervises. The standard markup in the trade is between 15 and 20 percent.

PRCASEBOOK

Olympics PR: The Greatest Show on Earth

Public relations firms often handle special events for clients, and the ultimate event may be representing a corporate sponsor at the Olympic Games. Amanda Kamin, an associate account director at Burson-Marstellar compiled the following diary of her work with Visa International at the Athens Olympics.

2004 Olympics Diary; Week One

Sunday 8 August
After months of phone calls, planning and preparation, the on-the-ground work begins even as we arrive at Heathrow for the flight to Athens. Waiting with the Visa team in the lounge, we bump into the Bermuda Olympic team and Sean Kerly, winner of a gold medal with the British hockey team in 1988. We invite him to our first media reception on Tuesday.

Monday 9 August
We arrive at the Visa press office, with every piece of communications kit—mobiles, Blackberries, laptops—and ring the media to get journalists to our press reception tomorrow evening. We then visit event venues to check the display materials we have designed, then back to the office to work the phones till 1 A.M.

Tuesday 10 August
We begin preparations for tonight's media reception. The journalists show up as soon as it kicks off—we have everyone from Shanghai TV to *The Wall Street Journal* and *EuroSport*. Many are hoping for interviews with athletes that we can organize. Others, from Bloomberg and Reuters, are looking for a business angle and we inform them about the special briefing on sponsorship we have organized.

Wednesday 11 August
Today we opened the Visa Olympians Reunion Center (VORC) at the Athens Tennis Club with 350 guests and camera crews. Even at night it's hot in Athens, so we organized for water misters for the terrace earlier on.

Carl Lewis turns up, as does Prince Albert of Monaco, much to the media's interest. We have to make sure the journalists have the proper accreditation before letting them in and facili-tate introductions to people such as Visa head of sponsorship Tom Shepard. There's one stressful moment: running around with two Italian journalists desperate to speak to Lewis, who left 20 minutes earlier. We track him down and the Carl Lewis story is on the front page of *La Gazzetta dello Sport* the next day.

Thursday 12 August
Today we have the first Team Visa lunch. Team Visa is a sponsorship and mentoring programme and the lunch features Sir Steve Redgrave, the mentor for the UK Team Visa athletes. My colleague disappears to VORC to help manage the event, while I hit the phones again to drum up media attendance for tomorrow's big event—the awards ceremony for the Visa Olympics of the Imagination (VOI) children's art contest. The finalists are from 17 countries, and even with five people it takes us hours to contact them all. I know the result of the contest and have to encourage the Chinese media to attend without revealing the winner. At 10 P.M. it's time for another meeting, over dinner, then back to the office at 1 A.M. to load up for tomorrow.

Friday 13 August
We spend two hours setting up the venue and by 11 A.M. It's 40°C, so we've organized to have 200 bottles of water sent to the venue. A journalist from *EuroSport* rings and asks if Prince Faisal of Jordan can attend with some guests. Redgrave and Prince Albert will be handling out medals to the kids and the VIP room also holds EU commissioner for culture and sport Viviane Reding, and about 12 bodyguards for both princes. Camera crews from Mexico, Greece, Poland, Russia, and China begin to arrive, as does a Polish radio station and UK journalists. We're pleased at the turnout because we were concerned the big story about the Greek sprinters would undermine all our efforts.

Saturday 14 August
My first day off. I've been given tickets for the swimming and men's gymnastics events, so I watch the sports for a while before heading to the beach. Hosting four major events in five days is no easy task and I'm glad we did so much preparation in London. Now it's begun, there are fewer sponsor events because the journalists are covering the sports.

I can see why it's important to reach them during the first week as we're beginning to build up a large clippings file, including hits in *The Daily Telegraph, The Sun*, and on ITN and Sky News.

2004 Olympics Diary; Week Two

Sunday 15 August

The finalists from VOI are scheduled to appear on *Rendezvous Athens*, a late-night talk show on Greek National Broadcast TV, so we head down to the TV station with the children and their guardians.

The program features their artwork, along with a B-roll of the grand opening of VORC, which is an excellent result.

Monday 16 August

It's time to get ready for tonight's event to celebrate the Torino 2006 Winter Games. The close contact we've had with the Torino organizing committee PR team will be very useful for us in two years. Turismo Torino has laid on Italy's premier bartender and an extensive Italian buffet, which pleases the business and travel journalists we've invited.

Tuesday 17 August

Visa is holding a briefing about the business of sponsorship for some of the nonsporting journalists who have been sent to Athens in case of a crisis. With little to report on so far, they are grateful for a business-based story. We now have good relationships with them all because we've seen them at our other events, and we're in a position to help Visa get positive coverage.

The rest of the second week is focused on preparation for the major events next week, although we still have to get hold of some national media for Team Visa lunches. We also get some time off and tickets for the Games.

2004 Olympics Diary; Week Three

Sunday 22 August

Swimmer Michael Phelps is sponsored by Visa USA and will be at VORC today for a press conference with Visa USA head of sponsorship Michael Lynch.

We've had less than a day to prepare, but it's been an easy sell. We focus on the stage dressing, getting Phelps to and from the event and how to handle all the questions we're expecting from the media.

Monday 23 August

Today we help Visa Europe with the Italian Team Visa lunch. Later Cherie Blair pays a visit to VORC.

Public relations does have its glamour moments. Amanda Karmin, an account executive for Burson-Marsteller (London) was assigned to the Athens Olympics on behalf of client Visa International. Here, she poses with Aldo Montano, Italian gold medal athlete in fencing.

Thursday 26 August

For the past couple of days, we've been preparing for the Team Visa party, which is held today for all the athletes and their mentors, including Rosa Mota, Sara Simeoni, Redgrave, and the media.

Friday 27 August

We get a call at short notice about former Olympic gymnastic gold medallist Nadia Comaneci visiting VORC. The team is fully occupied with calls for our Beijing 2008 event tomorrow, but fortunately I know from a contact at *The Times* that Alastair Campbell is looking for interviews with prominent Olympians. My colleague Sujit ends up chatting to Campbell over a drink while arranging an interview with Comaneci.

Saturday 28 August

Tonight is our last event. We've been working with the Visa China PR team and the Chinese National Tourism Agency on a press briefing for the next Olympic Games in Beijing. The Visa Olympians Reunion Center will be decorated throughout with red lanterns and there will be a Chinese dance performance after the briefing.

Although there will be a symbolic hand-over of the Games from Athens to Beijing at the closing ceremony tomorrow, tonight is the business hand-over and it's a great way to finish. We'll be heading home on Monday after three action-packed weeks, but we'll be doing it all again in mid-September at the Paralympics.

Source: Kamin, Amanda. "Event PR: The Greatest Show on Earth." *PRWeek*, September 20, 2004, www.prweek.com/us/.

Summary

Public Relations Departments

Most organizations have public relations departments. Such departments may be called by other names, such as corporate communications. Organizations, depending on their culture and the wishes of top management, structure the public relations function in various ways. Public relations professionals often serve at the tactical and technician level, but others are counselors to the top executive and have a role in policy making. In management theory, public relations is a staff function rather than a line function.

Public Relations Firms

Public relations firms come in all sizes and are found worldwide, providing a variety of services. In recent decades, many public relations firms have either merged with advertising agencies or become subsidiaries of diversified holding companies. Advantages of using outside firms include versatility and extensive resources, among other considerations; but they can also lack the full-time commitment of an in-house department, need a lot of direction, and are often more expensive.

CASE ACTIVITY >>

What Would You Do?

The Job Offer

You will graduate from college in several months and plan a career in public relations. After several interviews, you receive two job offers.

One is with a high-technology company that makes inkjet printers and scanners for the consumer market. The corporate communications department has about 20 professionals, and it is customary for beginners to start in employee publications or product publicity. Later, with more experience, you might be assigned to do marketing communications for a product group or work in a specialized area such as investor relations, governmental affairs, or even community relations.

The second job offer is from a local office of a large, national public relations firm. You would begin as an assistant account executive and work on several accounts, including a chain of fast-food restaurants and an insurance company. The jobs pay about the same, but the corporation offers better insurance and medical plans. Taking into consideration the pros and cons of working for public relations firms versus corporations, what job would best fit your abilities and preferences? Explain your reasons.

Questions for Review and Discussion

1. How have the role and function of public relations departments changed in recent years?
2. In what ways do the structure and culture of an organization affect the role and influence of the public relations department?
3. What kinds of knowledge does a manager of a public relations department need today?
4. Many departments are now called corporate communications instead of public relations. Do you think the first term is more appropriate? Why or why not?
5. What is the difference between a line and a staff function? To which function does public relations belong, and why?
6. Why is a compulsory-advisory role within an organization a good one for a public relations department to have?
7. What four areas of the organization cause the most potential for friction with public relations? Explain.
8. In your opinion, should public relations or human resources be responsible for employee communications? Why?
9. Public relations professionals often express a fear that they will lose influence and be relegated to purely technical functions if they are controlled by the marketing department. Do you think their fears are justified? Why or why not?

10. Name at least seven services that a public relations firm offers clients.
11. What are the three largest communications conglomerates in the world?
12. How important is international business to American public relations firms?
13. Why do large holding companies find the acquisition of public relations firms so attractive?
14. What are the pros and cons of using a public relations firm?
15. What are the standard methods used by a public relations firm to charge for its services?
16. Under what circumstances should a public relations firm resign from an account?

Suggested Readings

Berger, B. K. "Power Over, Power With, and Power to Relations: Critical Reflections on Public Relations, the Dominant Coalition, and Activism." *Journal of Public Relations Research* 17, no. 1 (2005): 5–28.

Bush, Michael. "The PR Industry From the Outside." *PRWeek*, September 11, 2006, 15.

Cody, Steve. "Taking the Lead: Communicators as Innovation Catalysts." *The Strategist*, Spring 2006, 8–11.

DuBrowa, Corey. "Breaking Through: Integrated Approaches to Communicating Innovation." *The Strategist*, Spring 2006, 14–17.

Heyman, W. C. "Study Shows Mix of Personal, Professional Patterns Combine to Signal Likely Success in PR Profession." *Public Relations Quarterly* 49, no. 3 (2004): 7–10.

LaMotta, Lisa. "Hiring in the Middle Ranks." *PRWeek*, September 25, 2006, 21.

Lewis, Tanya. "Wary Resignation: When to Quit an Account." *PRWeek*, August 25, 2003, 16.

Mitroff, Ian, Gerald, Swerling, and Jennifer Floto. "Study Proves Value of Public Relations and Finds Self-Doubt Within the Profession." *The Strategist*, Winter 2003, 32–34.

O'Neil, Julie. "An Investigation of the Sources of Influence of Corporate Public Relations Practitioners." *Public Relations Review* 29, no. 2 (2003): 159–169.

Plowman, K. D. "Conflict, Strategic Management, and Public Relations." *Public Relations Review* 31, no. 1 (2005): 131–138.

Rayburn, J., and V. Hazelton. "Survey Provides Profile of Independent Practitioner: Examines Practice Areas, Income and Profit." *Public Relations Tactics*, March 2005, 15–16.

Sha, B., and E. L. Toth. "Future Professionals' Perceptions of Work, Life, and Gender Issues in Public Relations." *Public Relations Review* 31, no. 1 (2005): 93–99.

Signorovitch, Dennis. "Handle with Care: Managing the Needs of Both Internal Customers and Corporate Communications Leaders." *The Strategist*, Spring 2006, 40–42.

Trickett, Eleanor. "Outside Look Shows PR's Role in Marketing Gaining Respect." *PRWeek*, September 11, 2006, 9.

Chapter Five

The Public Relations Process

Effective public relations is a process with four essential steps: (1) research, (2) planning, (3) communication, and (4) evaluation. Research provides the information required to understand the needs of publics and to develop powerful messages. Planning has been called the central function of management. It is the process of setting goals and objectives and determining ways to meet them. Communication, as we discuss it in this chapter, is related to message strategy. How do we make a message more appealing and persuasive to the public we need to reach? (Specific communication tactics are discussed in Chapter 10.) Evaluation is increasingly important in a profession that has too often complained that what we do cannot be measured. Executives justifiably demand accountability from public relations practitioners. Evaluation techniques provide a means for demonstrating to management that we achieved our objectives and contributed in a meaningful way to the organization. This chapter examines the roles each of these steps plays in an effective public relations program.

Research: The First Step

The crucial first step in the public relations process is research. Today, research is widely accepted by public relations professionals as an integral part of the planning, program development, and evaluation process.

Defining the Research Role

In basic terms, research is a form of listening. In their book *Using Research in Public Relations*, Glen Broom and David Dozier say, "Research is the controlled, objective, and systematic gathering of information for the purpose of describing and understanding."

Before any public relations program can be developed, information must be gathered and data must be collected and interpreted. This essential first step helps top management as they make policy decisions and map out strategies for effective communication programs. Research also provides a way to evaluate the program once it has been completed. Meaningful evaluation can lead to greater accountability and credibility with upper management.

There are different types of research to accomplish an organization's objectives and meet its information needs. The choice of research type really depends on the particular subject and situation. As always, time and budget are major considerations, as is the perceived importance of the situation. Consequently, many questions should be asked before formulating a research design:

> What is the problem?
> What kind of information is needed?
> How will the results of the research be used?
> What specific public (or publics) should be researched?
> Should the organization do the research in-house or hire an outside consultant?
> How will the research data be analyzed, reported, or applied?
> How soon will the results be needed?
> How much will the research cost?

These questions help public relations professionals determine the extent and nature of the research needed. Sometimes, only informal research is required, because of its low cost or the need for immediate information. At other times, a random scientific survey is appropriate, despite its costs and time requirement, because of the need for more precise data. The pros and cons of each research method is discussed later in the chapter.

Using Research

Research is involved in virtually every phase of a communications program. Studies show that public relations departments typically spend about 3 to 5 percent of their budget on research. Some experts say it should be 10 percent. Public relations professionals use research in a number of way.

Achieving Credibility with Management. Executives want facts, not guesses and hunches. A criticism of public relations practitioners is that they too often don't link communications issues to business outcomes. Research paves the way for such linkages. According to the findings of IABC's research on excellence in communication management, the inclusion of public relations personnel in an organization's policy and decision-making structure is strongly correlated with their ability to do research and link findings to the organization's objectives.

Defining Audiences and Segmenting Publics. Detailed information about the demographics, lifestyles, characteristics, and consumption patterns of audiences helps to ensure that messages reach the proper audiences. A successful children's immunization information campaign in California was based on State Health Department statistics showing that past immunization programs had not reached rural children and that Hispanic and Vietnamese children were not being immunized in the same proportion as other ethnic groups.

Formulating Strategy. Much money can be spent pursuing the wrong strategies. Officials of the New Hampshire paper industry, given bad press about logging and waterway pollution, thought a campaign was needed to tell the public what it was doing to reduce pollution. An opinion survey of 800 state residents by a public relations firm, however, indicated that the public was already generally satisfied with the industry's efforts. Consequently, the new strategy focused on reinforcing positive themes such as worker safety, employment, and environmental responsibility. In other words, through research that increased its understanding of stakeholder issues, the paper industry shifted its stance on the contingency continuum from accommodating what was incorrectly perceived as a public concern to an advocative stance for the organization. Research was extremely critical in appraising whether a threat existed and served to inform their strategy, and it helped them focus communication resources where they would do the organization the most good.

Testing Messages. Research is often used to determine what particular message is most salient with a target audience. According to one focus group study for a campaign to encourage carpooling, the message that resonated the most with commuters was saving time and money, not air quality or environmental concerns. Consequently, the campaign emphasized how many minutes could be cut from an average commute by using carpool lanes and the annual savings in gasoline, insurance, and car maintenance.

Helping Management Keep in Touch. Top management in many organizations is increasingly isolated from the concerns of employees, customers, and other important publics. Research helps bridge the gap by periodically surveying key publics about problems and concerns. This feedback is a "reality check" for top executives and often leads to better policies and communication strategies.

Preventing Crises. An estimated 90 percent of organizational crises are caused by internal operational problems rather than by unexpected natural disasters or external issues. Research can often uncover trouble spots and public concerns before they become news. Analyzing complaints made to a toll-free number or monitoring chat rooms on the Internet might tip off an organization that it should act before a problem attracts media attention. As you recall from Chapter 2, if you successfully engage in the proactive phase of the conflict management life cycle you can prevent a conflict or crisis through environmental scanning and other research tactics.

Monitoring the Competition. Savvy organizations keep track of what the competition is doing. And sometimes that competition is especially keen, as noted in the Global box about Nike and Adidas on page 118. Keeping track of the competition is done through surveys that ask consumers to comment on competing products, content analysis of the competition's media coverage, and reviews of industry reports in trade journals. Such research often helps an organization shape its marketing and communication strategies to counter a competitor's strengths and capitalize on its weaknesses.

Influencing Public Opinion. Facts and figures, compiled from a variety of primary and secondary sources, can change public opinion. Shortly before an election in Ohio, 90 percent of the voters supported a state ballot measure that would require cancer warnings on thousands of products from plywood to peanut butter. A coalition called Ohioans for Responsible Health Information, which opposed the bill, commissioned universities and other credible outside sources to research the economic impact of such legislation on consumers and major industries. The research, which was used as the basis of the grassroots campaign, led to the defeat of the ballot measure, with 78 percent of the voters voting "no."

Generating Publicity. Polls and surveys can generate publicity for an organization. Indeed, many surveys seem to be designed with publicity in mind. Simmons Bedding Company once polled people to find out if they slept in the nude. And KIWI, a shoe polish company, obtained extensive media coverage about a survey it commissioned that showed 97 percent of self-described "ambitious" young men believe that polished shoes are important.

— ON THE JOB >> —

World Cup Competition Is about More Than Soccer   *Global*

Adidas and Nike, the footwear and sporting goods behemoths, squared off during the 2006 FIFA World Cup. While U.S.-based Nike led German-based Adidas in other categories, Adidas had the lead in soccer footwear and apparel. Prior to the 2006 World Cup, Adidas had 48 percent of the U.S. soccer market and 36 percent of the European market, compared to Nike's 32 percent in each market. The competiton for the hearts, minds, and wallets of soccer fans is intense.

So, why all the fuss about soccer? Because it is a gateway sport into international markets. The World Cup had a global audience of about 2.8 billion in-home viewers; that is bigger than either the Olympics or the Super Bowl. The research organization Sponsorship Intelligence predicted that 79 percent of the world's population

would watch one match for at least 30 minutes. Therefore, Adidas sought to use soccer and soccer stars as a means of getting noticed in places like Japan and China.

As an official sponsor of the FIFA World Cup and its 64 games, Adidas paid for the rights to shut Nike out of U.S. television advertising for all the games, according to *Business Week*. Adidas also locked up all billboard advertising in Germany, the site of the 2006 World Cup games. Among Nike's novel public relations responses was its teaming with Google to develop an online social network of soccer fans—joga.com

PRWeek noted just before the games started in June 2006 that "the World Cup has already been won [by Adidas]—in terms of branded media coverage." In March 2006, *PRWeek*

found that Adidas had 50 percent more media mentions in connection with the World Cup than the next closest sponsoring brand—Coca-Cola.

Following the end of the tournament, *Marketing* magazine announced, "According to the latest figures, Adidas outperformed its bottom-line targets, selling a record number of 3 million replica shirts—of which half were for the German national team—double its sales at the 2002 tournament. Nike, meanwhile, sold 2.4 milion—a minor increase on its efforts four years ago. Adidas now holds a higher market share in Europe than its arch-rival, with 37% of all sporting-goods sales."

Herbert Hainer, CEO of Adidas, told the *Financial Times of London*, "There is no doubt that Adidas is the clear winner of this World Cup. We have more or less exceeded all of our targets."

Measuring Success. The bottom line of any public relations program is whether the time and money spent accomplished the stated objective. As one of its many programs to boost brand awareness, Miller Genuine Draft sponsored a "reunion ride" on Harley-Davidson Motor Company's 90th anniversary. Ketchum generated extensive media publicity about the "ride" and Miller's sponsorship that was 98 percent positive. Perhaps more importantly, sales increased in all but two of the cities included in the event. Evaluation, the last step of the public relations process, is discussed later in the chapter. In the following sections we discuss ways of doing research.

Research Techniques

When the term *research* is used, people tend to think only of scientific surveys and complex statistics. In public relations, however, research techniques are used to gather data and information.

In fact, a survey of practitioners by Walter K. Lindenmann, former senior vice president and director of research for Ketchum, found that three-fourths of the respondents described their research techniques as casual and informal rather than scientific and precise. The technique cited most often was literature searches/database information retrieval.

This technique is called secondary research, because it uses existing information in books, magazine articles, electronic databases, and so on. In contrast, with primary research, new and original information is generated through a research designed to answer a specific question. Examples of primary research are in-depth interviews, focus groups, surveys, and polls.

Another way to categorize research is by distinguishing between qualitative and quantitative research. Lindenmann contrasts the basic differences between qualitative and quantitative research in Table 5.1. In general, qualitative research affords researchers rich insights and understanding of situations or target publics. It also provides "red flags," or warnings, when strong or adverse responses occur. These responses may not be generalizability to a larger population, but they provide practitioners with early warnings of potential problems. Quantitative research is often more expensive and complicated, but it allows for greater generalizabity to large populations. If enormous amounts of money are to be spent on a national campaign, an investment in quantitative research may be important.

The following sections briefly describe the most common research techniques.

Organizational Materials. Robert Kendall, in his book *Public Relations Campaign Strategies*, calls researching organizational materials *archival research*. Such materials may include an organization's policy statements, speeches by key executives, past issues of employee newsletters and magazines, reports on past public relations and marketing efforts, and news clippings. Marketing statistics, in particular, often provide the baseline data for public relations firms that are hired to launch a new product or boost awareness and sales of an existing product or service. Archival research also is a major component in most audits that are intended to determine how an organization communicates to its internal and external publics.

TABLE 5.1

Qualitative versus Quantitative Research

Qualitative Research	Quantitative Research
"Soft" data	"Hard data"
Usually uses open-ended questions, unstructured	Usually uses close-ended questions, requires forced choices, highly structured
Exploratory in nature; probing, fishing-expedition type of research	Descriptive or explanatory type of research
Usually valid, but not reliable	Usually valid and reliable
Rarely projectable to larger audiences	Usually projectable to larger audiences
Generally uses nonrandom samples	Generally uses random samples
Examples: Focus groups; one-on-one, in-depth interviews; observation; participation; role-playing studies; convenience polling	Examples: Telephone polls, mail surveys, mall-intercept studies, face-to-face interviews, shared cost, or omnibus, studies; panel studies

Library and Online Database Methods. Reference books, academic journals, and trade publications are found in every library, oftentimes on CD-ROM. Online databases such as Proquest (www.proquest.com) and INFOTRAC (infotrac .thomsonlearning.com) contain abstracts or full-text of thousands, or even millions, of articles.

Some common reference sources used by public relations professionals include the *Statistical Abstract of the United States* (http://www.census.gov/statab/www/), which summarizes census information; the Gallup Poll (http://poll.gallup.com/), which provides an index of public opinion on a variety of issues; *American Demographics* magazine, which reports on population shifts and lifestyle trends; and *Simmons Study Media and Markets*, an extensive annual survey of households on product usage by brand and exposure to various media.

Literature searches, the most often used informal research method in public relations, can tap an estimated 1,500 electronic databases that store an enormous amount of current and historical information.

Public relations departments and firms use online databases in a number of ways:

> To research facts to support a proposed project or campaign that requires top management approval
> To keep up-to-date with news about clients and their competitors
> To track an organization's media campaigns and competitors' press announcements
> To locate a special quote or impressive statistic for a speech or report
> To track press and business reaction to an organization's latest actions
> To locate an expert who can provide advice on an issue or a possible strategy
> To keep top management apprised of current business trends and issues
> To learn about the demographics and attitudes of target publics

Online databases are available on a subscription basis and usually charge by how many minutes the service is in use. The following are some of the online databases commonly used in public relations:

> *Burrelle's Broadcast Database.* This database contains the full-text transcripts of radio and television programs within 24 hours after they are transmitted. Sources include ABC, NBC, CBS, CNN, National Public Radio, and selected syndicated programs.
> *Dow Jones News/Retrieval.* This massive business library electronically transmits up-to-the-second global coverage of business news, economic indicators, and industry and market data.
> *LexisNexis.* This database, available at www.lexisnexis.com, includes millions of full-text articles from magazines, newspapers, and news services as well as the full text of the *New York Times* and the *Washington Post*.

Public relations practitioners must follow current events and public affairs issues so that they can provide thoughtful counsel in their organizations. Reading newspapers and watching television news programs is a habit that young professionals must embrace.

A number of relatively new delivery systems are appearing that offer magazines (zinio.com) or newspapers (pressdisplay.com and newsstand.com) that are formatted like their print counterparts, but also include online Links and video. These services may appeal to the next generation of professionals. Other new media include services such as Audible.com, which delivers audio to MP3 players, including the daily reading of the *New York Times*. This enables commuters to multitask. Innovative newspapers are developing interactive versions of their daily editions that can be read to car commuters through satellite radio. Users can then save or forward the stories to colleagues. Listeners of National Public Radio (NPR) can forward stories or order transcripts or broadcasts.

This wide array of information resources, both on- and off-line, enables public relations practitioners to be current and knowledgeable about their own organization and its place in the larger world.

The Internet and World Wide Web.

The Internet is a powerful research tool for the public relations practitioner. Any number of corporations, nonprofits, trade groups, special interest groups, foundations, universities, think tanks, and government agencies post reams of data on the Internet, usually in the form of home pages on the World Wide Web (see the Insights box on this page).

Online search engines are essential for finding information on the Internet. With literally millions of possible Web sites, search engines make it possible for a researcher to simply type in a key word or two, click "Go," and in a few seconds receive all of the links that

the search engine has found that relate to a given topic. Search engines such as Google also have become locations for sharing expertise and problem-solving skills regarding a wide array of topics. In the Google Groups section of the Google Web site (www.groups.google.com), helpful information can be found on everything from recreation to business to the arts.

Google is one of the most popular search engine. Other popular engines include Yahoo!, Go.com, MSN Search, AOL Search, and Ask. Researchers also can use specialized search engines or search tools to locate audio and video content or content of topical interest, such as sports or business news. Reviews and directories of search engines are available at searchenginewatch.com. Public relations professionals should visit such sites from time to time to stay current on search capabilities as well as to monitor changes in search engines' policies, such as fees required for high placement in search results.

Researchers can use newsgroups such as PRFORUM, a newsgroup dedicated to public relations topics, to request information from others. Discussion groups and blogs are increasingly common sources of information for public relations practitioners. There are several Yahoo!-based PR discussion groups—PRSA_Discussion, PRBytes, PRMindshare, PRQuorum, and YoungPRPros are examples. Professional organizations such as the Public Relations Society of America and the International Association of Business Communicators have members-only discussion groups, PRCOnline and MemberSpeak, respectively. IABC has blogs addressing branding, employee communications, measurement, and media relations, which are open to nonmembers at commons.iabc.com. An extensive discussion of the Internet's development and operation appears in Chapter 9.

Content Analysis. Content analysis is the systematic and objective counting or categorizing of content. In public relations, content often is selected from media coverage of a topic or organization. This research method can be relatively informal or quite scientific in terms of random sampling and establishing specific subject categories. It is often applied to news stories about an organization.

At a basic level, a researcher can assemble news clips in a scrapbook and count the number of column inches. Don Stacks, University of Miami professor and author of *Primer of Public Relations Research*, writes that content analysis "is particularly appropriate for the analysis of documents, speeches, media releases, video content and scripts, interviews, and focus groups. The key to content analysis is that it is done objectively..., content is treated systematically..., [and] messages are transformed from qualitative statements to numbers, data that can be quantified and compared against other data."

A good example of content analysis is the way one company evaluated press coverage of its publicity campaign to celebrate its 100th anniversary. The campaign's success was measured by a low-budget content analysis of 427 references to the client and their product in newspapers, magazines, radio, and television. The content analysis revealed that the client's themes and copy points were included in the media coverage.

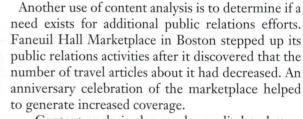

Another use of content analysis is to determine if a need exists for additional public relations efforts. Faneuil Hall Marketplace in Boston stepped up its public relations activities after it discovered that the number of travel articles about it had decreased. An anniversary celebration of the marketplace helped to generate increased coverage.

Content analysis also can be applied to letters and phone calls. They can provide good feedback about problems with an organization's policies and services. A pattern of letters and phone calls pointing out a problem is evidence that something should be done.

Interviews. As with content analysis, interviews can be conducted in several different ways. Almost everyone talks to colleagues on a daily basis and calls other organizations to gather information. In fact, public relations personnel faced with solving a particular problem often "interview" other public relations professionals for ideas and suggestions.

If information is needed on public opinion and attitudes, many public relations firms will conduct short interviews with people in a shopping mall or at a meeting. This kind of interview is called an

Surveys of public opinion, often taken by researchers on the street or in shopping malls, help public relations practitioners target audiences they wish to reach and to shape their messages.

intercept interview, because people are literally intercepted in public places and asked their opinions.

The intercept interview does not use a rigorous sampling method, but it does give an organization a sense of current thinking or exposure to certain messages. For example, a health group wanted to find out if the public was actually receiving and retaining crucial aspects of its message. To gather such information, intercept interviews were conducted with 300 adults at six malls. Both unaided and aided recall questions were asked to assess the overall impact of the publicity.

Intercept interviews last only two to five minutes. At other times, the best approach is to do in-depth interviews to get more comprehensive information. A major fund-raising project by charitable groups, for example, may require in-depth interviews of community and business opinion leaders to determine support for the campaign. The success of any major fund drive, depends on the support of key leaders and wealthy individuals. This more in-depth approach is called purposive interviewing, because the interviewees are carefully selected based on their expertise, influence, or leadership in the community.

Focus Groups. A good alternative to individual interviews is the focus group. The focus group technique is widely used in advertising, marketing, and public relations to help identify the attitudes and motivations of important publics. Another purpose of focus groups is to formulate or pretest message themes and communication strategies before launching a full campaign. Focus groups usually consist of 8 to 12 people who represent the characteristics of a target audience, such as employees, consumers, or community residents.

During the interview, a trained facilitator uses nondirective interviewing techniques that encourage group members to talk freely about a topic or give candid reactions to suggested message themes. The setting is usually a conference room, and the

Focus groups are an effective tool that can be utilized to collect qualitative data about public opinion and attitudes about products and services.

discussion is informal. A focus group may last one or two hours, depending on the subject matter.

A focus group, by definition, is an informal research procedure that develops qualitative information rather than hard data. Results cannot be summarized by percentages or even projected to an entire population. Nevertheless, focus groups are useful in identifying the range of attitudes and opinions among the participants. Such insights can help an organization structure its messages or, on another level, formulate hypotheses and questions for a quantitative research survey.

Increasingly, focus groups are being conducted online. This technique can be as simple as posing a question to an online chat or interest group. Researchers also are using more formal selection processes to invite far-flung participants to meet in a pre-arranged virtual space. In the coming years, techniques and services will be further developed for cost-effective, online focus group research.

In another adaptation of new media, engineering management professor Hal Nystrom conducted focus groups for a Monsanto subsidiary that were then Webcast to the client. The focus group files remained available for review via password on the Web. Time and location are becoming less relevant to conducting focus groups, increasing the potential of this research method.

Copy Testing. All too often, organizations fail to communicate effectively because they produce and distribute materials that a target audience can't understand. In many cases, the material is written above the educational level of the audience. Consequently, representatives of the target audience should be asked to read or view the material in draft form before it is mass-produced and distributed. This can be done one-on-one or in a small-group setting.

A brochure about employee medical benefits or pension plans, for example, should be pretested with rank-and-file employees for readability and comprehension. Executives and lawyers who must approve the copy may understand the material, but a worker with a high school education might find the material difficult to follow.

Another approach to determine the degree of difficulty of material is to apply a readability formula to the draft copy. Fog, Flesch, and similar techniques relate the number of words and syllables per sentence or passage with reading level. Highly complex sentences and multisyllabic words require an audience with a college education.

The Internet provides an increasing array of ways to test copy. Just two examples are Web surveys and Wikis. Web survey systems such as Survey Artisan (www .surveyartisan.com) now allow attachment of video or photo files that can be critiqued by a target audience across many locations. Wikis can provide a way for clients or audience members to critique and correct copy. A Wiki is a Web site that allows users to easily edit content. Wikis essentially turn audience members into copy collaborators.

Scientific Sampling

The research techniques discussed thus far can provide public relations personnel with good insights and help them formulate effective programs. Increasingly, however, public relations professionals need to conduct polls and surveys, as well as more rigorous content analyses, using highly precise scientific sampling methods. Such sampling is based on two important factors: randomness and a large number of respondents.

Random Sampling. Effective polls and surveys require a random sample. In statistics, this means that everyone in the targeted audience (as defined by the researcher) has an equal or known chance of being selected for the survey. This is also called a probability sample.

In contrast, a nonprobability survey is not random at all. For example, a number of factors can influence who is interviewed using the mall-intercept method. The time of day or location of the intercept interviews may affect the sample. Researchers doing interviews in the morning may have a disproportionate number of homemakers or senior citizens, whereas interviews after 5 P.M. may include more high school students and office workers. If the researcher stands outside a record store or athletic shoe outlet, the average age of those interviewed may be much younger than that of the general population. Improper sampling can lead to misleading results (see the Ethics box on this page).

The most precise random sample is one generated from lists that have the name of every person in the target audience. This is simple if you're conducting a random survey of an organization's employees or members, because the researcher can randomly select, for example, every 25th name on a list. However, care must be taken to avoid patterns in the lists based on rank or employee category. It is always advisable to choose large intervals between selected names so that the researcher makes numerous passes through the list. Computerized lists may allow for random selection of a specified number of names.

Another common method to ensure representation is to draw a random sample that matches the characteristics of the audience. This is called quota sampling. Human resource departments usually have breakdowns of employees by job classification, and it is relatively easy to proportion a sample accordingly. For example, if 42 percent of the employees work on the assembly line, then 42 percent of the sample should be assembly-line workers. A quota sample can be drawn on any number of demographic factors—age, sex, religion, race, income—depending on the purpose of the survey.

Random sampling becomes more difficult when comprehensive lists are not available. In those cases, researchers surveying the general population often use telephone directories or customer lists to select respondents at random. A more rigorous technique employs random generation of telephone numbers, ensuring that new and unlisted numbers are included in the sample.

Sample Size. In any probability study, sample size is an issue that must be addressed. National polling firms usually sample 1,000 to 1,500 people and get a highly accurate idea of what the U.S. adult population is thinking. A national poll sample of 1,500 people provides a margin of error within 3 percentage points 95 percent of the time. In other words, 19 out of 20 times that the same questionnaire is administered, the results should be within the same 3 percentage points and reflect the whole population accurately.

ON THE JOB >>

Is This News Release Misleading?

Ethics

Organizations often publicize the favorable findings of survey research, and the International Franchise Association (IFA) is no exception. It sent out a news release quoting a Gallup survey with the headline, "Gallup Survey: 92 Percent of Franchise Owners Successful." The text continued, "Whether you're serving burgers or bagels, tending to taxes or helping the bereaved select a casket, franchise owners consider themselves successful."

The news release didn't include the fact that the survey involved only those still operating and not those who failed. It also didn't specify how the sample was derived or whether bagel owners were even sampled. The IFA also grouped two categories of the survey results together—those who said "very successful" and those who said "somewhat successful"—to come up with the 92 percent.

If you were the public relations director for IFA, would you have allowed this news release to be distributed? Why or why not?

In public relations, the primary purpose of poll data is to get indications of attitudes and opinions, not to predict elections. Therefore, it is not usually necessary or practical to do a scientific sampling of 1,500 people. A sample of 250 to 500 will give relatively accurate data—with a 5 or 6 percent margin of error—that will help determine general public attitudes and opinions. A sample of about 100 people, accurately drawn according to probability guidelines, will include about a 10 percent margin of error.

This percentage of error would be acceptable if a public relations person, for example, asked employees what they want to read in the company magazine. Sixty percent may indicate that they would like to see more news about opportunities for promotion. If only 100 employees were properly surveyed, it really doesn't matter if the actual percentage is 50 or 70 percent. The larger percentage, in either case, would be sufficient to justify an increase in news stories about advancement opportunities.

Questionnaire Guidelines.

The following are some general guidelines for the construction of questionnaires:

> Determine the type of information that is needed and in what detail.
> State the objectives of the survey in writing.
> Decide which group(s) will receive the questionnaire.
> Decide on the size of the sample.
> State the purpose of the survey and guarantee anonymity.
> Use closed-ended (multiple-choice) answers as often as possible. Respondents find it easier and less time-consuming to select answers than to compose their own.
> Design the questionnaire in such a way that answers can be easily coded for statistical analysis.
> Strive to make the questionnaire no more than 25 questions. Long questionnaires put people off and reduce the number of responses, particularly in print questionnaires, because it is easy to see how long the survey will take to complete.
> Use categories when asking questions about education, age, and income. People are more willing to answer when a category or range is used. For example, what category best describes your age? (a) Under 25, (b) 26 to 40, and so on.
> Use simple, familiar words. Readability should be appropriate for the group being sampled. At the same time, don't talk down to respondents.
> Avoid ambiguous words and phrases that may confuse the respondents.
> Edit out leading questions that suggest a specific correct response or bias an answer.
> Remember to consider the context and placement of questions. A question placed before another can influence responses to the later question.
> Provide space at the end of the questionnaire for respondents' comments and observations. This allows them to provide additional information or elaboration that may not have been covered in the main body of the questionnaire.
> Pretest the questions for understanding and possible bias. Representatives of the proposed sampling group should read the questionnaire and be asked to make comments as to how it can be improved.

Designing a questionnaire and analyzing the results can be time-consuming, but software programs are available that can make the task much easier. One such program, Publics PR Research Software, was developed by Glen T. Cameron at the University of Missouri and Tim Herzog of Kno Technology. The software helps the public relations personnel create questionnaires by providing ready-made questions that can be tailored to fit any situation. In addition, the program also helps conduct data analysis to identify target publics. This component is a modest artificial intelligence module that draws on judgments from statistics to generate advice. Cameron describes it as artificial intelligence, but with a low IQ.

Reaching Respondents

Once a sample has been identified and a questionnaire has been developed, it must be delivered to prospective respondents. There are pros and cons to each method of delivery—(1) mail questionnaires, (2) telephone surveys, (3) personal interviews, (4) piggyback, or omnibus, surveys, and (5) Web and e-mail surveys.

Mail Questionnaires. Questionnaires may be used in a variety of settings. However, for four different reasons, most survey questionnaires are mailed to respondents:

1. Because the researchers have better control as to who receives the questionnaire, they can make sure that the survey is representative.
2. Large geographic areas can be covered economically.
3. It is less expensive to administer paper-based questionnaires than to hire interviewers to conduct personal interviews.
4. Large numbers of people can be included at minimal cost.

However, mail questionnaires do have some disadvantages. The biggest is the low response rate. A mail questionnaire by a commercial firm sent to the general public usually produces a response rate of 1 to 2 percent. If the survey concerns issues considered highly relevant to the general public, the response rate might increase to 5 to 20 percent. A much better response rate would be generated, however, if a questionnaire were mailed by an organization to its members. In this case, the response rate may be 30 to 80 percent. The more closely people identify with the organization and the questions, the better the response.

The response rate to a mail questionnaire can be increased, say the experts, if all the guidelines of questionnaire construction are followed. In addition, researchers should keep the following suggestions in mind:

> Include a stamped, self-addressed return envelope and a personally signed letter explaining the importance of participating in the survey.

> Provide an incentive. Commercial firms often encourage people to fill out questionnaires by including a token amount of money or a discount coupon. Other researchers promise to share the results of the survey with the respondents.

> Mail questionnaires by first-class mail. Some research shows that placing special issue stamps on the envelope attracts greater interest than simply using a postage meter.

> Mail a reminder postcard three or four days after the questionnaire has been sent.

> Do a second mailing (either to nonrespondents or to the entire sample) two or three weeks after the first mailing. Again, enclose a stamped, self-addressed return envelope and a cover letter explaining the crucial need for the recipient's participation.

Telephone Surveys. Surveys by telephone, particularly those that are locally based, are used extensively by research firms. The telephone survey has several advantages:

> The response or nonresponse is immediate. A researcher doesn't have to wait several weeks for responses to arrive by mail.

> A telephone call is personal. It is effective communication, and it is much cheaper than a personal interview.

> A telephone call is less intrusive than going door-to-door and interviewing people. Surveys have found that many people are willing to talk on the phone for up to 45 minutes, but they will not stand at a door for more than 5 or 10 minutes and are unwilling to admit strangers to their homes.

> The response rate, if the survey is properly composed and the phone interviewers trained, can reach 80 to 90 percent.

The major disadvantage of telephone surveys is the difficulty in getting access to telephone numbers. In many urban areas, as many as one-third to one-half of all numbers are unlisted. Although researchers can let a computer program pick numbers through random dialing, this method is not as effective as actually knowing who is being called. The dominance of cellular telephones whose numbers are not listed is an increasingly difficult hurdle. Because cell phone numbers are portable, it is difficult to know whether the 212 prefix you dialed belongs to a current or former resident of New York City or someone who simply wants to appear to be from New York. Another barrier is convincing respondents that a legitimate poll or survey is being taken. Far too many salespeople attempt to sell goods by posing as researchers.

Personal Interviews. The personal interview is the most expensive form of research because it requires trained staff and travel. If travel within a city is involved, a trained interviewer may only be able to interview 8 or 10 people a day, and salaries and transportation costs make it expensive. Considerable advance work is required to arrange interviews and appointments and, as previously noted, residents are reluctant to admit strangers into their homes.

However, in some instances personal interviews can be cost-effective. They can generate a wealth of information if the setting is controlled. Many research firms conduct personal interviews at national conventions or trade shows, where there is a concentration of people with similar interests.

Piggyback Surveys. An alternative method of reaching respondents is the piggyback survey, also known as the omnibus survey. In basic terms, an organization "buys" a question in a national survey conducted by a survey organization such as Gallup or Harris. For example, General Mills may place one or two questions in a national poll that ask respondents what professional athlete they most admire as a way to find new endorsers for its breakfast foods. In the same survey, the American Cancer Society may place a question asking how the public feels about sporting events sponsored by tobacco companies.

This method is attractive to public relations people for two reasons. One is cost. An organization pays much less to participate in a piggyback poll than to conduct its own survey. A second reason is expertise. Firms such as Gallup or Harris have the skill and organization to conduct surveys properly and efficiently.

Piggyback surveys, however, do have limitations. An organization can only get a small snapshot of public opinion with one or two questions, and the subject matter must be relevant to the general public.

Web and E-Mail Surveys. The newest way to reach respondents is through electronic communications. One such method is to post a questionnaire on an organization's Web site and then ask visitors to complete it online. The advantage of this is that once the visitor completes the survey, his or her response is immediately available and the results can be added to the running tabulation. For example, an undergraduate campaign team sought to test messages about the National Wildlife Foundation's travel program, which was targeted at those over age 50. The students sampled from an e-mail list of university alumni by year of graduation so that they reached the appropriate age group. They invited the alumni to visit a Web site and rate several of the travel program's message strategies.

Researchers use several methods to attract respondents to a Web site, including (1) banner ads announcing the survey on other Web sites or online networks, (2) sending e-mail invitations to members of the target audience, (3) telephoning individuals with an invitation to participate, and (4) sending a postcard. The major disadvantage of Web surveys is that it is difficult to control the exact characteristics of the respondents, because a Web site is accessible to virtually anyone with a computer and an Internet connection. It is also very important to control repeated participation by the same respondent by identifying the unique identifying number of the computer (called the IP address) and only allowing one submission. One of the biggest problems for online surveys is the low response rate due to the impersonal nature of the survey and the ease of leaving the survey's Web site with a single mouse click. For this reason, many online surveys begin with the most crucial questions to be asked and the key demographics needed for analysis.

If reaching the exact audience is important, another approach is an e-mail survey that is sent to a list of known respondents. Organizations can compile e-mail lists of clients or customers, but now it's also possible to purchase e-mail address lists from a variety of sources. Full-service Web survey companies can target populations, collect responses, and deliver data to the client. The costs of such surveys can be low if an online survey service such as freeonlinesurveys.com, which is more of a do-it-yourself service, is used. Zoomerang (info.zoomerang.com) and Harris Interactive recruit and maintain pools of respondents to fit profiles that clients want to survey. Gender, income, and political persuasion are examples of characteristics that can be selected for Web survey purposes.

Planning: The Second Step

The second step of the public relations process, following research, is program planning. Before any public relations activity can be implemented, it is essential that considerable thought be given to what should be done and in what sequence steps should be taken to accomplish an organization's objectives.

A good public relations program should be an effective tool to support an organization's business, marketing, and communications objectives. As senior consultant Larry Werner points out, "No longer are we simply in the business of putting press releases out; we're in the business of solving business problems through communications."

In other words, public relations planning should be strategic. As Broom and Dozier say in their text *Using Public Relations Research*, "Strategic planning is deciding where you want to be in the future (the goal) and how to get there (the strategies). It sets the organization's direction proactively, avoiding 'drift' and routine repetition of activities." A practitioner must think about a situation, analyze what can be done about it, creatively conceptualize the appropriate strategies and tactics, and determine how the results will be measured. Planning also involves the coordination of multiple methods—news releases, special events, Web pages, press kits, CD-ROM distribution, news conferences, media interviews, brochures, newsletters, speeches, and so on—to achieve specific results.

Systematic planning prevents haphazard, ineffective communication. Having a blueprint of what is to be done and how it will be executed makes programs more effective and public relations more valuable to the organization.

Approaches to Planning

Planning is like putting together a jigsaw puzzle. Research provides the various pieces. Next, it is necessary to arrange the pieces so that a coherent design, or picture, emerges. The best planning is systematic; that is, gathering information, analyzing it, and creatively applying it for the specific purpose of attaining an objective.

Following are two approaches to planning. In both cases, the emphasis is on asking and answering questions to generate a road map for success.

Management by Objective. One popular approach to planning is a process called management by objective (MBO). MBO provides focus and direction for formulating strategy to achieve specific organizational objectives.

In their book *Public Relations Management by Objectives*, Norman R. Nager and T. Harrell Allen discuss nine basic MBO steps that can help a practitioner conceptualize everything from a simple news release to a multifaceted communications program. The steps can serve as a planning checklist that provides the basis for strategic planning.

1. *Client/Employer Objectives.* What is the purpose of the communication, and how does it promote or achieve the objectives of the organization? Specific objectives such as "to make consumers aware of the product's high quality" are more meaningful than "to make people aware of the product."

2. *Audience/Publics.* Who exactly should be reached with the message, and how can that audience help achieve the organization's objectives? What are the characteristics of the audience, and how can demographic information be used to structure the message? The primary audience for a campaign to encourage carpooling consists of people who regularly drive to work, not the general public.

3. *Audience Objectives.* What is it that the audience wants to know, and how can the message be tailored to audience self-interest? Consumers are more interested in how a new computer will increase their productivity than in how it works.

4. *Media Channels.* What is the appropriate channel for reaching the audience, and how can multiple channels (news media, brochures, special events, and direct mail) reinforce the message among key publics? An ad may be best for making consumers aware of a new product, but a news release may be better for conveying consumer information about the product.

5. *Media Channel Objectives.* What is the media gatekeeper looking for in a news angle, and why would a particular publication be interested in the information?

6. *Sources and Questions.* What primary and secondary sources of information are required to provide a factual base for the message? What experts should be interviewed? What database research should be conducted? A quote from a project engineer about a new technology is better than a quote from the marketing vice president.

7. *Communication Strategies.* What environmental factors will affect the dissemination and acceptance of the message? Are the target publics hostile or favorably disposed to the message? What other events or pieces of information negate or reinforce the message? A campaign to conserve water is more salient if there has been a recent drought.

8. *Essence of the Message.* What is the planned communication impact on the audience? Is the message designed merely to inform, or is it designed to change attitudes and behavior? Telling people about the values of physical fitness is different from telling them how to achieve it.

9. *Nonverbal Support.* How can photographs, graphs, films, and artwork clarify and visually enhance the written message? Bar graphs or pie charts are easier to understand than columns of numbers.

A Strategic Planning Model. By working through the checklist adapted from Nager and Allen's book, a practitioner has in place the general building blocks for assembling a public relations plan. These building blocks serve as background to create a specific plan. Ketchum offers more pointed questions in its "Strategic Planning Model for Public Relations." Ketchum's organizational model, outlined below, makes sense to professionals and clients alike, moving both parties toward a clear situation analysis needed to make planning relevant to the client's overall objectives.

Facts

> *Category Facts*—What are recent industry trends?
> *Product/Service Issues*—What are the significant characteristics of the product, service, or issue?
> *Competitive Facts*—Who are the competitors, and what are their competitive strengths, similarities, and differences?
> *Customer Facts*—Who uses the product and why?

Goals

> *Business Objectives*—What are the company's business objectives? What is the time frame?
> *Role of Public Relations*—How does public relations fit into the marketing mix?
> *Sources of New Business*—What sectors will produce growth?

Audience

> *Target Audiences*—What are the target audiences? What are their "hot buttons"?
> *Current Mind-Set*—How do audiences feel about the product, service, or issue?
> *Desired Mind-Set.* How do we want them to feel?

Key Message

> *Main Point.* What one key message must be conveyed to change or reinforce mind-sets?

These two approaches to planning, MBO and Ketchum's model, lead to the next important step—writing a strategic public relations plan. The elements of such a plan are explained in the following section.

The Eight Elements of a Program Plan

A public relations program plan identifies what is to be done, why, and how to accomplish it. By preparing such a plan, either as a brief outline or as an extensive document, the practitioner can make certain that all the elements have been properly considered and that everyone involved understands the "big picture."

It is common practice for public relations firms to prepare a program plan for client approval and possible modification before implementing a public relations campaign. At that time, both the public relations firm and the client reach a mutual understanding of the campaign's objectives and how to accomplish them. Public relations departments of organizations also map out particular campaigns or show the departments' plans for the coming year.

Although there can be some variation, public relations plans include eight basic elements:

1. Situation
2. Objectives
3. Audience
4. Strategy
5. Tactics
6. Calendar/Timetable
7. Budget
8. Evaluation

This section elaborates on these elements and gives examples from campaigns that received PRSA Silver Anvil Awards for excellence. The PR Casebook on page 133 illustrates the elements of a public relations plan.

Situation. Valid objectives cannot be set without a clear understanding of the situation that led to the conclusion that a public relations program was needed. Three situations often prompt a public relations program: (1) The organization must conduct a remedial program to overcome a problem or negative situation; (2) the organization needs to conduct a specific one-time project; or (3) the organization wants to reinforce an ongoing effort to preserve its reputation and public support.

Loss of market share and declining sales often require a remedial program. Mack Trucks, for example, initiated an extensive public relations campaign after seeing its market share decline from 21 percent in the 1980s to less than 9 percent in the 1990s. Other organizations launch such campaigns to change public perceptions. The Turkish government conducted an extensive tourism campaign designed to combat negative public perceptions that the country was "uncivilized" and an "underdeveloped, Third-World Middle Eastern country."

Specific one-time events often lead to public relations programs. One such campaign was for the grand opening of San Antonio's new public library. It was important to plan a celebration that showcased the facility as an educational, cultural, and entertainment resource for everyone. The introduction of Microsoft's Vista operating system was also a one-time event; it required a program plan that covered many months of prelaunch activities.

In the third situation, program plans are initiated to preserve and develop customer or public support. Department 56, a leading designer and manufacturer of miniature lighted village collectibles, already had a successful business, but it wanted

PRCASEBOOK

The 100th Anniversary of Jell-O

A public relations plan contains eight basic elements. The following is an outline of a plan that Kraft Foods and its public relations firm, Hunter & Associates, developed for Jell-O's 100th anniversary celebration.

1. Situation

Sales of this famous dessert were flat. Brand research showed that Jell-O, on the eve of its 100th anniversary celebration, was not top-of-mind with consumers, who were moving to "newer" desserts. Research in company archives provided extensive historical information and graphics about the use and promotion of Jell-O through the years.

2. Objectives

> Increase brand awareness in order to increase sales.

> Generate widespread awareness of Jell-O's 100th anniversary in high-profile media.

3. Target Audience

> Current and lapsed Jell-O consumers; women, age 25–44, with families.

4. Strategies

> Use the nostalgic appeal of the brand to capture major media interest.

> Develop many story angles around three key messages for a broad range of media.

> Introduce a new Jell-O product to convey the idea that the brand is still in sync with the times.

> Involve LeRoy, New York, where Jell-O was invented, in the anniversary celebration

> Involve Kraft Food employees with anniversary celebrations at each plant and corporate location.

> Generate stories emphasizing three key messages: (1) Jell-O is fun, (2) Jell-O is contemporary, and (3) Jell-O is an American and Canadian icon.

5. Tactics

> Host a gala event with Bill Cosby, Jell-O spokesperson, as master of ceremonies.

> Introduce a new flavor—champagne.

> Publish a new cookbook.

> Open a new museum and tour exhibits around the country.

> Use Jell-O's hometown, LeRoy, New York, to host a Jell-O Jubilee.

> Establish a new Web site.

> Provide print and broadcast media with press kits that include historical backgrounders and artwork.

6. Calendar

> Eighteen months for the entire campaign

> Three months for research, planning

> Four months for preparing press kits, media lists, etc.

> Eleven months of scheduled events and news releases at quarterly intervals:

> First Quarter—Jell-O celebrates its 100th anniversary.

> Second Quarter—Champagne flavor is introduced, cookbook is promoted.

> Third Quarter—Jell-O museum opens and begins touring the nation.

> Fourth Quarter—Jell-O builds new float for Macy's Thanksgiving Parade.

7. Budget

> $450,000 for 18 months

8. Evaluation

> Brand awareness was established through much extensive media coverage. Research showed 6,617 positive stories, 7,893 minutes of TV time, and 101 minutes of radio time. This included extensive stories in the *New York Times,* inclusion of Jell-O in a Jay Leno monologue, and a Jell-O feature on Oprah Winfrey's mother's day special.

> Survey research showed 48 percent of respondents heard about the anniversary from television, while another 37 percent found out about it from newspapers or magazines.

> Sales of Jell-O increased more than 5 percent from the previous year.

Planning a public relations program requires conferences like this one, at which participants weigh information on such diverse topics as objectives, graphics, media selection, demographics, and timing.

new customers. Its public relations program to accomplish this included distribution of brochures on home decoration for the Christmas holidays and participation by its dealers in local efforts to decorate Ronald McDonald houses.

Relevant research often is included as part of the situation in a program plan. In the case of Department 56, consumer market analysis revealed a strong link between consumers interested in home decorating and those involved in collecting. In the Turkish campaign, research showed little public awareness of Turkey as a European travel destination, and a content analysis of press clippings disclosed a large percentage of negative stereotypes. Other research portrayed the typical American traveler to Turkey as a sophisticated person over the age of 40 with an income of at least $50,000. For the repositioning of Levi jeans for the college market, media-use patterns of students were analyzed using secondary research, including data collection about college students' use of computers. Such research provides the foundation for setting program objectives and shaping other elements of the program plan.

The program plan is informed by proactive research, as noted in the conflict management life cycle in Chapter 2. The proactive phase of the conflict management life cycle suggests that issues are tracked to assess potential competition or threats. When an imminent threat is identified through issues tracking, the threat appraisal model helps determine how much of a threat the issue is to the organization. The greater the threat, the more important the strategizing, planning, and development of objectives.

Objectives. Once the situation or problem is understood, the next step is to establish objectives for the program. A proposed objective should be evaluated by asking three questions:

1. Does it really address the situation?
2. Is it realistic and achievable?
3. Can success be measured in meaningful terms?

An objective is usually stated in terms of program outcomes rather than inputs. Or, put another way, objectives should not be the "means" but the "end." A poor objective, for example, is to "generate publicity for a new product." Publicity is not an "end" in itself. The actual objective is to "create consumer awareness about a new product." This is accomplished by such tactics as news releases, special events, and brochures.

It is particularly important that public relations objectives complement and reinforce the organization's objectives. Professor David Dozier of San Diego State University expressed the point well in a *Public Relations Review* article: "The prudent and strategic selection of public relations goals and objectives linked to organizational survival and growth serves to justify the public relations program as a viable management activity."

Basically, objectives are either informational or motivational.

Informational Objectives. Many public relations plans are designed primarily to expose audiences to information and to increase awareness of an issue, an event, or a product. The five objectives of public relations activity are discussed later in the chapter. The first two of these—message exposure and accurate dissemination of messages— are the most common. Many communication and marketing professionals believe that the major criteria for public relations effectiveness are (1) an increase in public awareness and (2) delivery of key messages.

The following are some examples of informational objectives:

> Mack Trucks: "Increase awareness and understanding of Mack highway vehicles and engine technology."

> Travelocity: "Increase consumers' overall awareness and excitement for the brand."

> National Association of Manufacturers (NAM): "Educate target audiences on the fundamental importance of manufacturing to our nation's current competitiveness and future prosperity."

One difficulty with informational objectives is measuring how well a particular objective has been achieved. Public awareness and the extent of education that takes place are somewhat abstract and difficult to quantify. Survey research often is required, which is explained in the evaluation section of this chapter; many organizations, however, infer "awareness" by counting the number of media placements. In reality, message exposure doesn't necessarily mean increased public awareness.

Motivational Objectives. Although changing attitudes and influencing behavior are difficult to accomplish in a public relations campaign, motivational objectives are easier to measure. That's because they are bottom-line oriented and are based on clearly measurable results that can be quantified. This is true whether the goal is an increase in product sales, a sellout crowd for a theatrical performance, or expanded donations to a charitable agency.

The following are some examples of motivational objectives:

> Duracell Batteries: "Distribute all of the branded 'guidebooks' [Together We Can Become Safe Families] and coupons to consumers in the major metropolitan cities."

> DaimlerChrysler: "Provide [teens] tools and tactics to survive the high-risk [driving] years."

> Puerto Rico Federal Affairs Administration voter registration campaign: "Registering 300,000 mainland Puerto Ricans by the 2004 election."
> Levi's Jeans: "Reverse Levi's stodgy image with young consumers by generating upbeat media coverage."

A public relations program will often have both informational and motivational objectives. A good example is the Fighting Hunger in Wisconsin campaign. Its objectives were to (1) increase public awareness of hunger in Wisconsin, (2) enlist additional volunteers, and (3) raise more money than in the previous year to support hunger relief programs around the state.

Objectives, and how to measure their accomplishment, are discussed later in the chapter.

Audience. Public relations programs should be directed toward specific and defined audiences or publics. Although some campaigns are directed to a general public, such instances are the exception. Even the M&M's Candy national "election" campaign to select a new color (blue) for its famous mix was designed to reach consumers 24 years of age or younger.

In other words, public relations practitioners target specific publics within the general public. This is done through market research that identifies key publics by such demographics as age, income, social strata, education, existing ownership or consumption of specific products, and where people live. For example, market research told M&M's Candy that young people were the primary consumers of its product. On a more basic level, a water conservation campaign defines its target audience by geography—people living in a particular city or area.

In many cases, common sense is all that is needed to adequately define a specific public. Take, for example, the Ohio vaccination program for children under the age of two. The primary audience for the message is parents with young children. Other audiences are pregnant women and medical professionals who treat young children. Perhaps a more complex situation involves a company that wants to increase the sale of a CD program on home improvement for do-it-yourselfers. Again, the primary audience is not the general public, but those persons who actually have computers with CD-ROM drives and enjoy working around the house. Such criteria exclude a large percentage of the American population.

The following are examples of how some of the organizations already mentioned have defined target audiences:

> Puerto Rico Federal Affairs Administration: "Puerto Ricans residing on the U.S. mainland of voting age who were unregistered to vote"
> DaimlerChrysler: "New drivers age 15–18 and their parents"
> Duracell: "[W]omen, ages 25–54 with children, who are the primary shoppers for their households"
> Levi's Jeans: "(1) College-age consumers; (2) youth-focused media"

As previously noted, some organizations identify the media as a "public." On occasion, in programs that seek media endorsements or that try to change how the media report on an organization or an issue, editors and reporters can become a legitimate "public." In general, however, mass media outlets fall in the category of a "means to an end." They are channels to reach defined audiences that need to be informed, persuaded, and motivated.

A thorough understanding of the primary and secondary publics is essential if a program's objectives are to be accomplished. Such knowledge also provides guidance on the selection of appropriate strategies and tactics that would reach these defined audiences.

The manufacturer of the CD on home improvement, for example, might completely bypass the general press and concentrate on specialized publications in the home improvement and computer fields. Cost is a driving factor; spending large sums to reach members of the general public on matters in which they have no stake or interest is nonproductive and a waste of money.

Strategy. A strategy statement describes how, in concept, an objective is to be achieved, providing guidelines and themes for the overall program. Strategy statements offer a rationale for planned actions and program components. One general strategy may be outlined or a program may have several strategies, depending on the objectives and the designated audiences.

The public relations programs for Help Heal Florida's Healthcare and Levi's Jeans illustrate the basic concept of formulating and writing a strategy. Note that the following strategies are broad statements; specific activities are part of tactics, covered in the next section. The health care reform group summarized its strategies as follows:

1. Convert feelings of discontent with healthcare costs into a willingness to listen and support medical liability reform.

2. Focus on problem consensus before offering solution specifics.

3. Build a broad-based coalition that includes the insurance industry, but don't walk hand-in-hand with them.

4. Avoid turning off consumers by resorting to the "same old fight between doctors and lawyers."

5. Communicate impact on patients rather than health-care providers, but insist on credible fact-based communications without resorting to "scare tactics" over access.

The following were Levi's Jeans' strategies:

1. Build an online community for college-age kids about college-age kids that's entertaining and interactive.

2. Creatively capitalize on the e-commerce explosion to engage target media.

3. Stimulate ongoing coverage via newsworthy moments-in-time.

The anchor for these three strategies was the Levi's Online Challenge: Levi's would select three college students who would purchase everything online that they needed to live for one semester.

Key Messages/Themes. The strategy element of a program plan should state key themes and messages to be reiterated throughout the campaign on all publicity materials. The Ohio juvenile immunization program, for example, was based on the concept that parents love their children and want them to be healthy. Thus, a key message was to tell parents how important vaccinations were to keep their children out of danger. Carrying out this message was the theme of the campaign, "Project L.O.V.E.," with the subhead "Love Our Kids Vaccination Project."

In the Turkish tourism campaign, the strategy of combating "negative stereotypes and lack of knowledge about Turkey" included key messages designed to reinforce historical/cultural sites, natural beauty, upscale accommodations, great shopping, excellent cuisine, ideal weather, and friendly people. In an effort to position Turkey as part of Europe instead of the Middle East, the themes "Center of World History" and "Where Europe Becomes Exotic" were used.

Tactics. Tactics is the nuts-and-bolts part of the plan that describes, in sequence, the specific activities that put the strategies into operation and help to achieve the stated objectives. Tactics use the tools of communication to reach primary and secondary audiences with key messages. Chapter 10 discusses communication tools in greater detail.

The Tactics of Levi's Jeans.   Levi's used a number of tactics to support the objectives and strategies of its program to reposition Levi's Jeans as a desirable brand in the college-age market. The Levi's Online Challenge kick-off was a contest to select three "point-and-click pioneers" who would make all necessary purchases online for a semester. Contestants answered questions such as, "What was the wackiest online purchase you ever made?" and "If you named your computer and mouse, what would you call them?" Other tactics included:

> Announcement of winners and "freshman orientation" for publicity.
> The semester of online shopping, including Levi's outfits, was documented on the personal Web pages of the three shoppers with digital photos, virtual diaries, and personal anecdotes.
> Creation of a weekly Web show using Webcams and headsets to broadcast online shopping experiences as well as chat on issues from cars to safe sex with thousands of teens logged on to Levi.com.
> Levi's Jeans made a $1 donation to the brand's ongoing beneficiary, the music industry's cause against AIDS called LIFEbeat, for every viewer who logged on to the final show.

The Tactics of KFC.   When KFC wanted to introduce its new line of oven-roasted chicken product, the company decided to take advantage of a popular culture event. NBC television's *The Apprentice* attacted young adults (ages 18 to 49), who were the target market for KFC's new food line. When Donald Trump made his final "you're fired" prouncement and hired his apprentice, KFC wanted to be positioned to hire the runner-up. Through press releases KFC and its public relations firm, Edelman, made the offer of an executive job as chief sales officer at KFC to *The Apprentice* runner-up. This tactic took advantage of the popularity of the television program. Other tactics included:

> A press release announced a one-week $25,000 job for the runner-up of *The Apprentice*. The release was distributed 10 days before the live finale of the popular television program.
> The story was pitched to top print, entertainment, television, radio, and lifestyle publications.
> KFC kept in contact with the show's NBC producers to make sure that the runner-up received the offer immediately following the finale.

> *The Apprentice* runner-up Kwame Jackson announced he was considering the offer.
> A second release was distributed that named Jackson and reiterated the job offer.
> Both Trump and Jackson were quoted in the media referring to the offer
> Whether the offer was accepted or not, as Trump told the *New York Times*: KFC "is getting millions of dollars' worth of publicity for something that is only going to cost them $25,000." "Maybe I should hire their marketing person," he told the *Times*.

Calendar/Timetable. The three aspects of timing in a program plan are (1) deciding when a campaign should be conducted, (2) determining the proper sequence of activities, and (3) compiling a list of steps that must be completed to produce a finished product. All three aspects are important to achieving maximum effectiveness.

The Timing of a Campaign. Program planning should take into account the environmental context of the situation and the time when key messages are most meaningful to the intended audience. A campaign to encourage carpooling, for example, might be more successful if it follows a major price increase in gasoline or a government report that traffic congestion has reached gridlock proportions.

Some subjects are seasonal. Department 56, the designer and manufacturer of miniature lighted village collectibles and other holiday giftware, timed the bulk of its campaign for November to take advantage of the Christmas holidays, when there was major interest in its product lines. Charitable agencies, such as the Wisconsin hunger project, also gear their campaigns around Christmas when there is increased interest in helping the unfortunate.

By the same token, strawberry producers increase public relations efforts in May and June, when a crop comes to market and stores have large supplies of the fruit. Similarly, a software program on income tax preparation attracts the most audience interest in February and March, just before the April 15 filing deadline. In another situation, a vendor of a software program designed to handle personal finances launched a public relations–marketing program in January. The timing was based on research indicating that people put "getting control of personal finances" high on their list of New Year's resolutions.

Other kinds of campaigns depend less on an environmental or seasonal context. The Mack Trucks and Levi's Jeans campaigns, for example, could be conducted at almost any time.

Scheduling of Tactics. The second aspect of timing is the scheduling and sequencing of various tactics or activities. A typical pattern is to concentrate the most effort at the beginning of a campaign, when a number of tactics are implemented. The launch phase of a campaign, much like that of a rocket, requires a burst of activity just to break the awareness barrier. After the campaign has achieved orbit, however, less energy and fewer activities are required to maintain momentum.

To further the rocket analogy, public relations campaigns often are the first stage of an integrated marketing communications program. Once public relations has created awareness and customer anticipation of a new product, the second stage may be an advertising and direct mail campaign.

Compiling a Calendar. An integral part of timing is advance planning. A video news release, a press kit, or a brochure often takes weeks or months to prepare. Arrangements for special events also take considerable time. Practitioners must take into account the deadlines of publications. Monthly periodicals, for example, frequently

FIGURE 5.1

A page from the April calendar used to plan an event.

Wednesday, April 12

M   Begin development of invitation, RSVP, envelopes, tickets, program, nametags, placards, etc.

J/M   Review printing costs and options

T   Investigate possibility of having palette tasting trays

T   Reserve Stars' Grill Room for evening of event (asking Jess)

T   Determine RSVP voice mail #

ALL   2 p.m. Committee Meeting at SF War Memorial and Performing Arts Center

need information at least six to eight weeks before publication. A popular talk show may book guests three or four months in advance.

In other words, the public relations professional must think ahead to make things happen in the right sequence, at the right time. One way to achieve this goal is to compile time lines and charts that list the necessary steps and their required completion dates.

Calendars and time lines take various forms. One simple method is to post activities for each day on a large monthly calendar. The public relations manager of Kendall-Jackson Winery used this method to plan a luxury wine tasting and dinner. Figure 5.1 shows an excerpt from one day of the April calendar (initials in the left column indicate the person responsible for the activity).

Gantt charts are also used for planning purposes. Essentially, a Gantt chart is a column matrix that has two sides. The left side has a vertical list of activities that must be accomplished, and the top has a horizontal line of days, weeks, or months. Figure 5.2 is a simplified example of a Gantt chart.

Budget. No program plan is complete without a budget. Both clients and employers ask, "How much will this program cost?" In many cases, the reverse approach is taken. Organizations establish an amount they can afford and then ask the public relations staff or firm to write a program plan that reflects the amount allocated.

A budget can be divided into two categories: staff time and out-of-pocket (OOP) expenses. Staff and administrative time usually takes the lion's share of any public relations budget. In a $100,000 campaign done by a public relations firm, for example, it is not unusual for 70 percent to be salaries and administrative fees. Information about how public relations firms charge fees is presented in Chapter 4. Some budgets of campaigns already discussed were as follows:

> Turkish Tourism: $650,000 for 15-month program; $450,000 in public relations firm fees and $200,000 in expenses.

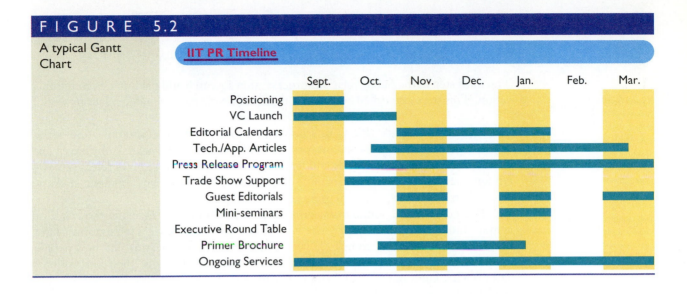

FIGURE 5.2

A typical Gantt Chart

IIT PR Timeline

	Sept.	Oct.	Nov.	Dec.	Jan.	Feb.	Mar.
Positioning							
VC Launch							
Editorial Calendars							
Tech./App. Articles							
Press Release Program							
Trade Show Support							
Guest Editorials							
Mini-seminars							
Executive Round Table							
Primer Brochure							
Ongoing Services							

> Florida Health Care: $585,000 (excluding paid advertising) for 11 months.

> Duracell: $600,000, including both the agency fee and OOP expenses. Program budget skewed heavily toward OOP expenses, because it accounted for production of 150,000 guidebooks and 300,000 coupons, Web site development, market research, the 10-city preparedness survey, a $250,000 donation to the American Red Cross, and all other miscellaneous expenses related to the program.

> Levi Jeans: $600,000; $460,000 in public relations firm fees and $140,000 in OOP expenses.

One method of budgeting is to use two columns. The left column will list the staff cost for writing a pamphlet or compiling a press kit. The right column will list the actual OOP expense for having the pamphlet or press kit designed, printed, and delivered. Internal public relations staffs, whose members are on the payroll, often complete only the OOP expenses. It is good practice to allocate about 10 percent of the budget for contingencies or unexpected costs.

In a program plan, budgets are usually estimated on the basis of experience and requests from vendors for estimates. After the program is completed, part of the evaluation is to compile a form that shows estimated expenses versus actual expenses.

Evaluation. The evaluation element of a plan relates directly back to the stated objectives of the program. As discussed earlier, objectives must be measurable in some way to show clients and employers that the program accomplished its purpose.

Consequently, evaluation criteria should be realistic, credible, specific, and in line with client or employer expectations. The evaluation section of a program plan should restate the objectives and then name the evaluation methods to be used.

Evaluation of an informational objective often entails a compilation of news clips and an analysis of how often key message points were mentioned. Other methods include determining how many brochures were distributed or the estimated number of viewers who saw a video news release. Motivational objectives often are measured and evaluated by increases in sales or market share, the number of people who called an 800 number for more information, or by benchmark surveys that measure people's perceptions before and after a campaign.

Communication: The Third Step

The Goals of Communication

The third step in the public relations process, after research and planning, is communication. This step, also called *execution*, is the most visible part of public relations work.

Implementing the Plan. In a public relations program, communication is the implementation of a decision, the process and the means by which objectives are achieved. A program's strategies and tactics may take the form of news releases, news conferences, special events, brochures, viral marketing, speeches, bumper stickers, newsletters, Webcasts, rallies, posters, and the like.

The goals of the communication process are to inform, persuade, motivate, or achieve mutual understanding. To be an effective communicator, a person must have basic knowledge of three things: (1) what constitutes communication and how people receive messages, (2) how people process information and change their perceptions, and (3) what kinds of media and communication tools are most appropriate for a particular message.

Concerning the last point, Kirk Hallahan of Colorado State University makes the point that today's communication revolution has given public relations professionals a full range of communication tools and media, and the traditional approach of simply obtaining publicity in the mass media—newspapers, magazines, radio, and television—is no longer sufficient, if it ever was. He writes:

> PR program planners need to reexamine their traditional approaches to the practice and think about media broadly and strategically. PR media planners must now address some of the same questions that confront advertisers. What media best meet a program's objectives? How can media be combined to enhance program effectiveness? What media are most efficient to reach key audience?

Hallahan's concept of an integrated public relations media model, which outlines five categories of media, is shown in Table 5.2.

A Public Relations Perspective. A number of variables must be considered when planning a message on behalf of an employer or client. Patrick Jackson, who was editor of *pr reporter* and a senior counselor, believes that communicators should ask whether proposed messages are (1) appropriate, (2) meaningful, (3) memorable, (4) understandable, and (5) believable to the prospective recipient. According to Jackson, "Many a wrongly directed or unnecessary communication has been corrected or dropped by using a screen like this."

In addition to examining the proposed content, a communicator should determine exactly what objective is being sought through the communication. James Grunig, emeritus professor of public relations at the University of Maryland, lists five possible objectives for a communicator:

1. *Message Exposure.* Public relations personnel provide materials to the mass media and disseminate other messages through controlled media such as newsletters and brochures. Intended audiences are exposed to the message in various forms.

2. *Accurate Dissemination of the Message.* The basic information, often filtered by media gatekeepers, remains intact as it is transmitted through various media.

TABLE 5.2

An Integrated Public Relations Media Model The variety and scope of media and communication tools available to public relations professionals runs the spectrum from mass media (public media) to one-on-one communication (interpersonal communication). Here, in chart form, is a concept developed by Professor Kirk Hallahan at Colorado State University.

Characteristic	Public Media	Interactive Media	Controlled Media	Events/Groups	One-On-One
Key use	Build awareness	Respond to queries; exchange information	Promotion; provide detailed information	Motivate attendees; reinforce attitudes	Obtain commitments; resolve problems
Examples	Newspapers, magazines, radio, television	Computer based: World Wide Web, databases, e-mail listservs, newsgroups, chat rooms, bulletin boards	Brochures, newsletters, sponsored magazines, annual reports, books, direct mail, point-of-purchase displays, video-brochures	Speeches, trade shows, exhibits, meetings/conferences, demonstrations, rallies, sponsorships, anniversaries	Personal visits, lobbying, personal letters, telephone calls, telemarketing
Nature of communication	Nonpersonal	Nonpersonal	Nonpersonal	Quasi-personal	Personal
Direction of communication	One-way	Quasi–two-way	One-way	Quasi–two-way	Two-way
Technological sophistication	High	High	Moderate	Moderate	Low
Channel ownership	Media organizations	Common carrier or institution	Sponsor	Sponsor or other organization	None
Messages chosen by	Third parties and producers	Receiver	Sponsor	Sponsor or joint organization	None
Audience involvement	Low	High	Moderate	Moderate	High
Reach	High	Moderate-low	Moderate-low	Low	Low
Cost per impression	Extremely low	Low	Moderate	Moderate	High
Key challenges to effectiveness	Competition, media clutter	Availability, accessibility	Design, distribution	Attendence, atmosphere	Empowerment, personal
dynamics					

3. *Acceptance of the Message.* Based on its view of reality, the audience not only retains the message, but accepts it as valid.

4. *Attitude Change.* The audience not only believes the message, but makes a verbal or mental commitment to change behavior as a result of the message.

5. *Change in Overt Behavior.* Members of the audience actually change their current behavior or purchase the product and use it.

Grunig says that most public relations experts usually aim at the first two objectives: exposure to the message and accurate dissemination. The last three objectives depend in large part on a mix of variables—predisposition to the message, peer reinforcement, feasibility of the suggested action, and environmental context, to name a few. The first two objectives are easier to accomplish than attitude change.

Although the communicator cannot always control the outcome of a message, researchers recognize that effective dissemination is the beginning of a process that leads to opinion change and adoption of products or services. Therefore, it is important to review all components of the communication process.

David Therkelsen, CEO of the American Red Cross in St. Paul, Minnesota, succinctly outlines the process:

> To be successful, a message must be received by the intended individual or audience. It must get the audience's attention. It must be understood. It must be believed. It must be remembered. And ultimately, in some fashion, it must be acted upon. Failure to accomplish any of these tasks means the entire message fails.

Therkelsen appropriately places the emphasis on the audience and what it does with the message. The following sections elaborate on the six elements he enumerates.

Receiving the Message

Several communication models explain how a message moves from the sender to the recipient. Some are quite complex, attempting to incorporate an almost infinite number of events, ideas, objects, and people that interact among the message, channel, and receiver.

Five Communication Elements.

Most communication models, however, incorporate four basic elements. David K. Berlo's model is an example. It has a sender/source (encoder), a message, a channel, and a receiver (decoder). A fifth element—feedback from the receiver to the sender—is now incorporated into modern models of communication.

Mass media researcher Wilbur Schramm's early models (see Figure 5.3) started with a simple communication model (top), but he later expanded the process to include the concept of "shared experience" (middle diagram). In other words, little or no communication is achieved unless the sender and the receiver share a common language and even an overlapping cultural or educational background. The importance of this "shared experience" becomes apparent when a highly technical news release about a new computer system causes a local business editor to shake his or her head in bewilderment.

Schramm's third model (bottom) incorporates the idea of continuous feedback. Both the sender and the receiver continually encode, interpret, decode, transmit, and receive information. The loop process also is integral to models that show the public relations process of research, planning, communication, and evaluation. This concept was illustrated in Chapter 1, which showed public relations as a cyclical process. Communication to internal and external audiences produces feedback that is taken into consideration during research, the first step, and evaluation, the fourth step. In this way, the structure and dissemination of messages are continuously refined for maximum effectiveness.

The Importance of Two-Way Communication.

Another way to think of feedback is as two-way communication. One-way communication, from sender to receiver, only disseminates information. Such a monologue is less effective than two-way communication, which establishes a dialogue between the sender and receiver.

Grunig goes even further to postulate that the ideal public relations model is two-way symmetric communication. That is, communication is balanced between the sender and the receiver. He says: "In the symmetric model, understanding is the principal objective of public relations, rather than persuasion."

In reality, research shows that most organizations have mixed motives when they engage in two-way communication with targeted audiences. Although they may employ dialogue to obtain a better sense of how they can adjust to the needs of an

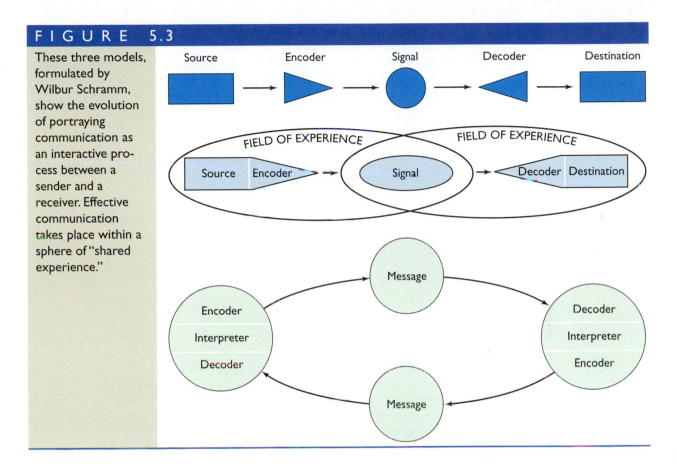

FIGURE 5.3

These three models, formulated by Wilbur Schramm, show the evolution of portraying communication as an interactive process between a sender and a receiver. Effective communication takes place within a sphere of "shared experience."

audience, their motive often is asymmetrical—to convince the audience of their point of view through dialogue. While two-way symmetric communication with targeted audiences is ideal and the default mode for most practitioners, understanding the complexity of practice is essential. As noted elsewhere in this text, the practice of public relations is dynamic. Motives and strategic goals change depending on a variety of factors. For example, while as a public relations practitioner you may advocate providing a new benefit for employees, your motives are mixed. Of course, employees will be pleased with the new benefit, but your real objective is to save the organization money through limiting employee turnover. In short, effective public relations practitioners need to make decisions about different stances on issues for different audiences and circumstances. Most of the time, practitioners' motives are mixed.

The most effective two-way communication, of course, is interpersonal or face-to-face, such as two people talking to each other. Small-group discussion also is effective. In both forms, the message is fortified by gestures, facial expressions, intimacy, tone of voice, and the opportunity for instant feedback. If a listener asks a question or appears puzzled, the speaker has an instant cue and can rephrase the information or amplify a point.

Barriers to communication grow as one advances to large-group meetings and, ultimately, to the mass media. Organizational materials can reach thousands and, through the mass media, even millions of people at the same time, but the psychological and physical distance between sender and receiver is considerably lengthened. Communication is less effective because the audience no longer is involved with the source. No immediate feedback is possible, and the message may undergo distortion as it passes through mass media gatekeepers.

Models of communication emphasize the importance of feedback as an integral component of the process. As they implement communication strategies, public relations personnel need to give feedback careful attention.

Paying Attention to the Message

Sociologist Harold Lasswell has defined the act of communication as "Who says what, in which channel, to whom, with what effect?"

Although in public relations much emphasis is given to the formation and dissemination of messages, this effort is wasted if the audience pays no attention. It is therefore important to remember the axiom of Walt Seifert, a pioneer public relations educator at Ohio State University. He said: "Dissemination does not equal publication, and publication does not equal absorption and action." In other words, "All who receive it won't publish it, and all who read or hear it won't understand or act upon it."

Some Theoretical Perspectives. We have proposed that in public relations, strategy should be based on more than common sense or rote learning of routines. The management of competition and conflict requires a sophisticated understanding of the climate in which an organization operates and the dispositions of its publics on a variety of matters. Seifert and social psychologists recognize that, at any given time, the majority of an audience are not particularly interested in a message or in adopting an idea. This doesn't mean, however, that audiences are merely passive receivers of information. Werner Severin and James Tankard, in their text *Communication Theories*, quote one researcher as saying:

> The communicator's audience is not a passive recipient—it cannot be regarded as a lump of clay to be molded by the master propagandist. Rather, the audience is made up of individuals who demand something from the communication to which they are exposed, and who select those that are likely to be useful to them.

This is called the media uses and gratification theory of communication. Its basic premise is that the communication process is interactive. The communicator wants to inform and even persuade; the recipient wants to be entertained, informed, or alerted to opportunities that can fulfill individual needs.

In other words, audiences come to messages for very different reasons. People use mass media for such purposes as (1) surveillance of the environment to find out what is happening, locally or even globally, that has some impact on them; (2) entertainment and diversion; (3) reinforcement of their opinions and predispositions; and (4) decision making about buying a product or service.

The media uses and gratification theory assumes that people make highly intelligent choices about which messages require their attention and fulfill their needs. If this is true, as research indicates it is, the public relations communicator must tailor messages that focus on getting the audience's attention.

One approach is to understand the mental state of the intended audience. In *Managing Public Relations*, James Grunig and Todd Hunt suggest that communication strategies be designed to attract the attention of two kinds of audiences: those who actively seek information and those who passively process information.

Passive audiences may initially pay attention to a message only because it is entertaining and offers a diversion. They can be made aware of the message through brief encounters: a billboard glimpsed on the way to work, a radio announcement heard in the car, a television advertisement broadcast before a show begins, and information available in a doctor's waiting room. In other words, passive audiences use communication channels that can be utilized while they are doing something else.

For this reason, passive audiences need messages that have style and creativity. The person must be lured by photos, illustrations, and catchy slogans into processing information. Press agentry, the dramatic picture, the use of celebrities, radio and television announcements, and events featuring entertainment can make passive audiences aware of a message. The objectives of communications, therefore, are simply exposure to and accurate dissemination of messages. In most public relations campaigns, communications are designed to reach primarily passive audiences.

A communicator's approach to audiences that actively seek information is different. These people are already at the interest stage of the adoption process (discussed later) and seek more sophisticated supplemental information. The tools may include brochures, in-depth newspaper and magazine articles, slide presentations, video presentations, symposiums and conferences, major speeches before key groups, and demonstrations at trade shows.

At any given time, of course, an intended audience contains both passive and active information seekers. It is important, therefore, that multiple messages and a variety of communication tools be used in a full-fledged information campaign.

Public relations personnel have two primary ways by which to determine strategies. First, research into audience attitudes can give insight into the extent of group interest in, or apathy toward, a new product or idea. But it's important to note that any issue likely has multiple audiences, oftentimes with competing rather than complementary interests. Research by skilled public relations practitioners accounts for these varied interests. Perhaps you plan to announce an organization-wide recycling initiative to prove to environmental activists that your company is "green." But if you've failed to note that the activists' real concerns are your factory emissions, you've missed the mark by a substantial margin. Second, more efficient communication can be achieved if the intended audience is segmented as much as possible. After dividing an audience into segments, a practitioner can select the appropriate communication tools. Even within a public category, demands may be different. For example, factory-line workers don't have the same concerns as senior vice presidents, but they're all employees and should be addressed by employee communications. How do you meet the needs of such diverse categories within a public?

Understanding the Message

Communication is the act of transmitting information, ideas, and attitudes from one person to another. Communication can take place, however, only if the sender and receiver have a common understanding of the symbols being used.

Effective Use of Language. Words are the most common symbols. The degree to which two people understand each other depends heavily on their common knowledge of word symbols. Anyone who has traveled abroad can readily attest that very little communication occurs between two people who speak different languages. Even signs translated into English for tourists often lead to some confusing and amusing messages. A brochure for a Japanese hotel, for example, said, "In our hotel, you will be well fed and agreeably drunk. In every room there is a large window offering delightful prospects." Even if the sender and receiver speak the same language and live in the same country, the effectiveness of their communication depends on such factors as education, social class, regional differences, nationality, and cultural background.

Employee communication specialists are particularly aware of such differences as a multicultural workforce becomes the norm for most organizations. One major factor is the impact of a global economy in which organizations have operations and employees in many countries. A second factor is the increasing multicultural composition of the American workforce. One study says that 85 percent of new entrants in the workforce are now white women, immigrants, African Americans, Hispanics, and Asians. For many of these workers, English will be a second language.

These trends will require communicators to be better informed about cultural differences and conflicting values in order to find common ground and build bridges between various groups. At the same time, a major task will be to communicate in clear and simple terms. A national survey by the Educational Testing Service found that 42 million American adults fall within the lowest category of literacy. Other studies show that one in eight employees reads at no better than a fourth-grade level.

Writing for Clarity. The nature of the audience and its literacy level are important considerations for any communicator. The key is to produce messages that match, in content and structure, the characteristics of the audience.

The Illinois Public Health Department had the right idea when it commissioned a song in rap music style as one way to inform low-income, poorly educated groups about the dangers of AIDS. The words and music of the "Condom Rag," however, were offensive to elected officials, who cancelled the song.

This example poses a classic dilemma for the expert communicator: Should the message be produced for supervisors, who may be totally different in background and education from the intended audience, or should it be produced with the audience in mind? The obvious answer is the latter, but it is often difficult to convince management of this. One solution is to copy-test all public relations materials on a target audience. This helps convince management—and communicators—that what they like isn't necessarily what the audience wants, needs, or understands.

Another approach is to apply readability and comprehension formulas to materials before they are produced and disseminated. Learning theory makes the case that the simpler the piece of writing, the easier it will be for audiences to understand.

The most widely known readability formula is by Rudolph Flesch. It is based on average sentence length and the number of one-syllable words per 100 words. If a randomly selected sample of 100 words contains 4.2 sentences and 142 syllables, it is ranked at about the ninth-grade level. This is the level for which most news releases and daily newspapers strive. In other words, long, complex sentences (more than 19 words) and multisyllabic words ("compensation" instead of "pay") reduce comprehension for the average reader.

The Cloze procedure, developed by William Taylor, also tests comprehension. The concept comes from the idea of closure, the human tendency to complete a familiar but incomplete pattern. In the Cloze procedure, copy is tested for comprehension and redundancy by having test subjects read passages in which every fifth or ninth word is removed. Their ability to fill in the missing words determines whether the pattern of words is familiar and people can understand the message.

Audience understanding and comprehension also can be increased by applying some of the following concepts.

Use Symbols, Acronyms, and Slogans. Clarity and simplicity of message are enhanced by the use of symbols, acronyms, and slogans. Each is a form of shorthand that quickly conceptualizes an idea and travels through extended lines of communication.

The world is full of symbols, such as the Christian cross, the Jewish Star of David, and the crusading sword of the American Cancer Society. Corporate symbols such as the Mercedes Benz star, the Nike swoosh, and the apple of Apple Computer are known throughout the world. The concept is called *branding*, and corporations invest considerable time and money to make their names and logos a symbol for quality and service.

A symbol should be unique, memorable, widely recognized, and appropriate. Organizations spend significant time and energy searching for unique symbols that convey the essence of what they are or what they hope to be. Considerable amounts of money are then spent on publicizing the symbols and creating meanings for them.

Acronyms are another shorthand for conveying information. An acronym is a word formed from the initial letters of other words. The Group Against Smokers' Pollution goes by the acronym GASP; Juvenile Opportunities in Business becomes JOB. And the National Organization for Women has the acronym NOW, which says a great deal about its political priorities.

In many cases, the acronym—because it is short and simple—becomes the common name. The mass media continually use the term *AIDS* instead of acquired immune deficiency syndrome. And UNESCO is easier to write and say than United Nations Educational, Scientific, and Cultural Organization.

Slogans help condense a concept. *Advertising Age* listed the top five slogans of the century as "Diamonds Are Forever" (De Beers), "Just Do It" (Nike), "The Pause That Refreshes" (Coca-Cola), "Tastes Great, Less Filling" (Miller Lite), and "We Try Harder" (Avis). Massive advertising and promotion have made these slogans readily identifiable with their organization and its products.

Avoid Jargon.　One source of blocked communication is technical and bureaucratic jargon. Social scientists call it *semantic noise* when such language is delivered to a general audience. Jargon interferes with the message and impedes the receiver's ability to understand it. An example of a useless news release is the following, which was actually sent to business editors of daily newspapers. This is how it began:

> Versatec, a Xerox Company, has introduced the Graphics Network Processor-SNA (Model 451). The processor, operating as a 377× RJE station, sends and receives EBCDIC or binary data in IMB System Network Architecture (SNA) networks using Synchronous Data LINK Control (SDLC) protocol.

This news release may be perfectly appropriate for an engineering publication serving a particular industry, but the information must be written in simple terms for the readers of a daily newspaper. Failure to understand the audience is a failure in communication.

Avoid Clichés and Hype Words.　Highly charged words with connotative meanings can pose problems, and overuse of clichés and hype words can seriously undermine the credibility of a message.

The *Wall Street Journal*, for example, mocked the business of high-technology public relations with a story titled, "High-Tech Hype Reaches New Heights." A reporter analyzed 201 news releases and compiled a "Hype Hit Parade" that included the 11 most overused and ineffective words. They were *leading, enhanced, unique, significant, solution, integrated, powerful, innovative, advanced, high performance*, and *sophisticated*.

Similar surveys have uncovered overused words in business and public relations. A New York firm, John Rost Associates, compiled a list of words and phrases used excessively in business letters and reports. The list included: *agenda, proactive, interface, networking, finalize, done deals, impact, bottom line, vis-à-vis, world class, state-of-the-art, user-friendly, competitive edge, know-how, win-win, breakthrough, fast track, hands-on, input, dialogue,* and *no-brainer.*

A survey of corporate annual reports also revealed the overuse of certain words. Robert K. Otterbourg, president of a company that does annual reports for corporations, said the most overused words were *challenge, opportunity, fundamental achievements, pioneering efforts,* and *state-of-the-art.*

Avoid Euphemisms.   According to Frank Grazian, founding editor of the business newsletter *Communication Briefings,* a euphemism is "an inoffensive word or phrase that is less direct and less distasteful than the one that represents reality."

Public relations personnel should use positive, favorable words to convey a message, but they have an ethical responsibility not to use words that hide information or mislead. Probably little danger exists in substituting positive words, such as saying a person has a disability rather than using the word *handicapped.* Some euphemisms can even cause amusement, such as when luxury cars are called "preowned" on the used car lot.

More dangerous are euphemisms that actually alter the meaning or impact of a word or concept. Writers call this *doublespeak*—words that pretend to communicate but really do not. Governments are famous for doublespeak. U.S. military briefing officers have described civilian casualties and destruction as "collateral damage." And the term *ethnic cleansing* was used in the Balkans to describe the murder of thousands in Kosovo. A government economist once called a recession "a meaningful downturn in aggregate output."

Corporations also use euphemisms and doublespeak to hide unfavorable news. Reducing the number of employees, for example, is often called right-sizing, skill mix adjustment, or career assignment and relocation. An airline once called the crash of a plane "the involuntary conversion of a 727."

Use of euphemisms to hide or mislead obviously is contrary to professional public relations standards and the public interest. As William Lutz writes in *Public Relations Quarterly,* "Such language breeds suspicion, cynicism, distrust, and, ultimately, hostility."

Avoid Discriminatory Language.   In today's world, effective communication also means nondiscriminatory communication. Public relations personnel should double-check every message to eliminate undesirable gender, racial, and ethnic connotations.

With regard to gender, it is unnecessary to write about something as being man-made when a word like synthetic or artificial is just as good. Companies no longer have manpower, but rather employees, personnel, and workers. Most civic organizations have chairpersons now, and cities have firefighters instead of firemen and police officers instead of policemen.

Writers also should be careful about descriptive phrases for women. *Bulldog Reporter,* a West Coast public relations newsletter, once criticized a Chicago public relations firm for describing a female company president as "a tall, attractive blonde who could easily turn heads on Main Street [but] is instead turning heads on Wall Street."

Nor is it appropriate in professional settings to say that a woman is the wife of someone also well known. A female vice president of a public relations firm cried foul, and received a published apology, when a local newspaper columnist described her as the wife of a prominent journalist.

Messages should not identify any individual by ethnic designation, but it may be necessary in some situations to designate a particular ethnic or racial group. Although fashions and preferences change, today's writers use *Asian American* instead of the now-pejorative *Oriental*. And the term *Hispanic* is now more acceptable than the politically charged *Spanish-speaking*. The term *Latino*, however, raises some controversy; some women say that it is sexist because the "o" in Spanish is male.

The term *black* seems to be making a comeback, according to the U.S. Department of Labor, which surveyed 60,000 households several years ago about the names of race and ethnic categories to use in job statistics. Forty-four percent of the blacks preferred this designation, whereas another 28 percent preferred African American and 12 percent chose Afro-American. As a matter of policy, many newspapers use *African American* on first reference and *black* on second reference. Headlines almost always use *black* because it is short.

Believing the Message

One key variable in the communication process, discussed further in Chapter 6, is source credibility. Do members of the audience perceive the source as knowledgeable and expert on the subject? Do they perceive the source as honest and objective or as representing a special interest? Audiences, for example, ascribe lower credibility to statements in an advertisement than to the same information contained in a news article, because news articles are selected by media gatekeepers.

Source credibility is a problem for any organizational spokesperson because the public already has a bias. In a study conducted for the GCI Group, Opinion Research Corporation found that more than half of those surveyed were likely to believe that a large company is probably guilty of wrongdoing if it is being investigated by a government agency or if a major lawsuit is filed against the company. Only one-third would trust the statements of a large company. The problem of source credibility is the main reason that organizations, whenever possible, use respected outside experts or celebrities as representatives to convey their messages.

The sleeper effect also influences source credibility. This concept was developed by Carl Hovland, who stated: "There is decreased tendency over time to reject the material presented by an untrustworthy source." In other words, even if organizations are perceived initially as not being very credible sources, people may retain the information and eventually separate the source from the opinion. On the other hand, studies show that audiences register more constant opinion change if they perceive a source to be highly credible in the first place.

A second variable in believability is the context of the message. Action (performance) speaks louder than a stack of news releases. A bank may spend thousands of dollars on a promotion campaign with the slogan, "Your Friendly Bank—Where Service Counts," but the effort is wasted if employees are not trained to be friendly and courteous.

Incompatible rhetoric and actions can be somewhat amusing at times. At a press briefing about the importance of "buying American," the U.S. Chamber of Commerce passed out commemorative coffee mugs marked in small print on the bottom, "Made in China."

Another barrier to the believability of messages is the audience's predispositions. This problem brings to mind the old saying, "Don't confuse me with the facts, my mind is already made up" (see the Insights box on truthiness an page 152 about the role of predispositions).

In this case, Leon Festinger's theory of cognitive dissonance is applicable. In essence, it says that people will not believe messages contrary to their predispositions unless communicators can introduce information that causes them to question their beliefs.

— ON THE JOB >> —

"Truthiness" Affects a PR Pro's Job

Insights

The American Dialect Society made news when it selected "truthiness" as its 2005 Word of the Year. The truthiness trend influences how the public relations practitioner manages public opinion. The term was coined and promoted by Comedy Central satirist, Stephen Colbert.

In reporting the story, the Associated Press defined *truthiness* as "the quality of stating concepts one wishes or believes to be true, rather than the facts." Truthiness, some experts suggest, is taking the U.S. by storm. As Professor Michael Adams, lexicologist at North Carolina State University, told the AP, "'truthiness' means 'truthy, not facty.'"

So, how does this concept affect public relations practitioners? PR pros work to influence public opinion to achieve competitive objectives or manage conflict. But ethical public rela-

tions practitioners demand that their organizations or clients are honest in representing themselves, their products, their ideas to their publics.

Peter Pitts, SVP at Manning Selvage & Lee, told *PRWeek*, "Broadly, when it comes to life, in general, the truth does not necessarily set you free. Sometimes the truth is complicated and counterintuitive." He explained, "What people in PR have to understand. . . is not only do you have to have the facts on your side, you have to know how to communicate them."

When political or religious views color how members of the public understand economic policy or science—for example, the use of stem cells in health research—public relations practitioners need to understand that the concept of truthiness may be at play. *PRWeek* suggested that public relations practitioners not only must

communicate clearly and in a consumable way, but also understand the other drivers that influence how people define what is true.

MS&L's Pitts told *PRWeek*, "People understand how to manipulate the media in ways so stories are not necessarily based on the facts." He said that people increasingly understand that public opinion can be swayed by pithy soundbites as much as by facts.

Mark Rozeen, SVP of research for GolinHarris, told *PRWeek*, "Facts have emotional connotations as well."

So, being right and proving it are not the only considerations that public relations practitioners must make in a world where "truthiness" is such a prevalent concept that it becomes the Word of the Year. In short, positions taken by PR people for organizations must "ring true" with the targeted publics, not just be an accumulation of facts.

Dissonance can be created in at least three ways. First, make the target audience aware that circumstances have changed. Second, give information about new developments or discoveries. This is an unthreatening way to break through a person's opinions. Third, use an unexpected spokesperson. Chevron, for example, sought to overcome opposition to some of its oil exploration policies by getting endorsements from several respected leaders in the conservation movement.

Involvement is another important predisposition that impacts how messages are processed by audience members. Involvement can be described in simple terms as interest in or concern about an issue or a product. Those with higher involvement often process persuasive messages with greater attention to detail and to logical argument (central processing), whereas those with low involvement in a topic are impressed more by incidental cues, such as an attractive spokesperson, humor, or the number of arguments given. The public relations professional can use the involvement concept to devise messages that focus more on "what is said" for high-involvement audiences and more attention to "who says it" for low-involvement audiences.

Remembering the Message

For several reasons, many messages prepared by public relations personnel are repeated extensively:

> Repetition is necessary because all members of a target audience don't see or hear the message at the same time. Not everyone reads the newspaper on a particular day or watches the same television news program.

> Repetition reminds the audience, so there is less chance of a failure to remember the message. If a source has high credibility, repetition prevents erosion of opinion change.

> Repetition helps the audience remember the message itself. Studies have shown that advertising is quickly forgotten if not repeated constantly.

> Repetition can lead to improved learning and increase the chance of penetrating audience indifference or resistance.

Researchers say that repetition, or redundancy, also is necessary to offset the "noise" surrounding a message. People often hear or see messages in an environment filled with distractions—a baby crying, the conversations of family members or office staff, a barking dog—or even while daydreaming or thinking of other things.

Consequently, communicators often build repetition into a message. Key points may be mentioned at the beginning and then summarized at the end. If the source is asking the receiver to call for more information or write for a brochure, the telephone number or address is repeated several times. Such precautions also fight entropy, which means that messages continually lose information as media channels and people process the information and pass it on to others. For example, one study about employee communications found that rank-and-file workers got only 20 percent of a message that had passed through four levels of managers.

The key to effective communication and message retention is to convey information in a variety of ways, using multiple communication channels. This helps people remember the message as they receive it through different media and extends the message to both passive and active audiences.

Acting on the Message

The ultimate purpose of any message is to have an effect on the recipient. Public relations personnel communicate messages on behalf of organizations to change perceptions, attitudes, opinions, or behavior in some way. Marketing communications, in particular, has the objective of convincing people to buy goods and services.

The Five-Stage Adoption Process. Getting people to act on a message is not a simple process. In fact, research shows that it can be a somewhat lengthy and complex procedure that depends on a number of intervening influences. One key to understanding how people accept new ideas or products is to analyze the adoption process. The five stages are summarized as follows:

1. *Awareness.* A person becomes aware of an idea or a new product, often by means of an advertisement or a news story.

2. *Interest.* The individual seeks more information about the idea or the product, perhaps by ordering a brochure, picking up a pamphlet, or reading an in-depth article in a newspaper or magazine.

3. *Evaluation.* The person evaluates the idea or the product on the basis of how it meets specific needs and wants. Feedback from friends and family is part of this process.

4. *Trial.* Next, the person tries the product or the idea on an experimental basis, by using a sample, witnessing a demonstration, or making qualifying statements such as, "I read. . . ."

5. *Adoption.* The individual begins to use the product on a regular basis or integrates the idea into his or her belief system. The "I read. . . " becomes "I think. . . ," if peers provide support for and reinforcement of the idea.

It is important to realize that a person does not necessarily go through all five stages with any given idea or product. The process may end after any step. In fact, the process is like a large funnel. Although many are made aware of an idea or a product, only a few will ultimately adopt it.

A number of factors affect the persuasion stage of the adoption process. Everett Rogers, author of *Diffusion of Innovation*, lists at least five:

1. *Relative Advantage*—the degree to which an innovation is perceived as better than the idea it replaces

2. *Compatibility*—the degree to which an innovation is perceived as being consistent with the existing values, experiences, and needs of potential adopters

3. *Complexity*—the degree to which an innovation is perceived as difficult to understand and use

4. *Trialability*—the degree to which an innovation may be experienced on a limited basis

5. *Observability*—the degree to which the results of an innovation are visible to others

The communicator should be aware of these factors and attempt to implement communication strategies that will overcome as many of them as possible. See Figure 5.4 for the stages of the decision process. Repeating a message in various ways, reducing its complexity, taking into account competing messages, and structuring the message to meet the needs of the audience are ways to do this.

The Time Factor. Another aspect that confuses people is the amount of time needed to adopt a new idea or product. Depending on the individual and situation, the entire adoption process can take place almost instantly if the result is of minor consequence or requires low-level commitment. Buying a new brand of soft drink or a bar of soap is relatively inexpensive and often done on impulse. On the other hand, deciding to buy a new car or vote for a particular candidate may involve an adoption process that takes several weeks or months.

Rogers's research shows that people approach innovation in different ways, depending on their personality traits and the risk involved. "Innovators" are venturesome and eager to try new ideas, whereas "laggards" are traditional and the last to adopt anything. Between the two extremes are "early adopters," who are opinion leaders; "early majority," who take the deliberate approach; and "late majority," who are often skeptical but bow to peer pressure.

Psychographics, discussed in Chapter 6, can often help communicators segment audiences that have "innovator" or "early adopter" characteristics and would be predisposed to adopting new ideas.

FIGURE 5.4

This graph shows the steps through which an individual or other decision-making unit goes in the innovation-decision process from first knowledge of an innovation to the decision to adopt it, followed by implementation of the new idea and confirmation of the new decision.

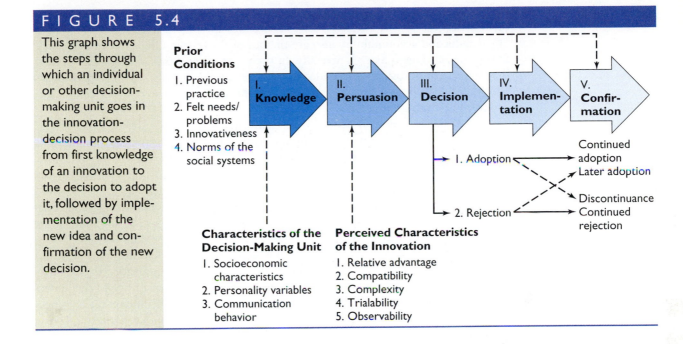

Prior Conditions
1. Previous practice
2. Felt needs/ problems
3. Innovativeness
4. Norms of the social systems

I. **Knowledge** → II. **Persuasion** → III. **Decision** → IV. **Implementation** → V. **Confirmation**

1. Adoption
2. Rejection

Continued adoption
Later adoption
Discontinuance
Continued rejection

Characteristics of the Decision-Making Unit
1. Socioeconomic characteristics
2. Personality variables
3. Communication behavior

Perceived Characteristics of the Innovation
1. Relative advantage
2. Compatibility
3. Complexity
4. Trialability
5. Observability

How Decisions Are Influenced. Of particular interest to public relations people is the primary source of information at each step in the adoption process. Mass media vehicles such as advertising, short news articles, feature stories, and radio and television news announcements are most influential at the awareness stage of the adoption process. A news article or a television announcement makes people aware of an idea, event, or new product. They also are made aware through such vehicles as direct mail, office memos, and simple brochures.

Individuals at the interest stage also rely on mass media vehicles, but they are actively seeking information and pay attention to longer, in-depth articles. They rely more on detailed brochures, specialized publications, small-group seminars, and meetings to provide details. At the evaluation, trial, and adoption stages, group norms and opinions are the most influential. Feedback, negative or positive, from friends and peers may determine adoption. If a person's friends generally disapprove of a candidate, a movie, or an automobile brand, it is unlikely that the individual will complete the adoption process even if he or she is highly sold on the idea. If a person does make a commitment, mass media vehicles become reinforcing mechanisms. Studies show, for example, that owners of a new car are the most avid readers of that car's advertising. The complexities of the adoption process show that public relations communicators need to think about the entire communication process—from the formulation of the message to the ways in which receivers ultimately process the information and make decisions. By doing so, communicators can form more effective message strategies and develop realistic objectives for what can actually be accomplished.

Evaluation: The Fourth Step

The fourth step of the public relations process is evaluation. It is the measurement of results against established objectives set during the planning process.

Evaluation is well described by Professor James Bissland, formerly of Bowling Green State University, who defines it as "the systematic assessment of a program and its results. It is a means for practitioners to offer accountability to clients—and to themselves."

Results and accountability also are themes of Professors Glen Broom and David Dozier of San Diego State University. In their text *Using Research in Public Relations*, they state, "Your program is intended to cause observable impact—to change or maintain something about a situation. So, after the program, you use research to measure and document program effects."

Frank Wylie, emeritus professor at California State University in Long Beach, summarizes: "We are talking about an orderly evaluation of our progress in attaining the specific objectives of our public relations plan. We are learning what we did right, what we did wrong, how much progress we've made and, most importantly, how we can do it better next time."

The desire to do a better job next time is a major reason for evaluating public relations efforts, but another equally important reason is the widespread adoption of the management by objectives system by clients and employers of public relations personnel. They want to know if the money, time, and effort expended on public relations are well spent and contribute to the realization of an organizational objective. Furthermore, evaluation or monitoring throughout a campaign may suggest that tactics or organizational stances should change. Evaluation helps practitioners make appropriate adjustments in the dynamic, ever-changing reality that is public relations practice.

Objectives: A Prerequisite for Evaluation

Before any public relations program can be properly evaluated, it is important to have a clearly established set of measurable objectives. These should be part of the program plan, but first some points need to be reviewed.

First, public relations personnel and management should agree on the criteria that will be used to evaluate success in attaining objectives. A Ketchum monograph simply states, "Write the most precise, most results-oriented objectives you can that are realistic, credible, measurable, and compatible with the client's demands on public relations."

Second, don't wait until the end of the public relations program to determine how it will be evaluated. Albert L. Schweitzer of Fleishman-Hillard public relations in St. Louis makes the point that "evaluating impact/results starts in the planning stage. You break down the problem into measurable goals and objectives, then after implementing the program, you measure the results against goals."

If an objective is informational, measurement techniques must show how successfully information was communicated to target audiences. Such techniques fall under the rubrics of "message dissemination" and "audience exposure," but they do not measure the effect on attitudes or overt behavior and action.

Motivational objectives are more difficult to accomplish. If the objective is to increase sales or market share, it is important to show that public relations efforts caused the increase rather than advertising or other marketing strategies. Or, if the objective is to change attitudes or opinions, research should be done before and after the public relations activity to measure the percentage of change.

Although objectives may vary, the following list contains the basic evaluation questions that every practitioner should ask:

> Was the activity or program adequately planned?
> Did the recipients of the message understand it?

> How could the program strategy have been more effective?
> Were all primary and secondary audiences reached?
> Was the desired organizational objective achieved?
> What unforeseen circumstances affected the success of the program or activity?
> Did the program or activity fall within the budget set for it?
> What steps can be taken to improve the success of similar future activities?

Current Status of Measurement and Evaluation

In the last decade, public relations professionals have made considerable progress in evaluation research and the ability to tell clients and employers exactly what has been accomplished. Sophisticated techniques are being used, including computerized news clip analysis, survey sampling, quasi-experimental designs in which the audience is divided into groups that see different aspects of a public relations campaign, and attempts to correlate efforts directly with sales.

Today, the trend toward more systematic evaluation is well established. Katherine Delahaye Paine, founder of her own public relations measurement firm, says that the percentage of a public relations budget devoted to measurement and evaluation was about 1 percent a decade ago, but is now closer to 5 percent. By 2010, it is projected that the amount will increase to 10 percent. One reason: There is increasing pressure on all parts of the organization—including public relations—to prove their value to the "bottom line."

There are, however, still those who say that public relations is not an exact science and is extremely difficult to measure. Walter K. Lindenmann, a former senior vice president and director of research at Ketchum, takes a more optimistic view. He wrote in *Public Relations Quarterly*: "Let's get something straight right off the bat. First, it is possible to measure public relations effectiveness. . . . Second, measuring public relations effectiveness does not have to be either unbelievably expensive or laboriously time-consuming."

Lindenmann suggests that public relations personnel use a mix of evaluation techniques, many borrowed from advertising and marketing, to provide more complete evaluation. In addition, he notes that there are at least three levels of measurement and evaluation (see Figure 5.5).

On the most basic level are compilations of message distribution and media placement. The second level, which requires more sophisticated techniques, deals with the measurement of audience awareness, comprehension, and retention of the message. The most advanced level is the measurement of changes in attitudes, opinions, and behavior.

The following sections outline the most widely used methods for evaluating public relations efforts. These include measurement of production, message exposure, audience awareness, audience attitudes, and audience action. Supplemental activities such as communication audits, readability tests, event evaluation, and split messages also are used. In most cases, a skilled practitioner will use a combination of methods to evaluate the effectiveness of a program.

Measurement of Production

One elementary form of evaluation is simply to count how many news releases, feature stories, photos, letters, and the like are produced in a given period of time. This kind of evaluation is supposed to give management an idea of a staff's productivity and

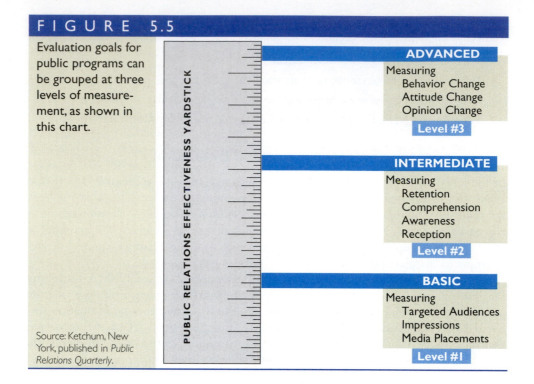

FIGURE 5.5

Evaluation goals for public programs can be grouped at three levels of measurement, as shown in this chart.

PUBLIC RELATIONS EFFECTIVENESS YARDSTICK

ADVANCED

Measuring
   Behavior Change
   Attitude Change
   Opinion Change

Level #3

INTERMEDIATE

Measuring
   Retention
   Comprehension
   Awareness
   Reception

Level #2

BASIC

Measuring
   Targeted Audiences
   Impressions
   Media Placements

Level #1

Source: Ketchum, New York, published in *Public Relations Quarterly*.

output. Public relations professionals, however, do not believe that this evaluation is very meaningful because it emphasizes quantity instead of quality. It may be more cost-effective to write fewer news releases and spend more time on the few that really are newsworthy. It may, for example, be more important for a staff person to spend five weeks working on an article for the *Wall Street Journal* or *Fortune* than to write 29 routine personnel releases.

Another side of the production approach is to specify what the public relations person should accomplish in obtaining media coverage. Perhaps your boss says you will be evaluated based on the number of feature stories that run in the top newspapers in your region or the number of news releases picked up by local media outlets.

Such evaluation criteria not only are unrealistic, they are almost impossible to guarantee, because media gatekeepers—not the public relations person—make such decisions. Management may argue, however, that such placement goals provide incentive to the public relations staff and are tangible criteria in employee performance evaluation.

Closely allied to the production of publicity materials is their distribution. Thus, a public relations department might report, for instance, that a total of 756 news releases were sent to 819 daily newspapers, 250 weeklies, and 137 trade magazines within one year or that 110,000 copies of the annual report were distributed to stockholders, security analysts, and business editors.

Measurement of Message Exposure

The most widely practiced form of evaluating public relations programs is the compilation of press clippings and radio or television mentions. Public relations firms and company departments working primarily on a local basis often have a staff member scan and clip the area newspapers. Large companies with regional, national, or even international outreach usually hire clipping services to scan large numbers of publications. It also is possible to have electronic clipping services monitor and tape major radio and television programs on a contractual basis. Burrelle's, for example, monitors nearly 400 local TV stations in 150 cities. Web tracking systems and firms are discussed in Chapter 9.

Strategic research by Hallmark Cards and its public relations firm, Fleishman-Hillard, identified the need for a reinvigoration and reintroduction of its 18-year-old Shoebox card line. Customers expressed affection for the humorous line, but said it had grown stale and sometimes offensive. The line was revamped and relaunched. Hallmark used media clips as one measure of its Shoebox relaunch campaign. According to Fleishman-Hillard's report, which was the basis for the firm's receipt of a Silver Anvil award from PRSA:

> PR strategies and tactics generated nearly 141 million trackable impressions. Radio outreach resulted in more than 100 million impressions. . . . Television outreach resulted in 17 million impressions nationwide, including WB's "The Daily Buzz," (seen in 134 markets), "ABC World News Weekend," The Weather Channel, WE cable network, CNN, and more than 80 local stations.

Similar analysis was provided for print coverage. Such a compilation measures media acceptance of the story and shows that Hallmark received massive coverage. Clearly, the publicity effort accomplished the first stage of the adoption process by making people aware of changes in the Shoebox line of cards.

Media Impressions. In addition to the number of media placements, public relations departments and firms report how many people may have been exposed to the message. These numbers are described as media impressions, the potential audience reached by a periodical or a broadcast program.

If, for example, a story about an organization appears in a local daily that has a circulation of 130,000, the media impressions are 130,000. If another story is published the next day, this counts for 130,000 more impressions. Estimated audiences for radio and television programs, certified by auditing organizations, also are used to compile media impressions.

A regional or national news story can generate millions of impressions by simple multiplication of each placement by the circulation or audience of each medium. Two examples:

1. DaimlerChrysler developed a public service campaign titled Road Ready Teens, which aimed at coordinating with other driver-safety programs to educate teenagers about automobile safety issues. The public relations campaign generated more than 29,000 news stories, which added up to 240 million media impressions.

2. M&M's Candy conducted a national contest to name a new color for M&M's. Public relations activities generated 1.06 billion impressions from 10,000 TV, radio, and print placements; these included 36,000 print column inches, 12 hours of television news coverage, and 74 hours of radio broadcast time.

Media impressions (see the Ethics box on page 160) are commonly used in advertising to document the breadth of penetration of a particular message. Such figures give a rough estimate of how many people are exposed to a message. They don't, however, disclose how many people actually read or heard the stories and, more important,

how many absorbed or acted on the information. Other techniques needed for this kind of evaluation are discussed later in this chapter.

Hits on the Internet. A cyberspace version of media impressions is the number of people reached via an organization's Web site or home page. Each instance of a person accessing a site is called a hit or a visit.

A good example is Purple Moon, a software developer of girls' interactive entertainment. It used a Web site to promote its CD-ROM product, "Friendship Adventures." According to the company and its public relations firm, Ketchum, "Media relations and grassroots online programs helped drive traffic resulting in 700,000 visitors in the first six months and an average of 6 million impressions per month, equaling or surpassing those of top kids' sites including Disney.com and Sports Illustrated for Kids."

A second example is the Florida health care reform campaign designed by Hill & Knowlton. The campaign included coordination of Floridians to send daily e-mail messages to legislators with a "headline of the day so they (legislators) were aware of the kind of coverage the issue was receiving in different areas of the state. The effect was one of a brush fire that could not be extinguished without reform." The Web-based system generated 163,128 constituent e-mails to legislators.

In another example, the Smithsonian Institution promoted the grand opening of its new National Museum of the American Indian (NMAI) in Washington, D.C. The museum's Web site was mentioned in media relations material. Hill & Knowlton, the museum's public relations firm, noted "25% of print coverage referenced the NMAI Web site, contributing to 1.2 million hits (17,025 visits) per day (prior average was 233,000 hits / 4,298 visits per day)."

Advertising Equivalency. Another approach is to calculate the value of message exposure. This is done by converting stories in the regular news columns or on the air into equivalent advertising costs. In other words, a five-inch article in a trade magazine that charges $100 per column inch for advertising would be worth $500 in publicity value.

Mack Trucks, for example, evaluated its public relations campaign to improve its image in the trucking industry by using advertising equivalency. It reported, "The program generated more than 9,000 inches of editorial coverage with an advertising equivalency of more than $1.2 million—more than five times the company's investment in the program."

Some practitioners even take the approach of calculating the cost of advertising for the same amount of space and then multiplying that total three to six times to reflect a number of research studies which show that a news story has greater credibility than an advertisement. Consequently, if Mack Trucks multiplied the equivalent advertising space by three, it could say that the editorial space was worth $3.6 million in publicity.

Although such dollar amounts may impress top management, the technique of calculating advertising equivalency is really comparing apples with oranges. In fact, Ron Levy, former president of North American Precis Syndicate, told *O'Dwyer's Public Relations Newsletter* that he thought the technique was "blatantly ridiculous."

One reason why the two can't be compared is the fundamental difference between advertising and publicity. Advertising copy is directly controlled by the organization and can be oriented to specific objectives. The organization also controls the size and placement of the message. News mentions, on the other hand, are determined by media gatekeepers and can be negative, neutral, or positive. In addition, a news release can be edited to the point that key corporate messages are deleted. In other words, the organization can't control size, placement, or content.

It thus becomes a question of what is being measured. Should an article be counted as equivalent advertising space if it is negative? It also is questionable whether a 15-inch article that mentions the organization only once among six other organizations is comparable to 15 column inches of advertising space. And the numbers game doesn't take into account that a 4-inch article in the *Wall Street Journal* may be more valuable in reaching key publics than a 20-inch article in the *Denver Post*.

In summary, the dollar-value approach to measuring publicity effectiveness is somewhat suspect, and there has been a rapid decline of such statistics in PRSA award entries. The equating of publicity with advertising rates for comparable space also does not engender good media relations. The technique reinforces the opinion of many media gatekeepers that all news releases are just attempts to get free advertising.

Systematic Tracking. As noted earlier, message exposure traditionally has been measured by sheer volume. Advances in computer software and databases, however, now make it possible to track media placements in a more sophisticated way.

Computer databases can be used to analyze the content of media placements by such variables as market penetration, type of publication, tone of coverage, sources quoted, and mention of key copy points. Ketchum, for example, can build up to 40 variables into its computer program, including the tracking of reporter bylines to determine if a journalist is predisposed negatively or positively to the client's key messages. Other firms, such as Carma International and Delahaye Medialink, do extensive analysis for clients using databases such as Lexis/Nexis. Table 5.3, prepared by Delahaye Medialink for a client, illustrates the type of analysis that can be done.

The value of systematic tracking is manifested in several ways. One is continuing, regular feedback during a campaign to determine if an organization's publicity efforts

TABLE 5.3

Total Coverage

Total Coverage	Total
Total impressions	89,641,378
Percent of positive impressions	26.98%
Percent of negative impressions	19.85%
Total articles	1,049
Percent of positive articles	35.65%
Percent of negative articles	16.02%
Percent of articles containing one or more positive messages	52.43%
Percent of articles containing one or more negative messages	18.78%

are paying off in terms of placements and mention of key messages. Tracking coverage and comparing it over a period of time is called *benchmarking*.

An example of benchmarking is the campaign that Capitoline/MS&L public relations conducted on behalf of the Turkish government to make Americans more aware of Turkey as a travel destination. By comparing the number of stories before and after the campaign was launched, Carma International found that articles with Turkey as the primary destination increased 400 percent. Favorable articles on Turkey increased 90 percent from the previous year.

At other times, an organization may wish to do a systematic analysis comparing its media coverage with the competition's. Is a major competitor getting more favorable publicity? Is the company being portrayed as an innovative leader, or is its size the only major message being mentioned? Such evaluation allows an organization to fine-tune its public relations efforts and concentrate on problem areas.

Another form of analysis is comparing the number of news releases sent with the number actually published and in what kinds of periodicals. Such analysis often helps a public relations department determine what kinds of publicity are most effective and earn the most return on investment (ROI). As Katharine Paine, former president of Delahaye Medialink, says, "The world doesn't need more data. What it needs is analyzed data."

Requests and 800 Numbers.

Another measure of media exposure is to compile the number of requests for more information. A story in a newspaper or an appearance of a company spokesperson on a broadcast often provides information as to where people can get more information about a subject.

In many cases, a toll-free number is provided. Dayton Hudson Corporation, owner of several department store chains, used a toll-free hotline number as part of its "Child Care Aware" program to help educate parents about quality child care and how to get it. In a six-month period, 19,000 calls were received from people seeking advice and copies of a brochure. Dole Food Company, through its toll-free number, got requests for more than 100,000 copies of its brochure titled "Fun with Fruits and Vegetables: Kid's Cookbook."

Requests for materials also can show the effectiveness of a public relations program. An information program by the U.S. Centers for Disease Control on AIDS prevention, for example, received nearly 2,000 phone calls on its information hotline after its *Safe Sex* program on the Public Broadcasting Service (PBS). In addition, the program and resulting publicity generated 260 requests for videotapes and 400 requests for "Smart Sex" organization kits.

Cost per Person.

Another way to evaluate exposure to a message is to determine the cost of reaching each member of the audience. The technique is commonly used in advertising to place costs in perspective. Although a 30-second commercial during the 2007 Super Bowl telecast cost $2.6 million, advertisers believed it was well worth the price because an audience of more than 140 million would be reached for less than two cents each. This was a relatively good bargain, even if several million viewers probably visited the refrigerator while the commercial played. Professor Dean Krugman at the University of Georgia conducts viewer behavior research that suggests that television ratings used in advertising offer a false precision. His findings indicate that public relations professionals should use caution in adapting such ratings to estimates of media coverage.

Cost-effectiveness, as this technique is known, also is used in public relations. Cost per thousand (CPM) is calculated by taking the cost of the publicity program and dividing it by the total media impressions (discussed earlier). SkyTel, for example, spent $400,000 to publicize its new two-way paging and messaging system and obtained 52 million impressions, about seven-tenths of a cent per impression. According to counselor Ford Kanzler, "CPMs for print publicity programs usually fall well below media space advertising and about 100 percent above direct mail promotions."

In another example, a campaign by the Virginia Department of Tourism to attract Canadian visitors cost $5,500, but generated 90,000 consumer inquiries. This made the cost per inquiry only six cents. The same approach can be done with events, brochures, and newsletters. Nike produced a sports video for $50,000, but reached 150,000 high school students, for a per-person cost of 33 cents.

Audience Attendance Counting attendance at events is a relatively simple way of evaluating the effectiveness of pre-event publicity. The New York Public Library centennial day celebration, for example, attracted a crowd of 10,000 for a sound and laser show and speeches. In addition, 20,000 visitors came to the library on the designated centennial day and more than 200,000 people from around the world visited the library's exhibitions during the year.

Poor attendance at a meeting or event can indicate inadequate publicity and promotion. Another major cause is lack of public interest, even when people are aware that a meeting or event is taking place. Low attendance usually results in considerable finger-pointing; thus, an objective evaluation of exactly what happened—or didn't happen—is a good policy.

Measurement of Audience Awareness

Thus far, techniques of measuring audience exposure and accurate dissemination have been discussed. A higher level of evaluation is to determine whether the audience actually became aware of the message and understood it. PR measurement expert Walter Lindenmann calls this the second level of public relations evaluation. He notes:

> At this level, public relations practitioners measure whether target audience groups actually received the messages directed at them: whether they paid attention to those messages, whether they understood the messages, and whether they have retained those messages in any shape or form.

The tools of survey research are needed to answer such questions. Members of the target audience must be asked about the message and what they remember about it. Public awareness of what organization sponsors an event also is important. BayBank found that only 59 percent of the spectators recognized the bank as sponsor of the Head of the Charles Regatta. Through various innovations, increased publicity efforts, and more signage at the following year's regatta, BayBank raised public awareness to 90 percent. (The bank has since been absorbed by another banking firm.)

Another way of measuring audience awareness and comprehension is day-after recall. Under this method, participants are asked to view a specific television program or read a particular news story. The next day they are interviewed to learn which messages they remembered.

Ketchum, on behalf of the California Prune Board, used this technique to determine if a 15-city media tour was conveying the key message that prunes are a high-fiber food source. Forty women in Detroit considered likely to watch daytime television shows were asked to view a program on which a Prune Board spokesperson would appear. The day after the program, Ketchum asked the women questions about the show, including their knowledge of the fiber content of prunes. Ninety-three percent remembered the Prune Board spokesperson, and 65 percent, on an unaided basis, named prunes as a high-fiber food source.

Measurement of Audience Attitudes

Closely related to audience awareness and understanding of a message are changes in an audience's perceptions and attitudes. A major technique to determine such changes is the *baseline study*. Basically, a baseline study is a measurement of audience attitudes and opinions before, during, and after a public relations campaign. Baseline studies, also called benchmark studies, graphically show the percentage difference in attitudes and opinions as a result of increased information and publicity. A number of intervening variables may account for changes in attitude, of course, but statistical analysis of variance can help pinpoint how much the change is attributable to public relations efforts.

The insurance company Prudential Financial regularly conducts baseline studies. One survey found that the company scored high in respondent familiarity, but achieved only a 29 percent favorable rating in fulfilling its corporate social responsibilities. As a result, the company launched "The Prudential Helping Hearts Program." This effort provided $2 million in matching grants to volunteer emergency medical service (EMS) squads to help purchase portable cardiac arrest equipment used to treat heart attack victims before they reach the hospital. After a year of publicizing the program and making grants, Prudential found that its overall corporate image had risen to 29 percent.

The American Iron and Steel Institute did a baseline study to determine the effectiveness of its campaign to inform the public about the industry's recycling efforts. Before the program, only 52 percent of the respondents in Columbus, Ohio, were aware that steel cans are recyclable. After the campaign, the percentage had risen to 64 percent.

The value of the baseline survey is underscored by Frank R. Stansberry, former manager of guest affairs for Coca-Cola. He once said, "The only way to determine if communications are making an impact is by pre-and posttest research. The first survey measures the status quo. The second one will demonstrate any change and the direction of that change."

Measurement of Audience Action

The ultimate objective of any public relations effort, as has been pointed out, is to accomplish organizational objectives. As David Dozier of San Diego State University aptly points out, "The outcome of a successful public relations program is not a hefty stack of news stories. . . . Communication is important only in the effects it achieves among publics."

The objective of an amateur theater group is not to get media publicity; the objective is to sell tickets. The objective of an environmental organization such as Greenpeace is not to get editorials written in favor of whales, but to motivate the public (1) to write elected officials, (2) to send donations for its preservation efforts, and (3) to get protective legislation passed. The objective of a company is to sell its products and services, not get 200 million media impressions. In all cases, the tools and activities of public relations are a means, not an end.

Thus, public relations efforts ultimately are evaluated on how they help an organization achieve its objectives. Cingular Wireless and its public relations firm, Ketchum, employed a variety of primary and secondary research methods, including data analysis of highway traffic safety statistics that showed that teens are four times more likely to be in distraction-related accidents and focus groups with educators to better understand how to communicate with teens. In their winning PRSA Silver Anvil award application, Ketchum recounted how the measurable objectives that were developed for the "Be Sensible! Cingular Wireless Helps Teens Manage Driving

Distractions" were addressed. The evaluation recap illustrates rigorous measurement of both awareness and audience actions:

Evaluation

Objective One: Create awareness of the dangers of distracted driving among 3 million teens over a three-year period (2002–2004):

> More than 10,000 high schools and 4,200 private driving schools have requested and received the teen-driving program.
> We have reached 5.6 million teens to date, significantly surpassing our three-year goal with 11 months still to go!
> From the 1,000 educator surveys received to date:
>> 93 percent of teachers strongly agree/agree that this program gives students a new perspective on the role of driver distraction in vehicle collisions.
>> 92 percent strongly agree/agree that the program generated student interest in the topic of driver distraction.
>> 99 percent of instructors said they would use the program again.

Objective Two: Integrate Be Sensible: Don't Drive Yourself to Distraction video into five state driver education programs by 2004:

> Maryland, Virginia, Maine, Ohio, Georgia, New Jersey, New York, Indiana, Kansas, Alabama, and Florida state driver education administrators have embraced the Be Sensible teen program by distributing the program to all driver education teachers statewide.

Cingular's Be Sensible: Don't Drive Yourself to Distraction program has been the recipient of several awards, including the CINE Golden Eagle and U.S. International Film and Video Festival Silver Screen.

PRCASEBOOK

Changing Health Behaviors in Hispanic Communities

The American Heart Association (AHA) launched "The Heart of Diabetes: Understanding Insulin Resistance" (THOD) to educate at-risk Hispanics on how insulin resistance, cardiovascular disease, and diabetes are related. To reach the Hispanic community, THOD used bilingual patient materials and publicity, a Hispanic celebrity, and bilingual physicians to drive patient enrollment in the program.

The goal of the campaign was to inform people with Type-2 diabetes and their families about the link between diabetes and cardiovascular disease. THOD provided participants with educational materials and a free subscription to *Diabetes Positive*, which people could request by telephone or over the Internet.

With the help of Rita Moreno and bilingual physicians, in 2003 more than 76 million media impressions drove 58,000

calls to the AHA call center, putting more than 15,000 Hispanic patients on the path to better health.

Research

The objectives for the campaign were based on varied and extensive research:

> *Web-Based Research.* No pharmaceutical companies or competing patient groups, such as the American Diabetes Association, were prepared to develop a program focused on cardiovascular disease and diabetes.
> *Media Audits.* Reporters were not focusing on the disease triangle of insulin resistance, diabetes, and cardiovascular disease.

(continued)

> *Industry Analysis.* Because the Hispanic population is a high-risk group for diabetes and related cardiovascular complications, the team consulted with a Hispanic/Latino healthcare consulting firm to better understand this community and plot an approach to effectively reach the target population.

> *Roper Starch Survey.* Roper Starch Worldwide was commissioned to conduct a telephone survey of people with diabetes (with an oversampling of Hispanics) to determine specific levels of awareness/behavior. Results showed that:

> > Patients were frustrated by a lack of bilingual materials.

> > More than 60 percent of patients surveyed had cardiovascular disease, but only 33 percent considered it among the most serious diabetes-related complications.

> > Many patients did not know what insulin resistance was or how it related to diabetes and cardiovascular disease.

Planning

Audience

Hispanic men and women with Type-2 diabetes who are at risk for cardiovascular disease.

Objectives

1. Education: Increase awareness of the relationship between insulin resistance/diabetes/cardiovascular disease among the at-risk population (Goal: 50 million media impressions).
2. Action: Help at-risk patients recognize and reduce their risk of cardiovascular disease (Goal: 7,500 enrollees) and drive traffic to the Spanish-language Web site.

Strategies

1. Leverage survey results to demonstrate the need for increased awareness.
2. Offer free Spanish–English health information (handbook, journal, Web site) through the AHA.
3. Engage a celebrity with ties to the Hispanic community.

Messages

1. Heart disease and stroke are the leading causes of death for people with diabetes, particularly Latinos/Hispanics.

2. Diabetes dramatically increases a person's risk for heart disease. Common underlying risk factors for diabetes are obesity, elevated cholesterol levels, high blood pressure, and physical inactivity. An emerging risk factor is insulin resistance, a condition in which the body doesn't efficiently respond to the insulin that it makes.

3. The American Heart Association's "The Heart of Diabetes: Understanding Insulin Resistance" program can help people with Type-2 diabetes learn more about the connection between diabetes and heart disease and understand what they can do to minimize their risks.

Execution

Patient Education Materials

Produced and distributed patient education materials in both Spanish and English. Patient education materials included the following:

> The handbook "Getting to the Heart of Diabetes," which was widely distributed through an alliance of organizations (i.e., American Association of Diabetes Educators, National Black Nurses Association, and the American Stroke Association).

> The "Thriver" journal, which patients could use to track blood glucose, blood pressure, cholesterol, diet, and exercise routines.

> The "Shape Your Family History" chart, which was designed to encourage families to map out their health problems and discuss them with their health care providers.

> The THOD consumer Web site at americanheart.org/diabetes.

The National Campaign Launch

The national campaign launch featured the following:

> Rita Moreno joined THOD as the national celebrity spokesperson, sharing her personal story of losing her mother and sister-in-law to diabetes-related heart disease.

> As part of the national launch, a reception was held at Restaurant Noche in New York City where Ms. Moreno revealed the Hispanic-specific survey statistics.

> A national radio public service announcement (available in English and Spanish) featuring Ms. Moreno was produced and distributed.

> Ms. Moreno and the national physician spokesperson were featured in a three-hour television satellite media tour and a two-hour radio media tour.

Local Activities

The following activities were conducted at the local/regional level:

> Ms. Moreno toured cities with high Hispanic populations, including Chicago, Los Angeles, Miami, and San Antonio, teaming up with local bilingual cardiologists to reach Hispanic patients with Type-2 diabetes.

> Worked with local AHA chapters to generate excitement in the market by tapping their local media contacts and coordinating special appearances for Ms. Moreno in heavily populated settings (e.g., Hispanic senior centers).

Evaluation

The evaluation component of the campaign focused on two major objectives: one on message outputs, with concomitant media exposure, and the other on the impacts of the campaign.

Objective 1

1. Education: Increase awareness of the relationship between insulin resistance/diabetes/cardiovascular disease among the at-risk population (GOAL: 50 million media impressions).
2. Results: Through targeted media outreach, the program generated 76 million media impressions, exceeding the goal by more than 50 percent. Coverage included Telemundo, Univision's national morning show *Despierta America*, *Newsday*, the *Chicago Sun-Times*, and the *San Antonio Express-News*.

Objective 2

1. Action: Help at-risk patients recognize and reduce their risk of cardiovascular disease (Goal: 7,500 enrollees) and drive traffic to the Spanish-language Web site.
2. Results: (1) More than 15,000 people enrolled in the program in 2003, doubling the goal set at the beginning of the year, representing the strongest determinant for the program's effectiveness. (2) In 2002, the total number of participation cards returned by Hispanics was 287. In contrast, the 2003 Hispanic program resulted in 1,631 returned cards, representing more than a 500 percent response increase. (3) The Rita Moreno radio public service announcement reached more than 62 million listeners, with more than 15 percent of the total number of airings in top-10 local markets. (4) More than 58,000 people contacted the AHA call center, and 246,000 patient education handbooks were distributed. (5) Numerous "Thrivers" have posted their personal testimonials on how following the program's guidelines has helped them live a healthier lifestyle.

Note the large numbers from the target audience who actually took action as a result of the campaign—enrolling in programs, returning participation cards, making calls to a help center, and posting testimonials. It is one thing to estimate the size of the audience that was exposed to the message, with some purported increased awareness resulting from the exposure, but the documentation of Objective 2 makes a far more impressive case for the good done by the campaign in improving the health of at-risk Hispanics.

Sources: The American Heart Association, in partnership with Takeda Pharmaceuticals North America, Eli Lilly and Company, and Manning Selvage & Lee, garnered a highly prized Public Relations Society of America Silver Anvil Award for this campaign.

Summary

Defining the Research Role

Research is the basic groundwork of any public relations program. It involves the gathering and interpretation of information. Research is used in every phase of a communications program.

Research Techniques

Secondary research uses information from library sources and, increasingly, from online and Internet sources. Primary research involves gathering new information through interviews or sampling procedures.

Sampling

The sampling method used constrains the extent to which the findings can be analyzed in detail and generalized to a larger population. When possible, probability samples generate the best results, particularly when doing quantitative research.

Reaching Respondents

Survey respondents may be reached by mail, e-mail, telephone, the Internet, personal interviews, or through piggyback (omnibus) surveys.

The Value of Planning

After research, the next step is program planning. Such planning must be strategic.

Approaches to Planning

Two approaches to planning are management by objective (MBO) and Ketchum's strategic planning model. Both involve asking and answering many questions.

Elements of a Program Plan

A program plan is either a brief outline or an extensive document identifying what is to be done and how. Firms prepare these for client approval. They usually include the eight elements of situation, objectives, audience, strategy, tactics, a calendar or timetable, budget, and evaluation.

The Goals of Communication

Communication, also called execution, is the third step in the public relations process. Five possible objectives at this stage are message exposure, accurate dissemination of the message, acceptance of the message, attitude change, and change in overt behavior.

Receiving the Message

Successful communication involves interaction, or shared experience, because the message not only must be sent but also received. The larger the audience, the greater the number of barriers to communication.

Paying Attention to the Message

Because audiences have different approaches to receiving messages, communicators must tailor messages to get recipients' attention. Communicators need to understand an audience's mental state. Messages for passive audiences must have style and creativity, whereas messages for an audience actively seeking information must have more sophisticated content. In either case, the effective message will raise the audience's "need" level by providing some obvious benefit.

Understanding the Message

The most basic element of understanding between communicator and audience is a common language. This is becoming a greater issue with the emphasis on multiculturalism. Public relations practitioners must consider their audiences and style their language appropriately, taking into consideration literacy levels, clarity and simplicity of language, and avoidance of discriminatory language.

Believing the Message

Key variables in believability include source credibility, context, and the audience's predispositions, especially their level of involvement.

Remembering the Message

Messages are often repeated extensively to reach all members of the target audience and to help them remember and enhance their learning. One way to do this is to convey information in several ways, through a variety of channels.

Acting on the Message

The success of a message is in its effect on the recipient. Five steps in acceptance of new ideas or products are awareness, interest, evaluation, trial, and adoption. The adoption process is affected by relative advantage, compatibility, complexity, trialability, and observability. The time needed to adopt a new idea or product can be affected by the importance of the decision as well as the personality of the person receiving the message. The primary source of information varies at each step of the adoption process.

The Purpose of Evaluation

Evaluation is the measurement of results against objectives. This can enhance future performance and also establish whether the goals of management by objective have been met.

Objectives: A Prerequisite for Evaluation

Objectives should be part of any program plan. There must be agreed-upon criteria used to evaluate success in obtaining these objectives.

Current Status of Measurement and Evaluation

The proportion of public relations budgets devoted to measurement and evaluation grew over the 1990s to about 5 percent. On the most basic level, practitioners can measure message distribution and media placements. The second level would be measurement of audience awareness, comprehension, and retention. The most advanced level is the measurement of changes in attitudes, opinions, and behaviors.

Measurement of Production

Measurement of production gives management an idea of a staff's productivity and output.

Measurement of Message Exposure

Several criteria can be used to measure message exposure, including the compilation of press clippings and radio/television mentions; media impressions, or the potential audience reached; hits on a Web site; advertising equivalency, which is calculated by converting news stories to the cost of a comparable amount of paid space; systematic tracking by use of computer databases; requests for additional information, often through a toll-free phone number; and audience attendance at special events. Sometimes exposure is evaluated by determining how much it cost to reach each member of the target audience.

Measurement of Audience Awareness

The next level of evaluation is whether the audience became aware of and understood the message. Audience awareness can be measured through survey research.

Measurement of Audience Attitudes

Changes in audience attitudes can be evaluated through a baseline or benchmark study, measuring awareness and opinions before, during, and after a public relations campaign.

Measurement of Audience Action

Ultimately, public relations campaigns are evaluated based on how they help an organization achieve its objectives through changing audience behavior, whether it involves sales, fund-raising, or the election of a candidate.

CASE ACTIVITY >>
What Would You Do?

Sunshine Cafe, a chain of coffee houses, did some market research and found that college students would be an excellent audience to reach. To this end, Sunshine Cafe has contacted your public relations firm and asked that you develop a comprehensive plan to do two things: (1) create brand awareness among college students and (2) increase walk-in business at their local stores in college towns.

Using the eight-point planning outline described in this chapter, write a public relations program for Sunshine Cafe. You should consider a variety of communication tools, including campus events. However, no money has been allocated for advertising.

Questions for Review and Discussion

1. What questions should a person ask before formulating a research design?
2. Identify at least five ways that research is used in public relations.
3. How can survey research be used as a publicity tool?
4. What is the procedure for organizing and conducting a focus group? What are the pros and cons of using focus groups?
5. What guidelines should be followed when releasing the results of a survey to the media and the public?
6. Name the eight elements of a program plan.
7. Explain the difference between an informational objective and a motivational objective.
8. What is the difference between a strategy and an objective?
9. Kirk Hallahan lists five categories of media and communication tools. What are they, and what are some of the pros and cons of each?
10. Why is two-way communication (feedback) an important aspect of effective communication?
11. What kinds of messages and communication channels would you use for a passive audience? An active information-seeking audience?
12. Why is it necessary to use a variety of messages and communication channels in a public relations program?

13. Explain the five steps of the adoption process. What are some of the factors that affect the adoption of an idea or product?

14. What is the role of stated objectives in evaluating public relations programs?

15. List four ways that publicity activity is evaluated. What, if any, are the drawbacks of each one?

16. How does measurement of message exposure differ from measurement of audience comprehension of the message?

17. What methods can be used to evaluate a company newsletter or magazine?

Suggested Readings

Beardsley, John. "Get Smart: Using the Right Words at the Right Time." *The Strategist*, Spring 2006, 29–31.

Cameron, Glen T. "Does Publicity Outperform Advertising? An Experimental Test of the Third-Party Endorsement." *Journal of Public Relations Research* 6, no. 3 (1994): 185–207.

Charland, Bernie. "The Mantra of Metrics: A Realistic and Relevant Approach to Measuring the Impact of Employee Communications." *The Strategist*, Fall 2004, 30–32.

Cobb, Chris. "YouTube and Beyond: How PR Pros Discover and Create Buzz with Online Video." *Public Relations Tactics*, June 2006, 21.

Hallahan, Kirk. "Strategic Media Planning: Toward an Integrated Public Relations Media Model." In *Handbook of Public Relations*, edited by Robert Heath. Thousand Oaks, CA: Sage, 2000, pp. 461–470.

Hood, Julia. "Companies Must Grasp Fact That Media Are Stakeholders." *PRWeek*, October 2, 2006, 9.

Hon, Linda Childers. "What Have You Done for Me Lately? Exploring Effectiveness in Public Relations." *Journal of Public Relations Research* 9, no. 1 (1997): 1–30.

"How to Measure Relationships? Grunig/Hon Study for Institute Measurement Commission Lays Groundwork." *pr reporter* 42, no. 40, October 11, 1999, 1–3.

Jo, Samsup. "Effect of Content Type on Impact: Editorial vs. Advertising." *Public Relations Review* 30, no. 4 (2004): 503–512.

Kim, Yungwook. "Measuring the Bottom-Line Impact of Corporate Public Relations." *Journalism and Mass Communication Quarterly* 77 (Summer 2000): 273–291.

Lindenmann, Walter K., editor. *Guidelines and Standards for Measuring and Evaluating PR Effectiveness.* Gainesville: Institute for Public Relations Research, University of Florida, 2003. (www.instituteforpr.com)

Newman, Kelli B. "A Strategic Subspeciality: Defining the Comprehensive Value of Broadcast Public Relations." *Public Relations Tactics*, June 2006, 18.

Nolan, Hamilton. "Today's Media Relations Rules." *PRWeek*, September 4, 2006, 14–15.

Oates, David B. "Measuring the Value of Public Relations: Tying Efforts to Business Goals," *Public Relations Tactics*, October 2006, 12.

Obston, A. "The Eight Words You Can't Say in a Press Release." *Public Relations Quarterly* 49, no. 3 (2004): 9–11.

Smuddle, P. "The Five P's for Media Interviews: Fundamentals for Newbies, Veterans and Everyone in Between. *Public Relations Quarterly* 49, no. 2 (2004): 29–34.

Stacks, Don W. *Primer of Public Relations Research.* New York: Guilford, 2002.

Steward, Joan. "More TV Stations Turning to Pay for Play: The Line Between Ads and Editorial Continues to Blur." *Public Relations Tactics*, June 2006, 26.

Ward, David. "Master of All Whom You Survey." *PRWeek*, September 25, 2006, 22.

Wylie, Ann. "Make Your Copy Clear and Concise: The Easier Your Story is to Read, the More People Will Read It." *Public Relations Tactics*, June 2006, 15.

Chapter Six

Public Opinion and Persuasion

What Is Public Opinion?

Editorial cartoonists often humanize public opinion in the form of John or Jane Q. Public, characters who have come to symbolize what people think about any given issue. The reality is that public opinion is somewhat elusive and extremely difficult to measure at any given moment. For example, 2004 polls in Cardiff, Wales, showed that 78 percent of the public favored a ban on smoking in restaurants and 76 percent agreed that it also should be banned in the workplace. However, just 26 percent believed that smoking should be banned in licensed pubs. Aware that public opinion varies, the Welsh government responded accordingly. Based on the results of the poll, Health Minister Jane Hutt defended her go-slow approach to banning smoking: "I want to [set policy], as much as possible, in partnership—listening and learning from others." Hutt implied that if public opinion on the issue changed, her ministry would reflect the evolving viewpoints.

On a more basic level, people constantly form and revise their opinions about public figures, like Donald Trump or Paris Hilton, often based on recent television appearances or Internet gossip. The court of public opinion is fickle and variable. Yesterday's superstars may be tomorrow's has-beens, until they release a ghost-written tell-all biography and are again thrust into the public spotlight. Accurately predicting the future direction of public opinion is extremely difficult because of the number of contingent variables involved.

In fact, public opinion as represented by John and Jane Q. Public is a number of monoliths, all existing simultaneously. Few issues create unanimity of thought, and public opinion on any issue is usually split in several directions that may be in conflict with one another. Even when members of an identifiable group share common beliefs and interests, the opinions of individuals or subgroups may vary widely. For example, the issue of immigration in the United States arouses a variety of perspectives among Christian groups. Fundamentalists tend to perceive the question of immigration from the vantage of biblical laws, whereas liberal Christian demoninations are likely to perceive the issue in relation to Christ's teachings on tolerance. Likewise, there will always be various conflicting public opinions about hot-button issues such as abortion, gay marriage, euthanasia, homeland security, and war.

It may come as a surprise that only a small number of people at any given time take part in public opinion formation on a specific issue. However, once people and the press begin to speak of public opinion on an issue as an accomplished fact, it can take on its own momentum. According to Irving Crespi, who has done much research on public opinion, public opinion can be an almost tangible force that affects all kinds of people, altering their beliefs or attitudes about controversial issues.

There are three reasons for the profound influence of vocal segments of society and public opinion momentum. First, psychologists have found that the public by and large tends to be passive. It is often assumed that there is a consensus when, in reality, it is more accurate to say that the majority of the people are apathetic because an issue doesn't interest or affect them. Thus, "public" opposition to such issues as nuclear power, gay marriage, abortion, and gun control may really be the view of a small but vocal group. Elizabeth Noelle-Neumann, an originator of the spiral of silence theory, defines public opinion as views that individuals can express in public without risking social alienation or isolation.

Second, one issue may engage the attention of a part of the population with a particular vested interest, whereas another arouses the interest of another segment. Parents, for example, may form public opinion on the need for improved secondary education, whereas senior citizens constitute the better part of public opinion on the need for increased Social Security benefits.

Third, people have some opinions that may conflict or compete with others around the same issue. For example, college students and their parents who advocate increased federal spending for education have come into conflict with proponents of smaller government who argue for fiscal restraints. People sometimes have contradictory opinions or attitudes. A person who vigorously complains about federal spending on pork barrel projects in one breath may in the other bemoan government's inability to repave streets or provide enough public parks in his or her neigborhood. Understanding and assessing the dynamics of competing or conflicting opinions is a crucial dimension of public relations work.

The examples provided here illustrate the following elements of public opinion that appear in public opinion research:

> Public opinion is the collective expression of the opinions of many individuals bound into a group by common aims, aspirations, interests, needs, beliefs, and ideals.

> People who are interested in or who have a vested or self-interest in an issue, or who can be affected directly by the outcome of the issue, form public opinion on that particular item.

> Opinion is generally related to specific events that have an impact on the population at large or a particular segment of society. Events, words, or other stimuli affect opinion only insofar as their relationship to self-interest or a general concern is apparent.

> Opinion does not remain aroused for a long period of time unless people feel acutely that their self-interest is involved or unless opinion—aroused by words— is sustained by events.

Gary Markstein's cartoon suggests the dimension of vested interest in public opinion. Cartoon, Gary Markstein, *Milwaukee Journal Sentinel*, 2004.

The "Public" Embedded in Public Opinion

The formation of public opinion is a constantly evolving process, and should not be regarded as static by public relations professionals. The public is often noncommittal about an issue, but once motivated, they form attitudes, beliefs, and take action to achieve their interests throughout the life cycle of the issue. Public relations professionals should identify and track identifiable public opinions and even strive to create or boost these opinions to affect public relations outcomes.

Public opinion plays a role in activating a group of people around an issue. Awareness and discussion leads to crystallizing of opinions and consensus building among the public. Unless people are aware of an issue, they are not likely to be concerned or have an opinion about it. As awareness grows, the issue becomes a matter of public discussion and debate, often garnering extensive media coverage. Through media coverage, the issue is placed on the public agenda and even more people become aware of it.

Suppose for example, activist and special interest groups organize a protest against scenic areas being threatened by logging or strip mining. These groups may have no formal power but they serve as "agenda stimuli" for the media that crave controversy and conflict. Opportunities for vivid television coverage occur when activists stage rallies and demonstrations. As is often the case, the issue gets simplified by the media into an us-versus-them stance. Opinion leaders begin to discuss the issue, perhaps viewing it as being symbolic of broader environmental and societal issues.

Public relations professionals often identify key audiences or publics through analysis of public opinion and thereby resolve the issue from their standpoint. For example, news in February 2006 that the U.S. government was going to contract with DP World, a company owned by the state of Dubai in the United Arab Emirates, to operate 21 American ports swiftly led to a massive public outcry. Public opinion was further aroused when it was learned that President George W. Bush's administration had not informed Congress of the deal until a short time before it was to be finalized. In March 2006, a CNN/USA Today/Gallup poll revealed that 66 percent of respondents were opposed to the deal and only 17 percent were in favor of it. Even though port security was to remain under U.S. control, it struck many Americans as highly suspect that a corporation owned by an Arab country would be in charge of operations. Because of the outcry from the public, which was an important audience, the deal soon fell victim to congressional opposition and the pressure of overwhelming negative public opinion.

Public relations professionals arouse public opinion in order to proactively generate positive opinions about an organization or issue. For example, James Dobson's radio program *Focus on the Family* has been notably successful in framing and affecting public opinion on a wide range of issues of concern to evangelical Christians. Through his widely syndicated radio program, Dobson's message also reaches an audience that is not necessarily religious but does share his opinions on moral concerns and family values.

Opinion Leaders as Catalysts

According to research in *Roper Reports*, 10 to 12 percent of the population, identified by the magazine as "influentials," drive public opinion and consumer trends. Knowledgeable experts who articulate opinions about specific issues in public discussion are called *opinion leaders*. Sociologists describe opinion leaders as (1) highly interested in a subject or issue, (2) better informed on an issue than the average person, (3) avid consumers of mass media, (4) early adopters of new ideas, and (5) good organizers who can get other people to take action.

Sociologists Elihu Katz and Paul Lazarsfeld defined opinion leaders as people who, because of their interest in and knowledge of a subject, become experts and inform others either formally as spokespeople or informally through daily interaction with family members, colleagues, and peers. Opinion leaders are not necessarily highly visible in the community, nor are they always leaders in other regards—it is as common to find an opinion leader among a group of coal miners or housewives as it is among a group of politicians or Fortune 500 company executives. Opinion leaders seem evenly distributed among the social, economic, and educational strata within their community. Opinion leaders frequently act as catalysts in the formation of public opinion. Through discussion or more formal presentations, they help frame and define issues that often have their roots in individuals' self-interests. It is through the influence of opinion leaders that public opinion often crystallizes into a measurable entity (see Chapter 2, pages 42–46 for detailed discussion of the life cycle of an issue). The PR Casebook on page 176 discusses the influence of opinion leaders in the wake of Hurricane Katrina.

Types of Leaders

There are two types of opinion leaders. First are the formal opinion leaders such as elected officials, presidents of companies, or heads of membership groups. News reporters often ask them for statements when specific issues relate to their areas of responsibility or concern. People with official titles are sometimes referred to as formal leaders. For example, Representative Nancy Pelosi (D-California) and Senator John McCain (R-Arizona) speak to issues from their respective positions of power on a wide

PRCASEBOOK

Bush and Team Weather a PR Crisis after the Storm

Prevention is always better than response, but an appropriate and timely response can still be effective in the ongoing process of crisis communication. Often, the public forms an opinion based on their first impressions and evaluates whether a crisis response was timely and effective regardless of the outcome.

Late-night talk show hosts got a great deal of mileage out of comparing the disaster of Hurricane Katrina, which ravaged the coasts of Mississippi and Louisiana in the fall of 2005, with the catastrophic failure of the Bush administration's public relations efforts to address the aftermath. In the immediate wake of the storm, it appeared to the American public that CNN and other news networks were better informed about the situation than was the president. When he did make public statements, Bush at first seemed out of touch. "I don't think anybody anticipated the breach of the levees," he told Diane

Sawyer on ABC's *Good Morning America* a few days after the storm. His praise for FEMA director Michael Brown for doing a "heck of a job" appeared incomprehensible to the public when set against images of suffering broadcast from the New Orleans Superdome.

Tim Goodman, writing for the *San Francisco Chronicle* on September 11, 2005, assessed the media feeding frenzy: "Bush and his administration have come under withering attack not only from a lengthy and bipartisan list of other politicians but also from anchors on nearly every channel—opinion-makers in the heat of the moment—whose voices abandoned objectivity and rose up in questioning tones as they took Bush and federal department heads to task." Journalists were less emphatic about pointing out that New Orleans mayor Ray Nagin and Louisiana governor Kathleen Blanco delayed asking for help from the federal government for several days and

variety of issues affecting the public. They appear frequently on television news to express their opinions about the Iraq War, the confirmation of Supreme Court justices, tax reform, and a host of other issues directly affecting constituents.

Second are the informal opinion leaders, those who have clout with peers because of some special characteristic. They may be role models who are admired and emulated or opinion leaders who can exert peer pressure on others to go along with something. In general, informal opinion leaders exert considerable influence on their peer groups by being highly informed, articulate, and credible on particular issues. U2 lead singer Bono is a current example of an informal leader who has had a worldwide impact on public opinion regarding issues such as world hunger and poverty. Actor George Clooney has emerged as another opinion leader on a wide range of social issues. Although many Americans find his ideas about the political process controversial, Clooney's advocacy to end genocide in the Darfur region of western Sudan in Africa is generally admired.

People seldom make a decision on their own but are influenced by their friends, parents, educators, supervisors, church leaders, physicians, public officials, celebrities, and the media in general when deciding to vote for a president or city mayor, or to purchase a car or even toothpaste. Public relations professionals attempt to influence these leaders just as they seek to influence the public at large.

The Flow of Opinion

Many public relations campaigns, particularly those in the public affairs arena, concentrate on identifying and reaching key opinion leaders who are pivotal to the success

President Bush works to counter negative public opinion after Hurricane Katrina in New Orleans, with Mayor Ray Nagin.

failed to make adequate plans for the evacuation of residents before, during, and after the storm.

Behind the scenes, the administration worked to change the public's perception. Their strategy had three components. First, chief political advisor Karl Rove and communications director Dan Bartlett arranged for key Republican leaders to visit the affected area. Second, they encouraged officials in the administration to keep silent regarding Democrat's criticism of the administration. Third, Rove and Bartlett attempted to shift some of the blame to Nagin and Blanco.

Many thought the administration's response was too little, too late, however. Opinion leaders were quick to point out the contrast between the post-Katrina Bush public relations campaign and the one that followed the events of September 11, 2001. A poll taken by CBS News found that only 38 percent of the public approved of Bush's handling of Hurricane Katrina in September 2005, while 58 percent disapproved and 48 percent believed that he had demonstrated strong leadership qualities. By comparison, 83 percent of Americans approved of Bush's leadership in the immediate wake of the 9/11 attacks and 66 percent had "a lot" of confidence in the president's ability to handle future crises at that time.

or failure of an idea or project. In 1948, sociologists Paul Lazarsfeld, Bernard Berelson, and Hazel Gaudet published a paper entitled "The People's Choice" that analyzed how people choose candidates in an election. They found that the mass media had minimal influence on electoral choices, but voters did rely on person-to-person communication with formal and informal opinion leaders.

These findings, later refined by Lazarsfeld and Katz, became known as the two-step flow theory of communication. Although later research confirmed that it really was a multiple-step flow, the basic concept remains valid. Public opinion is generally formed around the views of people who have taken the time to sift information, evaluate it, and form an opinion that is expressed to others. According to Lazarsfeld and Katz, information often is disseminated through the media (print, radio, and television) to opinion leaders who interact with other less informed members of the public. It is through the filter of face-to-face interactions between opinion leaders and others, rather than directly from the media itself, that public opinion is formed.

Multiple-step flow theory indicates that some people eventually become interested in, or at least aware of, an issue through a chain of two-step flow processes. The multiple-step flow model is graphically illustrated by a series of concentric circles. In the epicenter of action are "opinion makers." They derive large amounts of information from the mass media and other sources and then share that information with people in the adjoining concentric circle, who are labeled the "attentive public." Attentive publics are interested in the issue but rely on opinion leaders to synthesize and interpret information. The outer ring of the model consists of the "inattentive public." They are unaware of or uninterested in the issue and remain outside the opinion-formation process.

Another variation of the two-step model is N-step theory. Individuals are seldom influenced by only one opinion leader but interact with different leaders around an issue. For example, patients can seek information from their primary care physician but may also turn to close relations, such as parents or children, when forming a significant opinion or making a decision about a health issue.

Mass media effects are limited by personal influences. Diffusion theory explains that individuals adopt new ideas or products through five stages: awareness, interest, trial, evaluation, and adoption, as discussed in Chapter 5. According to Everett Rogers, author of *Diffusion of Innovations*, individuals are often influenced by media in the first two steps and by friends and family members in the third and fourth steps. And each individual is a decision maker who will adopt a new idea or product in reaching the final step.

The Role of Mass Media

Public relations personnel reach opinion leaders to influence key publics and also reach targeted publics directly via the mass media such as radio, television, newspapers, and magazines. *Mass media*, as the term implies, means that information from a source can be efficiently and rapidly disseminated to masses of people, sometimes literally millions. Cultivation theories suggest that reality is mediated by media selecting and repackaging of events to fit its audience interest. Uses and gratification theorists propose that, based on their needs, people use and respond differently to mass media, which competes with other information sources that also gratify these needs. Whether it is powerful or limited, mass media influences and at least informs people through news or entertainment in our daily lives. Thus, it is important to understand who controls the media and sets the media agenda.

Oscar H. Gandy, Jr., of the University of Pennsylvania, and other theorists have concluded that public relations professionals are major players in forming public opinion because they are often the first to provide mass media with information. Although journalists often argue that they rarely use public relations materials, one has only to look at the daily newspaper to see the quote from the press officer at the sheriff's department, the article on a new computer product, the statistics from the local real estate board, or even the postgame interview with the winning quarterback. In almost all cases, a public relations source at the organization provided the information directly or arranged the interview. Indeed, Gandy estimates that up to 50 percent of what the media carry comes from public relations sources in the form of "information subsidies." To better understand how public relations people inform the public and shape public opinion via the mass media, it is necessary to review briefly some theories about mass media effects.

Agenda Setting

One of the early theories, pioneered by mass communications researchers Max McCombs and Don Shaw, contends that media content sets the agenda for public discussion. People tend to talk about what they see or hear on the television news programs or read on the front pages of newspapers. Media, through the selection of stories and headlines, tell the public what to think about, but not necessarily what to think. The war on terrorism, for example, has been high on the media agenda for several years, but public opinion polls indicate a variety of viewpoints on the subject. Social scientist Joseph Klapper calls this the limited-effects model of mass media. He postulates, "Mass media ordinarily does not serve as a necessary and sufficient cause for audience effects, but rather functions among and through a nexus of mediating factors and influence." Such factors include the way that opinion leaders analyze and interpret the information provided by the mass media.

More recently, Wayne Wanta of the University of Missouri–Columbia and other scholars of agenda-setting theory have explored second-level agenda-setting effects, finding evidence that the media not only set agendas but also convey a set of attributes about the various subjects in the news. These positive or negative attributes are internalized and color public opinion. For example, a number of news stories regarding the disappearance of Alabama high school student Natalee Holloway focused on the potential danger for tourists in Aruba, when in fact the island has a relatively low crime rate compared to other countries in the region. This led to the public perception in the United States that travel to Aruba might be ill-advised.

From a public relations standpoint, even getting a subject on the media agenda is an accomplishment that advances organizational goals. Sales of Apple's iPod rose as the media reported its success and the public became aware of this "hot" item. Research is ongoing in terms of documenting how public relations efforts can build the media agenda, and thus affect public opinion.

Framing

Media content is influenced by a broad array of forces ranging from the professionalism of individual journalists to corporate ownership of media outlets to cultural and ideological factors, according to Pamela J. Shoemaker at Syracuse University and Steve Reeves at the University of Texas–Austin. Traditionally, framing theory was related to how journalists selected certain facts, themes, treatments, and even words to "frame," or shape, a story. This goes beyond journalists' simple selection of potential news stories in their role as gatekeepers and involves their interpetation of issues or creation of subtle nuances. According to researchers Julie L. Andsager at the University of Iowa and Angela Powers at Northern Illinois University, "Mass media scholars have long argued that it is important to understand the ways in which journalistic framing of issues occurs because such framing impacts public understanding and, consequently, policy formation." For example, how media frame the debate over health care and the role of health maintenance organizations often plays a major role in public perceptions of the issues involved.

Increasingly, scholars and professionals are applying framing theory to public relations efforts. In a paper titled "PR Goes to War: The Effects of Public Relations Campaigns on Media Framing of the Kuwait and Bosnian Crises," James Tankard and Bill Israel of the University of Texas found that the governments involved in the conflicts used public relations professionals to help frame the issues involved. The issues, as framed by public relations professionals, were then reflected in press coverage and thus influenced the public's opinion regarding the crisis. Tankard and Israel point out that the media dependency of most Americans—who often have little direct knowledge of such faraway places or the complex issues involved—means that they accept the media's version of reality, which originally came from what the two researchers describe as "special interest groups or other groups with particular causes."

Most public relations personnel rarely find themselves framing the issues of an international conflict, but they do exercise framing or positioning strategies for any number of products and services. For example, when Edelman was considering strategy for the launch of Apple's iMac computer, one of the strong themes (or frames) they developed was that Apple was on the way back to prosperity after several years of massive losses and erosion of customer support. Indeed, one headline in a daily news-paper proclaimed, "Apple Regains Its Stride." Such framing obviously bolsters investor and consumer confidence in the company.

Dietram Scheufele at the University of Wisconsin–Madison suggests that there are two types of framing: media framing and audience framing. He argued that fram-ing is a continuous process and that the behavioral, attitudinal, cognitive, and affective statuses of individuals are also involved in how they intrepret issues. For example, vot-ers in Florida may be less likely to respond favorably to a story about increased school funding. A number of Floridians are over the age of 65 (16.7 percent) and have already raised their children. Conversely, voters in Georgia, a state with fewer people over the age of 65 (9.2 percent), might react more favorably to school funding increases. However, a range of variables, beliefs, and attitudes simultaneously affect how individ-uals interpret an issue.

Political science professors Shanto Iyengar and Donald Kinder focus on the media's power to prime people in a more subtle but significant form of persuasive effect. They note how public relations professionals working for political campaigns seek to emphasize considerations that will help voters decide in their favor, often enlisting the expertise of a popular leader, and to downplay those considerations that will hurt their cause or candidate. Ultimately, the goal is to encourage voters to change the bases on which they make decisions about voting rather than simply change their choices about a given candidate or issue. The Insights box on page 181 takes a look at media framing in political campaigns.

Crucial Role of Conflict in Public Discourse

The process of public discourse is often rooted in conflict. Social scientists and legal scholars have defined conflict as any situation in which two or more individuals, groups, organizations, or communities perceive a divergence of interests. They have developed conflict theory, which offers insight into differences among individuals or groups and explains conflicting interests, goals, values, or desires. Public opinion often reflects such different, or even conflicting, views, attitudes, and behaviors.

According to conflict resolution scholars Morton Deutsch and Peter Colman, conflict in the public arena does not necessarily yield negative outcomes but creates a constructive process that builds toward consensus. Indeed, conflict or consensus is an actual theme of court opinions, which regulate and help ensure social stability and peaceful change within a democratic society. Conflict itself is an inherent constraint within social structures.

Controversies often serve to shape public opinion more intensively and exten-sively. Public relations professionals frequently have the challenging role of trying to minimize or resolve controversy in conflict situations. For example, MIT introduced a controversial radio-frequency transmitting ID-tag system in 2003. Many people on campus and from the nonprofit group Consumers Against Supermarket Privacy and Invasion and Numbering raised concerns about potential abuse of the system. MIT hired PR firm Fleishman-Hillard to "neutralize opposition," according to an article in *PRWeek*. Part of their strategy was "conveying the inevitability of technology."

At other times public relations practitioners may generate or promote contro-versy to engender positive or supportive public opinion. The Western Fuels Association, for example, hired Jack Bonner in essence to manufacture a "grassroots" public rela-tions campaign between 1997 and 2001. The Web site www.globalwarmingcost.org posed as an informational site, but surreptitiously generated e-mails signed by those

— ON THE JOB >>

Howard Dean: The "I Have a Scream" Speech

Insights

Public appearances and media framing are important aspects of public relations work. An unflattering action or malapropism by a public figure during a public appearance can fan the flames of gossip and rumor, and leave a deep impression on the public consciousness, particularly if broadcast repeatedly. In a real sense, it is the responsibility of candidates and their public relations personnel to anticipate how the media can take advantage of such mistakes and take care not to provide such opportunities. A quick response to reframe a misfortunate incident and impress a positive image on the public's mind is a necessary aspect of public relations.

On January 20, 2004, Howard Dean addressed a group of about 3,500 supporters after a disappointing third-place finish in the Iowa Caucuses. Dean had been the Democratic front-runner and was attempting to rally the troops by listing the primaries that he expected to win, followed by an enthusiastic "Yeeaaahhhh!" Dean's outburst is often cited as the reason that the Vermont governor's momentum as a contender suddenly came to a halt.

Television news quickly picked up on Dean's miscalculation—his failure to recognize that his voice was being recorded by a unidirectional microphone that suppressed crowd noise. By one count, the scream was aired no less than 633 times on CNN alone over the course of the next four days. Virtually all neworks aired a heavily edited version of the speech showing the ten seconds leading to Dean screaming and gesturing wildly. Yale historian David Greenburg noted in the *Washington Post* on January 29, "[The media] turned the 'scream' from an amusing, if slightly weird, sidelight into a four-day front-page story that may seriously damage his chances." Indeed, by February 18 Dean had called it quits.

In an article in the *Miami Herald* entitled "Dean Scream' Clip Was Media Fraud," Edward Wasserman argues that the way the story was presented represents "probably the clearest instance of media assassination in recent U.S. political history." The framing effect of repeatedly showing a 10-second video clip focusing on Dean's enthusiastic reaction, Wasserman argues, decontextualized Dean's message and even suggested that he was mentally unbalanced.

Joe Trippi, Dean's campaign manager, complained that the story was "totally unfair." Media executives were a bit more coy. Roger Ailes, chairman of Fox News and a Republican campaign consultant, noted that it may have been "overplayed a bit." Paul Slavin, senior vice president of ABC News, pointed to the vicious cycle of such news stories. "It took on such a life," he said, "the amount of attention it was receiving necessitated more attention." Of course, it is entirely possible that the speech had little real effect on Dean's campaign, and merely signaled an unpresidential manner to the public.

Howard Dean's infamous scream during a campaign rally is often cited as the reason his presidential bid ground to a halt. Media framing may have exaggerated the seriousness of Dean's outburst. Cartoon, Walt Handelsman, *Newsday*, 2004.

who answered questions about their heating costs to congressional representatives supporting his clients' views.

Mass media play a role in the unfolding of a conflict and serve to promote public debate by engaging the widest public involvement, a process known as *escalation*. The media also mediate among parties and de-escalate the conflict. Often, increasing direct communication between parties does more harm than good as the same arguments are repeated in a destructive way and nonnegotiable positions are confirmed over again. Mediated communication and shuttle diplomacy can be an effective means of resolving conflict, particularly at the early stages of a dispute. The role of the media is to interpret the issue, deliver the position of the other party, and even suggest avenues for resolution. George Will's "The Last Word" columns and Fareed Zakaria's editorials in *Newsweek* provide excellent examples of the media's ability to interpret competing positions and offer avenues for resolution. Not infrequently, they provide well-reasoned counterpoints in the same issue. Analysis of their articles also demonstrates how the media can be active in both escalation and de-escalation of conflicts.

Conflict is inherent in news frames. Public opinion is very often shaped by how a reporter frames an issue. A reporter's story on a conflict can be the sole information available to an audience. For example, a news story by an investigative reporter with special access to information about a controversial secret program at the Pentagon may represent the only perspective seen by the public. How that reporter frames the conflict can bias the public in favor of one party, or one solution, over another. Because the media are so crucial not only to presenting and explaining conflicts but also to keeping them from escalating, it is necessary for the parties and public relations practitioners involved to know how to work effectively with the media. Similarly, the media play a central role when public relations professionals want a conflict to escalate, to bring the issue to the fore.

All too often conflict is regarded as more newsworthy than resolution. Details about a volatile political election or corporate malfeasance are far more interesting to the public than the reporting of an amicable settlement or an acquittal. Conflict, as a component of news, ranges from wars to philosophical differences of opinion. Daily news stories and op-ed pieces include people criticizing government agencies or policies, a company's fraud, or celebrity scandals. Given the public's penchant for pleasure in the tribulations of others and voyeurism, it is little wonder that the daily news is filled with stories of conflict and turmoil.

The media's inclination to focus on tribulation posing as human interest often creates a conflict with sources. To maintain their credibility as objective judges of information, journalists are primed to conflict as part of their strategic approach to dealing with sources, while public relations practitioners, as advocates for favorable coverage, have a tendency to be accommodative or cooperative with reporters, according to researchers Jae-Hwa Shin and Glen T. Cameron. Public relations professionals should understand the nature of conflict as it exists in news coverage and the strategic orientations of journalists to escalate the conflict with sources for their own interest. The relationships between public relations professionals and journalists moves on a continuum from conflict to cooperation, much as they do with any other public (see Chapter 2 for detailed discussion of contingency stance and communication strategy). Laura M. Arpan, professor at Florida State University, has made an interesting point about the relationship in a crisis situation: "When the organization stole their thunder [broke the news about the crisis], journalists rated the practitioner as more credible, but also indicated greater interest in the story [than when they learned about the crisis from another party]." Journalists' tend to frame stories in terms of conflict and, to a lesser degree, the conflict resolution process. Nevertheless, bringing conflict management techniques to news making through the agenda-setting process is necessary for a wrangle in the marketplace of ideas to occur. Shin noted that the strategic conflict management of sources and reporters can benefit the ongoing agenda-setting process. Public relations professionals should understand journalists' orientation to escalate conflict as a means of maintaining balance and independence. Public relations practitioners should also try to transform conflicts in constructive ways. Rather than reporting only from the perspective of a dominant power such as governments and delivering the ideology of media conglomerates, the public interest can best be served by healthy competition among public relations sources and the media. From this perspective, public relations serves as a social force in the ongoing creation of news and news trends or agendas.

The PR Casebook box on this page looks at how Wal-Mart has negotiated a stream of negative publicity through crisis management public relations.

PR CASEBOOK

War Over Wal-Mart: Retail Giant Fights Back

The retail giant Wal-Mart has been under fire from critics who claim they exploit their workers by paying low wages and paltry benefits, contribute to the trade deficit by encouraging overseas sweatshops in places such as China, and destroy neighborhood business through uncompetitive pricing. Negative publicity has been exacerbated by a series of lawsuits calling attention to the alleged poor treatment of their employees, a dramatic 2005 documentary entitled *Wal-Mart: The High Cost of Low Price*, and pressure from activist groups including Wal-Mart Watch and Wake-Up Wal-Mart.

To counter the negative public opinion, executives for the company have fought back. In January 2005, they bought full-page ads in more than 100 newspapers across the country touting the company's record on opportunity for advancement. Once reticent executives, including CEO Lee Scott, now regularly talk about the company's policies with journalists and the Wal-Mart PR department sends out letters to the editor challenging the claims of their critics. "No one likes to hear someone say something negative about their family," said Sara

The film *Wal-Mart: The High Cost of Low Price*, directed by Robert Greenwald galvanzied criticism against the retail giant. Wal-Mart has taken an aggressive stance to counter its critics. Photo by Daniel Morduchowicz, 2005.

(continued)

Clark, a Wal-Mart spokesperson. "There are some things out there that are totally inaccurate, and we're looking to set the record straight," she told MSNBC News on February 1, 2004.

The company is quick to point out that opinion polls show that working families support Wal-Mart. Recent polls conducted by Quinnipiac University, and the Pew Charitable Trusts reported that 69 to 70 percent of American families have a favorable opinion of the retailer. Nevertheless, Wal-Mart has reason for concern and continued public relations efforts. The Pew Charitable Trust poll revealed that 31 percent of respondents have a negative opinion of the retailer, a figure that is higher than other comparable companies. As reported by Michael Barbaro in the *New York Times*, a 2004 internal report prepared by McKinsey & Company for Wal-Mart suggested that between 2 and 8 percent of consumers said that they would no longer patronize the retailer because of negative publicity.

Wal-Mart also hired the PR firm Edelman, who brought in their "big guns"; Michael K. Deaver, former communications director for Ronald Reagan, and Leslie Dach, an advisor to Bill Clinton, led the team. Six other former political advisors assisted, including David White, who worked on the Kerry campaign, and Nancy Johnson, who was the national political director for President Bush's 2004 campaign. A conference room on the second floor of Wal-Mart's corporate headquarters was turned into a war room, or as the team calls it, "Action Alley." Each morning the team began by scanning newspaper articles and television transcripts for anything that mentioned the company's name. If potentially harmful information was found, the team sought to counter it with press releases, telephoning reporters, and posting answers on the Web.

The Wal-Mart PR team also has tried to counter the negative publicity generated by *Wal-Mart: The High Cost of Low Price* by promoting *Why Wal-Mart Works & Why That Drives Some People Crazy*, a film that casts the retailer in a more favorable light. When activist groups announced a convention, the team held a press conference at which local suppliers, officials, and a few employees spoke about the positive effects that Wal-Mart has brought to communities. The team's goal is circumvent criticism from the outset, to make the company appear more responsive and community-oriented, and to convince "swing voters" that the company is moving in the right direction.

The Pervasiveness of Persuasion in Public Opinion

Persuasion has been around since the dawn of human history. It was formalized as a concept more than 2,500 years ago by the Greeks, who instituted rhetoric, the art of using language effectively and persuasively, as a central part of their educational system. Aristotle was the first to set down the ideas of ethos, logos, and pathos, which roughly translate as "source credibility," "logical argument," and "emotional appeal."

More recent scholars, such as Richard Perloff, author of *The Dynamics of Persuasion*, offer updated definitions: "Persuasion is an activity or process in which a communicator attempts to induce a change in the belief, attitude, or behavior of another person or group of persons through the transmission of a message in a context in which the persuadee has some degree of free choice."

Such a definition is consistent with the role of public relations professionals in today's society. Indeed, Professor Robert Heath of the University of Houston says:

> [P]ublic relations professionals are influential rhetors. They design, place, and repeat messages on behalf of sponsors on an array of topics that shape views of government, charitable organizations, institutions of public education, products and consumerism, capitalism, labor, health, and leisure. These professionals speak, write, and use visual images to discuss topics and take stances on public policies at the local, state, and federal levels.

The Dominant View of Public Relations

The dominant view of public relations, in fact, is one of persuasive communication actions performed on behalf of clients, according to Professors Dean Kruckeberg at the University of Northern Iowa and Ken Starck at the University of Iowa. Oscar Gandy, Jr., adds that "the primary role of public relations is one of purposeful, self-interested communications." And Edward Bernays even called public relations the "engineering" of consent to create "a favorable and positive climate of opinion toward the individual, product, institution, or idea which is represented."

A degree of advocacy on the part of the persuader exists in communication intended for the target audience. Most public relations efforts are viewed as persuasive communication management and ultimately seek to change the attitudes and behavior of people. For example, public relations professionals disseminate information about their products or services to potential customers in an effort to persuade them to recognize or buy those products or services. They also try to persuade legislators and other politicians in seeking favorable tax or regulatory actions. Politicians, on the other hand, use public relations to attract votes or raise money. Nonprofit organizations such as Greenpeace or the Red Cross persuade people to become aware of social or environmental issues, take actions, and donate money.

The Uses of Persuasion

Persuasion is used to (1) change or neutralize hostile opinions, (2) crystallize latent opinions and positive attitudes, and (3) maintain favorable opinions. The most difficult persuasive task is to turn hostile opinions into favorable ones. There is much truth to the adage, "Don't confuse me with the facts; my mind is made up." Once people have decided, for instance, that oil companies are making excessive profits, they tend to ignore or disbelieve any contradictory information. The public may overlook information pointing to geopolitical factors or increased demand from countries such as China and India as affecting the price of oil, and instead believe that executives at Exxon-Mobil and the Shell Group are conspiring to gouge consumers. Each of us, as Walter Lippmann has described, has pictures in his or her head based on an individual perception of reality. People generalize from personal experience, what they read in the newspaper or see on television, and what peers tell them. For example, if a person has an encounter with a rude clerk, the inclination is to generalize that the entire department store chain is not very good.

Persuasion is much easier if the message is compatible with a person's general disposition toward a subject. If a person tends to identify Toyota as a company with a good reputation, he or she may express this feeling by purchasing one of its cars. Nonprofit agencies usually crystallize the public's inherent inclination to aid the less fortunate by asking for donations. Both examples illustrate the reason that organizations strive to have a good reputation—it is translated into sales and donations.

The easiest form of persuasion is communication that reinforces favorable opinions. Public relations people, by providing a steady stream of reinforcing messages, keep the reservoir of goodwill in sound condition. More than one organization has survived a major problem because public esteem tended to ameliorate its current difficulties. Continual efforts to maintain the reservoir of goodwill is called preventive public relations, and it is the most effective type of public relations.

Persuasion and Negotiation

Persuasion is comparable to negotiation. Negotiation is the process in which two or more parties attempt to settle disputes, reach agreement about courses of action, and bargain for individual or collective advantage. Negotiation is sometimes used in lieu of the courts as a form of alternative dispute resolution, whereas persuasion conspicuously occurs in the marketplace as a form of communicative action, according to professor Jae-Hwa Shin at the University of Southern Mississippi. In nearly all cases, some degree of conflict exists between parties both in persuasion and negotiation. Like negotiators, a persuader and the persuadee intentionally or unconciously bargain according to their interests, values, or needs and, ideally, are willing to compromise on the differences. There is always some degree of resistance on the part of the persuadee based on their inclination to accept or reject the persuader's message and terms. For example, in negotiating the price of a used car, the seller attempts to persuade the buyer that the car is in good condition and worth the asking price. The seller's interest is to get the highest possible price. The buyer, whose best interest is to purchase the car for the lowest possible price, is inclined to point out defects that affect the value. In order for the sale to be successfully completed, both parties must reach agreement or compromise about a reasonable price that the buyer is willing to pay and the seller is willing to accept.

How parties position themselves before negotiations begin can be crucial to how the give and take unfolds. Public relations can play a major role in this positioning. Persuasion is an integral component of the public relations effort to bring parties into ultimate agreement. For example, using persuasion to put your organization on an equal footing with a competitor could lead to the realization that the two parties need to talk. In other words, public relations can be used as a tool leading to the alternative dispute resolution (ADR) process. ADR takes place outside the traditional courtroom and has gained acceptance among public relations professionals, the legal profession, and the public at large. ADR is typically much less expensive and often much more efficient than a traditional lawsuit.

Researchers Bryan Reber, Fritz Cropp, and Glen Cameron noted, "Public relations, based on the contingency theory, can be viewed as a constructive creator of antecedent conditions for alternative dispute resolution." They illlustrated this with a case in which public relations and legal professionals worked cooperatively to negotiate the hostile takeover bid of Conrail Inc. by the Norfolk Southern Corporation in the mid-1990s. Conrail resisted Norfolk Southern's bid to buy the company, favoring a deal tendered by the CSX Corporation that was less favorable to Conrail's stockholders. With the help of a public relations campaign coordinated by Fleishman-Hilliard, Norfolk Southern effectively persusaded their target audiences that their offer was more fiscally sound, preserved competition, and best served shipping clients. The public relations campaign, which helped sway public opinion in Norfolk Southern's favor, facilitated the negotiation process. The three companies reached a mutually beneficial agreement—CSX would purchase Conrail and immediately sell 58 percent of the rail routes and assets to Norfolk Southern.

Factors in Persuasive Communication

A number of factors are involved in persuasive communication, and public relations practitioners should be knowledgeable about each component embedded in the communication process: sender, message, channel, and receiver. The following section is a brief discussion of 10 factors related to these components: (1) audience analysis, (2) appeals to self-interest, (3) audience participation, (4) suggestions for action, (5) source credibility, (6) clarity of message, (7) content and structure of messages, (8) channels, (9) timing and context, and (10) reinforcement.

Audience Analysis

Knowledge of audience characteristics such as beliefs, attitudes, values, concerns, and lifestyles is an essential part of persuasion. It helps communicators tailor messages that are salient, answer a felt need, and provide a logical course of action. Since demographics cannot be changed and psychographics are not easily affected to a great degree by a public relations campaign, understanding such predisposing characteristics is critical to creating messages that do not conflict with those characteristics.

Basic *demographic* information, readily available through census data, can help determine an audience's age, gender, ethnicity, income, education, and geographic residence groupings. Other data, often prepared by marketing departments, provide information on a group's buying habits, disposable income, and ways of spending leisure time. Polls and surveys tap a target audience's attitudes, opinions, and concerns. Such research can reveal much about the public's resistance to some ideas, as well as its predisposition to support others.

For example, baby boomers born between the 1946 and 1964 have established their careers and are planning for impending retirement. Primary concerns include their health status and financial security. They are politically active and are heavy consumers of print media and television. Generation X, most often defined as people born between the mid-1960s and the early 1980s, on the other hand, are heavy users of new media and tend to make purchases based on technological appeal and perceptions of style. Because of their predisposition to novel, technological innovation, Generation Xers are more likely to be interested in purchasing a revolutionary automobile during the first model year than boomers or seniors.

Another audience-analysis tool is *psychographics*. This method attempts to classify people by lifestyle, attitudes, values, and beliefs. The Values and Lifestyle Program, popularly known as VALS, was developed by SRI International, a research organization in Menlo Park, California. VALS is routinely used in public relations to help communicators structure persuasive messages to different elements of the population. A good illustration is the way Burson-Marsteller used VALS for the National Turkey Foundation. The client's problem was simple: how to encourage turkey consumption throughout the year, not just at Thanksgiving and Christmas.

One element of the public was called "sustainers and survivors"; VALS identified them as low-income, poorly educated, often elderly people who ate at erratic hours, consumed inexpensive foods, and seldom ate out. Another element was the "belongers," who were highly family oriented and served foods in traditional ways. The "achievers" were those who were more innovative and willing to try new foods.

Burson-Marsteller tailored a strategy for each group. For survivors and sustainers, the message stressed bargain cuts of turkey that could be stretched into a full meal. The message for belongers focused on cuts traditionally associated with turkey, such as drumsticks. Achievers, who were better educated and had higher income levels, received messages about gourmet cuts and new, innovative recipes.

This segmentation of the consumer market into various VALS lifestyles enabled Burson-Marsteller to select appropriate media for specific story ideas. An article placed in *True Experience*, a publication reaching a population with the demographic characteristics of survivors and sustainers, was headlined "A Terrific Budget-Stretching Meal." Articles in *Better Homes and Gardens* with such titles as "Streamlined Summer Classics" and stories about barbecued turkey on the Fourth of July were used to reach belongers. Articles for achievers in *Food and Wine* and *Gourmet* magazines included recipes for turkey salad and turkey tetrazzini.

Other key characteristics include positioning and preferences of the public concerning an issue. Some audience characteristics are situational and specific to a given time point. Public relations professionals usually analyze the audience as a component of situational analysis at the beginning of public relations programs. For example, alumni are likely to support the university's football team if the team has had a winning season. If it has been a losing season, the university's public relations department may want to build support by stressing how it was a rebuilding year and demonstrate how promising recruits or changes in the coaching staff bode well for next season.

Appeals to Self-Interest

Self-interest was discussed earlier with regard to the formation of public opinion. Publics become involved in issues or pay attention to messages that appeal to their psychological, economic, or situational needs. For example, a cosmetics company may want to emphasize the antiaging effects of a new face cream. The company's messages may include testimonials from a well-known actress who appeals to the demographic group that they wish to target. If they wish to market the product to younger women, they might seek to employ Halle Berry as spokesperson, or Meryl Streep if they wish to reach an older demographic.

Appeals to self-interest are also used by charitable organizations to increase donations. While charities don't sell products, they do need volunteers and donations. Charities increase effectiveness of their appeals by carefully structuring their messages to highlight what volunteers or donors might receive in return. This is not to say that altruism is dead. Thousands of people give freely of their time and money to charitable organizations, but they do receive something in return. The "something in return" may be self-esteem, ego gratification, recognition from peers and the community, a sense of belonging, the opportunity to make a contribution to society, or even a tax deduction. Public relations people understand these psychological needs and rewards, and that is why there is always recognition of volunteers in newsletters and at award banquets.

Sociologist Harold Lasswell says that people are motivated by eight basic appeals. They are power, respect, well-being, affection, wealth, skill, enlightenment, and physical and mental vitality. Psychologist Abraham Maslow, in turn, says that any appeal to self-interest must be based on a hierarchy of needs. The first and lowest level involves basic needs such as food, water, shelter, and even such things as transportation to and from work. The second level consists of security needs. People need to feel secure in their jobs, safe in their homes, and confident about their retirement. At the third level are "belonging" needs—people seek association with others. This is why individuals join organizations or communities. "Love" needs comprise the fourth level of the hierarchy. Humans have a need to be wanted and loved—fulfilling the desire for self-esteem. At the fifth and highest level in Maslow's hierarchy are self-actualization needs. Once the first four need levels have been met, Maslow says that people are free to achieve maximum personal potential; for example, through traveling extensively or perhaps becoming a recognized expert on orchids.

Maslow's hierarchy helps to explain why some public information campaigns have difficulty getting their messages across to people classified in the VALS categories as "survivors" and "sustainers." Efforts to inform low-income groups about AIDS provide an example of this problem. For these groups, the potential danger of AIDS is less compelling than the day-to-day problems of poverty and satisfying the basic needs of food and shelter.

The challenge for public relations personnel, as creators of persuasive messages, is to tailor information to create, fill, or reduce a need. Social scientists have said that success in persuasion largely depends on accurate assessment of audience needs and their self-interests.

Audience Participation

A change in attitude or reinforcement of beliefs is enhanced by audience involvement and participation. Nineteenth-century showman P. T. Barnum recognized the power of audience participation. He observed that many people were willing to pay admission to see obvious hoaxes, such as the "Feejee mermaid" (a stuffed monkey sewn to the tail of a fish), because they enjoyed the process of exposing the "humbuggery" to their presumably less sophisticated companions.

Today, audience participation can take many forms. For example, an organization may have employees discuss productivity in a quality-control circle. Management may already have figured out what is needed, but if workers are involved in the problem solving, they often come up with the same solution or even a better one. Employees are more committed to making the solution work because they participated in the decision-making process—instead of in response to a policy or order handed down by higher management.

Participation also takes the form of samples that companies distribute to let consumers try a product without expense. Consumers who sample a product and make a judgment about its quality are more likely to purchase it. Many companies distribute product samples through the mail. Procter & Gamble distributed a small box of Tide laundry detergent with new washing machines so consumers could conveniently try it for free. Computer manufacturers are particularly attuned to this strategy. Dell Inc., for example, offers a trial version of Microsoft Office with its home computers and laptops. The software works for a limited period of time before the consumer must pay to register it.

Activist groups use participation as a way of helping people actualize their beliefs. Not only do rallies and demonstrations give people a sense of belonging, but the act of participation also reinforces their beliefs. The 1995 Million Man March held in Washington, D.C., provides an excellent example of grassroots participation. The event, modeled on the historic March on Washington at which Martin Luther King, Jr. addressed the nation a generation earlier, mobilized African American men around a variety of social justice issues. Asking people to do something, such as conserve energy, collect donations, or picket, activates a form of self actualization and commitment.

Suggestions for Action

A principle of persuasion is that people endorse ideas and take actions only if they are accompanied by a proposed action from the sponsor. Recommendations for action must be clear to follow. Public relations practitioners not only must ask people to conserve energy, for instance, but also furnish detailed data and ideas about how to do it.

A campaign conducted by Pacific Gas & Electric Company provides an example. The utility inaugurated a Zero Interest Program (ZIP) to offer customers a way to implement energy-saving ideas. The program involved several components:

> *Energy Kit*. A telephone hotline was established and widely publicized so interested customers could order an energy kit detailing what the average homeowner could do to reduce energy use.
> *Service Bureau*. The company, at no charge, sent representatives to homes to check the efficiency of water heaters and furnaces, measure the amount of insulation, and check doors and windows for drafts.
> *ZIP*. The cost of making a home more energy efficient was funded by zero-interest loans to qualified customers.

Source Credibility

A message is more believable to an intended audience if the source has credibility with that audience. This recalls Aristotle's concept of ethos, mentioned earlier, and it explains why organizations use a variety of spokespeople, depending on the message and intended target audience. Such consistency theories as balance theory or congruity theory suggest that attitude change can be stimulated by information that leads people to recognize conflicting attitudes. The persuasiveness of the source is a major factor in stimulating a revised attitude

Source credibility is based on three factors. One is *expertise*. Does the audience perceive the person as an expert on the subject? The California Strawberry Advisory Board, for example, arranged for a home economist to appear on television talk shows to discuss nutrition and to demonstrate easy-to-follow strawberry recipes. The viewers, primarily homemakers, identified with the representative and found her highly credible. By the same token, a manufacturer of sunscreen lotion used a professor of pharmacology and a past president of the State Pharmacy Board to discuss the scientific merits of its sunscreen versus other suntan lotions.

The second component is *sincerity*. Does the person come across as believing what he or she is saying? Christopher Kennedy Lawford's book *Symptoms of Withdrawal* has been widely hailed as an honest portrayal of drug and alcohol addiction. On the other hand, author James Frey's memoir on a similar subject, *A Million Little Pieces*, was exposed as containing fabrications. Nevertheless, the apparent sincerity of his descriptions of his struggle with drug addiction made the book a best seller before the fraud was exposed.

The third component, which is even more elusive, is *charisma*. Is the individual attractive, self-assured, and articulate, projecting an image of competence and leadership? President Bill Clinton is an excellent example. His commanding presence and polished public speaking made him a charismatic figure. Clinton's approval rating remained high even in the midst of several scandals, including impeachment over the Monica Lewinsky affair. Throughout his presidency, Clinton projected an aura of authenticity.

Expertise is less important than sincerity and charisma if celebrities are used as spokespersons. Their primary purpose is to call attention to a product or service rather than provide the audience with in-depth information. Another purpose is to associate the celebrity's popularity with the product. This technique is called *transfer*, which is a propaganda device.

Using celebrities has its problems, however. One is sheer number of celebrity endorsements, to the point that the public sometimes can't remember who endorses what. A second problem can be overexposure of a celebrity, such as Tiger Woods, who earns millions of dollars annually from endorsing more than a dozen products.

The third problem occurs when an endorser's actions undercut the product or service. When basketball star Kobe Bryant was charged with sexual assault in 2003, he failed to heed the advice of public relations professionals that he keep a low public profile. Instead, Bryant immediately held a press conference. With his wife by his side, he made an emotional public appeal proclaiming his innocence. Lawyer Roy Black commended Bryant's sincerity and apparent honesty, something that apparently helped convince the jury to rule in his favor. Even though Bryant was eventually acquitted of rape, the subsequent negative publicity, compounded by his numerous public appearances outside the courtroom, led McDonald's to drop him as a spokesperson for the company. Bryant also signed a $40 million contract to promote Nike athletic wear shortly before he was accused of sexual assault. Nike honored the contract after his acquittal, yet it was more than two years before the first ad for the shoe company featuring Bryant appeared.

"Anytime an advertiser pins its image to a star, whether an athlete or an actor, it takes a chance that reality won't live up to the storyboard," says Christina White, a reporter for the *Wall Street Journal*. Even when celebrities have not been involved in scandals, their endorsements can have negative effects on the marketing of products. The NPD Group, a consumer marketing company, reported that Donald Trump and Paris Hilton had very high recognition factors, but tended to negatively affect the public's decision to buy products that they endorsed. Sometimes, celebrities weather controversy relatively unscathed. For example, Martha Stewart's reputation as a domestic diva has remained intact despite conviction for perjury and a prison stay. Although sales of her magazine and products bearing her name suffered briefly, they have since rebounded. See Case Study in Chapter 7 about Martha Stewart Michael Jordan continues to endorse products even after being accused of adultery, illegal gambling, and a disastrous turn as a major league baseball player.

Studies show that the impact of a persuasive message will generally tend to decrease over time. The sleeper effect predicts that a message from a low-credibility source can actually increase in persuasiveness under the right circumstances. Low credibility may be caused by a discounting cue, such as when a government official predicts improving economic conditions, because he or she is presumed to be biased. However, the message may gain credibility when dissociated from its source.

Clarity of Message

Many messages fail because the audience finds them unnecessarily complex in content or language. The most persuasive messages are direct, simply expressed, and contain only one primary idea. Management expert Peter Drucker once said, "An innovation, to be effective, has to be simple and it has to be focused. It should do only one thing, otherwise it confuses." The same can be said for the content of any message.

Public relations personnel should always ask two questions: Will the audience understand the message? and What do I want the audience to do with the message? Although persuasion theory says that people retain information better and form stronger opinions when they are asked to draw their own conclusions, this doesn't negate the importance of explicitly stating what action an audience should take. Is it to buy the product, visit a showroom, write a member of Congress, make a $10 donation?

If an explicit request for action is not part of the message, members of the audience may not understand what is expected of them. Public relations firms, when making a presentation to a potential client, always ask specifically for the account at the end of the presentation.

Content and Structure of Messages

A number of techniques can make a message more persuasive. Persuasive messages emphasize some information while downplaying or omitting other pieces of information. Thus, both the content and structure of messages is important. Expert communicators continue to use a number of devices, including drama, surveys and polls, statistics, examples, mass media endorsements, and emotional appeals.

Drama and Stories. The first task of a communicator is to get the audience's attention. Because everyone likes a good story, this is often accomplished by graphically illustrating an event or situation. Newspapers often dramatize a story to generate reader interest in an issue. Drama also is used in public relations. Relief organizations, in particular, attempt to galvanize public concern and donations through stark black-and-white photographs and emotionally charged descriptions of suffering and disease. The Red Cross used dramatic images of relief efforts in the wake of Hurricane Katrina to encourage donations.

Surveys and Polls. Airlines and auto manufacturers, in particular, use the results of surveys and polls to show that they are first in "customer satisfaction," "service," and even "leg room" or "cargo space." The most credible surveys are those conducted by independent research organizations, but readers still should read the fine print to see what is being compared and rated. Is an American-made auto, for example, being compared only with other U.S. cars or with foreign cars as well?

Statistics. People are often impressed by statistics. Use of numbers can convey objectivity, size, and importance in a credible way that can influence public opinion. Caterpillar, for example, got considerable media publicity for its new 797 mining dump truck by combining statistics and some humor. In the news release for the largest truck in the world, it announced that the bed of the truck was so large that it could haul the following payloads: 4 blue whales, 217 taxicabs, 1,200 grand pianos, or 23,490 Furby dolls.

Examples. A statement of opinion can be more persuasive if some examples are given. A school board can often get support for a bond issue by citing examples of how present facilities are inadequate for student needs. Environmental groups tell how other communities have successfully established greenbelts when requesting a city council to do the same. Automakers promote the durability of their vehicles by citing performance data on a test track or in a road race.

Endorsements. In addition to endorsements by paid celebrities, products and services benefit from favorable statements by experts in what is called a third-party endorsement. A well-known medical specialist may publicly state that a particular brand of exercise equipment is best for general conditioning. Organizations such as the American Dental Association and the National Safety Council also endorse products and services. Media endorsements, usually unpaid, can come through editorials, reviews, surveys, and news stories. A daily newspaper may endorse a political candidate, review restaurants and entertainment events, and even compile a survey ranking the best local coffee houses. The media also produce news stories about new products and services that, because of the media's perceived objectivity, are considered a form of third-party endorsement.

Causes and Rationales. People tend to accept social ideas, norms, or practices in a group or society, forging a psychological connection to the community or society. Public relations professionals should assess and understand the social norms of a target audience to provide messages that emphasize tangible social benefits. By advocating a cause that taps into social norms and one that an audience is passionate about, public relations personnel can reach the audience and generate tremendous goodwill. Positive media attention benefiting the public relation professional's client is, in effect, a side effect. For example, an athletic footwear company that sponsors a breast cancer awareness event such as a walkathon builds good faith with potential consumers whose norms support better health.

Emotional Appeals. Fund-raising letters from nonprofit groups, in particular, use this persuasive device. Amnesty International, an organization dedicated to human rights and fighting state terrorism, began one direct mail letter with the following message in large red type:

> We Are God in Here . . .
> . . . That's what the guards taunted the prisoner with as they applied electrical shocks to her body while she lay handcuffed to the springs of a metal bed. Her cries were echoed by the screams of other victims and the laughter of their torturers.

Such emotional appeals can do much to galvanize the public into action, but they also can backfire. They raise ego defenses, and people don't like to be told that in some way they are responsible. A description of suffering makes many people uncomfortable, and, rather than take action, they may tune out the message.

Compared with other appeals such as humor or homespun familiarity, fear causes a stronger emotional reaction. However, strong fear appeals also can cause people to tune out, especially if they feel that they can't do anything about a problem anyway. Research indicates, however, that moderate fear appeal, accompanied by a relatively easy solution, is effective. An example of a moderate fear appeal is: What would happen if your child were thrown through the windshield in an accident? The message concludes with the suggestion that a baby, for protection and safety, should be placed in a secure infant seat.

Humor appeals are also effective at enhancing attention, message comprehension, and recall. For example, Miller Lite's "Brought to you by Dick" campaign revitalized the brand by poking fun at commercials that use traditional tactics such as Unique Selling Proposition (USP). Consumers view self-deprecating humor, a tactic pioneered in the mid-1980s by the car manufacturers VW in England and by Isuzu in the United States, as a refreshing change from advertisements that tout their wares with a serious tone.

Channels

Different media with different features can be used for diverse public relations purposes. Television is visual, sensational, and entertaining. Newspapers offer a lot of in-depth information and discuss conflicting views. Radio offers talks shows, is flexible or adaptable in format and content, and is accessible to people almost any place any time. Radio reaches target audiences quickly, making it an effective means of communication in crisis situations. However, face-to-face communication is often more effective than mass media. According to communication scholar, Steve H. Chaffee, people seek information from available sources, and interpersonal sources often are effective ways to reach people, even through word of mouth. For example, a company president speaking with employees who are threatening to strike may encourage a compromise through a personal appeal, whereas a mass-media message could make the employees angrier by interrupted messages, confused interpretation or the impersonal nature of the statements.

A variety of channels can also help messages penetrate to the audience and reinforce their persuasiveness. For example, news releases in print can be delivered to journalists or editors by carrier, fax, mail, and e-mail, while calls can be used to confirm that the messages are reaching media personnel.

Timing and Context

A message is more persuasive if environmental factors support the message or if the message is received within the context of other messages and situations with which the individual is familiar. These factors are called *timing* and *context*.

Information from a utility on how to conserve energy is more salient if the consumer has just received the January heating bill. A pamphlet on a new stock offering is more effective if it accompanies an investor's dividend check. A citizens' group lobbying for a stoplight gets more attention if a major accident has just occurred at the intersection in question.

Political candidates are aware of public concerns and avidly read polls to learn what issues are most important to voters. If the polls indicate that crime and unemployment are key issues, the candidate begins to use these issues—and to offer his or her proposals—in the campaign.

Timing and context also play an important role in achieving publicity in the mass media. Public relations personnel should read newspapers and watch television news programs to find out what media gatekeepers consider newsworthy. A manufacturer of a locking device for computer files got extensive media coverage about its product simply because its release followed a rash of news stories about thieves' gaining access to bank accounts through computers. Gatekeepers found the product newsworthy within the media's agenda resulting from actual news events. The value of information and its newsworthiness are based on timing and context. Public relations professionals should disseminate information at the time when it is most highly valued.

Reinforcement

Public relations professionals working on campaigns that attemp to influence public opinion on controversial and emotional issues will find cognitive dissonance a serious barrier. People tend to ignore or react negatively to messages that conflict with their value or belief systems. It is unlikely that a public relations campaign that is out of sync with an audience's core beliefs will be successful. Thus, it is important for public relations professionals to have a firm understanding of core values and design messages that reinforce the audience's outlook.

The concept of selective exposure, which suggests that people seek and support messages that support currently held beliefs and avoid those that challenge these attitudes, should be kept in mind as well. Beliefs and attitudes that are not fully formed can be affected by persuasive messages; however, long-established values are particularly resistant to change. Attitudes that have been tested are more resistant to change.

— ON THE JOB >>

Motivation–Ability–Opportunity Model for Enhancing
Message Processing

Insights

The following chart summarizes the various communication strategies that can be used to reach publics who have little knowledge or interest in a particular issue, product, or service. The object, of course, is to structure persuasive messages that attract their attention.

ENHANCE MOTIVATION	ENHANCE ABILITY	ENHANCE OPPORTUNITY
Attract and Encourage Audiences to Commence, Continue Processing	**Make It Easier to Process the Message by Tapping Cognitive Resources**	**Structure Messages to Optimize Processing**

Attract and Encourage Audiences to Commence, Continue Processing

Create attractive, likable messages (create affect)

Appeal to hedonistic needs (sex, appetite, safety)

Use novel stimuli:
> Photos
> Typography
> Oversized formats
> Large number of scenes, elements
> Changes in voice, silence, movement

Make the most of formal features:
> Format size
> Music
> Color

Include key points in headlines

Use moderately complex messages

Use sources who are credible, attractive, or similar to audience

Involve celebrities

Enhance relevance to audience—ask them to think about a question

Use stories, anecdotes, or drama to draw into action

Stimulate curiosity: Use humor, metaphors, questions

Vary language, format, source

Use multiple, ostensibly independent sources

Make It Easier to Process the Message by Tapping Cognitive Resources

Include background, definitions, explanations

Be simple, clear

Use advance organizers (e.g., headlines)

Include synopses

Combine graphics, text, and narration (dual coding of memory traces)

Use congruent memory cues (same format as original)

Label graphics (helps identify which attributes to focus on)

Use specific, concrete (versus abstract) words and images

Include exemplars, models

Make comparison with analogies

Show actions, train audience skills through demonstrations

Include marks (logos, logotypes, trademarks), slogans, and symbols as continuity devices

Appeal to self-schemas (roles, what's important to audience's identity)

Enhance perceptions of self-efficacy to perform tasks

Place messages in conducive environment (priming effects)

Frame Stories Using Culturally Resonating Themes, Catchphrases

Structure Messages to Optimize Processing

Expend sufficient effort to provide information

Repeat messages frequently

Repeat key points within text—in headlines, text, captions, illustrations, etc.

Use longer messages

Include multiple arguments

Feature "interactive" illustrations, photos

Avoid distractions:
> Annoying music
> Excessively attractive spokespersons
> Complex arguments
> Disorganized layouts

Allow audiences to control pace of processing

Provide sufficient time

Keep pace lively and avoid audience boredom

Source: Kirk Hallahan. "Enhancing Motivation, Ability, and Opportunity to Process Public Relations Messages." *Public Relations Review* 26, no. 4 (2000): 463–480.

— ON THE JOB >> —

Propaganda

Insights

No discussion of persuasion would be complete without mentioning propaganda and the techniques associated with it. In their book *Propaganda and Persuasion*, Garth S. Jowett and Victoria O'Donnell say, "Propaganda is the deliberate and systematic attempt to shape perceptions, manipulate cognitions, and direct behavior to achieve a response that furthers the desired intent of the propagandist." Its roots go back to the 17th century, when the Roman Catholic Church set up the Congregatio de Propaganda Fide ("congregation for propagating the faith"). During World Wars I and II, propaganda was associated with the information activities of the enemy. Nazi Germany even had a State Ministry for Public Englightenment and Propaganda headed by Dr. Joseph Goebbels. The U.S., of course, had its own propaganda operations during the wars.

Today, propaganda connotes falsehood, lies, deceit, disinformation, and duplicity—practices that opposing groups and governments accuse each other of employing. Advertising and public relations messages for commercial purposes do use several techniques commonly associated with propaganda. Patricia Curtin at the Univeristy of Oregon and T. Kenn Gaither at Elon University trace the historical definition of public relations from propaganda to strategic counsel. She implies that propaganda is a strong form of public relations for the invested interest of organization or individuals. The most common propaganda techniques are the following:

> *Plain Folks.* An approach often used by individuals to show humble beginnings and empathy with the average citizen. Political candidates, in particular, are quite fond of telling about their "humble" beginnings. Haley Barbour, governor of Mississippi, was particularly effective in contrasting his humble beginnings in Yazoo City with those of his opponents, whom he cast as careerists and insiders.

> *Testimonial.* A frequently used device to achieve source credibility, as discussed earlier. A well-known expert, popular celebrity, or average citizen gives testimony about the value of a product or the wisdom of a decision. For example, Omega associates the stylishness of their watches with the image of a high-fashion model, indicating in a print ad that their Constellation model is "Cindy Crawford's Choice." The controversial Scientology movement relies largely on celebrity testimonials from actors such as Tom Cruise and John Travolta to recruit converts.

> *Bandwagon.* The implication or direct statement that everyone wants the product or that the idea has overwhelming support encourages people to agree with the idea; for example, "Millions of Americans support a ban on abortion" or "Four out of five dentists agree. . . "

> *Card Stacking.* The selection of facts and data to build an overwhelming case on one side of the issue, while concealing the other side. For instance, the advertising industry had argued a ban on beer advertising would lead to enormous reductions in network sports programming and a ban on cigarette advertising would kill many magazines.

> *Transfer.* The technique of associating the person, product, or organization with something that has high status, visibility, or credibility. Many corporations, for example, have paid millions to be official sponsors of the 2008 Olympic Games, hoping that the public would associate their products with excellence and the spirit of the games.

> *Glittering Generalities.* The technique of associating a cause, product, or idea with favorable abstractions such as freedom, justice, democracy, and the American way. The White House named its military action in the Middle East "Operation Iraqi Freedom" and American oil companies argue for offshore drilling to "keep America energy independent."

Public relations professionals should be aware of these techniques to make certain that they don't intentionally use them to deceive and mislead the public. Ethical responsibilities exist in every form of persuasive communication.

Public relations professionals can use such innoculated attitudes to create resistance to potentially opposing arguments or negative publicity. In a crisis situation, such innoculation accompanied by tested beliefs will help a public figure or a company get through a crisis and maintain their prior reputation.

Limitation of Persuasion

In reality, the effectiveness of persuasive techniques is greatly exaggerated. Persuasion is not an exact science, and no surefire way exists to predict that people or media gatekeepers will be persuaded to believe a message or act on it. If persuasive techniques were as refined as the critics say, all people would be driving the same make of automobile, using the same soap, and voting for the same political candidate. In practice, the ability to persuade is contingent on a complex set of factors as opposed to persuasive messages that translate directly into behavior. Conflicting and competing messages frequently interrupt or cancel one another through a course of ongoing communication, given the freedom of receivers to be selective or even apathetic regarding particular messages.

For purposes of discussion, the limitations on effective persuasive messages can be listed as lack of message penetration, competing messages, self-selection, and self-perception.

Lack of Message Penetration

Despite modern communication technologies, the diffusion of messages is not pervasive. Not everyone, of course, watches the same television programs or reads the same newspapers and magazines. Not everyone receives the same mail or attends the same meetings. Not everyone the communicator wants to reach will be in the eventual audience. Despite advances in audience-segmentation techniques, communicators cannot ensure that 100 percent of their intended audiences will be reached. There is also the problem of message distortion as messages pass through media gatekeepers such as reporters and editors. Key message points often are left out, buried among less relevant information or placed in ineffective contexts, or even delivered in an unintended or negative way.

Competing or Conflicting Messages

Today, communication experts realize that no message is received in a vacuum. Messages are filtered through receivers' entire social structures and belief systems. Nationality, race, religion, gender, cultural patterns, family, and friends are among the variables that filter and dilute persuasive messages. Social scientists say a person usually conforms to the standards of his or her family and friends. Consequently, most people do not believe or act on messages that are contrary to the norms of their peer group. In addition, people receive countless competing and conflicting messages daily, which often diffuses the persuasiveness of the message.

Self-Selection

The people most wanted in an audience are often the least likely to be there. Vehement supporters or loyalists frequently ignore information from the other side. They do so by being selective in the messages that they want to hear. They read

Insights

Don'ts in Persuasion

Public relations professionals, by definition, are advocates for clients and employers. The emphasis is on persuasive communication that presents a selective message so as to influence a particular public in some way. At the same time, public relations practitioners must conduct their activities in an ethical manner.

Persuasive messages require truth, honesty, and candor for two practical reasons. First, as noted by Robert Heath, a professor at the University of Texas–Houston, a message is already suspect because it is advanced on behalf of a client or organization. Second, half-truths and misleading information do not serve the best interests of the public or the organization. The use of persuasive techniques, therefore, calls for some additional guidelines. Professor Richard L. Johannesen of Northern Illinois University, writing in *Persuasion:*

Reception and Responsibility, a text by Charles Larson, lists the following ethical criteria for using persuasive devices that should be kept in mind by every public relations professional:

> Do not use false, fabricated, misrepresented, distorted, or irrelevant evidence to support arguments or claims.
> Do not intentionally use specious, unsupported, or illogical reasoning.
> Do not represent yourself as informed or as an "expert" on a subject when you are not.
> Do not use irrelevant appeals to divert attention or scrutiny from the issue at hand. Among the appeals that commonly serve such a purpose are smear attacks on an opponent's character and appeals to hatred and bigotry or innuendo.
> Do not ask your audience to link your idea or proposal to emotion-laden values, motives, or goals to which it actually is not related.

> Do not deceive your audience by concealing your real purpose, your self-interest, the group you represent, or your position as an advocate of a viewpoint.
> Do not distort, hide, or misrepresent the number, scope, intensity, or undesirable features of consequences.
> Do not use emotional appeals that lack a supporting basis of evidence or reasoning or that would not be accepted if the audience had time and opportunity to examine the subject itself.
> Do not oversimplify complex situations into simplistic, two-valued, either–or, polar views or choices.
> Do not pretend certainty when tentativeness and degrees of probability would be more accurate.
> Do not advocate something in which you do not believe yourself.

books, newspaper editorials, and magazine articles and view television programs that support their predispositions. This is why social scientists say that the media are more effective in reinforcing existing attitudes than in changing them.

Self-Perception

Self-perception is the channel through which messages are interpreted. People will perceive the same information differently, depending on predispositions and preexisting opinions. The newsletter *Inside PR* describes how people react to news stories: "If they believe something to be true and see a story affirming that belief, their belief is strengthened. If they believe something to be true and see a story challenging that belief, they assume the story is biased or just plain wrong." Thus, depending on a person's views, an action by an organization may be considered a "great contribution to the community" or a "self-serving gimmick." Social judgment theory suggests that these internal factors such as beliefs, attitudes, or values will limit the extent to which an individual accepts or rejects a persuasive message.

ON THE JOB >>

Censorship of Google, Yahoo!, and Microsoft in China

Global

Launching into a global market poses public relations opportunities and challenges because of the different and often conflicting cultures, values, norms, rules, and laws. Should entry into a market lead to a compromise of one's existing values? Is freedom of expression, for example, an ethical obligation or should public relations professionals respect the sovereignty and laws of a host country? Google, Yahoo!, and Microsoft have expanded operations into the emerging Chinese market, a step complicated by the country's strict censorship rules. Each company has been criticized in the media. In order to restore their images, each company will need to demonstrate that their presence can have a beneficial effect on China's censorship laws. The companies can hardly succeed in a foreign market unless they can win the court of public opinion at home.

The market for Internet service in China holds enormous profit potential for U.S. computer software and support corporations. With 110 million current Internet users (second only to the United States) and a population estimated at over 1.3 billion as of July 2006, the potential for growth in China is staggering. Thus, it is comes as little surprise that Yahoo!, Google, and Microsoft were eager to sign deals with the Chinese government to provide Internet service and support. However, the decision comes at a cost.

At the crux of the issue is the Chinese government's insistence that all online activity be subject to scrutiny by the Public Security Bureau, composed of 30,000 "Internet police." Yahoo! and Google have been accused of censoring search results and "naming names," and Microsoft has taken fire for shutting sites deemed offensive by the Chinese government. As a result of the public relations crisis, Google stock lost 25 percent of its value in Feburary 2006 and the reputations of all three companies have been tar-nished. According to its critics, Google's motto, "Do No Evil," may now require a footnote.

Yahoo!, Google, and Microsoft remain adamant about their decisions to enter the Chinese market, although each has responded to public criticism and slightly amended their policies and procedures. The companies first defended their actions by arguing that Internet service with restrictions is better than no Internet service at all. Although "very distressed" by the conditions imposed by the Chinese government, Yahoo! cofounder Jerry Yang contended that the company could have great impact just by being in the market. Microsoft's stance was similar. "We think the benefits far outweigh the downside, in terms of promoting freedom of expression," said Microsoft associate general counsel Jack Krumholtz, whose sentiments were echoed by Microsoft founder Bill Gates. To help with the public relations implications, Yahoo! recently hired Porter Novelli.

Summary

What Is Public Opinion?

Public opinion can be difficult to measure; there are few if any issues on which the public (which is in fact many publics) can be said to have a unanimous opinion. In fact, only a small number of people will have opinions on any given issue. Engaging the interest of a public will involve affecting its self-interest. Publics also react strongly to events.

Opinion Leaders as Catalysts

The primary catalyst in the formation of public opinion is public discussion. People who are knowledgeable and articulate on specific issues can be either formal opinion leaders (power leaders) or informal opinion leaders (role models). Opinion "flows" from these leaders to the public, often through the mass media.

Role of Mass Media

Information from public relations sources often reach the public through mass media, defined as radio, television, newspaper, magazines, and electronic media. Agenda setting, or what people think about, affects which issues the public considers; however, agenda setting does not always determine what opinions the public holds. The mass media also frame issues insofar as journalists select certain facts and disregard others. Journalists and public relations professionals frequently use the agenda-setting process in public discourse and act as gatekeepers, subtly affecting how the public interprets issues through selectiveness and nuance.

Crucial Role of Conflict in Public Discourse

Conflict has been defined as a situation in which two or more factions perceive a divergence of interests. In public relations, conflict theory offers insight into the differences among individuals and groups and analyzes conflicts of interest, goals, desires, and values. How the media frame a conflict can influence the public toward one position or the other and escalate or de-escalate the conflict. The media play a role in unfolding conflicts and can promote public debate regarding the issue. The media also mediate or resolve conflicts in the court of public opinion by offering directions for conflict resolution.

Persuasion: Pervasive in Our Profession

The concept of persuasion has been around at least since the time of the ancient Greeks. The dominant view of public relations is of persuasive communications on behalf of clients. Persuasion can be used to change or neutralize hostile opinions, crystallize latent opinions and positive attitudes, and conserve favorable opinions.

Factors in Persuasive Communication

Factors involved in persuasion include audience analysis, audience participation, suggestions for action, source credibility, appeal to self-interest, message clarity, content and structure of messages, timing and context, and channels.

The Limitation of Persuasion

There are two practical reasons for an ethical approach to persuasive messages. First, publics will automatically have a level of suspicion because they know the communicator is promoting a client or organization. Second, the interests of that client or organization will not be well served by false or misleading communications.

CASE ACTIVITY >>
What Would You Do?

The school system of a major city wants to draw attention to the need for more volunteer adult tutors in the city's 200 public schools. Budget cutbacks in teaching staff and other resources have made it a vital necessity to recruit volunteers who will work with students on an individual basis to improve reading and math skills.

Your public relations firm has volunteered to organize a public information campaign. Explain what you would do in each of the following categories that relate to the structure and content of persuasive messages: drama, statistics, examples, testimonials, endorsements, and emotional appeals.

Questions for Review and Discussion

1. Public opinion is highly influenced by self-interest and events. What are these concepts?
2. What is the importance of opinion leaders in the formation of public opinion?
3. What is the role of media in the formation of public opinion?
4. What are the stages of public opinion?
5. Name the three objectives of persuasion in public relations work. What objective is the most difficult to accomplish?
6. Can you name and describe the nine factors involved in persuasive communication?
7. What are three factors involved in source credibility?
8. What are the pros and cons of using celebrities for product endorsements?
9. What are the levels of Maslow's hierarchy of needs? Why is it important for public relations people to understand people's basic needs?
10. Why is audience involvement and participation important in persuasion?

11. What techniques can be used to write persuasive messages?
12. Name several propaganda techniques. Should they be used by public relations people?
13. What are some ethical responsibilities of a person who uses persuasion techniques to influence others?

Suggested Readings

Arpan, Laura, M., and David R. Rosks-Ewodsen. "Stealing Thunder: Analysis of the Effects of Proactive Disclosure of Crisis Information." *Public Relations Review* 31, no. 3 (2005): 425–433.

Curtin, Patricia A., and Eric Rhodenbaugh. "Building the News Media Agenda on the Environment: A Comparison of Public Relations and Journalistic Sources." *Public Relations Review* 27, no. 2, (Summer 2001): 179–296.

De Burton, Simon. "Fancy a Touch of Start Status: The Relationship Between Brands and Celebrities." *Financial Times,* November 14, 2004, 5.

Dougall, Elizabeth. "Revelations of an Ecological Perspective: Issues, Inertia, and the Public Opinion Environment of Organizational Populations." *Public Relations Review* 31, no. 4 (2005): 534–543.

Glynn, C. J., S. Herbst, G. J., O'Keefe, R. Y. Shapiro, and J. Lindeman. *Public Opinion.* Boulder, CO: Westview, 2004.

Gower, Karla, K. "The Fear of Public Relations in Foreign Affairs: An Examination of the 1963 Fulbright Hearings into Foreign Agents." *Public Relations Review* 31, no. 1 (2005): 37–46.

Hiebert, Ray E. "Public Relations and Propaganda: Framing the Iraq War: A Preliminary Review." *Public Relations Review* 29, no. 4 (2003): 243–255.

Keller, Ed, and Jon Berry. *The Influentials: One American in Ten Tells the Other Nine How to Vote, Where to Eat, and What to Buy.* New York: Free Press, 2003.

Newman, Kelli B. "The Power of Emotion." *Public Relations Tactics,* July 2001, 27.

Perloff, Richard M. *The Dynamics of Persuasion,* 2d ed. Mahwah, NJ: Erlbaum, 2003.

Reber, Bryan, Fritz Cropp, and Glen Cameron. "Public Relations Practitioners in a Hostile Bid for Conrail Inc. by Norfolk Southern Corporation." *Journal of Public Relations Research* 15, no. 1 (2003): 1–26.

Shin, Jae-Hwa, and Glen T. Cameron. "Different Sides of the Same Coin: Mixed Views of Public Relations Practitioners and Journalists for Strategic Conflict Management." *Journalism and Mass Communication Quarterly* 82, no. 2 (Autumn 2005): 318–338.

Chapter Seven

Ethics and the Law

> *Avoiding Libel Suits*
> *Fair Comment Defense*

> **> Protecting Employee Privacy**
> *Employee Newsletters*
> *Photo Releases*
> *Product Publicity and Advertising*
> *Media Inquiries about Employees*

> **> Copyright Law**
> *Fair Use versus Infringement*
> *Photography and Artwork*
> *The Rights of Freelance Writers*
> *Copyright Issues on the Internet*
> *Copyright Guidelines*

> **> Trademark Law**
> *Protection of Trademarks*
> *The Problem of Trademark Infringement*
> *Misappropriation of Personality*

> **> Regulations by Government Agencies**
> *Federal Trade Commission (FTC)*
> *Securities and Exchange Commission (SEC)*
> *Other Regulatory Agencies*

> **> Corporate/Employee Free Speech**
> *Employee Free Speech*

> **> Liability for Sponsored Events**
> *Plant Tours and Open Houses*
> *Promotional Events*

> **> Working with Lawyers**

Today's public relations practitioners are faced with myriad ethical dilemmas and legal issues. A well-prepared professional grapples continually with these issues. In this chapter, we examine some of the ethical concerns and legal issues facing public relations practitioners.

What Are Ethics?

James Jaksa and Michael Pritchard provide a good definition of ethics in their book *Communication Ethics: Methods of Analysis*. "Ethics," they say, "is concerned with how we should live our lives. It focuses on questions about what is right or wrong, fair or unfair, caring or uncaring, good or bad, responsible or irresponsible, and the like."

A person's conduct is measured not only against his or her conscience but also against some norm of acceptability that has been determined by society, professional groups, or even a person's employer. The difficulty in ascertaining whether an act is ethical lies in the fact that individuals have different standards and perceptions of what is "right" or "wrong." Most ethical conflicts are not black or white, but fall into a gray area.

A person's belief system can also determine how that person acts in a specific situation. Philosophers say that the three basic value orientations are

1. *Absolutist*. The absolutist believes that every decision is either right or wrong, regardless of the consequences.
2. *Existentialist*. The existentialist, whose choices are not made in a prescribed value system, decides on the basis of immediate practical choice.
3. *Situationalist*. The situationalist believes that each decision is based on what would cause the least harm or the most good. This often is called the *utilitarian approach*.

Public relations professionals have the burden of making ethical decisions that satisfy (1) the public interest, (2) their employer, (3) their professional organization's code of ethics, and (4) their personal values. In an ideal world, these four spheres would not conflict. In reality, however, they often do.

In her book *Legal and Ethical Restraints on Public Relations*, University of Alabama professor Karla Gower wrote:

> Ethics is the study of right and wrong behavior. When faced with an ethical dilemma, the first step is to determine the values in competition or paradigms at work, such as truth versus loyalty, individual versus community. The second step is to decide which of three approaches would be the best one in the circumstances: a rule-based, an ends-based, or a care-based approach.

The Ethical Advocate

What would you do if you're asked to keep news about a planned layoff from your coworkers? What if your supervisor asked you to defend your company's questionable environmental practices? What if your client asked you to make positive, but unsubstantiated, claims about a new product. Because public relations practitioners serve as advocates for their organizations or clients, these actions might seem appropriate. But because practitioners also strive to represent the interests of various stakeholders in their organizations, difficult ethical issues are bound to arise.

Students, as well as public relations critics, are often concerned about whether a public relations practitioner can ethically communicate at the same time he or she is serving as an advocate for a particular client or organization. To some, traditional ethics prohibit a person from taking an advocacy role because that person is "biased" and trying to "manipulate" people.

David L. Martinson of Florida International University makes the point in a monograph published by the public relations division of the Association for Education in Journalism and Mass Communications, however, that the concept of role differentiation is important. This means that society, in general, expects public relations people to be advocates, just as they expect advertising copywriters to make a product sound attractive, journalists to be objective, and attorneys to defend someone in court. Because of such expectations, Martinson believes that "[P]ublic relations practitioners are justified in disseminating persuasive information so long as objective and reasonable persons would view those persuasive efforts as truthful." Martinson continues,

> Reasonable persons recognize that public relations practitioners can serve important societal goals in an advocacy (role defined) capacity. What reasonable persons require, however, is that such advocacy efforts be directed toward genuinely informing impacted publics. Communication efforts . . . will not attempt, for example, to present

false/deceptive/misleading information under the guise of literal truth no matter how strongly the practitioner wants to convince others of the merits of a particular client/organization's position/cause. . . . Role differentiation is not a license to "lie, cheat, and/or steal" on behalf of clients whether one is an attorney, physician, or public relations practitioner.

Some public relations theorists have argued that pure advocacy—that is, unwavering support for the organization's or client's position—is unethical. They suggest that the most ethical way to practice public relations is to consider accommodating the needs of both organizations and their publics.

Contingency theory (Chapter 2) takes a more nuanced view. From this perspective, public relations practitioners sometimes face a categorical imperative, or moral obligation, to advocate purely for the organization's position. For example, what would the ethical advocate representing the cattle industry do when faced with demands from People for the Ethical Treatment of Animals (PETA) to stop producing beef products? Would the ethical advocate, a person who works for the cattle industry because he or she believes in modern agriculture's role in feeding the world, attempt to find ways to accommodate PETA's demands or would he or she continue to purely advocate for cattle-raising clients? Instances frequently arise when conflict between an organization and its publics is unavoidable due to a clash of worldviews. To accommodate the demands of a public, such as PETA, would be unethical when a categorical moral imperative to advocate for your organization or client drives professional decisions.

The Role of Professional Organizations

Professional organizations such as the Public Relations Society of America (PRSA) and the International Association of Business Communicators (IABC) have worked to develop standards of ethical, professional public relations practice and to help society understand the role of public relations. See examples of codes of ethics in the Insights boxes on pages 206 and 207. Professionals and public relations scholars alike suggest that professional organizations can play a key and powerful role in advancing ethical practice.

Professional Codes of Conduct

Nearly every national public relations organization has a code of ethics, and the codes of such organizations as the Canadian Public Relations Society (CPRS), the Public Relations Institute of Southern Africa (PRISA), and the Public Relations Institute of Australia (PRIA) are very similar to the PRSA code.

Most national organizations place heavy emphasis on educating their members on professional standards rather than having a highly structured grievance process in place. They do exercise the right, however, to censure or expel members who violate the organization's code or who are convicted of a crime in a court of law.

The IABC's code is based on the principle that professional communication is not only legal and ethical but also in good taste and sensitive to cultural values and beliefs. Members are encouraged to be truthful, accurate, and fair in all of their communications.

The code is published in several languages, and IABC bylaws require that articles on ethics and professional conduct be published in the organization's monthly publication, *Communication World*. In addition, the organization includes sessions on ethics at its annual meeting, conducts workshops on ethics, and encourages chapters to

ON THE JOB >>

PRSA's Code of Ethics

Insights

The Public Relations Society of America (PRSA) has a fairly comprehensive code of ethics for its members. The group believes that "professional values are vital to the integrity of the profession as a whole."

Its six core values are as follows:

1. *Advocacy:* Serving the public interest by acting as responsible advocates for clients or employers.
2. *Honesty:* Adhering to the highest standards of accuracy and truth in advancing the interests of clients and employers.
3. *Expertise:* Advancing the profession through continued professional development, research, and education.
4. *Independence:* Providing objective counsel and being accountable for individual actions.
5. *Loyalty:* Being faithful to clients and employers, but also honoring an obligation to serve the public interest.
6. *Fairness:* Respecting all opinions and supporting the right of free expression.

The following is a summary of the major provisions and the kinds of activities that would constitute improper conduct.

Free Flow of Information

The free flow of accurate and truthful information is essential to serving the public interest in a democratic society.

You should not give an expensive gift to a journalist as a bribe so that he or she will write favorable stories about the organization or its products/services. Lavish entertainment and travel junkets for government officials, beyond the limits set by law, also are improper.

Competition

Healthy and fair competition among professionals should take place within an ethical framework. An employee of an organization should not share information with a public relations firm that is in competition with other firms for the organization's business. You should not disparage your competition or spread malicious rumors about them to recruit business or to hire their employees.

Disclosure of Information

Open communication is essential to informed decision making in a democratic society. You should not conduct grassroots and letter-writing campaigns on behalf of undisclosed interest groups. In addition, you should not deceive the public by employing people to pose as "volunteers" at a public meeting. This also applies to booking "spokespersons" on talk shows without disclosing that they are being paid by an organization or special interest for their appearance. Intentionally leaving out essential information or giving a false impression of a company's finan-

cial performance is considered "lying by omission." If you do discover that inaccurate information has been given out, you have a responsibility to correct it immediately.

Safeguarding Confidences

Client trust requires appropriate protection of confidential and private information. You should not leak proprietary information that could adversely affect some other party. If you change jobs, you should not use confidential information from your previous employer to benefit the competitive advantage of your new employer.

Conflicts of Interest

Avoid real, potential, or perceived conflicts of interest among clients, employers, and the public. A public relations firm should inform a prospective client that it already represents a competitor or has a conflicting interest. A firm, for example, should not be doing public relations for two competing fast-food restaurant chains.

Enhancing the Profession

Public relations professionals should work constantly to strengthen the public's trust in the profession. You should not say a product is safe when it isn't. If it's unsafe under certain usage or conditions, you have an obligation to disclose this information.

ON THE JOB >>

IPRA's Code of Ethics

Insights

The following code of professional conduct, based on the charter of the United Nations, has been published in 20 languages:

IPRA Members Shall Endeavor:

1. To contribute to the achievement of the moral and cultural conditions enabling human beings to reach their full stature and enjoy the indefeasible rights to which they are entitled under the "Universal Declaration of Human Rights."

2. To establish communication patterns and channels which, by fostering the free flow of essential information, will make each member of the group feel that he/she is being kept informed, and also gives him/her an awareness of his/her own personal involvement and responsibility, and of his/her solidarity with other members.

3. To conduct himself/herself always and in all circumstances in such a manner as to deserve and secure the confidence of those with whom he/she comes in contact.

4. To bear in mind that, because of the relationship between his/her profession and the public, his/her conduct—even in private—will have an impact on the way in which the profession as a whole is appraised.

IPRA Members Shall Undertake:

1. To observe, in the course of his/her professional duties, the moral principles and rules of the "Universal Declaration of Human Rights."

2. To pay due regard to, and uphold, human dignity, and recognize the right of each individual to judge for himself/herself.

3. To establish the moral, psychological, and intellectual conditions for dialogue in its true sense, and to recognize the right of the parties involved to state their case and express their views.

4. To act, in all circumstances, in such a manner as to take account of the respective interests of the parties involved: both the interests of the organization which he/she serves and the interests of the publics involved.

5. To carry out his/her undertakings and commitments, which shall always be so worded as to avoid any misunderstanding, and to show loyalty and integrity in all circumstances so as to keep the confidence of his/her employers, past or present, and of all the publics that are affected by his/her actions.

IPRA Members Shall Refrain From:

1. Subordinating the truth to other requirements.

2. Circulating information which is not based on established and ascertainable facts.

3. Taking part in any venture or undertaking which is unethical or dishonest or capable of impairing human dignity or integrity.

4. Using any manipulative methods or techniques designed to create subconscious motivation which the individual cannot control of his/her own free will and so cannot be held accountable for the action taken on them.

---

include discussions of ethics in their local programs. PRSA and other organizations have similar programs.

Critics often complain that such codes of ethics "have no teeth" because there's really no punishment for being unethical and unprofessional. Even if a practitioner is expelled from the organization they can continue to work in public relations.

Problems with code enforcement are not unique to public relations groups. Professional organizations, including the Society for Professional Journalists, are voluntary organizations, and they don't have the legal authority to ban members from the field because no license is required to practice. Such organizations run a high risk of being sued for defamation or restricting the First Amendment guarantee of free speech if they try to expel members or restrict their occupations.

ON THE JOB >>

Ford–Firestone
Tire Recall

Ethics

Can public relations gloss over a lack of corporate responsibility? The Firestone–Ford tire recall controversy, detailed in Chapter 2, (see page 57), raises serious ethical questions about each company's failure to take action until the glare of publicity apparently forced them to admit there was a problem.

For nearly two years before the recall, for example, Ford had received complaints from overseas in such nations as Venezuela and Saudi Arabia about possible problems with Firestone tires on its Explorers. Yet, Ford continued to sell Explorers with Firestone tires in the U.S. market. Firestone also had indications that the tread was separating from some of its models as early as 1994, because there already was a pattern of lawsuits.

Even when the National Highway Traffic Safety Administration (NHTSA) launched an investigation in May of 2000 after receiving numerous reports of accidents and fatalities, it took another three months before Firestone voluntarily recalled 6.5 million tires. This has led many critics to charge that both Firestone and Ford were more interested in preserving their images and corporate reputations than in saving lives.

But hiding information, or refusing to act swiftly in the public interest, is no doubt the worst public relations strategy. Both Firestone and Ford saw their reputations and credibility plummet in the wake of disclosures about what they knew and when. Corporate credibility also declined when both companies actively blamed each other for the problem. Kirk O. Hanson, a senior lecturer in business ethics at the Stanford Business School, wrote: "In the long run, sound ethical behavior makes good business sense, allowing companies to protect their reputations and their bottom line. Acting ethically is also the right thing to do."

Consequently, most professional groups believe that the primary purpose of establishing codes of ethics is not enforcement, but rather education and information. They seek to enunciate standards of conduct that will guide members in their professional lives. It seems to work. Several studies have shown that the members of PRSA and other organizations have a much higher awareness of ethics and professional standards than nonmembers. Raising awareness about ethical dilemmas is important for professionals because such dilemmas are part of the fabric of public relations practice (see Ethics box on this page).

Ethics in Individual Practice

Despite codes of professional practice and formalized accreditation, ethics in public relations boils down to deeply troubling questions for the individual practitioner: Would I lie for my employer? Would I rig a doorprize drawing so a favorite client can win? Would I deceive in order to gain information about another agency's clients? Would I cover up a hazardous condition? Would I issue a news release presenting only half the truth? Would I seek to bribe a reporter or a legislator? Would I withhold some information in a news conference and provide it only if a reporter asks a specific question? Would I quit my job rather than cooperate in a questionable activity? In other words, to what extent, if any, would I compromise my personal beliefs?

These and similar questions plague the lives of many public relations people, although a number hold such strong personal beliefs and/or work for such highly principled employers that they seldom need to compromise their personal values. If employers make a suggestion that involves questionable ethics, the public relations person often can talk them out of the idea by citing the possible consequences of such an action—adverse media publicity, for example.

"To thine own self be true," advised New York public relations executive Chester Burger at an IABC conference, echoing Shakespeare. A fellow panelist, Canadian politician and radio commentator Stephen Lewis, commented: "There is a tremendous jaundice on the part of the public about the way things are communicated. People have elevated superficiality to an art form. Look at the substance of what you have to convey, and the honesty used in conveying it." With the audience contributing suggestions, the panelists formulated the following list of commendable practices:

> Be honest at all times.
> Convey a sense of business ethics based on your own standards and those of society.
> Respect the integrity and position of your opponents and audiences.
> Develop trust by emphasizing substance over triviality.
> Present all sides of an issue.
> Strive for a balance between loyalty to the organization and duty to the public.
> Don't sacrifice long-term objectives for short-term gains.

Adherence to professional standards of conduct—being truly independent—is the chief measure of a public relations person. Faced with such personal problems as a mortgage to pay and children to educate, practitioners may be strongly tempted to become yes-men or women and decline to express their views forcefully to an employer, or to resign. J. Kenneth Clark, vice president of corporate communications, Duke Power Company, Charlotte, North Carolina, once gave the following advice to an IABC audience:

> If the boss says newspapers are no damn good, the yes-man agrees.
> If the boss says to tell a reporter "no comment," the yes-man agrees.
> If the boss says the company's employees get a paycheck and don't really need to be informed about anything else, the yes-man agrees.
> If the boss says the public has no right to pry into what's going on inside a company—even though that company is publicly held and is dependent upon public support and public sales—the yes-man nods his head agreeably. . . .
> The fate of the yes-man is as inevitable as it is painful. Although your boss may think you're the greatest guy in the world for a while, you're going to lose your internal credibility because you never really state your professional opinions. And you're talking to a person who dotes on strong opinions and does not think highly of people who fail to offer them.

Thus, it can be readily seen that ethics in public relations really begins with the individual—and is directly related to his or her own value system as well as to the good of society. Although it is important to show loyalty to an employer, practitioners must never allow a client or an employer to rob them of their self-esteem.

Ethical Dealings with the News Media

The most practical consideration facing a public relations specialist in his or her dealings with the news media is that anything less than total honesty will destroy credibility and, with it, the practitioner's usefulness to an employer.

Trust can be maintained even when practitioners say "no comment" and refuse to answer questions that go beyond information reported in the news releases, according to a study by Professors Michael Ryan and David L. Hartinson, published in *Journalism and Mass Communication Quarterly*. Practitioners and journalists tend to agree on how they define lying; both, for example, believe that giving evasive answers to reporters' questions constitutes lying.

— ON THE JOB >>

Cash for News Coverage Raises Ethical Concerns

Global

In Russia and Eastern Europe, it's not uncommon for companies and public relations practitioners to pay journalists to get a news release or a product photo published in the news columns of a newspaper or mentioned on a television news program. The Russians call this practice "zakazukha."

A survey by the IPRA also found that "pay-for-play" was practiced extensively in Africa, the Middle East, and Southern Europe. To a much lesser extent, it occurs in Asia, Western Europe, Australia, and the United States.

IPRA and five other global organizations have joined forces to support a set of principles designed to foster greater transparency between public relations professionals and the media in an attempt to end bribery for media coverage throughout the world. The other organizations are the Inter-

national Press Institute, the International Federation of Journalists, Transparency International, the Global Alliance for Public Relations and Communications Management, and the Institute for Public Relations Research and Education.

The guidelines call for the following:

> News material should appear as a result of the news judgment of journalists and editors, not as a result of any payment in cash or in kind or any other inducements.
> Material involving payment should be clearly identified as advertising, sponsorship, or promotion.
> No journalist or media representative should ever suggest that news coverage will appear for any reason other than its merit.
> When samples or loans of products or services are necessary for a journalist to render an objective opinion, the length of time should

be agreed in advance and loaned products should be returned.
> The media should institute written policies regarding the receipt of gifts or discounted products and services, and journalists should be required to sign the policy.

"In too many countries, bribery of the news media robs citizens of truthful information that they need to make individual and community decisions," said Don Wright, then president of IPRA. He continued, "We started this campaign with the goal of creating greater transparency and eliminating unethical practices in dealings between news sources and the media."

IPRA and the Institute for Public Relations Research and Education (IPR) have also started a biennial international index of bribery and the media to monitor progress in the reduction of media corruption around the world.

Gifts

Achieving trust is the aim of all practitioners, and it can only be achieved through highly professional and ethical behavior. It is for this reason that public relations practitioners should not undermine the trust of the media by providing junkets of doubtful news value, extravagant parties, expensive gifts, and personal favors for media representatives. Journalists, for the most part, will think you are trying to bribe them to get favorable coverage. Gifts of any kind, according to PRSA, can contaminate the free flow of accurate and truthful information to the public (see PR Casebook on page 211).

Another area of ethical concern is when a company or organization pays a reporter's expenses for covering its event or news conference. U.S. journalists, as a rule, don't expect their expenses to be paid for by the company or organization that they are covering. However, the practice is quite common in other nations (see the Global box on this page). In one survey, almost a third of European journalists expected public relations people to pay their expenses. The percentage rises to almost 60 percent in Asian nations.

PRCASEBOOK

Political Pay-offs or Relationship Building?

Should a public relations firm interested in government contracts give gifts and political contributions to elected officials? And, if they do, does it raise any ethical concerns?

At least three public relations firms have received negative publicity and criticism because of gift giving and political contributions. For example, in Chicago Edelman received intense media scrutiny after it was revealed that it had contributed $32,600 to Governor Rod Blagojevich (D-Illinois) and had been successful in receiving the renewal of a $6.2 million state tourism contract.

In Colorado, Peter Webb Public Relations had a three-year $400,000 annual contract with the state lottery, but it was also revealed by the *Rocky Mountain News* that the firm had given 23 gifts to lottery officials, which included meals and sports tickets. In the uproar, the Colorado Lottery cancelled the contract with the public relations firm and the state legislature considered a bill that would bar vendor gifts to lottery employees.

Meanwhile, in Los Angeles, the mayor cancelled all contracts with public relations firms working for various city agencies because Fleishman-Hillard's $3 million contract with the LA Department of Water and Power also involved the firm's contributions to elected officials. It is not illegal to make such contributions, as long as they are publicly reported, but the media and the public often perceive such contributions as influence peddling to get government contracts.

Doug Downie, general manager of the Fleishman office in Los Angeles, was unapologetic. He told *PRWeek*, "The way to understand this dynamic is that contributions allow you to build relationships with elected officials and while they are not necessarily required in order to do public affairs work, they are door openers, and they are certainly something that is appreciated by people who need to raise money in order to seek higher office or to win office in the first place. . . . This is how our political system works."

Edelman Chicago general manager Cathleen Johnson agrees that contributions are a valid strategy. She told *PRWeek*, "It's really part of doing business. We have made contributions throughout the history of the company really because we're a part of the community."

What do you think? Should government agencies hire public relations firms in the first place? Are political contributions, legally reported, part of pursuing government business? Do you think it is a part of "relationship building" or simply a method to get favorable treatment for contracts? What do such controversies do to the image of public relations as a whole?

Shades of Gray in the News Business

Although it may be presumed that public relations representatives would benefit from being able to influence journalists with gifts or offers of paid advertising, this is not the case. A major selling point of public relations work is the third-party credibility of reporters and editors. The public trusts journalists to be objective and to be basically impartial in the dissemination of information. If the public loses that trust because they feel the media can be "bought," the information provided by public relations sources also becomes less trusted. Professional organizations such as PRSA often weigh in on this subject (see the Insights box on page 213).

The relationship between automotive journalists and car manufacturers is already questionable, according to the *Wall Street Journal*. It is not unusual, for example, for an editor at *Car and Driver* to write reviews for autos made by an automaker that also employs the journalist as a consultant. As the author of the *Wall Street Journal* article notes, "Welcome to the world of automotive enthusiast journalism where the barriers that separate advertisers from journalists are porous enough for paychecks to pass through." There's also considerable suspicion that the maker of the Car of the Year on the cover of an auto magazine has placed extensive paid advertising in that particular

When operating in any nation, public relations professionals, must be familiar with local laws that can affect
their activities. In China, for example, press reports
can be introduced as evidence to prove claims of product liability.

So, if a person wants to sue a company for a faulty product, one
common strategy is to get the story in the press. Defendants in
such cases have no choice but also to get press coverage or convince Chinese editors not to run a story.

A *Wall Street Journal* article on product liability in China notes:
"Building good relations with the press is one way to head off potential lawsuits. When a Shanghai fast-food customer took a fly in his fish
fillet to the newspaper because the U.S. restaurant chain refused to
compensate him, the restaurant's manager called local editors to
explain his side of the story. No article ran and no suit was filed."

issue. Is this just coincidence, or part of an
"understanding"? Magazines, in particular,
are increasingly blurring the line between
news features and advertisements.

Transparency is another problem. Should
a spokesperson on a television talk show
reveal his or her employer? This question
came to the forefront when it was revealed
in the press in 2005 that Armstrong Williams,
a conservative political commentator, had
been paid $240,000 by the U.S. Department
of Education to promote the government's
"No Child Left Behind" education program.
Williams was paid to promote the U.S.
Department of Education program on his
syndicated television and radio show, *The
Right Side*, as well as in op-ed pieces. His
contract also stipulated that he interview
Education Secretary Rod Paige and encourage other journalists to promote the education initiative, according to *USA Today*.
Williams told *USA Today*, "I wanted to do it
because it's something I believe in," but he
understood why some might call it unethical.

The incident led to loud objections on Capitol Hill and elsewhere. Congressman
George Miller of California told the *Washington Post* that the Williams contract "is propaganda, it's unethical, it's dangerous and it's illegal" Media scholar Alex Jones, director
of Harvard's Shorenstein Center, told the *Washington Post* that Williams' promotion of
the government program was "propaganda masquerading as news, paid by government,
truly a recipe from hell." Jones told the *Post*, "It would make any thinking person hearing any pundit speak want to say, 'Okay, how much did they pay you to say that?'"

When Williams' newspaper syndication company, Tribune Media Services, learned
about the contract between the journalist and the government they dropped his column.
Tribune Media Services released a statement saying, "Accepting compensation in any
form from an entity that serves as a subject of his weekly newspaper columns creates, at
the very least, the appearance of a conflict of interest." The statement further argued
that readers of his column would wonder whether his opinions "have been purchased
by a third party."

In the midst of the controversary was the public relations firm Ketchum. The
Department of Education had contracted with Ketchum for promotional services and
Ketchum, in turn, wrote the contract for Williams. *USA Today* reported that "Williams'
contract was part of a $1 million deal with Ketchum that produced 'video news releases'
designed to look like news reports."

Public Relations and the Law

Public relations practitioners deal with ethical issues on a regular basis. So, too, are
they faced with issues that can get themselves or their clients into legal hot water.
Depending on the field of practice, regulatory and legal demands can be a part of
everyday life for a public relations professional. Globalization adds to the complexity

ON THE JOB >>

PRSA Addresses Ethics of Paying for News Placement in Iraq

In late 2005, when accusations were made that the U.S. military was paying Iraqi journalists for a positive spin on the U.S. operations in Iraq, the Public Relations Society of America saw a need and an opportunity to address the ethical relationships between PR practitioners and journalists. Judith T. Phair, president and CEO of PRSA, released a statement regarding the "pay for play" articles. She noted in her prepared statement that "leaders of the Public Relations Society of America overwhelmingly adopted a resolution that condemns in the strongest possible terms, any lack of transparency in communications with the media that hides the origin of the communications." Phair's statement continued:

> PRSA has consistently voiced concerns about the blurring of lines between tactical disinformation campaigns and straightforward communications from military spokespersons in time of war. PRSA

advocates complete disclosure of sources and sponsorship of all information provided to the media.

PRSA takes very seriously its responsibility to provide leadership and guidance on matters affecting the flow of information in a free society. It is clearly a violation of the PRSA code and contrary to the basic principles of the ethical practice of our profession for a public relations professional to pay a news outlet to run stories that are presented as editorial content produced by that news organization.

PRSA acknowledged in its statement that an entity as large as the U.S. government may have a hard time maintaining control over its activities and messaging strategies. It also noted that there is very real temptation to do whatever it takes to get a positive message out about your organization, especially in times of crisis and conflict. However, Phair wrote:

Judith T. Phair, president and CEO of PRSA

There are no shortcuts in those endeavors. Open, two-way communications remains paramount—even in the face of frustration and failure. . . .

PRSA's leaders are calling for communications based upon openness, honesty and candor as the best, most effective way to demonstrate the principles of freedom for which the United States stands.

Source: PRSA press release. http://media.prsa.org/article_display.cfm?article_id=651

of dealing with these demands. No matter the field of practice, public relations professionals will often find themselves faced with legal questions regarding copyright, privacy, liability, and other related issues.

A Sampling of Legal Problems

The law and its many ramifications are somewhat abstract to the average person. Many people may have difficulty imagining exactly how public relations personnel can run afoul of the law or generate a suit simply by communicating information.

To bring things down to earth, we provide here a sampling of recent government regulatory agency cases and lawsuits that involved public relations materials and the work of practitioners:

> Public relations firm Porter Novelli sued two employees who left to start another public relations firm, claiming that they had planned the new firm on company time and took a client with them.

> The *Baltimore Sun* newspaper sued the governor of Maryland when he instructed state employees not to talk to specific *Sun* reporters. The newspaper claimed that the governor was violating its First Amendment rights. The *Sun* lost the suit.

> Bonner & Associates and client Pharmaceutical Research and Manufacturers of America were charged with violating Maryland's lobbying disclosure laws. A citizens group claimed that the firm used "deceptive tactics in the guise of a consumer-based organization to do the bidding of the pharmaceutical industry."

> An investor relations executive for former energy giant Enron pleaded guilty to charges of fraud and testified against his former bosses in hopes of receiving a more lenient sentence.

> The Federal Trade Commission (FTC) filed charges against three national diet firms after they failed to provide factual evidence in their advertising and publicity that clients actually achieved weight-loss goals or maintained them.

> A Chicago man sued for invasion of privacy after he appeared in a video news release for a cholesterol-lowering drug because the company and video producer didn't tell him the actual purpose of the taping.

> The Los Angeles city attorney filed a civil suit against Fleishman-Hillard charging that the LA office inflated invoices, claimed work that was not done, and double-charged for other activities when the firm worked for the city's Department of Water and Power.

> A San Francisco public relations practitioner who was fired by his employer for refusing to write misleading news releases won a lawsuit against his former employer for "unlawful dismissal."

> An 81-year-old man sued the United Way of America for using his picture on campaign posters and brochures without his permission.

These examples provide some idea of the legal pitfalls that a public relations person may encounter. Many of the charges were eventually dismissed or settled out of court, but the organizations paid dearly for the adverse publicity and the expense of defending themselves.

Public relations personnel can be held legally liable if they provide advice or tacitly support an illegal activity of a client or employer. This area of liability is called conspiracy. A public relations professional can be named as a coconspirator with other organizational officials if he or she:

> Participates in an illegal action such as bribing a government official or covering up information of vital interest to the public health and safety

> Counsels and guides the policy behind an illegal action

> Takes a major personal part in the illegal action

> Helps establish a "front group" whereby the connection to the public relations firm or its clients is kept hidden

> Cooperates in any other way to further an illegal action

These five concepts also apply to public relations firms that create, produce, and distribute materials on behalf of clients (see the Ethics box on page 215). On more than one occasion, the courts have ruled that public relations firms cannot hide behind the defense of "the client told me to do it." Public relations firms have a legal responsibility to practice "due diligence" in the type of information and documentation supplied

ON THE JOB >>

Use of Front Groups Poses Ethical Concerns

Ethics

The proliferation of so-called front groups waging purported "grassroots" campaigns to achieve public relations goals has created much debate in the field in recent years. The establishment of dozens of such groups evoked a strongly worded statement from the board of directors of the PRSA.

PRSA specifically condemns the efforts of those organizations, sometimes known as "front groups," that seek to influence the public policy process by disguising or obscuring the true identity of their members or by implying representation of a much more broadly based group than exists.

Almost every "save the environment" organization has spawned a counter group. For example, the Forest Alliance of British Columbia posed as a grassroots movement opposing the International Coalition to Save British

Columbia's Rainforests, composed of 25 "green" groups. It was later revealed that the Canadian timber industry paid Burson-Marsteller $1 million to create the alliance, whose aim was to convince the public that environmental destruction has been exaggerated and to persuade lawmakers to abolish unprofitable environmental regulations.

Names given to many of the organizations are confusing, if not downright deceptive. Northwesterners for More Fish was the name chosen for a "grassroots" coalition of utilities and other companies in the Northwest under attack by environmental groups for depleting the fish population. In California's Riverside County, a public relations firm organized Friends of Eagle Mountain on behalf of a mining company that wanted to create the world's largest landfill in an abandoned iron ore pit. A prohunting group that works to convince people that wildlife

is so plentiful that there is no reason not to kill some of it is known as the Abundant Wildlife Society of North America.

A Gallup Poll once showed that the majority of Americans considered themselves environmentalists. In the face of such findings, "People sometimes create groups that try to fudge a little bit about what their goals are," said Hal Dash, president of Cerrell Associates, a Los Angeles public relations firm that has represented clients with environmental problems.

Questioned about the tactics used in so-called grassroots campaigns, more than half of professionals surveyed by *PRNews* said that it is unethical for parties to fail to mention that their impetus for contacting a government official or other organization is due to a vested interest or membership in another organization sponsoring the campaign.

by a client. Regulatory agencies such as the Federal Trade Commission have power under the Lanham Act to file charges against public relations firms that distribute false and misleading information.

Defamation

Public relations professionals should be thoroughly familiar with the concepts of libel and slander. Such knowledge is crucial if an organization's internal and external communications are to meet legal and regulatory standards with a minimum of legal complications.

Traditionally, libel was a printed falsehood and slander was an oral statement that was false. Today, as a practical matter, there is little difference in the two, and the courts often use *defamation* as a collective term.

Essentially, *defamation* is any false statement about a person (or organization) that creates public hatred, contempt, or ridicule, or inflicts injury on reputation. A person filing a libel suit usually must prove four things:

1. The false statement was communicated to others through print, broadcast, or electronic means.
2. The person was identified or is identifiable.
3. There is actual injury in the form of money losses, loss of reputation, or mental suffering.
4. The person making the statement was malicious or negligent.

Private citizens usually have more success winning defamation suits than public figures or corporations. With public figures—government officials, entertainers, political candidates, and other newsworthy personalities—there is the extra test of whether the libelous statements were made with actual malice (*New York Times v. Sullivan*). Actual malice was defined by the Supreme Court as making the libelous statement knowing the information was false or publishing the information with "reckless disregard" as to whether it was false.

Corporations, to some degree, also are considered "public figures" by the courts for three reasons:

1. They engage in advertising and promotion offering products and services to the public.
2. They are often involved in matters of public controversy and public policy.
3. They have some degree of access to the media—through regular advertising and news releases—that enables them to respond and rebut defamatory charges made against them.

This is not to say that corporations don't win lawsuits regarding defamation. A good example is General Motors, which filed a multimillion-dollar defamation suit against NBC after the network's *Dateline* news program carried a story about gas tanks on GM pickup trucks exploding in side-impact collisions.

In a news conference, GM's general counsel meticulously provided evidence that NBC had inserted toy rocket "igniters" in the gas tanks, understated the vehicle speed at the moment of impact, and wrongly claimed that the fuel tanks could be easily ruptured. Within 24 hours after the suit was filed, NBC caved in. It agreed to air a nine-minute apology on the news program and pay GM $2 million to cover the cost of its investigation.

Increasingly, corporations are using fraud and contract law to sue news organizations, instead of pursuing harder-to-prove libel claims. In *Food Lion v. Capital Cities/ABC* (1995), for example, the grocery chain was awarded $315,000 after it sued *ABC News* for fraud and trespassing; two TV producers had lied on job applications and hidden cameras in their wigs to report an exposé on alleged health violations at several stores.

Avoiding Libel Suits

There is little investigative reporting in public relations. However, libel suits can be filed against organizational officials who make libelous accusations during a media interview, send out news releases that make false statements, or injure someone's reputation.

Some executives have been sorry that they lost control during a news conference and called the leaders of a labor union "a bunch of crooks and compulsive liars." Suits have been filed for calling a news reporter "a pimp for all environmental groups." Such language, although highly quotable and colorful, can provoke legal retaliation, merited or not.

Accurate information, and a delicate choice of words, must be used in news releases. For example, a former employee of J. Walter Thompson advertising agency claimed she was libeled in an agency news release that stated she had been dismissed because of financial irregularities in the department she headed. Eventually, the $20 million lawsuit was dismissed because she couldn't prove that the agency acted in a "grossly irresponsible manner."

In situations involving personnel, organizations often try to avoid lawsuits by saying that an employee left "for personal reasons" or to "pursue other interests," even if the real reason was incompetence or a record of sexual harassment. News releases and product publicity should also be written in accordance with FTC and SEC regulations, to be discussed shortly.

Another potentially dangerous practice is making unflattering comments about the competition's products. Although comparative advertising is the norm in the United States, companies walk a narrow line between comparison and "trade libel," or "product disparagement." Statements should be truthful, with factual evidence and scientific demonstration available to substantiate them. Companies often charge competitors with overstepping the boundary between "puffery" and "factual representation."

An organization can offer the opinion that a particular product or service is the "best" or "a revolutionary development" if the context clearly shows that the communication is a statement of opinion attributed to someone. Then it is classified as "puffery" and doesn't require factual evidence. Along the same line, a statement of opinion also has a degree of legal protection through the First Amendment guarantee of freedom of speech.

Don Sneed, Tim Wulfemeyer, and Harry Stonecipher, in a *Public Relations Review* article, say that a news release should be written to indicate clearly statements of opinion and statements of fact. They suggest that (1) opinion statements be accompanied by the facts on which the opinions are based, (2) statements of opinion be clearly labeled as such, and (3) the context of the language surrounding the expression of opinion be reviewed for possible legal implications.

The Fair Comment Defense

Organizations can do much to ensure that their communications avoid materials that could lead to potential lawsuits. By the same token, organizations are somewhat limited in their ability to use legal measures to defend themselves against criticism.

Executives are often incensed when an environmental group includes their corporation on its annual "dirty dozen" polluters or similar lists. Executives are also unhappy when a broadcast consumer affairs reporter flatly calls a product a "rip-off."

A corporate reputation may be damaged and product sales may go down, but a defamation case is difficult to win because, as previously mentioned, the accuser must prove actual malice. Also operating is the concept of fair comment and criticism.

This defense is used by theater and music critics when they lambaste a play or concert. *Fair comment* also means that when companies and individuals voluntarily display their wares to the public for sale or consumption, they have no real recourse against criticism done with honest purpose and lack of malicious intent.

Protecting Employee Privacy

An area of law that particularly applies to employees of an organization is invasion of privacy. Public relations staff must be particularly sensitive to the issue of privacy in at least four areas:

1. Employee newsletters
2. Photo releases
3. Product publicity and advertising
4. Media inquiries about employees

Let's explore each of these areas individually.

Employee Newsletters

It is no longer true, if it ever was, that an organization has an unlimited right to publicize the activities of its employees. In fact, Morton J. Simon, a Philadelphia lawyer and author of *Public Relations Law*, wrote, "It should not be assumed that a person's status as an employee waives his right to privacy." Simon correctly points out that a company newsletter or magazine does not enjoy the same First Amendment protection that the news media enjoy when they claim "newsworthiness" and "public interest." A number of court cases, he says, show that company newsletters are considered commercial tools of trade.

This distinction does not impede the effectiveness of newsletters, but it does indicate editors should try to keep employee stories organization-oriented. Indeed, most lawsuits and complaints are generated by "personals columns" that may invade the privacy of employees. Although a mention that Joe Doaks honeymooned in Hawaii or that Mary Worth is now a great-grandmother may sound completely innocent, the individuals involved—for any number of reasons—may consider the information a violation of their privacy. The situation may be further compounded into possible defamation by "cutesy" editorial asides in poor taste.

In short, one should avoid anything that might embarrass or subject an employee to ridicule by fellow employees. Here are some guidelines to remember when writing about employee activities:

> Keep the focus on organization-related activities.
> Have employees submit "personals" in writing.
> Double-check all information for accuracy.
> Ask: Will this embarrass anyone or cause someone to be the butt of jokes?
> Don't rely on secondhand information; confirm the facts with the person involved.
> Don't include racial or ethnic designations of employees in any articles.

Photo Releases

Ordinarily, a public relations practitioner doesn't need a signed release if a person gives "implied consent" by posing for a picture and is told how it will be used. This is particularly true for "news" photographs published in internal newsletters.

Public relations departments, however, should take the precaution of (1) filing all photographs, (2) dating them, and (3) giving the context of the situation. This precludes the use of old photos that could embarrass employees or subject them to ridicule. It protects against using photographs of persons who are no longer employed or have died, and against using newsletter photographs for advertising purposes. If a photo of an employee or customer is used in product publicity, sales brochures, or advertisements, the standard practice is to obtain a signed release.

Product Publicity and Advertising

As just noted, an organization must have a signed release on file if it wants to use the photographs or comments of employees and other individuals in product publicity, sales brochures, and advertising. An added precaution is to give some financial compensation to make a more binding contract.

Chemical Bank of New York unfortunately learned this lesson the hard way. The bank used pictures of 39 employees in various advertisements designed to "humanize" the bank's image, but the employees maintained that no one had requested permission to use their photos in advertisements. Another problem was that the pictures had been taken up to five years before they began appearing in the series of advertisements.

An attorney for the employees, who sued for $600,000 in damages, said, "The bank took the individuality of these employees and used that individuality to make a profit." The judge agreed and ruled that the bank had violated New York's privacy law. The action is called misappropriation of personality, discussed later in this chapter.

Written permission also should be obtained if the employee's photograph is to appear in sales brochures or even in the corporate annual report. This rule also applies to other situations. A graduate of Lafayette College sued the college for using a photo of his mother and him at graduation ceremonies, without their permission, in a financial aid brochure.

Media Inquiries about Employees

Because press inquiries have the potential of invading an employee's right of privacy, public relations personnel should follow basic guidelines as to what information will be provided on the employee's behalf. In general, employers should give a news reporter only basic information. This may include

> Confirmation that the person is an employee
> The person's title and job description
> Date of beginning employment or, if applicable, date of termination

Unless it is specified by law or permission is given by the employee, a public relations person should avoid providing information about an employee's (1) salary, (2) home address, (3) marital status, (4) number of children, (5) organizational memberships, and (6) job performance. If a reporter does seek any of this information, because of the nature of the story, a public relations person can volunteer to contact the employee and have the person speak directly with the reporter. Many organizations do provide additional information to a reporter if it is included on an optional biographical sheet that the employee has filled out. In most cases, the form clearly states that the organization may use any of the information in answering press inquiries or writing its own news releases. A typical biographical form may have sections in which the employee can list his or her (1) honors and awards, (2) professional memberships, (3) marital status and names of any children, (4) previous employers, (5) educational background, and (6) hobbies or interests. This sheet should not be confused with the person's official employment application, which must remain confidential.

If an organization uses biographical sheets, it is important that they be dated and kept current. A sheet compiled by an employee five years previously may be hopelessly out of date.

Copyright Law

Should a news release be copyrighted? How about a corporate annual report? Can a *New Yorker* cartoon be used in the company magazine without permission? What about reprinting an article from *Fortune* magazine and distributing it to the company's sales staff? Are government reports copyrighted? What constitutes copyright infringement?

These are some of the bothersome questions that a public relations professional should be able to answer. Knowledge of copyright law is important from two perspectives: (1) what organizational materials should be copyrighted and (2) how to utilize correctly the copyrighted materials of others.

In very simple terms, copyright means protection of a creative work from unauthorized use. A section of the U.S. copyright law of 1978 states: "Copyright protection subsists . . . in the original works of authorship fixed in any tangible medium of expression now known or later developed." The word *authorship* is defined in seven categories: (1) literary works; (2) musical works; (3) dramatic works; (4) pantomimes and choreographic works; (5) pictorial, graphic, or sculptural works; (6) motion pictures; and (7) sound recordings. The word *fixed* means that the work is sufficiently permanent or stable to permit it to be perceived, reproduced, or otherwise communicated.

The shield of copyright protection was reduced somewhat in 1991 when the Supreme Court ruled unanimously that directories, computer databases, and other compilations of facts may be copied and republished unless they display "some minimum degree of creativity." The court stated, "Raw facts may be copied at will."

Thus, a copyright does not protect ideas, but only the specific ways in which those ideas are expressed. An idea for promoting a product, for example, cannot be copyrighted—but brochures, drawings, news features, animated cartoons, display booths, photographs, recordings, videotapes, corporate symbols, slogans, and the like that express a particular idea can be copyrighted.

Because much money, effort, time, and creative talent are spent on organizational materials, copyright protection is important. By copyrighting materials, a company can prevent competitors from capitalizing on its creative work or producing a facsimile brochure that tends to mislead the public.

The law presumes that material produced in some tangible form is copyrighted from the moment it is created. This is particularly true if the material bears a copyright notice, for which one of the following methods may be employed:

> Using the letter "c" in a circle (©), followed by the word copyright
> Citing the year of copyright and the name of the owner

This presumption of copyright is often sufficient to discourage unauthorized use, and the writer or creator of the material has some legal protection if he or she can prove that the material was created before another person claims it.

A more formal step, providing full legal protection, is official registration of the copyrighted work within three months after creation. This is done by depositing two copies of the manuscript (it is not necessary that it has been published), recording, or artwork with the Copyright Office of the Library of Congress. Copyright registration forms are available from U.S. post offices. Registration is not a condition of copyright protection, but it is a prerequisite to an infringement action against unauthorized use by others. The Copyright Term Extension Act, passed in 1998 and reaffirmed by the U.S. Supreme Court (*Eldred v. Ashcroft*) in 2003, protects original material for the life of the creator plus 70 years for individual works and 95 years from publication for copyrights held by corporations.

Copyright has implications internationally, too. The Recording Industry Association of America (RIAA) has launched a public relations and lobbying effort to convince European Union (EU) nations to extend the length of time that music can be copyrighted. Copyright protection lasts only 50 years in Europe, compared with 95 years in the United States. That means that 1950s recordings by Elvis Presley and such jazz greats as Ella Fitzgerald are in the public domain. This doesn't please American record companies; they believe that European recordings of these artists will enter the United States and the international market at cheaper prices, thus undercutting their profits. If the American recording industry is unsuccessful in getting copyright terms extended in Europe, the next step is to convince U.S. Customs to seize such products and block them from the U.S. market.

The duration of copyright protection in Europe does not affect only American recordings—in 2012 the Beatles first hit "Love Me Do" will be 50 years old, thereby facing the same problem.

Fair Use versus Infringement

Public relations people are in the business of gathering information from a variety of sources, so it is important to know where fair use ends and infringement begins (see the Insights box on page 222). *Fair use* means that part of a copyrighted article may be quoted directly, but the quoted material must be brief in relation to the length of the original work. It may be, for example, only one paragraph in a 750-word article and up to 300 words in a long article or book chapter. Complete attribution of the source must be given regardless of the length of the quotation. If the passage is quoted verbatim, quote marks must be used.

It is important to note, however, that the concept of fair use has distinct limitations if part of the copyrighted material is to be used in advertisements and promotional brochures. In this case, permission is required. It also is important for the original source to approve the context in which the quote is used. A quote out of context often runs into legal trouble if it implies endorsement of a product or service.

The copyright law does allow limited copying of a work for fair use such as criticism, comment, or research. However, in recent years, the courts have considerably narrowed the concept of fair use when multiple copies of a copyrighted work are involved.

Even the unauthorized photocopying of newsletters and published articles can cost an organization large sums of money. Texaco, for example, lost a lawsuit filed by publishers of scientific journals, who claimed that the company violated the copyright law by permitting employees to photocopy articles for their files.

Organizations that have a single subscription to a newsletter and then circulate it via in-house e-mail also violate the law. Atlas Telecom paid a $100,000 settlement after admitting that it electronically distributed about a dozen telecommunications newsletters to its employees.

Lawsuits can be avoided if an organization orders quantity reprints from the publisher and pays a licensing fee that permits it to make paper or electronic copies. Dow Jones, publisher of the *Wall Street Journal*, has a whole department (www.djreprints.com)

ON THE JOB >>

Plagiarism versus Copyright Infringement

Insights

Copyright infringement and plagiarism differ. You may be guilty of copyright infringement even if you attribute the materials and give the source, but don't get permission from the author or publisher to reproduce the materials.

In the case of plagiarism, the author makes no attempt to attribute the information at all. As the guide for Hamilton College says, "Plagiarism is a form of fraud. You plagiarize if you present other writer's words or ideas as your own." Maurice Isserman, writing in the *Chronicle of Higher Education,* further explains, "Plagiarism substitutes someone else's prowess at explanation for your own efforts."

The World Wide Web has increased the problems of plagiarism because it is quite easy for anyone, from students to college presidents, to cut and paste entire paragraphs (or even pages) into a term paper or speech and claim it as their own creation. Of course, students also can purchase complete term papers online, but that loophole is rapidly shrinking as more sophisticated software programs, such as www.turnitin.com, can scan the entire Internet for other sources that use the same phrases used in a student's research paper.

John Barrie, founder of Turnitin, told the *Wall Street Journal* that "85 percent of the cases of plagiarism that we see are straight copies from the Internet—a student uses the Internet like a 1.5 billion-page cut-and-paste encyclopedia." Most universities have very strong rules about plagiarism, and it is not uncommon for students to receive an F in a course for plagiarism. In the business world, stealing someone else's words and expression of thought is called theft of intellectual property and lawsuits are filed.

Source: Dennis L. Wilcox. *Public Relations Writing and Media Techniques,* 5th ed. Boston: Allyn & Bacon, 2005, 77.

that arranges reprints which can be used in print, e-mail, PDF, or Web link formats. The same concept applies to videotaping television shows or news programs for widespread distribution.

Government documents (city, county, state, and federal) are in the public domain and cannot be copyrighted. Public relations personnel, under the fair use doctrine, can freely use quotations and statistics from a government document, but care must be exercised to ensure that the material is in context and not misleading.

Photography and Artwork

The copyright law makes it clear that freelance and commercial photographers retain ownership of their work. In other words, a customer who buys a copyrighted photo owns the item itself, but not the right to make additional copies. That right remains with the photographer unless transferred in writing.

In a further extension of this right, the duplication of copyrighted photos is also illegal. This was established in a 1990 U.S. Federal District Court case in which the Professional Photographers of America (PP of A) sued a nationwide photofinishing firm for ignoring copyright notices on pictures sent for additional copies.

Freelance photographers generally charge for a picture on the basis of its use. If it is used only once, perhaps for an employee newsletter, the fee is low. If, however, the company wants to use the picture in the corporate annual report or on the company calendar, the fee may be considerably higher. Arrangements and fees then can be determined for (1) one-time use, (2) unlimited use, or (3) the payment of royalties every time the picture is used.

Computer manipulation of original artwork can also violate copyright. One photographer's picture of a racing yacht was used on a poster after the art director electronically changed the numbers on the sail and made the water a deeper blue. In another case, a photo distribution agency successfully sued *Newsday* for unauthorized use of a color image after the newspaper reconstructed the agency's picture using a computer scanner, then failed to credit the photographer. FPG International was awarded $20,000 in damages, 10 times the initial licensing fee of $2,000.

In sum, slightly changing a copyrighted photo or a piece of artwork can be considered a violation of copyright if the intent is to capitalize on widespread recognition of the original art. This was the case when the estate of the late children's author Dr. Seuss won a $1.5 million judgment against a Los Angeles T-shirt maker for infringement of copyright. The manufacturer had portrayed a parody of Dr. Seuss's Cat in the Hat character smoking marijuana and giving the peace sign. In another situation, the Rock and Roll Hall of Fame filed a copyright suit against a freelance photographer who snapped a picture of the unique building at sunset and sold posters of his work without paying a licensing fee.

Similarly, sports logos are registered trademarks, and a licensing fee must be paid before anyone can use logos for commercial products and promotions. Teams in the National Football League and the National Basketball Association earn more than $3 billion annually selling licensed merchandise, and the sale of college and university trademarked goods is rapidly approaching that mark. Schools such as Notre Dame, Michigan, and Ohio State rake in more than $3 million a year in royalties from licensing their logos to be placed on everything from beer mugs to T-shirts.

The penalty for not paying a licensing fee is steep. During Super Bowl week, the NFL typically confiscates about $1 million in bogus goods and files criminal charges against the offending vendors.

The Rights of Freelance Writers

Although the rights of freelance photographers have been established for some years, it was only recently that freelance writers gained more control over the ownership of their work. In the now famous case of *Community for Creative Non-violence v. Reid*, the U.S. Supreme Court in 1989 ruled that writers retained ownership of their work and that purchasers of it simply gained a "license" to reproduce the copyrighted work.

Prior to this ruling, the common practice was to assume that commissioned articles were "work for hire" and the purchaser owned the copyright. In other words, a magazine could reproduce the article in any number of ways and even sell it to another publication without the writer's permission. Under the new interpretation, ownership of a writer's work is subject to negotiation and contractual agreement. Writers may agree to assign all copyright rights to the work they have been hired to do or they may give permission only for a specific one-time use.

In a related matter, freelance writers are pressing for additional compensation if an organization puts their work on CD-ROM, online databases, or the World Wide Web. They won a major victory in 2001 when the Supreme Court (*New York Times v. Tasini*) ruled that publishers, by making articles accessible through electronic databases, infringed the copyrights of freelance contributors.

Public relations firms and corporate public relations departments are responsible for ensuring compliance with the copyright law. This means that all agreements with a freelance writer must be in writing, and the use of the material must be clearly stated. Ideally, public relations personnel should negotiate multiple rights and even complete ownership of the copyright.

Copyright Issues on the Internet

The Internet and World Wide Web have raised new issues about the protection of intellectual property. Two issues regarding copyright are: (1) the downloading of copyrighted material and (2) the unauthorized uploading of such material.

Downloading Material. In general, the same rules apply to cyberspace as to more long-standing methods of disseminating ideas. Original materials in digital form are still protected by copyright. The fair-use limits for materials found on the Internet are essentially the same as for materials disseminated by any other means.

Related to this is the use of news articles and features that are sent via e-mail or the Web to the clients of clipping services. An organization may use such clips to track its publicity efforts, but it can't distribute the article on its own Web site or intranet without permission and a royalty payment to the publication in which the article appeared. One national clipping service, Burrelle's, has already made an agreement with more than 300 newspapers to have their customers pay a small royalty fee in exchange for being able to make photocopies of clippings and make greater use of them.

Uploading Material. In many cases, owners of copyrighted material have uploaded various kinds of information with the intention of making it freely available. Some examples are software, games, and even the entire text of *The Hitchhiker's Guide to the Galaxy*. The problem comes, however, when third parties upload copyrighted material without permission. Consequently, copyright holders are increasingly patrolling the Internet and World Wide Web to stop the unauthorized use of material.

Copyright Guidelines

A number of points have been discussed about copyright. A public relations person should keep the following in mind:

> Ideas cannot be copyrighted, but the expression of those ideas can be.

> Major public relations materials (brochures, annual reports, videotapes, motion pictures, position papers, and the like) should be copyrighted, if only to prevent unauthorized use by competitors.

> Although there is such a thing as fair use, any copyrighted material intended directly to advance the sales and profits of an organization should not be used unless permission is given.

> Copyrighted material should not be taken out of context, particularly if its use will imply endorsement of the organization's services or products.

> Quantity reprints of an article should be ordered from the publisher.

> Permission is required to use segments of television programs or motion pictures.

> Permission must be obtained to use segments of popular songs (written verses or sound recordings) from a recording company.

> Photographers and freelance writers retain the rights to their works. Permission and fees must be negotiated to use works for other purposes than originally agreed on.

> Photographs of current celebrities or those who are now deceased cannot be used for promotion and publicity purposes without permission.

> Permission is required to reprint cartoon characters, such as Snoopy or Garfield. In addition, cartoons and other artwork or illustrations in a publication are copyrighted.

> Government documents are not copyrighted, but caution is necessary if the material is used in a way that implies endorsement of products or services.

> Private letters, or excerpts from them, cannot be published or used in sales and publicity materials without the permission of the letter writer.

> Original material posted on the Internet and the World Wide Web has copyright protection.

> The copyrighted material of others should not be posted on the Internet unless specific permission is granted.

Trademark Law

What do the names Coca-Cola, Marlboro, and IBM, the Olympic rings, and the logo of the Dallas Cowboys have in common? They are all registered trademarks protected by law.

A *trademark* is a word, symbol, or slogan, used singly or in combination, that identifies a product's origin. According to Susan L. Cohen, writing in *Editor & Publisher's* annual trademark supplement, "It also serves as an indicator of quality, a kind of shorthand for consumers to use in recognizing goods in a complex marketplace." Research indicates, for example, that 53 percent of Americans say brand quality takes precedence over price considerations. Consequently, branding is important to companies and organizations.

There has been a proliferation of trademarks and service marks in modern society. Coca-Cola may be the world's most recognized trademark, according to some studies, but it is only one of almost 1 million active trademarks registered with the federal Patent and Trademark Office. This proliferation can lead to problems as you see in the Insights box on this page.

The Protection of Trademarks

Trademarks are always capitalized and are never used as nouns. They are always used as adjectives modifying nouns. For example, the proper terms are Kleenex tissues, Xerox copies, and Rollerblade skates. A person who "uses a Kleenex," "makes a Xerox," or "goes Rollerblading" is violating trademark law.

In addition, organizations take the step of designating brand names and slogans with various marks. The *registered trademark symbol* is a superscript, small capital "R" in a circle—®. "Registered in U.S. Patent and Trademark Office" and "Reg. U.S. Pat. Off" may also be used. A "TM" in small capital letters indicates a trademark that isn't registered. It represents a company's common-law claim to a right of trademark or a trademark for which registration is pending.

A *service mark* is like a trademark, but it designates a service rather than a product, or is a logo. An "SM" in small capitals in a circle—SM—is the symbol for a registered service mark. If registration is pending, the "SM" should be used without the circle.

FedEx® Is Not Synonymous With Overnight Shipping.

That's why you can't FedEx or Federal Express your package. Neither FedEx® nor Federal Express® are nouns, verbs, adverbs or even participles. They are adjectives and identify our unique brand of shipping services. So if you want to send a package overnight, ask for FedEx® delivery services.

When you do, we think you'll know why we say "Why Fool Around With Anyone Else?"® After all, FedEx is "Absolutely, Positively the Best in the Business."® Help us protect our marks. Ask us before you use them, use them correctly, and, most of all, only ask for FedEx® delivery services.

FedEx.
Be absolutely sure.

© 1998 Federal Express Corporation

www.fedex.com

These symbols are used in advertising, product labeling, news releases, company brochures, and so on to let the public and competitors know that a name, slogan, or symbol is protected by law.

Public relations practitioners play an important role in protecting the trademarks of their employers. They safeguard trademarks and respect other organizational trademarks in the following ways:

> Ensure that company trademarks are capitalized and used properly in all organizational literature and graphics. Lax supervision can cause loss of trademark protection.

> Distribute trademark brochures to editors and reporters and place advertisements in trade publications, designating names to be capitalized.

> Educate employees as to what the organization's trademarks are and how to use them correctly.

> Monitor the mass media to make certain that trademarks are used correctly. If they are not, send a gentle reminder.

> Check publications to ensure that other organizations are not infringing on a registered trademark. If they are, the company legal department should protest with letters and threats of possible lawsuits.

> Make sure the trademark is actually being used. A 1988 revision of the Trademark Act no longer permits an organization to hold a name in reserve.

> Ensure that the trademarks of other organizations are correctly used and properly noted.

> Avoid the use of trademarked symbols or cartoon figures in promotional materials without the explicit permission of the owner. In some cases, a licensing fee is required.

Organizations adamantly insist on the proper use of trademarks in order to avoid the problem of having a name or slogan become generic. Or, to put it another way, a brand name becomes a common noun through general public use. Some trade names that have become generic include *aspirin, thermos, cornflakes, nylon, cellophane,* and *yo-yo.* This means that any company can now use these names to describe a product.

The Problem of Trademark Infringement

Today, when there are thousands of businesses and organizations, finding a trademark not already in use is extremely difficult. The task is even more frustrating if a company wants to use a trademark on an international level.

A good example is what happened to Nike at the 1992 Olympic Games in Barcelona. The athletic shoe manufacturer paid millions to be an official sponsor of the games, and it planned to introduce a new line of clothing at the event. There was a snag, however. A Spanish high court ruled that the Beaverton, Oregon, firm's trademark infringed on the trademark of a Barcelona sock company that had registered "Nike" more than 60 years ago. The court barred Nike from selling or advertising its sports apparel in Spain, an action that cost the company about $20 million in sales potential.

The complexity of finding a new name, coupled with the attempts of many to capitalize on an already known trade name, has spawned a number of lawsuits claiming trademark infringement. For example,

> *Entrepreneur* magazine was awarded $337,000 in court damages after filing a trademark infringement lawsuit against a public relations firm that changed its name to "EntrepreneurPR."

> *Fox News* filed a suit against satirist and author Al Franken because the title of his book was *Lies and the Lying Liars Who Tell Them: A Fair and Balanced Look at the Right.* Fox claimed that the phrase "fair and balanced" was trademarked.

> The widow of the man who said "Let's roll" when he and others tried to overpower the hijackers of Flight 93 over Pennsylvania on September 11 petitioned the federal government to trademark the phrase. She wanted to license the phrase to fund a foundation to assist children who had lost a parent.

> Phi Beta Kappa, the academic honor society, filed a $5 million trademark infringement suit against Compaq Computer Corp. after the company launched a "Phi Beta Compaq" promotion targeted at college students.

> MADD (Mothers Against Drunk Driving) filed a trademark suit against an organization calling itself DAMMADD, a nonprofit group established to spread antidrug messages. MADD said the similar name would confuse the public.

In these cases and many others, organizations claimed that their registered trademarks were being improperly exploited for commercial or organizational purposes. Some guidelines used by courts to determine if there has been trademark infringement include the following:

> Has the defendant used a name as a way of capitalizing on the reputation of another organization's trademark—and does the defendant benefit from the original organization's investment in popularizing its trademark?

> Is there an intent (real or otherwise) to create confusion in the public mind? Is there an intent to imply a connection between the defendant's product and the item identified by trademark?

> How similar are the two organizations? Are they providing the same kinds of products or services?
> Has the original organization actively protected the trademark by publicizing it and by actually continuing to use it in connection with its products or services?
> Is the trademark unique? A company with a trademark that merely describes a common product might be in trouble.

Misappropriation of Personality

A form of trademark infringement also can result from the unauthorized use of well-known entertainers, professional athletes, and other public figures in an organization's publicity and advertising materials. A photo of Reese Witherspoon may make a company's advertising campaign more interesting, but the courts call it "misappropriation of personality" if permission and licensing fees have not been negotiated.

Deceased celebrities also are protected. To use a likeness or actual photo of a personality such as Elvis Presley, Marilyn Monroe, or even Princess Diana, the user must pay a licensing fee to an agent representing the family, studio, or estate of the deceased. Elvis, even 30 years after his death, is still the "King," and his estate generates about $40 million in income annually. The estate of Peanuts comic strip creator Charles Schulz collects about $30 million annually. The estates of NASCAR icon Dale Earnhardt and Beatle John Lennon each garner about $20 million a year.

The legal doctrine is the right of publicity, which gives entertainers, athletes, and other celebrities the sole ability to cash in on their fame. The legal right is loosely akin to a trademark or copyright, and many states have made it a commercial asset that can be inherited by a celebrity's descendents.

Legal protection also extends to the use of "sound-alikes" or "look-alikes." Bette Midler won a $400,000 judgment against Young & Rubicam (later affirmed by the Supreme Court on appeal) after the advertising agency used another singer to do a "sound-alike" of her singing style in a rendition of the song "Do You Wanna Dance?" for a Ford commercial. The court ruled: "When a distinctive voice of a professional singer is widely known and is deliberately imitated in order to sell a product, the sellers have appropriated what is not theirs."

Regulations by Government Agencies

The promotion of products and services, whether through advertising, product publicity, or other techniques, is not protected by the First Amendment. Instead, the courts have traditionally ruled that such activities fall under the doctrine of commercial speech. This means that messages can be regulated by the state in the interest of public health, safety, and consumer protection.

Consequently, the states and the federal government have passed legislation that regulates commercial speech and even restricts it if standards of disclosure, truth, and accuracy are violated. One consequence was the banning of cigarette advertising on television in the 1960s. Public relations personnel involved in product publicity and the distribution of financial information should be aware of guidelines established by such government agencies as the Federal Trade Commission and the Securities and Exchange Commission.

The Federal Trade Commission (FTC)

The Federal Trade Commission (FTC) has jurisdiction to determine if advertisements are deceptive or misleading. Public relations personnel should also know that the commission has jurisdiction over product news releases and other forms of product publicity, such as videos and brochures. In the eyes of the FTC, both advertisements and product publicity materials are vehicles of commercial trade—and therefore subject to regulation. In fact, Section 43(a) of the Lanham Act makes it clear that anyone, including public relations personnel, is subject to liability if that person participates in the making or dissemination of a false and misleading representation in any advertising or promotional material. This includes advertising and public relations firms, which also can be held liable for writing, producing, and distributing product publicity materials on behalf of clients.

An example of an FTC complaint is one filed against Campbell Soup Company for claiming that its soups were low in fat and cholesterol and thus helpful in fighting heart disease. The commission charged that the claim was deceptive because publicity and advertisements didn't disclose that the soups also were high in sodium, a condition that increases the risk of heart disease.

The Campbell's case raises an important aspect of FTC guidelines. Although a publicized fact may be accurate in itself, FTC staff also consider the context or "net impression received by the consumers." In Campbell's case, advertising copywriters and publicists ignored the information about high sodium, which placed an entirely new perspective on the health benefits of the soup.

Hollywood's abuse of endorsements and testimonials to publicize its films also has attracted the scrutiny of the FTC. It was discovered that Sony Pictures had concocted quotes from a fictitious movie critic to publicize four of its films. And Twentieth Century Fox admitted that it had hired actors to appear in "man in the street" commercials to portray unpaid moviegoers.

Excerpts in ads from regular reviewers also can be misleading and in violation of FTC guidelines. David Ansen, movie critic for *Newsweek*, was quoted that a film starring Chevy Chase and Goldie Hawn was "good fun." The context was much different. He told the *Wall Street Journal*, "I had written that though it was all intended as good fun, it's about as much fun as getting hit by a bus."

FTC investigators are always on the lookout for unsubstantiated claims and various forms of misleading or deceptive information. Some of the words in promotional materials that trigger FTC interest are: *authentic, certified, cure, custom-made, germ-free, natural, unbreakable, perfect, first-class, exclusive,* and *reliable*.

In recent years, the FTC also has established guidelines for "green" marketing and the use of "low-carb" in advertisements and publicity materials for food products. The following general guidelines, adapted from FTC regulations, should be taken into account when writing product publicity materials:

> Make sure the information is accurate and can be substantiated.

> Stick to the facts. Don't "hype" the product or service by using flowery, nonspecific adjectives and ambiguous claims.

> Make sure celebrities or others who endorse the product actually use it. They should not say anything about the product's properties that cannot be substantiated.

> Watch the language. Don't say "independent research study" when the research was done by the organization.

ON THE JOB >>

Investor Relations Group Adopts New Code

Ethics

The National Investor Relations Institute (NIRI) has adopted a new code of ethics in the wake of corporate financial scandals such as Enron, WorldCom, and Tyco. NIRI (www.niri.org) requires all its members to affirm the code in writing. Members sanctioned for violating laws or SEC regulations will be expelled from the organization. The 12-point code is as follows:

1. Maintain the highest legal and ethical standards.
2. Avoid even the appearance of professional impropriety.
3. Ensure full and fair disclosure.
4. Provide fair access to corporate information.
5. Serve the interests of shareholders.
6. Keep track of company affairs and all investor relations (IR) laws and regulations.
7. Keep confidential information confidential.
8. Do not use confidential information for personal advantage.
9. Exercise independent professional judgment.
10. Avoid relationships that might affect ethical standing.
11. Report fraudulent or illegal acts within the company.
12. Represent oneself in a reputable and dignified manner.

> Provide proper context for statements and statistics attributed to government agencies. They don't endorse products.

> Describe tests and surveys in sufficient detail so the consumer understands what was tested under what conditions.

> Remember that a product is not "new" if only the packaging has been changed or the product is more than six months old.

> When comparing products or services with a competitor's, make certain you can substantiate your claims.

> Avoid misleading and deceptive product demonstrations.

Companies found in violation of FTC guidelines are usually given the opportunity to sign a consent decree. This means that the company admits no wrongdoing but agrees to change its advertising and publicity claims. Companies may also be fined by the FTC or ordered to engage in corrective advertising and publicity.

The Securities and Exchange Commission (SEC)

The megamergers and the IPOs (initial public offerings) of many new companies that began in the 1990s and continue today have made the Securities and Exchange Commission (SEC) a household name in the business world. They have also made the practice of investor relations increasingly important (see the Ethics box on this page). The SEC closely monitors the financial affairs of publicly traded companies and protects the interests of stockholders.

SEC guidelines on public disclosure and insider trading are particularly relevant to corporate public relations staff members who must meet the requirements. The distribution of misleading information or failure to make a timely disclosure of material information may be the basis of liability under the SEC code. A company may even be liable if, despite satisfying regulations by getting information out, it conveys crucial information in a vague way or buries it deep within the news release.

A good example is Enron, the now-defunct Houston-based energy company that became the largest corporate failure in U.S. history. The company was charged with a number of SEC violations, including the distribution of misleading news releases about its finances. According to congressional testimony, the company issued a quarterly earnings news release that falsely led investors to believe that the company was "on track" to meet strong earnings growth in 2002. Three months later, the company was bankrupt.

The SEC has volumes of regulations, but the three concepts most pertinent to public relations personnel are as follows:

1. *Full information must be given on anything that might materially affect the company's stock.* This includes such things as (1) dividends or their deletion, (2) annual

and quarterly earnings, (3) stock splits, (4) mergers or takeovers, (5) major management changes, (6) major product developments, (7) expansion plans, (8) change of business purpose, (9) defaults, (10) proxy materials, (11) disposition of major assets, (12) purchase of own stock, and (13) announcements of major contracts or orders.

2. *Timely disclosure is essential.* A company must act promptly (within minutes or a few hours) to dispel or confirm rumors that result in unusual market activity or market variations. The most common ways of dispensing such financial information are through use of electronic news release services, contact with the major international news services (Dow Jones Wire), and bulk faxing.

3. *Insider trading is illegal.* Company officials, including public relations staffs and outside counsel, cannot use inside information to buy and sell company stock (see the PR Casebook on page 232).

Maureen Rubin, an attorney and professor at California State University, Northridge, explains that a court may examine all information released by a company, including news releases, to determine whether, taken as a whole, they create an "overall misleading" impression. As a result, investor relations personnel must also avoid such practices as:

> Unrealistic sales and earnings reports

> Glowing descriptions of products in the experimental stage

> Announcements of possible mergers or takeovers that are only in the speculation stage

> Free trips for business reporters and offers of stock to financial analysts and editors of financial newsletters

> Omission of unfavorable news and developments

> Leaks of information to selected outsiders and financial columnists

> Dissemination of false rumors about a competitor's financial health

In 1998, the SEC passed new regulations supporting the use of "plain English" in prospectuses and other financial documents. The new rules are supposed to make information understandable to the average investor by removing sentences littered with "lawyerisms" such as aforementioned, hereby, therewith, whereas, and hereinafter. According to then-SEC Chairman Arthur Levitt, the cover page, summary, and risk factor sections of prospectuses must be clear, concise, and understandable.

The SEC's booklet on "plain English" gives helpful writing hints such as (1) make sentences short; (2) use *we* and *our*; *you* and *your*; and (3) say it with an active verb. More information about SEC guidelines can be accessed at its Web site: www.sec.gov/.

Fair Disclosure Regulation. In 2000, the SEC issued another regulation regarding Fair Disclosure (known as Reg FD). Although regulations already existed regarding "material disclosure" of information that could affect the price of stock, the new regulation expanded the concept by requiring publicly traded companies to broadly disseminate "material" information via a news release, Webcast, or SEC filing. According to the SEC, Reg FD ensures that all investors, not just brokerage firms and analysts, will receive financial information from a company at the same time.

Sarbanes-Oxley Act. The Sarbanes-Oxley Act was enacted in 2002 in response to the Enron and WorldCom financial scandals. The Enron scandal alone cost

PRCASEBOOK

A Suggested Recipe for Martha Stewart: Litigation Public Relations

The practice of litigation public relations started in the 1990s. The O. J. Simpson murder trial gave the practice high visibility as both sides extensively used public relations to influence public perceptions—and even the jury pool—about the character of the defendant.

Since then, a number of public relations firms have started litigation practices to help both celebrities and organizations deal with criminal charges and class-action suits that can severely damage reputations and even the bottom line. In essence, litigation public relations is a form of reputation management.

As James Haggerty, author of *Winning Your Case with Public Relations*, writes "Communication is now central to the management of modern litigation. It can mean communicating to external audiences, such as the media, or to internal audiences, like employers, investors, shareholders, and others with a vested interest in the organization." He continues, "while you can have a victory in the court of law, your legal victory doesn't amount to much if, in the process, you sacrifice reputation, corporate character, and all of the other elements that make up an organization's goodwill in the marketplace."

Martha Stewart, the queen of home decorating and cooking, didn't win in a court of law or in the court of public opinion. She was sentenced to five months in prison (plus five months home confinement) for lying to federal investigators about a stock sale and possible insider trading. On the courthouse steps after the conviction, Stewart told the press, "Whatever happened to me personally shouldn't have any effect whatsoever on the great company Martha Stewart Living Omnimedia."

Unfortunately, that wasn't the case. Stewart didn't realize that the whole business was based on her persona. As crisis communication consultant Steven Fink noted, "People are buying her products because they have a positive impression of the public image of Martha Stewart. If that image becomes damaged, it can hurt her business in a serious way."

And it was serious. Although the revenues and stock price of her company declined during the pretrial period, total revenues dropped 33 percent in the three months following the conviction. The television program *Martha Stewart Living* lost half of its viewers after the verdict, and revenues from the program dropped 50 percent, causing the show to be suspended.

Martha Stewart reads a prepared statement after being convicted of lying to federal prosecutors about a stock sale based on insider information.

Public relations experts say that the basic concepts of litigation public relations practice could have saved Stewart, or at least resulted in a less painful outcome. Stewart, for example, stonewalled the media, even though there was intense public interest because of her celebrity status. Indeed, the public relations firm Hill & Knowlton found that 80 percent of Americans are willing to suspend judgment if an organization responds quickly to an accusation. Other studies have found that nearly three times as many people presume an organization to be innocent when the company responds to all allegations, as opposed to saying "no comment."

Stewart did employ a rather uncommon litigation public relations tactic—she developed a personal litigation public relations Web site (www.marthatalks.com). On this Web site

Stewart was quoted, "As part of my promise to keep you informed about key developments, my attorneys and I will do our best to post relevant items from the trial and related op-eds, as soon as they become available." In a study of Stewart's and other personal litigation public relations Web sites, professors Bryan Reber, Karla Gower, and Jennifer Robinson identified four standards for personal litigation public relations Web sites:

1. They are monologic, not dialogic.
2. They embrace long-standing litigation public relations standards.
3. They reflect the public persona of the defendant.
4. They serve as the official voice of the defendant.

But Stewart was faulted for not following any of the basic rules of crisis communications. According to *PRWeek*, Stewart "resisted making even the slightest apologetic gesture as she was accused, tried, and convicted of Wall Street shenanigans."

It also didn't help her reputation and image when she showed up for court with a $5,000 designer purse, about which the media gleefully reported in full.

Despite the fact that Stewart has strong and vocal critics regarding her public relations strategies, the company that bears her name, Martha Stewart Living Omnimedia, seems to be thriving. In the second quarter of 2006 it announced its revenues were up 47 percent compared to the same quarter in 2005.

When she was a guest on *Fox News* in April 2006, David Asman summarized her comeback, "Well, if you thought Martha Stewart was down for the count, think again. Since her release from prison, her business is back, and so is her stock, scoring deal after deal, with Sirius Satellite Radio, a new magazine, designing upscale homes, also grabbing six Emmy nominations for daytime TV. Now the Martha Stewart brand will be in Macy's, inking a deal to stock a line of home furnishings."

investors an estimated $90 billion. Officially known as the Public Company Accounting Reform and Investor Protection Act, the law's purpose is to increase investor confidence in a company's accounting procedures. Chief executive officers (CEOs) and chief financial officers (CFOs) must now personally certify the accuracy of their financial reports and are subject to criminal proceedings if they are not accurate.

The law also forbids companies from giving personal loans to officers and directors, and it places more independent fiscal responsibility on boards of directors to ensure that companies are adhering to good corporate governance and accounting practices. One of the first executives to be charged under the act was Richard Scrushy, former CEO of HealthSouth Corp. Prosecutors claimed he was involved in a $2.7 billion accounting fraud at the company, but he was acquitted on all charges.

The jury is still out, however, as to whether the Sarbanes-Oxley Act will ensure that the public actually receives more detailed financial information from public companies. The act is still being clarified and challenged in the courts, and attorneys have a powerful role in deciding what can and can't be released. Woody Wallace, head of an investor relations firm, told *O'Dwyer's PR Services Report*, "Most attorneys are conservative and are going to cut down what's being said. Less information and less useful information is being given out. News releases become cursory."

One fall-out of the act, from a public relations standpoint, is the decision by communication conglomerates not to give a financial break-out of their different divisions, including public relations firms. Consequently, it has become practically impossible to say with any certainty what public relations firm is the largest in the world based on revenues. See the discussion on communications conglomerates in Chapter 4.

Other Regulatory Agencies

Although the FTC and the SEC are the major federal agencies concerned with the content of advertising and publicity materials, the Food and Drug Administration (FDA) and the Bureau of Alcohol, Tobacco and Firearms (BATF) have also established guidelines.

The Food and Drug Administration (FDA). The FDA oversees the advertising and promotion of prescription drugs, over-the-counter medicines, and cosmetics. Under the federal Food, Drug, and Cosmetic Act, any "person" (which includes advertising and public relations firms) who "causes the misbranding" of products through the dissemination of false and misleading information may be held liable under provisions of the law.

The FDA has specific guidelines for video, audio, and print news releases on health care topics. First, the release must provide "fair balance" by telling consumers about the risks as well as the benefits of the drug or treatment. Second, the writer must be clear about the limitations of a particular drug or treatment, for example, that it may not help people with certain conditions. Third, a news release or media kit should be accompanied by supplementary product sheets or brochures that give full prescribing information.

Because the FDA places major curbs on advertising and promotion of prescription drugs, drug companies sometimes try to sidestep the regulations in various ways. The FDA is increasingly scrutinizing celebrities who are paid by drug companies to mention a drug's name when they are talking about their own disease on the talk show circuit.

The Bureau of Alcohol, Tobacco, and Firearms (BATF). The BATF administers the Federal Alcohol Administration Act. Any advertising or publicity about products with alcohol must conform to various regulations regarding the risk and supposed benefits of such products.

Wineries, in particular, have run into problems by implying that there are health benefits associated with drinking wine. After intense lobbying by the $9 billion California wine industry, the BATF finally agreed to let wineries label bottles with such statements as "The proud people who made this wine encourage you to consult your family doctor about the health benefits of wine consumption."

"Food Slander" Laws. A recent development in state legislation is "food slander" laws. A dozen states have put "agricultural product disparagement" laws, making it a crime to criticize or denigrate food with information that is not based on scientific fact.

The legislation, which resulted from the U.S. apple industry's losing almost $100 million because of the Alar scare, is designed to curtail activist groups that often use scare tactics and faulty information to disparage a particular food product. Millions of Americans learned about such laws when popular television celebrity Oprah Winfrey was sued by several Texas cattlemen for allegedly disparaging beef on her talk show. The trial, held in San Antonio, was a publicity bonanza for Oprah—and the jury acquitted her.

In summary, public relations personnel have the responsibility to know, or at least be familiar with, all pertinent regulatory guidelines. A number of court cases have determined that you can be liable for disseminating false and misleading information on behalf of a client or employer.

Corporate/Employee Free Speech

The First Amendment of the U.S. Constitution guarantees "freedom of speech," but exactly what speech is protected has been defined by the courts over the past 200 years, and is still being interpreted today. However, there is a well-established doctrine that commercial speech does not enjoy the same First Amendment protections as other forms of speech.

Essentially, the government may regulate advertising that is false, misleading, deceptive, or advertising for unlawful goods and services. The courts also have ruled that product news releases, brochures, and other promotional vehicles intended to sell a product or service constitute commercial speech.

Another area, however, is what is termed *corporate free speech*. The courts, for the most part, have upheld the right of corporations and other organizations to express their views on public policy, proposed legislation, and a host of other issues that may be of societal or corporate concern. Organizations often do so through opinion articles in magazines and newspapers, letters to the editor, postings on their Web sites, and even news releases.

Some landmark Supreme Court cases have helped establish the concept of corporate free speech. In 1978, for example, the Court struck down a Massachusetts law that prohibited corporations from publicizing their views on issues subject to the ballot box. Then, in 1980, the Court ruled that a New York Public Utilities Commission regulation prohibiting utilities from making statements of public policy and controversy was unconstitutional. Six years later, the Court ruled that the California Public Utilities Commission could not require Pacific Gas & Electric Company to include messages from activist consumer groups in its mailings to customers. The utility argued that inclusion of such messages (called "bill stuffers") impaired the company's right to communicate its own messages. A more recent corporate free speech issue involved Nike (see the Insights box on page 236).

Employee Free Speech

A modern, progressive organization encourages employee comments and even criticisms. Many employee newspapers carry letters to the editor because they breed a healthy atmosphere of two-way communication and make company publications more credible.

Yet, at the same time, recent developments have indicated that not all is well for employee freedom of expression. A *Time* magazine essay by Barbara Ehrenreich, for example, gives startling examples of organizations that deny free speech to employees. A grocery worker in Dallas was fired for wearing a Green Bay Packers T-shirt to work when the Dallas Cowboys were scheduled to play Green Bay in the conference playoffs. A worker at Caterpiller, Inc., was suspended for wearing a T-shirt titled "Defending the American Dream," a slogan of the union that had bitterly fought the company in a strike.

Employee freedom of expression and the issue of privacy have also been raised by court decisions that give employers the right to read employees' e-mail. Pillsbury, for example, fired a worker who posted an e-mail message to a colleague calling management "back-stabbing bastards." The employee sued, but the court sided with the company.

Although employee privacy is still an issue, the trend line is for increased monitoring of employee e-mail by employers. Employers are concerned about being held liable if an employee posts a racial slur, engages in sexual harassment online, and even transmits sexually explicit jokes that would cause another employee to feel that the workplace was a "hostile" environment. In other words, you should assume that any e-mails you write at work are subject to monitoring and that you can be fired if you violate company policy. Complicating this further is the fact that government employees may have their e-mails made public if some interested party files a Freedom of Information Act request. E-mails produced by a public employee on a government-owned computer are considered requestable documents under the FOIA.

Two other aspects of employee free speech are whistle-blowing and protection of an organization's trade secrets. State and federal laws generally protect the right of employees to "blow the whistle" if an organization is guilty of illegal activity.

ON THE JOB >>

Nike's Free Speech Battle

Insights

The Supreme Court again became involved with corporate free speech in 2003 when it was petitioned by Nike, the shoe and sports clothes manufacturer, to redress a California Supreme Court decision that had ruled that the company's efforts to explain its labor policies abroad was basically "garden variety commercial speech."

The case, *Nike v. Kasky*, raised the thorny question of how to deal with the blurred lines that often separate free speech and commercial speech. Marc Kasky, an activist, had sued Nike, claiming that the company had made false and misleading statements that constituted unlawful and deceptive business practices. Nike, on the other hand, claimed that it had the right to express its views and defend itself against allegations by activist groups that it operated sweatshop factories in Asia and paid subpar wages.

The California Supreme Court disagreed. In its deci-

sion, it wrote "when a corporation, to maintain and increase its sales and profits, makes public statements defending labor practices and working conditions at factories where its products are made, those public statements are commercial speech that may be regulated to prevent consumer deception."

The U.S. Supreme Court, however, was less certain about the "commercial" nature of Nike's public relations campaign. Although it didn't make a decision and sent the case back to the California courts, Eugene Volokh, professor of law at UCLA, noted in a *Wall Street Journal* op-ed piece that Justice Stephen Breyer made an important point. According to Volokh, "Because the commercial message (buy our shoes) was mixed with a political mes-

sage (our political opponents are wrong), and was presented outside a traditional advertising medium, it should have been treated as fully protected."

Rather than face the California courts again, Nike decided to settle the case with Kasky for $1.5 million that would go to the Fair Labor Association to monitor American factories abroad, particularly in Asia. A number of groups that had supported Nike's effort to defend corporate free speech, including PRSA and the Arthur W. Page Society, were somewhat disappointed that the conclusion of the case left many unanswered questions about the right of corporations to speak out on issues and even defend themselves against the charges of activist groups.

Does a corporation have the right of free speech? Nike took its case to the U.S. Supreme Court after the California courts ruled that Nike's defense of its labor practices abroad was simply "commercial speech." Here, protesters unfurl banners opposing Nike's position.

Whistle-blowing can occur in corporate, nonprofit, and government organizations. For example, an employee might blow the whistle on his or her organization by reporting to the Environmental Protection Agency the illegal release of a toxic substance from the employer's manufacturing plant.

It also is well established that an organization has a legal right to fire employees or sue former employees if they reveal proprietary information to the competition. For example, in 2006 an employee at Coca-Cola headquarters in Atlanta was arrested for allegedly attempting to sell Coke's trade secrets to competitor Pepsi-Cola. In this case, Pepsi reported the incident to Coke and the FBI who set up a sting to catch the employee. These laws also apply to public relations firms, which usually have employees sign agreements that they will not divulge proprietary information about clients to outsiders or, if they leave the firm, to their new employers.

Liability for Sponsored Events

Public relations personnel often focus on the planning and logistics of events. Consequently, they must also take steps to protect their organizations from liability and possible lawsuits.

Plant Tours and Open Houses

Plant tours should not be undertaken lightly. They require detailed planning by the public relations staff to guarantee the safety and comfort of visitors. Consideration must be given to such factors as (1) logistics, (2) possible work disruptions as groups pass through the plant, (3) safety, and (4) amount of staffing required.

A well-marked tour route is essential; it is equally important to have trained escort staff and tour guides. Guides should be well versed in company history and operations, and their comments should be somewhat standardized to make sure that key facts are conveyed. In addition, guides should be trained in first aid and thoroughly briefed on what to do in case of an accident or heart attack. At the beginning the guide should outline to the visitors what they will see, the amount of walking involved, the time required, and the number of stairs. This warning tells visitors with heart conditions or other physical limitations what they can expect.

Many of the points about plant tours are applicable to open houses. The added problem with open houses is having large numbers of people on the plant site at the same time. Such an event calls for special logistical planning by the public relations staff, including the following possible measures: (1) arranging for extra liability insurance, (2) hiring off-duty police for security and traffic control, (3) arranging to have paramedics and an ambulance on site, (4) making contractual agreements with vendors selling food or souvenirs, and (5) ordering portable potties.

Such precautions will generate goodwill and limit the company's liability. It should be noted, however, that a plaintiff can still collect if negligence on the part of the company can be proved.

Promotional Events

These events are planned primarily to promote product sales, increase organizational visibility, or raise money for charitable causes. Events that attract crowds require the same kind of planning as does an open house. Public relations personnel should be concerned about traffic flow, adequate restroom facilities, signage, and security. Off-duty police officers are often hired to handle crowd control, protect celebrities or government officials, and make sure no disruptions occur.

Liability insurance is a necessity. Any public event sponsored by an organization should be insured against accidents that might result in lawsuits charging negligence. Organizations can purchase comprehensive insurance to cover a variety of events or a specific event. The need for liability insurance also applies to charitable organizations if they sponsor a 10-K run, a bicycle race, or a hot-air balloon race. Participants should sign a release form that protects the organization against liability in case of a heart attack or an accident. An organization that sponsored a 5-K "fun run" had the participants sign a statement that stated in part, "I assume all risk associated with running in this event, including, but not limited to, falls, contact with other participants, the effects of the weather, including high heat/or humidity, traffic, and other conditions of the road."

Promotional events that use public streets and parks also need permits from the appropriate city departments. A 10-K run or a parade, for example, requires permits from the police or the public safety department to block streets. Sponsors frequently hire off-duty police to control traffic.

A music store in one California city found out about these considerations the hard way. It allowed a popular rock group to give an informal concert in front of the store as part of a promotion. Radio DJs spread the word and, as a result, a crowd of 8,000 converged on the shopping center, causing a massive traffic jam. The city attorney filed charges against the store for creating a public disturbance and billed the store $80,000 for police overtime pay to untangle the mess.

A food event, such as a chili cook-off or a German fest, requires a permit from the public health department and, if liquor is served, a permit from the state alcohol board. If the event is held inside a building not usually used for this purpose, a permit is often required from the fire inspector. In addition, a major deposit may be required as insurance that the organization will clean up a public space after the event.

Working with Lawyers

This chapter has outlined a number of areas in which the release of information (or the lack of release) raises legal issues for an organization. Public relations personnel must be aware of legal pitfalls, but they are not lawyers. By the same token, lawyers aren't experts in public relations and often lack sufficient understanding of how important the court of public opinion is in determining the reputation and credibility of an organization.

In today's business environment, with its high potential for litigation, it is essential for public relations professionals and lawyers to have cooperative relationships. Although much is written about the tug-of-war between public relations people and lawyers concerning the release of information, a survey by Kathy R. Fitzpatrick, a public relations professor at DePaul University, found that almost 85 percent of the public relations respondents said their relationship with legal counsel was either "excellent" or "good." Researchers at the University of Houston and the University of Missouri, in separate studies, found that lawyers and public relations practitioners report cooperative relationships.

Though both professions express respect for the colleagues with whom they work, they show less respect for members of the opposite profession generally. A lawyer told the Missouri researchers, "They [public relations practitioners] are a necessary evil. Contemporary distrust of institutions has resulted from people putting a favorable spin on messages. I think so much of [public relations practitioners'] work product is blatantly manipulatively." Nonetheless, both professions acknowledge that working as a team is in the best interest of their organization.

The relationship between lawyers and public relations practitioners is such an important issue that both professions regularly deal with it in publications and seminars. *PR News* has an online newsletter, *Crisis and Legal PR Bulletin*, and provides publications and programming that address the intersection of law and public relations. The University of Georgia School of Law provided practicing lawyers with a day-long continuing education program titled, "Winning in the Court of Public Opinion." Lawyers and public relations professionals are increasingly recognizing the important skills each party brings to communications and litigation planning.

PRSA's monthly tabloid *Tactics* suggests six "keys to winning in the court of law—and public opinion." They are

1. Make carefully planned public comment in the earliest stages of a crisis or legal issue.
2. Understand the perspective of lawyers and allow them to review statements when an organization is facing or involved in litigation.
3. Public relations practitioners need to guard against providing information to the other side of the legal case.
4. Public relations professionals should counsel and coach the legal team.
5. Build support from other interested parties, such as industry associations or chambers of commerce.
6. Develop a litigation communication team before you need it.

Because the collaboration between lawyers and public relations practitioners is so important, a number of steps can be taken by an organization to ensure that the public relations and legal staffs have a cordial, mutually supportive relationship:

> The public relations and legal staffs should report to the same top executive, who can listen to both sides and decide on a course of action.
> Public relations personnel should know basic legal concepts and regulatory guidelines in order to build trust and credibility with the legal department.
> Both functions should be represented on key committees.
> The organization should have a clearly defined statement of responsibilities for each staff and its relationship to the other. Neither should dominate.
> Periodic consultations should be held during which materials and programs are reviewed.
> The legal staff, as part of its duties, should brief public relations personnel on impending developments in litigation, so press inquiries can be answered in an appropriate manner.

Summary

What Are Ethics?

Ethics refers to a person's value system and how he or she determines right or wrong. The three basic value orientations are (1) absolutist, (2) existentialist, and (3) situationalist. Even if one is an advocate for a particular organization or cause, one can behave in an ethical manner. Because of the concept of role differentiation, society understands that the advocate is operating within an assigned role, much like a defense lawyer or prosecuting attorney in court.

The Role of Professional Organizations

Groups such as PRSA, IABC, and IPRA provide an important role in setting the standards and ethical behavior of the profession. Most professional organizations have published codes of conduct and educational programs.

Professional Codes of Conduct

True public relations professionals have a loyalty to a higher standard and to the public interest. They are more than "careerists" and practice public relations with more than a "technician mentality." They are not hired guns who just parrot whatever the client or organization wants them to say.

Defamation

There is now little practical difference between libel and slander; the two are often collectively referred to as *defamation*. The concept of defamation involves a false and malicious (or at least negligent) communication with an identifiable subject who is injured either financially or by loss of reputation or mental suffering. Libel suits can be avoided through the careful use of language. Some offensive communications will fall under the "fair comment" defense; an example of this would be a negative review by a theater critic.

Invasion of Privacy

Companies cannot assume when publishing newsletters that a person waives his or her right to privacy due to status as an employee. It is important to get written permission to publish photos or use employees in advertising materials, and to be cautious in releasing personal information about employees to the media.

Copyright Law

Copyright is the protection of creative work from unauthorized use. It is assumed that published works are copyrighted, and permission must be obtained to reprint such material. The doctrine of fair use allows limited quotation, as in a book review. Unless a company has a specific contract with a freelance writer, photographer, or artist to produce work that will be exclusively owned by that company (a situation called "work for hire"), the freelancer owns his or her work. New copyright issues have been raised by the popularity of the Internet and the ease of downloading, uploading, and disseminating images and information.

Trademark Law

A trademark is a word, symbol, or slogan that identifies a product's origin. These can be registered with the U.S. Patent and Trademark Office. Trademarks are always capitalized and used as adjectives rather than nouns or verbs. Companies vigorously protect trademarks to prevent their becoming common nouns. One form of trademark infringement is "misappropriation of personality," the use of a celebrity's name or image for advertising purposes without permission.

Regulations by Government Agencies

Commercial speech is regulated by the government in the interest of public health, safety, and consumer protection. Among the agencies involved in this regulation are the Federal Trade Commission, the Securities and Exchange Commission, the Food and Drug Administration, and the Bureau of Alcohol, Tobacco, and Firearms.

Corporate/Employee Free Speech

Organizations, in general, have the right to express their opinions and views about a number of public issues. However, there is still some blurring of lines between what is considered "commercial speech" and "free speech," as illustrated by the Nike case. Employees are limited in expressing opinions within the corporate environment. E-mail, for example, is company property and subject to monitoring. Employees can be fired (or former employees sued) for revealing trade secrets. At the same time, whistle-blowers have protection against retaliation.

Working with Lawyers

Because of all the issues discussed in this chapter, a cooperative relationship must exist between public relations personnel and legal counsel. It helps if both groups report to the same top executive and both are represented on key committees. Public relations practitioners should also be aware of legal concepts and regulatory guidelines and receive briefings from the legal staff on impending developments.

CASE ACTIVITY >>

What Would You Do?

Tough Ethical Choices—To Accept or Reject a Client

Here's hypothetical situation. A well-known professional baseball player is suspected of having used steroids and other performance-enhancing drugs. He has not been charged. His agent asks you to advise and assist him in handling the intense media interest in the case. He wants you to try to place favorable stories about the baseball star in the media and create a positive environment for him. If formally accused, it could mean irreparable damage to his baseball career.

You are not asked to do anything unethical. The money is quite good, and you know the publicity from working on the case will probably help your public relations consulting career, especially if the athlete is exhonorated. Would you take the account? The agent tells you confidentially that the athlete has admitted that he took some substance that was unknown to him, but may have been steroids. Does this information affect your decision? What are the ethics of the situation as you see them?

Questions for Review and Discussion

1. What is ethics? How can two individuals disagree about what constitutes an ethical dilemma or concern?

2. Some critics say voluntary codes of ethics "have no teeth" because they can't be enforced. Are there other reasons for having codes of ethics?

3. Some argue that there is such a thing as an "ethical advocate." What reasons do they give?

4. Public relations practitioners often have conflicting loyalties. Do they owe their first allegiance to their client or employer or to the standards of their professional organization, such as PRSA?

5. Why are gifts to the media considered unprofessional and, at times, unethical?

6. Why do public relations staff and firms need to know the legal aspects of creating and distributing messages?

7. How can a public relations person take precautions to avoid libel suits?

8. What is the concept of fair comment and criticism? Are there any limitations?

9. What precautions should a public relations person take to avoid invasion of privacy lawsuits?

10. If an organization wants to use the photo or comments of an employee or a customer in an advertisement, what precautions should be taken?

11. What basic guidelines of copyright law should public relations professionals know about?

12. When the media call about an employee, what kinds of information should the public relations person provide? What other approaches can be used?

13. How do public relations people help an organization protect its trademarks?

14. What should be the relationship between public relations staff and legal counsel in an organization?

Suggested Readings

Bowen, Shannon A. "A Practical Model for Ethical Decision Making in Issues Management and Public Relations." *Journal of Public Relations Research* 17, no. 3 (2005): 191–216.

Bunker, Matthew D., and Bethany Bolger. "Protecting a Delicate Balance: Facts, Ideas, and Expression in Compilation Copyright Cases." *Journalism & Mass Communications Quarterly* 80, no. 1 (2003): 183–197.

Gower, Karla K. *Legal and Ethical Restraints on Public Relations*. Long Grove, IL: Waveland Press, 2003.

Haggerty, James F. *Winning Your Case with Public Relations*. New York: Wiley, 2003.

Kim, Yungwook, and Youjin Choi. "Ethical Standards Appear to Change with Age and Ideology: A Survey of Practitioners." *Public Relations Review* 29, no. 1 (2003): 79–89.

Langston, R. Carter. "Public Relations and the Law: Six Keys to Winning in the Court of Law—and Public Opinion." *Public Relations Tactics*, March 2006, 14.

Nolan, Hamilton. "Press Subpoenas Are Wake-up Call for PR." *PRWeek*, May 15, 2006, 10.

Reber, Bryan, Karla Gower, and Jennifer Robinson. "The Internet and Litigation Public Relations." *Journal of Public Relations Research* 18, no. 1 (2006): 23–44.

Chapter Eight

Reaching the Audience

Books

> The Spoken and Visual Media
> *Radio*
> *Television*
> *Sponsored Films and Videotapes*

> Online Media

Nature of the Public Relations Audience

If the audience on which public relations practitioners focused their messages was a monolithic whole, their work would be far easier—and far less stimulating. In reality, an audience is a complex intermingling of groups with diverse cultural, ethnic, religious, and socioeconomic attributes whose interests coincide at times and conflict at others.

A successful public relations campaign must take into account the shifting dynamics of audiences and target those segments of an audience that are most desirable for its particular purpose, in addition to employing the mass media most effective in reaching those segments. Some audience segments are easily identifiable and reachable as "prepackaged publics." For example, advocacy, civic, educational and charitable ogranizations are generally well-organized groups whose members are bound by common interests; thus, they constitute ready-made targets for public relations practitioners.

Diversity is the most significant aspect of the mass audience, or general public, in the United States. Differences in geography, history, culture, and economy among the regions of this sprawling country are striking; ranchers in Montana have different attitudes than residents in the heavily populated Eastern seaboard cities. Yet people in the two areas often share national interests. Ethnicity, generational differences, and socioeconomic status also shape the audience segments that public relations practitioners address. For example, the American Heart Association (AHA) provides resources aimed at African American and Latino populations. The Power to End Stroke movement is an AHA initiative targeted to African Americans. *Soul Food Recipies*, a publication subsidized by the AHA, encourages healthy eating habits as part of the effort to prevent the likelihood of stroke.

The international audience for public relations has expanded swiftly. Growth of global corporations and expanded foreign marketing by smaller firms creates new public relations challenges, as does increased foreign ownership of U.S. companies. International audiences are a diverse and significant target for public relations campaigns. For example, Xerox Corporation has a Worldwide Strategic PR division that serves markets in countries ranging from Afghanistan to Zimbabwe. Each nation has separate, culturally sensitive public relations initiatives including customer support, crisis management, media relations, and other forms of publicity.

Technology can be used to segment a mass audience and complie valuable demographic information. Computer and related technologies can be used to conduct both primary and secondary research to identify target audiences. Geographic and social statistics found in Census Bureau reports provide a rich foundation. Much of this data can be broken down by census tract and ZIP code. Data on automobile registrations, voter registrations, sales figures, mailing lists, and church and organization memberships also can be merged into computer databases. One marketing research organization, Claritas Inc., has divided the Chicago metropolitan area into 62 lifestyle clusters.

It has assigned a name to each cluster; for example, "Boomers & Babies," whose buying habits, Claritas says, include "rent more than five videos a month, buy children frozen dinners, read parenting magazines." The Internet and World Wide Web also provide an efficient and effective way to move beyond geographical limits in public relations messages, but they require quicker responses to their swiftly changing audiences.

People are becoming more visually oriented and seem to have shorter attention spans. At our computer screens, we are exposed to dynamic multimedia content including Web sites with streaming videos, regularly updated blogs, instant messaging, and Web forums. The enormous impact of television on daily life has increased visual orientation, with many people now obtaining virtually all of their news from their TVs. Television news and entertainment programs increasingly are presented as discrete and quickly shifting images. The swift pace of presentation may lead to viewers' shortened attention spans. Political leaders now reach the public largely in 10-second "sound bites." Television also serves as a potent communicator of manners, mores, and aspirations. *American Idol* and reality shows, for example have made the dream of becoming famous seem tangible, if only, as artist Andy Warhol predicted in 1968, for a figurative 15 minutes.

Audiences sometimes coalesce around single issues. Some individuals become so zealously involved in promoting or opposing a single issue that they lose the social and political balance so necessary in a democracy. Animal rights and right-to-life activists frequently have been accused of going too far. For example, in 2004, a New Jersey grand jury indicted the militant animal rights group Stop Huntingdon Animal Cruelty for demonstrating against the biological research company Huntingdon Life Sciences. Their tactics included physically assaulting workers, firebombing cars, harassing communications, and bomb threats.

Society now places a heavy emphasis personality and celebrity. Sports stars, television and movie actors, and musical performers are virtually worshipped by some fans. When stars embrace causes, people will often take note of those causes. Increasingly, celebrities are used as spokespersons and fund-raisers, even though their expertise as performers does not necessarily qualify them as experts or opinion leaders for complex issues. Actors Richard Gere, George Clooney, Charlton Heston, and Susan Sarandon and musician Bono have all been outspoken advocates of political causes; other stars such as Paul Newman, Robert Redford, and Don Henley have worked for causes more quietly behind the scenes. Actors Ronald Reagan and Arnold Schwarzenegger, and professional wrestler Jesse Ventura, all capitalized on their fame to rise to political office with varying degrees of success.

Another modern development with implications for public relations practice is that strong distrust of authority and suspicion of conspiracy have arisen from sensationalistic investigative reporting. Especially since Richard Nixon resigned the presidency in the wake of the Watergate scandal, many Americans have become quick to suspect their leaders of wrongdoing. The unethical business practices of executives at Enron, Tyco, WorldCom, Arthur Andersen, and other large corporations has led to a general distrust of businesses. People are so inundated with exaggerated political promises, see so much financial chicanery, and are exposed to so much misleading or even contradictory information that many of them now distrust what they read and hear in the news. They suspect evil motives, and tend to enjoy gossip and believe rumors. The need for public relations programs to develop an atmosphere of justifiable, rational trust is obvious.

Public relations has become more strategic in practice; audiences are targeted precisely and in some instances messages are customized at the individual level. In health care settings, for example, e-mail messages can be tailored to the individual patient based on his or her most recent examination. Not only can the public relations professional target a precise public, but in many cases the professional can actually bypass the mass media and communicate directly with the preselected audience through customized mailings or other direct means such as personalized e-mails or broadcast faxes. The use of communication channels that directly reach an audience is called controlled media. Examples of controlled media include sponsored films or videotapes and events, which are discussed later in this chapter.

Target Markets and Other Emerging Audiences

As the demographic makeup of the United States continues to change dramatically, three major target audiences have emerged that deserve special attention. One is senior citizens, or seniors. This group frequently is defined as men and women 65 years or older, although some sociologists, marketing experts, and organizations such as AARP (formerly the American Association of Retired Persons), include everyone over age 50. A comparable group is the so-called tween market consisting of youths age 7 to 12, in addition to the well-defined teenage demographic group. The third group consists of racial and ethnic minorities, particularly audiences of African American and Hispanic descent. Beyond the diversity of ethnic markets in the United States, similar trends are evident in an international context and global markets have obviously risen. Other emerging audiences with unique profiles include religious groups and the gay community.

Senior Audience

Medical advances and better living conditions have improved life expectancy to the point that today 36.3 million Americans, or 12 percent, are age 65 or older, according to the 2004 U.S. Census. By 2050, the Census Bureau projects that 21 percent of the population will be 65 or older. The heavy upsurge in the senior population will peak at 50 million by 2010, when the post–World War II baby boomers begin to reach age 65.

These older citizens form an important opinion group and a consumer market with special interests. As with other demographic groups, they are not a monolithic audience, but display many differences in personality, interest, financial status, health concerns, and lifestyles. Nevertheless, public relations professionals should not overlook the following general characteristics of the senior audience:

> With the perspective of long experience, they often are less easily convinced than young adults, demand value in the things they buy, and pay little attention to fads.

> They vote in greater numbers than their juniors and are more intense readers of newspapers and magazines. Retirees also watch television heavily.

> They form an excellent source of volunteers for social, health, and cultural organizations because they have time and often are looking for something to do.

> According to Neilson/NetRating, seniors over the age of 65 were the fastest-growing segment of the population using the Internet in 2003, increasing at 25 percent. They accounted for 5.6 percent of Internet users. Seniors are also among the largest consumers of television, magazines, and newspapers.

> They are extremely health conscious, out of self-interest, and want to know about medical developments. A Census Bureau study showed that most people over age

65 say they are in good health; not until their mid-80s do they frequently need assistance in daily living.

> They are financially better off than the stereotypes suggest. In 2004, the poverty rate among older Americans was 9.8 percent, compared to 12.5 percent for the population at large. The Census Bureau found that people age 65 to 74 have more discretionary income than any other group. Median assets of older Americans were $108,885, with an annual income of $23,787 in 2003, and they hold 70 percent of the country's assets. In many instances, seniors' homes are completely paid for.

> Although they are poor customers for household goods, they eat out frequently and do a lot of gift buying. They also travel frequently. In fact, seniors account for about 80 percent of commercial vacation travel.

Youth Audience

Public relations professionals recognize the importance of the youth market. Children and teenagers represent an important demographic to marketers because they influence their parents' buying decisions, have their own purchasing power, and will mature into adult consumers. According to consumer market research company Packaged Facts, today's youth market (15- to 24-year-olds) has over $350 billion of purchasing power.

In a *PR Reporter* article, Marianne Friese of Ketchum succinctly stated the importance of the youth audience: "They rival the baby boom in sheer size and their global purchasing power is enormous." Smaller families, dual incomes, and postponing having children until later in life have led to greater disposable income. Likewise, greater attention to the importance of child rearing, advocated on television talk shows, Web sites targeted to parents, self-help books, and magazine articles, combined with advertising messages associating brand loyalty with good parenting have led to increased spending. Guilt can play a role as well. Parents pressed for time may substitute material goods for time spent with children and teenagers.

Today's children have greater autonomy and decision-making power within the family than in previous generations. Children often pester or nag their parents into purchasing items they would not otherwise buy. *Kidfluence*, a 2001 marketing publication, notes how pestering can be divided into two categories—"persistence" and "importance." Persistence nagging (a plea, that is repeated over and over again) is less sophisticated than importance nagging, which appeals to parents' desire to provide the best for their children. Like every new generation before them, they cause adults to fret about their character but show signs that they, too, will rise to the challenges that come with maturity.

The youth market has been labeled as *Generation Y* (Gen Y), a term used for those born between 1976 and 2003; they succeed *Generation X* (Gen X).

Because they are such voracious consumers of electronic media, some pundits have labeled Generation Y the e-Generation. The Fortino Group (Pittsburgh) projects that Generation Y will spend 23 years online. Spending one-third of their lives online will have interesting impacts:

> They will spend as much time interacting with friends online as in person.
> Initial interaction online will precede most dating and marriages.
> They will spend 10 times more time online than in interaction with parents.
> They will be more reserved in social skills.
> They will be savvy and skeptical about online identities such as chat participants.
> They will not tolerate print forms, slow application processes, and archaic systems.

Generation Y values relationships and trust. In a survey of 1,200 teens worldwide, Ketchum's Global Brand Marketing Practice found:

> Parents still rule when it comes to advice about careers and drugs, and even for product decisions.

> Trust in information is derived from relationships.

> The top five sources of advice are parents, doctors, clergy, friends, and teachers.

> As avid and skilled Internet users, Gen Y remains savvy about unfiltered and unpoliced content.

> Teens also recognize the credibility of editorial content compared to ads and even public service announcements, with television being the most trusted medium for them.

> Garnering publicity for products and issues will impact Gen Y, whether directed at them or at those to whom they look for advice.

Ethnic Audiences

Historically, the United States has welcomed millions of immigrants and assimilated them into the cultural mainstream. Immigrants have given the United States an eclectic mixture of personal values, habits, lifestyles, and perceptions that have been absorbed slowly, sometimes reluctantly. Two minorities have a long history in the United States: African Americans and Native Americans.

Recently, ethnic groups, primarily Hispanics, African Americans, Asian Americans, and Native Americans, as a whole have been growing five times faster than the general population, with nonwhite ethnic groups now comprising a majority in some states such as California. The U.S. Census Bureau predicts that by the year 2010 Hispanics and African Americans will make up 14.6 and 12.5 percent of the U.S. population respectively, for a total of 27.1 percent, with Caucasians accounting for 67.3 percent. Asian Americans and Native Americans comprise the remaining percentage. According to the Census Bureau, even greater changes will occur by 2050. Notably, Hispanics will comprise nearly one-fourth of the U.S. population.

A basic point for public relations professionals to remember is that minority populations form many target audiences, not a massive monolithic group whose members have identical interests. Hispanics in Miami have different cultures and concerns from Asian Americans in San Francisco. To be more precise, even the common terms for minority groups, such as Asian American, miss the cultural diversity among that racial group. For example, the lifestyles, values, and interests of fourth-generation Japanese Americans in Los Angeles are dramatically different from what is found among recent immigrants from the Philippines. Thus, the public relations professional must identify and define the audience with particular care and sensitivity, not only taking race into account but also increasingly considering the cultural and ethnic self-identity of many target audience segments.

The number and reach of the minority media through which messages can be delivered has increased just as the number of constituents has expanded. The *Gale Directory of Publications and Broadcast Media* lists 162 Hispanic publications and 245 African American publications. Spanish-language and African American radio stations also have increased in number. According to Arbitron, there were 678 radio stations across the country broadcast in Spanish in 2005. Two Spanish-language TV networks, Univision and Telemundo, serve millions of viewers. The Black Entertainment Television Network (BET) has a large national audience. Newscasts on KTSF reach

82,000 Cantonese speakers each night in the area around San Francisco, a region with an Asian population of 19.2 percent. Many cable and satellite providers offer special packages in a variety of native languages. A substantial number of outlets exist for public relations messages, provided news releases and story pitches are translated and culturally appropriate. Business Wire, a major distributor of public relations messages, recognizes this diversity of interest among racial and ethnic minority groups by operating separate Hispanic, African American, and Asian American media circuits within the United States.

The expansion of the Hispanic population represents a challenge for public relations practitioners. Merely translating messages into Spanish is not sufficient. Public relations practitioners must shape communications to be responsive to the Hispanic culture. According to New America Strategies Group and DemoGraph Corporation, Hispanic culture places great emphasis on family and children, spending three times more on health care and entertainment than white households.

Radio is an especially important way to reach this ethnic group. Surveys show that the average Hispanic person listens to the radio 26 to 30 hours a week, about 13 percent more than the general population. Hispanic station KLVE-FM has the largest audience in Los Angeles, more than any English-language station.

Television also has a large, rapidly expanding Hispanic audience. In 2004, the Nielsen rating service estimated the number of Hispanic households (those in which the head of the household is of Hispanic descent) in the United States with television sets at 10.57 million. Univision, the predominant Spanish-language TV network, claims to reach three-fourths of Hispanic viewers. Since it signed up to be rated in early 2006, Univision consistently has ranked fourth or fifth among all broadcast networks in the 18–34 demographic according to the Nielsen's National Television Index. The Spanish language TV network Telemundo is also making impressive market share gains. The Insights box on page 249 looks at the film industry's appeal to the Hispanic market.

Public relations people need to pay particular attention to the sensitivities of racial and ethnic minority audiences. For example, the iconic figure of Aunt Jemima on packages of breakfast food products was widely regarded in the black community as a patronizing stereotype. To change this perception, Quaker Oats company cooperated with the National Council of Negro Women to honor outstanding African American women in local communities, who then competed for a national award. At the local award breakfasts, all of the foods served were Aunt Jemima brands, and Quaker Oats officials participated in the programs. The project helped generate an atmosphere of mutual understanding.

Public relations practitioners also should be aware of mixed-race individuals whose representation in the media is perhaps more complex. This complexity was lampooned recently by comedian Dave Chappelle in a 2004 sketch entitled "The Racial Draft," which compared the media's obsession with racial identity with a professional sports players' draft. Tiger Woods is one high-profile, mixed-race individual who has built a positve image.

Accomplished mixed-race individuals sometimes feel that their racial identity is exploited or treated like a carnival attraction in the media. Pittsburg Steeler Hines Ward received notoriety in South Korea after being voted the Most Valuable Player in Super Bowl XL. President Roh Moo-hyun invited the star athlete to visit Korea in April 2006, promising that the country would welcome him as a hero. Ward, who is of Korean and African American heritage, was angered during the visit by what he considered the commerical exploitation and violations of his privacy by the competitive

— ON THE JOB >>

Paramount Reaches Out to Hispanic Audiences

Insights

Although about 25 million Hispanics go to the movies annually, each seeing an average of 10 films a year, the film industry has been slow to produce films tailored to this market.

Paramount Studios, however, sought to address this situation by the producing a comedy *Nacho Libre*, during the summer of 2006. The film features Jack Black as a cook in a Mexican monastery/orphanage who turns to *lucha libre*—Mexico's popular form of pro wrestling—to raise money for the orphans. Shot in Mexico with a local cast and crew, the film co-stars Mexican telenovela star Ana de la Reguera as Sister Encarnación, Nacho's love interest.

The studio launched an extensive advertising and public relations campaign to promote the movie among Hispanics. It hired HM Communications, a consultant in Hispanic marketing, to focus mainly on the Mexican American market. Although about two-thirds of U.S. Hispanics are of

Mexican heritage, one of the "don'ts" of marketing is treating the audience as homogeneous.

With this in mind, Paramount took Ms. de la Reguera on a media and promotional tour of cities with large Mexican American populations. Her status as a Mexican soap star drew considerable media attention and large audiences in such cities as San Antonio and Dallas.

The film's advertising campaign was segmented to various elements of the Hispanic population. For young males, the ads focused on the more ridiculous, comic moments. For families, they featured the heroic nature of the lead, Nacho. In one poster, orphans surround Nacho. For television, the studio made trailers for Spanish-language networks, including Univision and Telemundo.

In selecting other marketing partners, Paramount avoided stereotypes like tie-ins with the American fast-food chain Taco Bell. Julia Pistor, one of the film's producers, told the *Wall Street Journal*, "We didn't want it to be the

'Three Amigos! A Mexican Movie,' referring to the 1986 Mexican bandit farce starring Steve Martin, Chevy Chase, and Martin Short.

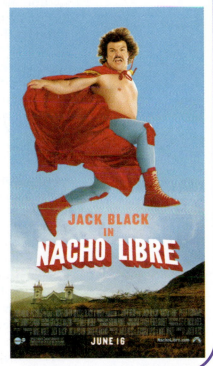

South Korean media. He canceled several scheduled appearances, cut his trip short, and has prepared to file a lawsuit against a Korean publishing company that released a book about him without his consent.

Global Audiences

Audiences in places such as Russia, China, India, Latin America, and Europe are getting the attention of public relations professionals as trade (and public relations) expands on a global basis. Public relations professionals must overcome language barriers and consider social differences to practice culturally appropriate and locally acceptable public relations. Differences in lifestyles, customs, values, and cultures are not the only challenges. Differences associated with political, economic, and industrial structures also affect the strategic planning and execution of public relations campaigns.

When McDonald's opened its first restaurant in Russia immediately after the fall of the Soviet Union in 1991, the press embraced the fast-food restaurant as a symbol of all that was positive about Western culture in contrast to Soviet culture. As the novelty of Western-style capitalism wore thin, however, public relations in Russia reincorporated old-style Soviet propaganda tools. Corruption was common as so-called public relations "technologists" funnelled millions of dollars into journalists' hands in exchange for favorable press. Overloading the press with rumor and hearsay about rival politicians or corportions, a technique known as "black public relations," was also a frequent strategy.

With the new millenium, however, Russian public relations professionals began to recognize the benefit of modern public relations approaches. They assisted the German manufacturer Bosch, for example, launched a major campaign to convince Russians of the advantage of owning a dishwasher. By enlisting artists and musicians as advocates, Bosch increased sales by 70 percent in a brief period. An art installation entitled "A Monument to the Amount of Time Wasted on Washing Up," was particulary successful at helping define public need for a dishwasher. An art installation in the United States or Canada would probably be ineffective in convincing consumers to buy such a product, but because of cultural differences, it was successful in Russia.

China is another growing market undergoing revolutionary political, social, and industrial changes. Since it reopened to Western markets in 1978, the growth of business opportunites in China has been phenomenal. Despite the dark shadow of corruption and government regulation as an ongoing concern (see box on page 199 about Google, Yahoo!, and Microsoft in China in Chapter 6), American and European companies have embraced the Chinese market. Awareness of local customs and business practices is critical, however. "There are cultural differences that you have to become attuned to," said Cynthia He, an investment relations manager with the search engine company Baidu in China during an interview with *Time* magazine Asia edition reporter Bill Powell. "I've been at meetings when I've been very blunt in pointing something out, and there will be an awkward second or two of silence, and then someone will politely say, 'Well, that's a very American way of looking at it,' which is another way of saying, hey, will you tone it down a bit!" Chinese value their long tradition and personal influence is important in every aspect of the business, social, and media systems. For example, if public relations practitioners want to send out news releases, they may need to get to know the reporters personally as part of the process.

Companies occasionally misstep when entering intenational markets. Budweiser's decision to purchase the exclusive rights for beer sales at the 2006 World Cup held in Germany is illustrative. The Germans are fiercely proud of their native beers, and the notion that an American company woud infringe on this has created an uproar. According to an article in *Forbes* magazine by Marc E. Babej and Tim Pollack, "the European press danced on the head of the mega-brewer, expressing disdain for the Budweiser brand." German politician Fritz Maget made headlines by proclaiming that Budweiser was the "worst beer in the world," and that the Germans "have a duty of public welfare and must not poison visitors to the World Cup." Whether risking derision from German consumers will hurt Budweiser's global reputation in the long run remains to be seen. Because the media relish conflict, Budweiser garnered more exposure than if the German beer loyalists had not gone on the attack. In the short term, the sponsorship deal appears ill-conceived if not arrogant, but time will tell whether the American company actually gains brand recognition from the controversy.

with their religious faith, the GLBT community may be offended by conventional or normative principles that conflict with their values and lifestyles. As with any target audience, public relations professionals need consider the identities of Christian and GLBT audience groups when undertaking public relations efforts.

PR CASEBOOK

You Can't Have Your Cake, and Eat It Too

Ford Ads in Gay Media Draw Fire

It is often impossible to satisfy multiple publics simultaneously. The Ford Motor Company recognized this after experiencing a public relations crisis in the wake of a campaign to extend their market to specific groups.

In 2005, Ford ran print ads for Jaguar, Land Rover, and Volvo targeted to gay, lesbian, bisexual, and transgendered (GLBT) individuals in gay and lesbian publications. The American Family Association and other conservative groups condemned the decision. Interestingly, gay-themed ads were not produced for other lines such as Ford and Lincoln-Mercury. The American Family Alliance (AFA) threatened a six-month boycott of Ford unless it pulled the ads, and stopped sponsoring gay events. Faced with a boycott, Ford pulled the ads—at least for a time.

Gay and lesbian activist groups protested Ford's decision. After meeting with members of seven gay and lesbian rights groups, Ford recanted their position and agreed to run ads for all eight of their car lines. Joe Layton, Ford's head of human resources, explained, "It is my hope that this will remove any ambiguity about Ford's desire to advertise to all important audiences and put this particular issue behind us." A statement issued jointly by nineteen GLBT rights groups on December 15, 2005, praised Ford's decision to reinstate the ads: "We welcome today's statement from Ford Motor Company and commend their firm stance in support of inclusion." The issue entered into a convoluted cycle of crisis, with actions and the reactions of AFA and GLBT to the other party (see the conflict management life cycle in Chapter 2).

The issue was far from resolved. Although the AFA briefly ended calls for a boycott after meeting with executives at Ford, it was reinstated in 2006. A petition on the AFA Web site called for a boycott because of the company's continued "extensive promotion of homosexuality." Donald Wildmon, president of the AFA, claimed that the boycott has been effective because Ford stock had dropped 13 percent since the campaign began.

Ford Motor Company ran ads in gay-themed publications in 2005, prompting conservative groups to protest. In response, Ford pulled the ads, only to reverse its decision after meeting with gay and lesbian leaders. Ad, Jaguar, Ford Motor Company, 2005, Witeck-Combs Communication.

The situation puts Ford at the center of a wider political controversy over gay marriage and the rights of GLBT individuals. With the prospect of a constitutional amendment defining marriage as the union between a man and a woman, Ford has defined its position in a manner that could have repercussions. "Advertising all of its brands in the gay, lesbian, bisexual and transgendered press makes a strong statement," said David Smith, vice president of policy and strategy at the Human Rights Campaign, in a statement to the *Detroit News*. "We believe this represents more than what was asked for. Ford did a really good job of clearing the air."

Ford has taken the stance that it values its target customers, even if it comes at the expense of sales to other segments. It seems you can't have your cake, and eat it too.

Source: Jeremy W. Peters, "U.S.: Ford, Reversing Decision, Will Run Ads in Gay Press," *The New York Times*, December 15, 2005.

Matching the Audience with the Media

This section explains the major media—how each one functions and ways in which it can be used for public relations purposes. With the broad array of print, audio, visual, and new media outlets available, public relations practitioners must make wise choices to use their time and budgets efficiently and effectively to produce desired outcomes.

Before we look at each medium in more detail, some general guidelines can be given for matching audiences with the media:

> Print media are the most effective for delivering a message that requires absorption of details and contemplation by receivers. Printed matter can be read repeatedly and kept for reference. Newspapers are fast and have the most widespread impact of the print outlets. Magazines, although slower, are better for reaching special-interest audiences. Books take even longer but can generate strong impact over time. Increasingly, traditional media primarily appeals to older or more highly educated audiences.

> Television has the strongest emotional impact of all media. Its visual power makes situations seem close to the viewer. The vividness and personality of the TV communicator creates an influence that print media cannot match. Television currently has the largest and broadest audience. The Insights box about *American Idol* on page 255 speaks to the force of television.

> Radio's greatest advantages are flexibility and the ability to reach specific target audiences. Messages can be prepared for and broadcast on radio more rapidly than on television, and at a much lower cost. Because there are nine times as many radio stations as TV stations, audience exposure is easier to obtain, but the audiences reached are smaller.

> Use of online media, once thought of as a supplemental method of reaching a generally well-educated, relatively affluent audience, is expanding exponentially. Currently, somewhere between 70 and 75 percent of U.S. households have Internet access. About 16 percent of the world's population has Internet access, and that number grew at a rate of about 183 percent between 2000 and 2005. In the foreseeable future, it is likely that electronic media delivery systems, such as the Internet and wireless communications, will overtake print media and even television as the primary source of information.

The Print Media

Newspapers

Newspapers are designed for family reading, with something for men, women, and children, and newspaper material is aimed at an audience of varying educational and economic levels. Newspaper editors cast a wide net to capture the reading interests of as many people as possible. Newpapers have a broad appeal among adults and are effective at handling complex or in-depth material that television cannot adequately cover. While hard copies of newspapers such as the *New York Times*, the *Washington Post* or the *Wall Street Journal* reach older public opinion leaders, young people tend to use newspapers in print less as sources of information and favor online media instead.

Approximately 1,500 daily newspapers and 7,200 weekly newspapers are published in the United States. Although some metropolitan newspapers have circulations

— ON THE JOB >> —

Star Today, Sold Tomorrow: American Idol

Insights

Popular culture phenomena such as *American Idol* can be good public relations outlets. The winner of *American Idol* can lend their fame, however brief, to sell a product, advocate for a cause, or boost the ratings of a television show. This form of instant celebrity, constantly renewed and recycled, offers opportunities to frequently redesigned public relations campaigns that will be perceived by the public as novel, while at the same time familiar.

American Idol is one of the most successful television programs of all times. Created by Simon Fuller, each episode of the talent show series achieves stellar market share ratings. It has been nominated for 14 Emmy awards and has spin-offs in nearly a hundred countries, including an *Indonesian Idol* and a Swiss version (*MusicStar*). To be fair, the American version is a spin-off of the original *Pop Idol*, also created by Fuller, in the United Kingdom.

The winners, and even the finalists, become instant celebrities. Many, most notably finalists Kelly Clarkson, Clay Aikens, and Taylor Hicks, signed lucrative record deals and appear regularly talk shows, awards ceremonies, and in guest spots on sitcoms. Clarkson, for example, was featured on the NBC series *American Dreams*, while finalist Vonzell Solomon appeared on *The Tyra Banks Show*. Hicks and runner-up Katherine McPhee appeared on *Larry King Live*. The finalists also do a lucrative summer tour, "American Idols Live." In July 2006, President Bush took time away from his schedule to meet with ten of the Idols, including Hicks and McPhee.

American Idol's success and media attention has not failed to capture the attention of corporations eager to tap into the huge potential market for their goods. Several companies, such as the Ford Motor Company and Coca-Cola, have signed agreements to have their name associated with the show. Much of the marketing and public relations takes the form of product placements, exclusive agreements, or through stealth. Simon Cowell and the other judges sip from Coca-Cola cups during the judging as contestants nervously await their decisions in the Coca-Cola Red Room in each episode. Winners have driven off in new Ford Mustangs or SUVs. The partnerships recall the marketing and public relations campaigns of the 1950s and 1960s, when corporations hawked their wares through exclusive contracts with game shows.

Success on *American Idol* is no guarantee of future success, however. Runner-up Justin Guarini was dropped from his record label after disappointing sales from his 2004 album. A film starring Guarini and Clarkson proved an abysmal box office flop. The

American Idol judge Paula Abdul toasts the launch of Coca-Cola C2 with Don Knauss, (right), president and chief operating officer, and Javier Benito (left), chief marketing officer for Coca-Cola North America. Image courtesy of Coca-Cola Corporation.

American Idol industry must also contend with public backlash. The film *American Dreamz* mercilessly satirized the show, primarily through Hugh Grant's thinly disguised parody of judge Simon Cowell, was much more successful than "From Justin to Kelly."

American Idol and, by extension, the sponsored campaigns have at least the illusion of a personalized appeal. After all, the audience participates in the decision of who will become a star today (and commodity tomorrow).

of more than 1 million copies a day, approximately two-thirds of daily newspapers have circulations of 20,000 or less. Most cities today have only one daily newspaper, resulting in little competition between newspapers. Television, direct mail, and the Internet now pose the main challenges to newspapers.

Every edition of a newspaper contains hundreds of news stories and pieces of information, in much greater number than even the largest news staff can gather by itself. More than most readers realize, and more than many editors care to admit, newspapers depend on information brought to them voluntarily. The *Columbia Journalism Review* noted, for example, that in one edition the *Wall Street Journal* had obtained 45 percent of its 188 news items from news releases. Although the *Journal's* use of news releases may be higher than that of general-interest daily newspapers, some don't think so. Albert Scardino, press secretary for former Mayor David N. Dinkins, estimated that 50 percent of the material in the New York dailies comes from public relations sources.

Competition among public relations professionals and firms for limited resources is fierce. Many more press releases are sent to news outlets than can be printed or broadcast. Newspapers receive nearly 80 percent of their income from advertising and about 20 percent from selling papers to readers. They cannot afford to publish press releases that are nothing more than commercial advertising; to do so would cut into their largest source of income. To be published, a release submitted to a newspaper must contain information that an editor regards as news of interest to a substantial number of readers.

Editors resist pressure to suppress material they consider to be newsworthy and, conversely, to print material they do not believe to be newsworthy, although the definitions of *newsworthiness* are abstract and fluctuating. Because newspapers are protected by the First Amendment to the Constitution, they cannot be forced to publish any material, including news releases, nor do they need to receive permission from the government or anyone else to publish whatever they desire.

Public relations professionals should understand the role of editors in the news process. The editor heads the news and editorial departments. The associate editor conducts the editorial and opinion pages and deals with the public concerning the paper's content. The managing editor is the head of news operations to whom the city editor and the editors of sections such as sports, business, entertainment, and family living answer. The city editor directs the staff of local news reporters. Some members of the city staff cover beats such as the police and city hall; others are on general assignment, meaning that they are sent to cover any type of story the city editor deems to be potentially newsworthy. See Chapter 10 for guidelines on how to prepare materials for newspapers.

Magazines

Magazines differ markedly from newspapers in terms of content, time frame, and methods of operation. Therefore, they present different opportunities and problems to public relations practitioners. In contrast with daily newspapers, with their tight deadlines, magazines are published weekly, monthly, or sometimes quarterly. Because these publications usually deal with subjects in greater depth than newspapers do, magazine editors may allot months for the development of an article. Public relations professionals who seek to supply subject ideas or ready-to-publish material to magazines must plan much further ahead than is necessary with newspapers.

Magazine editors in most instances aim carefully at special-interest audiences. They target a specific, well-defined readership groups. The more than 75,000 periodicals published in the United States may be classified in several ways. Periodicals generally are grouped into categories such as news magazines, women's interest, men's interest, the senior market, and trade journals. Each magazine has its own specialty interest and its special formula. Examination of the monthly periodical Writer's Digest will provide abundant information about individual magazines and the kinds of material each publishes. While some magazines struggle for readership in the marketplace, sports-, home- or health-related magazines tend to have growing audiences.

The size and nature of a magazine determines its content. Most common is a formula of several major articles, one or two short articles, and special departments. These may be personal commentaries or compilations of news items in specific categories. Short items about new products in a trade journal, for example, or miscellaneous short notices that may interest the magazine's audience often appear interspersed among the advertisments and features.

Operating with much smaller staffs than newspapers have, magazines are heavily dependent on material submitted from outside their offices. Some, especially the smaller ones, are almost entirely staff written. The staffs create ideas and cover some stories; they also process public relations material submitted to them. The more carefully the submitted material is tailored to the particular periodical's audience, editorial perspective, and writing style, the more likely it is to be published, with or without rewriting by the staff. Many magazine articles have their origins in suggestions submitted by public relations practitioners. An article in a women's magazine on preventing sunburn, for example, may have resulted from a letter and a media kit sent to an editor by a sunscreen manufacturer or its public relations firm.

Many magazines purchase part or almost all of their material from freelance writers. An editor may buy a submitted article for publication if it fits the magazine's formula or the editor may commission a writer to develop an idea into an article along specified lines. Editors are always looking for ideas. Public relations professionals may find opportunities for story development by working with editors or freelance writers.

A public relations practitioner has four principal approaches for getting material into a periodical:

1. Submit a story idea that would promote the practitioner's cause, either directly or subtly, and urge the editor to have a writer, freelance or staff, develop the story on assignment.

2. Send a written query to the editor outlining an article idea and offering to submit the article in publishable form if the editor approves the idea.

3. Submit a completed article, written either by the practitioner or by an independent writer under contract, and hope that the editor will accept it for publication. In this and the two previously mentioned instances, however, the editor should be made fully aware of the source of the suggestion or article.

4. For trade journals and other periodicals that use such material, submit news releases in ready-to-publish form.

Books

Because their writing and publication is a time-consuming process, often involving years from the conception of an idea until the appearance of the volume, books are not popularly recognized as public relations tools. Yet they can be. A book, especially a hardcover one, has stature in the minds of readers, even if the content proves to be fabricated—such as was the case of James Frey's so-called memoir, *A Million Little Pieces*.

Books promulgate ideas—usually complex concepts that require greater detail and analysis than news stories or magazine peices. As channels of communication, books reach thoughtful audiences, including opinion leaders, willing to devote time to their study. Publication of a book often starts a trend or focuses national discussion on an issue.

Paperback books attained popularity during World War II, when they were, published for soldiers to read in the field. The growth of paperback publishing since the 1940s has opened new avenues for using books as public relations vehicles. An examination of nonfiction titles on the paperback shelves will show the range of opportunity that exists to promote products or services, ideological movements, intellectual trends, personalities, and fads. Books as public relations tools, both hardcover and paperback, usually are best suited to promote ideas and create a favorable state of mind. For example, the books by Conrad Hilton and J. Willard Marriott, placed in hotel rooms, have helped establish the character and tradition of both the Hilton and Marriot hotels. Political movements often are publicized through books by their proponents, and sometimes for nefarious ends. Nazi dictator Adolf Hitler's *Mein Kampf* (1925–26), often translated "My Struggle," or Chinese communist chairman Mao Zedong's so-called *Little Red Book* (1964) are notorious examples.

Although the fact is seldom mentioned publicly, companies and nonprofit organizations sometimes pay subsidies to both hardcover and paperback publishers to help defray production costs of a book they wish to see published. Often, the subsidy is subtle and takes the form of a guarantee to purchase a specific number of copies. In other cases, it is explicit. Encouragment and financial support for a beautifully illustrated book on New England, to cite an example, might come from a state travel agency, which approaches the publisher either directly or through an author. The state agency subsidizes the production costs, knowing that the book will bring returns by drawing visitors to the area.

Books have also taken a page from the tactics of product placement on television and in movies. The trend started when Bulgari, the Italian jewelry company, paid author Fay Weldon and undisclosed amount to feature the brand prominently in her latest book, which—naturally—was titled *The Bulgari Connection*. More recently, Procter & Gamble made a deal with the publisher of teenage books to place the names of its Cover Girl cosmetics in various books. In return, P&G will prominently promote the books on its Beinggirl.com Web site directed at adolescent girls.

Because a published book often takes a year from acceptance of the manuscript to publication, public relations efforts must be long-range in nature and represent a broad stroke at influencing public opinion. Long before it hits bookshelves, public relations professionals should publicize a book's upcoming publication and arrange for the author to make personal appearances or give interviews on talk shows to discuss the book's content.

The Spoken and Visual Media

Radio, television, motion pictures, sponsored films, video, and multimedia have strong impact on virtually everyone. The messages they contain usually have a more immediate and visceral impact on the intended audience than print media. As early as 1936, in an essay entitled "The Work of Art in the Age of Mechanical Reproduction," the philosopher and critic Walter Benjamin compared film to hieroglyphics, calling it a new form of pictorial expression that is at once poetical and incomparably powerful. And Benjamin's pronoucement has come true!

Radio

Speed and mobility are the special attributes that make radio unique among the major media, though Internet communications such as blogs and podcasting threaten to unseat radio's unique position. If urgency justifies such action, messages can be placed on the air almost instantly upon their receipt at a radio station. They need not be delayed by the time-consuming production processes of print. Because radio programming is more loosely structured than television programming, interruption of a program for an urgent announcement can be done with less internal decision making.

Although most public relations material does not involve such urgency, moments of crisis do occur when quick on-the-air action helps companies or other organizations get information to the public swiftly. Perhaps more importantly, radio communication is often the only available media for disseminating information during times of crisis or emergencies such as hurricanes or terrorist acts, when the electricity is out for large segments of the population. Hurricane Katrina revealed how fragile communications through newspapers, television, or electronic media are during a time of crisis and offered an insight into the usefulness of radio.

Radio benefits, too, from its ability to be broadcast and heard almost anywhere. Reporters working from mobile trucks can broadcast from the scene of a large fire within minutes after it has been discovered. Compared to video crews, they can hurry from a press conference to a luncheon speech, carrying only a small amount of equipment. A disc jockey can broadcast an afternoon program from a table in a neighborhood shopping center. Radio has great flexibility.

That flexibility extends to listeners as well. Radios in automobiles reach captive audiences, generating the popularity of drive-time disc jockeys. Radio brings news, programs, music, talk, and opinion to mail carriers on their routes, carpenters on construction sites, and homeowners pulling weeds in their gardens. In fact, according to *PRWeek*, radio is a pervasive medium, with 97 percent of adults listening to an AM or FM station at least once a week.

In many markets, a media company will own a group of stations, including both AM and FM formats, with perhaps one news director and one weathercaster serving all of the stations in the market. Both AM and FM stations in the group attempt to develop distinctive "sounds" by specializing in a particular kind of music or talk format. A public relations practitioner should study each station's format and submit material suitable to it.

Commercial radio is highly promotional in nature and provides innumerable opportunities for public relations specialists to further their causes. Radio programs may be divided into two general categories: news–talk and entertainment. The news director for a station or station group is responsible for the former, the program director for the latter. At least eight possible targets exist in radio programs:

1. *Newscasts.* Many stations have frequent newscasts, most often regularly spaced five-minute segments. If the station has a network affiliation, some of the newscasts it carries will be national in content. National Public Radio is one example. Of much more interest to the public relations practitioner are the local newscasts. News releases sent to a radio station should cover the same newsworthy topics as those sent to a newspaper; they should follow identical rules of accuracy and timeliness. Brevity is fundamental on radio, though. See Chapter 10 for how to write a radio news release.

2. *Actualities.* Radio news directors "brighten" their newscasts by including *actualities*. These are brief reports from scenes of action, either live or on tape. Public relations

representatives may supply stations with actualities from events or speeches to be used on newscasts.

3. *Editorials.* Radio stations in larger markets or AM talk stations often broadcast editorials, comparable to newspaper editorials, that are usually delivered by the station manager. Public relations specialists may be able to persuade a station to carry an editorial of endorsement for their causes. They should stay alert, too, for editorials that condemn a cause they espouse. The practitioner should request equal time on the air for a rebuttal, usually given by a leading executive of the organization or company under attack. Hundreds of smaller stations, however, do not carry editorials.

4. *Community Calendars.* Many smaller stations broadcast a daily program called the "Community Bulletin Board" or a similar title. This listing of upcoming events is an excellent way to circulate information about a program or schedule the practitioner is handling.

5. *Community Events.* Radio stations sometimes sponsor community events such as outdoor concerts, art shows, festivals, or long-distance runs. Repeated mention of such events on the air for days or weeks usually turns out large crowds. Here, too, is an opportunity for the public relations professional to convince a station either to sponsor or to develop tie-ins with such events.

6. *Talk Shows.* Placement of a client on a talk show provides exposure for an individual or a cause, while avoiding the filtering of information by news staff. Talk shows may be news-oriented, such as a discussion of a controversial issue, and produced by the news director; or they may be entertainment-oriented, controlled by the program director and handled by a staff producer. Midmorning homemaker hours have numerous spots for guest appearances. Talk radio allows listeners to call in to voice their opinions at various times throughout the day.

7. *Disc Jockey Shows.* On the entertainment side, disc jockeys frequently air material provided by public relations sources on their programs. The DJs conduct on-the-air contests and promotions, give away tickets to shows, peform satirical skits, discuss coming local events, offer trivia quizzes—whatever they can think of to make their programs distinctive, entertaining, and lively. A disc jockey on the air several hours a day devours large amounts of material. After studying a program's style, an able public relations practitioner can supply material that a DJ would welcome.

8. *Public Service Announcements (PSAs).* These commercials promoting public causes such as health care and civic programs are run free of charge by stations, usually in unsold time slots during scheduled commercial breaks. PSA scripts should be written to run 20, 30, or 60 seconds. Use of celebrity voices is common. See Chapter 10 for how to write a PSA.

Television

According to estimates provided by the A. C. Nielsen Company, the major rating firm for national programming, more than 102 million American households own television sets. Nielson also reports that the average American family watches television about seven hours a day despite the advent of the Internet. Little wonder that public relations specialists look upon television as an enormous arena in which to tell their stories.

The fundamental factor that differentiates television from other media and gives it such pervasive impact is the visual element. Producers of entertainment shows, newscasts, and commercials regard movement on the screen as essential. Something must happen to hold the viewer's attention. The single "talking head" set against a simple backdrop once common to television news programs has given way in recent years to bold graphics, running headlines, sports scores, and stock quotes—sometimes to the detriment of the central message.

Because of this visual orientation, television emphasizes personality. Only on television do news reporters achieve "star status." Entertainment programs are built around stars. When public relations people plan material for television, they should remember the importance of visual impact and personality.

Television shows live and die by their ratings. A scorecard mentality dominates the selection of programs and program content, especially on the networks. The viewing habits of a few thousand Americans, recorded by the Nielsen, Arbitron, and other rating services, determine what programs all TV watchers can see. Networks and local stations determine the prices they charge to show commercials by the estimated size of the audience watching a program when the commercial is shown. Even nonprofit television stations keep a close watch on the size of their audiences, because their income comes in part from the grants that corporations give them to show certain programs.

A tremendous battle for admission to the home viewer's screen has developed among satellite dish, cable TV, and the traditional broadcast stations and networks. In the mid-1970s, the three basic commercial networks were viewed by 92 percent of the audience during the prime-time evening hours. This figure has fallen to below one-third of the total television audience. The fragmenting of the television audience has led to the rise of cable news and programming competitors that are challenging the supremacy of the network.

This turmoil has opened up enormous programming potential and produced a consequent increase in public relations opportunities. When a cable system offers hundreds of channels, the need for program material is voracious. However, the number of viewers for an individual cable channel is often relatively small, because the total TV audience is fragmented among so many competing channels. On the plus side, the public relations specialist faces fewer editing and management barriers in getting a program or short segment broadcast. Public relations directors for cultural, social, and other nonprofit agencies, and even for commercial interests, can use these so-called PEG channels effectively to promote public service causes by creating interesting programs. Municipal authorities have the right to demand that cable systems to which they grant operating franchises include an access channel for public, educational, or government programming, without advertising.

The possibilities for the public relations specialist to use television are so numerous that they are worth examining on two levels: network and local.

Guest Appearances on News and Talk Shows.
Placement on such programs as the *Tonight* and *Today* shows allows clients to plug new products, books, films, and plays and to advocate their causes. For entertainment personalities in particular, interviews on such shows provide a setting in which to display their skills. National leaders are interviewed in depth on the Sunday discussion panel shows such as *Meet the Press*. On the local or niche programming level, visiting experts in such fields as homemaking crafts, sponsored by companies and trade associations, demonstrate their skills for the moderator and audience. National public relations firms send such clients around well-established circuits of local television shows in each city they visit on a local level.

News Releases and Story Proposals.
The process of submitting news releases to television network news departments is identical to that followed with radio stations. Video news releases (VNRs) are ready-to-broadcast tapes or satellite feeds with background footage for use in news programs. News story suggestions or

letters often are sent directly to popular TV personalities. If a story or an idea is accepted, the assignment editor gives it to a reporter for development. When a client is criticized in a controversial news situation or editorial, a representative should submit the client's response and urge that it be used on-air. If the response is submitted in concise videotape form, the likelihood of a quick airing is increased. Smaller TV stations, in particular, lack enough staff to cover all potentially newsworthy events in their areas. Public relations practitioners can fill the gaps by delivering videotapes of events they handle for inclusion in newscasts. Excerpts from a local speech by a prominent client may be incorporated into an evening news show. Arrival or departure at the local airport of a client in the news might be used as well, if the person says something newsworthy on camera. Local cable channels sometimes will show films of 15- or 20-minute duration produced by corporations in which the direct commercial message is nonexistent or muted. The purpose of such films is to strengthen a company's image as a good community citizen. Films explaining large civic programs by nonprofit organizations also may be used.

Program Ideas. The representative of an important cause may propose to a network that it build an episode in a dramatic or comedy series around the cause. Activist groups apply considerable pressure on television producers and the networks to include social issues such as environmental problems, drunk driving, and AIDS in their program scripts. Characters in situation comedies or dramas quite frequently take strong advocacy positions in their plotlines, thus delivering messages to viewers.

Protest Demonstrations. Stations show demonstrations primarily because they involve movement and have high visual impact. However, demonstrations are such a staple on some large-city television stations that they have become a visual cliché. A group supporting or opposing a cause notifies a station that it will march at a certain time and place. Carrying placards, the marchers parade before the camera, and a representative is shown explaining the group's cause. Although, for fairness, stations should put on an advocate for the other side in the same sequence, some stations neglect this responsibility, and so the marching group's point of view dominates. Many group demonstrations are so much alike, however, that their impact is minimized.

Silent Publicity. Much has been written about the subliminal impacts of product placement/mention in entertainment programs that publicize a client's product or cause. In a detective show, for example, the star might be shown chasing the villain through an airport terminal past a Delta sign. Or the automobiles used by the lead characters might be exclusively Ford products. Or a program's credits might include a mention such as, "Transportation provided by American Airlines." Another way to generate silent publicity, especially valuable for the tourist industry, is to convince network show producers to shoot their programs in a client's city or region. For example, the network series *Las Vegas* has provided the city with much publicity. New Orleans chef Emeril's cooking shows did much to bolster the city's tourism industry, casting the Crescent City as a gourmet destination, at least before Hurricane Katrina struck.

Mention of motion pictures brings to mind, first and inevitably, the commercial entertainment films turned out by that entity known as Hollywood. From a public relations point of view, possibilities for influencing the content of commercial motion pictures for client purposes are relatively limited. Public relations professionals who know their way through the labyrinth of Hollywood financing and production can make deals for silent publicity through use of brand-name merchandise, negotiating how the product will be used and whether there will be a fee. Firms such as Pepsi and Coca-Cola make deals to show their products in a movie, often tied in with an off-screen promotion of the item. Public relations professionals often negotiate for a brand's logo or favorable appearance of a product in films, music videos or video games. For example, the 2006 film *Fantastic Four* featured no less than 50 product placements ranging from Aleve to Xbox.

Public relations counselors and corporate departments occasionally serve as advisers on films that involve their areas of expertise. Filmmakers seek this advice to prevent embarrassing technical errors on the screen and to protect themselves from inadvertently angering a group that might retaliate by denouncing the picture. In terms of specific public relations results similar to those obtainable from the other mass media, however, commercial films are a minor channel.

Sponsored Films and Videotapes

Video is an important public relations tool. Corporations and nonprofit organizations use films and videotapes for internal purposes as part of audiovisual programs to train and inform their employees or for external purposes to inform and influence the public, the financial community, or visitors touring their facilities. When, for example, Levi Strauss & Co. needed to explain to its employees a new personnel management program called Teamwork, it prepared a video for them. Like some other corporations, San Diego Gas & Electric Company produces a periodic *Employee Video News Magazine*. The topics covered range from the company's annual meeting to an employees' campaign against graffiti.

Activist groups have been using films and videotapes for advocacy and to publicize their causes since at least the early 1990s. These films and videotapes, as a form of popular culture, have a powerful effect on public mood and can generate controversy. For example, America's Voice, a cable network operated by National Empowerment Television, frequently broadcasts VNRs produced by the National Rifle Association and the American Life League, an antiabortion group. Popular culture can also have a profound effect on public perceptions, which suggests avenues and opportunities for public relations campaigns. Although not directly sponsored by activist groups, films such as Michael Moore's *Fahrenheit 9/11* (2004), Morgan Spurlock's Super Size Me (2004), and Davis Guggenheim's *An Inconvenient Truth* (2006), starring and based on a book by Al Gore, each presented strong points of view critical of big corporations, government, and consumerism. Because each film reached a wide audience, public relations professionals had great concern about their impact. The retail giant Wal-Mart has undertaken a major public relations campaign to counter charges leveled by the 2005 film *Wal-Mart: The High Cost of Low Price* (see the PR Casebook box on page 183 about Wal-Mart in Chapter 6).

Online Media

The personal computer represents a significant and swiftly expanding tool for public relations practitioners. Today, more than 70 percent of U.S. households have home computers. E-mail and the Internet's ability to deliver information about clients' projects, to establish contacts with reporters, and to exchange ideas has drastically altered the intellectual and entertainment landscape in the brief span of 15 years: It is hard to imagine that e-mail was not widely used before the early 1990s and that the first World Wide Web page appeared in 1991.

The Internet and World Wide Web offer unusual opportunities to reach audiences with messages in the exact form that public relations practitioners conceive them. Millions of companies, nonprofit organizations, and individuals maintain sites on the World Wide Web, from which they explain their companies and brands, promote their products and services, and often sell merchandise directly to consumers. They post text, audio, and video news releases and other company materials on their Web site so that anyone can easily access them. Most sites are readily accessible to the public but some require access codes or have other access limitations. By participating in online discussion groups, chat rooms, and similar online interchanges, public relations people often reach opinion leaders in specific fields with facts and opinions favorable to their cause. They even directly reach target consumers, investors, community members, and employees without having to pass through any media gate keepers. Using e-mails and listservs, public relations practitioners can deliever a specially tailored message to a precise target audience.

Recently, blogs and podcasting have emerged as a viable medium to initiate public discussion on small to large scales. Howard Dean effectively used these tools to build support during his presidential campaign in 2003–2004. Bloggers and podcasters increasingly offer breaking news faster than print or broadcast outlets. The pace of media relations has increased as public relations professionals monitor online news, striving for what Professor Stephen Thomsen of Brigham Young University calls "real-time response." Public relations professionals hope to catch errors or offer balancing comments for stories as they break online and before they pick up momentum through print and broadcast dispersion. In conflict or crisis situations, online media are becoming more important in terms of the diffusion of stories and expression of opinions. Public relations practitioners should note that online media can help them resolve conflicts or amplify crises rapidly, depending on their contingency stance. Increasingly, success or failure depends on the ability of public relations practitioners to appropriately use online media.

Public relations professionals especially depend on online media for communicating with *Generations X* and *Y*. Gen Xers and Gen Yers spend a lot of time in front of computers, searching the Web, chatting with their friends, playing videogames, or shopping online. The computer world allows them to multitask, perhaps doing research for a paper while also making friends who they may never meet face-to-face, ultimately even dating and getting married to someone from the other side of the world. Sites such as Facebook.com, YouTube.com, or MySpace.com provide a forum for young people to exchange ideas, make virtual friends, and pursue romantic relationships. The downside, of course, is potential for abuse. As with the Internet in general, it is often difficult to accertain the accuracy of sources and disclosure of personal information poses potentially dangerous consequences.

Summary

The Nature of the Public Relations Audience

The public relations practitioner must reach a diverse and constantly changing audience. One of the most important aspects of the job is identifying the target audience in order to appropriately and effectively customize communications and public relations efforts. Current trends include an increase in the public's diversity, use of technology, visual orientation, fervent support for single issues, emphasis on personality and celebrity, a strong distrust of authority, and expanding international audiences.

Senior, Youth, Ethnic Audiences

Increasingly important publics are youth, seniors, and ethnic minorities. The senior group has grown in number as life span has increased. It has also grown in affluence. Young people comprise another growing audience with a changing face. Their values, lifestyle, interests, and consumption patterns are conspicuously different from other demographic groups. The population of ethnic groups is increasing at five times the rate of the general population, and such groups constitute many different target audiences.

Global and Other Emerging Audiences

Language and cultural differences are the primary challenges in reaching global audiences. The public relations practitioner must be sensitive to the special issues, concerns, or interests of different national and ethnic audiences. This is also true for emerging audiences such as religious groups or the gay community.

Matching the Audience with the Media

Each of the media has different strengths for different types of communication. Public relations practitioners must be careful to use the appropriate media (or, sometimes, single medium) for each public relations campaign.

The Print Media

Print media—newspapers, magazines, other periodicals, and books—are appropriate for communications that take time and benefit from rereading. Both newspapers and magazines are commercial institutions that depend heavily on advertising for their income. While newspapers reach a wide range of audiences on a daily or weekly basis, magazines are published less frequently and often deal with subjects at greater length and in greater depth than is possible in a daily newspaper. Magazines also are more likely to be targeted at a special-interest audience.

Books are published on much longer schedules than either magazines or newspapers and require more long-term public relations efforts, but can still be useful as public relations tools.

The Spoken and Visual Media

Radio is one of the quickest and most flexible means of communicating a message, reaching a variety of audiences through such types of programming as newscasts, community calendars or events, talk shows, and public service announcements. It can be an especially effective medium for reaching a large audience in a crisis or emergency. Television has a tremendous influence on society because of its pervasiveness and visual impact. The growth of cable television has provided new venues for public relations with access channels and local-origination programming. Public relations opportunities exist in television on both the network and the local levels. Popular culture can have a profound effect on public perceptions and attitudes. Product placement is an example of public relations at work in the motion picture industry. Sponsored films and videotapes can also be effective public relations tools.

Online Media

The Internet and World Wide Web provide a opportunities for public relations practitioners to communicate directly with audiences without the filter of editors and journalists. Young people are easily targeted through online media because they spend more time in front of a computer than other groups, and the medium is ingrained in their lifestyle and behavioral pattern. Online news sources are growing in stature, especially when big stories are breaking and developing throughout the workday. In conflict or crisis situations, online media are becoming more important in terms of diffusion of stories and public relations professionals should understand the strengths and limitations of the media.

CASE ACTIVITY >>
What Would You Do?

The latest innovation in sun care is spray-on sunscreens that come in cannisters that spray a clear mist to completely coat the skin without damaging the ozone layer. Dermatologists claim that spray-on sunscreens offer the same protection as lotions. They also have the additional advantage of being easy to apply, which means that individuals will be more likely to to coat every part of the body rather than just dabbing a little lotion on their arms, nose, or shoulders.

Banana Boat brand is currently marketing its UltraMist sunblock, but it's in competition with other major brands such as Coppertone's Continuous Spray and Neutrogena's Fresh Cooling Body Mist Sunblock. In addition, Target and Wal-Mart are planning to market their own brands of spray-on sunscreens.

Market research indicates that a major demographic group for spray-on sunscreens are college students who, whenever they can, spend a lot of time sun tanning and going to the beach. Indeed, spring break finds thousands of college studens crowding the beaches of Florida, Mexico, Texas, and California.

Banana Boat retains your public relations firm to develop a product publicity program for its UltraMist

sunblock aimed directly at the college audience. One suggestion for making Banana Boat the market leader is positioning the company as the leading authority on sunscreens and how to use them effectively, including educating the public about SPF ratings, and so on.

Plan a campaign that would reach college students through traditional media (newspapers, magazines, radio, television) and the Internet. Also, what kind of special events or promotions would you plan?

Questions for Review and Discussion

1. Why is the senior audience so important in the United States? What are some of the characteristics of this audience?
2. What are the characteristics of the youth market? What are their media use habits?
3. What are some of the markets for ethnic groups? How do you think the various changes in the racial and ethnic makeup of the United States will affect future practice of public relations?
4. What are some challenges facing public relations in dealing with global audiences?
5. What are some of the opportunities for public relations professionals regarding emerging audiences?
6. On what basis do newspaper editors select the news releases they publish?

7. Why are special-audience magazines and trade journals such important targets for many public relations people?
8. What two special attributes make radio distinctive among the major media of mass communication?
9. Do local radio newscasts have good potential as an outlet for news releases? If so, why?
10. What are some attractive features of television in terms of reaching audiences? What are some possibilities for the public relations specialist to use television?
11. Can you describe three ways in which public relations practitioners use online media?
12. A good public relations person knows how to create news events. Why is this important?

Suggested Readings

Cameron, Glen T., and Jae-Hwa Shin. "The Potential of Online Media: A Coorientational Analysis of Conflict between PR Professionals and Journalists in South Korea." *Journalism and Mass Communication Quarterly* 80 (Autumn 2003): 583–602.

Galloway, Chris. "Cyber-PR and 'Dynamic Touch.'" *Public Relations Review* 31, no. 4 (2005): 572–577.

"Getting Beyond Stereotypes: Grassroots PR Campaign Works to Give Media a Truer Picture of Native Americans." *Ragan's Media Relations Report*, January 2005, 3, 7.

Iacono, Erica. "Web Audience Could Offset Print Decline." *PRWeek*, April 10, 2006, 10.

Maceluch, Dan. "Drive Your Business and Boost Value." *Communication World* 23, no. 4 (2004): 32–33.

McGuire, Craig. "PSAs That Speak the Right Language." *PRWeek*, May 27, 2006, 18.

Morton, Linda P. "PRSA Publication Managers' Preferences for Graphic Designs." *Public Relations Review* 31, no. 2 (2005): 281–283.

Nolan, Hamilton. "Paths toward Global Growth." *PRWeek*, April 3, 2006, 13.

Pringle, Shelley. "Hallmark Puckers Up for Valentine's Day." *Communication World* 23, no. 1 (2006): 42–43.

"Target Practice." *Economist* 375, no. 8420 (2006): 13–15.

Chapter Nine

Tech Tools and Trends

The Communications Explosion

The explosive growth of the Internet and the World Wide Web has created a form of mass communication unlike any other. Technological advances and innovations merit a chapter dedicated to the tools of the profession, but from the outset, it is important to keep in mind that the key to success with any tool remains a smart, highly skilled user. The communications explosion of digital technologies offers fascinating opportunities for success in public relations that will be covered throughout the chapter, but such tools should never replace thoughtful strategic planning and carefully crafted communication of program elements.

In 1990, the Internet was used only by scientists to exchange information. Today, the Internet is a household word and a global communications tool for millions of people. According to a study commissioned by *pr reporter*, use of the new technology is the leading trend in public relations. This should not be surprising, given the definition of public relations as strategic management of competiltion and conflict. Digital devices of all kinds enable the more advanced and ambitious practitioner to stay on top of the latest events in the external communication environment. And new technologies provide more precise and instantaneous delivery of messages to those publics, thereby impacting competitive success or stemming crisis costs for the practitioner's employer.

Through the Internet's World Wide Web, thousands of companies, organizations, media outlets, and individuals tell the world about themselves, sell their wares, and promote their ideas. By posting pages of printed words, graphics, photographs, and sounds, these people and organizations communicate with tens of millions of "netizens" worldwide.

ON THE JOB >>

Who Is Concerned about the Digital Divide?

Ethics

The following editorial in *Monde Diplomatique* expresses concern about the global digital divide. Read the statement and consider the questions presented.

The Internet became available to the public only a decade ago. In that short time, it has revolutionized political, economic, social, and cultural life to such an extent that we can now reasonably speak of the new Internet world order in telecommunications. Nothing is as it was before. For a large proportion of the world's people the speed and reliability of computer networks has changed their manner of communication, study, shopping, news, entertainment, political organization, cultural life, and work. The growth of Internet-based activities and e-mail has put the computer at the center of a network, relayed via a new generation of do-everything phones, that has transformed all areas of social activity.

But this remarkable transformation has largely been to the advantage of Western countries, already the beneficiaries of previous industrial revolutions. It is now exacerbating the digital gap between those who have an abundance of information technologies and the many more who would have none. Two figures give a sense of the inequality: 91 percent of the world's users of the Internet are drawn from only 19% of the world's population. The digital gap does as much to accentuate and aggravate the North-South divide as the traditional inequality between rich and poor—20 percent of the population of the rich countries own 85 percent of the world's wealth. If nothing is done cyber technologies will leave the inhabitants of the least advanced countries outside, especially in sub-Saharan Africa, where scarcely 1 percent of people have access, and those are mostly men.

Who is responsible for this digital divide? Should we really be concerned about the lack of Internet access in countries that have so many other basic infrastructure problems? Can the Internet be used as a development tool, offering developing countries a way to leapfrog forward in making progress toward filling basic needs?

Most importantly, what role can you envision for public relations professionals as part of the solution to the digital divide?

Despite the ubiquity of the Internet, a huge digital divide exists across the globe, which poses a strategic problem if communication resources are devoted exclusively or predominantly to new media channels. Key publics may be missed altogether. The Ethics box on this page looks at the implications of the digital divide.

Caveats aside, the Internet is the most intriguing of the new electronic technologies that are changing mass communication in general and providing public relations practice with innovative tools. According to the Middleberg/Ross Survey of journalists nationwide, the Internet is a rapidly growing means of receiving news releases, story ideas, and even audio and photo files from public relations sources. Other digital technologies have revolutionized the management of public relations.

This chapter examines how such recent developments and new technologies can be applied to accomplish public relations objectives in a highly competitive and sometimes conflict-ridden environment. As you can see in Table 9.1, these new technologies have had an impact on the media, and consequently on public relations practice.

The Computer

The computer processor is no longer exclusive to personal computers. Many of the smart devices used by public relations professionals employ computer processors.

TABLE 9.1

Pros and Cons of New Media in Public Relations

Traditional Mass Media	New Media
Geographically constrained: Local or regional targets	Distance insensitive: Topic, need, or interest targeting worldwide
Hierarchical: Series of gatekeepers/editors	Flattened: One to many and many to many
Unidirectional: One-way dissemination	Interactive: Feedback, discussion, debate, and response to requests by person or machine
Space/time constraints: Limited pages and airtime	Fewer space/time constraints: Large, layered capacity for information
Professional communicators: Highly trained to professional standards	Nonprofessional: Anyone with limited training or professional values may participate
High access costs: Startup and production costs prohibitive	Low access costs: More affordable, but expensive computer programming talent required initially
General interest: Large audiences and broad coverage	Customized: Narrowcasts, even individually tailored
Linearity of content: News hierarchy	Nonlinearity of content: Hypertext links enable nonlinear navigation
Feedback: Slow, effortful, and limited	Feedback: E-mail and online chat are immediate and easy
Ad-driven: Big audiences and revenue	Diverse funding sources: Varied but limited revenue
Institution-bound: Corporate ownership	Decentralized: Grassroots efforts
Fixed format: Predictable in format, time and place	Flexible format: Emerging but fluid formats; multimedia
News, values, journalistic standards: Conventional	Formative standards: Currently obscure

Source: Adapted from *pr reporter*, May 17, 1999.

Personal organizers, calendars, and contact lists reside on personal digital assistants (PDAs) such as Palm, BlackBerry, or many smartphones, and even on computerized wristwatches. Computers enable the automation of office procedures so that tasks can be completed more quickly and extensively than the old do-it-by-hand methods were capable of accomplishing.

As a research tool, computers make an immense amount of information easily accessible through secondary analysis of data. E-mail and chat forums enhance environmental scanning and issues management. Three skills that are essential to success in public relations—project management, time billing, and digital presentation—all are made more efficient and flexible through the use of computers.

Most importantly, the computer is the vehicle that can carry the practitioner into the universe of the Internet and World Wide Web. Communication and information resources abound in the online world, making life for public relations professionals more interesting and efficient.

The Internet

Created in the late 1960s by researchers who were seeking a way to link computers in separate cities, the Internet was initially an academic–government tool. It came into public use in the early 1990s; tie-ins developed between the American system and those in more than 150 other countries.

An example of how public relations firms use the Internet is the home page of Edelman Worldwide. It offers a variety of information about clients.

Internet use increased when graphics and sound were added, forming what came to be called the World Wide Web. Aware of the Web's commercial possibilities but not quite sure how to exploit them, tens of thousands of companies established sites on the Web. The Internet has no official central control headquarters, so obtaining valid statistics on use of the global system is difficult. However, the number of hits, the number visitors to a site, can be determined. Because many hits are by "surfers" just searching to see what they can find, this figure is of limited commercial value. Figures for hits can be wildly inflated, because complex Web pages may generate hits for each major component of the pages rather than counting only one hit per page. Furthermore, each time a user returns to a page during a visit, another hit is recorded. Several organizations, including the Audit Bureau of Circulations (ABC), are working on more sophisticated tracking methods that can count the number of unique visitors to a site.

The Internet and Public Relations

The Internet gives public relations practitioners a multifaceted form of worldwide communication, primarily involving message exchange by e-mail, information delivery and persuasion through the Web, and extensive access to audiences for strategic research opportunities. The following section outlines the primary uses of the Internet by public relations professionals.

E-mail Distribution. E-mail includes messages to individuals; newsletters to staff members; transmission of news releases, photos, and pitch letters to media offices; and dispatch and receipt of copy between public relations firms and clients,

— ON THE JOB >> —

Creating Winning Web Sites

Insights

A Web site can serve as a controlled, yet credible, tool for organizations to disseminate messages. National surveys indicate that audiences hold Web-based information in high regard. Internet information, according to one survey of over 1,000 respondents by professors at the University of California at Santa Barbara, was as credible as TV, radio, and magazines, but less credible than newspapers. Researchers say that this high credibility perhaps explains why Web information is seldom double-checked with other sources by the audience.

Web sites also enable strategic targeting of messages to audiences. Responsible practitioners can get the word out to key publics using links to customized Web pages tailored to the particular public. However, according to Stuart Esrock and Greg Leichty, most corporate Web sites are used to service investors, customers, and, to a lesser extent, the media. Consequently, the communication potential of Web sites has not yet been fully tapped.

To date, according to Candace White and colleagues at the University of Tennessee, most Web site planning is done by trial and error, with little formal research and evaluation. Practitioners report Web site development as a low priority on to-do lists because of skepticism about the site's effectiveness, inefficient evaluation methods, and lack of control over the site.

Opportunities for a broader range of publics should be developed as support for Web sites increases and public relations practitioners become more assertive in taking control of Web sites. Given the enormous and burgeoning audience for Web sites, as well as key target audiences, creating more effective Web sites will be essential for public relations departments.

Louis Falk of Florida International University offers some no-nonsense advice for Web site development:

> Make it fast. Be sure that a page loads in less than eight seconds.
> Use a functional, balanced design. Make sure that the site works on all major Web browsers, such as Internet Explorer and Netscape. Place the most important information on the left side of the page. Use standard colors that work consistently on many different browsers and machines. Offer an easy and logical interaction, making good use of internal search engines.
> Make sure there are no dead links.
> Include contact information.
> Identify your purpose(s). Public information differs dramatically from e-commerce, for instance.
> Keep it fresh. Not only should information be current, you also should check the site's performance on a regular basis.
> Register with major search engines. This ensures that you can be found.

including fully formatted documents using software such as Adobe Acrobat. Most e-mail systems now accept hypertext e-mail that presents images in full color when the e-mail is opened. Professional Training Associates, a newsletter publisher, was able to send its direct mail postcard on the Internet to selected editors and reporters. The postcard announced a new Web site entitled Hard@Work with a whimsical shot of the publisher and editor perched on a rock in the middle of a stream.

World Wide Web Sites. These sites provide a way for organizations to tell Internet users what they do, to publicize projects, and to advocate policies. Edelman Worldwide, for example, gives information about its clients. Ketchum offers recipes from its food-product clients. The Insights box on this page discusses the elements of winning Web sites.

RSS—Really Simple Syndication. An emerging technology may very well supplant the majority of printed news releases sent to reporters and editors. RSS is a

Web-based process of searching and gathering together news and information that is then fed to the user's computer or wireless device such as a cell phone. Essentially, software called an RSS reader is loaded onto the device and preferences for topics and sources are set. The reader then searches for and delivers information to the user. Journalists increasingly look to RSS as a customized source that enables them to reduce irrelevant media pitches. Many recommend that any good public relations person will set up an RSS feed to put releases and stories out there for journalists' RSS readers to find. Many Web sites do not offer RSS feeds, but major news organizations and companies offer their content in RSS format so that the readers can obtain it for delivery to users. Strategic communictors not only deliver RSS feeds but also make wise use of the RSS platform to track the activities of competitors and to monitor issues that might grow into conflicts of crisis dimensions for their employers or clients. Two recommended, free RSS readers are NewsDesk (www.wildgrape.net) and Dogpile Search Tool (www.dogpile.com). NewsGator is an inexpensive RSS feeder that integrates RSS news into your e-mail program if you use Microsoft Outlook for e-mail. With NewsGator, a public relations professional can readily set up a news watch using key words, with stories on the watch topic delivered as e-mail.

Podcasting. In the same way that text content such as online newspaper and magazine stories can be delivered electronically to users, so too can radio, television, and even film content make their way to digital devices. A computer or a PDA or an MP3 player can play audio or video files when it is convenient for users. The term *podcast* is associated with the Mac Ipod, but the range of devices capable of playing podcasts runs the gamut. The podcast consumer can either select a particular program for download or set up a regular delivery of a program automatically whenever a new content is available. The term refers to both the content and the process, with the author of the product called the podcaster. Public relations professionals increasingly will become podcasters by making files available on Web sites. Those who are able to create audio news releases or video products that can then be delivered to highly targeted audiences will have an additional tool for reaching key publics with compelling multimedia content.

Brochureware. Although this term is used ironically by those who envision Web sites as a unique new channel, much of the content on Web sites is little more than an online version of the brochures and collateral materials that organizations provide to stakeholders. Public relations professionals should increasingly capitalize on the interactive and multimedia characteristics that distinguish Web communication from traditional print materials. Over time, interactivity and video clips will distinguish brochureware from its print predecessor, adding to the mix of communication tools available to the public relations professional.

Here are specific examples of how the Internet is used in public relations practice:

> Organizations increasingly set up Web sites to serve the informational needs of reporters, especially during a crisis or a breaking news situation. The *Starr Report* investigation of President Clinton's affair with Monica Lewinsky was released to the Web for wide and immediate dissemination. News organizations then made it available on their own Web sites, where an estimated 24.7 million people read parts of it in a matter of days—still one of the most galvanizing Web events to date.

> Xerox's public relations Web site offers answers to any question—any question at all. In response to an online question, the offbeat site reported its calculation that it would take 33,661 years to vacuum the state of Ohio! A mention in *People* magazine and various TV news features resulted.

Greenpeace, the activist environmental organization, uses its Web site to publicize its confrontations at sea with vessels whose work it opposes. Here, a Greenpeace ship tries to block passage of a Norwegian whaling vessel. The Web site carries news reports and back-ground information from the Greenpeace point of view.

> At least 400 health care organizations and companies distribute medical information over their Web sites. Two examples are the American Medical Association, which provides information for physicians and patients about treatments, medical developments, and other health care news, and the National Alliance of Breast Cancer Organizations (NABCO), which provides current information about breast cancer research and treatment, events, and links to other Web sites.

> Companies such as Boeing and HP/Compaq have used Webcasting to increase coverage of important news conferences by broadcasting video footage over the Web via Medialink's media portal.

> The University of Wisconsin's Technology Enhancing Cancer Communication (TECC) (http://chess2.chsra.wisc.edu/tecc) offers support for cancer patients and their loved ones who provide care for them. Interactive technologies link people facing similar cancer challenges across distance and time and facilitate effective cancer communication between patient, partner/caregiver, and clinical teams. TECC explores how computers can be used to help those dealing with cancer or caring for loved ones with cancer.

> The governor of Hawaii used a Webcast to address critics and field questions from concerned citizens regarding a teachers' strike and lockout. At a minimal direct cost of $100, the governor reached an enormous direct audience, estimated at 30,000. Facing a crisis in the schools, Governor Cayetano communicated directly to the audience, generating both advanced and follow-up coverage and ongoing access to the archived Webcast online.

Key Aspects of the Internet

Public relations professionals should keep in mind the following important facts about the Internet:

> *Its reach is worldwide.* A message intended for local or regional use may draw reactions, good or bad, from unexpected places.

> *The content of the Internet is virtually uncontrolled.* Anyone can say or show anything without passing it through "gatekeepers," the editors and producers who approve the material that reaches the public through traditional media channels. Lack of editorial control permits unfettered freedom of speech, but it also permits distribution of unconfirmed, slanted, or even potentially libelous material. *Tactics*, which is published by PRSA, welcomes this freedom from editorial control. It asserts: "PR pros can now get messages out without passing them through the filter of editors and journalists. Traditional media gatekeepers have lost their power in today's point-and-click world."

> Issue tracking, one of the major components of the life cycle of conflict management discussed in Chapter 2, can be more thorough and far more immediate using the Internet. Services such as NewsEdge monitor Web-based news and wire services and alert users when relevant topics appear in Internet news sources. By monitoring the Internet, practitioners can keep track of what competitors, opponents, and the general audience are saying. Thus informed, practitioners can better shape their own

tactics and messages as well as respond in real time to forestall erroneous or unbalanced stories from gaining momentum without correction. A PR Newswire executive recalled how a story released by his service at 7:30 A.M. prompted an e-mail response by a public relations person. The result was a factually corrected release on PR Newswire by 7:35 A.M.

Internet Problems

In addition to its multiple benefits, the global spiderweb of interlocking computer networks also offers some challenges. The following should be kept in mind when planning Internet-based communication programs:

> The difficulty in finding desired information frustrates some users. Increasingly, search engines are prioritizing search results based on fee payments from companies and organizations, biasing search results.

> Controversial security problems and legal questions of copyright infringement, libel, invasion of privacy, and pornography remain unsolved.

> Time-consuming procedures for online transactions or product registrations can be terminated by an error message that the procedure was not successful, generating skepticism about the efficiency of the Web and its reliability as a communication tool.

> Malicious and irritating practices nag at online users. The Internet offers many opportunities for spammers to clutter e-mail channels with bogus or dubious offers. Unsolicited advertising on the Web adds to this clutter, making the messages sent by public relations professionals less effective. Online users are perhaps most decisively impacted by those who program viruses to take down servers or disrupt personal computer systems.

In sum, the Internet is an evolving form of mass communication. Public relations tools based on the Internet are frequently conceived, developed, and hyped for their features. Many will end up on the tech scrap heap; however, the winners can equip the adept professional with a competitive edge.

Other Computer Applications

Computers store, codify, analyze, and search out information at speeds far beyond human capabilities. They transmit information over long distances at fantastically high speeds. The variety of tasks that computers can be used to accomplish make them powerful tools for public relations practice. Still more astounding is the anticipated development of the "thinking" computer. The well-known physicist and thinker Stephen Hawking predicts that artificial intelligence will one day universally supercede human brainpower. The dazzling future aside, immediate application of the new technologies in public relations are well worth adopting right now. Promising new media tools are listed in Table 9.2 on page 276.

Dictation and Voice Generation

Most computers sold today have the memory and processing speed needed to recognize human speech. The software program Dragon Naturally Speaking not only

TABLE 9.2

Some New Tools in Public Relations Practice. A wide range of technologies serve important functions of modern public relations and often are directed at particular audiences. Some of these technologies are just emerging, others are more commonly used.

New Tech Tool	PR Function	Typical Audience	Techniques/Features
Internet	Media relations	Media contacts	Pitching stories and sending digital media kits
	Activism	Media	Evens the resource field for activist groups
	Crisis management	Media and internal audiences	Preemptive tool against investigative hatchet job
	Event or product promotion	Widespread, often teens or trendsetters	Guerrilla (subtle) and viral (self-generating) dissemination
Intranet	Internal communication	Employees and password-access outsiders	Enables confidential communication and rumor research
Online newswires, (e.g., Newstream.com)	Investor relations	Investors and financial media in 6,000 online news-rooms	Submit to Business Wire and index with Yahoo! company news
Webcasting services such as Medialink	Meetings and media relations	Varied	Enables a large, geographically dispersed audience to participate online
Web searching	Issues tracking	Management	Search by client or industry name
Web site development	E-commerce and public information	Customers and constituents	Offer products and services
Online monitoring services, (e.g., Dialog NewsEdge, and Briefme.com)	Issues and crisis management	Practitioner receives news alerts	Enables monitoring of both slow-boil and breaking news about own organization
CD-ROM	Media relations	Media	Digital media kit or reporter's resource
	Employee communication	Employees	Interactive, audiovisual training and notification
Satellite and radio media tours	Publicity	Viewers and listeners	Overcomes distance barriers in media appearances
Web research	Audience analysis and message testing	Colleagues and clients	Online surveys, focus groups, secondary research, and usability studies
Media database software (e.g., prPowerBase)	Release distribution/ tracking	Media	Access and use Bacon's and other major databases
Research software (e.g., Publics, SPSS)	Formative and evaluative research	Client	Enables targeted audiences and tailored messages
Presentation software (e.g., PowerPoint)	Briefings	Varied	Multimedia features and last-minute changes
Calendar software (e.g., Sidekick, Outlook)	Project and event coordination	Varied	Set up team meetings and recurring appointments
Project management software (e.g., Microsoft Project)	Production and campaign planning/tracking	Colleagues and clients	Enables control of complex projects
Time tracking and billing software (e.g., Timeslips)	Management	Colleagues and clients	Track time for productivity analysis and billing of services
Media management software (e.g., Vocus, Spinware)	Media relations	Media	Track media contacts and coverage, online press center
Creativity tools (e.g., Visio, Photoshop, Quark)	Materials production	Readers and viewers	Design and layout of materials
Netbusiness card	Firm visibility and marketing	Clients	Registered users appear in all major online Yellow Pages

recognizes the user's speech but also improves its recognition accuracy by taking into account corrections the user makes in the dictated text on the computer screen. Over time, the program becomes more accurate in converting speech to word processing, presentation, Web, database, or spreadsheet content. Computer commands also may be spoken, including the command "Read Text," which prompts the computer to generate speech by reading the written text to the user. One of the important benefits of this new technology may well be a reduction in painful repetitive motion syndrome injuries caused by hours of keyboarding. Conversational exchanges with Web sites will create a virtual presence for organizations that offer counseling or other special interactive services to users.

In general, professionals capitalizing on dictation and voice generation should use these new tools to create a positive virtual presence, a more personal and responsive experience for members of the public. However, most such uses remain in the imaginations of cutting-edge practitioners at this point.

Expert Systems

One modest form of artificial intelligence—expert system programming—has made its mark in the business world. Expert systems identify a limited domain of expertise and then emulate the decision making that an expert would undertake. Someday public relations professionals will use expert systems to assist with special-event planning, issue evaluation, and other domains of expertise in the field.

Public Relations Management Tools

Public relations professionals can use project-scheduling software such as Microsoft Project and MacProject to quickly create and modify Gantt charts, track resources, and monitor progress toward the completion of a project. See Figure 5.2 in Chapter 5 for an example an a Gantt chart. Special software such as Timeslips streamlines the time-billing process and allows professionals to use the computer as a timer and recorder of billable hours. Particularly in the public relations agency world, time tracking to capture precious billable hours is an essential task that can be made less burdensome with software. Programs such as Spin Control and Vocus are used in public relations to manage the media relations process. Such programs help the public relations professional develop media contact databases, track mail and phone pitches to those contacts, and record news coverage obtained from the media relations effort.

Processing of News Releases

Word processing programs are invaluable in creating news releases for different types of publications, including trade magazines, daily newspapers, and the business press. A draft document can be attached to e-mail for delivery to a client or supervisor. Changes made by others can be highlighted automatically in the text with the editor identified. Professionals can use mail merge features to customize or even localize releases to increase news value for individual editors in a distribution list.

However, when such batch-processing tools are used, care must be taken to ensure that the merge is done correctly. It can be irritating, and even insulting, to get a misaddressed message that appears to be personalized. In addition, unless care is taken, different versions of a document can be confused, leading to the distribution of an earlier draft. For example, a branch of the Centers for Disease Control and Prevention e-mailed an advisory to medical doctors that had comments and draft language embedded but hidden in the file. The hidden back-channel discussion of the draft was not deleted or locked, thus the physicians were able to view the comments. No harm was done because the comments were mostly text edits, but what if confidential deliberations had been included?

E-Mail

The frequent collaboration of public relations professionals with clients and colleagues has been greatly enhanced through the sharing of draft documents via e-mail. When compatible word processing, graphics, or desktop publishing software is used by both parties, documents attached to e-mail can be opened, edited, and returned, even when one person uses a Mac and the other is on a PC machine. Even incompatible systems can communicate using software such as Adobe Acrobat to view documents and attach the equivalent of sticky notes to the document without actually being able to open and change the document.

Desktop Publishing

Computers can be used to create professional-looking newsletters and illustrated material on a machine right in the office. This "just-in-time" printing enables a sense of immediacy in content without sacrificing appearance. Desktop publishing saves both money and time. Less than $5,000 will buy all the components necessary to produce high-quality newsletters and graphics in-house: a personal computer, a word processing program, a graphics program, page layout software, and a magazine-quality laser printer. Producing materials in-house reduces the time and expense of involving a commercial printer, especially when turnaround times are short and production standards are not excessively high. For the best possible publication quality, however, the advisable approach is to deliver the files to a professional printer for production using a suite of design, photo, and layout tools such as those included in Adobe In-Design.

Mailing Lists

Up-to-date mailing lists are vital in public relations work. Lists of names are typed into database programs such as Microsoft Works or ACT! contact management software and stored in computer memory. The capability to select groups of names from a master list assists practitioners in reaching target audiences. For example, when introducing its new models, Ford sought to generate ample publicity for more than 2,000 of its dealers located in rural areas. As reported in *Public Relations Journal*, the automaker created a computer file on each dealer that included the addresses, phone numbers, and names of local spokespersons. By combining this file with its standard news release, Ford created 9,600 customized news releases. Every release mentioned a local dealer by name and used local dealer data. The releases also were sent to customers based on a carefully culled mailing list of potential customers in each dealer's territory.

Public relations departments and firms may compile their own computer lists of media contacts or purchase databases from press-directory companies, such as Bacon's MediaSource software, which provides postal addresses, e-mail addresses, and phone data for nearly 30,000 editors on CD-ROM or at a password-protected Web site. Online services are now the norm because of the need to update the contact information for reporters and editors who regularly change news beats, positions, or even employers.

Online Conferences

Online conferences, which can be likened to a chat room or instant messaging session, that is, a series of typed messages exchanged among members of a work group, are increasingly valuable in public relations. Practitioners use their computers to "converse" with clients and suppliers or participate in forums on professional matters with their peers. Importantly, transcripts of exchanges can be retained in computer memory or printed to document negotiations with clients or establish common ground with publics.

Because of the ubiquity of personal computers, online conferences are becoming commonplace. Mobile computing with laptops, notebook computers, and palm-sized PDAs makes out-of-office conferences during business travel an important part of the business communication landscape. Free software such as Netmeeting is available for online conferencing. More sophisticated applications are available for those with more advanced needs.

With the rise in telephone services over the Internet, named VoIP for Voice over Internet Protocol, voice conferences have become less expensive. Traditionally, conference participants would call in to a toll-free phone number, which charges the conference host a significant fee. Callers provide a passcode and enter the conversation. Now, VoIP services such as Skype (www.skype.com) enable computer-to-computer voice calls as well as computer chat for no charge. Recently, Skype released its own conference calling function, enabling up to 100 participants to call in using Skype. This is an excellent tool for functions such as briefing public relations teams and clients about emerging issues, conducting problem-solving sessions, and gaining consensus on the stance along the contingency continuum the organization will take regarding a public.

Graphics, Design, and Photography

The use of computers to design eye-catching graphics—illustrations, graphs, charts, and text—has emerged as a stellar new technology in public relations practice. Recent developments in computer software make such graphics feasible and widely available, even in one-person public relations offices.

Attractive graphics give visual impact to annual reports and employee publications, as well as to video programs and presentations. Imaginative visual effects may be obtained with only a modest investment of time and money. Representations of people, designs, and charts add visual zest that stimulates audiences. Increasingly, public relations departments and firms employ such graphics to dress up transparencies or digital presentations.

High-quality digital cameras, easily identified by their larger camera bodies and compatibility with conventional SLR lenses, generate images at 8 megabytes each for professional-quality shots that can be manipulated in virtually the same ways as conventional film processing in terms of special effects and retouching. For as little as $2,000, a camera and excellent specialized lenses and sophisticated flash systems enable small public relations firms to deliver superb photos to Web and print platforms. Even large-scale posters can be printed in high resolution and saturated color by specialty photoprint services from digital files. Specifications, technical proofing, and final print orders can all be accomplished online.

Fax Transmission

Increasingly, the lines between fax and e-mail have blurred. It is now possible to use services that will convert an e-mail message into a broadcast fax that can be delivered to the actual fax machines of the target public. Similarly, incoming faxes to a professional's phone number can be received and forwarded as e-mail to the traveling professional. Public relations professionals use faxes, or the equivalent in the form of a scanned document attached to an e-mail, to send news releases, drafts of a client's newsletter, instructions from headquarters to a branch office, or any number of documents. Using a broadcast fax, a sender can transmit a single document to hundreds of recipients simultaneously. A corporation, for example, can distribute a news release swiftly and equally to competing news media. In another application, a customer can call a major vendor such as PR Newswire or Business Wire via toll-free number, request a piece of information, and receive it by fax within minutes.

A word of caution: Discretion should be used in faxing news releases to editors. Send only those you consider to be truly important and urgent. Editors complain, often quite sharply, about the amount of "junk" faxes they receive.

News Release Delivery

More than a dozen American companies deliver news releases electronically to large newspapers and other major news media offices. The news releases are fed into computers at the receiving newsrooms and examined by editors.

The difference between news release delivery firms and the traditional news services such as the Associated Press is this: Newspapers, radio, and television stations pay large fees to receive the reports of the news services, which maintain staffs of editors and reporters to gather, analyze, select, and write the news in a neutral style. In contrast, the news release delivery companies are paid by creators of news releases to distribute the news releases to the media, who pay nothing to receive them. These delivery services are prepaid transmission belts, not selectors of material. However, they do enforce editing standards and occasionally reject releases as unsuitable.

Electronically delivered news releases have an advantage over the conventional variety. Releases transmitted by satellite tend to receive closer, faster attention from media editors than those arriving by mail.

One of the largest news release delivery companies is Business Wire. Using electronic circuits and satellite communications, the company can simultaneously reach more than 1,600 media points in the United States and Canada and more than 500 in Europe, Latin America, East Asia, and Australia. In addition, Business Wire provides rapid dissemination of financial news releases to more than 600 securities and investment firms worldwide. The company sends an average of 175 news releases daily for a roster of more than 9,000 clients.

Another large news release delivery company, PR Newswire, was the first to distribute its releases by satellite. PR Newswire's computers distribute releases and official statements from more than 7,500 organizations directly into newsroom computers. Each day, PR Newswire transmits approximately 150 such releases. PR Newswire releases are entered into several commercial databases.

Video and Audio News Release Distribution

Satellite transmission also makes the fast distribution of video news releases (VNRs) possible. The picture-and-voice releases are sent primarily to cable television networks, local cable systems, and local television stations. Nearly 30 companies produce and distribute hundreds of VNRs for clients. Only relatively few of the most newsworthy, technically superior VNRs succeed in obtaining airtime. (See Chapter 10 for a discussion of VNRs.) Successful VNRs usually feature video footage that would be difficult for a station to obtain, as demonstrated by the following examples:

> A VNR sponsored by OshKosh B'Gosh bib overalls quotes the winner of its Search for the Oldest Bib Overall contest, 89-year-old Claude Mehder, who owns a pair of c. 1901 bibs: "We'll keep having kids, as long as the bib overalls hold up."

> Ringling Bros. and Barnum & Bailey circus clowns helped PC Computing magazine conduct the Notebook Torture Test of laptop computers.

> "The Car of the Future," a VNR distributed by D. S. Simon Productions, included DVD video screens, on-board message systems, global positioning, and a home security monitor.

Voice-and-sound news releases for use on radio also are distributed by satellite.

Teleconferencing

The most spectacular use of satellite transmission for public relations purposes is teleconferencing, which is also called videoconferencing. A public relations professional can easily arrange a teleconference by employing a firm that specializes in this service. In the United States, some 20,000 sites are equipped to handle such events.

With teleconferencing, groups of conferees separated by thousands of miles can interact instantaneously with strong visual impact, saving time and transportation costs. In one 5-year period, the Boeing Company used teleconferencing for 5,699 meetings and eliminated the need for more than 1.5 million travel miles.

Figure 9.1 is a schematic showing how satellite transmission works. Guests at receiving locations view the presentation on large screens. Regular telephone circuits back to the point of origin enable the guests to ask follow-up questions.

Here are examples of teleconferencing in operation:

> Ford Motor Company has installed a $10 million system connecting more than 200 Ford locations in North America. It provides customer and vendor relations as well as regular sales training events. Other companies have similar systems.

> A Midwestern magazine company incurred major costs for expensive executive travel on short notice to its parent company in New York, with as many as five flights a week. The costs for installation of a Picturetel system were recovered in a matter of months. The system's robotic camera can switch from a wide angle shot of all participants at a large conference table to a full-screen shot of each speaker. The speaker's microphone activates the camera to "zero-in" on him or her while speaking, providing a fairly naturalistic meeting environment in all locations.

> The Whirlpool Corporation in the United States and an N. V. Philips division in the Netherlands needed to explain their new $2 billion joint-venture agreement. So they held an international teleconference for their respective stockholders and employees, the media, and financial analysts.

> Hill & Knowlton, on behalf of several government agencies, arranged a two-hour conference between Cairo, Egypt, and five U.S. cities that permitted several hundred U.S. investors to talk directly with high-ranking Egyptian officials about private investment in that nation.

FIGURE 9.1

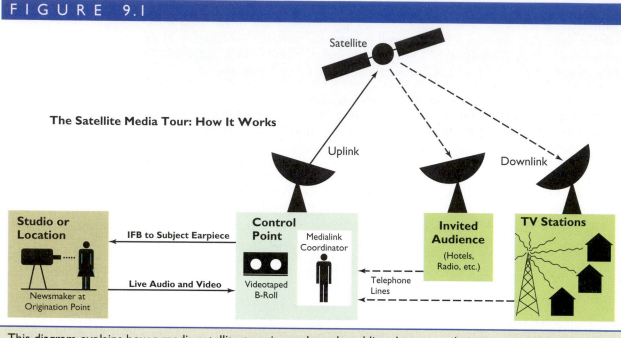

The Satellite Media Tour: How It Works

This diagram explains how a media satellite tour is conducted, enabling the person being interviewed to remain in one place while appearing on screens in other cities.

Source: Medialink, Inc.

> To introduce a newly developed hepatitis B vaccine, Merck Sharp & Dohme used a teleconference beamed to more than 400 locations where doctors, health care workers, and reporters had gathered. After watching the presentation, the invited guests telephoned questions to a panel of experts.

Webconferencing

The Web has become a less expensive alternative for videoconferencing. In its most basic form, Webconferencing is a "see-you-see-me" technology. Users with cameras and microphones mounted on their computers can engage in an Internet version of videophone.

Increasingly, professionals are able to use the Web for interactive Webcasts that primarily serve for the dissemination of information. For example, a press conference might be Webcast to any one who logs on to the event online. The participants can ask questions of the news source during the conference by e-mail. Seminar-style events can attract a worldwide audience.

The Center for Communications Health Research at the University of Michigan (www.chcr.umich.edu) regularly offers real-time Webcast seminars about cancer research. Past Webcasts are stored in an archive and can be viewed on demand. Discussion among participants takes place using AOL Instant Messenger. A recent Webcast topic was "Fractional Factorial Designs," suggesting that the term *narrowcast* also may be appropriate, given that the topics are sometimes quite specialized.

Satellite Media Tours

Instead of having a celebrity—an actor or author, for example—crisscross the country on an expensive, time-consuming promotional tour, public relations sponsors increasingly use the so-called satellite tour. In a time of crisis, imagine the value in having a leader make a personal plea for calm or for consideration of all the facts in a case by interacting with trusted local media figures.

With a satellite tour, the personality is stationed in a television studio, and TV reporters interview the personality by satellite from their home studios. Two-way television is used, permitting a virtual dialogue. Each station's reporter is put through to the personality at a specified time; thus a series of interviews, 5 to 10 minutes each, can be done in sequence. Corporations also employ satellite media tours to promote their products or services, often using a well-known performer or other "name" figure as a spokesperson.

Before his paralyzing spinal injury, actor Christopher Reeve, most famous for his film role as Superman, set an endurance record by doing 45 consecutive interviews at one sitting. Tiresome mentally and physically, no doubt, but much faster and cheaper than visiting all those cities!

Other Tools

Numerous other electronic tools also are used regularly in public relations practice. New instruments based on digital transmission appear frequently.

Cell Phones

Using cell phones, public relations professionals can be available anytime and at any place. This is a double-edged sword, meaning that work matters are only a ringtone away.

In health care public relations, cell phones are being used to provide treatment reminders and to organize activist and support groups. In addition, the nearly ubiquitous presence of cell phones in teen and young adult populations affords opportunities for clever public relations professionals to reach this important target audience. (See page 285, for a discussion of cell phones and flash mob activity.)

Personal Digital Assistants

In business settings, the Palm Pilot, BlackBerry, and Treo, along with smartphones and pocket PCs running a full software suite, provide portable management of traditional information such as e-mail, calendars, tasks, and contacts. The Windows Mobile 2005 operating system enables the latest generation of these wireless devices to use PowerPoint for presentations and Excel to review/revise budgets and spreadsheets on the fly. In addition, PDAs also offer striking new business functions such as the electronic exchange of business cards by infrared beam between Bluetooth-enabled handhelds. Most of these devices also offer Web browsing and Instant Messaging (IM) capabilities. Because developing nations do not have extensive landlines and electrical infrastructure, PDAs are one "leapfrog technology" to enable professionals to skip earlier technologies. One of the text book's authors is working in South Africa on health and risk communication efforts delivered through PDAs to traditional healers serving HIV-AIDS patients. (The Global box on page 284 looks at how the United Nations is utilizing new technologies to reach global audiences.)

ON THE JOB >>

The United Nations High Commission for Refugees Draws on the Web for Global Reach

Global

The global digital divide does not cause the human tragedies that result in refugee camps. However, the digital revolution may be part of the solution by making the world small enough that we all become aware and involved with the plight of refugees.

The United Nations High Commissioner for Refugees (UNHCR) Website seeks to increase public awareness of the global refugee problem. The site includes maps, photographs, and print and video news about people who have abandoned their homes to escape war and persecution. A *Refugees Magazine* is available as well as UNHCR screensavers. Interviews with the Director of UNHCR can be viewed on demand.

International sponsors are helping local newspapers mount Web editions of their papers so that refugees can assess when conditions are favorable for a return to their homelands. Spokespersons provide testimonials and

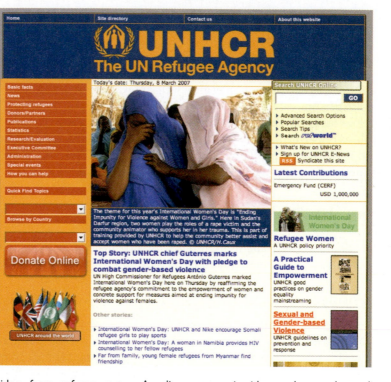

video from refugee camps. Angelina Jolie has been particularly active in the work of the UNHCR, taking time to

appear in videos and to conduct online chat sessions with interested persons around the world.

Source: Courtesy of UNHCR Public Information Section.

Memory: The CD-R/RW, DVD-R/RW, and Flash Memory

The multimedia versions of the familiar music CD and movie DVD offer an enormous capacity for message delivery in public relations; up to 300,000 pages of text, color pictures, and graphics can be stored on a single DVD. Because of their high storage capacity, CDs and DVDs have been the common "coinage" in public relations firms for the transfer of Web pages, graphics, and entire publications among account or project team members.

CDs and DVDs with an "/RW" notation are rewritable and can be used to backup professional work. It only takes one computer crash for overly confident young professionals to realize the importance of backing up creative copy and irreplaceable records that a public relations client is expecting to use. More recently, dedicated backup systems, essentially huge external hard drives holding hundreds of gigabytes of memory are a wise investment for one-click backup of an entire computer.

Now that materials can be delivered digitally to customers over the Internet or other wireless communication networks, some question the utility of CDs and DVDs. However, many people prefer a tangible product over virtual information. Public relations practitioners should keep this human need for tangible communication products in mind when deciding how much information to provide exclusively in digital form. A "press disc," the CD/DVD version of a media kit, is being used, but reporters make little use of the novelty. A more efficient use of the disc technique is to distribute information to specific target audiences. For example, corporations may distribute their annual reports to stockholders on CD or DVD.

Informational brochures can be placed on discs and mailed to target audiences. Buick, for example, mailed 20,000 discs to users of Apple computers to tell them about its new models. Recipients of the Buick disc were able to interact with the information presented. By pushing a few buttons, a user could load a virtual trunk with luggage and ask questions about mileage, standard equipment, and how the Buick compared with other auto makes.

Even business cards have joined the digital age. Up to 600 megabytes of information can be placed on a small, circular CD that fits in the tray of the computer's CD-ROM drive. An agency can use a CD business card to present all collateral materials about the firm as well as sample campaigns, including video and audio clips, on one 25-megabyte business card (e-businesscards.co.uk).

New technologies often have a limited life span. Increasingly, discs are being supplanted by flash memory sticks the size of a five-pack of gum that plug into the USB port of most modern computers. These memory sticks serve as portable, external hard drives that hold enormous amounts of data, the equivalent of DVD capacity. Flash memory can be used to read and write large amounts of data for backups or for the delivery of very large files, such as multimedia presentations and photo layouts, to clients.

Blogs, Moblogs, and Vlogs

The term *blog* is a contraction of two words, *Web* and *log*. A blog is a regularly updated online diary that also features links to news items and stories on the Web. The individual running the site is called a blogger. This person typically is a pundit who wishes to express his or her views on the news. Some bloggers are professional journalists. A blog also serves as a public forum for active give-and-take with the blogger, serving as an excellent forum for public discourse about an issue such as in the Dixie Chicks case covered in Chapter 1. Moblogging using cell phones with cameras is the latest rage. With moblogging, content is posted to the Internet from a mobile or portable device, such as a cell phone or PDA. One of the latest developments in the online diary/forum area is video logs, or vlogs. For example, the Natural Resources Defense Council and Environmental Countdown recently hired a highly appealing video personality, Amanda Congdon of the vlog Rocketboom, to anchor its environmental Web site. She will make a coast to coast trip documenting and discussing environmental issues. (See Chapter 10 for more information on blogs.)

A Peek at Future Technologies

Although it is unwise to predict the future in general, it is even more questionable in the fast-changing world of new media technologies. Nevertheless, it can be useful to anticipate what imminent technological advances may mean for public relations professionals.

> *Think Digital, but Not Necessarily Online.* Many public relations tools will involve specialized digital devices or media that are not online or that are used more frequently offline. For example, digital tablets and digital ink enable online content to be downloaded overnight so that the user can carry the lightweight device on a commuter train. Page loads are instantaneous because there is no download delay, and voice recognition/generation features enable commands and replies. News and other content can be read to the user by the tablet, making better use of professional travel time.

> *Forget Papyrus—And Even Drop Paper.* As already noted, computer processing is not limited to traditional devices. Thin, lightweight tablets hardly larger than a yellow notepad can link to the Internet and carry the computing power of full-sized desktop computers. These devices recognize the user's handwriting and respond to touch commands on the screen, enabling note taking and small-group activity in public relations offices. An even more portable medium is reaching the consumer market. E-ink enables computer functions on a sheet of material the size and thickness of a typical plastic placemat at a dining table. Applications for public relations remain to be realized, but as a portable computer and a reading device, the potential communication angles should be very interesting.

> *Wireless Broadband.* Cable and other high-capacity services such as satellite and DSL service often are collectively referred to as broadband services. Broadband enables online public relations professionals to meet the eight-second rule for loading Web pages while offering broadcast-quality video and unlimited information stores to media, investors, and other publics. Cell and dish satellite companies have now broken the broadband barrier, meaning that wireless computers and cell devices will browse and communicate at speeds comparable to desktop machines currently on cable or DSL service. These broadband speeds enable the Internet to offer the previously mentioned that telephone service called VoIP (Voice over Internet Protocol) at low cost, especially for international calling.

> *Virtual Presence.* Increased online capacity through broadband services will enable public relations professionals and Webmasters to create virtual environments and emulate the bricks-and-mortar presence of their organizations. Special boxes are becoming commercially available that will generate scents to accompany other elements of virtual reality to give users a sense of presence in a world created by the organization. Activist groups could convey pollution conditions. E-commerce sites could offer a restaurant atmosphere (sounds, aroma, clientele, layout, view) to help users decide where to make a reservation or what food suits their fancy for takeout.

> *Processing speed and memory capacity.* With continuing increases in computer chip capacity and speed, public relations professionals will enjoy digital tools in the future that are unimagined now. According to a National Public Radio program entitled *Talk of the Nation, Science Friday,* computer processors will be 25 times faster within five years. Quantum computing researchers are manipulating the spin of electrons in atoms to compute and record data at rates 1,000 times what we know today. Artificial intelligence to assist with crises, issues management, complex event management, and visual design will become commonplace. Multimedia and unusual hybrid media will meet public relations objectives such as on-demand information and virtual presence, which are currently constrained by machine limitations.

The future promises many changes and advances in communication tools and channels. However, each tool requires an "operator" with good managerial judgment and excellent people skills. In the midst of a new age of electronic wonders, most public relations triumphs will continue to hinge on human creativity.

PRCASEBOOK

HP Leads in Video Communication

HP, formerly Hewlett-Packard, headquartered in Palo Alto, California, spends more than $20 million annually on video communications and produces some of the nation's most sophisticated business television.

The company began live interactive broadcasts in 1981, using a transmitter to reach more than 80 plant and sales sites nationwide. This enabled an executive to address many audiences simultaneously. By 1996, HP had 127 sites linked to its video communications network, including several in Canada, South America, and Europe.

HP also has 48 teleconference rooms at 44 locations in the United States, Europe, and Asia. These facilities allow participants to hold meetings with people in as many as eight locations. Two-way audio and video allow a truly interactive meeting format; participants can also share information, including files and graphics on personal computers.

HP is developing an interactive multimedia network so that employees eventually will be able to view live videos, including the company president's semiannual address, on their personal computers. "Until the majority of employees can view video on their PCs or workstations, I don't think business television is going to advance much," said Mary Anne Easley, manager of HP's employee communications.

To communicate with employees, HP also produces a high-quality in-house video magazine. Released four times a year at a cost of $50,000 an issue, it is formatted after television's entertainment and lifestyle programs. According to Easley, "Television is an effective medium for reaching the baby boomers, the production and clerical workers."

Recently, HP was shaken by a scandal involving unethical, if not illegal, behavior by top officers of the company. They were complicit in ordering a private investigation of phone records and behavior of HP board members who were thought to be leaking confidential HP information to news reporters. HP endured the firing or resignation under duress of three of its top officers. HP's CEO, who was not directly involved in the scandal, sought to restore the company's reputation, as outlined by the cycle of conflict management presented in Chapter 2. He called a news conference and made an apology to company employees, the stockholders, and to the reporters whose phone records were investigated. In addition, he promised that HP would implement board policies and procedures that would preclude any future scandals. The news conference, as well as follow-up information and background, were relayed to HP employees via its video communications network.

Summary

The Communications Explosion
In the 1990s, the Internet grew from a means of exchanging scientific information within a relatively small community to become a global communications tool for the masses, blending telephone, television, and the computer into an information superhighway. Three key factors that have contributed to the communication explosion: fiber-optic cable, the digital transmission of sound and pictures, and wireless technologies.

The Computer
The computer is not just a tool to handle office procedures; it is also the on-ramp to the Internet.

The Internet
One of the primary uses of the Internet is for communication, both in the form of e-mail and in information delivery and research opportunities. Its reach is worldwide, but keep in mind that Internet content is virtually uncontrolled. Users can become frustrated in trying to find information online. There are also problems with security and copyright infringement.

Other Computer Uses
Public relations practitioners use computers in the following tasks: dictation and voice generation, expert system programming, processing of news releases, e-mail, desktop

publishing, mailing list generation, online conferencing, graphics production, and facsimile transmission. They also use computers as management tools.

Satellite Transmission

Major newspapers use satellites to transmit material to regional printing plants. A number of companies deliver news releases via satellite, including audio and video releases. Teleconferencing is a rapidly growing application of satellite transmission; approximately 20,000 U.S. sites are equipped to use this technology, saving companies time and money on business travel.

Other Tools

Other electronic tools include cell phones, personal digital assistants, CDs and DVDs, and electronic blackboards.

A Peek at Future Technologies

Future trends may include the use of offline digital devices, the growth of broadband and wireless broadband services, the development of "virtual presence" capabilities, and expanded processing speeds and memory capacity. All of these wonders will still require traditional managerial judgment and people skills.

CASE ACTIVITY >>
What Would You Do?

Ashland Community Hospital is deeply involved in health education as part of its approach to preventive care. In the past, the hospital has distributed leaflets about various diseases and conducted community seminars on such topics as how to stop smoking, the importance of physical fitness, and how to detect early signs of cancer.

The hospital can use new technologies to expand its potential in health education. Write a proposal on how the hospital could use the Internet, the World Wide Web, e-mail, CDs and DVDs, podcasts, and blogs to disseminate health care information to the community.

Questions for Review and Discussion

1. What part of the Internet has home pages? What does the term *home page* mean?
2. What is the Internet, and what are some of its most promising uses in public relations?
3. Define the following terms: broadband, virtual presence, brochureware, listservs, Webcasting, and artificial intelligence.
4. How do you think public relations professionals should address the tangibility factor when pitching stories to reporters?
5. What is the difference between a news release delivery system such as Business Wire and a news service such as the Associated Press?
6. Teleconferencing is growing in popularity. Explain how it operates. How does it differ from Webconferencing?

How do you think the two will merge as a result of broadband Internet service?
7. Celebrities frequently participate in satellite media tours. How do SMTs work, and why do many spokespersons prefer them to traditional promotion tours?
8. What impact do you think the tailoring of messages to individual audience members will have on public relations? Will it make our work more difficult? Noticeably more effective? Less ethically sound?
9. As a public relations practitioner, how might you use online computer conference calls?
10. Do you think that new technologies will facilitate or hamper creativity in public relations?

Suggested Readings

Altus, Celeste. "Intranets Keep Teams on Same Page Worldwide." *PR Week,* September 4, 2006, 9.

Barkow, Tim. "Blogging for Business: Do You Really Want Your Employees to Have Their Own Blogs At Work?" *The Strategist,* Fall 2004, 40–42.

Frank, John N. "Blogs Offer New Way for PR Pros to Speak with Clients," *PR Week,* October 18, 2004, 9.

Hazley, Greg. "Digital Age that Hit PR, Now Proves Its Worth." *O'Dwyer's PR Services Report,* June 2005, 1, 14, 16, 40.

Hiebert, Ray E. "Commentary: New Technologies, Public Relations, and Democracy." *Public Relations Review,* 31 (2005): 1–9.

Iacono, Erica. "Newswires 2.0." *PR Week,* September 11, 2006, 17.

Kiousis, Spiro, and Daniela V. Dimitrova. "Differential Impact of Web Site content: Exploring the Influence of Source (Public Relations versus News), Modality, and Participation on College Student's Perceptions." *Public Relations Review* 32, no. 2 (2006): 177–179.

McKenna, Ted. "Popular Vlogger Joins Environmental Effort." *PRWeek,* September 25, 2006, 2.

"More Abuse for the Much-Maligned Press Release: Is RSS Becoming the Preferred Way to Receive News?" MRR Online, Ragan's eNewsstand, October 13, 2006, www.raganenewsstand.com.

O'Brien, Keith. "Growth of MVNOs Making 'Third Screen' More Targeted." *PR Week,* April 10, 2006, 6.

Parker, Laura. "Courts Are Asked to Crack Down on Bloggers, Websites. Those Attacked Online Are Filing Libel Lawsuits." *USA Today,* October 3, 2006, p. 1A.

Porter, Lance V., and Lynne M. Sallot. "Web Power: A Survey of Practitioners' World Wide Web Use and Their Perceptions of Its Effects on Their Decision-Making Power." *Public Relations Review* 31 (2005): 111–119.

Quain, John R. "Fine Tuning Your Filter for Online Information." *New York Times Circuits,* October 13, 2006, www.nytimes.com/ref/technology/circuits/03basi.html.

Regalado, Antonio, and Dionne Searcey. "Where Did That Video Spoofing Gore's Film Come From?" *The Wall Street Journal Online,* August 3, 2006. http://online.wsj.com

Taylor, Maureen, and Danielle C. Perry. "Diffusion of Traditional and New Media Tactics in Crisis Communication." *Public Relations Review,* 31 (2005): 209–217.

Chapter Ten

Public Relations Tactics

Public relations professionals rely on a toolbox of varied tactics. News releases, public service announcements, press conferences, and special events are just some of the best-known and time-honored tactics. In this chapter, we introduce you to those tactics and others. Filling your public relations toolbox with a variety of tactics is essential to entry-level practice, when most public relations professionals will be applying those tactics directly. As you advance in your practice, you will need a well-developed understanding of tactics as you develop communications strategies to meet your organization's business objectives.

The News Release

The news release, also called a press release, is the most commonly used public relations tactic. Basically, a news release is a simple document whose primary purpose is the dissemination of information to mass media such as newspapers, broadcast stations, and magazines.

A great deal of the information that you read in your weekly or daily newspaper originates from a news release prepared by a publicist or public relations practitioner on behalf of a client or employer. Gary Putka, the Boston bureau chief of the *Wall Street Journal*, admits that "a good 50 percent" of the stories in the newspaper come from news releases. Another study, by Bennett & Company (Orlando), found that 75 percent of the responding journalists said they used public relations sources for their stories.

The media rely on news releases for several reasons. First, the reality of mass communications today is that reporters and editors spend most of their time processing information, not gathering it. Second, no media enterprise has enough staff to cover every single event in a community. Consequently, a lot of the more routine news in a newspaper is processed from information provided by public relations practitioners. As one editor of a major daily once said, public relations people are the newspaper's "unpaid reporters."

It must be remembered, however, that a news release is not paid advertising. News reporters and editors have no obligation to use any of the information from a news release in a news story. News releases are judged solely on newsworthiness, timeliness, interest to the readers, and other traditional news values. Consequently, it is important for any news release to be well written, formatted correctly, and contain accurate, timely information.

Planning a News Release

Before writing a news release, a number of questions should be answered to give the release direction and purpose. A planning worksheet should be used to answer the following questions:

> What is the key message? This should be expressed in one sentence.

> Who is the primary audience for the release? Is it for consumers who may buy a product or service? Or is it for purchasing agents in other companies? The answer to this question also affects whether the release is sent to a daily community newspaper or to a trade magazine.

> What does the target audience gain from the product or service? What are the potential benefits and rewards?

> What objective does the release serve? Is it to increase product sales, to enhance the organization's reputation, or to increase attendance at an event?

These planning questions are answered from a public relations perspective, but the next step is to think like a journalist and write a well-crafted news story that includes the traditional five Ws and H: who, what, when, where, why, and how. This is discussed further in the next several sections.

The Format of a News Release

News releases follow a standard, traditional format. You should use the following tips when crafting your own news releases (other tips are given in the Insights box on page 294):

> Use standard 8.5-by-11 inch paper. It should be white or on the organization's letterhead.

> Identify the sender (contact) in the upper-left-hand corner of the page and provide the sender's name, address, and telephone number. Many releases also include a fax number and an e-mail address.

> After the contact information, write "For Immediate Release" if the material is intended for immediate publication, which is usually the case. Some practitioners discard the phrase because they say that all news releases are automatically assumed to be for immediate release.

> Leave two inches of space for editing convenience before starting the text.

> Provide a boldface headline that gives the key message of the release so the editor knows exactly what the release is about at a glance.

> Provide a dateline, for example: Minneapolis, MN: January 21, 2007. This indicates where the news release originated.

> Start the text with a clearly stated summary that contains the most important message you want to convey to the reader, even if he or she only reads the first paragraph. Lead paragraphs should be a maximum of three to five lines.

> Leave at least a 1.5-inch margin. Double-space the copy to give editors room to edit the material.

> Use a 10 or 12 point standard type, such as Times Roman or Courier, because they are easy to read.

> Never split a paragraph from one page to the next. Place the word *more* at the bottom of each page.

> Place an identifying slug line and page number at the top of each page after the first one.

News releases that are prepared for Web news sites or e-mail have a somewhat different format. See the Insights box on page 295 for some guidelines.

The Content of a News Release

A news release, as already noted, is written like a news story. The lead paragraph is an integral and important part of the text, because it forms the apex of the journalistic "inverted pyramid" approach to writing. This means that the first paragraph succinctly summarizes the most important part of the story and succeeding paragraphs fill in the details in descending order of importance.

There are three reasons why you should use the inverted pyramid structure. First, if the editor or reporter doesn't find anything interesting in the first three or four lines of the news release, it won't be used. Second, editors cut stories from the bottom. In fact, Business Wire estimates that more than 90 percent of news releases are rewritten in much shorter form than the original text. If the main details of the story are at the

ON THE JOB >>

Rules for Writing a News Release

Insights

All news releases should be "news centered," according to Schubert Communications, a Pennsylvania public relations firm. Lisa Barbadora, director of public relations and marketing content for Schubert, gives these rules for writing news releases:

> Use short, succinct headlines and subheads to highlight main points and pique interest. They should not simply be a repeat of the information in the lead-in paragraph.

> Don't use generic words such as "the leading provider" or "world-class" to position your company. Be specific, such as "with annual revenues of."

> Don't describe products using phrases such as "unique" or "total solution." Use specific terms or examples to demonstrate the product's distinctiveness.

> Use descriptive and creative words to grab an editor's attention, but make sure they are accurate and not exaggerated.

> Don't highlight the name of your company or product in the headline of a news release if it is

not highly recognized. If you are not a household name, focus on the news instead.

> Tell the news. Focus on how your announcement affects your industry and lead with that rather than overtly promoting your product or company.

> Critique your writing by asking yourself, "Who cares?" Why should readers be interested in this information?

> Don't throw the whole kitchen sink into a release. Better to break your news into several releases if material is lengthy.

> Don't use lame quotes. Write like someone is actually talking— eliminate the corporatese that editors love to ignore. Speak with pizzazz to increase your chances of being published.

> Target your writing. Create two different tailored releases that will go out to different types of media rather than a general release that isn't of great interest to either group.

> Look for creative ways to tie your announcement in with current news or trends.

> Write simply. Use contractions, write in active voice, be direct,

avoid paired words such as "clear and simple," and incorporate common action-oriented phrases to generate excitement. Sentences should be no longer than 34 words.

> Follow the Associated Press Stylebook and specific publications' editorial standards for dates, technical terms, abbreviations, punctuation, spellings, capitalization, and so on.

> Don't use metaphors unless they are used to paint a clearer picture for the reader.

> Don't overdo it. It's important to write colorfully, to focus on small specific details, to include descriptions of people, places, and events—but do not write poetry when you want press.

> Don't be formulaic in your news release writing. Not every release must start with the name of the company or product. Break out of the mold to attract media attention.

> Don't expect editors to print your entire release. Important information should be contained in the first two paragraphs.

> Make it clear how your announcement is relevant for the editors' readers.

Source: Jerry Walker. "18 Simple Rules for Writing a News Release." *O'Dwyer's PR Services Report,* November 2002, 32–33.

beginning, the release will still be understandable and informative even if most of the original text has been deleted.

A third reason for using the inverted pyramid is that readers don't always read the full story. Statistics show, for example, that the average reader spends less than 30 minutes a day reading a metropolitan daily newspaper. This means that they read a lot of headlines and first paragraphs, and not much else.

Here are some other guidelines for the content of a news release:

> Use Associated Press (AP) style. The vast majority of newspapers and broadcast stations use this stylebook as a guide for word usage, punctuation, and capitaliza-

tion. A news release written in AP style makes the job of editors much easier and often makes a difference whether the release is used at all.

> Be concise. Edit the copy to remove excess words and "puff" words. Few news releases need to be more than two pages long. A reporter can obtain additional details by telephoning or e-mailing the source and checking for additional background information on the organization's Web site.

> Avoid clichés and fancy phrases. When editors get a release that uses terms such as *unique, revolutionary,* and *state-of-the-art,* they are likely to throw it away.

> Avoid technical jargon. Releases, for the most part, are written for general audiences unfamiliar with the terms and jargon used within an organization. The objective is to write for understanding, not confusion.

> Double-check all information. Be absolutely certain that every fact and title in the release is correct and that every name is spelled properly. Check the copy for errors in grammar, punctuation, and sentence structure. Make sure trademarks are noted.

> Eliminate boldface and capital letters. Avoid boldfacing key words or sentences and don't place the name of the organization in all capital letters.

> Include organization background. A short paragraph at the end of the news release should give a thumbnail sketch of the organization. It may be a description of what the organization does or manufactures, how many employees it has, or whether it is a market leader in a particular industry.

> Localize whenever possible. Most studies show that news releases with a local angle get published more often than generic news releases giving a regional or national perspective. Airlines, for example, "localize" news releases about the total number of passengers and revenues by breaking down such figures by specific cities and making that the lead paragraph for releases sent to journalists in those cities. Insurance companies also do "hometown" releases by mentioning local agents in the copy. The news release shown on page 296 is good example of the format and copy for a news release.

Beyond the technical questions of contents and format are sometimes ethical questions surrounding news releases.

ON THE JOB >>

How to Write An Internet-Ready News Release

Insights

The format and content of news releases for distribution via e-mail and the Internet is somewhat different than the traditional 8.5-by-11, double-spaced format that is mailed or faxed to media outlets. B. L. Ochman, writing in the *Strategist,* suggests that you should "think of the electronic news release as a teaser to get a reporter or editor to your Web site for additional information." He makes the following suggestions:

> Use a specific subject line that identifies exactly what the news release is about.

> Make your entire release a maximum of 200 words or less, in five short paragraphs. The idea is brevity so that reporters see the news release on one screen and don't have to scroll. If a journalist has hundreds of e-mails in his or her inbox, scrolling becomes a real chore.

> Write only two or three short sentences in each of the five paragraphs.

> Use bulleted points to convey key points.

> Above the headline or at the bottom of the release be sure to provide a contact name, phone number, e-mail address, and URL for additional information.

> Never send a release as an attachment. Journalists, because of possible virus infections, rarely open attachments.

Ochman concludes, "Write like you have 10 seconds to make a point. Because online, you do."

FOR IMMEDIATE RELEASE

Contacts:
Mike Duggan, Golden Valley Microwave Foods
952-832-3439
-OR-
Bernice Neumann, Morgan&Myers
612-825-0050

**ACT II INTRODUCES FIRST AND ONLY KETTLE CORN
MICROWAVE POPCORN**

MINNEAPOLIS, Minn. – July   – Sweet and salty, two classic flavor combinations, have long been paired in all-time favorite foods. Now, Golden Valley Microwave Foods (GVMF) has made microwave popcorn – one of America's favorite snacks – available in delicious slightly sweet, slightly salty ACT II® Kettle Corn.

An American tradition introduced by settlers in the 1700-1800s, kettle corn was first made outdoors by popping corn in large cast-iron kettles with rendered lard and sweeteners, such as molasses, honey or sugar. In the past decade, this tasty snack started being served again at outdoor gatherings, such as fairs, concerts, carnivals and flea markets, primarily in the Midwestern states.

-more-

-2-

"Kettle Corn doesn't have to be just for special occasions anymore," says Mike Duggan, Golden Valley Microwave Foods marketing manager. "We wanted to make this a fun flavor combination conveniently available to families whenever they want hot, fresh, great-tasting popcorn."

ACT II Kettle Corn is the first of its kind in a microwave form. The company spent eight years researching and developing an authentic kettle corn flavor. "We had to develop the process and source a natural sweetener that withstands high-temperature microwave heating without burning, and we succeeded," says Jim Montealegre, vice president of product development at GVMF.

ACT II Kettle Corn is available in a 3-, 5- and 6-pack carton and contains three 1-cup servings per bag. Suggested retail price ranges from $2.19 for a 3-pack to $2.99 for a 6-pack carton.

GVMF, based in Minneapolis, Minn., is the largest manufacturer of microwave popcorn in the world, selling its ACT II®, Orville Redenbacher's® and Healthy Choice® brands in 30 countries around the globe. Microwave popcorn, ready-to-eat sweet popcorn, popcorn balls, soft pretzels and snack mix are included in GVMF's product line. GVMF is the first and only microwave popcorn manufacturer to control all selecting of seed, growing, sorting and processing of corn, as well as bag manufacturing, used in its popcorn products.

XXXX

GOLDEN VALLEY MICROWAVE FOODS • 7450 Metro Boulevard, Edina MN 55439 • Tel 800.328.6286 • Fax 952.835.9635

The news release is the workhorse of public relations. This is an example of a well-written and -formatted news release from Kettle Corn, which was prepared by Morgan&Myers public relations.

Publicity Photos

News releases are often accompanied by a photo. News releases about personnel often include a head-and-shoulder picture (often called a mug shot) of a person named in the release. New product news releases often include a photo of the product in an attractive setting. See the publicity photo on page 297 for an example.

Studies show that more people "read" photographs than read articles. The Advertising Research Foundation found that three to four times as many people notice the average one-column photograph as read the average news story. In another study, Wayne Wanta of the University of Missouri found that articles accompanied by photographs are perceived as significantly more important than those without photographs.

Like press releases, publicity photos are not published unless they appeal to media gatekeepers. Although professional photographers should always be hired to take the photos, public relations practitioners should supervise their work and select which photos are best suited for media use. Some additional suggestions follow.

Quality. Photos must have good contrast and sharp detail so that they reproduce in a variety of formats, including grainy newsprint. Digital photography is the norm, and in many cases editors download digital photos from an organization's Web site. But a beautiful photo on the computer screen may not come out the same way when it is printed. Most Web sites use images at 72 dpi (dots per inch) for fast download, but newspapers need photos at 150 to 200 dpi, and magazines need at least 300 dpi. Consequently, organizations usually have an online news or press room that provides high-resolution photos for journalists. Photos also are supplied to editors on CD to ensure maximum reproduction quality.

Subject Matter. A variety of subjects can be used for publicity photos. Trade magazines, weekly newspapers, and organizational newsletters often use the standard "grip-and-grin" photo of a person receiving an award or the CEO shaking hands with a visiting dignitary. This has been a staple of publicity photos for years, and there is no sign that they are going out of fashion despite being tired clichés. Another standard approach is the large group photograph, which is appropriate for the club newsletter, but almost never acceptable for a daily newspaper. A better approach is to take photos of groups of three or four people from the same city and send only that photo to editors in that specific city.

Composition. The best photos are uncluttered. Photo experts recommend (1) tight shots with minimum background, (2) an emphasis on detail, not whole scenes, (3) and limiting wasted space by reducing gaps between individuals or objects. At times, context also is important. Environmental portraits show the subject of the photo in his or her normal surroundings—for example, a research scientist in a lab.

Action. Too many photos are static, with nothing happening except someone looking at the camera. It's better to show people doing something—talking, gesturing, laughing, running, or operating a machine. Action gives a photo interest.

Scale. Another way to add interest is to use scale. Apple, for example, might illustrate its newest iPod by having Steve Jobs hold the device while surrounded by a large stacks of CDs, showing how much music could be stored on it.

Camera Angle. Interesting angles can make the subject of a photo more compelling. Some common methods are shooting upward at a tall building to make it look even taller or an aerial shot giving viewers an unusual perspective.

Lighting. Professional photographers use a variety of lighting techniques to ensure that the subject is portrayed, quite literally, in the best light. Product photos, for example, always have the light on the product and the background is usually dark or almost invisible. Background is an important

Media kits often include photos and color slides of the product. This is the color slide that accompanied the media kit for Kettle Corn, Act II.

consideration. If the executives at a banquet are all wearing dark suits, the photographer shouldn't line them up in front of a dark red curtain, because there will be no contrast. Also, outdoor shots require using the sun to advantage.

Color. In the past, most publicity photos were black and white for economic reasons. Today, with digital cameras and flash cards, almost all publicity photos are color. Because of new printing technologies, many publications now use color on a regular basis. Daily newspapers, for example, regularly use color publicity photos in the food, business, sports, and travel sections. Publications have differing requirements. Some want photos that can be downloaded via Web sites; others want 35-mm slides, and still others want a color photograph that can be scanned.

Media Advisories and Fact Sheets

On occasion, public relations staff will send a memo to reporters and editors about a news conference or upcoming event that they may wish to cover. Such memos also are used to let the media know about an interview opportunity with a visiting expert or alert them that a local person will be featured on a network television program. These media advisories also are referred to as media alerts. A sample media alert is shown below. Advisories may be sent with an accompanying news release or alone.

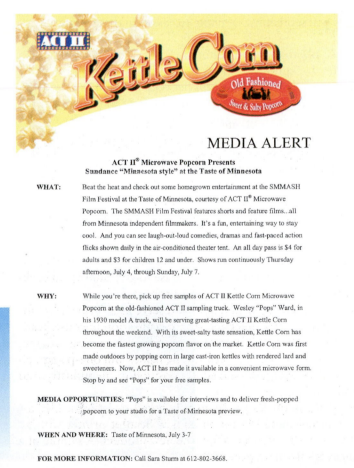

> A media alert is a thumbnail sketch of a product and the special events surrounding its launch. As the name implies, it is an "alert" to the media in case they would like cover the announcement or event.

The most common format for media advisories to use is short, bulleted items rather than long paragraphs. A typical one-page advisory might contain the following elements: a one-line headline, a brief paragraph outlining the story idea, some of journalism's five Ws and H, and a short paragraph telling the reporter whom to contact for more information or to make arrangements. The following is the text of a media advisory from Old Bay Seasonings.

Media Alert

Who:	Old Bay Seasoning, a unique blend of a dozen herbs and spices and a Chesapeake Bay cooking tradition for over 60 years, conducted a search for America's seafood lovers and Old Bay fans.
	More than 1,600 people across the country entered the contest by briefly describing in 100 words or less why they are America's biggest seafood fanatics and Old Bay fans and providing their favorite unusual uses for Old Bay.
What:	Ten lucky finalists from across the country were selected to vie for a $10,000 grand prize in the first-ever Old Bay Peel and Eat Shrimp Classic—a 10-minute, timed tournament to see who can peel and eat the most Old Bay-seasoned shrimp.
When:	The contest will kick off Labor Day Weekend on Friday, August 30, from 11:30 A.M. to 12:30 P.M.
Where:	Harborplace Amphitheater (outdoors) 200 East Pratt Street Baltimore, Maryland
Special Guest:	Tory McPhail, executive chef at Commander's Palace restaurant in New Orleans and rising star in the culinary industry, will be master of ceremonies for the event.
Contact:	Amanda Hirschhorn, Hunter Public Relations 212/679.666X, ext. 239, or ahirschhorn@hunterpr.com Event-day cell: 212/555.555x

SATELLITE FEED INFORMATION FOLLOWS
Friday, August 30
Feed Time: 3:30–3:45 P.M. ET (Fed in Rotation)
Coordinates: C-Band: Telstar 4 (C)/Transponder 11/AUDIO 6.2 & 6.8
DL FREQ: 3920 (V)

Fact sheets are another useful public relations tool. Fact sheets are often distributed to the media as part of a media kit or with a news release to give additional background information about the product, person, service, or event.

Fact sheets are usually one to two pages in length and serve as a "crib sheet" for journalists when they write a story. A fact sheet about an organization may use headings that provide (1) the organization's full name, (2) products or services offered, (3) its annual revenues, (4) the number of employees, (5) the names and one-paragraph biographies of top executives, (6) the markets served, (7) position in the industry, and (8) any other pertinent details.

A variation on the fact sheet is the FAQ (frequently asked questions). HP, for example, supplemented an Internet news release on its new ScanJet printer with an FAQ that answered typical consumer questions about the new product. A sample of a product information fact sheet is shown on page 300.

Fact sheets concentrate on a product or service's strengths and capabilities. Some give ingredients; others discuss how to prepare the product.

July 2001

Contact: Bernice Neumann or
Heather Behnke
612-825-0050

FACT SHEET

ACT II® Kettle Corn

Product Description: The leader in microwave popcorn, ACT II introduces a truly unique popcorn flavor combination – slightly sweet, slightly salty – in all-new ACT II® Kettle Corn. This new popcorn is the result of exclusive technology, bringing Americans a centuries-old tradition in a convenient microwave form. ACT II Kettle Corn is first of its kind in the microwave popcorn category.

Net Weight: 3.5 oz. bag (99 g)

Servings: 3 servings per bag

Preparation: 1) Place unfolded bag in the center of microwave oven with the instructions facing up.

2) **Pop on HIGH at full power in the microwave until bag expands and popping slows 1-2 seconds between pops. LISTEN to popping rate and do not leave microwave unattended.** Overcooking may cause scorching. Normal popping time is 2-5 minutes.

3) Remove from microwave. Carefully open bag at top by pulling diagonally at corners.

4) Enjoy!

GOLDEN VALLEY MICROWAVE FOODS • 7450 Metro Boulevard, Edina MN 55439 • Tel 800.328.6286 • Fax 952.835.9635

Media Kits

A media kit, which is sometimes referred to as a press kit, is usually prepared for major events and new product launches. Its purpose is to give editors and reporters a variety of information and resources that make it easier for reporters to write about the topic.

The basic elements of a media kit are (1) the main news release; (2) a news feature about the development of the product or something similar; (3) fact sheets on the product, organization, or event; (4) background information; (5) photos and drawings with captions; (6) biographical material on the spokesperson or chief executives; and (7) some basic brochures. All information should be clearly identified; it's also important to prominently display contact information such as e-mail addresses, phone numbers, and Web site URLs.

The contents of a media kit are usually placed inside a custom-designed folder. The folder will vary based on the size of budget. Pillsbury designed a folder that was the shape of a large chocolate chip cookie with a bite taken out of it to launch its new Big DeLuxe Classics cookies. Other organizations, such as Cirque du Soleil, just use a standard folder with its name emblazoned on it.

The typical media kit folder is 9 by 12 inches and has four surfaces: a cover, two inside pages (with pockets to hold news releases, etc.), and a back cover that gives the name and address of the organization. Another common feature is to have a slot on the inside page that holds a business card of the public relations contact person. The PR Casebook on this page discusses a media kit for an award-winning public relations campaign.

PRCASEBOOK

It's Corny, but It Worked

Product publicity is one of the most difficult assignments in public relations because media gatekeepers are always sensitive about giving away "free advertising" to a company that's promoting a particular product.

Morgan&Myers, a public relations firm in Minneapolis, was able to surmount media skepticism with a creative media campaign for a relatively mundane product—microwave popcorn. Golden Valley Microwave Foods, another Minnesota firm, wanted to introduce its new product, Act II Kettle Corn, that combined salt and a sweet taste in the same product. It already was the world's largest manufacturer of microwave popcorn, selling its Act II, Orville Redenbacher's and Healthy Choice brands in 30 nations around the world.

Morgan&Myers came up with a media kit that attracted considerable media interest. Research showed that a large percentage of people eat microwave popcorn while watching rented videos at home, so the firm decided to package the media kit in a standard video case with the typical movie packaging.

The cover art on the case was a couple on a beach holding hands at sunset and the title, "When Sweet Met Salty." The subhead added, "Two unlikely opposites make one delicious couple." There was even the film reviewer comment, "This tasty romance had me craving more—Juliet Cruncher, Boston Popper." On the back cover, more reviews: "A delicious pair—Roger Corn, Los Angeles Grocery News."

The media kit was inside the video box. It contained (1) a pitch letter to editors; (2) a news release about the new product; (3) a fact sheet about the nutritional qualities of the product; (4) two 35-mm color slides showing a bowl of popcorn and the product package; (5) a media advisory about sponsorship of a civic event, "The Taste of Minnesota," where the company dispensed samples from a 1930 model A truck; and (6) a CD of all the media materials in digital form. These media materials are shown throughout this chapter.

The result: Nearly a third of the media in cities where Act II brands were strongest covered the story. Stories also appeared in major online and print media in 10 of the top

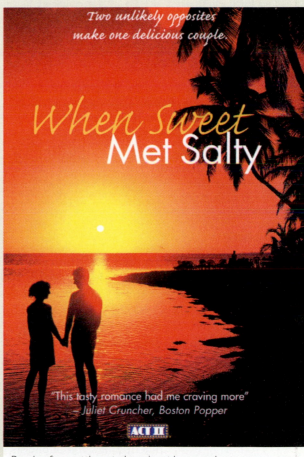

Two unlikely opposites make one delicious couple.

When Sweet Met Salty

"This tasty romance had me craving more"
— Juliet Cruncher, Boston Popper

ACT II

People often watch rented movies at home and eat popcorn, so Kettle Com designed a media kit in the shape of a VHS movie box.

major media markets, including *Newsday* and the *Chicago Tribune*. Virtually all news stories communicated two company messages: (1) Act II Kettle Corn was the first product of its kind on the market and (2) the distinctive sweet-salty flavor was the hallmark of kettle corn.

The campaign received the Bronze Anvil for Product Media Kits from the PRSA.

— ON THE JOB >>

Electronic press
kits becoming
the standard

Insights

Press kits are a staple among public relations tactics, but technology has allowed, indeed required, that press kits' delivery and contents be reconsidered.

Traditional press kits often include a fact sheet, overview press release, bios, some photos or graphics, frequently asked questions, and so forth. These press kits are usually contained in a themed folder and are mailed or handed out to journalists. Electronic press kits can be delivered via the Internet or by CD.

Electronic press kits, like their predecessors might, depending on the subject, include:

> Fact sheets
> Newsworthy press releases
> Bios
> Backgrounders
> Testimonials
> Links to archived information
> Contact information
> Charts or graphs
> Photos or illustrations
> Audio
> Video
> Animation

The flexibility of electronic press kits is illustrated by Jennifer McAndrew, senior publicist for the publicity division of BookPros. She told *PRWeek,* "When pitching our authors for interview opportunities with national television programs, such as *Today,* we always include a DVD of video clips from the author's past television interviews. This helps the producer gauge an author's interview style and talent as a guest."

Source: Craig McGuire, "The New, Lightweight Press Kit," *PRWeek,* May 15, 2006, 18.

A good example of a well-designed media kit that fits an organization's products and personality was created by Crayola to celebrate its 100th anniversary with a 25-city bus tour. The kit was a self-mailer that unfolded into a large round sheet 2 feet in diameter that featured artwork done with a rainbow of crayon colors. The kit also included a colorful news release (localized for each city) and two background articles on the history of the company. One piece of interesting trivia: "Since 1903, more than 120 billion crayons have been sold throughout the world. End-to-end they would circle the earth 200 times."

Compiling and producing a media kit is time-consuming and expensive. It's not uncommon for media kits to cost $8 to $10 each by the time all of the materials have been produced. Much of the cost is in printing the kits. Consequently, Weber Shandwick has predicted the end of paper media kits. A poll of 1,500 media outlets in 2004 found that 70 percent of them prefer electronic communications. HP is part of the growing trend of organizations using online media kits (see the Insights box on this page). It issued a media kit online for a trade show instead of spending the money to print kits for editors covering the event. The cost savings was almost $20,000 over mailing printed kits to about 200 reporters.

Pitch Letters

As previously noted, getting the attention of media gatekeepers is difficult because they receive literally hundreds of news releases and media kits every week.

Consequently, many public relations practitioners and publicists will write short letters or notes to editors that try to grab their attention. In the public relations industry, this is called a *pitch*. A generic pitch is shown on page 303. It simply lets the editor know, in brief form, about the contents of the media kit. In many cases, the letter will be accompanied by a sample of the product. Public relations people also use pitches—either mailed, e-mailed, or phoned—to ask editors to assign a reporter to a particular event, to pursue a feature angle on an issue or trend, or even to book a spokesperson on a forthcoming show.

Pitching is a fine art, however, and public relations personnel must first do some basic research about the publication or broadcast show that they want to contact. It's important to be familiar with the kinds of stories that a publication usually publishes

July

Dear Editor:

Gorp, chocolate covered nuts, salted nut rolls. The list of traditional sweet and salty foods that make for great flavor is long. Now, Golden Valley Microwave Foods is adding to that tradition with all-new ACT II® Kettle Corn, an early-American favorite style of popcorn available for the first time for microwave popping.

Although sweetened popcorn is a staple enjoyed from Europe to South America and Asia, Americans have only been able to find the old-fashioned slightly sweet, slightly salty popcorn – known as kettle corn – at local fairs, markets or other outdoor events mainly in the Midwest. A treat from pioneer days, kettle corn has traditionally been popped in large, black kettles with various oils, sweeteners and salt.

Enclosed you'll find further information on ACT II Kettle Corn Microwave Popcorn, along with a sample. Once you've tasted this first and only microwave kettle corn, we think you'll agree it's a delicious snack completely unique to the existing buttered and salted popcorn category.

We've also included a CD with media materials, photos and additional illustrated information about ACT II Kettle Corn.

Please call me at 612-825-0050 if you have any questions.

Sincerely,

Bernice Neumann

Bernice Neumann
Public Relations Counsel to Golden Valley Microwave Foods

GOLDEN VALLEY MICROWAVE FOODS • 7450 Metro Boulevard, Edina MN 55439 • Tel 800.328.6286 • Fax 952.835.9635

or the kinds of guests who appear on a particular talk show. Knowing a journalist's beat and the kinds of stories he or she has written in the past also is helpful.

The media expresses great interest in trends, so it's also a good idea to relate a particular product or service with something that is already identified as part of a particular fashion or lifestyle. Fineberg Publicity, a New York firm, convinced *Hard Copy* to do a 3-minute segment on its client Jockey International. The news hook was the "slit skirt" trend in the fashion industry and how women were buying stylish hosiery to complement their skirts. The segment showed celebrities wearing Jockey's hosiery products.

The best pitch letters show a lot of creativity and are successful in grabbing an editor's attention. *Ragan's Media Relations Report* gives some opening lines that generated media interest and resulting stories:

> "How many students does it take to change a light bulb?" (A pitch about a residence hall maintenance program operated by students on financial aid)

> "Would you like to replace your ex-husband with a plant?" (A pitch about a photographer who is expert at removing "exes" and other individuals out of old photos)

ON THE JOB >>

Guidelines for Pitching Stories by E-Mail

Insights

Publicists frequently pitch story ideas by e-mail. In fact, many editors prefer this method compared to letters, faxes, or even phone calls. However, it's important to remember some guidelines:

> Use a succinct subject line that tells the editor what you have to offer; don't try to be cute or gimmicky.
> Keep the message brief; one screen at the most.
> Don't include attachments unless the reporter is expecting you to do so. Due to virus attacks, many reporters never open attachments unless they personally know the source.
> Don't "blast" e-mails to large numbers of editors. E-mail systems are set up to filter messages with multiple recipients in the "To" and "BCC" fields, a sure sign of spam. If you do send an e-mail to multiple editors, break the list into small groups.
> Send tailored e-mail pitches to specific reporters and editors; the pitch should be relevant to their beats and publications.
> Personally check the names in your e-mail database to remove redundant recipients.
> Give editors the option of getting off your e-mail list; it will make your list more targeted to those who are interested. By the same token, give editors the opportunity to sign up for regular updates from your organization's Web site. If they cover your industry, they will appreciate it.
> Establish an e-mail relationship. As one reporter said, "The best e-mails come from people I know; I delete e-mails from PR people or agencies I don't recognize."

Source: Dennis L. Wilcox. *Public Relations Writing and Media Techniques*, 5th ed. Boston: Allyn & Bacon, 2005, 207.

> "Our CEO ran 16 Boston Marathons . . . and now he thinks we can walk a mile around a river." (A pitch about a CEO leading employees on a daily walk instead of paying for expensive gym memberships or trainers)

See the Insights box on this page for information on pitching stories via e-mail.

Newsletters and Magazines

Most organizations, whether the local Rotary Club or IBM, publish newsletters for their members, employees, retirees, and vendors and even for community opinion leaders. Subscription newsletters offer expert advice and inside information to individuals and organizations with specific interests in a particular topic or industry.

The typical newsletter is four to eight pages and printed on 8.5-by-11 paper. For the most part, newsletters emphasize short articles and have few graphic elements. A good example of a newsletter is *O'Dwyer's PR Newsletter*. It has a two-column format, and short articles are announced with boldface, underlined headlines one size larger than the text copy. In sum, newsletters are economical, easy to design, and can be used to convey information in a straightforward manner.

Newsletters for employees typically report personnel promotions, forthcoming events, policy announcements, news from field offices, the introduction of new products, productivity achievements by employee teams, opportunities to attend workshops and seminars, and the typical announcements from human resources. The objective is to inform employees about company affairs.

An organizational newsletter aimed at an outside audience, members of the organization, or both, may contain items about political trends that could affect the organization, announcements of new programs, brief human interest stories, and features on community involvement. Many nonprofit groups have newsletters for their contributors to let them know how the organization is using their money and what programs are being funded. A newsletter is a brisk compilation of highlights and tidbits, not a place for contemplative essays or discussion.

The next step up from the newsletter is a newspaper, usually in tabloid format, that has a masthead, a number of photos, and the type of headlines that one would see in a regular weekly or daily newspaper. Many of these publications use extensive color throughout and can run up to 16 pages.

A magazine is the apex of organizational publications. It is the most elaborate in terms of color, graphics, paper stock, and design. And it's always the most expensive to produce. Accenture's glossy magazine has an annual budget of $700,000. Boeing spends $500,000 on its quarterly *Aero* magazine. In general, magazines are written for specific audiences, which can include (1) employees and retirees, (2) stockholders and investors, (3) wholesalers of company products, and (4) consumers. See page 000 for the cover of Z, the magazine of the Cleveland Zoological Society.

The writing and designing of organizational periodicals is a multifaceted process. The Insights box on page 306 gives some tips that are applicable for newsletters, newspapers, and magazines.

Electronic Newsletters

Many organizations supplement their printed publications with electronic newsletters and magazines. In many instances, organizations are completely eliminating print publications. Electronic publications are known as *e-zines*, and their primary advantage is the instant dissemination of information to employees or members via a listserv.

Another major advantage of electronic newsletters, of course, is cost. An average print newsletter might cost up to 50 cents per copy, whereas an e-zine typically costs less than 5 cents per copy. Most e-zines rely on a simple format, which means text only, limited use of color, limited graphics, no photos, and no fancy design effects. This is because e-zines, which are sent via e-mail, are received on a variety of different e-mail systems around the world, many with limited graphics capabilities.

Electronic newsletters should be kept to three to five window panes at maximum. Individual news items should also be short, about 10 to 12 lines each. The writing style should be punchy and somewhat more informal than regular print publications. Most people don't like to scroll through a long newsletter. Most readers will only scan the newsletter for items of interest.

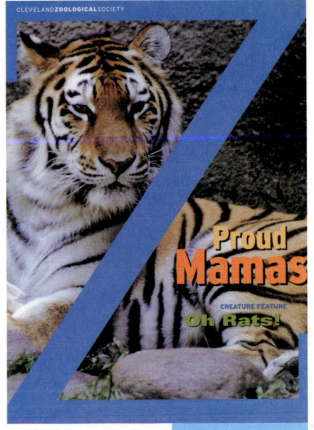

The Cleveland Zoological Society reaches its members and prospective contributors through a well-designed four-color magazine, simply titled Z. (Design: Nesnadny + Schwartz: Cleveland + New York + Toronto)

E-zines on Intranets

Many organizations, particularly large corporations, have established intranets for their employees. Essentially, an intranet works on the same principle as the Internet, but it is a private network within an organization for the exclusive use of employees and management. Because they are closed systems and the technical standards are set by the organization, intranets are able to handle much more sophisticated electronic newsletters.

A good example of what is possible on an intranet is HP's online publication, which is sent daily to 140,000 HP employees in 37 nations. HPNow is an attractive newsletter that includes color, graphics, photos, and links to thousands of archived pages that contain everything from past issues to news releases, speeches, organizational charts, position papers, and employee awards.

— ON THE JOB >> —

How to Create Newsletters and Brochures

Insights

Newsletters and brochures should be designed to convey information in an attractive, uncluttered way. Here are some guidelines:

Copy

> Less is better. Use short, punchy sentences. Keep paragraphs short.
> Use informative subheads to break up copy blocks.
> Use bullets to list key points.
> Summarize and repeat the two or three main points.
> Tell the complete story in headlines or pull-out quotes.
> Keep readers in mind; what do they need to get out of the story?
> Use quotes from credible, outside sources.

Layout

> Don't try to fill every space; allow for plenty of white space.

> Organize layout from left to right and top to bottom. Most people read in this sequence.
> Avoid large blocks of reverse type (white on black background). It's difficult to read.
> Avoid photos and artwork as background screens for copy; it's also difficult to read.
> Facing pages should be composed as two-page spreads; that's how readers see them.
> Use graphics and photos to balance blocks of copy.
> Make photos and illustrations as large as possible. Whenever possible, use action-oriented photos.

Type

> The best type size for text is 10 or 11 point with 2 points of leading. If the audience is older, increase the type size to 12 or 14 point.
> Use serif type for text. It is easier to read. Headlines can be set in sans serif type.

> Use a minimum number of fonts and type families. A three-ring circus of type is poor design and just confuses people.
> Use boldface sparingly. Use for subheads and for a few key words. Don't use it for an entire paragraph.
> Use italic type for emphasis sparingly, if at all.
> Avoid all caps in headlines. Capital and lowercase letters are more readable.

Color

> Use black ink for text. If you use a second color, apply it as a highlight to frame a story, a pull-quote (set in larger type), or an entire page.
> Headlines can use color, but the ink should be on the dark side rather than pastel.
> Avoid using extensive color on low-quality paper. If you have color, use coated stock (glossy) to get maximum color reproduction.

Source: Adapted from Dennis L. Wilcox. *Public Relations Writing & Media Techniques,* 5th ed. Boston: Allyn & Bacon, 2005, 352.

Brochures

Writing brochures, like producing newsletters and magazines, requires the coordination of several elements. These include message content, type selection, graphics layout, and design. Public relations personnel, who are often charged with writing content, work with designers and printers to make the final product.

Brochures are often called booklets, pamphlets, or leaflets, depending on their size and content. A pamphlet or booklet, for example, is characterized by a booklike format and multiple pages. An example of a booklet is a corporate annual report. A leaflet is often described as a single piece of paper printed on both sides and folded into three panels, giving it a 4-by-9-inch format. Handbills and flyers are printed on one side of a page and are often placed on bulletin boards. For the purposes of this section, however, the term *brochure* will be used for all of these formats.

Brochures are used primarily to provide information about an organization, a product, or a service. Organizations mail brochures or hand them out to potential customers, place them in information racks, hand them out at conferences, and generally distribute them to anyone who wants basic information. Whenever an organization needs to explain something to a large number of people—employees, constituents, or customers—a brochure is a good way to do it.

The following are some basic questions to answer when planning a brochure:

> Who is the audience? What are its characteristics? Is it a particular demographic in terms of education, income, or ethnic background?

> What is the brochure supposed to accomplish? Is it to impress, entertain, sell, inform, or educate?

> What is the best format for getting the message across? Should it be a simple flyer, a pocket-sized brochure, a cheaply printed leaflet, or a four-color brochure?

Factors such as budget, the number of copies needed, and the intended distribution method also must be considered. Whatever the format, the writer should keep it in mind as copy is developed. The most common mistake is to write more than the proposed format can accommodate. A second mistake is to cram everything in by reducing the type size or margins, making it difficult to read the text. In other words, less is best so that there is adequate room for white space and graphics.

The concept of good writing also applies to brochures. Short, declarative sentences are better than compound sentences. Short paragraphs are better than long ones. Major points should be placed in headlines, bulleted, or boldface. See the Insights box on page 306 for tips on how to write an effective brochure.

The Reach of Radio and Television

Broadcasting and its various forms, which now includes Webcasting, are important because they reach the vast majority of the American public on a daily basis. Each week, it is estimated that radio reaches 94 percent of Americans ages 12 and older, with a total audience of 223 million. With the average American now commuting nearly 50 minutes each workday, a large percentage of this audience is reached in their cars.

Television also reaches a mass audience. The National Association of Broadcasters (NAB) says that local TV news attracts 150 million viewers. Network news reaches 30 million, and another 34 million are reached through regional and national cable shows.

Writing and preparing materials for broadcast and digital media, however, requires a special perspective. Instead of writing for the eye, a practitioner has to shift gears and think about adding audio and visual elements to the story. This section discusses the tactics employed by public relations personnel, when they use radio, television, and the Web on behalf of their employers and clients.

Radio

News releases prepared for radio differ in several ways from releases prepared for print media. Although the basic identifying information is the same (letterhead, contact, subject), the standard practice is to write a radio release using all uppercase letters in a double-spaced format.

The length of the radio release should also be indicated. For example, "RADIO ANNOUNCEMENT: 30" or "RADIO ANNOUNCEMENT: 60." This indicates that the announcement will take 30 or 60 seconds to read.

The timing is vital, because broadcasters must fit their messages into a rigid time frame that is measured down to the second. Most announcers read at a rate of 150 to 160 words per minute. Of course, word lengths vary, so it's not feasible to set the timing based on the number of words in a message. Instead, the general practice is to use an approximate line count. With word processing software set for 60 spaces per line, the following standard can be applied:

2 lines = 10 seconds (about 25 words)

5 lines = 20 seconds (about 45 words)

8 lines = 30 seconds (about 65 words)

16 lines = 60 seconds (about 125 words)

The writing style of radio releases also differs. A news release for a newspaper uses standard English grammar and punctuation. Sentences often contain dependent and independent clauses. In a radio release, a more conversational style is used, and the emphasis is on strong, short sentences. This allows the announcer to breathe between thoughts and the listener to follow what is being said. An average sentence length of about 10 words is a good goal.

The following is an example of a 60-second news feature (153 words) distributed to radio stations by the North American Precis Syndicate for the National Automotive Parts Association (NAPA):

Car Care Corner

YOU CAN KEEP YOUR CAR, AND YOUR FAMILY ON THE ROAD TO SAFETY EVEN IN ROUGH WEATHER, IF YOU HEED A FEW HINTS. FIRST, HAVE YOUR BATTERY AND CHARGING SYSTEM TESTED BY A CERTIFIED TECHNICIAN. AN OLD BATTERY MAY FAIL IF IT HAS TO RUN LIGHTS, HEATER, DEFROSTER, DEFOGGER, AND WIPERS WHEN THE TEMPERATURE IS LOW. HAVE YOUR ANTIFREEZE CHANGED BY AN AUTOMOTIVE TECHNICIAN EVERY TWO YEARS. STEER CLEAR OF LOW TIRE INFLATION. A 30-DEGREE DROP IN TEMPERATURE CAN MAKE A FOUR TO FIVE POUND DIFFERENCE IN PRESSURE. LOW PRESSURE TIRES DON'T MEET THE ROAD PROPERLY OR SHED WATER EFFECTIVELY. CHECK TIRE WEAR. PUT A PENNY IN THE TREAD WITH LINCOLN'S HEAD DOWN. IF THE TOP OF HIS HEAD SHOWS, YOU NEED NEW TIRES. YOU CAN LEARN MORE FROM THE EXPERTS AT THE NATIONAL AUTOMOTIVE PARTS ASSOCIATION AT W-W-W—DOT—N-A-P-A—ON-LINE—DOT-COM.

Notice the spaces in the Web site address. This alerts the news announcer to read the URL slowly so people can remember it. The same rule is applied to telephone numbers, and oftentimes an address or telephone number is repeated a second time for listeners who are in the process of grabbing a pencil and pad.

Audio News Releases

Although broadcast-style news releases can be sent to radio stations for announcers to read, the most common and effective approach is to send the radio station a recording of the news announcement.

An audio news release, commonly called an *ANR*, can take two forms. One simple approach is for someone with a good radio voice to read the entire announcement; the person doing the reading may not be identified by name. This, in the trade, is called an *actuality*. In a second approach, an announcer is used, but a quote called a *soundbite* is included from a satisfied customer or a company spokesperson. This approach is better than a straight announcement because the message comes from a "real person" rather than a nameless announcer. This type of announcement is also more acceptable to stations; because the radio station's staff can elect to use the whole recorded announcement or take the role of announcer and just use the soundbite.

Format. The preferred length for an ANR is one minute. However, shorter ones can be used. The audio recording should also be accompanied by a paper copy of the script. This enables the news director to judge the value of the tape without having to listen to it.

Here is a 60-second script for an ANR that includes a soundbite from a spokesperson. It was produced by Medialink for its client, Cigna Health Systems, and distributed to radio stations via satellite.

Worried at Work

New Survey Shows American Workers Are Stressed Out but Can

Take Simple Steps to Ease Workplace Tension

SUGGESTED ANCHOR LEAD: If you're feeling stressed out at work, you're not alone. A new survey shows economic uncertainty, dwindling retirement savings, and ongoing terrorist concerns have American workers increasingly stressed out. But as Roberta Facinelli explains, employees and employers alike can do things to counteract all this tension.

SCRIPT: If you're like most American workers, you're facing increased stress on and off the job. In fact, according to a new nationwide study conducted by employee assistance experts at CIGNA Behavioral Health, almost half of employees surveyed have been tempted to quit their jobs over the past year, have quit, or are planning to soon, given the series of pressures they're facing. But according to CIGNA's Dr. Jodi Aronson Prohofsky, there are things you can do to ease workplace tension.

CUT (Aronson Prohofsky): Simple changes in your lifestyle can help reduce stress. Exercising more often, volunteering, making time to read or engaging in a favorite hobby are all easy steps we can take. Many of us also take time out for reflection and meditation to deal with daily pressures.

SCRIPT: Employees often find workplace support programs a good place to start, so check with your employer. Many provide programs such as counseling services, flexible work schedules as well as nutrition and health programs—all of which can help reenergize stressed out workers to achieve a better work–life balance. I'm Roberta Facinelli.

SUGGESTED ANCHOR TAG: If you're interested in learning more about workplace stress reduction tips, visit www.cignabehavioral.com.

The Cigna script is an example of an ANR that gives information and tips to the listener in a conversational way. It contains helpful information about how to reduce stress and is not overly commercial. Cigna is mentioned in the context of the story, but primarily as a source of information. A station newsperson, no doubt, would find the subject current and newsworthy for the station's audience.

Production and Delivery. Every ANR starts with a carefully written and accurately timed script. The next step is to record the words. When recording, it is imperative to control the quality of the sound. A few large organizations have complete recording studios, some hire radio station employees as consultants, but most organizations use a professional recording service.

Professional recording services have state-of-the-art equipment and skilled personnel. They can take a script, edit it, eliminate words or phrases that will not be understandable, record it at the proper sound levels, and produce a finished tape suitable for broadcasting.

Radio news stories and features can be produced in multiple copies on cassette or CD. The most common method, and the most economical, is to burn the recording to CD. In addition, the MP3 or iPod format for digital files is increasingly popular.

Radio stations, like newspapers, have preferences about how they want to receive audio news releases. One survey by DWJ Television found that almost 75 percent of radio news directors prefer to receive actualities by phone. This is particularly true for late-breaking news events in the station's service area. When a forest fire threatened vineyards in California's Napa Valley, a large winery contacted local stations and offered an ANR with a soundbite from the winery's president telling everyone that the grape harvest would not be affected. About 50 stations were called, and 40 accepted the ANR for broadcast use.

Organizations sending ANRs for national distribution usually use satellite or the World Wide Web.

Use of ANRs. Producing ANRs is somewhat of a bargain compared with producing materials for television. Ford Motor Company, for example, spent $3,500 for national distribution of a news release on battery recycling as part of Earth Day activities. More than 600 radio stations picked up the ANR, and about 5 million people were reached. Despite its cost-effectiveness, an ANR should not be sent to every station. Stations have particular demographics. A release about the benefits of vitamin supplements for senior citizens isn't of much interest to a rock music station.

The use of ANRs is increasingly popular with radio stations. Thom Moon, director of operations at *Duncan's American Radio Quarterly*, told *PRWeek* that he thinks the major reason for this is the consolidation of ownership in radio broadcasting (Clear Channel now owns 1,200 stations), which has resulted in cost cutting and fewer news personnel.

Jack Trammell, president of VNR-1 Communications, echoed this thought when he told *pr reporter*, "They're telling us they're being forced to do more with less. As long as radio releases are well produced and stories don't appear to be blatant commercials, newsrooms are inclined to use them." Trammell conducted a survey of radio stations and found that 83 percent of them use radio news releases (RNRs). And 34 percent said such releases give them ideas for local stories. The news editors look for regional interest (34 percent), health information (23 percent), and financial news (11 percent). They also like technology stories, children's issues, politics, seasonal stories, and local interest issues.

Additional tips about writing radio news releases are given in the Insights box on page 311.

Radio Public Service Announcements

Public relations personnel working for nonprofit organizations often prepare public service announcements (PSAs) for radio stations.

A PSA is defined by the FCC as an unpaid announcement that promotes the programs of government or voluntary agencies or that serves the public interest. In general, as part of their responsibility to serve the public interest, radio and TV stations provide airtime to charitable and civic organizations to make the public aware of and educate them about such topics as heart disease, mental illness, and AIDs.

Profit-making organizations do not qualify for PSAs despite their claims of providing "public service," but sometimes an informational campaign by a trade group qualifies. For example, the Aluminum Association received airtime on a number of stations by producing a PSA about how to recycle aluminum cans. Before the announcement was released, the association received an average of 453 calls a month. Five months after the PSA began appearing, the association had received 9,500 calls at its toll-free number. The PSA was used in 46 states, and 244 stations reported 16,464 broadcasts of the announcement.

Format and Production. Radio PSAs, like radio news releases, are written in uppercase and double-spaced. Their length can be 60, 30, 20, 15, or 10 seconds. And, unlike radio news releases, the standard practice is to submit multiple PSAs on the same subject in various lengths.

ON THE JOB >>

Guidelines for Writing a Radio News Release

Insights

The following are tips from the Broadcast News Network, which writes and distributes news releases for a number of clients:

> Time is money in radio. Stories should be no longer than 60 seconds. Stories without actualities (soundbites) should be 30 seconds or less.
> The only way to time your story is to read it out loud, slowly.
> A long or overly commercial story is dead on arrival. Rather than editing it, a busy radio newsperson will discard it.
> Convey your message with the smallest possible number of words and facts.
> A radio news release is not an advertisement; it is not a sales promotion piece. A radio news release is journalism—spoken.
> Announcers punctuate with their stories; not all sentences need verbs or subjects.
> Releases should be conversational. Use simple words and avoid legal-speak.
> After writing a radio news release, try to shorten every sentence.
> Listeners have short attention spans. Have something to say and say it right away.
> Never start a story with a name or a vital piece of information. While listeners are trying to figure out the person speaking and the subject matter, they don't pay attention to the specific information.

The idea is to give the station flexibility in using a PSA of a particular length to fill a specific time slot. DWJ Television explains: "Some stations air PSAs in a way that relates length to time of play, for example, placing one length in their early news shows and another in the late news shows. Supplying both lengths allows a campaign to be heard by those who only watch one of these shows."

PSAs can be delivered in the same way as radio news releases. Scripts can simply be mailed to the station for reading by announcers. Another popular approach is to mail stations a cassette or CD with announcements of varying lengths. Once a recording is made, it also can be transmitted via telephone.

Here is a basic PSA produced by the American Red Cross, which shows how the same topic can be treated in various lengths:

20 seconds

Ever give a gift that didn't go over real big? One that ended up in the closet the second you left the room? There is a gift that's guaranteed to be well received. Because it will save someone's life. The gift is blood, and it's desperately needed. Please give blood. There's a life to be saved right now. Call the American Red Cross at 1-800-GIVE LIFE.

— ON THE JOB >> —

Adding Music and Sound to a PSA

Insights

You can make your radio PSA more interesting if you take the time to incorporate music and other sounds (SFX) into the speaker's script (VO). The Santa Clara County (California) Network for a Hate Free Community distributed the following PSA in a CD format to radio stations in the area.

Don't Teach Hate (60 Seconds)

MUSIC: MUSIC BOX VERSION OF "WHEELS ON THE BUS"
SFX: BABY TALK, CHILDREN LAUGHING
VO: AT SIX WEEKS BABIES LEARN TO SMILE.
SFX: BABY COOING

VO: BY SIX MONTHS THEY WILL RESPOND TO DIFFERENT COLORS.
SFX: BABY LAUGHING
VO: AT SIXTEEN MONTHS, THEY DEVELOP A SENSE OF SELF.
SFX: BABY SAYS "MINE!"
VO: AT WHAT AGE DO THEY LEARN TO HATE?
SFX: (PAUSE—MUSIC STOPS)
SFX: HORN HONKS, BRAKES SLAM.
ANGRY MAN'S VOICE: JEEZ, FREAKIN' FOREIGNERS, TOO DAMN STUPID TO OPERATE A CAR. YOU OKAY, BACK THERE, SPORT?
(MUSIC UP)
BABY'S VOICE: "M OKAY DADDY.

VO: THEY LEARN TO HATE WHEN YOU TEACH THEM. YOUR CHILDREN ARE LISTENING AND THEY'RE LEARNING FROM YOU. INSULTS AND SLURS BASED ON RACE, RELIGION, DISABILITY, GENDER OR SEXUAL ORIENTATION TEACH CHILDREN IT'S OKAY TO HATE. HATE IS THE ENEMY IN SANTA CLARA COUNTY AND YOU ARE ON THE FRONT LINE.

To report a hate crime or to receive services, call the Santa Clara County Network for a Hate Free Community at (408) 792–2304.

---

60 seconds

We want you to give a gift to somebody, but it's not a gift you buy. We want you to give a gift, but not necessarily to someone you know. Some of you will be happy to do it. Some of you may be hesitant. But the person who receives your gift will consider it so precious, they'll carry it with them the rest of their life. The gift is blood and, every day in America, thousands of people desperately need it. Every day, we wonder if there will be enough for them. Some days, we barely make it. To those of you who give blood regularly, the American Red Cross and the many people whose lives you've saved would like to thank you. Those of you who haven't given recently, please help us again. There's a life to be saved right now. To find out how convenient it is to give blood, call the American Red Cross today at 1-800-GIVE-LIFE. That's 1-800-GIVE-LIFE.

Another PSA script, showing sound and music, is shown in the Insights box on this page.

Use of Radio PSAs. Almost any topic or issue can be the subject of a PSA. Stations, however, seem to be more receptive to particular topics. A survey of radio station public affairs directors by West Glen Communications, a producer of PSAs, found that local community issues and events were most likely to receive airtime, followed by children's issues. The respondents also expressed a preference for PSAs involving health and safety, service organizations, breast cancer, and other cancers.

The majority of respondents also prefer PSAs that include a local phone number rather than a national toll-free number. Therefore, many national groups distribute scripts to chapters that can be "localized" before they are sent to radio stations.

Other studies have shown that an organization needs to provide helpful information in a PSA and not make a direct pitch for donations. PSAs often tell people about the organization and direct listeners to a phone number or Web site where they can obtain more information—and make a donation.

Radio Media Tours

Another public relations tactic for radio is the radio media tour (RMT). Essentially, a spokesperson conducts a series of around-the-country, one-on-one interviews with radio announcers from a central location. A public relations practitioner (often called a publicist in such a situation) prebooks telephone interviews with DJs, news directors, or talk show hosts around the country, and the personality simply gives interviews over the phone that can be broadcast live or recorded for later use.

A major selling point of the RMT is its relatively low cost and the convenience of giving numerous short interviews from one central location. Laurence Mosowitz, president of Medialink, told *PRWeek*, "It is such an easy, flexible medium. We can interview a star in bed at his hotel and broadcast it to the country. Radio is delicious."

A major multinational pharmaceutical concern, Schering-Plough, used an RMT to point out that most smokers in the United States fail to recognize the warning signs of chronic bronchitis. Of course, the company makes a drug for such a condition. The RMT was picked up by 88 stations with an audience of more than 2.8 million. The RMT was part of a campaign that also used a satellite media tour (SMT) for television stations. SMTs are discussed in the next section.

Television

There are four approaches for getting an organization's news and viewpoints on local television. The first approach is to simply send the same news release that the local print media receive. If the news director thinks the topic is newsworthy, the item may become a brief 10-second mention by the announcer on a news program. A news release may also prompt the assignment editor to consider visual treatment of the subject and assign the topic to a reporter and a camera crew for follow-up.

A second approach is a media alert or advisory informing the assignment editor about a particular event or occasion that would lend itself to video coverage. Media alerts, which were discussed earlier in the chapter, can be sent via e-mail, fax, or even regular mail.

The third approach is to phone or e-mail the assignment editor and make a pitch to have the station do a particular story. The art of making a pitch to a television news editor is to emphasize the visual aspects of the story.

The fourth approach is to produce a video news release (VNR) that, like an ANR, is formatted for immediate use with a minimum of effort by station personnel. The VNR also has the advantage of being used by numerous stations on a regional, national, or even global basis.

Video News Releases

An estimated 5,000 VNRs are produced annually in the United States. Large organizations seeking enhanced recognition for their names, products, services, and causes are the primary clients for VNRs. The production of VNRs can be more easily justified if there is potential for national distribution and multiple pickups by television stations and cable systems.

A typical 90-second VNR, says one producer, costs a minimum of $20,000 to $50,000 for production and distribution. Costs vary, however, depending on the number of location shots, special effects, the use of celebrities, and the number of staff required to produce a high-quality tape that meets broadcast standards.

Because of the cost, a public relations department or firm must carefully analyze the news potential of the information and consider whether the topic lends itself to a fast-paced, action-oriented visual presentation. A VNR should not be produced if there's nothing but talking heads, charts, and graphs. Another aspect to consider is whether the topic will still be current by the time the video is produced. On average, it takes four to six weeks to script, produce, and distribute a high-quality VNR. In a crisis situation or for a fast-breaking news event, however, a VNR can be produced in a matter of hours or days. The VNR for the launch of the Segway Human Transporter was produced in 10 days by Burson-Marsteller.

Another example of a fast response with a VNR is Pepsi. Within a week of news reports that syringes and other sharp objects had been found in cans of Diet Pepsi, the soft-drink company produced and distributed a VNR showing that the insertion of foreign objects into cans on their high-speed bottling lines was virtually impossible. This VNR, because of its timely nature and high public interest, reached a total of 186 million viewers and helped avoid a massive sales decline of Pepsi products.

Format. Writing a script for a VNR is a bit more complicated than writing one for an ANR because the writer has to visualize the scene, much like a playwright or screenwriter. Adam Shell, in *Public Relations Tactics*, describes the required skills:

> Producing a VNR requires expert interviewing skills, speedy video editing, creative eye for visuals, and political savvy. The job of the VNR producer is not unlike that of a broadcast journalist. The instincts are the same. Engaging soundbites are a result of clever questioning. Good pictures come from creative camera work. A concise, newsworthy VNR comes from good writing and editing. Deadlines have to be met, too. And then there's all the tiny details and decisions that have to be made on the spot. Not to mention figuring out subtle ways to make sure the client's signage appears on the video without turning off the news directors.

Perhaps the best way to illustrate some of Shell's comments is to show a typical VNR script. See pages 315 to 316 for a script prepared by Medialink for Beringer Vineyards.

Production. Although public relations writers can easily handle the job of writing radio news releases and doing basic announcements for local TV stations, the production of a VNR is another matter. The entire process is highly technical, requiring trained professionals and sophisticated equipment.

Consequently, public relations departments and firms usually outsource production to a firm specializing in scripting and producing VNRs. Public relations personnel, however, usually serve as liaison and give the producer an outline of what the VNR is supposed to accomplish. The public relations person also will work with the producer to line up location shots, props, and the individuals who will be featured.

Medialink, a major producer and distributor of VNRs, gives some tips about the production of VNRs that best meet the needs of TV news directors:

> Give TV news directors maximum flexibility in editing the tape using their own anchors or announcers. This can be done by producing the VNR on split audio (the announcer track on one audio channel and the natural sound of the VNR on another). This way, the news director has the option of "stripping" the announcer's voice and inserting the voice of a local reporter or announcer.

Medialink

As these extracts from a video news release illustrate, the script of a VNR requires thinking about the visuals at the same time that you write copy and plan for interview excerpts. This two-column format, showing visual and audio components, how a script is written.

VISUAL	AUDIO
FADE IN:	
Suggested Anchor Lead-in:	Despite the economy and world events, things are going "GRAPE" in California's wine country. The "CRUSH," officially underway in the heart of wine country, is the most exciting time of year. Grapes generate (help generate) billions of dollars in travel, tourism, jobs and sales. Especially in the Napa Valley where wine makers consistently create some of the world's finest wine. The buzz this year? A later than usual harvest may produce even higher quality wines.
	As Mother nature places the finishing touches on this year's grape harvest, wine lovers are out in force, pursuing their passion in restaurants, hotels and wine tasting rooms. If the bottom line is good taste, Elizabeth Anderson uncorks some vintage secrets.
	NAT SOT (:04 approx)
	NARRATION
	Coming to a glass near you…
Pour Nouveau-Beringer	The grapes of California's crush.
Crush, picking-harvest	92% of America's wine is produced in California...some of the world's best in Napa Valley.
Wine, grapes	Beringer's Nouveau, the first wine of the 2002 vintage, will beat all California wines to market. Of the Golden State's 847 wineries, this landmark is the oldest in Napa Valley...bottling award-winning magic for 125 years.
Napa beauty shot	
Wine picking, crush-harvest.	
Nouveau, Beringer beauty shots, famous	**NAT SOT Beringer Winemaker**
Exteriors, wine is poured.	"The grapes are ready...just the right sugar content."
See Beringer name of famous real estate	
Historical video (from tv cmxl)	
B-roll to complement what he says	
Continuously show various vineyards – St. Clements, Stags Leap	
Barrels, caves	
Dissolve to: Beringer and awards <u>See</u> 4	

> Produce the VNR with news footage in mind. Keep soundbites short and to the point. Avoid commercial-like shots with sophisticated effects.

> Never superimpose your own written information on the actual videotape. TV news departments usually generate their own written notes in their own typeface and style.

> Never use a stand-up reporter. Stations do not want a reporter who is not on their own staff appearing in their newscast.

(continued)

Medialink

VISUAL	AUDIO
in their language	This all American industry is wining, dining and growing!
Shopping and buying wine	
Scenery, tourism, wine tasting, etc.	**SOT: Napa Valley Wine Association Expert**
ON CAMERA *See this person in her own vineyard, as talks*	"Sales go up despite a volatile stock market or the economy. More people are cocooning.staying home…and what is better to enjoy at home than a good wine? Loyal consumers still spend for their favorite brand. Wine remains one of life's pleasures that is still affordable, you have a fabulous tourist destination…and a lot of history and art…all in one glass…it's magical"
Begin **Montage** of beauty shots	**NAT SOT (:01)**
Recapping what we've seen, visually	**NARRATION**
Cave gates open, see rare wines	
Gate has Beringer Logo on it.	It's a complex recipe of earth, light, air, hidden caves, historical vineyards and oak barrels of TLC…
Tourists mill thru barrels and caves, dissolves	**NAT SOT (glasses clink-toast) :02**
To caves, vineyards, barrels, etc.	**NARRATION**
Dissolve to:	The easy part….
Conclude with sunset, beauty shots	**NAT SOT (couple pours, sips Nouveau)**
Tasting and purchasing wine, closeup	**NARRATION**
Couple toasts, Pour wine. Beauty shot	..is up to you.
Wide shot winery, sunset, happy ending visual	**ELIZABETH ANDERSON REPORTING**
	SUGGESTED ANCHOR TAG
	This year's California harvest shows more Chardonnay grapes being crushed and bottled than anything else…followed by Cabernet, Zinfandel, Merlot, Chenin Blanc, Syrah-Shiraz and Sauvignon Blanc.
	Beringer's finest costs about $125.00. But, you can pay as little as $8-dollars and still have a 4-star experience.
	To find out more, click onto www.Beringer.com

> Provide TV stations with a local angle. This can be done by sending supplemental facts and figures that reflect the local situation. This can be added to the VNR when it is edited for broadcast.

> Good graphics, including animation, are a plus. Stations are attracted to artwork that shows things in a clear, concise manner.

Delivery. The VNR package should also include two or three minutes of B-roll, or background pictures, for use by TV news producers in repackaging the story. Typical B-roll includes additional interviews, soundbites, and file footage. A Nielsen Media Research survey of 130 TV news directors, for example, found that 70 percent preferred VNRs with B-roll attached.

An advisory should accompany the VNR package or be sent to news directors before the actual satellite transmission of the video to the station. The advisory, in printed form, should contain the basics: the key elements of the story, background and description of the visuals, editorial and technical contacts, satellite coordinates, and the date and time of the transmission. Many stations prefer to receive this advisory by fax instead of e-mail or wire service. A fax is on printed paper and can be passed around the newsroom so many staffers can see it.

Satellite transmission is the most cost-effective way to distribute VNRs nationally or even globally. In addition, it is the preferred method of most news directors. Virtually every television station in the country has at least one satellite receiving dish. The old method was analog transmission, but increasingly stations are now receiving digital transmissions via satellite.

Ethical Uses of VNRs. Video news releases come under fire from time to time because television stations use the content without revealing the source. The Public Relations Society of America promotes a standard for VNRs: "All prepackaged materials should contain a complete disclosure of the sources of information, the transparent identification of individuals or ogranizations who paid for, sponsored or initiated the production of the materials, and an explicit revelation of interests/points of view represented in the materials." Unfortunately, even when public relations practitioners apply these standards, they can come under fire if television stations choose not to include the source and, in effect, represent the VNR as their own reporting.

The Center for Media and Democracy, a watchdog group based in Madison, Wisconsin, conducted a 10-month study during 2005 and 2006 in which they tracked 36 VNRs to determine whether they were used and, if so, whether their source was revealed. The center reported that

> Of the 36 VNRs the study tracked, 69 television stations aired at least one VNR.
> The VNRs were used in both large and small markets.

ON THE JOB >>

VNRs Reach Millions of People

Insights

Here's a list of the top 10 VNRs that, according to Nielsen Media Research, were used by television stations in a recent year:

> Insurance Institute for Highway Safety (IIHS): The crashworthiness of large pickup trucks (213 million viewers, 1,855 airings)
> British Airways: Improvements to the Concorde (191 million viewers, 214 airings)
> Buena Vista film studio: Pearl Harbor world premiere (190 million viewers, 204 airings)
> Insurance Institute for Highway Safety (IIHS): SUV bumper crash test (157 million viewers, 1,332 airings)
> Motorola: The role of mobile phones (146 million viewers, 92 airings)
> Insurance Institute for Highway Safety (IIHS): Crash-test results of Dodge Grand Caravan/Hyundai Elantra (139 million viewers, 1,309 airings)
> Ericsson: Consumer-oriented technology products (130 million viewers, 181 airings)
> European Space Agency: The first European astronaut (121.6 million viewers, 298 airings)
> Taco Bell: The reentry of 15-year-old space station Mir as part of a product promotion (121 million viewers, 1,615 airings)
> Novartis: FDA approval of Gleevec oral therapy drug (120 million viewers, 1,062 airings)

Overall, these 10 VNRs reached a total audience of more than 1.5 billion viewers in the United States, Canada, Europe, Asia, and Australia.

> Of 87 VNR broadcasts, not one of those broadcasts included full disclosure of the source of the VNR.

> The stations included their specific graphics to make the VNRs indistinguishable from station-generated news.

> Stations included their independently gathered footage in only 7 of the 87 VNR broadcasts documented by the center.

The Center for Media and Democracy findings led the Federal Communications Commission to conduct an investigation into the use of VNRs. These findings provide ample evidence that public relations practitioners must be vigilant about including full disclosure on any press materials, including VNRs. Whether broadcasters use or delete that disclosure is something that practitioners cannot control.

Satellite Media Tours

The television equivalent to the radio media tour is the satellite media tour (SMT). Essentially, an SMT is a series of prebooked, one-on-one interviews from a fixed location (usually a television studio) via satellite with a series of television journalists or talk show hosts. (See also Chapter 9.)

The SMT concept started several decades ago when companies began to put their CEOs in front of television cameras. The public relations staff would line up reporters in advance to interview the CEO via satellite feed during allocated time frames of one to five minutes. This way, journalists throughout the country could personally interview a CEO in New York even if they were based in San Francisco. For busy CEOs, the satellite was a time-efficient way to give interviews.

Today, the SMT is a staple of the public relations and television industry. In fact, a survey by WestGlen Communications found that nearly 85 percent of the nation's television stations participate in satellite tours.

The easiest way to do an SMT is to simply make the organization's spokesperson available for an interview at a designated time. Celebrities are always popular, but an organization also can use articulate experts. In general, the spokesperson sits in a chair or at a desk in front of a television camera. Viewers usually see the local news anchor asking questions and the spokesperson on a large screen, via satellite, answering them in much the same way that anchors talk to reporters at the scene of an event.

Another popular approach to SMTs is to get out of the television studio and do the interviews on location. When the National Pork Producers Council wanted to promote outdoor winter grilling, its public relations staff hired a team from News Broadcast Network to fire up an outdoor grill in Aspen, Colorado, and have a celebrity chef in a parka give interviews, via satellite, while he cooked several pork recipes.

Personal Appearances

Radio and television stations increasingly operate on round-the-clock schedules. They require vast amounts of programming to fill the time available.

Thus far, this chapter has concentrated on how to prepare and generate timely material for newscasts. This section focuses on how to get spokespersons on talk and magazine shows. In these cases, your contact is no longer the news department, but the directors and producers of such programs. The most valuable communication tools in reaching these people are the telephone and the persuasive pitch litter, as discussed earlier in this chapter.

Before contacting directors and producers, however, it is necessary for the public relations staff to do their homework. They must be totally familiar with a show's format and content, as well as the type of audience that it reaches. Media directories are available, such as Bacon's, that give key information about specific programs, such as the names and addresses of producers, the program format, audience demographics, and the purpose of the show.

A second approach, and one that is highly recommended, is to actually watch the program and study the format. In the case of a talk or interview show, what is the style of the moderator or host? What kinds of topics are discussed? How important is the personality or prominence of the guest? How long is the show or a segment? Does the show lend itself to product demonstrations or other visual aids? The answers to such questions will help determine whether a particular show is appropriate for your spokesperson and how to tailor a pitch letter to achieve maximum results.

Talk Shows

Radio and television talk shows have been a broadcast staple for many years. KABC in Los Angeles started the trend in 1960, when it became the first radio station in the country to convert to an all-news-and-talk format. Today, more than 1,110 radio stations have adopted the format. Stations that play music also may include talk shows as part of their programming. In fact, it is estimated that there are now more than 4,000 radio talk shows in the United States.

The same growth applies to television. Phil Donahue began his show in 1967. Today, there are more than 20 nationally syndicated talk shows and a number of locally produced talk shows. For the past decade, the number one syndicated daytime talk show has been the *Oprah Winfrey Show*, attracting about 8 million viewers on a daily basis. On the network level, three shows are the Holy Grail for publicists: NBC's *Today*, ABC's *Good Morning America*, and CBS's *Early Show*. Collectively, these three shows draw about 14 million viewers between 7 and 9 A.M. every weekday.

The advantage of talk shows is the opportunity to have viewers see and hear the organization's spokesperson without the filter of journalists and editors interpreting and deciding what is newsworthy. Another advantage is the opportunity to be on air longer than the traditional 30-second soundbite in a news program.

When thinking about booking a spokesperson on a local or syndicated talk show, there's a checklist of questions to consider:

> Is the topic newsworthy? Is there a new angle on something already in the news?

> Is the topic timely? Is it tied to some lifestyle or cultural trend?

> Is the information useful to viewers? How-to and consumer tips are popular.

> Does the spokesperson have viewer appeal? A celebrity may be acceptable, but there must be a natural tie-in with the organization and the topic to be discussed.

Jay Leno's *Tonight Show* is a highly desirable venue for politicians like House Speaker Nancy Pelosi (D-California) on which to get their positions heard.

The Ideal Talk
Show Guest

Insights

What constitutes a killer TV guest? Senior producer for *Your World with Cavuto,* Gresham Strigel, shared his thoughts with *Bulldog Reporter,* a media placement newsletter:

> Guests should be personable and approachable when producers conduct preinterviews on the phone. They are forthright but not aggressive. "If you're wishy-washy, non-committed, or stilted, you're not going much further."

> Guests should have strong opinions. "We don't call certain people back because they have been trained not to say anything. The stronger your position is, and the higher up it is, the more media attention you're going to get. Nobody likes guests who play it safe."

> Guests should be passionate about the subject. "We don't want people who are robotic—who just spit out facts. If you convey passion about what you're talking about, you jump off the screen."

> Guests should be able to debate without getting personal or mean-spirited. "Smile. . . . Audiences like to see someone who is comfortable on-screen—someone who is happy to be there."

> Guests should have engaging, outgoing personalities. "Talking heads and ivory-tower types don't do well on television. They're better suited for print, where their personality—or lack of it—can't turn audiences off."

> Can the spokesperson stay on track and give succinct, concise statements. The spokesperson must stay focused and make sure that the key messages are mentioned.

> Can the spokesperson refrain from getting too commercial? Talk show hosts don't want guests who sound like advertisements.

See the Insights box on this page for more information on what makes an ideal talk show guest.

Magazine Shows

The term *magazine* refers to a television program format that is based on a variety of video segments in much the same way that print magazines have a variety of articles. These shows may have a guest related to the feature that's being shown, but the main focus is on a video story that may run from 3 to 10 minutes. At the network level, CBS's *60 Minutes* and NBC's *Dateline* are examples of a magazine program.

Many human-interest magazine shows are produced at the local level. A sampling of magazine shows in one large city featured such subjects as a one-pound baby who survived, a treatment for anorexia nervosa, a couple who started a successful cookie company, remedies for back pain, tips on dog training, a black-belt karate expert, blue-collar job stress, and the work habits of a successful author. Most, if not all, of these features came about as the result of someone making a pitch to the show's producers. The objective of the segments, at least from the perspective of the people featured, is exposure and the generation of new business. The tips on dog training, for example, featured a local breeder who also operated a dog obedience school. The karate expert ran a martial arts academy, and even the story of the one-pound baby was placed by a local hospital touting its infant care unit.

Booking a Guest

The contact for a talk show may be the executive producer or assistant producer of the show. If it is a network or nationally syndicated show, the contact person may have the title of talent coordinator or talent executive. Whatever the title, these people are known in the broadcasting industry as *bookers* because they are responsible for booking a constant supply of timely guests for the show.

ON THE JOB >>

How to Place a Client on a TV Talk Show

Insights

Television stations are looking for interesting, articulate guests for their talk shows. The larger the station, the more stringent are its requirements for accepting a guest. This summary of needs and procedures for *AM/San Francisco*, the morning show on KGO-TV, the ABC network outlet in San Francisco, is typical of those for metropolitan stations. The information is from an article published in *Bulldog Reporter*, a West Coast public relations newsletter.

The station wants guests "who will provide information that will help our viewers to save money and save time, helpful hints around the house, consumer-type things." The station also uses guests from the business community who can comment on money, taxes, the stock market, and similar topics.

KGO-TV defines the audience for this show as primarily nonworking women, 18 to 49, married, with at least one child. The show also attracts working viewers before they leave for their jobs.

Segments on the one-hour show run from 6 to 10 minutes. The usual pattern is to open with a celebrity–entertainer, then offer two segments on consumer topics. Segments 4, 5, and 6 cover "more serious subjects."

The production staff will normally consider for appearance only those who have appeared on television previously. Usually it asks to see a video clip of a prior TV appearance; an effective clip is an important way to gain acceptance.

"TV is a visual medium and a lot of our audience isn't just sitting there watching. They're folding clothes or ironing, so we need a voice that will grab their attention."

The public relations practitioner should submit a brief written query to the show's producer—"a one-page letter getting straight to the basics: whom you're offering, what their experience is, exactly what their topic would be, what shows they've been on previously, a bio (biographical statement) and all other information available on the person, as well as clippings, copies of articles on the person or topic."

Staff members try to answer queries in about a week, perhaps sooner. The show is booked at least a week in advance but sometimes has last-minute openings.

One common approach in placing a guest is to phone the booker to briefly outline the qualifications of the proposed speaker and why this person would be a timely guest. Publicists also can write a brief one-page letter or send an e-mail telling the booker the story angle, why it's relevant to the show's audience, and why the proposed speaker is qualified to talk on the subject. In many cases, the booker will ask for video clips of the spokesperson's appearances on previous TV shows or newspaper clips of press interviews. It's important to be honest about the experience and personality of the spokesperson, so the booker isn't disappointed and your credibility is intact. See the Insights box on this page for further discussion about booking tactics.

In recent years, there has been some controversy over guests who are invited because they are celebrities and have large audience appeal. However, once they get on the show, it turns out that they are endorsers of various products. (See the Ethics box on page 322.)

In general, talk shows book guests three to four weeks in advance. Unless a topic or a person is extremely timely or controversial, it is rare for a person to be booked on one or two day's notice. Public relations strategists must keep this in mind as part of overall campaign planning.

— ON THE JOB >> —

Should Guests on TV Talk Shows Reveal Their Sponsors?

Ethics

Actress Lauren Bacall, appearing on NBC's *Today* show, talked about a dear friend who had gone blind from an eye disease and urged the audience to see their doctors to be tested for it. She also mentioned a drug, Visudyne, that was a new treatment for the disease.

Meanwhile, over at ABC's *Good Morning America* show, actress Kathleen Turner was telling Diane Sawyer about her battle with rheumatoid arthritis and mentioned that a drug, Enbrel, helped ease the pain. A month later, Olympic gold medal skater Peggy Fleming appeared on the show to talk about cholesterol and heart disease. Near the beginning of the interview, Fleming said, "My doctor has put me on Lipitor and my cholesterol has dropped considerably."

What the viewing audience didn't know was that each of these celebrities was being paid a hefty fee by a drug company to mention its product in prime time. Indeed, even the talk show hosts apparently didn't know until the *New York Times* wrote an investigative piece on drug companies using "stealth marketing" tactics to get product mentions on regular news and talk shows.

This raises a dilemma for public relations personnel who often book guests on various radio and television talk shows. Should you tell the show's producer up-front that a celebrity is under contract as an endorser of a particular product? If you do, it may mean that your spokesperson won't be booked, because programs such as NBC's *Today* show tend to shy away from "stealth marketing."

What are your responsibilities? What is the responsibility of the talk show hosts? Should the public know that Peggy Fleming is appearing as an endorser of a product?

Product Placements

Television's drama and comedy shows, as well as the film industry, are good vehicles for promoting a company's products and services. It is not a coincidence that the hero of a detective series drives a Dodge Viper or that the heroine is seen boarding a United Airlines flight.

Such product placements, sometimes called *plugs*, are often negotiated by product publicists and talent agencies. This is really nothing new. *IPRA Frontline* reports, "In the early 1900s, Henry Ford had an affinity for Hollywood and perhaps it is no coincidence that his Model T's were the predominant vehicle appearing in the first motion pictures of the era."

Product placements, however, came of age with the movie *ET* in the early 1980s. The story goes that M&M's Candies made a classic marketing mistake by not allowing the film to use M&M's as the prominently displayed trail of candy that the young hero used to lure his big-eyed friend home. Instead, Hershey's Reese's Pieces jumped at the chance, and the rest is history. Sales of Reese's Pieces skyrocketed, and even today, more than 20 years after the film's debut, the candy and the character of ET remain forever linked in popular culture and the minds of a whole generation of *ET* fans.

The use of Reese's Pieces in *ET*, according to marketing experts, was one of the most famous product placements of all time. And it spawned a whole new industry of product placements in television shows and movies. Clothing manufacturers and retailers are particularly active in product placements because studies show that today's youth gets most of their fashion ideas from watching television shows. This is why Simon, Paula, and Randy have Coca-Cola glasses sitting in front of them on *American Idol*, and Buffy the Vampire Slayer wore jeans from the Gap. It also explains why Tom Cruise wore Ray-Bans in *Risky Business* and used an Apple computer in *Mission Impossible*, James Bond drives a BMW, the characters in *Swordfish* drank Heineken beer, and *Alias*'s Agent Bristow used a Nokia phone.

The *Wall Street Journal* explained how America's number one show, *American Idol*, engages in product placement:

"The series launched in summer 2002 with a few sponsors, namely Coca-Cola Co., which paid to have a big Coke cup sitting in front of the three judges in every episode. . . . In the current season, Fox abandoned any pretense at subtlety. The Coke cups are still there. . . , but now Coca-Cola's famous logo appears prominently onscreen for part of each show; fizzy bubbles fill a screen behind contestants as they describe what song they will sing each week. The contestants film a new commercial for Ford each week. And each episode is loaded with other hard sells for a truckload of other merchandise, ranging from Cingular phones and text-messaging services to Kenny Rogers' new CD."

Another opportunity for product exposure on television is on game shows. *The Price Is Right*, for example, uses a variety of products as prizes for contestants. In one episode, for example, the prize was a tent, a camp table and chairs, and lanterns. It was a great, low-cost product placement for Coleman for less than $200.

Public relations specialists should always be on the alert to opportunities for publicity on television programs and upcoming movies. If the company's service or product lends itself to a particular program, the normal procedure is to contact the show's producers directly or through an agent who specializes in matching company products with the show's needs.

Issues Placement

A logical extension of product placements is convincing popular television programs to write an issue or cause into their plotlines. Writers for issue-oriented shows such as *ER* and *Law & Order* are constantly bombarded with requests from a variety of nonprofit and special-interest groups. The most visible issues may be health related. For example, Fox's medical drama *House* even has a location on its Web site (http://www.fox.com/house/features/research/) that allows research into medical topics featured by episode.

The National Campaign to Prevent Teen Pregnancy, for example, works very hard to get the issue of teen pregnancy placed into television programming. The WB's *Seventh Heaven* included an episode in which the Camden family supported Sandy as she went into labor. *The George Lopez Show* on ABC discussed teen pregnancy when George and Angie's teenage daughter Carmen planned to get pregnant to keep her boyfriend. Many social and health organizations also lobby the producers of daytime soap operas to write scripts in which the major characters deal with cancer, diabetes, drug abuse, alcoholism, and an assortment of other problems.

The idea is to educate the public about a social issue or a health problem in an entertaining way. Someone once said, "It's like hiding the aspirin in the ice cream." Even the federal government works with popular television programs to write scripts that deal with the dangers and prevention of drug abuse. All of this has not escaped the notice of the drug companies; they are now exploring the opportunities for getting their products mentioned in plotlines, too. The Insights box on page 324 demonstrates how activist groups have begun to use films in their attempts to put issues on the national agenda.

— ON THE JOB >> —

Activists Use Films to Get Their Points Across

Insights

Some nontraditional public relations tactics have almost become mainstream. It's nothing new to support public relations campaigns with media relations, but even more subtle tactics are taking root—the documentary as public relations tactics is becoming almost commonplace.

Films have been most often used by activists or corporate critics to gain grassroots support for their campaigns. The documentary as a means of supporting a larger activist public relations campaign may have gotten its first broad notice when Michael Moore released the film *Fahrenheit 9/11* as a means of raising public awareness regarding what Moore argued were the misdeeds of the Bush administration. The politically partisan film was part of a larger campaign to reach like-minded voters prior to the 2004 presidential election. Like Moore, filmmaker Robert Greenwald has made a recent career of using film to critique business and political entities. His anti-Wal-Mart film, *Wal-Mart: The High Cost of Low Price,* was supported by a Web site (www.walmartmovie.com) that invited visitors to host a movie screening party. Community activist groups and church groups alike were listed as hosting screening parties. Likewise, Morgan Spurlock received attention and built anti-fast food fervor with his award-winning documentary *Super Size Me.*

Former Vice President and presidential candidate Al Gore made a splash in 2006 with a documentary about global warming titled, *An*

Al Gore brought attention to the environmental issue of global warming through a variety of public relations tactics including the film *An Inconvenient Truth,* a Web site, and talk show appearances.

Inconvenient Truth. The documentary was part of a larger public relations campaign that included personal appearances. In fact, the film and Gore's book of the same title are based on lectures he was giving to environmental activist groups. The film provided Gore and his environmental cause with a larger platform, including interviews on *The Daily Show with Jon Stewart,* reviews in the *New York Times* and the *Washington Post,* an issue of *Wired* magazine dedicated to the film and subject of global warming, and buzz at the Sundance Film Festival. To support the public relations campaign, a Web site (www.climatecrisis.net) invited site visitors to pledge to see the film; it provided information about the film and book, scientific facts related to global warming, news coverage of the issue, a

blog devoted to the subject, and tips on how individuals can limit their contribution to global warming. The public relations campaign surrounding the film was, of course, two-sided—raise awareness of the subject and sell tickets to the film.

The line between whether the public relations campaigns surrounding such films are aimed more at raising awareness for the cause or the film is pretty thin. But, without doubt, the public relations campaigns surrounding the films do raise awareness in support of a cause larger than simply seeing the film. Whereas films have always been used as means for promoting products through product placement, cause-related documentaries seem to be enjoying an upsurge as a grassroots public relations tactic.

The flip side of asking scriptwriters to include material is asking them to give a more balanced portrayal of an issue. The health care industry, for example, is concerned about balance in such programs as *ER*. The popular program deals with a variety of health issues and, in many cases, health maintenance organizations (HMOs) are portrayed in an unfavorable light. Even the American Bar Association gets upset about the portrayal of lawyers in some series. Consequently, these organizations often meet with writers to educate them about the facts so their programs are more balanced.

Ultimately, however, the programs are designed as entertainment. Scriptwriters, like newspaper editors, make their own evaluations and judgments.

Other Forms of Placement

Another form of product placement is agreements with radio stations to promote a product or event as part of their programming. The most common example is a concert promoter giving DJs 10 tickets to a "hot" concert that are then awarded as prizes to listeners who answer a question or call within 30 seconds.

A nonprofit group sponsoring a fund-raising festival also may make arrangements for a radio station (or television station) to cosponsor an event as part of the station's own promotional activities. This means that the station will actively promote the festival on the air through PSAs and DJ chatter between songs. The arrangement also may call for a popular DJ to broadcast live from the festival and give away T-shirts with the station's logo on them. This, too, is good promotion for both the festival and the radio station, because it attracts people to the event.

A station's director of promotions or marketing often is in charge of deciding what civic events to sponsor with other groups. Stations will usually agree to a certain number of promotional spots in exchange for being listed in an organization's news releases, programs, print advertising, and event banners as a sponsor of the event. Such terms are spelled out in a standard contract, which is often supplied by the radio or television stations.

Stations will not necessarily promote or cosponsor every event. They must be convinced that their involvement will benefit the station in terms of greater public exposure, increased audience, and improved market position.

The Internet

This section has emphasized radio and television, but it would be incomplete if the Internet was not mentioned as a major vehicle for distributing information and also reaching millions of people. See the Insights box on pages 326 and 327 for some illustrations of how public relations is adding online tools to its tactics.

One important development has been the advent of Web-based news sites. There are more than 6,000 news sites, and the number grows each day. In addition, according to WestGlen Communications, "more than 50 percent of the 110 million users of the Internet in the United States use this medium as a source of news and information."

MSNBC.com, for example, reaches 4 million viewers a day, which no daily newspaper in the United States can match. Dean Wright, editor-in-chief of MSNBC.com told *Jack O'Dwyer's Newsletter*, "No one would seriously suggest that the daily newspaper is irrelevant. But the Web is something that can't be ignored. The message I have for PR pros is, if you want to reach out to a highly desirable demographic—people at work—then you must include the Web in your plans."

— ON THE JOB >> —

Blogs, Pods, and Wikis Enter the PR Vernacular

Insights

Communication and research technologies are changing almost daily and certainly dramatically. Because communication and research are at the center of effective public relations practice, public relations pros must remain vigilant to these changes and embrace or eschew the technologies as appropriate to their organizations or clients.

E-mail is nothing new, but the volume of it continues to increase. Effective public relations practitioners need to manage the use and flow of e-mail. To effectively manage e-mail, PR pros might set aside time on a daily basis to read and reply to e-mail. You should also judiciously decide when e-mail is an adequate means of communication. E-mail should not replace face-to-face or voice-to-voice communication. Especially when building a relationship, electronic communication cannot replace interpersonal communication.

Blogs are an exploding phenomenon. The blog-tracking Web site Technorati.com was tracking 50 million blogs in mid-2006. In addition, Technorati data indicated 75,000 new blogs were created each day, with 50,000 blog updates each hour. Certainly, blogs are a communication form that public relations pros must understand. According to Technorati:

> The power of weblogs is that they allow millions of people to easily publish their ideas, and millions more to comment on them. Blogs are a fluid, dynamic medium, more akin to a "conversation" than to a

library—which is how the Web has often been described in the past. With an increasing number of people reading, writing, and commenting on blogs, the way we use the Web is shifting in a fundamental way. Instead of being passive consumers of information, more and more Internet users are becoming active participants. ("About Us" at www.technorati.com)

Blogs are increasingly used as sources of information for news, consumer goods, entertainment, and hobbies. Public relations practitioners view blogs as both a blessing and a curse. They are a blessing because they allow PR pros to post their own point of view unfettered by the editing process of the traditional mass media. They are a curse because their instant nature (remember the 50,000 hourly updates) means that an unanswered rumor about an organization can grow rapidly into a crisis. Jim Nall, chief strategy and marketing officer for Cymfony, wrote in *Public Relations Tactics* that digital camera shoppers posted warnings about dissatisfaction with a particular camera brand and model, automobile owners complained about the factory-installed tires on a new car, and homemakers suggested an alternative product to remove stains from clothes on the competition's blog.

Experts suggest that when PR practitioners use blogs to support their clients or organizations, they must listen to concerns, be honest and not phony, understand that in the

Purina is one company that provides a variety of podcasts for its customers—pet owners.

"blogosphere" everything's on the record, and make the message conversational and informal rather than a hard sales pitch.

Podcasting has become mainstream. It was initially an activity primarily aimed at distributing "radio" programs via the Internet to iPods for the consumers' convenience. Podcasts are now both audio and video and are commonly used to reach customers and prospective customers. Tom Biro, director of new media strategies at the MWW Group, wrote in *Public Relations Tactics*, "It's not about putting a 15- or 30-minute commercial on someone's iPod, though—it's about service marketing." He cited an example of the pet food maker Purina and that company's weekly podcast "where animal experts discuss anything from pet insurance to training."

Really simple syndication (RSS) is a means for public relations practitioners to do research by "subscribing" to multiple Web sources. The RSS file format allows practitioners to view content they preselect from a variety of sources. RSS essentially mines and delivers information to people who have indicated they are interested in the content. Public relations can use RSS in at least two ways: to monitor blogs and other Web sources for information about their company or client, and to provide a means of delivery of information to journalists, consumers, investors, employees or other interested publics.

Wikipedia (www.wikipedia.org) has become a favorite online information source. One of the authors overheard one student say to another, "I *love* Wikipedia." Wikipedia is an online encyclopedia of sorts. It contains about 1.3 million articles in its English language version. Wikipedia articles are available in 229 languages—from English to Kanuri. What makes Wikipedia especially important to public relations practitioners is that entries can be made by anyone and anyone can alter or correct an entry. Like many Web-based media, Wikipedia's rules are developed and enforced by the "Wikipedia community" or those registered users who contribute to and monitor Wikipedia content. The problem with this self-policing mechanism is that inaccuracies can be introduced to content. Brian Wasson, a communications professional writing in *Public Relations Tactics*, observed,

Unlike traditional encyclopedias, there is no formal editing process to assure that content in an article is accurate. An article can change in a second, and once-correct information can be replaced with fallacies. The site acknowledges this limitation, but maintains that, over time, Wikipedia will mature into a comprehensive, well-vetted informational resource.

The temptation for PR pros is to post promotional information about their companies, clients, products, or causes on Wikipedia. This sort of self-promotion is frowned on by the Wikipedia community, according to Wasson. While posting information about your organization or client is appropriate, it should stick to facts and refrain from puffery. It should also be identified as being written by a representative of your organization. The other important consideration for public relations practitioners and Wikipedia is to monitor information about your client or company and correct it, identifying yourself as a representative of the organization, when inaccurate information is posted.

From blogs to Wikipedia, the media landscape is being revolutionized and as communication professionals, public relations practitioners must work to make appropriate use of these media.

Elizabeth Shepard, editor-in-chief of Epicurious.com and Concierge.com, agrees. She says Epicurious.com, the longest-running and largest food site on the Internet, gets 20 million page views per month. She told *Jack O'Dwyer's Newsletter,* "People contact me about new restaurant openings or special tasting menus, new wines that are launching in the U.S., or special distribution of wines in certain areas." Needless to say, such a Web site is an excellent publicity opportunity for restaurants and wineries.

Of course, many Web sites are extensions of a particular newspaper, magazine, radio or television station, or even television network. That means that the materials used by these traditional media may also wind up on their Web sites. Articles from *Gourmet*, *Bon Appetit*, and *Parade*, for example, can be found on Epicurious.com, but most of these sites also have editors who are looking for original material. Public relations practitioners should not neglect such sites in today's world.

Podcasts

The editors of the *New Oxford American Dictionary* affirmed what many public relations practitioners already knew—podcasting is a hot and rapidly growing communication trend. That's why the dictionary's editors chose *podcasting* as their 2005 Word of the Year. The definition of podcasting, "a digital recording of a radio broadcast or similar program, made available on the Internet for downloading to a personal audio player," was included in the *New Oxford American Dictionary* beginning in its 2006 edition.

Podcasting had been the domain of techies and early adopters, but it got a boost into the mainstream in June 2005 when Apple added a podcast directory to its iTunes Web site. Podcasts are now listed in several online directories such as podcast.net, podcastdirectory.com, ipodder.org, and podcastingnews.com. They are also available at the Web sites of specific organizations. Podcasts are a valuable public relations tool because they allow organizations to link active and interested members of their publics to deliver an entertaining, unedited, and often long-format messages.

Podcasts are used by a variety of organizations to reach diverse audiences with highly targeted messages. For example, in May 2005, Disneyland Resort incorporated podcasts into its corporate communications plan, according to *PRWeek*. In five months, there were 64,000 downloads of its podcasts. *PRWeek* noted some advantages of podcasts include allowing listeners to download and listen at their convenience, reaching a highly targeted and involved audience, and providing a means of instant feedback from the audience.

The Propane Education & Research Council (PERC) also used podcasts for public education in its "Propane Days" event. In May 2006, following the devastation of Hurricane Katrina in 2005 and preceding the 2006 hurricane season, PERC decided to educate its audience on the role propane can play in the aftermath of a disaster. PERC made podcasts available at PropaneCast.com and featured stories such as homeowners who used propane generators to power their homes after Hurricane Katrina.

Another podcast phenomenon has been dubbed "momcasts," but the podcasts are really family-focused. Two mothers host an Internet show that is podcast on MommyCast.com. This podcast provides a forum for sponsorship by organizations that are targeting busy parents. Georgia-Pacific, for example, sponsored the podcast on behalf of its Dixie brand of paper goods. Uncle Ben's brand promoted the health benefits of whole grains on MommyCast.com. In a similar vein, Whirlpool brands sponsored a weekly American Family podcast that promised "The discussion-based podcast will address matters that impact families with diverse backgrounds and experiences. The podcast will feature real, everyday people and/or subject-matter experts." Audrey Reed-Granger, Whirlpool Brand's director of public relations, told *PRWeek*, "We're in touch with our consumers; we know what they need and want. For busy moms, there's more to life than appliances. Sometimes, women and families just want to commiserate. Sometimes, just laugh." Podcasts allow public relations pros to easily reach these niche targets.

Weblogs

Weblogs, or blogs, have become an integral part of the Internet. Essentially, blogs are regularly updated online personal journals with links to items of interest on the Web. In 2005, the Pew Internet and American Life Project found that more than 8 million Americans have created blogs. The number of blogs and bloggers has exploded in recent years.

Technorati, a blog tracking organization, estimated in 2006 that there were about 75,000 new blogs a day, about 1.2 million posts each day, and about 50,000 blog updates each hour. The blogosphere is changing so rapidly that it is hard for a textbook treatment to remain current. Between March 2003 and July 2005, according to Technorati, the number of blogs doubled every five and a half months.

Most bloggers are amateurs, but many are professional communicators who like to express their opinions, observations, and criticisms about almost everything. And, although the mass majority of bloggers are obscure, others have risen in prominence and have a large following. Democrats and the Republicans even issue press credentials to some of these bloggers to cover their conventions.

Increasingly, a number of public relations practitioners are becoming bloggers on behalf of their employers and clients because, as one professional says, "They [blogs] let businesses take their message right to the public without the TV network news or the local newspaper having to act as a mouthpiece." Jason Kottke, a San Francisco Web designer and blogger, told *PRWeek*:

> A clever Weblog can combine the information dissemination of a traditional Web site with the communication you get with direct mail, e-mail, or an e-mail newsletter. The frequent updates, along with looser writing style adopted by many Webloggers gives your customers the impression that you're having a conversation with them instead of just shoving information at them in a press release form.

Public relations personnel also are starting to pitch Weblogs. One public relations firm didn't think a client's minor software upgrade was worth a news release, but staff did send an e-mail to some bloggers covering the industry and got a favorable response. The Heritage Foundation, a conservative think tank, also took the time to e-mail 175 political bloggers and found that most of them would be interested in receiving information from the organization. According to Lloyd Trufelman and Laura Goldberg of Trylon Communications, who wrote in *Public Relations Tactics*:

> The most important thing a publicist can do before pitching a blogger is to carefully read his or her blog. Unlike beat reporters at typical news outlets, bloggers are extremely idiosyncratic in choice of subject matter and slant. In order to begin a conversation with one—and it should be viewed as a conversation, rather than a pitch—it is vital that you are well-acquainted with the interests of the blogger. Many of them still consider their sites to be personal forums for their views and perspectives, and are wary of corporate or PR interference.

Trufelman and Goldberg offer these tips for pitching to bloggers:

> - Do not spam bloggers
> - Be aware of their likes and dislikes before contacting them
> - Conventional pitch letters may be offensive
> - E-mail is the preferred means of contact
> - Be completely open and honest about why you are contacting bloggers
> - Disclose your affiliation
> - Keep pitches short and link any published story or item you might want the blogger to consider
> - Do not ask bloggers to link to your client's site or the latest press release

Another aspect of blogs, which causes headaches for public relations staffs, is what the writers may say about a company or its products. As *Ragan's Media Relations Report* says, "A prominent blogger who trashes a product, service, or company can do serious damage to sales or public image. Bloggers also frequently post links to mainstream or other news articles—making the reach of offending news coverage that much greater."

Consequently, it is recommended that public relations personnel monitor Weblogs that reach large numbers of consumers or that cover a particular industry. Oftentimes, the information being disseminated is untrue or distorted, and it's necessary for organizations to set the record straight. At other times, a blog site may be an excellent opportunity to place positive information about an organization.

Many organizations are setting up their own blogs as a means of answering critics or getting information out quickly. David Krejci, vice president of Web relations for Weber Shandwick, wrote in *Public Relations Tactics* that he recommends that his client inject their voice into the blog conversation by writing their own blogs. He poses the question, What if an explosion happens at your company's factory? "Any employee with a camera can shoot images of the occurrence anad have it online in minutes. How well and how quickly would your client respond? A company with a blog: minutes." He suggests letting your client or CEO know that "blogs represent a compelling alternative to mainstream media for some audiences, that media consumption is increasingly fragmented, that mainstream media often look to blogs for information."

Media Interviews

Another widely used method of publicizing an individual or a cause is the interview, which may appear in print form in newspapers and magazines or on television and radio. Satellite media tours (SMTs) are a popular method, which was discussed earlier in the chapter. The ability of the person being interviewed to communicate easily is essential to success. Although required to stay in the background, with fingers crossed that all goes well, a public relations specialist can do much to prepare the interviewee.

Andrew D. Gilman, president of CommCore Consulting Group in New York City, emphasizes the need for preparation. He says, "I would no more think of putting a client on a witness stand or through a deposition without thorough and adequate preparation than I would ask a client to be interviewed by a skillful and well-prepared journalist without a similar thorough and adequate preparation."

Purpose and Objective

In all interviews, the person being questioned should say something that will inform or entertain the audience. The practitioner should prepare the interviewee to meet this need. An adroit interviewer attempts to develop a theme in the conversation—to draw out comments that make a discernible point or illuminate the character of the person being interviewed. The latter can help the interviewer—and his or her own cause as well—by being ready to volunteer specific information, personal data, or opinions about the cause under discussion as soon as the conversational opportunity arises.

In setting up an interview, the public relations person should obtain from the interviewer an understanding as to its purpose. Armed with this information, the practitioner can assemble facts and data for the client to use in the discussion. The practitioner also can aid the client by providing tips about the interviewer's style.

Some interviewers on the radio talk shows that have proliferated in recent years ask "cream puff" questions, while others bore in, trying to goad the guest into unplanned admissions or embarrassment. Thus, it is especially important to be well acquainted with the interviewer's style, whether it be Larry King before a national audience of millions or a local broadcaster. Short, direct answers delivered without hesitation help a guest project an image of strength and credibility.

Print Differs from Broadcast

A significant difference exists between interviews in print and those on radio and television. In a print interview, the information and character impressions the public receives about the interviewee have been filtered through the mind of the writer. The person interviewed is interpreted by the reporter, not projected directly to the audience. On radio and television, however, listeners hear the interviewee's voice without intervention by a third party. During a television interview, in which personality has the strongest impact of all, the speaker is both seen and heard. Because of the intimacy of television, a person with a weak message who projects charm or authority may influence an audience more than one with a strong message who does not project well. A charismatic speaker with a strong message can have enormous impact.

Know When to Say No

When an organization or individual is advocating a particular cause or policy, opportunities to give newspaper interviews are welcomed, indeed sought after. Situations arise, however, when the better part of public relations wisdom is to reject a request for an interview, either print or electronic. Such rejection need not imply that an organization has a sinister secret or fails to understand the need for public contact.

For example, a corporation may be planning production changes that likely will have plants closing. Details are incomplete, and company employees have not been told. A reporter, suspecting something, requests an interview with the company's chief executive officer. Normally, the interview request would be welcomed, to give the executive public exposure and an opportunity to enunciate company philosophy. At this moment, however, public relations advisers fear that the reporter's questions might uncover premature information, or at least force the executive into damaging evasive answers. So the interview request is politely declined or delayed. The next week, when all is in place, the chief executive announces the changes at a news conference. Avoiding trouble is a hidden but vital part of a public relations adviser's role.

An alternative approach would be for the chief executive officer to grant the interview, with the understanding that only topics specified in advance would be discussed. Usually such an approach is unacceptable, however, because most reporters resent restrictions and want to uncover the reasons for them.

The Print Interview

An interview with a newspaper reporter may last about an hour, perhaps at lunch or over coffee in an informal setting. The result of this person-to-person talk may be a published story of perhaps 400 to 600 words. The interviewer weaves bits from the conversation together in direct and indirect quotation form, works in background material, and perhaps injects personal observations about the interviewee. The latter has no control over what is published, beyond the self-control he or she exercises in answering the questions. Neither the person being interviewed nor a public relations representative should ask to approve an interview story before it is published. Such requests are rebuffed automatically as a form of censorship.

Magazine interviews usually explore a subject in greater depth than those in newspapers, because the writer may have more space available. Most magazine interviews have the same format as those in newspapers. Others appear in question-and-answer form. These require prolonged taped questioning of the interviewee by one or more writers and editors. During in-depth interviews, the person interviewed must guard against saying something that can be taken out of context.

Radio and Television Interviews

The opportunities for public relations people to have their clients interviewed on the air are plentiful. The current popularity of talk shows, both on local stations and syndicated satellite networks, provides many opportunities for on-air appearances in which the guest expresses opinions and answers call-in questions. A successful radio or television broadcast interview appearance has three principal requirements:

1. *Preparation.* Guests should know what they want to say.
2. *Concise speech.* Guests should answer questions and make statements precisely and briefly without excessive detail or extraneous material. Responses should be kept to 30 seconds or less, because the interviewer must conduct the program under strict time restrictions.
3. *Relaxation.* "Mic fright" is a common ailment for which no automatic cure exists. It will diminish, if the guest concentrates on talking to the interviewer in a casual person-to-person manner. Guests should speak up firmly; the control room can reduce volume, if necessary.

A public relations adviser can help an interview guest on these points. Answers to anticipated questions may be worked out and polished during a mock interview in which the practitioner plays the role of broadcaster. A tape recording or videotape of a practice session will help the prospective guest to correct weaknesses.

All too often, talk show hosts know little about their guests for the day's broadcast. The public relations adviser can overcome this difficulty by sending the host in advance a fact sheet summarizing the important information and listing questions the broadcaster might wish to ask. On network shows such as David Letterman's, nationally syndicated talk shows such as Oprah Winfrey's, and local programs on metropolitan stations, support staffs do the preliminary work with guests. Interviewers on hundreds of smaller local television and radio stations, however, lack such staff resources. Hosts at these stations may go on the air almost "cold" unless provided with volunteered information.

News Conferences

At a news conference, communication is two-way. The person speaking for a company or a cause submits to questioning by reporters, usually after a brief opening statement. A news conference makes possible quick, widespread dissemination of the sponsor's information and opinions through the news media. It avoids the time-consuming task of presenting the information to the news outlets individually and ensures that the intensely competitive newspapers and electronic media hear the news simultaneously. From a public relations point of view, these are the principal advantages of the news conference. Against these important pluses must be weighed the fact that the person holding the conference is open to direct and potentially antagonistic questioning.

In public relations strategy, the news conference can be either an offensive or a defensive device, depending on the client's need. Most news conferences—or *press conferences*, as they frequently are called—are positive in intent; they are affirmative actions to project the host's plans or point of view. A corporation may hold a news conference to unveil a new product whose manufacture will create many new jobs, or a civic leader may do so to reveal the goals and plans for a countywide charity fund drive she or he will head. Such news conferences should be carefully planned and scheduled well in advance under the most favorable circumstances.

Public relations specialists also must deal frequently with unanticipated, controversial situations. If a business firm, an association, or a politician becomes embroiled in difficulty that is at best embarrassing, possibly incriminating, the press and public demand an explanation. A bare-bones printed statement is not enough to satisfy the clamor and may draw greater press scrutiny if the organization appears to be stonewalling. A well-prepared spokesperson may be able to achieve a measure of understanding and sympathy by issuing a carefully composed printed statement when the news conference opens.

No matter how trying the circumstances, the person holding the news conference should create an atmosphere of cooperation and project a sincere intent to be helpful. The worst thing he or she can do is to appear angry or resentful of the questioning. A good posture is to admit that a situation is bad and that the organization is doing everything in its power to correct it, the approach described by Professor Timothy Coombs at Eastern Illinois University as the "mortification" strategy. (Further discussion of crisis public relations appears in Chapter 2.)

Two more types of news conferences are held. One is spontaneous, arising out of a news event: the winner of a Nobel Prize meets the press to explain the award-winning work or a runner who has just set a world's record breathlessly describes his or her feelings. The other type is the regularly scheduled conference held by a public official at stated times, even when there is nothing special to announce. Usually this is called a *briefing*—the daily State Department briefing, for example.

Planning and Conducting a News Conference

First comes the question, "Should we hold a news conference?" Frequently, the answer should be no! Reporters and camera crews should not be summoned to a press conference to hear propaganda instead of news or information of minor interest to a limited group. When this happens, their valuable time has been wasted—and it is valuable. If the material involved fails to meet the criteria of significant news, a wise public relations representative will simply distribute it through a press release.

Every news outlet that might be interested in the material should be invited to a news conference. An ignored media outlet may become an enemy, like a person who isn't asked to a party. The invitation should describe the general nature of the material to be discussed so an editor will know what type of reporter to assign.

Timing of a press conference depends on the local media situation. If the city has only an afternoon newspaper, 9:30 or 10 A.M. is good, because this gives a reporter time to write a story before a midday deadline. If the city's newspaper publishes in the morning, 2 P.M. is a suitable hour.

Another prime goal of news conference sponsors is coverage on the early evening newscasts on local television stations, or even network TV newscasts if the information is important enough. A conference at 2 P.M. is about the latest that a television crew can cover and still get the material processed at a comfortable pace for inclusion in a dinner-hour show. This time period can be shortened a little in an emergency.

A warning: A public relations representative in a city with only an afternoon newspaper who schedules a news conference after that paper's deadline, yet in time for the news to appear on the early evening television newscasts, makes a grave blunder. Newspaper editors resent such favoritism to television and have long memories. Knowledge of, and sensitivity to, local news media deadlines are critical to public relations success.

Preparing the Location

At a news conference, public relations representatives resemble producers of a movie or television show. They are responsible for briefing the spokesperson, making arrangements, and ensuring that the conference runs smoothly. They stay in the background, however.

Bulldog Reporter, a West Coast public relations newsletter, suggests the following checklist for a practitioner asked to organize a news conference. The time factors given are normal for such events as new product introductions, but conferences concerning spot news developments for the daily press and electronic media often are called on notice of a few days or even a few hours.

> Select a convenient location, one that is fairly easy for news representatives to reach with minimal travel time.

> Set the date and time. Times between midmorning and midafternoon are good. Friday afternoons are deadly, as are days before holidays.

> When possible, issue an invitation to a news conference about six to eight weeks ahead of time, but one month is acceptable. The invitation should include the purpose of the conference, names of spokespersons, and why the event has significant news value. Of course, the date, time, and location must be provided.

> Distribute a media release about the upcoming news conference when appropriate. This depends on the importance of the event.

> Write a statement for the spokesperson to give at the conference and make sure that he or she understands and rehearses it. In addition, rehearse the entire conference.

> Try to anticipate questions so the spokesperson can readily answer difficult queries. Problem–solution rehearsals prepare the spokesperson.

> Prepare printed materials for distribution at the conference. These should include a brief fact sheet with names and titles of participants, a basic news release, and basic support materials. This is sometimes called a *media kit.*

> Prepare visual materials as necessary. These may include slides, transparencies, posters, or even a short videotape.

> Make advance arrangements for the room. Be sure that there are enough chairs and leave a center aisle for photographers. If a lectern is used, make certain that it is large enough to accommodate multiple microphones.

> Arrive 30 to 60 minutes early to double-check arrangements. Test the microphones, arrange name tags for invited guests, and distribute literature.

At some news conferences, still photographers are given two or three minutes to take their pictures before questioning begins. Some photographers complain that, thus restricted, they cannot obtain candid shots. If free shooting is permitted, as usually is the best practice, the physical arrangements should give the photographers operating space without allowing them to obstruct the view of reporters.

Practitioners should take particular care to arrange the room in such a way that the electronic equipment does not impede the print reporters. Some find it good policy for the speaker to remain after the news conference ends and make brief on-camera statements for individual TV stations, if their reporters request this attention. It is important that such statements do not go beyond anything the speaker has said to the entire body of reporters.

A final problem in managing a news conference is knowing when to end it. The public relations representative serving as backstage watchdog should avoid cutting off the questioning prematurely. To do so creates antagonism from the reporters. A moment comes when reporters run out of fresh questions. If the speaker does not recognize this, the practitioner may step forward and say something like, "I'm sorry, but I know some of you have deadlines to make. So we have time for just two more questions."

The Press Party and the Media Tour

In the typical news conference, the purpose is to transmit information and opinions from the organization to the news media in a businesslike, time-efficient manner. Often, however, a corporation, an association, or a political figure wishes to deliver a message or build rapport with the media on a more personal basis; then a social setting is desirable. Thus is born the press party or the press trip.

The Press Party

This gathering may be a luncheon, a dinner, or a reception. Whatever form the party takes, standard practice is for the host to rise at the end of the socializing period and make the "pitch." This may be a hard-news announcement, a brief policy statement followed by a question-and-answer period, or merely a soft-sell thank-you to the guests for coming and giving the host an opportunity to know them better. Guests usually are given press packets of information, either when they arrive or as they leave. Parties giving the press a preview of an art exhibit, a new headquarters building, and so forth are widely used. The press party is a softening-up process, and both sides know it.

The advantages of a press party to its host can be substantial under the proper circumstances. During chitchat over food or drink, officials of the host organization become acquainted with media people who write, edit, or broadcast material about them. Although the benefit from the host's point of view is difficult to measure immediately, the party opens the channels of communication.

Also, if the host has an important policy position to present, the assumption—not necessarily correct—is that editors and reporters will be more receptive after a social hour. The host who expects that food and drink will buy favorable press coverage may receive an unpleasant surprise. Conscientious reporters and editors will not be swayed by a free drink and a plate of prime rib followed by baked alaska. In their view, they have already given something to the host by setting aside a part of their day for the party. They accept invitations to press parties because they wish to develop potential news contacts within the host's organization and to learn more about its officials.

The Media Tour

There are three kinds of media tours. The most common is a trip, often disparagingly called a *junket*, during which editors and reporters are invited to inspect a company's

— ON THE JOB >> —

Special Events Generate "Buzz"

Insights

Special events are a common tactic for public relations practitioners and Hanes, the clothing company, held an unusual event to promote a new line of women's undergarments. In April 2006, Hanes and spokesperson Jennifer Love Hewitt hosted a "Panti-monium" launch party in Hollywood and declared 2006 the Year of Panti-monium to market a new line of underwear. The event was meant to help generate buzz about the new line. Invited guests included celebrities; consumer, entertainment, and lifestyle reporters; and producers, agents and other Hollywood types. Guests were treated to manicures, massages, and champagne as models exhibited Hanes intimate apparel.

Hanes mixed models, celebrities including the company's spokesperson Jennifer Love Hewitt, and the press at a launch party for a new product line.

Source: Michael Bush, "Hanes Goes Hollywood for Its 'Panti-monium' Launch Party," *PRWeek*, May 8, 2006, 3.

manufacturing facilities in several cities, ride an inaugural flight of a new air route, or watch previews of the television network programs for the fall season in Hollywood or New York. The host usually picks up the tab for transporting, feeding, and housing the reporters.

A variation of the media tour is the *familiarization trip*. "Fam trips," as they are called, are offered to travel writers and editors by the tourism industry (see Chapter 12). Convention and visitors bureaus, as well as major resorts, pay all expenses in the hope that the writers will report favorably on their experiences. Travel articles in magazines and newspapers usually result from a reporter's fam trip.

In the third kind of media tour, widely used in high-technology industries, the organization's executives travel to key cities to talk with selected editors; for example, top Apple executives toured the East Coast to talk with key magazine editors and demonstrate the capabilities of the new Apple iMac computer. Depending on editors' preferences, the executives may visit a publication and give a background briefing to key editors, or a hotel conference room may be set up so that the traveling executives can talk with editors from several publications at the same time.

The Ethics of Who Pays for What. In recent years, soul-searching by media members, as well as by professional public relations personnel who feel it is unethical to offer lavish travel and gifts, has led to increased self-regulation by both groups as to when a press tour or junket is appropriate and how much should be spent.

The policies of major dailies forbid employees to accept any gifts, housing, or transportation; the newspapers pay all costs associated with a press tour on which a staff member is sent. In contrast, some smaller dailies, weeklies, and trade magazines accept offers for an expense-paid trip. Their managers maintain that they don't have the resources of large dailies to reimburse an organization for expenses and such trips are legitimate for covering a newsworthy activity.

Some newspapers with policies forbidding acceptance of travel and gifts don't extend the restrictions to all departments. Reporters in the hard-news area, for example, cannot accept gifts or travel, but such policy may not be enforced for reporters who write soft news for sports, travel, and lifestyle sections. Few newspapers, for example, pay for the press box seats provided for reporters covering a professional football game, nor does the travel editor usually pay the full rate for rooms at beach resorts that are the focus of travel articles.

Given the mixed and often confusing policies of various media, public relations professionals must use common sense and discretion. First of all, they should not violate the PRSA code of ethics, which forbids lavish gifts and free trips that have nothing to do with covering a legitimate news event. Second, public relations professionals should be sensitive to the policies of news outlets and should design events to stay within them. A wise alternative is to offer reporters the option of reimbursing the company for travel and hotel expenses associated with a press tour.

Summary

The News Release
The news release is the most commonly used public relations tactic. News releases are sent to journalists and editors, and they are the source for a large percentage of articles that are published. News releases must be accurate, informative, and written in journalistic style.

Publicity Photos
Publicity photos often accompany news releases to make a story more appealing. Photos must be high-resolution and well composed. A photo can be made more interesting by manipulating the camera angle and lighting and by showing scale and action. Color photos are now commonly used in most publications.

Media Advisories and Fact Sheets
Advisories, or alerts, let journalists know about an upcoming event such as a news conference or photo or interview opportunities. Fact sheets give the 5 Ws and H of an event in outline form. Fact sheets also can be used to provide background on an executive, a product, or an organization.

Media Kits
A media kit, or press kit, is typically a folder containing news releases, photos, fact sheets, and features about a new product, an event, or other newsworthy projects undertaken by an organization. Many media kits are now produced in CD format to save costs.

Pitch Letters
Public relations personnel "pitch" journalists and editors with story ideas about their employers or clients. Such pitches can be letters, e-mails, or even telephone calls. A good pitch is based on research and a creative idea that will appeal to the editor.

Newsletters and Magazines
Newsletters are relatively economical to produce and are used to convey information in a relatively simple format. Many newsletters are now distributed via e-mail and listservs. Intranets allow organizations to distribute newsletters with highly sophisticated graphics on a daily basis. The second level of organizational publication is tabloid newspapers, which have more photos and graphics than

newsletters do. The apex of organizational publishing is the four-color magazine.

Brochures

The objective of brochures is to inform and educate. Brochures come in all sizes and formats. For mass distribution, a relatively simple brochure or flyer is the most economical. Annual reports for publicly owned corporations are mandated by the SEC, but most companies also use the annual report as a marketing tool.

The Reach of Radio and TV

In today's society, radio and television reach the vast majority of people on a daily basis.

Radio News Releases

These releases, unlike those for print media, must be written for the ear. A popular format is the audio news release (ANR) that includes an announcer and a quote (soundbite) from a spokesperson. Radio news releases should be no longer than 60 seconds.

Public Service Announcements

Both radio and television stations accept public service announcements (PSAs) from nonprofit organizations that wish to inform and educate the public about health issues or upcoming civic events. PSAs are like advertisements, but stations don't charge to air them. Television PSAs require visual aids.

Broadcast Media Tours

A radio media tour (RMT) and a television satellite media tour (SMT) happen when an organization's spokesperson is interviewed from a central location by journalists across the country. Each journalist is able to conduct a one-on-one interview for several minutes.

Video News Releases

The video news release (VNR) is produced in a format that television stations can easily use or edit based on their needs. VNRs are relatively expensive to produce, but they have great potential for reaching large audiences.

News Feeds

With a news feed, an organization arranges for coverage of a particular event, and television stations across the country can watch it in real time or receive an edited version of it for later use.

Personal Appearances

Public relations personnel often book spokespersons on radio and television talk shows. The guest must have a good personality, be knowledgeable, and give short, concise answers.

Product Placements

Producers are increasingly making deals with companies to feature their products on television shows or movies. Nonprofit organizations also lobby to have scripts mention key health messages and deal with various social issues.

The Internet

Public relations personnel should not overlook Web news sites for placement of publicity. Podcasts have quickly become a public relations campaign staple. In addition, the popularity of Weblogs, or blogs, means that public relations personnel should also harness them as a tactic for reaching an audience. Organizations are increasingly using Webcasts to transmit news conferences and interact with journalists.

Media Interviews

A face-to-face interview with a print or broadcast journalist is a good way to communicate an organization's perspective. Before being interviewed, however, the individual should have a clear idea of what the journalist needs and how key messages of the organization can be effectively communicated. Public relations personnel often brief and prepare executives for various interviews.

News Conferences

A news conference is a way that an organization can distribute information to multiple journalists at the same time. It is a format for journalists to ask questions. News conferences should only be held when there is news that requires elaboration and clarification.

CASE ACTIVITY >>

What Would You Do?

The public relations toolbox is expanding with the addition of online tactics. A local start-up company specializing in outdoor grilling supplies has hired you to help publicize its product.

The company produces supplies including grilling spices, wood planks for smoking seafood and vegetables, and grilling tools. The company cannot afford nationwide advertising, but wants to raise awareness of its products nationally. The company has a Web site from which it takes orders for its products. Using this existing resource, what online tactics would your recommend for this client? What media would your target? Would a podcast or blog make sense for this client? Should the client post news releases on its Web site? Write a memo to the client outlining your ideas and justifying them. Be as specific as possible so your ideas are clear to the client.

Questions for Review and Discussion

1. How should a news release be formatted? Why is the inverted pyramid structure used in news releases?
2. List at least six guidelines for writing a news release.
3. Why is it a good idea to include a photograph with a news release? What six factors should be considered with regard to a publicity photo?
4. Before pitching an item to a journalist or editor, why is it a good idea to first do some basic research on the individual, the publication, or the talk show?
5. Various methods can be used to deliver publicity materials to the media. Name the methods and compare their relative strengths and weaknesses. Some experts believe that e-mail is the ultimate distribution channel. Do you agree or disagree?
6. Radio news releases must be tightly written. What's the general guideline for the number of lines and words in a 30-second news release? What other guidelines should be kept in mind when writing a radio news release?

7. How does an audio news release differ from a standard radio news release?
8. What is the advantage of a radio media tour (RMT) or a satellite media tour (SMT) to an organization and to journalists? Are there any disadvantages?
9. List four ways that an organization can get its news and viewpoints on local television.
10. Companies increasingly are working with television programs and film studios to get their products featured as part of a program or movie. What do you think of this trend?
11. Why should public relations personnel pay attention to bloggers and their sites?
12. What are the benefits of one-on-one media interviews? Are there any pitfalls?
13. What are the logistics of organizing a news conference?

Suggested Readings

Biro, Tom. "Get the Blogging Started: Tech Tips for Newbies." *Public Relations Tactics*, March 2006, 26–27.

Callison, Coy. "Media Relations and the Internet: How Fortune 500 Company Web Sites Assist Journalists in News Gathering." *Public Relations Review* 29, no. 1 (2003): 29–41.

Eskridge, Amy Goldwert. "Getting Your Best Results from a Video News Release." *Public Relations Tactics*, June 2004, 27.

Fowler, Geoffrey A. "Product Placement Now Star on Chinese TV." *Wall Street Journal*, June 2, 2004, B1, B3.

Gonzalez-Herrero, A., and M. Ruiz de Valbuena. "Trends in Online Media Relations: Web-Based Corporate Press Rooms in Leading International Companies." *Public Relations Review*, 32, no. 3 (2006): 267–275.

Iacono, Erica. "Lights, Camera, and the Power of TV." *PRWeek*, May 29, 2006, 15.

Ketchner, Kathy. "Preparing for Better Presentations." *Public Relations Tactics*, February 2004, p. 27.

Krejci, David. "Answering the Commonly Asked Client Question: What Do We Do about the Blogs?" *Public Relations Tactics*, March 2006, 26.

Porter, L. V., and L. M. Sallot. "Web Power: A Survey of Practitioners' World Wide Web Use and Their Perceptions of Its Effects on Their Decision Making Power." *Public Relations Review* 31, no. 1 (2005): 111–119.

Praeger, Jane. "Ten Tips to Make Your Presentation Compelling." *Public Relations Tactics*, May 2004, 17.

Quenqua, Douglas. "A New Kind of Speech for a New Kind of CEO." *PRWeek*, April 5, 2004, 18.

Quenqua, Douglas. "How to Walk the Talk Shows." *PRWeek*, March 15, 2004, 18.

Schmelzer, Randi. "Gore's 'Truth' Finds Receptive Audience." *PRWeek*, May 29, 2006, 8.

Schneiders, Greg. "Blogs Just a Reflection of Overall Consumer Empowerment Trend." *PRWeek*, May 15, 2006, 9.

Sweeney, Katie. "Broadcast PR Executives: Controversy Aside, Stations Stand by VNRs." *Public Relations Tactics*, June 2004, 22.

Thompson, Clive. "Blogs to Riches: The Haves and Have-Nots of the Blogging Boom." *New York Magazine*, February 20, 2006.

Trammell, K. D., and A. Keshelashvili. "Examining the New Influencers: A Self-Presentation Study of A-List Blogs." *Journalism and Mass Communication Quarterly* (Winter 2005): 968–982.

Wallace, Michelle. "Budgeting for a Creative Satellite Media Tour." *Public Relations Tactics*, July 2004, 16.

Wasson, Brian. "The Wide World of Wikipedia and Why PR Practitioners Should Take Note." *Public Relations Tactics*, March 2006, 22.

Wilcox, Dennis L. *Public Relations Writing & Media Techniques*, 5th ed. Boston: Allyn & Bacon, 2005.

Chapter Eleven

Global Public Relations

> > The Rise of NGOs
> > Public Relations Development in Other Nations
> > Opportunities in International Work

What Is Global Public Relations?

Global public relations, also called international public relations, is the planned and organized efforts of a company, institution, or government to establish and build relationships with the publics of other nations. These publics, in turn, are the various groups of people who are affected by, or who can affect, the operations of a particular firm, institution, or government.

International public relations can also be viewed from the standpoint of its practice in individual countries. Although public relations is commonly regarded as a concept developed in the United States at the beginning of the 20th century, some of its elements, such as countering unfavorable public attitudes through publicity and annual reports, were practiced by railroad companies in Germany as far back as the mid-19th century, to mention only one such country. (See Chapter 3.)

Even so, it is largely U.S. public relations techniques that have been adapted nationally and regionally in countries throughout the world, including many totalitarian regimes. Today, although in some languages there is no term comparable to *public relations*, the practice has spread to most countries, especially those with industrial bases and large urban populations. This is primarily the result of worldwide technological, social, economic, and political changes and the growing understanding that public relations is an essential component of advertising, marketing, and public diplomacy.

International Corporate Public Relations

This section explores the new age of global marketing and addresses the differences in language, laws, and cultural mores that must be overcome when companies conduct business in foreign countries. We also discuss how U.S. public relations firms represent foreign interests in this country as well as U.S. corporations in other parts of the world. Aspects of public relations practice in some other countries are delineated.

The New Age of Global Marketing

For decades, hundreds of corporations based in the United States have been engaged in international business operations, including marketing, advertising, and public relations. All these activities exploded to unprecedented proportions during the 1990s, largely because of new communications technologies, development of 24-hour financial markets almost worldwide, the lowering of trade barriers, the growth of sophisticated foreign competition in traditionally "American" markets, and the shrinking cultural differences, which is bringing the "global village" ever closer to reality.

Today, almost one-third of all U.S. corporate profits are generated through international business. In the case of Coca-Cola, probably the best-known brand name in the world, international sales account for 70 percent of the company's revenues. In addition, large U.S. based public relations firms such as Burson-Marsteller and Edelman are now generating between 30 and 40 percent of their fees serving foreign clients (see Chapter 4).

At the same time, overseas investors are moving into American industries. It is not uncommon for 15 to 20 percent of a U.S. company's stock to be held abroad. The United Kingdom, for example, has a direct foreign investment in the United States exceeding $122 billion, followed by Japan and the Netherlands with nearly half that sum each, according to the U.S. Department of Commerce.

Fueling the new age of global public relations and marketing are satellite television, computer networks, electronic mail, fax, fiber optics, cellular telephone systems, and emerging technologies such as integrated services digital network (ISDN), which enable users to send voice, data, graphics, and video over existing copper cables. For example, Hill & Knowlton has its own satellite transmission facilities, and the General Electric Company has formed an international telecommunications network, enabling employees to communicate worldwide using voice, video, and computer data simply by dialing seven digits on a telephone. Using three satellite systems, Cable News Network (CNN) is viewed by more than 200 million people in more than 140 countries. England's BBC World Service also reaches an impressive number of nations, including the 40-plus members of the British Commonwealth. A number of newspapers and magazines are also reaching millions with international editions. *Reader's Digest*, to cite one example, reaches 60 nations and is published in 21 languages. And, of course, the *Wall Street Journal* and the *Financial Times* have daily editions in the United States, Europe, and Asia.

Much of the jousting for new business takes place on western European terrain, where a recently expanded European Union (EU) is attracting enormous interest. Although hampered by recession in recent years, public relations expenditures have increased significantly. This increase has been generated in part by expansion of commercial television resulting from widespread privatization, the desire of viewers for more varied programming, satellite technology, and slowly developing EU business connections. Satellite TV reaches well over 30 million people, mostly through direct transmission of programming to homes that bypasses conventional networks, local stations, and cable systems. On the print side, the business press has been growing about 20 percent every year, and there are about 15,000 trade publications in western Europe.

Although the EU promoted the phrase "a single Europe," corporations and public relations firms still face the complex task of communicating effectively to 400 million people in 25 countries speaking multiple languages. Differences in language, laws, and cultural mores among countries are a continuing challenge to culturally sensitive public relations practice. There also is a need for both managers and employees to learn to think and act in global terms as quickly as possible. Already, Burson-Marsteller, with offices in many countries, is spending more than $1 million a year on training tapes and traveling teams of trainers to foster a uniform approach to client projects.

Trade is now a global enterprise, but not everyone is happy about it. Here, protestors demonstrate against the World Trade Organization (WTO) and its policies. Today, as never before, international organizations and corporations must pay attention to public opinion on a global basis.

Language and Cultural Differences

Companies operating in other nations are confronted with essentially the same public relations challenges as those in the United States. Their objectives are to compete successfully and to manage conflict effectively, but the task is more complex on an international and intercultural level.

Public relations practitioners need to recognize cultural differences, adapt to local customs, and understand the finer points of verbal and nonverbal communication in individual nations. Experts in intercultural communication point out that many cultures, particularly non-Western ones, are "high-context" communication societies. In other words, the meaning of the spoken word is often implicit and based on the environmental context and personal relationships rather than on explicit, categorical statements. The communication styles of Asian and Arab nations, for example, are high context.

In contrast, European and American communication styles are considered low context. Great emphasis is placed on exact words, and receivers are expected to derive meaning primarily from the written or verbal statements, not from nonverbal behavior cues. Legal documents produced in the West are the ultimate in explicit wording.

The concept of low- and high-context communication styles is manifested in several ways. U.S. citizens, for example, tend to be very direct (and often blunt) in their communication style. In high-context cultures, Americans often are perceived as verbose, opinionated, and very focused on getting to the point as soon as possible. They also are clock watchers, get upset if meetings don't start on time, and carry day planners as if they were bibles.

The communication style in a high-context culture is quite different. Group harmony is more important than take-charge individualistic traits, a social relationship must be built before business is conducted, a handshake takes the place of a legal contract, and being on time to a meeting isn't all that important. One important aspect of high-context Asian cultures is "loss of face." Individuals don't want to offend, so a person will never say no outright. A Japanese executive, for example, will suck air through his or her teeth and exclaim, "Sa! That will be very difficult" when they really mean "no."

There also are other cultural differences. Geert Hofstede, a company psychologist for global giant IBM, studied national/cultural differences among employees around the world back in the 1970s and came up with five basic cultural dimensions. Today, students still rely on his typology to understand various national cultures. Professors David Guth and Charles Marsh of the University of Kansas summarized Hofstede's cultural dimensions in their book, *Adventures in Public Relations: Case Studies and Critiical Thinking*:

1. *Power distance* measures how tolerant a society is about unequally distributed decision-making power. Countries with a high acceptance of power distance include Mexico and France. Countries with a low acceptance include Austria and the United States.

2. *Individualism*, as contrasted with collectivism, pits loyalty to one's self against loyalty to a larger group. Countries in Asia and Latin America gravitate toward collectivism, while the United States, Canada, and most European countries gravitate toward individualism.

3. *Masculinity/femininity* contrasts competiveness (traditionally masculine) against compassionand nurturing (traditionally feminine). Masculine nations include Australia, Germany, and Japan. Feminine nations include Sweden and Spain.

4. *Uncertainty avoidance* measures how well a society tolerates ambiguity. Nations that have difficulty functioning in uncertainty include Japan, Belgium, and Greece. Nations that tolerate ambiguity include Great Britain, the United States, and Sweden.

5. *Long-term versus short-term orientation* measures a society's willingness to consider the traditions of the past and carry them into the future. China and other East Asian nations tend to have long-term orientations. The United States has a short-term orientation.

Language, of course, is another challenge. The following are some examples of the type of language problems that have been reported in various newspaper and magazine articles:

> A British executive staying at a hotel in New York was embarrassed because he asked the front desk for a "rubber," which is an eraser in England. The hotel staff thought he wanted a condom.

> A producer of calzones, which are cheese and meat-filled turnovers, had a major marketing problem in Spain because in Spanish *calzone* means "underwear."

> The Milk Processor Association found that the catchy phase "Got Milk?" didn't translate too well into Spanish. The literal translation was "Are You Lactating?"

> The thumbs-up gesture in the United States means "well done" or "good job." In other cultures, it can be considered offensive and should be avoided. Also, the thumb-and-forefinger "OK" sign is an obscene gesture in many cultures.

Cultural differences provide additional pitfalls, as shown by the following examples:

> In China, tables at a banquet are never numbered. The Chinese think such table arrangements appear to rank guests and that certain numbers are unlucky. It's better to direct a guest to the "primrose" or "hollyhock" table.

> Americans are fond of using first names, but it's not proper business etiquette in Europe and Asia unless you have been given permission.

> Early morning breakfast meetings are not done in Latin America; by the same token, a dinner meeting may not start until 9 or 10 P.M.

> In Thailand, patting a child on the head is seen as a grave offense because the head is considered sacred. Also, it's considered a crime to make disrespectful remarks about the royal family, particularly the king.

> In Latin America, greetings often include physical contact by hugging individuals or grabbing them by the arm. Men and women commonly greet each other with a kiss on the cheek in Argentina and Chile.

> News releases in Malaysia should be distributed in four languages to avoid alienating any segment of the press.

> Gift giving is common in Asian cultures. Executives, meeting for the first time, will exchange gifts as a way of building a social relationship.

> In Muslim nations, particularly the Middle East, men should not stand near, touch, or stare at any woman.

All of these illustrations indicate that Americans and others not only must learn the customs of the country in which they are working, but they also should rely on native professionals to guide them. See the Insights box on page 346 about cultural sensitivity in China. Media materials and advertising must be translated, and the best approach is to employ native speakers who have extensive experience in translating ad copy and public relations materials. For example, see the FedEx news releases on page 347.

Representing Foreign Corporations in the United States

Corporations and industries in other countries frequently employ public relations and lobbying firms to advance their products, services, and political interests in the United States. In fact, in a six-year period from 1998 to mid-2004, the Center for Public

ON THE JOB >>

Starbucks in China: Cultural Sensitivities and the Power of the Blog

Global

Should Starbucks have a shop in the Forbidden City, the hallowed 600-year-old home of China's emperors? In a classic case of conflict management, Starbucks became the topic of a Web crusade to be expelled from China's national icon because many Chinese believe it offends their national culture to have a U.S.-based company selling coffee in the compound.

Although Starbucks has had a small outlet in the Forbidden City since 2000, the pressure to close the shop began in early 2007 when 29-year-old news anchor Rui Chenggang wrote on his blog that Starbucks "is really too inappropriate for the world's impression of the Forbidden City. This isn't globalization, this is the erosion of Chinese Culture." In the space of a week, his posting had been viewed more than a half-million times, and his demand to shut the café turned into a national cause. Indeed, the Chinese use

of the Internet to express their opinions is giving foreign corporations major headaches. China is home to 132 million Internet users, second only to the United States. And according to one government estimate, there are 20 million Chinese bloggers, of whom more than 3 million write actively.

Rui Chennggang even e-mailed the president of Starbucks suggesting that the store be removed from the Forbidden City. Starbuck's CEO Jim McDonald responded, "We have shown and continue to show our respect for local history, culture, and social customs, and have made a serious effort to fit within the environment of the Forbidden City." According to the *Wall Street Journal,* the Starbucks shop doesn't even display its logo on a sign outside the shop, which is housed next to the national museum store.

Starbucks officials declined further comment, but Geoffrey Fowler, a re-

porter for the *Wall Street Journal,* wrote that government officials often heed online protests and makes changes. A KFC store at Beihai Park, a scenic imperial garden north of the Forbidden City, was closed after a local political advisory board objected.

In sum, Starbucks is going though the continuency continuum outlined in Chapter 2. Should the company be a strong advocate for keeping its café open in the Forbidden City, or should it move toward more accommodation and resolution? According to *Wall Street Journal* reporter Fowler, "Even blog crisis advisors don't entirely agree on how companies should respond to bloggers in these cases." He quoted Sam Flemming, the chief executive of Shanghai-based blogging consultancy CIC, which works for Pepsi and Nike. "And then you should react quickly. Consumers feel like they should be listened to. If they feel like they're being ignored, it makes things even worse"

Source: Fowler, Geoffrey. "It's Called the Forbidden City for a Reason." *Wall Street Journal,* January 19, 2007, B1.

Integrity (a nonprofit watchdog group) reported that 700 companies with headquarters in about 100 nations, spent more $520 million lobbying the U.S. government. The center's analysis continued, "Over that time, those companies employed 550 lobbying firms firms and teams of 3,800 lobbyists, more than 100 of whom were former members of Congress."

Companies from the United Kingdom (UK) top the list, spending more than $180 million betweeen 1998 and 2004. This included BP (British Petroleum) and the pharmaceutical giant GlaxoSmithKline, which have extensive operations in the United States. GlaxoSmithKline, for example, consistently lobbies on Medicare and Medicaid reform issues. BP, on the other hand, lobbies on matters relating to environmental standards and oil and gas issues. Companies from Germany were

International public relations requires the translation of news releases into several languages. Here, the first part of this FedEx announcement is in English. Also shown is the same announcement in Thai. (MDK Consulting/Bangkok)

second on the list, spending about $70 million on lobbying. The major spender is DaimlerChrysler Corporation. Swiss corporations were third with about the same expenditures, and Japanese companies were fourth with about $60 million during that six-year period.

Even companies that don't directly operate in the United States engage in lobbying. They seek to ensure an advantageous trade policy in international trade agreements of which the United States is a major player. According to the Center for Public Integrity, "Not surprisingly, international trade was by far the most common issues foreign companies reported lobbying on, followed by defense and taxation."

Foreign companies in the defense industry were particularly successful, according to the watchdog group. In the six-year period under analysis, 16 foreign companies lobbied the U.S. Department of Defense and received, in return, $16.4 billion in Pentagon contracts, $5.6 billion of which were awarded without competition.

Carl Levin, vice president and senior consultant, Burson-Marsteller, Washington, D.C., gives five major reasons for foreign corporations to retain public relations counsel in the United States:

1. To hold off protectionist moves that threaten their companies or industries.

2. To defeat legislation affecting the sale of their products.

3. To provide ongoing information on political, legal, and commercial developments in the United States that could bear on their business interests.

4. To support expansion of their markets in the United States. See the PR Casebook box on page 348 for a description of Unilever's Dove campaign in the U.S.

5. To deal with a crisis situation that threatens the financial health or reputation of their organization. See Chapter 2 for a description of the Bridgestone tire crisis in the United States.

PRCASEBOOK

Unilever Brings "Real Beauty" Campaign to the United States

Unilver, headquartered in the UK and the Netherlands, wanted to generate sales for its beauty products and its new Dove Firming product line in various nations including the United States. To this end, they worked with Edelman Worldwide to develop a new theme that rejected the stereotypical use of the "perfect woman" as a beauty role model.

Strategy One, Edelman's opinion research division, conducted a survey of more than 3,000 women in 10 nations (including the United States) and found that women would respond to a campaign that featured actual women. Titled the "Campaign for Real Beauty" (CFRB). Dove became a sponsor of American Women in Radio and Television to increase exposure among key influentials. The Dove Self-Esteem Fund was then launched in partnership with the Girl Scouts of America and young girls were encouraged to participate in a photo and essay tour contest to capture "real beauty."

According to *PRWeek*, which named the Dove program the Consumer Launch Campaign of the Year 2006, "The PR program was timed to coincide with the launch of the Dove Firming ad campaign—which featured six real women posing—untouched—in their underwear. Consumers were given an opportunity to meet the women at a photo shoot in Times Square where they could sign a Dove Self-Esteem Fund pledge banner. For each name signed, a dollar was donated to the "Uniquely Me!" program designed to help build self-esteem in young girls.

The six women were featured on the season premiere of *The Ellen DeGeneres Show* and *The Oprah Winfrey Show*. The media coverage was impressive; 650 million impresssions and nearly four hours of broadcast time, including 10 minutes on the *Today* show. In addition, more than 1 million visitors logged into the CFRB Web site.

Representing U.S. Corporations in Other Nations

Many U.S. corporations are global in scope, with employees, products, manufacturing plants, and distribution centers around the world. The largest U.S. giants in terms of 2006 sales, according to *Forbes* magazine, are (1) Wal-Mart, $348 billion; (2) ExxonMobil, $335 billion; (3) Chevron, $199 billion; (4) General Electric, $163.3 billion, and (5) Citigroup, $146.5 billion.

These giant corporations, including hundreds of other U.S. companies, also engage in extensive public relations and lobbying activities in other nations for virtually the same five reasons that Levin lists in the previous section. The total amount expended on public relations and lobbying abroad, however, is not known because the U.S. companies don't have to report such expenditures to the U.S. government.

Public relations professionals who work for these giants, as well as a host of other American companies, are automatically in the field of international public relations, because their work involves many nations. Many of these corporations also retain global public relations firms such as Burson-Marsteller and Hill & Knowlton to provide services from offices in major cities around the world. The global scope of public relations firms was discussed in Chapter 4.

At the start of the 21st century and in the aftermath of the 9/11 terrorist attack in 2001, American companies face a number of challenges abroad in terms of competing with other large corporations headquartered in other nations, dealing with sustainable development, being boycotted by nations that disagree with American foreign policy, and being good corporate citizens at the local and national level. David Drobis, a former senior partner and chair of Ketchum, outlined some of these challenges in a speech before the International Communications Consultancy Organization (ICCO). According to Drobis, one major challenge is to better communicate the economic advantages of globalization to the world's people. The *Economist*, for example, has called globalization a massive communications failure because the public and private sectors have done such a poor job communicating globalization's benefits, being transparent about their activities, and building important alliances.

Drobis believes that public relations professionals are best-suited to explain the benefits of globalization. These benefits must be communicated to three key groups. The first group is the companies themselves. Companies must realize that international capitalism has a bad connotation in many parts of the world because it is perceived as nothing more than "a byword for oppression, exploitation, and injustice by rapacious multinationals."

Companies, Drobis says, have done little to correct this view despite the efforts of a few highly responsible companies who have outstanding programs. He continues, "companies must take into consideration a broad group of stakeholders as they pursue their business goals globally. And by doing so, there are tangible and intangible business benefits. In this way, good corporate citizenship is not a cost of doing business, but rather a driver of business success. What's good for the soul is also good for business."

Studies show, says Drobis, "that companies that pursue initiatives—be they related to the environment, labor standards, or human rights—are rewarded with improved business success in a number of areas, including shareholder value, revenue, operational efficiencies, higher employee morale and productivity, and corporate reputation."

The second group that must be informed of the benefits of globalization is nongovernmental organizations (NGOs). Although many NGOs are outright hostile to all private enterprise, American companies must realize that NGOs can become an important seal of approval and branding. Indeed, major mainstream NGOs such as the World Wildlife Federation and Greenpeace are working with corporations on sustainable development programs. The *Financial Times* notes, "A new type of relationship is emerging between companies and NGOs, where NGOs act as certification bodies, vertifying and, in many cases, permitting the use of their logos, showing that products and services are being produced in a socially responsible and environmentally friendly ways."

The third group is international institutions such as World Trade Organization (WTO), the World Bank, the International Monetary Fund (IMF), or even the United Nations. Drobis says these organizations are unfairly criticized as being undemocratic, but fairly criticized for being nontransparent. An article in *Foreign Affairs* puts it this way: "To outsiders, even within the same government, these institutions can look like closed and secretive clubs. Increased transparency is essential. International organizations can provide more access to their deliberations, even after the fact."

Drobis, in giving advice to American companies doing business abroad, concludes that the era of "relationship building" is over. Instead, he says, the 21st century is one of "confidence building" in the international arena so various publics not only trust corporations to do the right thing, but also believe globalization is a benefit to hundreds of millions of poor people around the globe.

On a more basic level, American corporations use public relations as part of the marketing mix to promote their products and services around the globe.

International Government Public Relations

This section explores how and why the governments of most nations seek to influence the opinions and actions of governments and people in other countries. Many employ U.S. public relations firms for this purpose. Conflict and war also generate efforts by nations to make their cases in the court of world opinion.

Influencing Other Countries

The governments of virtually every country have one or more departments involved in communicating with other nations. Much effort and millions of dollars are spent on the tourism industry, attracting visitors whose expenditures aid the local enomomy. Even larger sums are devoted to lobbying efforts to obtain favorable legislation for a country's products; for example, Costa Rica urged the U.S. Congress to let its sugar into the nation at favorable rates. Conflict and war also lead to public relations efforts. See the Global box on Israel and Palestine on page 351. Israel has also been active on the public relations front as a result of the Lebanon conflict in 2006.

Information Efforts by the United States. The American government is the major disseminator of information around the world. This is called *public diplomacy*, because it is an open communication process primarily intended to present American society in all its complexity so citizens and governments of other nations can understand the context of U.S. actions and policies. Another function is to promote American concepts of democracy, free trade, and open communication around the world.

The United States Information Agency (USIA), created in 1953 by President Dwight Eisenhower, was the primary agency involved in shaping America's image abroad. USIA, in many ways, was the direct descendant of George Creel's Committee on Public Information (CPI) during World War I and Elmer Davis's Office of War Information during World War II (see Chapter 3).

Following World War II, the new threat, of course, was the outbreak of the Cold War with the Soviet Union and the Communist bloc nations in Eastern Europe. The Cold War was a war of words on both sides to win the "hearts and minds" of governments and their citizens around the world. Some USIA activities included (1) the stationing of public affairs officers (PAOs) at every American embassy to work with local media, (2) publication of books and magazines, (3) distribution of American films and TV programs, (4) sponsorship of tours by American dance and musical groups, (5) art shows, (6) student and faculty exchange programs such as the Fulbright Program, and (7) sponsorship of lecture tours by American authors and intellectuals.

At the height of the Cold War, USIA had a budget of about $900 million and 12,000 employees. When the Soviet Union imploded in the early 1990s, the fortunes of the USIA began to fall as Congress and other critics decided that the United States didn't need such a large public profile in the world. As a result, the agency was abolished in 1999 and most of its functions were transferred to the U.S. Department of State under an undersecretary of state for public affairs and diplomacy. The staff was cut 40 percent and funding for projects decreased sharply.

The 9/11 terrorist attacks on the United States created a new impetus to "sell" America and the U.S. decision to invade Afghanistan and Iraq. Once again, the cry was to "win the hearts and minds" of the world's people and to gain public, as well as international support, for U.S. actions. The effort, however, was somewhat diffused

ON THE JOB >>

The Image War: Israel vs. the Palestinians

Global

The Israeli–Palestinian conflict has produced any number of news stories and photos showing Israeli soldiers, tanks, helicopters, and guided missiles being used against a relatively unarmed Palestinian population. As Israeli's minister of information Nachman Shai said, "We looked like Goliath and they looked like David."

This has caused some concern for the Israeli government, particularly as it affects opinion in the United States, because it is important to have the continuing support of the American population and the government. That support is in danger if public opinion shifts to increased sympathy for the Palestinian cause.

Consequently, Israel has been active, encouraging the Jewish community in the United States to be more proactive

in explaining the Israeli side of the conflict. In addition, a New York public relations firm has been hired to place Israel's representatives in various media outlets. According to Steve Rubenstein, from Rubenstein Associates, "We felt people were missing the whole truth and that if we could show a fuller picture visually, it would be easier to make the Israeli case."

The Palestinians are also beginning to realize how decisive the battle for public opinion is, and various Arab groups, such as the Arab-American Anti-Discrimination Committee (ADC), have stepped up publicity efforts to inform Americans about the Palestinian side of the conflict. The group has taken out full-page ads in daily newspapers across the country and written op-ed articles. Another group, the Council of

American-Islamic Relations (CAIR) also places ads in American publications to improve the image of Arabs living and working in the United States.

More recently, when the Hamas organization won the Palestinian general election in 2006, it immediately signed a $180,000 contract with a public relations consultant to persuade Europeans and Americans that it was not a group of religious fanatics who promoted suicide bombings and hatred of Israel. Nashat Aqtash, the public relations consultant and also a teacher at Birzeit University in Ramalah, told the *Manchester Guardian*, "Hamas has an image problem. The Israelis were able to create a very bad image of the Palestinians in general and particularly Muslims and Hamas. My contract is to project the right image."

and confused because the Pentagon and the White House undertook public diplomacy efforts rather than the U.S. State Department.

The 9/11 Commission, in its 2004 final report, called for centralization of U.S. diplomacy efforts, a more robust and targeted program, and a drastic increase in funding of diplomatic exchanges and campaigns. The 2006 budget for the State Department's public diplomacy programs included $450 million for educational and cultural exchange programs and $646 million for VOA and its related broadcast operations. Both programs were allocated even less money in the 2007 budget, which critics said was already a miniscule budget for global public diplomacy. It represents, in comparative terms, the cost of about five F-22 combat planes recently delivered to the Air Force. See the PR Casebook on pages 352–353 for more information on U.S. public diplomacy efforts abroad.

Broadcast Efforts. The Voice of America (VOA), created in 1942, was part of USIA for several decades. When USIA was dismantled and moved to the State Department, VOA was placed under the control of an independent federal agency, the Broadcasting Board of Governors (BOG). The idea was to have a firewall between the agency and the administration to ensure that VOA would continue to be an objective

PRCASEBOOK

U.S. "Public Diplomacy" Faces Major Obstacles

Perhaps the easiest part of the War on Terrorism was the toppling of the Taliban regime in Afghanistan and the removal of Saddam Hussein's government in Baghdad. Most experts agree, however, that the toughest part is winning the war of worldwide public opinion.

The U.S. government is now engaged in a war of ideas. As the *Economist* points out, "It has to persuade America, its allies and Muslims around the world that its fight is against terror, not Islam." Many experts are less optimistic about winning this part of the war. One Arab expert told the Associated Press, "The U.S. point of view is not unknown to the Arab people, they just don't buy it." According to the *New York Times*, "Many Muslims say American policy favors Israelis over Palestinians and needs to be altered before sentiments will change."

John Paluszek, senior counsel of Ketchum, puts it more bluntly. He wrote in *PRWeek*, "It's the policy, stupid." He continues, "It is policy—and related action—that matters most in successful PR. Recent opinion polls tell us that it's current American foreign policy, not traditional American values, that is unacceptable to many people in the Middle East." Indeed an Advisory Group on Diplomacy for the Arab and Muslim World appointed by Congress concluded, "much of the resentment toward America stems from our policies" and "[i]n this time of peril, public diplomacy is absurdly and dangerously underfunded."

Although funding is a major problem, critics also say that the limited monies available have been poorly spent. One project that received considerable criticism was a multimillion dollar advertising campaign initiated by Charlotte Beers, a former CEO of two major advertising agencies. She was named Undersecretary of Public Diplomacy and Public Affairs for the State Department in 2001. Almost immediately she decided on using advertising as a major tool to win "hearts and minds." Her idea was a series of television commercials with the theme "shared values" that would show Muslim men and women leading happy and productive lives in a religion-tolerant America. As one critic dryly noted, "It was like this was the 1930s and the government was running commercials showing happy blacks in America."

Although the ads were used in Indonesia, the world's largest Muslim nation, most television stations in the Middle East refused to accept the ads because they were considered nothing but "propaganda." Also, of the Muslims featured in the

American public diplomacy abroad has taken a severe beating since the invasion of Iraq. Here, Lebanese demonstrators protest outside the U.S. embassy in Beirut.

ads, none of them were Arabs. After about five weeks, the State Department suspended the advertising program, and Charlotte Beers, barely 18 months into her job, resigned for "health reasons." Her successor, Margaret Tutwiler, lasted only five months.

President Bush, in 2005, then appointed Karen Hughes to the public diplomacy and public affairs position. She is one of the president's most trusted confidantes and most observers believed her access to the president was a positive development for a renewed—and more effective—public diplomacy effort on the part of the United States to win favorable worldwide public opinion. Her high status in the Bush administration was evident at her swearing in ceremony. On hand were the president, Laura Bush, Condoleezza Rice, four cabinet secretaries, and the chair of the Joint Chiefs of Staff.

Shortly after her appointment, Ms. Hughes took a three-country "listening tour" of the Middle East that met with mixed results. She also initiated rapid-response teams of State Department specialists to monitor the Arab press and electronic media for the purpose of countering misinformation and distortions. Other initiatives include meeting with Muslim leaders in the United States and even doing an interview on Al Jazeera, the popular Arabic satellite television station often accused by administration officials of being anti-American.

Meanwhile, global opinion polls show that the image of the United States abroad continues to decline. The Pew Research Center, a group based in Washington, D.C., has conducted an annual survey since 2002 to access America's image abroad. In its 2006 survey of 16,700 citizens in 15 nations, it found approval of American policies continued to drop. In Spain, for example, only 23 percent of the respondents had a favorable view of America, down from 41 percent the previous year. In Turkey, only 12 percent said they had a favorable opinion, down from 23 percent the previous year. There were also declines in India, Russia, and Indonesia. According to the *New York Times*, "Although strong majorities in several nations expressed worries about Iran's nuclear intentions, in 13 of 15 countries polled, most people said the war in Iraq posed more of a danger to world peace. Russians held that view by a 2 to 1 margin."

A similar 2006 poll by the Harris opinion poll in association with the *Financial Times*, found that Europeans see the United States as the greatest threat to global stability. The newspaper, reporting the survey of 5,000 people in five western European nations (Britain, France, Germany, Spain, and Italy) continued, "Some 36 percent identified the U.S. as the greatest threat to global stability, while 30 percent named Iran and 18 percent selected China."

There is some good news, according to the *Economist*. It reported, "The Pew survey shows that respondents are able to distinguish between a country, its people, and its government. The American people are more popular than America the country, while Mr. Bush's ratings are far lower than both."

As America's chief image officer, Karen Hughes continues to be upbeat. She told the *New York Times*, "Ed Murrow [the legendary CBS newsman and former director of the United States Information Agency] once famously said that there's no cash register that rings when a mind is changed. But I think over the long haul we can begin to shape a better perception in the Middle East." The other major challenge, however, is to improve America's image throughout the rest of the world. That task may be next to impossible, according to the Pew survey, as long as American troops are in Iraq.

news service with credibility around the world. Article One of the VOA, for example, states that it should be a "reliable and authoritative source of news" and the news should be "accurate, objective, and comprehensive."

Its core work has traditionally been broadcasting news, sports, and entertainment around the world via shortwave. This is still done to a large extent, but VOA has also established AM and FM radio transmitters throughout the world to reach an even broader audience. In addition, the agency supplies many radio and television stations throughout the world with various news, music, and talk programs free of charge. The VOA also offers audio streaming on the World Wide Web. The worldwide audience for VOA is difficult to judge, given all the distribution methods but estimates are several hundred million listeners.

VOA is the major voice of the United States abroad, but the government isn't always happy with its strict adherence to journalistic standards and objectivity. Consequently, the government also operates radio and television services that are more proactive in advancing U.S. interests and foreign policy. Radio Free Europe was started in 1949 to reach the nations of Eastern Europe under the thumb of the Soviet Union. Radio Liberty was started, with CIA funding, to broadcast directly to the citizens of the Soviet Union. The Soviet response during the Cold War was to jam these broadcasts because they were American "propaganda." Although both services still exist, they have significantly fewer staff and do less broadcasting.

More recently, Congress set up radio and television services focusing on Iraq and the Middle East. Radio Sawa, for example, injects news tidbits written from an American perspective into a heavy rotation of American and Middle Eastern pop music. A similar radio service aimed at Iranian youth is Radio Farda. On the television side, the U.S. government started Al Hurra. According to the *New York Times*, Al Hurra is "a slickly produced Arab-language news and entertainment network that [is] beamed by satellite from a Washington suburb to the Middle East." It is the American government's answer to Al Jazeera, the popular pan-Arab television service.

It is worth repeating that VOA, and services such as Radio Sawa, are not directed at U.S. citizens. Under the United States Information and Educational Exchange Act of 1948, Congress prohibited the government from directing its public diplomacy efforts toward its own citizens, because of fears that the government would propagandize its own citizens.

U.S. Firms Working for Foreign Governments

For fees ranging upward of $1 million per year, several hundred American public relations firms work in this country for other nations. In recent years, for example, Hill & Knowlton has represented Indonesia and Morocco; Burson-Marsteller has represented Argentina, Costa Rica, Hungary, and Russia (the latter mainly in trade fairs); and Ruder Finn has represented El Salvador, Israel, and Japan. Especially active in representing other nations is Doremus & Company, whose clients have included Egypt, Iran, Jordan, the Philippines, Saudi Arabia, and Tunisia.

In many cases, the public relations objectives are to influence U.S. foreign policy, generate tourism, create favorable public opinion about the countries, or encourage trade.

The Countries' Goals. What do these countries seek to accomplish? Burson-Marsteller's Carl Levin says that they pursue several goals, including:

> To advance political objectives

> To be counseled on probable U.S. reaction to the client government's projected action

> To advance the country's commercial interests—for example, sales in the United States, increased U.S. private investment, and tourism

> To assist in communications in English

> To counsel and help win understanding and support on a specific issue undermining the client's standing in the United States and the world community

> To help modify laws and regulations inhibiting the client's activities in the United States

Under the Foreign Agents Registration Act (FARA) of 1938, all legal, political, fund-raising, public relations, and lobbying consultants hired by foreign governments to work in the United States must register with the Department of Justice. They are required to file reports with the attorney general listing all activities on behalf of a foreign principal, compensation received, and expenses incurred.

Action Programs. Normally hired by an embassy after open bidding for the account, the firm first gathers detailed information about the client country, including past media coverage. Attitudes toward the country are ascertained both informally and through surveys.

The action program decided on will likely include the establishment of an information bureau to provide facts and published statements of favorable opinion about the country. In many cases, a nation may also use paid issue advertising in publications such as the *New York Times*, *Washington Post*, *Wall Street Journal*, and the *Financial Times* that reach a high percentage of opinion leaders and elected officials. The Republic of Kazakhstan, for example, placed full-page ads in major American newspapers after its national elections to reinforce public perceptions that it was a democracy. The ad's headline: "Today, Kazakhstan has another asset besides oil, gas and minerals. Democracy."

Appointments also are made with key media people and other influentials, including educators, business executives, and leaders of various public policy groups. In many cases, the primary audiences are key members of congressional committees, heads of various governmental agencies, and even the White House staff. These people are often invited to visit the client country on expense-paid trips, although some news media people decline on ethical grounds. (Ethical questions will be discussed in more detail shortly.)

Gradually, through expert and persistent methods of persuasion (including lobbying), public opinion may be changed, favorable trade legislation may be passed, foreign aid may be increased, or there's an influx of American tourists to the country.

Problems and Rewards.
The toughest problems confronting the public relations firm are often as follows:

> Deciding whether to represent a country, such as Uzbekistan or Zimbabwe, whose human rights violations may reflect adversely on the agency itself

> Persuading the governments of such nations to alter some of their practices so that the favorable public image sought may reflect reality

> Convincing officials of a client country, which may totally control the flow of news internally, that the American press is independent from government control and that they should never expect coverage that is 100 percent favorable

> Deciding whether to represent a nation such as Belarus, in which the autocratic head the state, Aleksandr Lukashenko, has drastically reduced civil liberties and crushed any opposition.

Why, then, do these firms work for other governments? Perhaps even those that are unpopular? Says Burson-Marsteller's Carl Levin: "I do not think it is overreaching to state that in helping friendly foreign clients we also advance our national interests. And we help in ways that our government cannot." A case in point is China, which has ramped up its public relations and lobbying efforts in recent years to counter criticisms (and fears) in the United States about its growing economic and military power. It hired the Patton Boggs firm, for example, to lobby on a wide range of issues before Congress, including trade tariffs, intellectual property, currency exchange rates, and Taiwan. Public relations firms were also retained to fend off congressional criticism in 2005 when China made a bid for Unocal, a small U.S. oil company. No amount of public relations, however, was able to stem public and congressional concern bordering on xenophobia that a "foreign company" was buying a "strategic resource." China withdrew its offer.

In another situation, Qorvis Communications has represented Saudi Arabia since 9/11 and earned about $13 million for its efforts in a recent 12-month period. The account, however, has not been without controversy. Several senior officers of Qorvis resigned, according to newspaper reports, because they were uncomfortable working on the Saudi account. Also, in 2005, the FBI raided the offices of Qorvis as part of an investigation to determine if the agency had met the requirements of the Foreign Agents Registration Act (FARA).

The following is a representative sample of contracts signed by American public relations firms to work on behalf of foreign clients, as reported in *O'Dwyer's Public Relations Newsletter*:

The Glover Park Group: $600,000 contract with the government of Turkey to devise an overall communications and media strategy aimed at the American public. The firm, according to *O'Dwyer's*, also "will advise the Turks on their relationship with the White House and Congress.

GoodWorks International: $180,000 contract with the government of Rwanda to promote U.S. investment in the country. According to the contract, the firm will "focus greater public attention on the tremendous improvements on the economic, political, and social aspects since 1994, when the genocide unfolded."

Fleishman-Hillard and its sister firm, DDB Advertising: $40 million contract with the Egyptian Tourist Agency to promote tourism and U.S. investment.

Fahmy Hudome International: $750,000 contract with the government of Libya to help develop long-term, U.S.-Libyan relations.

Ketchum: multimillion dollar contract with the Russian government to improve the country's image. According to the *Financial Times*, Ketchum will advise the Kremlin on communications with Western media during the 2006–2007 Kremlin presidency of the Group of Eight leading nations (G8).

A&R Partners: $250,000 contrtact with the Australian Tourism Commission to promote travel to the country.

Hill & Knowlton: $3.8 million contract with the U.S. State Department for work in Afghanistan to persuade farmers not to grow poppies; it's estimated that 85 percent of the world's heroin comes from Afghan poppies.

The Rise of NGOs

Hundreds of nongovernmental organizations (NGOs) depend on international support for their programs and causes. Such organizations as Greenpeace, Amnesty International, Doctors Without Borders, Oxfam, and a large number of groups opposed to globalization have been effective in getting their messages out via the World Wide Web, e-mail, and demonstrations.

One study by StrategyOne, the research arm of Edelman Worldwide, showed that media coverage of such organizations more than doubled over a four-year period, and NGOs were perceived by the public to be more credible than the news media or corporations when it came to issues such as labor, health, and the environment. Thought leaders, for example, trust NGOs more than government or corporations because they consider the NGOs' motivation to be based on "morals" rather than "profit." Public Affairs Council president Doug Pinkham said the StrategyOne report should be taken as a "wake-up call" by large corporations that have failed to embrace greater social responsibility and transparency. Pinkham told *PRWeek*, "The next five to ten years will be challenging for companies that operate on a world stage with the rise of technologically enabled activism."

Indeed, there is increasing evidence that giant corporations are adopting a more accommodative stance (see Chapter 2) cooperating with activist NGOs to form more socially responsible policies. Citigroup, for example, adopted new policies to reduce habitat loss and climate change after the Rainforest Action Network (RAN) urged customers to cut up their Citicards and plastered the Internet with nasty jibes against named executives.

Public Relations Development in Other Nations

Public relations as an occupation and a career has achieved its highest development in the industrialized nations of the world—the United States, Canada, western Europe, and parts of Asia. It emerges more readily in nations that have multiparty political systems, considerable private ownership of business and industry, large-scale urbanization, and relatively high per capita income levels, which also impacts literacy and educational opportunities.

China has experienced explosive growth in public relations as it has become industrialized and embraced a relatively free-market economy. As discussed in Chapter 1, public relations activity in China has grown tremendously in the past decade. Public relations revenues for the past several years have experienced double-digit gains, and China is now the second largest market in Asia after Japan.

The United States and other European nations began exporting their public relations expertise to the People's Republic of China during the mid-1980s. Hill & Knowlton, active in Asia for more than 30 years, began its Beijing operation in a hotel room with three U.S. professionals and a locally hired employee. Today, almost every global public relations firm has a Beijing office to represent U.S. and European companies in the Chinese market.

In addition, global public relations firms and advertising agencies are now buying stakes in successful Chinese firms. Omnicom Group of New York, for example, bought a majority stake in Unisono Fieldmarketing, which has 2,000 full- and part-time employees. The French advertising holding company, Publicis Groupe, purchased an 80 percent stake in the Shanghai-based Betterway Marketing Solutions. Geoffrey Fowler, a reporter for the *Wall Street Journal*, wrote, "Newly acquired Chinese agencies are likely to help the multinationals as they push beyond China's wealthy coastal cities into its interior, increasingly an important commercial battlefield. China has more than 100 cities with a population exceeding one million."

Indeed, homegrown Chinese firms in advertising, public relations, and marketing have developed to the point that they have lured business away from the large international firms. The Chinese firms offer low cost and wide reach. In the public relations area, Chinese firms have advanced beyond product publicity and now offer services in analysis, government, community relations, and even sports marketing. Other nations and regions, to varying degrees, also have developed larger and more sophisticated public relations industries within the past decade. Here are some thumbnail sketches from around the globe:

> *Thailand.* This nation has a great deal of foreign investment and is becoming an assembly center for automobiles. It's the primary hub in Southeast Asia for international tourism, and a number of public relations firms, advertising firms, and corporations have well-qualified staffs to handle media relations, product publicity, and special event promotion. However, Thailand lacks a cohesive national organization of public relations practitioners to promote professional development. More recently, the country has suffered image problems abroad as the result of a military coup in late 2006. The deposed prime minister, Thaksin Shinawatra, isn't giving up without a fight. He hired Edelman's New York office to help arrange meetings with the international news media to present his point of view.

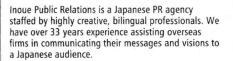
> *Japan.* Business and industry are still at the stage of perceiving public relations as primarily media relations. Public relations firms and corporate communications departments work very closely with the more than 400-plus reporters' clubs that filter and process all information for more than 150 newsgathering organizations. See above for an ad by a Japanese public relations firm.

> *Australia, Singapore, and Hong Kong.* These are relatively mature public relations markets, offering a variety of services ranging from financial relations to media

relations and special event promotion. More attention is given to overall strategic planning and integrating communications for overall corporate objectives. A major growth area in Singapore is in the hospitality and service industry as the island nation adds new resorts and casinos.

> *Mexico.* Traditionally, small public relations firms dominated the market and provided primarily product publicity. With the North American Free Trade Agreement, international firms have established operations with more sophisticated approaches to strategic communications.

> *India.* The Indian market, with more than 1 billion people, is a major market for products, services, and public relations expertise. There arc at least 1,000 large and small public relations firms serving the subcontinent, but training and educating qualified practitioners continues to be a major problem.

> *Brazil.* With the largest economy in South America, Brazil has about 1,000 public relations firms, primarily in the São Paulo area. To date, few global public relations firms have established a presence, primarily because Brazilian corporations still spend a disproportionate amount of their budgets on advertising campaigns. Issues management, public affairs, internal communications, and marketing communications remain somewhat undeveloped fields.

> *Russian Federation and the Former Soviet Republics.* The rise of a market economy and private enterprise has spurred the development of public relations activity, but the continuing stagnation of the Russian economy has stunted its development. The press and journalists are still very dependent on supplemental income, and news articles can be "bought" without much effort (see the Ethics box on page 360). In a more recent development, Russia's giant oil and energy company Gazprom signed a multimillion dollar contract with a consortium of several global public relations firms (including Moscow-based PBN) to improve the image of the state-controlled gas monopoly after it was badly dented by "gas wars" with the former Soviet Republics. Earlier, a group of PR firms led by U.S.-based Ketchum worked to improve the image of President Vladimir Putin when he assumed the presidency of the G8, an association of world's major economic powers.

> *Middle East.* The Middle East comprises 22 nations and more than 300 million people. In general, the public relations industry is relatively immature and unstructured, and lacks trained personnel. There is government-censored media and fear of transparent communications. Dubai, which is in the United Arab Emirates, in recent years has positioned itself as a major business center and has attracted many international companies. Consequently, it's expected that public relations services will expand in Dubai.

> *Africa.* South Africa is a relatively mature market with a long tradition of public relations education, professional development for practitioners, and large corporations with international outreach. Nigeria, the most populous nation in Africa, has made some strides in developing its public relations industry.

Opportunities in International Work

The 1990s, according to many experts, represented a new golden age of global marketing and public relations. The opening of the European market, coupled with economic and social reforms in the former Soviet Union hastened the reality of a global economy.

Got a News Release? Please Include Cash

Paying a reporter or an editor to publish or broadcast a news release has long been a common practice in many parts of the world, especially in emerging nations where salaries are low. In Russia, the practice of paying for placement is called *zakazukhi* ("bought articles"), and the International Public Relations Association (IPRA) has announced the formation of an international committee to eliminate the practice. According to IPRA president Alasdair Sutherland, "The credibility of any publication can only be based on its independent objectivity. As long as the practice of illicit paid-for-editorial continues in any marketplace, the local public can never have confidence in what they read."

The issue of *zakazukhi* in Russia was brought into the open when Promaco, a public relations firm in Moscow, issued a fictitious news release to see how much various publi-

cations would charge to publish it as a news item. According to the *Economist,* "Of the 21 publications tested, one published the news release for free (but without checking its accuracy). Four asked for more information, and did not run stories. Three said they would run the article as an advertisement. But 13 papers and magazines offered to run it as an article, for fees ranging from around $135 at *Tribuna,* a paper backed by Gazprom, the national gas company, to more than $2,000 in the official government newspaper, *Rossiskaya Gazeta.*"

Sutherland, who is an executive at Manning Selvage & Lee public relations, said, "IPRA has long been aware of this unethical practice in a number of marketplaces around the world, especially in some where the concept of a free press is comparatively 'new.' ... We urge both Russian and international public relations clients not to support

this illegal practice in the future. According to our code, no IPRA member is permitted to use such methods."

Russian editors were less than embarrassed. According to the *Economist,* "The editor of *Noviye Izvestiya* said it made no difference to readers whether articles were paid or not." Another editor suggested that public relations firms were really to blame. When the newspaper wants to run the news release as an advertisement, the public relations firms just take their business elsewhere.

What do you think? If you were doing public relations for an American or European firm in Moscow, would you go along with the local custom of *zakazukhi*? Or would you refuse to pay the media for using your news release? How about the common practice in China of giving reporters "transportation" money for attending a news conference?

All of these developments led Jerry Dalton, past president of the PRSA, to say: "I think more and more American firms are going to become part of those overseas markets, and I expect a lot of Americans in public relations will be living overseas." Indeed, Dalton believes that the fastest-growing career field for practitioners is international public relations. He adds: "Students who can communicate well and are fluent in a foreign language may be able to write their own ticket." But the coming of the "global village," as Marshall McLuhan once described it, still means that there will be a multiplicity of languages, customs, and values that public relations professionals will have to understand. (The Insights box on page 361 gives tips for American citizens traveling abroad.)

Gavin Anderson, chairman of Gavin Anderson & Company, a pioneer in international public relations penned the following observations some years ago—but the message is still relevant today:

Practitioners of either global or international public relations are cultural interpreters. They must understand the business and general culture of both their clients (or employers) and the country or countries in which they hope to do business. Whether

── ON THE JOB >> ─────────

Giving the "Ugly American" a Makeover

Insights

Business for Diplomatic Action Inc., a nonprofit organization, works with U.S. companies to improve the reputation of the United States around the world. To that end, it has compiled guidelines on how business travelers (as well as tourists) should behave abroad. Here are some tips from its brochure, "World Citizens Guide":

Read a map. "Familiarize yourself with the local geography to avoid making insulting mistakes." Knowledge of current events and public issues are a real plus.

Dress up. "In some countries, casual dress is a sign of disrespect."

Talk small. "Talking about wealth, power, or status—corporate or personal—can create resentment." Bragging about how great America is, is a real turnoff.

No slang. "Even casual profanity is unacceptable."

Slow down. "We talk fast, eat fast, move fast, live fast. Many cultures do not."

Listen as much as you talk. "Ask people you're visiting about themselves and their way of life."

Speak lower and slower. "A loud voice is often perceived as bragging."

Exercise religious restraint. "In many countries, religion is 'not a subject for discussion.'"

Exercise political restraint. "Steer clear. . . if someone is attacking U.S. politicians or policies. Agree to disagree."

Learn some words. Learning some simple phrases in the host country's language is most appreciated.

Source: McCarney, Scott. "Teaching Americans How to Behave Abroad." *Wall Street Journal*, April 11, 2006.

---

as an outside or in-house consultant, the first task is to tell a U.S. company going abroad (or a foreign party coming to the United States) how to get things done. How does the market work? What are the business habits? What is the infrastructure? The consultant also needs to understand how things work in the host country, to recognize what will need translation and adaptation. . . .

The field needs practitioners with an interest in and knowledge of foreign cultures on top of top-notch public relations skills. They need a good sense of working environments, and while they may not have answers for every country, they should know what questions to ask and where to get the information needed. They need to know where the potential dangers are, so as to not replenish the business bloopers book.

The decision to seek a career in international public relations should be made during the early academic years, so that a student can take multiple courses in international relations, global marketing techniques, the basics of strategic public relations planning, foreign languages, social and economic geography, and cross-cultural communication. Graduate study is an asset. Students should also study abroad for a semester or serve an internship with a company or organization in another nation as a desirable starting point. Students may also apply for the Fulbright Progam that funds travel and study abroad. Another opportunity is a student foreign study scholarship offered by Rotary International.

A note of caution. American students should not assume they have an "inside" advantage working for an Amercian-based global corporation. Increasingly, global

There are a number of employment opportunities in international public relations. Here, Hong Kong–based Cathay Pacific seeks a communications manager for North America.

CATHAY PACIFIC

COMMUNICATIONS MANAGER, AMERICAS

Cathay Pacific Airways, Asia's premier international airline, is now seeking candidates to fill the position based in Los Angeles.

Responsibilities:
- Effectively communicate and generate goodwill with key organizations to positively affect their behavior, especially toward purchasing our company's products and services.
- Maintain and develop key media relationships. Coordinate interviews between influential media contacts and company's key personnel.
- Act as the company's spokesperson. Create and distribute press releases.
- Increase visibility of our company in N. America through special events and activities.
- Maintain good internal staff communications. Handle crisis communications effectively.
- Effectively keep our company's name in front of key publics through innovative and concentrated community support opportunities.
- Support the company's N. America Marketing & Sales initiatives.

Requirements:
- Minimum 5 years experience in Public Relations with important projects involved.
- Ability to communicate effectively at all levels with superior oral and written skills.
- College degree with strong PC knowledge.
- Superior independent work capability.
- Excellent decision-making, problem-solving, time management and organization skills. Must be detailed oriented.

We offer a unique package of benefits including attractive salary plus profit sharing; company sponsored insurance, travel benefits, pension & 401k option.

Forward resume immed to Personnel & Administration Manager via Fax 1-310-615-0042 or email: usa#personnel@cathaypacific.com.

---

corporations are looking at a worldwide pool of young talent—and Europeans are often excellent candidates because they know several languages and are more accustomed to intercultual communications. Hewlett-Packard is one example; it prefers to hire European- or American-trained Russians for its corporate communications efforts in Moscow and the Russian Federation.

Taking the U.S. Foreign Service Officers' examination is the first requirement for international government careers. Foreign service work with the innumerable federal agencies often requires a substantial period of government, mass media, or public relations service in the United States before foreign assignments are made, however.

Summary

What Is Global Public Relations?

Public relations now takes place on a global scale, with relationships being built with the publics of all nations. Although some elements of public relations were being practiced in Europe over a hundred years ago, American techniques are those most commonly adapted for use throughout the world.

International Corporate Public Relations

In the new age of global marketing, public relations firms represent foreign interests in the United States as well as the interests of American corporations around the world.

This means that the practitioner must deal with issues of language and cultural differences, including subtle differences in customs and etiquette and even ethical dilemmas involving bribery.

International Government Public Relations

Most governments seek to influence the international policies of other countries as well as the opinions and actions of their publics. These communications can range from promoting tourism to attempts to influence trade policies. The U.S. government refers to its international information effort as "public diplomacy," the attempt to enhance understanding of our culture and promote our foreign policy objectives. The Voice of America radio broadcasts are part of this program. There are also U.S. public relations firms working for foreign governments, helping them advance their political objectives and commercial interests, counseling them on probable U.S. reactions to their proposed actions, and assisting in communications in English.

The Rise of NGOs

Among the nongovernmental organizations depending on international support for their causes are Greenpeace, Amnesty International, Doctors Without Borders, Oxfam, and the International Red Cross. Such organizations are widely believed to be more credible by the news media and the public on such issues as labor, health, and the envi-

ronment, partly because they are perceived to lack the self-interest ascribed to governments and corporations.

Public Relations in Other Nations

Public relations is a well-developed industry in many nations around the world. China, in particular, has a rapidly expanding industry that is getting more sophisticated every year.

Opportunities in International Work

As global marketing and communications have expanded in recent years, so too have opportunities for international public relations work. Fluency in foreign language is a valued skill but not a prerequisite; also important are backgrounds in international relations, global marketing techniques, social and economic geography, and cross-cultural communication.

CASE ACTIVITY >>
What Would You Do?

Turkey has a problem. The country was on track to becoming the fastest-growing destination for Americans prior to 9/11. That projection was derailed by the terrorist attacks and the subsequent invasions of Afghanistan and Iraq, which caused many Americans to think twice about visiting a Muslim nation—even if it had a secular government and a strong European orientation.

Yet, Turkey remains a virtual treasure-house of art, culture, and cuisine that would appeal to seasoned travelers looking for a new experience and destination. To this end, the Turkish Culture and Tourism Office has retained your public relations firm to conduct a media relations program in the American press (and to some extent the European media) to increase awareness of Turkey as a desirable tourist destination.

Research and interviews with Turkish tourism authorities indicate that segmentation of various audiences

would be more fruitful than a general campaign. Travelers interested in food and wine, for example, might be reached by articles about the cuisine of Turkey. Music lovers might be interested in the new jazz sounds coming from Turkish musicians, and even shoppers looking for vintage jewelry and exotic products such as carpets in the famous bazaars of Instanbul would be a good, specialized public. Then, of course, there are the history buffs who would be interested in visiting the sites of ancient civilizations.

Now that you know the possible interests of several target audiences, develop a public relations plan that will use appropriate media and events for these various audiences. Your plan should outline possible feature stories for print and broadcast media, as well as the venues for special events.

Questions for Review and Discussion

1. What is meant by international public relations? What are some of the reasons for its growth in recent decades?
2. How does public relations fit into the mix of global marketing operations?
3. What are some of the difficulties that a corporation is likely to encounter when it conducts business in another country?
4. What objectives do foreign nations seek to accomplish by hiring U.S. public relations firms to represent them in America?

5. International surveys indicate that citizens of other nations have low approval ratings of the United States and its policies. What "public diplomacy" efforts could the United States undertake to change these negative perceptions?

6. The U.S. government conducted an extensive program of "public diplomacy" as part of the War on Terrorism. Do you think it was effective? Why or why not? What suggestions do you have for U.S. public diplomacy efforts?

7. What is the Russian practice of *zakazukhi*? Why does the IPRA consider it a bad practice?

8. Why is Israel worried about its image in the United States and other nations?

9. International public relations requires knowledge of a nation's history and political sensitivities. It also requires a knowledge of proper manners and cultural sensitivity. What advice is given for business executives who travel abroad?

10. What kinds of ethical dilemmas do public relations firms face when they are asked to do work for a particular nation?

11. What does the abbreviation *NGO* mean? How has new information technology enabled NGOs to expand their influence?

12. What opportunities exist for someone who wants to specialize in international public relations as a career?

Suggested Readings

"Anti-Americanism: The View from Abroad." *Economist*, February 19, 2005, 24–25.

Badler, Dick. "10 Rules for Building a Successful Global Corporate Communications Organization." *The Strategist*, Winter 2004, 18–21.

Drobis, David R. "The New Global Imperative for Public Relations." *O'Dwyer's PR Services Report*, January 2002, 8, 26–28.

Freitag, Alan R. "Ascending Cultural Competence Potential: An Assessment and Profile of U.S. Public Relations Practitioners' Preparation for International Assignments." *Journal of Public Relations Research* 14, no. 3 (2002): 207–227.

"Global Special 2006." *PRWeek*, June 26, 2006, 16–22.

Gorney, Carole. "China's Economic Boom Brings a PR Explosion." *The Strategist*, Spring 2005, 35–38.

Kelly, William, Tomoko, Masumoto, and Dirk Gibson. "Kisha Kurabu and Koho: Japanese Media Relations and Public Relations." *Public Relations Review* 28, no. 3 (2002): 265–281.

Knowlton, Brian. "Global Image of the U.S. Is Worensing, Survey Finds." *New York Times*, June 14, 2006, A14.

Lee, Suman. "An Analysis of Other Countries International Public Relations in the U.S." *Public Relations Review* 32, no. 2, (2006): 97–103.

Mateas, Margo M. "Spotlight on Diversity: Managing Diversity in Virtual Teams across the Globe." *Public Relations Tactics* 11, no. 8 (2004): 20.

Paluszek, John. "How Do We Fit Into The World?" *The Strategist*, Winter 2004, 6–11.

Rieff, David. "Their Hearts and Minds? Why the Ideological Battle Against Islamists Is Nothing Like the Struggle Against Communism." *New York Times Magazine*, September 4, 2005, 11–12.

Stateman, Alison. "Diplomatic Link: The Private Sector's Role in U.S. Public Diplomacy." *The Strrategist*, Spring 2005, 40–42.

Wang, Jian. "Managing National Reputation and International Relations in the Global Era: Public Diplomacy Revisited." *Public Relations Review* 32, no. 2 (2006): 91–96.

Ward, David. "Rehearsing for the PR World Tour." *PRWeek*, January 31, 2005, 24.

Wei, Ran, and Jing Jiang. "Exploring Culture's Influence on Standardization Dynamics of Creative Strategy and Execution in International Advertising." *Journalism & Mass Communications Quarterly* 82, no. 4 (2005): 838–856.

Zhang, Juyan, and William L. Benoit. "Message Strategies of Saudi Arabia's Image Restoration Campaign after 9/11." *Public Relations Review* 30, no. 2 (2004): 161–167.

Chapter Twelve

Business, Sports, Tourism, and Entertainment

> ## Marketing Communications
> *Product Publicity*
> *Cause-Related Marketing*
> *Corporate Sponsorships*

> ## Environmental Relations

> ## Corporate Philanthropy

> ## The Entertainment Industry

> ## The Practitioner's Responsibility
> *Damage Control*
> *Ethical Problems for Publicists*

> ## Conducting a Personality Campaign
> *Interview the Client*
> *Prepare a Biography of the Client*
> *Plan a Marketing Strategy*
> *Conduct the Campaign*
> *Record the Results*

> ## Promoting an Entertainment Event
> *Publicity to Stimulate Ticket Sales*
> *The "Drip-Drip-Drip" Technique*
> *A Look at the Movie Industry*

> ## Sports Publicity

> ## Travel Promotion
> *Phases of Travel Promotion*
> *Appeals to Target Audiences*
> *Times of Crisis*

Public relations in the for-profit realm is generally thought of as corporate work. Certainly a large percentage of public relations practitioners working in for-profit organizations work for corporations. But there are other substantial for-profit segments of the public relations industry. You have been familiarized thus far with the public relations role, process, and tactics. In this chapter, we delve more deeply into some of the day-to-day issues that public relations practitioners face. In addition to examining the role of public relations in the corporation, we look at the specialties of entertainment, sports, and tourism public relations. Increasingly, public relations students express interest in sports, entertainment, and hospitality public relations. With a proliferation of major and minor league ball clubs, university teams that rival for-profit clubs in terms of personnel, a growing cult of celebrity, and a strong convention and tourism sector, these opportunities are available to persistent new graduates.

Today's Modern Corporation

Today, giant corporations have operations and customers around the world. International conglomerates control subsidiary companies that often produce a grab bag of seemingly unrelated products under the same corporate banner. These companies deal with a number of governments at many levels. Their operations affect the environment, control the employment of thousands, and have an impact on the financial and social well-being of millions.

The large size of these corporations, however, also distances them from stakeholders. A corporation has a "face" in terms of its products, logo, and brand being readily visible in advertising and billboards from Azerbaijan to Zimbabwe and all the nations in between. However, the average consumer really can't really comprehend organizations such as Wal-Mart, the world's largest retailer, with $348 billion in worldwide sales, or Exxon Mobil, with $335 billion in global sales. These figures boggle the mind, and they represent more than the combined gross national product (GNP) of many nations.

The public is distrustful of the power, influence, and credibility of such giant corporations and business in general. When U.S. gasoline prices rise rapidly, for example, suspicion spreads that the oil companies have conspired to gouge the public, a distrust that the oil companies never fully allay. Major corporate financial scandals and the misdeeds of corporate executives also take their toll.

For example, fewer than 3 in 10 Americans (27 percent) feel that most large U.S. corporations are trustworthy, according to a recent Roper survey. And a Gallup poll reveals that business leaders and stockbrokers have joined used car dealers in the category of "least trusted" individuals in American society. Gallup polls also indicate that 82 percent of the public believes that the top executives of larger corporations receive outrageous salaries in the millions of dollars and, at the same time, improperly use corporate funds to fund lavish lifestyles.

Public perceptions of greed and corporate misdeeds are reinforced by stories in the media. Hundreds of stories were written about celebrity CEO Martha Stewart's indictment, trial, and conviction for lying to federal investigators about a stock sale, and other executives from such corporations as Enron, WorldCom, Adelphia, and Tyco were also in the news for falsifying financial records or raiding the corporate treasury.

The Role of Public Relations

The extensive negative publicity about corporations and business in general over the past several years has made it imperative that companies make a special effort to regain their credibility and public trust. Thus, the concept of corporate social responsibility (CSR) is now high on the priority list of executives and their public relations staffs who are charged with improving the reputation and citizenship of their employers.

Indeed, the public relations profession has taken steps to outline a plan of action for rebuilding public trust in business. A coalition of 19 U.S.-based organizations—including the Council of Public Relations Firms, the International Association of Business Communicators, and the National Investor Relations Institute—published a white paper in 2003 titled *Restoring Trust in Business: Models for Action*.

"These are people who deal with trust issues all the time," says James Murphy, global managing director of communications for Accenture, and chair of the coalition. "Therefore, we're in a good position to address them." The 10-page white paper asked American businesses and their leaders to act in three main areas: (1) adopt ethical principles, (2) pursue transparency and disclosure, and (3) make trust a fundamental precept of corporate governance. Copies of the report were sent to Fortune 500 CEOs and to the 50,000 public relations professionals represented by member groups in the coalition.

The importance of public relations in CSR is explained by Jack Bergen, senior vice president of marketing and communications for Siemens Corporation. He told

PRWeek, "We are the eyes and ears of an organization. The best way to be socially responsible is to have your eyes and ears trained on all the stakeholders, to know what they want and need from the company. These are classic public affairs issues and the idea that they should be handled by anyone else would show a lack of understanding."

A number of strategies and tactics can be used to implement CSR, which involves corporate performance as well as effective communications. One of the more important ones is the role of the public relations executive in counseling the CEO. The public relations executive serves as a link between the chief executive and the realities of the marketplace and the organization, according to Mark Schumann, global communications practice leader with Towers Perrin. He told an international IABC conference that CEOs are often "disconnected" and surrounded by other executives who simply agree with whatever the CEO says. Schumann told *PRWeek*, "everyone sucks up and lies to them." Schumann believes corporate public relations professionals should be "playwright[s] and director[s], but we also need to be the toughest critics" to ensure that CEOs come across as concerned and involved with employees and customers.

Corporations seek a better reputation for a variety of reasons. First, responsible business practices ward off increased government regulation. As a result of major financial scandals such as the implosion of Enron, the U.S. Congress passed new laws regarding accounting practices and disclosure (see discussion of the Sarbanes-Oxley Act in Chapter 7). Second, there is the matter of employee morale; companies with good policies and good reputations tend to have less employee turnover. Corporate reputation also affects the bottom line. A survey of executives by the Center for Corporate Citizenship with the Hitachi Foundation, for example, found that 82 percent of the respondents believe that good corporate citizenship contributes to meeting an organization's financial objectives. In addition, 53 percent say corporate citizenship is important to their customers.

Being a good corporate citizen is an admirable goal, but corporations also face a number of pressures and counterpressures when making decisions and forming policies. General Electric once outlined four key factors that have to be considered at all times when making a decision:

1. *Political.* How do government regulations and other pressures affect the decision?
2. *Technological.* Do we have the engineering knowledge to accomplish the goal?
3. *Social.* What is our responsibility to society?
4. *Economic.* Will we make a profit?

The following sections discuss various facets of today's modern corporation and kinds of activities that require the expertise and counsel of public relations professionals.

Media Relations

Reporting by the media is a major source of public information and perceptions about the business world and individual companies. In recent years, the news hasn't been all that favorable.

Major financial scandals such as Enron, WorldCom, HealthSouth, and Tyco haven't helped the overall reputation of business, nor has the extensive coverage of criminal trials for CEOs such as Martha Stewart. Negative coverage can cause a corporation's reputation to plummet. Wal-Mart, once ranked number one in corporate reputation, saw its position drop to seventh in the space of six months after coverage regarding the hiring of illegal immigrants and the filing of a class-action suit that claimed the company discriminated against female employees.

As a result, corporate executives are somewhat defensive about how journalists cover business, because they feel that too much emphasis has been given to corporate misdeeds. One survey, by Jericho Communications, found that almost half of the respondents agreed with the statement that a "CEO must view the media as an enemy." Another 60 percent said an executive can best avoid controversy by "limiting exposure to the media" and through "secrecy and tighter control of information."

Many corporate executives take this approach because they have several ongoing complaints about media coverage. These include inaccuracy, incomplete coverage, inadequate research and preparation for interviews, and antibusiness bias. One survey by the American Press Institute, for example, found about a third of the CEOs polled were dissatisfied with the business news they found in their local newspapers.

In response, business editors and reporters state that often they cannot publish or broadcast thorough, evenhanded stories about business because many company executives, uncooperative and wary, erect barriers against them. Writers complain about their inability to obtain direct access to decision-making executives and being restricted to using news releases that don't contain the information they need. Journalists assert, too, that some business leaders don't understand the concept of objectivity and assume that any story involving unfavorable news about their company is intentionally bad.

Journalists also say it's a major mistake for corporate executives to slash public relations and communications during times of financial scandal and economic downturn. A survey of journalists conducted by Middleberg Euro RSCG, a public relations firm, and the Columbia University Graduate School of Journalism, found that journalists also believe corporations should focus on delivering more fact-driven messages. Don Middleberg, director of the survey, told PRWeek, "You [executives] should communicate factually, frequently, and consistently. Use this time wisely, say the journalists, to position yourself."

Public relations practitioners serving businesses stand in the middle. They must interpret their companies and clients to the media, while showing their chief executives and other high officials how open, friendly media relations can serve their interests. One major interest that executives have is corporate reputation, and this is often tarnished or enhanced by the type of media coverage that an organization receives.

Savvy public relations professionals understand that business reporters often don't have adequate business preparation. Therefore, public relations practitioners spend a great deal of time and energy providing background and briefing reporters on the business operations of their clients and employers. It's one way of ensuring that coverage will be more accurate and thorough.

One survey by Hill & Knowlton found that Canadian CEOs believe that print and broadcast media criticism is the biggest threat to their company's reputation; even ahead of such things as disasters and allegations by the government about employee or product safety. At the same time, surveys show that the media is probably the most effective way for an organization to get its message across and to achieve business goals. A PRWeek survey of CEOs, for example, found that more than 80 percent of the respondents said conducting media interviews was the most effective way for the company to spread its message, followed by attending or speaking at industry conferences and trade shows. In third place was meeting with key industry and financial analysts; fourth place was "authoring op-eds, bylined articles, or letters-to-the-editor."

Customer Relations

The day when a business could operate successfully on the Latin precept of *caveat emptor*—"let the buyer beware"—is long gone. In today's society, sellers are expected to deliver goods and services of safe, acceptable quality on honest terms. Consumers' rights are protected by the federal government, and federal and state agencies enforce those rights. The Federal Trade Commission (FTC) regulates truth in advertising, the National Highway Traffic Safety Administration sets standards for automakers, and the Consumer Product Safety Commission examines the safety of other manufactured goods.

Customer service, in many respects, is the front line of public relations. A single incident, or a series of incidents, can severely damage a company's reputation and erode public trust in its products and services. Customer satisfaction is important because of word of mouth. A person who has a bad experience, surveys indicate, shares his or her story with an average of 17 people, whereas a person with a good experience tells an average of 11 people.

The rapid growth of the Internet and blogs, however, has considerably changed the math. Today, a dissatisfied customer is capable of informing thousands, or even millions, of people in just one posting. One somewhat embarrassing example happened to Comcast: A customer videotaped a Comcast repairman sound asleep on the customer's couch and posted it on www.snakesonablog.com. The clip was then picked up by a technology blog and then was also shown on an MSNBC program. In no time flat, about 200,000 people saw the video and Comcast was embarrassed enough to immediately send a team of technicians to the customer's home to fix the problem. The incident, however, reached an even greater audience when a story about the video in the *New York Times* noted that the repairman had fallen asleep while he tried to get through to the cable company's repair office on the phone.

Further illustrating this problem, *Pittsburgh Post-Gazette* reporter Teresa Lindeman wrote:

> [C]ompanies that consider ignoring tales of dissatisfied customers might want to take a look at a study released. . . by the Wharton School of the University of Pennsylvania.
>
> "Researchers there found that more than 50 percent of Americans said they wouldn't go to a store if a friend had a bad shopping experience there. Even worse, when someone has a problem, it gets embellished with every retelling, and pretty soon that store has a really, really big problem.

Traditionally, customer service has been separate from the communications or public relations function in a company. Bob Seltzer, a leader in Ruder Finn's marketing practice, told *PRWeek*, "I defy anyone to explain the wisdom of this. How a company talks to its customers is among, if not the, most critical communications it has." Rande Swann, director of public relations for the Regional Airport Authority of Louisville, Kentucky, agrees. He says, "Our reputation is probably based more on how we serve our customers than any other single thing. If we don't have a reputation for great service, we don't have travelers."

Increasingly, however, corporations are realizing that customer relations serves as a telltale public relations barometer. Many public relations departments now regularly monitor customer feedback in a variety of ways to determine what policies and communications strategies need to be revised. One common method is to monitor customer queries to the organization's Web site. Indeed, most companies have a "Contact Us" link on their Web sites. Another method is the content analysis of phone calls to a company's customer service center.

Small companies can easily monitor the nature of customer comments and also respond in a timely manner. It gets more difficult, however, for a large company. Ford Motor Company, for example, receives about 7,500 phone calls to its national customer service center every day.

It is important for public relations professionals to be involved in active listening to customer feedback so they can strategize the steps companies should take to ensure their good reputations. As Andy Hopson, CEO of Burson-Marsteller's northeast region, told *PRWeek*, "Ignoring complaints can ultimately damage a company's reputation."

Public relations professionals also pay attention to consumer surveys. In particular, the American Customer Satisfaction Index is the definitive benchmark of how buyers feel about business practices. The index, which has been tracking customer satisfaction for 200 companies in 40 industries for over a decade, has found that offering the lowest prices may not necessarily get a company the highest satisfaction rating. Wal-Mart, for example, only scores 75 out of 100 points, compared with the national average of 74.4 for all companies.

Reaching Diverse Markets

The United States is becoming more diverse every year, a fact that is now being recognized by corporate marketing and communications departments. Reaching such diverse audiences was covered in Chapter 8, but it's worthwhile to summarize some key aspects.

According to the U.S. Census Bureau, the U.S. population by 2010 will be 12.5 percent African American; 14.6 percent Hispanic; and 4 percent Asian and Pacific Islander. As these groups continue to expand and become more affluent, they will constitute a larger share of the consumer marketplace. In 2007, for example, it was estimated that buying power among Hispanics would increase 315 percent. The increase among Asians was estimated to be 287 percent, and among African Americans 170 percent.

According to Gina Amaro, director of multicultural and international markets for *PR Newswire*, "Companies that focus solely on one audience when creating products are missing an enormous opportunity. Furthermore, companies that do not incorporate a multicultural marketing and PR campaign to communicate these products and services to their many niche audiences will miss even larger opportunities."

Many public relations firms have set up specialty practices for multicultural marketing and communications. Edelman Worldwide, for example, has a diversity practice that assists companies. One client, Unilever, hired Edelman to organize a Hispanic marketing communications campaign for six of its personal care products, including Dove Soap.

Companies also have set up departments to reach minority audiences. Wells Fargo Bank, for example, organized an Emerging Markets division to help increase home ownership among minority families. Part of this initiative is a Hispanic Customer Service Center in Las Cruces, New Mexico, which provides specialized services to Spanish-speaking homebuyers in 16 states. In addition to translating brochures and other information into Spanish, bilingual customer service representatives are available to answer e-mail and telephone inquiries.

Yahoo! also has recognized the potential of the Hispanic market. It began Yahoo! en Español and quickly merged with Telemundo to create Yahoo! Telemundo. The merger recognizes online trends. According to Nielsen/NetRatings, the number of Hispanics who went online increased by 11 percent between April 2005 and April 2006. Special features, such as music, television, news, and various promotions, are designed exclusively for this audience. Gina Amaro of *PR Newswire* agrees with this approach. She says that it is vitally important to build relationships with niche audiences by communicating to them in their language and culture.

Consumer Activism

Dissatisfied customers can often be mollified by prompt and courteous attention to their complaints or even an offer by a company to replace an item or provide discount coupons toward future purchases. A more serious and complex threat to corporate reputation, which can also affect sales, are consumer activists who demand changes in corporate policies.

Tyson Foods, a major American producer of meat and poultry products, was accused of inhumane treatment of animals by various animal rights groups, including People for the Ethical Treatment of Animals (PETA). The corporate response was to establish an office of animal well-being to assure retailers and consumers that Tyson takes humane animal handling seriously.

Ed Nicholson, Tyson's director of media and community relations, told *PRWeek*, "The people from PETA are not going to be satisfied unless we go out of business, but there are consumers less radical than PETA who are still concerned about animal-handling practices." The Tyson office, headed by a veterinarian, oversees audits of animal-handling practices and make those audits available to customers on request.

KFC also has been targeted by PETA and other animal rights groups, whose efforts have received extensive media publicity. The charges of inhumane animal treatment can and do affect consumer buying decisions, especially when activists stand outside franchises wearing T-shirts that say "KFC Tortures Animals." In such a situation, the public relations staff has the difficult job of defending the company against what it believes are unfounded allegations and, at the same time, to assure the public that KFC's policies do provide for the humane slaughter of its chickens.

Consequently, when it came to light that a KFC subcontractor was mistreating chickens, the company immediately called the abuse by workers appalling and told the subcontractor to clean up its act—or lose its contract. In this instance, because of the quick corporate response, the media was able to include KFC's actions in the story about the abuses, which were documented on videotape.

Coca-Cola also has had reputational problems raised by its customers. Some activist groups charged the giant bottler with contributing to childhood obesity by selling its products in schools. Karl Bjorhus, director of health and nutrition communications for Coca-Cola, told *PRWeek*, "We have been listening and trying to understand what people's concerns are."

As a result, the company partnered with the American Beverage Association and the Alliance for a Healthier Generation to voluntarily shift to lower calorie and healthier beverages in school vending machines. The change was announced in 2006 and is scheduled to be completed in the 2009–2010 school year.

In today's climate of media attention to such health-related topics as obesity, every food product company is suspect. McDonald's was the subject of a movie documentary, *Super Size Me*, in which the writer/director decided to eat three meals a day at McDonald's for one month. He details how all the "junk food" made him overweight and prone to major health problems.

In this case, McDonald's reaction was aggressive. Walt Riker, vice president of corporate communications, told *PRWeek*, "We're responding aggressively because the film is a gross misrepresentation of what McDonald's is about. The scam in the movie is that he has given the impression that he only ate three basic meals day, but the reality is that he stuffed himself with 5,000 to 7,000 calories, which is two or three times the recommended amount."

According to *PRWeek*, "McDonald's has been engaging the media in interviews and the company has made its global nutritionist, Cathy Kapica, available." Kapica appeared on CNN and CNBC, and gave a number of newspaper interviews about the film producer's "extreme behavior." The company also distributed a VNR and an ANR giving its views on smart choices in diet and exercise. It also sent briefing materials to its 2,700 franchises so they could talk to local media in an informed way.

At the strategic level, a company weighs the potential impact of the charges or allegations on potential customer reaction and possible effect on sales before deciding on a course of action. Activist consumer groups are a major challenge to the public relations staff of an organization. Do you accommodate? Do you stonewall? Do you change policy? Chapter 2 addressed issues management, but here are some general guidelines from Douglas Quenqua, which appeared in *PRWeek*, on how to be proactive.

ON THE JOB >>

Standing on Principle, or Bowing to Consumer Pressure?

Ethics

Procter & Gamble has a problem. Two influential conservative groups have called for a boycott of Crest toothpaste and Tide detergent. The boycott was called because the company posted a statement on its intranet telling employees that it opposes a proposed statute in Cincinnati, its headquarters, that would preclude protecting gays and lesbians from discrimination.

The leaders of the two groups, Focus on the Family and the American Family Association, contend that P&G is implicitly supporting same-sex marriage. "For Procter & Gamble to align itself with radical groups committed to redefining marriage in our country is an affront to its customers," says Dr. James C. Dobson, head of Focus on the Family. He has called for the boycott on his syndicated radio program, which claims to reach 9 million listeners a week.

P&G believes the two conservative Christian groups are distorting the issue by relating the issue of same-sex marriage with proposed legislation that exempts gays and lesbians from discrimination laws. However, the company has to consider what impact a boycott would have on sales. This poses an ethical dilemma. Should the company stand by its beliefs in this matter, or should it retract its opposition to the proposed statute and avoid being boycotted?

Do

> Work with groups who are more interested in solutions than getting publicity.
> Offer transparency. Activists who feel you're not open aren't likely to keep dealing with you.
> Turn their suggestions into action. Activists want results.

Don't

> Get emotional when dealing with advocacy groups.
> Agree to work with anyone making threats.
> Expect immediate results. Working with adversaries takes patience—establishing trust takes time.

Consumer Boycotts

The boycott—a refusal to buy the products or services of an offending company—has a long history and is a widely used publicity tool of the consumer movement. PETA, for example, announced that consumers should boycott Safeway until it improved conditions for farm animals. A key theater for this protest was Safeway's annual stockholders meeting at which activists would unfurl a banner saying, "Safeway means animal cruelty." It was, as *PRWeek* says, "all the makings of a PR person's worst nightmare."

Corporations face a variety of challenges today from advocacy groups quite adept at generating media coverage for their particular cause. Here, the People for the Ethical Treatment of Animals (PETA) demonstrate outside a Kentucky Fried Chicken restaurant in Hong Kong to protest what they claim is the restaurant chain's cruel treatment of chickens.

Safeway headed off a boycott by negotiating. Just days before the annual meeting, the company's public affairs staff began working with PETA and quickly announced new standards for monitoring conditions with meat suppliers. Instead of a protest, PETA supporters showed up at the annual meeting with a large "Thank You" sign for entering stockholders. In addition, PETA ended its 20-state boycott of the chain. The director of public affairs for Safeway said the boycott didn't have any effect on sales, but PETA took a different tact. Its director told *PRWeek*, "It's just a truism that you don't want your corporation targeted by activists. My hunch is the timing of the call [from Safeway public affairs] was not purely coincidental."

The success of consumer boycotts is mixed. Various activist groups have boycotted Procter & Gamble for years without much effect because the company makes so many products under a variety of brand names that consumers can't keep track of the complete P&G product line.

On the other hand, a single product name is more vulnerable. Back in 1995, Shell Oil Company decided to sink an aging oil platform in the Atlantic Ocean; environmental activists violently objected. Sales dropped by 70 percent in some European nations, prompting the company's decision to dispose of the oil platform in another way. During the 1980s, Barclays Bank continued to do business in South Africa during apartheid, but suffered a 10 percent drop in the bank's share of the student market within two years.

More recently, activists conducted a successful boycott against Triumph, a British underwear company that operated a plant in Myanmar, a country run by a military dictatorship. The activists' campaign featured a poster showing a woman wearing a barbed wire bra, with the slogan, "Support breasts, not dictators." Triumph was inundated with consumer complaints and, within eight days, closed its factory in Myanmar. "The fact that it was about bras helped," said the activist group director. "We knew it would appeal to the media."

Activists point out that a boycott doesn't have to be 100 percent effective in order to change corporate policies. Even a 5 percent drop in sales will often cause corporations to rethink their policies and modes of operation. Nike got serious about sweatshop conditions abroad only after activist groups caused its stock and sales to drop. Nike was losing market position, so it decided to formulate new policies for its subcontractors abroad and become active in a global alliance of manufacturers to monitor working conditions in overseas factories.

Employee Relations

Customers are a primary public for any profit-making organization, but so are employees. In many ways, employees are the front line of any effective public relations program. A company's reputation, for example, is often enhanced or damaged by how rank-and-file employees feel about their employer. One Internet survey of consumers by GolinHarris, for example, found that 70 percent of respondents believed that the number one criterion for good corporate citizenship was treating employees well.

Employees have been called an organization's "ambassadors" because they represent the company within a large circle of family, relatives, and friends. If morale is low or if employees feel the company is not treating them fairly, it's reflected in their comments to others. On the other hand, enthusiastic employees can do much to enhance an organization's reputation within a community as a good place to work. This, in turn, generates more job applicants and also enhances employee-retention rates.

Consequently, the public relations department, often working with the human resources department, concentrates on communicating with employees just as vigorously as it does on delivering the corporate story to the outside world. A workplace that respects its management, has pride in its products, and believes it is being treated fairly is a key factor in corporate success.

Surveys indicate, however, that the success of communication efforts varies widely among organizations. According to a survey of 1,000 U.S. workers by Towers Perrin, 20 percent believe their organizations do not tell them the truth. About half of the respondents say their companies generally tell employees the truth, and about the same percentage believe that their employers try too hard to "spin" the truth. Another finding: Almost half believe they get more reliable information from their direct supervisors than they do from senior executives.

The value of credible and trustworthy communications cannot be underestimated. Mark Schumann of Towers Perrin told *Public Relations Tactics*, "Regardless of the topic, an organization will find it difficult to motivate, engage, and retain their most talented employees if their messages are not believed."

Public relations professionals will tell organizations that effective employee relations is more than just a string of well-written and informative messages. A survey by Meta Group, for example, found that the majority of information technology (IT) companies admitted that they had an employee morale problem due to lack of job growth and curtailed budgets. At the same time, however, only about 10 percent of the companies polled saw employee communications as an answer. The top three solutions, according to *PRWeek*, were (1) employee recognition, (2) skill-development opportunities, and (3) career development. Communications ranked ninth, behind events, annual action plans, challenging work, and professional development.

Another issue is sexual harassment. This worries both employees and management for both legal and ethical reasons. The U.S. Supreme Court ruled in *Meritor Savings Bank v. Vinson* (1986) that a company may be held liable in sexual harassment suits even if management is unaware of the problem and has a general policy condemning any form of verbal or nonverbal behavior that causes employees to feel "uncomfortable" or consider the workplace a "hostile environment."

To protect themselves from liability and the unfavorable publicity of a lawsuit, organizations not only have to have a policy, they must also clearly communicate the policy to employees and conduct workshops to ensure that everyone thoroughly understands what might be considered sexual harassment. What about off-color jokes at the watercooler or via e-mail? What about a Playboy calendar in someone's cubicle? What about a coworker constantly asking you for a date? These are questions that might be answered through employee communications or workshops.

Layoffs and Outsourcing

Layoffs present a major public relations challenge to an organization. Julia Hood, editor in chief of *PRWeek*, says it best: "The way in which a company handles job reductions can have a significant impact on its reputation, its share price, and its ongoing ability to recruit and maintain good staff. And that presents a major challenge for communication departments."

Although human resource (HR) departments are most involved in layoffs, it's also a situation in which the expertise of the public relations department is harnessed to ensure employee understanding and support. One cardinal rule is that a layoff is never announced to the media before employees are informed. Another cardinal rule is that employees should be informed in person by their immediate supervisors—the traditional "pink slip" or an e-mail message is unacceptable. Employees who are being retained should also be called in by their immediate supervisors to let them know their status.

The rumor mill works overtime when there is uncertainty among employees about job security, so it's also important for the company to publicly announce the layoffs and the impact as quickly as possible. Companies should be forthright about layoffs; this is not the time to issue vague statements and "maybes" that just fuel the rumor mill.

Companies that are interested in their reputations and employee trust also make every effort to cushion the layoff by implementing various programs. Merrill Lynch, for example, laid off 6,000 employees by giving them the option of "voluntary separation" in exchange for one year's pay and a percentage of their annual bonuses. Other companies offer outplacement services, the use of office space, and other programs. Such programs do much to retain employee goodwill even as workers are being laid off.

A more contentious issue, which has become an emotional and political football in recent years, is the matter of outsourcing white-collar jobs to such nations as India. The practice is commonly called *offshoring*, and many American companies are now using lower-paid professionals in India and other Asian nations to do everything from customer service to software engineering and accounting.

The increasing practice of offshoring presents major internal communication challenges for public relations departments. How do you explain the corporate policy? How do you overcome employee suspicion that their jobs are vulnerable because a software engineer in India works for a fraction of what U.S. workers are paid?

Minorities in the Workforce

As discussed earlier, the United States is becoming more diverse. This can intensify problems of language and cultural difference in the workplace. Traditionally, senior executives have been white males, although there has been some advancement of females and minorities into the executive suite.

The greatest change, of course, has been in the composition of rank-and-file employees. As more minorities join the workforce, often coming from different cultures and religious faiths, employers must be sensitive to their needs. English as a second language is one hurdle; public relations staffs must be sure that employee communications are written in plain English and that basic words are used to communicate key messages.

Even menu selections in the employee cafeteria must be considered. Asians are used to eating rice instead of mashed potatoes and gravy. There is also the need to expand offerings for vegetarians, to make sure that pork alternatives are available, and that there are plenty of fresh fruits for people on health diets. Religious beliefs must be respected and accommodated. Devout Muslims pray to Mecca five times a day, and many organizations have provided space for prayer. Jews, on the other hand, have several holy days that require certain dietary restrictions and attendance at synagogue.

In today's world, companies must embrace diversity and also actively recruit ethnic minorities and people of color. A failure to do so can cause major public relations problems for an organization. If a large minority group in the community believes a company fails to hire enough of its members, the result may be a product boycott, rallies at corporate headquarters, and even lawsuits—which usually receive extensive coverage in the media. Such situations should never arise if a company has good policies in place and remains sensitive to employee concerns.

When it fails to do so, the cost in terms of money and corporate reputation can be great. Texaco, Inc., provides a notorious example. After lingering in federal court for more than two years, a suit against the oil company by 1,300 employees charging racial discrimination was blown wide open by disclosure of tapes recorded secretly at meetings of company executives. The executives were heard using racial slurs against employees and discussing the destruction of documents the employees might use in their suit. Eleven days later, Texaco agreed to pay $176 million to settle the case—the largest settlement ever in a racial discrimination suit.

Investor Relations

Another major component of keeping a company's health and wealth is communicating with shareholders and prospective investors. Investor relations (IR) is at the center of that process.

The goal of investor relations is to combine the disciplines of communications and finance to accurately portray a company's prospects from an investment standpoint. Some key audiences are financial analysts, individual and institutional investors, shareholders, prospective shareholders, and the financial media. Increasingly, employees are an important public, too, because they have stock options and 401K plans.

Individuals who specialize in investor or financial relations, according to salary surveys, are the highest-paid professionals in the public relations field. One reason for this is that they must be very knowledgeable about finance and myriad regulations set down by the SEC on initial public offerings (IPOs) of stock, mergers, accounting requirements, the contents of quarterly financial reports, and public disclosure of information. A company going public for the first time, for example, is required by the SEC to observe a "quiet time" when company executives are not allowed to talk about the offering to analysts or the financial press to avoid "hyping" the stock.

Mergers also require the expertise of investor relations experts in order to satisfy SEC rules and also to keep the various publics informed. Investor relations could have been better, the experts say, when Hewlett-Packard merged with Compaq Computer. On the day that the $20 billion deal was announced, both companies saw significant drops in the value of their stock. Lou Thompson, president of the National Investor Relations Institute (NIRI), said that both companies failed to convince skeptical market analysts that the merger was a good idea before going public with the announcement.

Market skepticism, however, was just the start of HP's problems. Walter Hewlett, son of the cofounder of the company, immediately denounced the merger and led a stockholder protest that gained national headlines. The family of cofounder David Packard also weighed in against the deal. There was an intense proxy fight that involved mass mailings to stockholders, full-page ads in the *Wall Street Journal*, and impassioned speeches at the annual meeting. The fight over the merger, which ultimately was approved, cost each side millions of dollars. In the bitter fight, most experts agreed that HP suffered damage to its reputation and brand.

In another situation, Google's IPO had to be delayed because cofounders Sergey Brin and Larry Page made some comments about the stock offering in a major magazine interview during the SEC's mandated "quiet period." The foul-up gave Google a rocky start in terms of positioning the stock and building a good reputation among Wall Street analysts.

Investor relations staff primarily communicate with institutional investors, individual investors, stockbrokers, and financial analysts. They are also sources of information for the financial press such as the *Wall Street Journal*, *Barron's*, and the *Financial Times*. In their jobs, they make many presentations, conduct field trips for analysts and portfolio managers, analyze stockholder demographics, oversee corporate annual reports, and prepare materials for potential investors.

Marketing Communications

Many companies use the tools and tactics of public relations to support the marketing and sales objectives of their business. This is called *marketing communications* or *marketing public relations*.

Thomas L. Harris, author of *The Marketer's Guide to Public Relations*, defines marketing public relations (MPR) as the "process of planning, executing, and evaluating programs that encourage purchase and consumer satisfaction through credible communication of information and impressions that identify companies and their products with the needs, wants, concerns, and interests of consumers."

In many cases, marketing public relations is coordinated with a company's messages in advertising, marketing, direct mail, and promotion. This has led to the concept of *integrated marketing communications (IMC)* in which companies manage all sources of information about a product or service in order to ensure maximum message penetration. This concept was first discussed in Chapter 1 as a major concept in today's modern public relations practice.

In an integrated program, for example, public relations activities are often geared to obtaining early awareness and credibility for a product. Publicity in the form of news stories builds credibility, excitement in the marketplace, and consumer anticipation. These messages make audiences more receptive to advertising and promotions about the product in the later phases of the campaign. Indeed, there is a growing body of research to support that public relations is the cornerstone of branding and positioning a product or service.

Take for example, the potato industry, which had taken a hit because of the popularity of low carb diets like the Atkins and South Beach diets. The United States Potato Board partnered with Fleishman-Hillard to launch an integrated communication campaign to reintroduce the potato. The campaign used advertising in the *New York Times*, *Washington Post*, and *USA Today* to generate interest within the media. The ads focused on the FDA nutrition label and endorsements by nutritionists who identified the potato's key nutritional benefits and introduced the "healthy potato" campaign theme. Simultaneously, press kits were distributed, an exclusive appeared in the *New York Times*, and a nutritionist briefed food and nutrition editors. The United States Potato Board's Web site was redesigned to be more consumer-friendly, its URL was changed to healthy-potato.com, and new recipes were featured. A partnership was developed with Weight Watchers to inform that organization's dieters of the potato as a health food and the two groups coreleased a VNR. Registered dieticians were enlisted as regional spokespersons, and a registered dietician testified before the congressional Dietary Guidelines Advisory Committee as the committee reviewed the nation's dietary standards.

The campaign was evaluated and deemed successful:

> It reached 140 million people with the combination of advertising and publicity.
> A senior editor at *Cooking Light* magazine commended the campaign before a meeting of the International Association of Culinary Professionals.
> The new congressional nutritional guidelines were favorable to the potato.

The objectives of marketing communications, often called *marcom* in industry jargon, are accomplished in several ways.

Product Publicity

The cost and clutter of advertising have mounted dramatically, and companies have found that creative product publicity is a cost-effective way to reach potential customers. Even mundane household products, if presented properly, can be newsworthy and capture media attention.

Clorox, for example, generated numerous news articles and broadcast mentions for its Combat cockroach killer by sponsoring a contest to find America's five worst cockroach-infested homes. And Dove Deodorant sponsored a Most Beautiful Underarms pageant at Grand Central Station in New York. Miss Florida won the crown. The contest received airtime on *Today* and *Fox & Friends*, and mention on the news shows of 400 television stations.

A company also can generate product publicity by sponsoring a poll. Polls, in order to get media attention, can be somewhat frivolous and even unscientific. *Food & Wine* magazine, along with AOL, did such a survey and announced to the world that the supermarket checkout line is the most popular choice for where to meet a mate. It also found that whipped cream is the sexiest food, but that chocolate mousse is better than sex.

Product publicity can be generated in other ways. Old Bay Seasoning sponsors a shrimp-eating contest; Briggs & Stratton, which makes lawnmowers, compiles an annual top ten list of beautiful lawns; Hershey Foods set a Guinness World Record by making the largest Kisses Chocolate, which weighed several tons.

Product Placement.
A product that appears as part of a movie or television program is a form of product placement. This was discussed in Chapter 8, so only a brief mention will be made here. Essentially, product placements help build brands by exposure in multiple films and television shows. The Corvette that the actors drive to the airport, the United flight that takes them to a destination, the Hilton they stay in, and the Grey Goose vodka martini they order in the bar are all examples of product placement.

Increasingly, product placements are the result of fees paid to film studios and television producers. At times, there is a trade-off; as when the Gap, for example, volunteers to provide the entire wardrobe for a television show, which reduces the cost of production for the producer and also gives the clothing firm high visibility.

On occasion, the filmmaker has a story line that requires a specific product. This is referred to as "product integration" because the product is not only seen but also integrated into the actual script and plot. Tom Hanks, for example, played a FedEx executive stranded on a deserted island in *Cast Away. Where the Heart Is* was a tale of a pregnant teen living in an Oklahoma Wal-Mart. Both corporations gave their permission for portrayal of its brand.

According to Stuart Elliott and Julie Bosman, writing in the *New York Times*, opportunities to promote products inside television shows "come in the form of what is called branded entertainment or product integration. They include mentioning brands in lines of dialogue, placing products in scenes so they are visible to viewers, and giving advertisers roles in plots of shows, whether it is a desperate housewife showing off a Buick at a shopping mall or a would-be apprentice trying to sell a new flavor of Crest toothpaste. . . . The goal of branded entertainment is to expose ads to viewers in ways that are more difficult to zip through or zap than traditional commercials. Devices like digital video recorders and iPods are making it easier than ever to avoid or ignore conventional sales pitches."

Product placement opportunities also are available on local and national game shows that give products to the winners.

Cause-Related Marketing

Companies in highly competitive fields, where there is little differentiation between products or services, often strive to stand out and enhance their reputation for CSR by engaging in cause-related marketing. In essence, this means that a profit-making company collaborates with a nonprofit organization to advance its cause and, at the same time, increase sales. A good example is Yoplait yogurt brand, which tells customers that 10 cents will be donated to support breast cancer research for each pink Yoplait lid consumers send in.

Companies supporting worthy causes have good customer support. One study, by Cone/Roper, found that 79 percent of Americans feel companies have a responsibility to support causes as part of its corporate citizenship. More important, 81 percent said they were likely to switch brands, when price and quality were equal, to support the cause.

American Express was not the first company to do cause-related marketing, but its success in raising money to restore the aging Statue of Liberty and Ellis Island in 1984 set a new benchmark for effectiveness. The company spent $6 million publicizing the fact that one penny of every dollar spent on its credit cards would go to the restoration. American Express raised $1.7 million for the cause. It also saw the use of its cards jump 28 percent, and applications for new cards increased 17 percent. In addition, it was an excellent branding strategy—the easy association in the public's mind between American Express and an American icon.

Selecting a charity or a cause event to support involves strategic thinking. Here are some tips for conducting cause-related marketing:

> Look for a cause related to your products or services or one that exemplifies a product quality.

> Consider causes that appeal to your primary customers.

> Choose a charity that doesn't already have multiple sponsors.

> Choose a local organization if the purpose is to build brand awareness for local franchises.

> Don't use cause-related efforts as a tactic to salvage your organization's image after a major scandal; it usually backfires.

> Understand that association with a cause or nonprofit is a long-term commitment.

> Realize that additional funds must be allocated to create public awareness and build brand recognition with the cause.

Corporate Sponsorships

A form of cause-related marketing is corporate sponsorship of various activities and events such as concerts, art exhibits, races, and scientific expeditions. The ultimate corporate sponsorship is the Olympics, which is discussed in the Insights box on page 382.

Companies spend about $10 billion annually sponsoring activities ranging from the Indianapolis 500, the Kentucky Derby, the Grammy Awards, PGA golf tournaments, and even the concert tours of Christina Aguilera or Kelly Clarkson. Many of these events, unlike causes, are money-making operations in their own right, but a large part of the underwriting often comes from sponsorships provided by other corporations.

The popularity of sponsored events is due to several reasons. These events (1) enhance the reputation and image of the sponsoring company through association, (2) give product brands high visibility among key purchasing publics, (3) provide a focal point for marketing efforts and sales campaigns, and (4) generate publicity and media coverage.

Sponsorships can be more effective than advertising. Visa International, for example, spends about $200,000 annually sponsoring the USA-Visa Decathlon Team, or about the price of a 30-second prime time TV commercial. Speedo, the swimwear manufacturer, sponsors the U.S. Olympic swim team, but also gets its name before millions of television viewers, because most of the swimmers from other nations also wear Speedo swim caps and suits. At the Sydney games, about 70 percent of the Olympic gold medalists in swimming wore Speedo gear. This translates to brand dominance in sales.

Local stadiums and concert halls almost everywhere now have corporate names. An obscure technology company, 3 COM, got reams of national publicity when Candlestick Park in San Francisco became 3 COM Park. After 3COM Corporation's naming contract expired, Monster Cable bought the rights and 3 COM Park became Monster Park (at least until Monster Cable's contract expires in 2007). Naming rights to the new baseball stadium in San Francisco went to SBC, the telephone company that is now AT&T. In Philadelphia, Lincoln Financial Group—not exactly a household name—snapped up naming rights for the new stadium for the Eagles pro football team. The company's reasoning: Its name becomes recognized as a major brand by those attending Eagle games and the 10 million television fans who watch games at home on television.

The demographic characteristics of potential customers determine, for the most part, what events a company will sponsor. Manufacturers of luxury products usually sponsor events that draw the interest of affluent consumers. That's why Lexus, a luxury car, sponsors polo championships. Tennis also has fairly affluent demographics, so Volvo sponsors tennis tournaments. General Motors GMC division, however, is interested in selling pickup trucks, so it sponsored a 15-city country and western tour. See the Insights box on page 383 for more guidelines on corporate sponsorships.

On occasion, a company will sponsor an event for the primary purpose of enhancing its reputation among opinion leaders and influential decision makers. Atofina Chemicals, for example, usually sponsors events that advance science education. However, it did agree to sponsor an exhibit of ballet-themed works by Degas at the Philadelphia Art Museum to highlight the company's history as a Paris-based corporation. One objective

ON THE JOB >>

Olympic Torch Visits Six Continents

Global

The 2004 Olympics marked the first time that the Olympic Torch went around the world—traveling 78,000 kilometers in 78 days—before a runner made the final lap and ignited the cauldron at the opening ceremonies in Athens before a live audience of 72,000 and a global TV audience of 4 billion.

Almost 4,000 torchbearers carried the flame to previous host cities and, for the first time, the flame visited Africa and Latin America. An estimated 260 million people saw the flame during the relay, which made Coca-Cola and Samsung Electronics, who paid hefty (though undisclosed) fees to the Athens 2004 Organizing Committee, very happy corporate sponsors.

Gabriel Kahn, a reporter for the *Wall Street Journal*, summarized what the two corporate sponsors received in return: "The sponsors . . . turn each stop along the relay into a golden marketing opportunity. Both Samsung and Coke get to choose some of the relay runners for each city. Their corporate logos emblazon all sorts of torch-related paraphernalia. And as the relay entourage winds its way through each city, Coke and Samsung trucks leave behind a stream of pennants, pins, and sodas."

Both Coca-Cola and Samsung also were official sponsors of the Olympic games, which runs about $40 million per sponsor. Samsung, for example, integrated its brand presence into interactive experiences, bus wraps, airport luggage carts, and other signage. Both sponsors also operated extensive hospitality centers for athletes and visiting dignitaries.

Elli Panagiotopoulou Giokeza, writing in IPRA's *Frontline*, explains why corporate sponsors are attracted to the Olympics: "The sponsorship of the Olympic Games is a great communication tool, which not only extends the corporate visibility of the companies involved, but also provides them with the possibility to increase their relationship with the consumer and their respective trade audiences."

Corporations sponsor a number of special events for public relations, marketing, and image-building purposes. Here, Olympic Ambassador Spiros Lambridis holds the Olympic flame on arrival at Beijing in the Olympic Torch relay that visited 34 cities on six continents before arriving in Athens. The relay was underwritten and sponsored by Coca-Cola and Samsung.

Another reason is given by Josh McCall in *PRWeek*: "The Olympics continue to be among the most prominent platforms for branding on the planet." One study, for example, showed that half of U.S. consumers thought Olympic sponsors were industry leaders.

was to increase employee pride. The company's 1,200 employees in Philadelphia and their families were invited to an exclusive showing at the museum before the exhibit was open to the public. In addition, the company used the exhibit and museum as a centerpiece for entertaining customers and their significant others. It also organized events for and donations of products to the Philadelphia High School for the Creative and Performing Arts.

Environmental Relations

Another aspect of CSR that is gaining momentum in the first decade of the 21st century is increased corporate concern for the environment and the maintenance of sustainable resources. The 1990s saw major clashes and confrontations between corporations and activist nongovernmental organizations (NGOs) about a host of environmental and human rights issues. The current trend line, however, is for more cooperation and partnerships among these former adversaries. Many companies, such as Shell, are now issuing annual corporate responsibility reports and working with environmental groups to clean up the environment, preserve wilderness areas, and even replace exploited natural resources.

Home Depot is a good case study. Between 1997 and 1999, the giant chain of homebuilding supplies was the target of environmentalists who picketed hundreds of Home Depot stores. They were concerned that the company, the world's largest retailer of lumber, was causing the massive destruction of forests around the world by not ensuring that its supplies didn't come from endangered forests. The protests received extensive media coverage and the company, quite frankly, was worried about a consumer backlash and sliding sales.

In 2001, Home Depot conducted an assessment of the "state of the world's forests." The company's wood-purchasing policy states: "To set our purchasing directives through 2010, we are conducting our second review of the state of the world's forests, to be completed in 2005–2006." The company says it has increased the number of products certified by the Forest Stewardship Council "whose mission is to promote environmentally appropriate, socially beneficial and economically viable management of the world's forests." In addition to working with the Forest Stewardship Council, Home Depot partners with the World Wildlife Fund, the Nature Conservancy, and other organizations "to promote responsible forestry and curb illegal logging."

The company correctly perceived the potential problem as an issue that needed to be addressed (see discussion of issues management in Chapter 2). As a first step, the company agreed to stop using products from endangered forests and backed up its decision by slashing its imports from Indonesia, where loggers were practically clear-cutting tropical forests by 90 percent. It also pressured Canada to declare logging off-limits in the Great Bear Rainforest in British Columbia. In another effort, it mediated an agreement between timber companies and environmentalists in Chile to preserve natural forests and establish guidelines for the sustainable farming of new trees.

ON THE JOB >>

Selection Criteria for Corporate Sponsorships

Insights

Corporations are inundated with requests from organizations to sponsor everything from rock concerts to museum exhibits to sporting events. Consequently, each corporation selects sponsorships that best support its marketing and public relations objectives. A company considering a sponsorship should ask the following questions:

> Can the company afford to fulfill the obligation? The sponsorship fee is just the starting point. Count on doubling it to have an adequate total event budget.
> Is the event or organization compatible with the company's values and mission statement?
> Does the event reach the corporation's target audience?
> Is there enough time before the event to maximize the company's use of the sponsorship?
> Are the event organizers experienced and professional?
> Is the event newsworthy enough to provide the company with opportunities for publicity?
> Will the event be televised?
> Will the sales force support the event and use it to leverage sales?
> Does the event give the company a chance to develop new contacts and business opportunities?
> Can the company live with the event on a long-term basis while its value builds?
> Is there an opportunity for employee involvement? Corporate sponsorships can be used to build employee morale and teamwork.
> Is the event compatible with the "personality" of the company's products?
> Can the company reduce the cash outlay and enhance the marketing appeal by trading off products and in-kind services?
> Will management support the event? If the answer is yes to the previous questions, the likelihood of management support of the sponsorship is fairly high.

The partnership between Home Depot and environmental groups is a win-win situation. The company gets credit for being environmentally concerned, which results in less negative publicity and more customer loyalty. The environmental groups, in turn, have more power to accomplish their objectives. Randy Hayes, president of the Rainforest Action Network, told the *Wall Street Journal*, "If you've got Home Depot carrying your water, you're going to get a lot farther than as just an environmental group."

Other large corporations around the world are forging alliances with various NGOs to preserve the environment, promote human rights, and provide social/medical services. The following are some examples of long-term CSR programs:

> The Royal Dutch/Shell Group has set the abolishment of child labor as its goal. Shell companies in 112 nations have procedures in place to prevent the use of child labor.

> Unilever, the food and consumer products company, is helping to restore a dying river estuary in the Philippines. The campaign is one of several programs by the company's global Water Sustainability Initiative.

> Volvo Corporation is working with the UN High Commissioner for Human Rights on a project addressing discrimination in the workplace.

> LM Ericsson, a Swedish telecommunications company, has a program to provide and maintain mobile communications equipment and expertise for humanitarian relief operations.

> Merck, the pharmaceutical giant, is a partner with the Bill and Melinda Gates Foundation on a five-year AIDS project in Botswana and is selling its drugs at cost in developing nations.

Corporate Philanthropy

Another manifestation of CSR is corporate philanthropy. This, in essence, is the donation of funds, products, and services to various causes, ranging from providing uniforms and equipment to a local Little League team to giving a university a multimillion dollar donation to upgrade its science and engineering programs. In many cases, an organization's public relations department handles corporate charitable giving as part of its responsibilities.

In 2006, American corporations gave $12.7 billion to a variety of causes. Although there is a common perception that corporate philanthropy provides the lion's share of all donations, the actual percentage is very small. Of the $295 billion total given in 2006, only 4.3 percent was from corporations. The largest amount of money given, 76.5 percent, was given by individuals. See Chapter 13 on nonprofits for more information on fund-raising.

Corporations, of course, have long used philanthropy to demonstrate community goodwill and to polish their reputations as good citizens. There's also evidence that corporate giving is good for business and retaining customers. As previously noted, the Hill & Knowlton survey found that 79 percent of Americans claim to take corporate citizenship into consideration when purchasing products. At the same time, 76 percent of the respondents believe that companies participate in philanthropic activities to get favorable publicity, whereas only 24 percent believe corporations are truly committed to the causes they support.

Getting good publicity, no doubt, is a factor, but this should not be a company's ultimate objective. Cone/Roper, a survey organization, says companies should be very

When the world's largest Aquarium—the Georgia Aquarium in Atlanta—needed to transport two Beluga whales from Mexico City to the Aquarium, Atlanta-based UPS came to the rescue with specially built tanks, a specially equipped cargo plane, and ground transportation. The safe and humane shipping of the 12-foot long, 1,600-pound whales gave UPS an opportunity to provide a public service for its hometown, but also garnered the package carrier with local, national, and international news coverage.

careful about touting their good deeds, because the public will be skeptical about the motivation. Instead, companies should concentrate on the people they help, and the programs they showcase should be more than "window dressing." The research firm further states, "Never do it for publicity. Do it for building your business, your brand equity, and your stakeholder relations."

Companies don't give to anything and everything. A series of small grants to a wide variety of causes doesn't really help any particular charity, and it dilutes the impact of the contributions. HomeBanc Mortgage Corporation, for example, used to give $300,000 annually in small grants to a variety of causes, but it decided that the available funds could have more impact (and visibility) if only one or two causes were significantly funded. Consequently, the company now gives most of its charitable funds to Habitat for Humanity, a nonprofit that builds homes for low-income families. In Home Banc's case, funding Habitat for Humanity is a strategic decision to funnel contributions into a cause directly related to home ownership, which is the business of the mortgage company.

Strategic philanthropy is defined by Paul Davis Jones and Cary Raymond of IDPR Group as "the long-term socially responsible contribution of dollars, volunteers, products, and expertise to a cause aligned with the strategic business goals of an organization." Such giving, they say, can reap a number of benefits for the corporation, including:

> Strengthened reputation and brand recognition
> Increased media opportunities
> Improved community and government relations
> Facilitation of employee recruitment and retention

ON THE JOB >>

The Value of Corporate Philanthropy

Insights

Corporate philanthropy is viewed favorably by employees, customers, and shareholders, according to a survey conducted by the Council on Foundations (COF) and the Walker Information Group. The following is a summary of the major findings.

Employees
One-third to two-thirds agree that (1) a good giving record is a main reason for remaining with an employer, (2) corporate generosity is one of the factors that differentiates a company, and (3) a company that does good deeds gains their admiration.

Customers
One-third say they would select a company based on its giving record.

Shareholders
One-third attest to the effect of corporate philanthropy programs on their

investment decisions and specifically say corporate generosity (1) affects the bottom line, (2) positively affects stock performance, and (3) affects where to invest.

Type of Program
Stakeholders rate companies highest for higher visibility efforts, such as providing sponsorship support for worthwhile nonprofit events and causes and having employee volunteers. Fewer stakeholders rate companies positively for contributing cash or donating in-kind products and services.

Recommendations
The following recommendations are based on the survey results:

> Set out a strategic plan for corporate philanthropy that is both focused and consistent with your overall corporate goals.

> Take stock of and quantify what the company does in the area of corporate philanthropy.

> Realize that of all a company's stakeholder groups, the employees are likely to know best the company and what it does in philanthropy.

> Ensure that the CEO and other senior leaders are aware of the significant role they play in how stakeholders form perceptions of a company's philanthropic programs.

> Ensure that an effective and realistic external communications effort is a key element of our philanthropic program.

> Develop and conduct a process to reassess the way the philanthropy function is delivered.

Source: *PRWeek*, May 5, 2003, 15.

> Enhanced marketing
> Access to research and development
> Increased corporate profitability

Corporate philanthropy, despite its potential benefits, does have its limitations. A large grant by a corporation, for example, cannot offset a major financial scandal or the negative publicity of a class-action suit for discrimination of female employees.

The Entertainment Industry

Business public relations is not confined to the corporate boardroom. Entertainment is also big business. Public relations in the entertainment business can involve serving as a publicist for a celebrity or sports figure or working for an athletic team or a sports or entertainment venue. Entertainment public relations also includes working in the travel industry, promoting specific sites or destinations or working for a travel business such as a cruise line. These are just a few examples of how public relations intersects with the business of entertainment.

A dominant factor in today's mass media is the glorification of celebrities. Sports heroes and television personalities in particular, along with radio talk-show hosts, members of the British royal family, movie stars, high-profile criminals, and some politicians are written about, photographed, and discussed almost incessantly. Indeed, the number and circulation of celebrity magazines continue to increase every year. *People*, the industry leader, is generally regarded as the most successful magazine in the country and has a circulation of almost 4 million copies a week.

In some cases, celebrity results from natural public curiosity about an individual's achievements or position in life. Frequently, however, it is carefully nurtured by publicists for the client's ego satisfaction or commercial gain.

The publicity buildup of individuals is outside the mainstream of public relations work, and some professional practitioners are embarrassed by the exaggerations and tactics used by promoters of so-called beautiful people. Nevertheless, all students of public relations should know how the personal publicity trade operates. At some point, knowledge of personal publicity techniques may be useful.

An illustration of the issue of celebrity image management is provided in the Insights box on page 388.

The Practitioner's Responsibility

Handling publicity for an individual carries special responsibilities. Often clients turn to their publicists for personal advice, especially when trouble arises.

Damage Control

A practitioner handling an individual client is responsible for protecting the client from bad publicity as well as generating positive news. When the client appears in a bad light because of misbehavior or an irresponsible public statement, the publicist must try to minimize the harm done to the client's public image. The objective is damage control.

Politicians who say something controversial in public, and then later wish they hadn't, try to squirm out of their predicaments by claiming they were misquoted. This is a foolish defense unless the politicians can prove conclusively that they were indeed quoted incorrectly. Reporters resent accusations of inaccuracy and may hold a grudge against the accusers. If an accused reporter has a politician's statement on tape, the politician appears even worse. A better defense is for the politicians to explain what they intended and to express regret for the slip of the tongue.

A similar approach is recommended for Hollywood celebrities who are caught in scandalous acts or are the targets of unfounded rumor. Experts suggest immediate response so that the momentum of subsequent stories is minimized. A brief, honest statement of regret for bad behavior or denial of rumors works well. Television's mass audience enjoys celebrity news. TV lends itself to a short statement that makes a perfect 20-second sound bite to fit in a brief story. Then the celebrity needs to disappear from sight and take care of personal matters.

— ON THE JOB >>

Celebrity Conflict Required Prompt Response

Insights

When actor Mel Gibson was picked up on charges of drunken driving in the summer of 2006 he was accused of making anti-Semitic comments to the arresting officers. While that offense alone would make a celebrity publicist cringe, it was intensified by the fact that Gibson, a devout Christian, had previously been accused of being anti-Semitic and had made apologies to members of the Jewish community and faith. It might have seemed like déjà vu for Gibson's publicist.

Gibson had come under fire by members of the Jewish community when he directed and produced *The Passion of the Christ.* Many believed the film portrayed Jews in a way that incited racism and hatred against them. In contrast, Christians made up the core of the film's audience, with Christian ministers urging their church members to attend screenings of *The Passion.* At the time of this conflict, in 2004, Gibson made the talk show rounds and denied all accusations that he was an anti-Semite. *The Passion of the Christ* was an enormous success, grossing more than $600 million worldwide.

Following his 2006 arrest on drunken driving charges and his reported tirade against Jews, Gibson made an apology saying the statements he made he did not "believe to be true" and called the statements "despicable." This first apology was rejected by many Jewish leaders, including the leadership of the Anti-Defamation League (ADL), as "insufficient" and "unremorseful."

Gibson made a more complete statement two days later, saying,

I want to apologize specifically to everyone in the Jewish community for the vitriolic and harmful words that I said to a law enforcement officer the night I was arrested on a DUI charge. . . . I am not an anti-Semite. I am not a bigot. . . . Hatred of any kind goes against my faith. I'm not just asking for forgiveness. I would like to take it one step further, and meet with leaders in the Jewish community, with whom I can have a one-on-one discussion to discern the appropriate path for healing.

ADL national director Abraham H. Foxman said, "We are glad that Mel Gibson has finally owned up to the fact that he made anti-Semitic remarks and his apology sounds sincere. Once he completes his rehabilitation for alcohol abuse, we will be ready and willing to help him with his second rehabilitation to combat this disease of prejudice."

PR experts at the time suggested that Gibson's fuller apology may have come too late to save him. Celebrity crisis expert Richard Levick told the Associated Press, "In the first 24 hours, people start forming opinions. He has constantly been behind the story and needs to get out front. What he's done through actions has turned perception into reality. People presume he is anti-Semitic." But celebrity publicist Michael Levine told the Associated Press, "The best defense is a good offense and the only offense is a relentless one." Levine said that Gibson's public relations team followed the four principles of

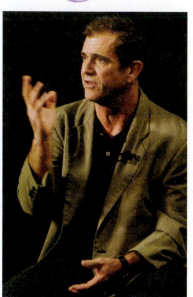

Actor Mel Gibson engaged in damage control after he was accused of making racist remarks.

celebrity crisis management—speed, humility, contrition, and personal responsibility. "If you go with those four things, you generally do pretty well in America," Levine said.

While the conventional wisdom suggests the stance Levine outlines and the one Gibson took, PR researcher Lisa Lyon found that pre-existing reputation should affect response strategy. She found that if you have a bad reputation, apology can actually backfire or boomerang. Because of Gibson's pre-existing reputation within the Jewish community, time will tell whether the court of public opinion will reward Gibson's conventional strategy or whether he would have been better served by a more defensive strategy.

Ethical Problems for Publicists

Personal misconduct by a client, or the appearance of misconduct, strains a practitioner's ingenuity and at times his or her ethical principles. Some practitioners will lie outright to protect a client, a dishonest practice that looks even worse if the media show the statement to be a lie. On occasion, a practitioner acting in good faith may be victimized because the client has lied.

Issuing a prepared statement to explain the client's conduct, while leaving reporters and their editors dissatisfied, is regarded as safer than having the client call a news conference, unless the client is a victim of circumstances and is best served by talking fully and openly. The decision about holding a news conference also is influenced by how articulate and self-controlled the client is. Under questioning, a person may say something that compounds a problem.

Conducting a Personality Campaign

A campaign to generate public awareness of an individual should be planned just as meticulously as any other public relations project. Practitioners conducting such campaigns follow a standard step-by-step process.

Interview the Client

The client should answer a detailed personal questionnaire. The practitioner should be a dogged, probing interviewer, digging for interesting and possibly newsworthy facts about the person's life, activities, and beliefs. When talking about themselves, individuals frequently fail to realize that certain elements of their experiences have publicity value under the right circumstances.

Perhaps, for example, the client is an actress playing the film role of a midwestern farmer's young wife. During her get-acquainted talks with the publicist, she mentions that while growing up in a small town she belonged to the 4-H Club. The publicist struck gold. When she was a member of the youth organization, she actually did the farm jobs she will perform in the film.

Not only must practitioners draw out such details from their clients, they must also have the ingenuity to develop these facts as story angles. When the actress is a guest on a television talk show, the publicist should prompt her to recall incidents from her 4-H experience. Two or three humorous anecdotes about mishaps with pigs and chickens, tossed into the interview, give it verve.

Prepare a Biography of the Client

The basic biography should be limited to four typed pages, perhaps fewer. News and feature angles should be placed high in the "bio," as it is termed, so an editor or producer can find them quickly. The biography, a portrait and other photographs of the client, and, if possible, additional personal background items should be assembled in a media kit for extensive distribution. Usually the kit is a cardboard folder with inside pockets.

Plan a Marketing Strategy

The practitioner should determine precisely what is to be sold. Is the purpose only to increase public awareness of the individual, or is it to publicize the client's product, such as a new television series, motion picture, or book? Next, the practitioner should decide which audiences are the most important to reach. For instance, a politician trying to project himself or herself as a representative of minority groups should be scheduled to speak before audiences in minority neighborhoods and placed on radio stations whose demographic reports show that they attract minority listeners.

Conduct the Campaign

In most cases, the best course is to place the client on multiple media simultaneously. Radio and television appearances create public awareness and often make newspaper feature stories easier to obtain. The process works in reverse as well. Using telephone calls and pitch letters to editors and program directors, the publicist should propose print and on-air interviews with the client. Every pitch should include a news or feature angle for the interviewer to develop. Because magazine articles require longer to reach print, the publicist should begin efforts to obtain them as early as feasible.

An interview in an important magazine—a rising female movie star in *Cosmopolitan* or *In Style*, for example—has major impact among women readers. Backstage maneuvering often takes place before such an interview appears. Agents for entertainers on their way up eagerly seek to obtain such interviews. When a personality is "hot," however, magazine editors compete for the privilege of publishing the interview. The star's agent plays them against each other, perhaps offering exclusivity but demanding such rewards as a cover picture of the star, the right to choose the interviewer (friendly, of course), and even approval of the article. Editors of some magazines yield to publicists' demands; other publications refuse to do so.

News Releases. News releases are an important publicity tool, but the practitioner should avoid too much puffery. *Bulldog Reporter*, a West Coast public relations newsletter, once gave a "fireplug" award to a press agent who opined about a cable-televised concert in a tropical setting. According to the news release, "The historical event, in a balmy night that could only rival, not surpass, the audience's decibel level for enthusiasm, should overshadow any in-person star appearance ever offered on subscription television."

Photographs. Photographs of the client should be submitted to the print media as often as justifiable. Media kits usually include the standard head-and-shoulders portrait, often called a "mug shot." Photographs of the client doing something interesting or appearing in a newsworthy group may be published merely with a caption, without an accompanying story. The practitioner and the photographer should be inventive, putting the client into unusual situations. The justification for a successful submission may be thin if the picture is not colorful and/or timely. If the client seeks national attention, such pictures should be submitted to the news services so that, if newsworthy, they will be distributed to hundreds of newspapers. (Requirements for photographs are discussed in Chapter 10.)

Sharply increased awareness among newspaper editors of women's concern about sexual exploitation has largely eliminated "cheesecake" pictures—photographs of nubile young women in which the news angle often is as skimpy as their attire—from newspaper pages. At one time such pictures were published frequently as editors tried to spice up their pages. Such photos, blatantly contrived and often in bad taste, still show up in print today.

Cheesecake photographs still are printed in the trade press, even though they are seldom seen in daily newspapers in America. Certain British and Australian newspapers,

Sports figures and their teams receive considerable publicity by appearing on various sports and game shows. Here, Diane Taurasi *(right)* of the Phoenix Mercurys (National Basketball Association) appears on ESPN after receiving the Rookie of the Year award.

however, continue to publish large photos of skimpily clad young women, who are often topless.

Public Appearances. Another way to intensify awareness of individual clients is to arrange for them to appear frequently in public places. Commercial organizations at times invite celebrities of various types or pay them fees to dress up dinner meetings, conventions, and even store openings. A major savings and loan association employed a group of early-day television performers to appear at openings of branch offices. Each day for a week for two hours an entertainer stood in a guest booth, signing autographs and chatting with visitors, who received a paperback book of pictures recalling television's pioneer period. Refreshments were served. A company photographer took pictures of the celebrity talking to guests. Visitors who appeared in the pictures received copies as souvenirs. These appearances benefited the sponsor by attracting crowds and helped the entertainers stay in the public eye.

Awards. A much-used device, and a successful one, is to have a client receive an award. The practitioner should be alert for news of awards to be given and nominate the client for appropriate ones. Follow-up communications with persuasive material from the practitioner may convince the sponsor to make the award to the client. In some instances, the idea of an award is proposed to an organization by a practitioner, whose client then conveniently is declared the first recipient. The entertainment business generates immense amounts of publicity for individuals and shows with the Oscar, Golden Globe, and Emmy awards. Winning an Academy Award bolsters a performer's career.

Psychologists believe that televised awards ceremonies give viewers a sense of structure in life. This return to normalcy partly explains why the Emmy awards ceremony was rescheduled twice after the September 11 attack on the World Trade Center and Pentagon so that "the show could go on."

Record the Results

Clients who employ practitioners want tangible results in return for their fees. Practitioners need to compile and analyze the results of personality campaigns to determine the effectiveness of the various methods used. Tearsheets, photographs, copies of news releases, and, when possible, videotape clips of their public appearances should be provided to clients. Clipping services can help practitioners assemble this material. At the end of campaigns, or at intervals in long-term programs, summaries of what has been accomplished should be submitted to clients.

Promoting an Entertainment Event

Attracting attendance at an event—anything from a theatrical performance to a fund-raising fashion show or a street carnival—requires a well-planned publicity campaign.

Publicity to Stimulate Ticket Sales

The primary goal of any campaign for an entertainment event is to sell tickets. An advance publicity buildup informs listeners, readers, and viewers that an event will occur and stimulates their desire to attend. Rarely, except for community events publicized in smaller cities, do newspaper stories and broadcasts about an entertainment event include detailed information on ticket prices and availability. Those facts usually are deemed too commercial by editors and should be announced in paid advertising. However, some newspapers may include prices, times, and so on in tabular listings of scheduled entertainments. Performance dates usually are included in publicity stories.

Stories about a forthcoming theatrical event, motion picture, rock concert, book signings, or similar commercial activities should concentrate on the personalities, styles, and popularity of the activities or products. Every time a product or show is mentioned, public awareness grows. Thus, astute practitioners search for fresh news angles to produce as many stories as possible.

The "Drip-Drip-Drip" Technique

Motion picture studios, television production firms, and networks apply the principle of "drip-drip-drip" publicity when a show is being shot. In other words, there is a steady output of information about the production. A public relations specialist, called a unit man or woman, is assigned to a film during production. That person turns out a series of stories for the general and trade press and plays host to media visitors to the set. The television networks mail out daily news bulletins about their shows to media television editors. They assemble the editors annually to preview new programs and interview their stars. The heaviest barrage of publicity is released shortly before the show openings.

Television is a high-stakes business with a great deal of uncertainty. The national television networks—ABC, CBS, NBC, Fox, and CW—offer dozens of pilot programs, most of which lack staying power. Some pilots survive near-death experiences, the way *Seinfeld* did in 1989 when ratings were dismal. A year later, the comedy series reappeared to begin a rise in popularity that culminated in the hype surrounding the final episode. An audience estimated at 80 million generated advertising revenues of $1.6 million for a 30-second spot. The publicity and suspense surrounding the final episode were so great that Jerry Seinfeld declared, "I'm sick of myself." The comedian's discomfort probably was relieved somewhat by his $1 million per episode salary.

A much-publicized device is to have a star unveil his or her star in the cement of the Hollywood Walk of Fame, just before the star's new film or show appears.

Videotaped recordings of these events turn up on TV stations across the country. *American Idol* host Ryan Seacrest unveiled his Walk of Fame star just before the top 12 contestants were named in the 2006 singing contest. Coincidence or *Idol* drip, drip, drip?

One danger of excessive promotion of an event, however, is that audience expectation may become too high, so that the performance proves to be a disappointment. A skilled practitioner will stay away from "hype" that can lead to a sense of anticlimax.

A Look at the Movie Industry

Motion picture public relations departments use market research, demographics, and psychographics to define the target audiences they seek to reach. Most motion picture publicity is predominantly aimed at 18- to 24-year-olds, where the largest audience lies. Seventy-five percent of the film audience is under age 39, although increased attendance by older moviegoers has become evident recently.

Professional entertainment publicity work is concentrated in New York and Los Angeles, the former as the nation's theatrical center and the latter as the motion picture center. (American television production is divided primarily between these two cities, with the larger portion in Los Angeles.)

A typical Los Angeles–area public relations firm specializing in personalities and entertainment has two staffs: one staff of "planters," who deliver to media offices publicity stories about individual clients and the projects in which they are engaged, and another staff of "bookers," whose job is to place clients on talk shows and set up other public appearances. Some publicity stories are for general release; others are prepared specifically for a single media outlet such as a syndicated Hollywood columnist or a major newspaper. The latter type is marked "exclusive," permitting the publication or station that uses it to claim credit for "breaking" the story.

Another device is to provide supplies of tickets for a new movie or show to radio stations, whose disc jockeys award them to listeners as prizes in on-the-air contests. In the process, these announcers mention the name of the show dozens of times. Glamorous premieres and trips for media guests to distant points so that they can watch the filming or attend an opening are used occasionally, too.

For such services to individual or corporate entertainment clients, major Hollywood publicists charge at least $3,000 a month, with a three-month minimum. The major studios and networks have their own public relations staffs.

Entertainment firms also may specialize in arranging product placement in movies and television programs. Usually movie or television producers trade visible placement of a product in a show or film in exchange for free use of the item.

The fast-food industry provides excellent opportunities for market-based public relations involving giveaways of character figures with meals. Movies such as *Over the Hedge* received huge boosts in visibility and ticket sales. Wendy's offered Kids' Meals with toys based on the movie's characters. Characters from a film can provide a key incentive to young customers in the highly competitive takeout business, providing a large but transitory advantage in the so-called burger wars. But, according to *Brandweek* the movie's integrated marketing effort moved well beyond children's toys. Act II Microwave Popcorn sported *Over the Hedge* packaging, and Trix yogurt included games based on the film. In addition, there were tie-ins with HP computers, which were promoted using the film's cuddly characters; Wal-Mart, which featured an in-store promotion of the movie; and Hallmark, which promoted *Over the Hedge* party goods.

Sports Publicity

The sports mania flourishing in the United States and in various forms around the world is stimulated by intense public relations efforts. Programs at both the big-time college and professional levels seek to arouse public interest in teams and players, sell tickets to games, and publicize the corporate sponsors who subsidize many events. Increasingly, too, sports publicists work with marketing specialists to promote the sale of booster souvenirs and clothing, a lucrative sideline for teams.

Sports publicists use the normal tools of public relations—media kits, statistics, interviews, television appearances, and the like—to distribute information about their clients. But dealing with facts is only part of their role—they also try to stir emotions. For college publicists, this means creating enthusiasm among alumni and making the school seem glamorous and exciting in order to recruit high school students. Publicists for professional teams work to make them appear to be hometown representatives of civic pride, not merely athletes playing for high salaries.

Sometimes these efforts succeed spectacularly, if the team is a winner. When a team is losing, however, the sports publicist's life turns grim. He or she must find ways to soothe public displeasure through methods such as having players conduct clinics at playgrounds and make sympathetic visits to hospitals.

Emerging sports increasingly compete for prominence and fan loyalty with more established sports. Soccer is widely popular among youth in America, leading to hopes among its promoters that the professional game will make inroads in the U.S. sports market. The Professional Golf Association (PGA) bought an 11-page advertising supplement in *Business Week* magazine to promote the professional golfer as a great athlete, philanthropic leader, and consummate professional in the face of rigorous travel and performance pressures.

Because the public yearns for heroes, publicists focus on building up the images of star players, sometimes to excess. They know that stars sell tickets.

Sports in America is big business, with $150 billion in gross annual revenues. Sometimes an unseemly side crops up in sports coverage. The impasse between players and owners in the National Hockey League (NHL) caused fans to lose patience with both the wealthy owners and the highly paid players. Intractable positions by both sides threatened the future of the professional league.

Public relations plays a critical role in sports, far beyond the promotion of celebrities. Two important areas are sports crisis management and sponsorship management. According to John Eckel of Hill & Knowlton Sports, professional communicators must deal with the media focus on issues ranging from player strikes to high ticket and concession costs to boorish athletes who deny that they are role models, even while they benefit from their visibility. Jay Rosenstein of Cohn & Wolfe attributes much of sports crisis public relations to the "human factor in the sports world, where egos are otherworldly, behavior is reminiscent of the entertainment world, and media focus is unrelenting."

The advertising agency DDB Worldwide studied the effectiveness of a very high-profile sponsorship—the Summer Olympics. The agency found that, for a company to benefit in terms of sales and goodwill, the Olympic Games require a huge commitment of $40 million per sponsor, plus extensive costs in marketing that sponsorship. See the Global box on page 395 about concerns relating to the Beijing games in 2008.

Soccer, however, is the world's most popular sport and the World Cup is the most costly of all sports sponsorships (see the Insights box on page 396). The 2006 World Cup, held in Germany, was a 64-game tournament seen by more than a billion viewers around the world. What they saw was the Adidas three-stripe logo on match balls, referee uniforms, outfits worn by volunteers, and billboards in and around the coun-

── ON THE JOB >> ──

Beijing Garners Sports and Travel Prize

Global

The selection of Beijing as the venue for the 2008 Olympic Games was both a sports and travel coup for the Chinese government. The *Beijing Morning Post* trumpeted the selection with the headline, "Smiles Everywhere, Joy Ignites." And indeed, China has received the opportunity to manage what Richard Yarbrough calls "one of the world's largest bullhorns" for displaying a city and country's achievements and character.

However, hosting the Olympic Games in Beijing is not without conflict, and some of the conflict management techniques described in Chapter 2 may have to be applied to travel and sports public relations surrounding the games. The following are prominent issues that the Olympic organizers must address:

> Taiwan has expressed fear that the games will fuel Chinese nationalism, leading to stronger moves to reincorporate the island nation into China.

> The Dalai Lama and his Tibetan government in exile have supported the games coming to China, provided that it is a stimulus for societal change and freedom.

> The United States has urged China to show a "modern" face to the world, which it appears to be striving to accomplish.

> Amnesty International has remained neutral about the games, urging China to improve its human rights record.

> Perhaps a sore loser, French officials argue that awarding the games to China flouts freedom and violates human rights, much like giving the 1936 Games to Nazi Germany.

> In Germany, the interior minister opines that the games will spur China's democratic development.

> Sponsors look on with concern that their enormous corporate contributions to the games in China will not besmirch their companies.

> Environmental activists look with interest at one of the three themes of the Olympics offered by Beijing: A Green Olympics that showcases environmental concerns for the globe and showcases the billions spent on environmental reform in China.

The Chinese government, in collaboration with its public relations firm Weber Shandwick Worldwide, has begun to address these issues proactively. A combination of effective communication and constructive behavior may enable "Smiles Everywhere, Joy Ignites" to be the headline once again at the close of the 2008 Olympic Games.

---

try's stadiums. Adidas also had exclusive rights to advertisements during broadcasts of games in the U.S. by ABC and ESPN.

The shoe and sports apparel manufacturer paid $315 million to the World Cup's governing body, the Federation Internationale de Football (FIFA) for sponsorship rights, which extend through 2014. In addition, the Adidas partnership gives it prominent marketing placement on FIFA's World Cup Web site, which organizers estimated would attract 4 billion visitors during the tournament alone. Nike, the archrival of Adidas, paid an estimated $144 million to be the official sponsor of the Brazilian team, which has won more World Cup championships than any other nation, until 2018.

Despite the estimated $8.9 billion annually spent on sponsoring sports events, tallying the benefits is still less than scientific. With that in mind, Publicis Groupe launched a new service in mid-2006 that uses optical-resolution technology to scan sports broadcasts for brand names and images. According to the *Wall Street Journal*, "The scan tracks the percentage of the TV screen that is taken up by an individual corporate logo, as well as the logo's location on the screen and whether there are other brands on the screen at the same time. The data are then used to calculate the financial value of the screen time, based on a formula loosely tied to the cost of TV ad time." The program, for example, found that Honda was the highest-scoring brand in

ON THE JOB >>

Soccer's Superstar: Did He Recover?

Insights

When French soccer star Zinedine Zidane head-butted an Italian opponent in the final game of the 2006 World Cup series he was ejected from the game—an extraordinary penalty. This was the final act of Zidane's career. He was set to retire after the game. Following a series of television interviews in which he apologized but expressed no regret for what he considered a provoked attack, Zidane's popularity was as strong as ever:

> Adidas posted its planned www.mercizidane.fr Web site, thanking the soccer star for his years as an Adidas brand ambassador.
> Sixty-one percent of French soccer fans in one poll said they forgave Zidane for what may have been the game-losing behavior.
> President Jacques Chirac publicly assured Zidane that France still "admires and loves him," according to Reuters.
> Sports journalists voted Zidane the best player of the World Cup and awarded him the Adidas Golden Ball award, despite the head-butting incident.

Zidane employed a defense that his act was justified because the Italian player, Marco Materazzi, insulted his

French soccer star Zinedine Zidane created an international incident that required an apology and image repair when he head-butted an Italian opponent in the final game of the 2006 FIFA World Cup.

family—seeking to shift the blame for the act to Materazzi. Zidane told an interviewer, "There was a serious provocation. My act is not forgivable. But they must also punish the true guilty party, and the guilty party is the one who provokes."

Zidane's case provides illustrations of the reputation management stage of the life cycle of conflict (see Chapter 2) and University of Missouri Professor Bill Benoit's theory of image restoration. Following Benoit's typology of image restoration strategies, it appears that Zidane employed several. He *apologized* (Benoit calls the strategy "mortification"), but expressed no regret as he *shifted the blame*, noted the *provocation*, and said that defending his family *transcended* the act. Perhaps Zidane's favorable appeal can be linked to his nearly running the spectrum of Benoit's typology of image restoration strategy.

terms of exposure during the Indy 500 broadcast. The data show the brand received 1,400 seconds of broadcast exposure on ABC, estimated to be worth $1.33 million.

Sponsorships may also have an effect on a company's stock price. Professor Lance Kinney at the University of Alabama researched 61 sports event sponsorships. He found a significant increase in stock price for companies sponsoring Olympic events and baseball. Although no direct causal link can be proven, the relationship between sports sponsorships and corporate net worth is an interesting area of continuing research.

Travel Promotion

With money in their pockets, people want to go places and see things. Stimulating that desire and then turning it into the purchase of tickets and reservations is the goal of the travel industry. Public relations has an essential role in the process, not only in attracting visitors to destinations but in keeping them happy once they arrive.

Like entertainment and sports, travel draws from the public's recreation dollars. Often its promoters intertwine their projects with those of entertainment and sports entrepreneurs (see the Insights box on this page for one approach).

Phases of Travel Promotion

Traditionally, the practice of travel public relations has involved three steps:

1. Stimulating the public's desire to visit a place
2. Arranging for the travelers to reach it
3. Making certain that visitors are comfortable, well treated, and entertained when they get there

Fear of terrorism has focused emphasis on a crucial new element—ensuring travelers' safety.

Stimulation is accomplished through travel articles in magazines and newspapers, alluring brochures distributed by travel agents and by direct mail, travel films and videos, and presentations on the World Wide Web. Solicitations of associations and companies to hold conventions in particular locations encourage travel by groups.

Some publications have their own travel writers; others purchase freelance articles and pictures. Well-done articles by public relations practitioners about travel destinations often are published, too, if written in an informational manner without resorting to blatant salesmanship and purple prose. Aware of public resistance to such exaggeration, *Condé Nast Traveler* magazine carries the slogan "Truth in Travel" on its cover. In fact, *O'Dwyer's PR Services Report* warns that "PR overkill" results from indiscriminate distribution of news releases, nagging follow-up calls to editors about releases, ignorance about the publication being pitched with a story, and excessive handling of writers on arranged trips so that they find it difficult to get a complete picture of the travel destination.

ON THE JOB >>

"Novel" Approach to Getting Attention for Resort

Insights

When a Caribbean resort wanted to garner some media attention, its public relations agency, Nike Communications, suggested a "novel" approach.

The Little Dix Bay luxury resort arranged with some of the leading publishing houses in the United States to make advance copies of novels available exclusively to the guests of Little Dix Bay and affiliated properties. In a March 2006 press release, the resort announced:

> Ladies and gentlemen, you read it here first: The final word in intellectual one-upmanship is at Little Dix Bay, a Rosewood Resort which has forged an exclusive relationship with America's top publishing houses entitling its pampered, privileged guests bragging rights to the latest wave of best sellers before they're even on sale.
>
> The program, called "Hot Type," puts an end to the high-class ennui of "been there, read that." Little Dix Bay in the stunning British Virgin Islands makes available advance copies of new fiction and non-fiction works by the world's most prominent authors, including Candace Bushnell, John Updike, Steve Martin, Stephen King, Annie Proulx, and many more. New titles will arrive monthly to the "Hot Type" library.
>
> "Little Dix Bay's guests—who have always been avid readers—have more than just new titles to inspire their reading pleasure. The resort's breathtaking, free-form pool entices with a misting waterfall—the perfect accompaniment to a special "book menu" from which guests may choose an advance book copy to devour during their stay.

The campaign, which was in its second year in 2006, garnered coverage in *Fortune*, the *New York Times*, the *Wall Street Journal*, *Travel & Leisure*, *Condé Nast Traveller*, and *USA Today*, according to a report in *PRWeek*.

In its second year, the campaign brought authors to the resort to speak about their new books with guests.

Source: Miller, Amanda Christine. "Resort Builds Buzz with Books." *PRWeek*, May 29, 2006, 19

ON THE JOB >>

How Many "Freebies" to Accept?

Ethics

Creation of newspaper and magazine stories about travel destinations, which are essential in tourism promotion, poses a problem for writers and public relations people. Who should pay the writers' expenses in researching these stories?

Some large newspapers forbid their travel writers to accept free or discounted hotel rooms, meals, and travel tickets. They believe that such subsidies may cause writers to slant their articles too favorably, perhaps subconsciously.

Many smaller publications and most freelance writers cannot afford such an expensive rule, however, and following it would prevent them from preparing travel articles. Freelance travel writer Jeff Miller took the publishing industry to task in *Editor & Publisher* magazine for paying $150 per newspaper story

and $500 to $1,000 per magazine story while banning writers from taking subsidized trips. Travel writers claim the hypocritical policy makes the publications look good, but that it is regularly ignored by travel writers who simply cannot make a living without subsidized trips. The writers contend that pride in their professional objectivity keeps them from being influenced by their hosts' "freebies." Some point to critical articles they have written on subsidized trips.

For the public relations director of a resort, cruise, or other travel attraction, the situation presents two problems: (1) How much hospitality can be given to the press before the "freebies" become a form of bribery? and (2) How does the director screen requests from self-described travel writers who request free housing or travel?

The Society of American Travel Writers (SATW) sets the following guideline:

Free or reduced-rate transportation and other travel expenses must be offered and accepted only with the mutual understanding that reportorial research is involved and any resultant story will be reported with the same standards of journalistic accuracy as that of comparable coverage and criticism in theater, business and finance, music, sports, and other news sections that provide the public with objective and helpful information.

What do you think of the SATW guidelines? Are they specific enough to guide you in your public relations position for a gorgeous Caribbean resort? What of the "no sponsored trips" policy at some newspapers and magazines? Do you believe that heavily discounted trips tend to buy writer loyalty in the same way that free trips do?

Arrangements for travel are made through travel agencies or by direct booking at airlines, airports, and railroad and bus stations. Complicated tours and cruises are arranged most frequently by travel agencies, which charge customers retail prices for accommodations and receive a 10 percent commission from the travel supplier. Wholesalers create package tours that are sold by travel agencies.

To promote sales, the 38,000 U.S. travel agencies distribute literature, sponsor travel fairs, and encourage group travel by showing destination films at invitational meetings. Cities and states operate convention and travel departments to encourage tourism. A widely used method of promoting travel is the familiarization trip, commonly called a "fam trip," in which travel writers and/or travel salespeople are invited to a resort, theme park, or other destination for an inspection visit. In the past, fam trips often were loosely structured mass junkets. Today they are smaller and more focused. See the Ethics box on this page regarding freebies to travel writers.

Good treatment of travelers is a critical element of travel promotion. If a couple spends a large sum on a trip, then encounters poor accommodations, rude hotel

There's always something new in the travel industry. Here, *Queen Mary 2* makes its way past the Statue of Liberty in New York on its maiden voyage from England. A public relations firm handled the logistics of media coverage. Media were interested because the luxury cruise ship was the largest, longest, tallest, and most expensive ($800 million) ship ever built to date.

clerks, misplaced luggage, and inferior sightseeing arrangements, they come home angry. And they will readily tell their friends how bad the trip was.

Even the best arrangements go awry at times. Planes are late, tour members miss the bus, and bad weather riles tempers. This is where the personal touch means so much. An attentive, cheerful tour director or hotel manager can soothe guests, and a "make-good" gesture such as a free drink or meal does wonders. Careful training of travel personnel is essential. Many travelers, especially in foreign countries, are uneasy in strange surroundings and depend more on others than they would at home.

Appeals to Target Audiences

Travel promoters identify target audiences, creating special appeals and trips for them. Great Britain's skillfully designed publicity in the United States is an example of a successful effort. Its basic appeal is an invitation to visit the country's historic places and pageants. It also offers London theatrical tours, golf expeditions to famous courses in Scotland, genealogical research parties for those seeking family roots, and tours of cathedrals. Special tours can be arranged for other purposes as well.

Packaging. *Packaging* is a key word in travel public relations. Cruises for family reunions or school groups, family skiing vacations, university alumni study groups, archaeological expeditions, even trips to remote Tibet are just a few of the so-called niche travel packages that are offered. A package usually consists of prepaid arrangements for transportation, housing, most meals, and entertainment, with a professional escort to handle the details. Supplementary side trips often are offered for extra fees.

Appeals to Seniors. The largest special travel audience is older citizens. Retired persons have time to travel, and many have ample money to do so. Hotels, motels, and airlines frequently offer discounts to attract this audience. As a means of keeping old-school loyalties alive, many colleges conduct alumni tours, heavily attended by senior citizens.

A large percentage of cruise passengers, especially on longer voyages, are retirees. Alert travel promoters design trips with them in mind, including such niceties as pairing compatible widows to share cabins and arranging shore trips that require little walking. Shipboard entertainment and recreational activities with appeal to older persons—nostalgic music for dancing rather than current hits, for example—are important, too.

Times of Crisis

Public relations in travel requires crisis management, just as in corporate work. Crises come in many forms, from those of dangerous magnitude to the small but embarrassing varieties.

The Caribbean island of Aruba, for example, is a popular destination for U.S. tourists (about 1 million annually) but its tranquil image of clear water, beautiful beaches, and swaying palm trees was considerbly shaken in May of 2005. That was the month that Natalee Holloway, a 18-year-old from Alabama on a class graduation trip disappeared from one of Aruba's resorts. The disappearance—and the strong inference of foul play—became a major story in the print and broadcast media. At one point, 60 foreign reporters were on the Dutch island covering the case. Howard Kutz, media critic for the *Washington Post*, noted, "Cable TV is treating this as the crime of the century, or at least, the obsession of the moment." He told the *Christian Science Monitor* that Aruba had garnered more media coverage over Holloway than it had received in the last 20 years.

The Holloway story was a major crisis for the Aruba tourism industry, and other Caribbean islands were also concerned that tourism would decline because of the negative coverage. The story continued to garner headlines as Holloway's mother gave extensive interviews and loudly complained about the lack of progress the Aruba police were making in finding her daughter. The Alabama legislature even got into the act and threatened a boycott of the island until the case was solved.

Aruba's public relations firm, Quinn & Co. in New York, originally retained to promote the island's beaches and resorts, had to immediately switch gears and do crisis management. One tactic was to centralize information about the police investigation and to give regular updates on progress in the case. The firm also worked with cruise lines, travel agents, and airlines to assure them that the Aruba was safe and still an attractive destination. The government also issued a statement saying, "This comes as a shock to Aruba where crime against tourists is almost non-existent," noting the island's repeat visitor rate of 40 percent, the highest in the Caribbean.

A year later, in 2006, no trace of Natalee Holloway had been found and no one had been charged with her alleged murder. The story, however, faded from the headlines and the media moved on. In Aruba, tourism is about back to normal.

On a different level, the luxurious liner *Queen Elizabeth 2* departed on a high-priced cruise before refurbishing was completed. Many passengers had unpleasant trips because some of the facilities were in disrepair, leading to one news report describing the ship as a floating construction project. Others had their reservations canceled because their cabins were not completed. After bad international publicity and a class-action suit by some passengers, the Cunard cruise line offered a settlement. It gave full refunds of cruise fares plus a travel credit for a future cruise.

Among numerous areas of concern, travel firms need to make certain that they provide equal facilities and service to all races. They also need to ensure that their facilities and practices are environmentally sound or risk negative publicity, as when a cruise ship had to pay a heavy fine after a passenger videotaped its crew members tossing debris overboard.

PRCASEBOOK

Viral Marketing—Word-of-Mouth Communication Updated

Long before the rise of the Internet, professional communicators recognized the value of favorable recommendations and "buzz" about a product or service. For public relations programs, the primary objective was often to enhance or maintain the reputation of a company or celebrity. Today, spreading the word can generate greater traffic to a Web site, where both marketing and public relations objectives can be met. The primary purpose of viral marketing is to stimulate impulse purchases or downloads, but increasingly pass-it-on techniques on the Web serve public relations objectives in reputation management and message dissemination. Generating excitement about the release of a musician's latest CD or the opening of a movie are two common uses of viral marketing in the entertainment business.

Viral marketing has adopted a new terminology and some special techniques that take advantage of new technology to stimulate the natural inclination of people to tell others about a good deal, a good service, or a good group. For example, Hotmail began to offer free e-mail in 1997, including a message on each e-mail: "get your free, private e-mail." Within a year and a half, Hotmail garnered 12 million subscribers with a total investment of a half million dollars.

Viral marketing firms devise ways to stimulate the natural spread of recommendations through financial incentives called *cohort communication*. Going beyond the relatively natural spread of information through tactics similar to Hotmail's inviting message, viral marketing specialists orchestrate dissemination of favorable reviews. Software systems track referrals to a Web site or recommendations sent to friends, chalking up cash or merchandise credits for the sender. Recommending a CD to friends can earn the recommender credit or free downloads of music tracks, for example.

Detractors worry that viral marketing is easily recognized as commercial manipulation, except among hard-core enthusiasts. Others say that it is deceptive and unethical to facilitate or reward what should be a natural process of trusted friends exchanging tips and links about great deals or great Web sites. For example, the music industry recruits fans to log on to chat rooms and fan Web sites to hype a band's new album. Some liken this to the questionable old practice of payola in the radio industry—payment to disk jockeys for air time.

Viral marketing companies argue that the technique will work only when the idea, the movement, or the product earns genuine support from the marketplace. Then, netizens take advantage of the convenience of the Web to forward what they like to others. Jupiter Communications found that over half of online users visit sites based on a recommendation and nearly all have forwarded a recommendation to another friend. Public relations professionals will need to make careful and ethical decisions to decide how best to use the Web to spread messages.

To explore viral marketing on your own and to consider how to adapt the techniques to your own public relations activities on campus, visit some of the Web sites of the following viral marketing companies:

> Caffeine Online Marketing Solutions at www.getcaffeinated.com

> Viralon Corporation at www.viralon.com

> EmailFactory.com at www.emailfactory.com

Summary

Today's Modern Corporation

Today, giant corporations have operations and customers around the globe. The public is often distrustful of these large entities because of their perceived wealth and power. Corporate financial scandals in recent years have further eroded public trust.

The Role of Public Relations

Corporations must make special efforts to win back public credibility and trust, and the concept of corporate social responsibility (CSR) should be high on the list of priorities. Public relations professionals are on the frontline in this effort, counseling companies to be more transparent in their operations, to adopt ethical standards of conduct, and to improve corporate governance.

Media Relations

The public's perception of business comes primarily from the mass media. Consequently, it is important for organizations to effectively tell their story and establish rapport with business editors and reporters by being accessible, open, and honest about company operations and policies.

Customer Relations

Customer service, in many ways, is the front line of public relations. Customer satisfaction is important for building loyalty, generating positive word of mouth for products, and maintaining the reputation of company. Public relations professionals solicit customer feedback as often as possible and act to satisfy customers' needs for communication and service.

Reaching a Diverse Market

The U.S. population is becoming more diverse, and companies are now establishing communication programs, as well as marketing strategies, to serve this changing audience.

Consumer Activism

In today's society, any number of special-interest groups exert pressure on corporations to be socially responsible. Companies cannot avoid activist groups; they must engage in dialogue to work out differences. Oftentimes, public relations staff serve as mediators. Consumer boycotts also require public relations expertise to deal effectively with a group's demands.

Employee Relations

Employees are the "ambassadors" of a company and are the primary source of information about the company for friends and relatives. Employee morale is important, and a good communications program—coupled with enlightened company policies—does much to maintain high productivity and employee retention.

Layoffs and Outsourcing

The cardinal rule, from a public relations standpoint, is to first talk to employees in person before announcing a layoff to the public. Many companies ease the impact of layoffs by providing severance packages. Offshoring is a growing concern of American workers, and companies must be sensitive to possible criticism.

Minorities in the Workplace

The American workforce is becoming increasingly diverse. Companies must take this into consideration when planning employee communication campaigns.

Investor Relations

Public relations professionals who work in investor relations must be knowledgeable about communications and finance. It's the highest-paying field in public relations, but practitioners must have extensive knowledge of government regulations.

Marketing Communications

Increasingly, companies take an integrated approach to campaigns. Public relations, marketing, and advertising staffs work together to complement each other's expertise. Product publicity and product placement are part of marketing communications. Cause-related marketing involves partnerships with nonprofit organizations to promote a particular cause. Another aspect of marketing communications is corporate sponsorships.

Environmental Relations

A new trend is for corporations and activist organizations to engage in dialogue and collaborative efforts to change situations that damage the environment or violate human rights.

Corporate Philanthropy

Companies give about $12 billion a year to worthy causes. It's important to select a charity that is complementary to an organization's business and customer profile. In general, corporate philanthropy is part of an organization's commitment to social responsibility.

The Practitioner's Responsibility

A big challenge for public relations practitioners who handle personalities is damage control when misbehaviors occur or irresponsible public statements are made. This may test a practitioner's ethical principles; it is never wise to lie to protect a client.

Conducting a Personality Campaign

A practitioner planning a campaign to generate public awareness of an individual must interview the client, prepare a biography, plan a marketing strategy, and conduct the campaign through news releases, photographs, and public appearances.

Promoting an Entertainment Event

Publicity campaigns to promote events include publicity to stimulate ticket sales. The "drip-drip-drip" technique involves a steady output of information as the event is being planned. The entertainment industry defines target audiences to promote motion pictures and television shows.

Sports Publicity

Sports publicists promote both college and professional teams. This effort becomes more difficult when a team isn't winning. Emerging sports must compete for prominence and fan loyalty with more established sports. Some publicity focuses on building images of star players. Publicity efforts also include both sports crisis and sponsorship management.

Travel Promotion

Travel promotion involves increasing the public's desire to visit a place, arranging for them to reach it, making sure they enjoy their trips, and ensuring their safety. Campaigns sometimes include familiarization trips to increase travel agents' awareness of destinations.

CASE ACTIVITY >>

What Would You Do?

The Dixie Chicks is one of the most successful recording and performing acts in recent times. The three-woman group has sold more than 24 million copies of their songs, and their 2003 tour generated box office sales of $60.5 million, an all-tme high for a country music tour.

But that was before the group's fortunes suffered a major setback when lead singer Natalie Maines told a London concert audience that she was "ashamed" of President Bush, also from Texas, for invading Iraq. That didn't sit well with the group's core audience, country music fans who tend to be conservative and patriotic. Fans were furious and stopped buying their records; country music stations across the country retaliated by refusing to air their music.

Then, in 2006, the Dixie Chicks came out with a new album that was heavily promoted by Columbia Records, the group's record label. The new album, *Taking the Long Way*, included the single "Not Ready to Make Nice," which addressed fans and programmers who boycotted the group in 2003. The group's feisty attitude and refusal to modify their political opinions despite audience backlash received considerable media coverage, including the cover

of *Time* Magazine and appearances on such programs as *60 Minutes*, *Larry King Live*, and *Good Morning America*. As a result, the album was at the top of the Billboard chart for the first two weeks after its release despite the decision by many country music stations to refuse to play it.

The Dixie Chicks, however, appear to be leaving their country music base and are now attempting to reach a broader audience base. The album did get good play at outlets such as Starbucks and Apple ITunes music service, as well as among their hard-core fans—which includes many in Europe and Australia. Indeed, music critics say *Taking the Long Way* leans more toward the 1970s country rock than the groups previous albums.

Your public relations firm, which specializes in entertainment, is retained by the Dixie Chicks and Columbia Records to forge a new personality and broader audience for the group. What objectives would you set? What strategies and tactics would you use to again make the Dixie Chicks one of the most successful musical groups on the market? Would you, in some way, incorporate their willingness to criticize the U.S. involvement in Iraq and other political beliefs? Why or why not?

Questions for Review and Discussion

1. What are the characteristics of today's modern corporation? Why is there so much public suspicion and distrust? Is there any evidence to support the public's perceptions?

2. What is the concept of corporate social responsibility (CSR), and why is it important to today's corporations? What is the role of public relations professionals in CSR?

3. Traditionally, customer relations and public relations have been separate corporate functions. Do you think the two functions should be merged? Why or why not?

4. How should companies consider diversity in their marketing and public relations strategies?

5. Consumer activists are very vocal about the misdeeds of corporations. How should a company react to charges and allegations from activist groups such as PETA? What factors would go into your decision making?

6. Why are employee relations efforts so important to a company's image and reputation?

7. Many companies give workers time off with pay to volunteer on local charitable projects. Would you be

more inclined to work for such a company? Why or why not?

8. Give some examples of product publicity and product placement.

9. Why is corporate sponsorship of concerts, festivals, and even the Olympics considered a good marketing and public relations strategy?

10. Corporate philanthropy is now very strategic; companies support organizations and causes that have a direct relationship to their business. Do you think all this makes corporate philanthropy too self-serving? Why or why not?

11. What is the first step in preparing a campaign to increase the public's awareness of an individual client?

12. Why do practitioners put emphasis on certain players on sports teams?

13. What are the basic phases of travel promotion?

Suggested Readings

Anderson, William B. "Crafting the National Pastime's Image: The History of Major-League Baseball Public Relations." *Journalism and Communication Monographs* 5, no. 1 (2003): 1–43.

Buffington, Jody. "Can Human Resources and Internal Communications Peacefully Coexist?" *The Strategist*, Fall 2004, 33–35.

Chabria, Anita. "Cause Survey 2005: Communication When It Matters." *PRWeek*, October 24, 2005, 18–26.

Daniels, Chris. "Roots Builds on Olympic Ties to Put Clothes on Map." *PRWeek*, June 20, 2005, 8.

Hazley, Greg. "Ford Is Latest Reversal in Culture War Clash." *O'Dwyer's PR Services Report*, January 2006, 24–25.

Herskovits, Beth. "The PR Road Show: Working with Touring Exhibitions Offers Rich and Varied Opportunities." *PRWeek*, May 2, 2005, 17.

Hood, Julia. "CEO Survey 2005: Banking on Your Team." *PRWeek*, November 7, 2005, 18–24.

Kang, Stephanie, and Mike Esterl. "At World Cup: Nike and Adidas Fight for Top Spot." *Wall Street Journal*, May 23, 2006, A1.

Landler, Mark. "The Hard Sell in Germany: Marketing Is Just as Intense as World Cup's Zealous Fans." *New York Times*, June 7, 2006, C1, C4.

Leeds, Jeff. "Chicks Sing New Song: Who Needs Airplay? *New York Times*, June 10, 2006, A15, A21.

Lukaszewski, James P. "Work with Me: With Low Trust Levels in Senior Management, You Need to Become an Employee Communications Strategist." *The Strategist*, Fall 2004, 18–21.

McQuade, George. "Bring Back Gimmicks, Tricks, Say Entertainment PR Legends." *O'Dwyer's PR Services Report*, January 2006, 93.

Nolan, Hamilton. "Corporate Survey 2005: Broadening Communications." *PRWeek*, June 27, 2006, 16–22.

Park, Dong-Jin, and Bruce K. Berger. "The Presentation of CEOs in the Press, 1990–2000: Increasing Salience, Positive Valence, and a Focus on Competency and Personal Dimensions of Image." *Journal of Public Relations Research* 16, no. 1 (2004): 93–125.

Voeller, Greg, and Kelly Groehler. "Employees: Always the Primary Audience." *The Strategist*, Fall 2004, 27–29.

Waxman, Sharon. "Celebrity Freebies: A Force Irresistible?" *New York Times*, February 15, 2006, B1, B7.

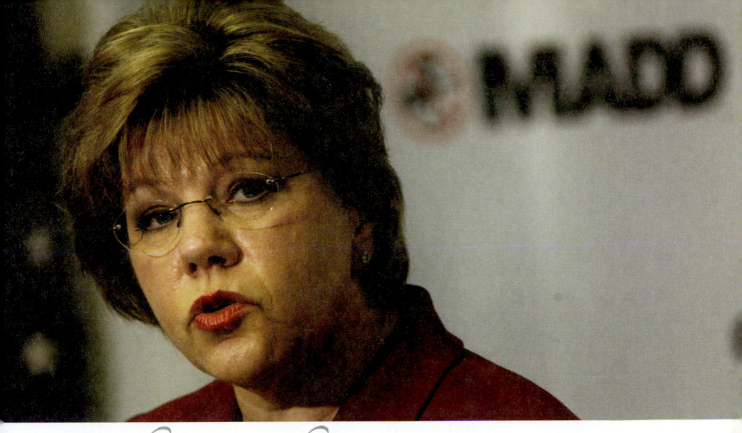

Chapter Thirteen

Nonprofit, Education, and Government

The Role of Public Relations in Nonprofit, Education, and Government Organizations

A broad area of public relations work, and the source of many jobs, is found in non-profit organizations, which are often called *charities*. In the United States, there are about 920,000 such groups, according to GuideStar, an organization that compiles information on nonprofits. The range of nonprofit institutions is astounding, from membership organizations, advocacy groups, social service organizations, and educational organizations to hospitals and health agencies and small city historical societies to global foundations that disperse million-dollar grants. Government agencies at the federal, state, and local levels are not exactly nonprofit organizations but share many of the characterisitics of nonprofits.

Nonprofit, or not-for-profit, organizations can be defined as organizations whose main purpose is to serve the public interest and are noncommercial. In other words, non-profit organizations do not distribute monies to shareholders or owners. This is not to say that non-profit organizations cannot generate income or hold assets, but there are a number of complicated restrictions regulating how income may be generated and finances are managed. Put very simply, no individual or organization can make a profit or use a nonprofit organization's assets for purposes not directly associated with its stated goals and activities. A crucial point about nonprofit is that they are generally set up to serve the public good. From public relations perspective, nonprofit organizations have been often represented as fostering goodwill, and as beacons of social responsibility.

Another important point about nonprofits is that they are tax exempt. The federal government grants them this status because they enhance the well-being of their members, as with trade associations, or enhance the human condition in some way, as with environmental work or medical research. Many nonprofit organizations could not survive if they were taxed. Nonprofit organizations do not have shareholders who invest in the organizations and buy and sell stocks. Thus, they face the unending public relations task of raising money to pay their expenses, finance their projects, and recruit volunteer workers as well as paid employees.

Basic Purposes and Functions of Nonprofit, Education, and Government Public Relations

Federal and state governments, state universities or colleges, and health and human services organizations or nonprofit hospitals would seem to have little in common with the Public Relations Society of America, the National Academy of Songwriters, Mothers Against Drunk Driving (MADD) and the American Red Cross, yet all engage in the same types of public relations tasks in order to succeed and thrive.

Because these organizations are not profit-oriented, the practice of public relations on their behalf differs somewhat from that in the business world. Traditionally, nonprofit social agencies have been seen as the "good guys" of society—high-minded, compassionate organizations whose members work to help people achieve a better life. Of course, in actual practice some nonprofits violate the public trust and their relationships with potential donors suffer as a result.

All nonprofit organizations create communication campaigns and programs, including special events, brochures, and radio and television appearances, and Web sites that stimulate public interest in organizational goals and invite further public involvement. Recruiting volunteers and keeping them enthusiastic are essential. Most of these organizations establish realistic fund-raising goals and plans to raise money, though government agencies are funded primarily through taxes.

Membership organizations advocate for their members rather than for society as a whole. Members of professional or trade associations and labor unions share similar interests and have particular issues and needs. The public relations efforts of these organizations primarily target their members but also advocate on behalf of their members in the larger social, political, and economic realms.

Advocacy groups perform a variety public relations functions and implement diverse strategies and tactics. They advocate social and environment causes and sometimes create conflict in order to effect social change. Such tactics as continuous publicity, demonstrations, or litigation are often used by these groups. They raise funds to support such efforts and recruit volunteer workers.

Philantrophic, cultural, and religious organizations, on the other hand, function as social service organizations. Their goals generally are to create a better society, reduce conflict, or support existing norms or values. Their public relations approaches are usually more accommodative, using tactics such as sponsored events, conferences, and letter-writing campaigns. They are often funded by corporations or wealthy people motivated by altruism, seeking public recognition and improved reputation, or some combination of both.

Health organizations such as hospitals and health agencies may be organized either as not-for-profit or for-profit institutions. This chapter focuses on those insititutions that function as nonprofit entities. While the daily operations of nonprofit hospitals closely resemble that of their for-profit brethren, the crucial difference is that no shareholders receive dividends, all excess funds are reinvested in the institution, and they are tax-exempt. All legitimate medical foundations and charities function as not-for-profit organizations. Depending on their emphasis and mission, the public relations efforts of health organizations target patients, specific demographic groups, or the community at large. Health education outreach campaigns, as a public relations function, promote public health and serve the public good. These organizations tend to be accomodative, though they sometimes compete for preeminence in situations of risk, emergency, or disaster.

Most educational institutions, on the other hand, operate as nonprofit organizations. Elementary and secondary schools, colleges and universities, and any number of trade and specialized schools, whether public or private, are devoted to enhancing the general public good through their programs. Most schools are tax exempt and do not have shareholders, but are generally regulated or licensed through a variety of accrediting bodies. Educational institutions focus on current and prospective students, faculty, teachers, and staff, though government and the community relations are important aspects of the public relations functions in educational institutions.

Although government agencies and adminstrations are not technically nonprofit organizations, they share characteristics such as tax exemption, serving the public good, and regulations against external distribution of funds to individuals or entities. The public relations functions of government agencies primarily consist of disseminating information. Government agencies often promote the policies of the current administration and seek support from people. Such public relations efforts frequently are associated with reelection campaigns.

Each of these areas—membership organizations, advocacy groups, social issue organizations, health organizations, educational institutions, and government entities—employ public relations specialists to promote their services, assist with fundraising, spread news of their successes or crises, assist with smooth daily operations or crisis management, implement campaigns that address social issus, and help develop long-range plans and visions. Opportunities for empolyment in these areas should not be overlooked by aspiring public relations professionals.

Competition, Conflict, and Cooperation in Nonprofit, Education, and Government Oranizations

For many nonprofit organizations, partnerships can be mutually beneficial. The United Way is a good case in point—many business and nonprofit organizations ranging from the National Football League to the Advertising Council to numerous local organizations partner with the United Way to maximize donations that are then distributed to hundreds of associated charities. However, the frustrating reality is that nonprofits often compete with each other for members, funds, and other resources.

Competition among nonprofit agencies for donations is intense. For many nonprofit groups, obtaining operating funds is a necessity that dominates much of their activities. Without generous contributions from companies and individuals, nonprofit organizations could not exist. As an indication of the scope of philanthropy in the United States, and of the money needed to keep voluntary service agencies operating, American contributions to charity were $260 billion in 2005, according to the Giving Institute (see the Insights box on page 409 for a breakdown of sources and category of

ON THE JOB >>

Charitable Contributions Reach a New Level

Insights

Charitable giving is a well-established American institution. A record $260 billion was given in 2005, a growth of 6 percent over the previous year, according to the Giving USA Foundation.

Accounting for about half of the increase were several disasters in 2005 that generated an additional $7.4 billion in contributions. Hurricane Katrina, which devastated New Orleans and surrounding areas, generated an outpouring of $5.3 billion in contributions.

The Asian tsunami, which cost thousands of lives in Indonesia and neighboring nations, received $1.9 billion in contributions from Americans, while the Pakistan earthquake generated about $200 million.

According to the research conducted by the Center for Philanthropy at Indiana University, the major sources of U.S. donations were rounded as follows:

Distribution of the $260 billion was in the following categories:

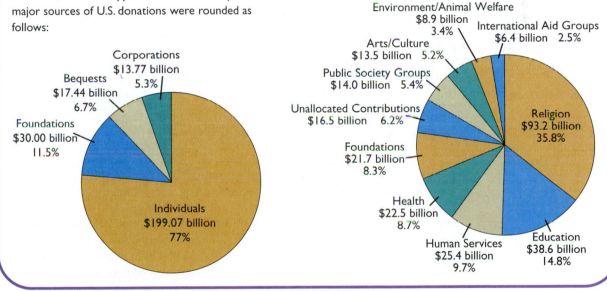

Corporations
$13.77 billion
5.3%

Bequests
$17.44 billion
6.7%

Foundations
$30.00 billion
11.5%

Individuals
$199.07 billion
77%

Environment/Animal Welfare
$8.9 billion
3.4%

International Aid Groups
$6.4 billion 2.5%

Arts/Culture
$13.5 billion 5.2%

Public Society Groups
$14.0 billion 5.4%

Unallocated Contributions
$16.5 billion 6.2%

Foundations
$21.7 billion
8.3%

Health
$22.5 billion
8.7%

Human Services
$25.4 billion
9.7%

Religion
$93.2 billion
35.8%

Education
$38.6 billion
14.8%

giving). Additional funds are donated to specialized nonprofit organizations that do not fall under the "charity" mantle, and still more are contributed by federal, state, and local governments.

Relationships among nonprofit organizations represent a conspicuous mix of parties who have a willingness to cooperate but must also compete for limited or scarce resources. Such partnerships are based on common interests, but in advocating their individual interests, they are no different from business organizations that must struggle for market shares.

For example, in addition to the Public Relations Society of America (PRSA), a number of public relations organizations or agencies compete with one another to promote the common interests of professionals in the field. Universities or colleges within the same state also compete for more funding from their respective state governments, even as they enter into collaborate partnerships to obtain more from the federal government. Hospitals also compete for "customers," but must work together to resolve shared concerns and issues. Government agencies also struggle for budget allocations but then must cooperate with respect to serving the public and sometimes with respect to the political climate.

Activist groups who espouse certain causes, on the other hand, can come into conflict with other organizations whose values are different. Such conflcts can be a high-profile. In recent years, a number of religious organizations have come into conflict with groups that advocate for secular values. For example, the American Civil Liberties Union (ACLU), a nonprofit organization founded in 1920 "to defend and preserve the individual rights and liberties guaranteed to every person in this country by the Constitution and laws of the United States," often comes into conflict with the American Center for Law and Justice, a conservative group founded by Pat Robertson to preserve "religious liberty, the sanctity of human life, and the two-parent, marriage-bound family." Although both organizations state that they are committed to preserving "liberty," their respective views of what constitutes "liberty" are often diametrically opposed.

Membership Organizations

Membership organizations are composed of people who share common business or social interests. Their purpose is mutual help and self-improvement. Membership organizations often use the strength of their common bond to develop the professionalism of their members, endorse legislation, and support socially valuable causes. Their main function is to advocate for the well-being of their members.

Professional Associations

Members of a profession or skilled craft organize for mutual benefit. In many ways, their goals resemble those of labor unions in that they seek improved earning power, better working conditions, and public appreciation of their respective roles in society. Professional associations place their major emphasis on setting standards for professional performance, establishing codes of ethics, determining requirements for admission to a field, and encouraging members to upgrade skills through continuing education. In some cases, they have quasi-legal power to license and censure members. In most cases, however, professional groups use the techniques of peer pressure and persuasion to police their membership.

In general, professional associations are national in scope. Larger organizations often have district, state, or local chapters. Many scientific and scholarly associations, however, are international, with chapters in many nations. The Public Relations Society of America (PRSA) and the International Association of Business Communicators (IABC) are examples of professional associations.

Public relations specialists for professional organizations use the same techniques as their colleagues in other branches of practice. And like their counterparts in trade groups and labor unions, many professional associations maintain offices near the seats of government in Washington, D.C., and the various state capitals and employ lobbyists to advocate for their positions. One of the most politically active and successful professional associations is the American Medical Association (AMA). With 220,000 physician members, the AMA has developed lobbying and grassroots efforts to influence medical liability, or "tort," reform to the association's advantage. The AMA argues that medical liability settlements are excessive. They provide Physician

Action Kits and talking points for members to use when speaking about medical liability reform. In addition, the AMA sponsors letter-writing campaigns and provides experts to testify before Congress.

Trade Associations

The membership of a trade association usually consists of manufacturers, wholesalers, retailers, or distributors in the same field. Memberships are held by corporate entities, not individuals. A few examples of trade associations include Electronic Industries Alliance, American Beverage Association, the Property Casualty Insurers Association, and National Association of Home Builders. At last count, there were about 6,000 trade and professional associations in the United States. Because federal laws and regulations often can affect the fortunes of an entire industry, about one-third of these groups are based in the Washington, D.C., area. There, association staffs can monitor congressional activity, lobby for or against legislation, communicate late-breaking developments to the membership, and interact with government officials on a regular basis.

Trade associations are often placed in situations where they must compete or collaborate with one another. Although individual members of trade associations may be direct rivals competing for market share, it is often to their advantage to work together promoting an entire industry, generating public support, and sharing information of common interest to the entire membership. By representing an entire industry, an association often is more effective as a news source than is an individual company. When a news situation develops involving a particular field, reporters often turn to the spokesperson of its association for comment. To promote their industry, many trade organizations create video news releases for broadcast on local and national news outlets. Some controversy surrounds this practice because VNRs are often presented by television stations as "straight news" without proper attribution, so it is not always clear to the public that the VNRs were underwritten or developed by a trade organization.

Labor Unions

Like trade assocations, labor unions represent the interests of an entire industry. However, labor unions advocate on behalf of employees, whereas trade associations typically represent the interests of management. As with other membership organizations, labor unions lobby for better working conditions, higher wages, increased safety regulations, better benefits, and education for their memberships. Since their apex in the late 1970s, labor unions have suffered serious membership losses and, as a consequence, political clout. The United Auto Workers, for example, saw membership decline from 1.5 million in 1979 to less than half that number in 2004. Today, total union membership accounts for less than 15 percent of all American workers, with the figure dropping to about 10 percent in the private sector. About 20 states, including Mississippi and Kansas, have adopted so-called right-to-work statutes that weaken or, in some cases, actively discourage union activity. Partially owing to the efforts of management and to a changing political climate, labor unions have suffered an image crisis.

Media portrayals often suggest that unions are corrupt, inflexible, and lack concern for anyone except their members. Nevertheless, labor unions have largely been been responsible for many things that Americans today take for granted: the end of child labor, the 40-hour workweek, laws against discrimination in hiring and firing, and the minimum wage. Unions are still are very much a part of the American scene, representing teachers, players in the National Basketball Association, and UPS employees, among others.

Unions rely on public relations tools to assert strength and influence (see the Insights box on page 413). Unions must seek to build their memberships, protect members' job security, and improve their public images. Unions employ public relations when communicating with their internal audiences in various companies or organizations. They must keep their memberships informed about what they receive in return for their dues, including recreational and social programs and representation by union leadership on their behalf to company management. Labor unions are often in conflict with management, which is dominant in terms of both financial strength and political clout. In every national political campaign, unions spend millions of dollars to support of candidates they regard as friendly. Some of this money goes directly to candidates, but significant amounts are devoted to "issue ads" that do not explicitly endorse an individual. This practice, which despite rhetoric to the contrary represents a fraction of the money spent on issue ads supporting probusiness interests, enables support of candidates beyond individual campaign spending limits.

Chambers of Commerce

A chamber is an association of business professionals who work to improve their city's commercial climate and to publicize its attractions. Above all, chambers of commerce serve as boosters of local business growth. State chambers of commerce and, nationally, the U.S. Chamber of Commerce help guide local chambers and particularly speak for business interests before state legislatures and the federal government. In fact, according to the Center for Public Integrity, the national Chamber of Commerce spent a total of $181 million on lobbying between 1998 and 2004—more than any other single entity.

Local chambers of commerce play the role of community booster: Chambers spotlight the unique characteristics of their cities and sing their praises to anyone who will listen. Chambers often coin a slogan for a city, such as "Furniture Capital of Indiana" (Berne) or "Business at its Best since 1926" (Belfast, Maine).

Often, a chamber of commerce serves as the public relations arm of city government. The chamber staff generally produces the brochures and maps sent to individuals who seek information about visiting the city or who consider moving to the area. Chambers also conduct polls and compile statistics about the economic health of the city, including data on major industries, employment rates, availability of schools and hospitals, housing costs, and so on. Attracting conventions and new businesses to the city also is an important part of chamber work.

Advocacy Groups

Any number of pressing issues affect communities to varying degrees, from housing and social issues such as poverty, abortion, and racism to threats such as epidemic diseases and environmental degradation. Organizations that fight for social causes can have significant impact, both positive and negative. For example, the environment holds a high place on the public agenda, primarily because of vigorous campaigns by environmental organizations. By advocating for recycling, eliminating toxic waste sites, purifying the air and water, and preserving natural resources, such organizations strongly influence our collective conscience.

Advocacy groups include activist groups such as Greenpeace and People for the Ethical Treatment of Animals (PETA) and social issue organizations such as the National Rifle Association and American Family Association (AFA). They advocate to

— ON THE JOB >> —

Defining Labor's Continuing Relevance

Insights

Unions face numerous challenges, particularly the public's often negative perception of them as greedy, corrupt, and outdated. The AFL-CIO's public relations efforts to counter this negativity and maintain membership stress their unions' continuing relevance for the American worker.

The American Federation of Labor and the Congress of Industrial Organizations (AFL-CIO) is the parent group of 54 national and international labor unions. Founded in 1955 with the merger of two separate union groups, the AFL-CIO's mission is to "improve the lives of working families—to bring economic justice to the workplace and social justice to our nation." The AFL-CIO is one of the largest special-interest membership groups in the United States with over 10 million constituents. However, this is down sharply from its zenith in the late 1950s when nearly one out of every five American workers was a union member. Still, the AFL-CIO has sizeable influence on the political process, primarily through political action committees and direct lobbying of federal and state officials.

The union's public relations efforts have concentrated on maintaining membership and demonstrating that unions are still relevant in America. Members are barraged with a constant stream of mailings detailing the union's stand of timely issues such as trade deficits, living wage issues, Social Security, health care provisions, employment law, and safety regulations. In addition, the Web site www.aflcio.org/

The AFL-CIO has been in a period of decline, but is taking steps to revitalize its image by demonstrating its continuing relevance. 1995 Huck Labor Cartoons—UCS, (www.lafn.org/politics/gvdc/Labor.html).

provides figures documenting inequities, such as that women still earn 76 cents for every dollar made by a man. The Web site also points out that union workers earn an average of 28 percent more than their nonunion counterparts.

The union has been the target of fierce criticism. For example, Mark Tapscott, writing for the Heritage Foundation, a conservative think-tank, blasted the union leadership in 2005. "For years, unions have created trusts, which are little more than slush funds available only to selected officials who use the money to pay for campaign activities. . . ."

To stem such criticisms, and affect public opinion, the AFL-CIO Web site

provides media resources in the form of press releases, statistics, and links to public and member opinion research. One strategy has been to publish guest columns written by opinion leaders from outside the union. Several of these columns stress the historic gains won by labor in the past, connecting the labor movement to American democracy. University of Wisconsin–Green Bay professor Harvey J. Kaye, for example, traces the labor movement to the writings of Revolutionary War patriot Thomas Paine. The union also has recently added a blog to their Web site, http://blog.aflcio.org/, allowing users to send news stories and comment on labor issues.

promote their own causes, but often are perceived as lobbying for the good of the whole society. In fact, their causes are often in conflict with one another. For example, the AFA often expresses views that conflict with those of the Gay and Lesbian Alliance Against Defamation (GLAAD).

The principal ways in which advocacy groups work to achieve their goals are lobbying, litigation, mass demonstrations, boycotts, reconciliation, and public education. Some of these organizations work relatively quietly through lobbying or reconciliation. Others are stridently confrontational, using such hard tactics as litigation or mass demonstrations. For example, several years ago, demonstrators from Anti-Racist Action, the Ontario Coalition Against Poverty, and the New Socialist Group threw water balloons and eggs at participants in a conference sponsored by Human Life International, a Canadian pro-life group.

Activist Groups

Greenpeace, an organization that operates in 41 countries including the United States, is perhaps the best known of the confrontational groups. With 2.8 million members, Greenpeace is second among environmental groups to the much less flamboyant National Wildlife Foundation. Recently contributions to Greenpeace have declined; so has the group's political influence. However, their movement is still vital. Television viewers are familiar with the daredevil efforts of some members in small boats to stop nuclear warships and whaling vessels they regard as harmful to the public.

The Christian Coalition of America fights abortion with public statements, mailings, and telephone calls, and works closely with the right wing of the Republican Party. The group, along with other organizations that are pro-life, spent about $4.7 milllion between 1998 and 2004 on lobbying, while the pro-choice groups spent $4.9 million, according to the Center for Public Integrity. Christian denominations sometimes adopt an activist role. The Southern Baptist Convention mounted a boycott of Disney corporation and all of its subsidiaries in protest of sex and violence in Disney entertainment productions. The boycott was also motivated by "gay days" at Disney's theme parks.

Social Issue Organizations

Social issue organizations are similar to activist groups in structure, but often have more broadly defined social and behavioral goals. Mothers Against Drunk Driving (MADD) is one such group. Antiabortion right-to-life groups and the pro-choice Planned Parenthood and National Organization for Women (NOW) are bitter enemies, and frequently clash in public demonstrations. Animal rights groups such as PETA at times resort to extremely confrontational tactics such as raiding animal research laboratories and seeking to shame the wearers of fur with splashing them with red paint symbolizing blood. The group's campaign against the dairy industry takes a different tack, using humor and parody on the Web site at www.milksucks.com.

Other groups, such as the American Family Association, press advertisers to drop sponsorship of television shows that they consider contrary to family values. As a result of massive letter campaigns by this group, Coca-Cola and Procter & Gamble decided to cancel commercials on programs that the AFA considered objectionable. Members of the AFA also pressured Pepsi into canceling its Madonna ads after seeing the star's video clip for her song "Like a Prayer," which they considered sacrilegious. Kansas Action for Children, a child advocacy group in Topeka, Kansas, provides an exhaustive databook as well as a report card to assess child well-being in the state. As a result, the grades and the data influence policy and legislation concerning children and teens.

Public Relations Strategies and Tactics

This section describes the principal ways in which advocacy groups work to achieve their goals.

Lobbying. Much of this is done at state and local government levels. In just one example, approximately 150 organizations have campaigned for laws to forbid smoking in public places and to restrict the sale of tobacco around the country. The campaign has had numerous successes in most U.S. states.

The National Rifle Association (NRA) is among the most powerful and influential groups in the country. They expert enormous influence over Congress and state legislatures through lobbying and campaign contributions and have helped defeat legislation aimed at restricting handgun and automatic weapon sales. The NRA and other affiliated pro-gun groups spent about $5 million lobbying Congress in 2004, according to the Center for Public Integrity. In contrast, gun control groups had a lobbying budget one-fifth the size—about $1 million.

Litigation. Organizations file suits seeking court rulings favorable to their projects or attempting to block unfavorable projects. The Sierra Club did so in a multiyear action that resulted in a decision by the U.S. Fish and Wildlife Service declaring the northern spotted owl a endangered species.

Mass Demonstrations. Designed to demonstrate public support for a cause and in some cases to harass the operators of projects to which the groups object, mass demonstrations require intricate public relations work. Organizers must obtain permits, inform the media, and arrange transportation, housing, programs, and crowd control. A mass demonstration of farmers dependent on irrigation water from drought-threatened rivers in Klamath Falls, Oregon, culminated with the arrival on a truck trailer of a gigantic metal pail, the symbol of the grassroots movement.

Boycotts. "Hit them in the pocketbook" is the principle underlying use of the boycott to achieve a goal. Some boycotts achieve easily identifiable results. Others stay in effect for years with little evident success. One environmental success story occurred when the Rainforest Action Network boycotted Burger King for buying Central American beef raised in cleared rain forests. The fast-food chain agreed to stop such purchases.

Reconciliation. Some environmental organizations have achieved good results by cooperating with corporations to solve pollution problems. The Environmental Defense Fund joined a task force with McDonald's to deal with the fast-food chain's solid waste problem, leading to a company decision to phase out its polystyrene packaging.

Fund-Raising. Raising money to conduct their programs is an ongoing and costly problem for nonprofit organizations. In the 1990s, Greenpeace sent out 4.5 million pieces of mail a month for this purpose. With so many groups in the field, competition for donations is intense. Some professional fund-raisers believe that as a whole, nonprofit groups depend too much on direct mail and should place more emphasis on face-to-face contacts. Ironically, while some environmental groups advocate preservation of forests, they also create mountains of waste paper by sending out millions of solicitation letters to raise funds for their organization.

Social Service Organizations

The term *social* includes social service, philanthropic, cultural, and religious groups serving the public in various ways. Because communication is essential for their success, they require active and creative public relations programs.

Organizations frequently have dual roles, both service and advocacy. These organizations serve the social needs of individuals, families, and society in many ways. Among prominent national organizations of this type are Goodwill Industries, the American Red Cross, the Boy Scouts and Girl Scouts of America, and the YMCA. Their advocacy is rooted in as sense of social purpose and the betterment of society as a whole. Local chapters carry out national programs. Service clubs such as the Rotary, the Kiwanis, the Lions, and the Exchange Club also raise significant amounts of money for charitable projects. The New York Philharmonic, Metropolitan Museum of Art, Southern Baptist Convention also serve the interest of the community on the one hand, while advocating for their existence on the other.

Philathrophic Foundations

Hundreds of tax-free foundations in the United States control about 11.5 percent of total charitable giving, or $30 billion in 2005. Money to establish a foundation is provided by a wealthy individual or family, a group of contributors, an organization, or a corporation. The foundation's capital is invested, and earnings from the investments are distributed as grants to qualified applicants. The Bill and Melinda Gates Foundation, for example, made grants of $1.36 billion in 2005 on projects for education and global health.

The Gates Foundation was already the largest in the world but became what one writer described as a "behemoth" in June of 2006 when Warren Buffett, the world's second richest man, gave $30 billion—85 percent of his fortune—to the Gates Foundation. In a stroke of a pen, the Gates Foundation doubled its size to $60 billion. It completely eclipses all other foundations in terms of wealth; the Ford Foundation, the second largest foundation in the world, only has $11.6 bilion in assets. The third largest is the Robert Woods Johnson Foundation with $9.1 billion, followed by the Lilly Endowment with $8.4 billion. Although the public has often heard of the Rockefeller Foundation because its long history, it currently does not even rank in the top 10 foundations in terms of assets.

The public is familiar with these large, highly visible national foundations, which make grants to a variety of causes, but organizations such as the Susan G. Komen Breast Cancer Foundation, the Annenberg Foundation, and the Avon Foundation also are well known. Many smaller foundations, some of them extremely important in their specialized fields, distribute critical funds for research, education, public performances, displays, and similar purposes. Many of these organizations not only dispense money but also engage in numerous fund-raising activities to raise money for foundation efforts.

Corporations often set up their own foundations for handling philanthropic activities. Often the majority of their grants are not cash but involve the companies' products. The IBM Foundation, as well as HP and Apple, often make grants of computers and other high-tech equipment to educational institutions. When it became a public corporation, Google also set up a foundation (www.google.org) for the purpose of making grants in several areas, including global poverty, health, energy, and the environment. As of August 2006, the foundation had allocated more than $33 million in grants.

Cultural Organizations

Generating interest and participation in the cultural aspects of life falls heavily non-profit organizations. So too, in many instances, does the operation of libraries; musical organizations, such as symphony orchestras; and museums of art, history, and natural sciences. Such institutions frequently receive at least part of their income from government sources; many are operated by governments. Even government-operated cultural institutions such as the Smithsonian Institution depend on private support to raise supplementary funds. Cuts to government programs that subsidize the arts at the state and federal levels have placed an increased burden on private support for cultural institutions. For example, funding for the National Endowment for the Arts was cut 43 percent in fiscal year (FY) 1996 to $99.5 million. The proposed budget for FY 2007 is $124 million. To put that in perspective, this is less than the cost ($133 million) of one F-22 Raptor, the military's new fighter plane. In 2005, the Smithsonian Insititution received about $122 million in public support, mostly from a special congressional appropriation. The remaining portion of its $443 million operating budget came from private support given by individuals and corporations.

Cultural organizations have a great demand for public relations professionals. The constant need to publicize exhibitions, performances, and events, as well as supporting ongoing fund-raising efforts, presents many opportunities. Most institutions have in-house divisions of public relations and marketing, but some such as the Getty Museum or the New York Philharmonic use outside agencies. While crisis management is rarely an issue, scandals and natural disasters do occasionally affect cultural institutions.

Religious Organizations

The mission of organized religion, as perceived by many faiths today, includes much more than holding weekly worship services and underwriting parochial schools. Churches distribute charity, conduct personal guidance programs, provide leadership on moral and ethical issues in their communities, and operate social centers where diverse groups gather. On occasion, such groups also get involved in what is called "the cultural wars" (see the PRCasebook on pages 418–419 about religious protests against the movie *The DaVinci Code*).

Some denominations operate retirement homes and nursing facilities for the elderly. They also help newlyweds start their marriages, plan for family, and even assist with child care for working parents. Religious organizations mostly function to reduce conflict, while using soft tactics to compete with other religious organizations for membership. For example, while Baptist churches recruit members in direct competition with the outreach efforts of other protestant denominations, gentle, personal, and welcoming persuasion generally is favored over more direct appeals. In the same manner, different Baptist sects in the same town compete for membership.

At times, religious organizations assume political roles to further their goals at local, state, and federal levels. In many U.S. cities, churches have taken an active role in the debate about immigration, including establishing sanctuaries. The Catholic Charities USA provides the needy with shelter, food, and clothing. It has a vigorous public relations program that has helped it earn its place at the top of the fund-raising ranks, closely followed by the nondenominational Salvation Army (see the Insights box on page 420).

With regard to religious organizations, a recent study by the Brookings Institution, titled *Fiscal Capacity of the Voluntary Sector*, stated: "Because religion occupies a stable,

PRCASEBOOK

Value of Conflict in Public Relations: Protest Strategies and *The Da Vinci Code*

Creating controversies or conflicts can be an effective, if somewhat risky, public relations strategy. Perhaps *The Da Vinci Code*'s success demonstrates the old adage, "there is no such thing as bad press."

Works that confront deeply held religious beliefs have a long history of arousing conflict and controversy. *The Da Vinci Code*, a 2006 film based on the best-selling novel of the same title by Dan Brown, ignited a firestorm of criticism from Catholic and other Christian groups with its release on May 19, 2006. They protested what was perceived as an attack on their beliefs; namely, the film's contentions that Jesus was married to Mary Magdalene, that they had children, and that the Catholic Church has conspired to hide the existence of Jesus' heirs from the world.

Catholic nonprofit groups such as America Needs Fatima (ANF) and Opus Dei were among the most vocal critics. "The more Hollywood mocks our faith," said ANF director Robert Ritchie, "the more it demonstrates a brazen contempt for God." More than 100,000 people signed a petition sponsored by ANF and the American Society for the Defense of Tradition, Family, and Property.

Many churches and nonprofit groups have turned to direct action. The ANF helped orchestrate more than 1,700 protests in the United States in May 2006. In Rome, the Vatican called for a boycott of the film and members of the Christian groups picketed cinemas. South Korean Christian groups unsuccessfully sought to have *The Da Vinci Code* banned altogether. The Thai government censored the final 10 minutes of the film until Columbia Pictures reversed the decision upon appeal.

Opus Dei, which is cast as a sinister organization in the film, offered the following statement on the group's Web site: "We also want to point out that *The Da Vinci Code*'s depiction of Opus Dei is inaccurate, both in the overall impression and in many details, and it would be irresponsible to form any opinion of Opus Dei based on *The Da Vinci Code*." The group is pleased, however, that the movie has received so much attention, seeing it as an opportunity to capitalize on the public's interest in theological questions.

For the most part, the protests were peaceful. "Influencers in the Body of Christ have learned that it's not a good idea to protest in the way of anger and rage," said David Kirkpatrick, a Christian opinion leader and former producer at Paramount. Cardinal Camillo Ruini of Rome showed a sophisticated understanding of media buzz and indicated perhaps the best way to react when he stated, "If it is clear that [*The Da Vinci Code*] has nothing to do with truth and it amuses you to go see it, why not?"

Director Ron Howard and the film's star Tom Hanks tend to agree with Ruini. No one, Hanks suggested, is being forced to see or accept the movie's premises. Speaking before the movie's opening, Howard stated, "My advice, since virtually no one has really seen the movie yet, is to not go see the movie if you think you're going to be upset. Wait. Talk to somebody

The 2006 film *The Da Vinci Code* sparked worldwide protests, such as this demonstration in Pakistan. "Pakistan Bans '*Da Vinci Code*': '*Da Vinci Code*' Banned in Mostly Muslim Pakistan; Officials Site Blasphemous Material about Jesus." CBS News, June 3, 2006.

who has seen it. Discuss it. And then arrive at an opinion about the movie itself." He added, "This is supposed by be entertainment; its not theology." However, Sony Pictures, Hanks, and Howard have clearly benefited from the controversy.

As with the notorious statements about World Trade Center widows made in Ann Coulter's 2006 book *Godless: The Church of Liberalism*, contentiousness sometimes translates into ticket sales or cash register receipts.

central role in American life, religious institutions will be looked to as a backup finance and delivery mechanism by other subsectors. . . particularly. . . in the human service field."

Public Relations Strategies and Tactics

Emphases for public relations goals will vary depending on the purposes of social service organizations. In general, however, nonprofit social service organizations design their public relations to achieve the following objectives: (1) Develop public awareness of their missions and activities; (2) induce individuals to use their services; (3) recruit and train volunteer workers; (4) obtain operating funds.

The sections that follow discuss ways in which each of these obejctives can be pursued.

Publicity. The news media provide well-organized channels for stimulating public interest in nonprofit organizations and are receptive to newsworthy material from them. Newspapers usually publish stories and announcements about meetings, training sessions, and similar routine activities. Beyond that, much depends on the ingenuity of the public relations practitioner in proposing feature articles and photographs. Television and radio stations will broadcast important news items about organizations and are receptive to feature stories and guest appearances by organization representatives. Stories about activities are best told in terms of individuals, rather than in broad abstractions. Public relations practitioners should look for unusual or appealing personal stories, such as a retired teacher helping Asian refugee children to learn English.

Creation of Events. Events make news and attract crowds and are another way to increase public awareness. Such activities might include an open house in a new hospital wing or a concert by members of the local symphony orchestra for an audience of blind children.

Novel stunts sometimes draw more attention to a cause than their intrinsic value would seem to justify. For example, a bed race around a shopping center parking lot by teams of university students who are conducting a campus fund drive for the March of Dimes is bound to attract curious spectators. It would almost certainly draw local television and newspaper coverage and raise money, as well.

Use of Services. Closely tied to increasing overall public awareness are efforts to induce individuals and families to use an organization's services. Free medical examinations, free clothing and food for the needy, family counseling, nursing services for shut-ins, cultural programs at museums and libraries, offers of scholarships, and

— ON THE JOB >> —

Insights

"Doing the Most Good": The Salvation Army's Mission

The American Marketing Association has identified the Salvation Army's public relations departments as among the most successful in the country. Although their budget for publicity is small compared to nonprofits such as the United Way or the Sierra Club, they make efficient use of their resources. "Writing and disseminating press releases and newsworthy items to the appropriate media is the first step," says Virginia Knor, a Salvation Army public relations specialist, "and they need to be distributed in a timely fashion." The news releases are sent via satellite to more than 80,000 registered journalists on PRNewswire for Journalists. Regular, cost-efficient, rapid dissemination of information, combined with a clear and consistent message about the efficient and wide-ranging

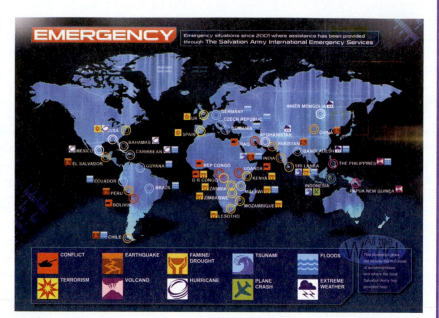

"Emergency Situations Since 2001 Where Assistance Has Been Provided Through the Salvation Army International Emergency Services," Salvation Army Emergency Relief Map.

mission of the organization, continue to make the Salvation Army among the most visible and successful international nonprofit organizations.

Founded in 1865 by Methodist minister William Booth and his wife, Catherine, the Salvation Army is one of the oldest social service organizations in the world. Its original mission, to evangelize London's poor, has evolved into a multifaceted operation that pro-

vides disaster services, shelters for battered women, services for the aging, family counseling, and countless other programs. Today, the Salvation Army helps nearly 30 million needy individuals in over 100 nations and preaches its message in more than 160 languages.

Public relations is an essential component of the Salvation Army's mission. Using the campaign message "Doing the Most Good," their public relations efforts target small donors who con-

tribute change to the familiar Christmas Red Kettle drives at shopping centers as well as major corporate sponsors. A recent Christmas campaign raised $104 million. A consistent message and impeccable reputation also helps the Salvation Army raise substantial funds for relief efforts in disaster areas around the world, such as the recent tsunami in Indonesia or earthquake in Pakistan.

Source: "How the Salvation Army Uses News Releases," *PRNewswire*, August 22, 2005, www.marketingpower.com/content28971.php.

many other services provided by nonprofit organizations are worthless unless potential users know about them. Because of shyness or embarrassment, persons who would benefit from available services sometimes hesitate to use them. Written and spoken material designed to attract these persons should emphasize ease of participation and privacy of services in matters of health, financial aid, and family. An example of this approach is the American Cancer Society's widely publicized campaign to encourage people to have colonoscopies to screen for colon cancer.

Creation of Educational Materials. Public relations representatives of nonprofit organizations spend a substantial portion of their time preparing written and audiovisual materials to educate the public. Such materials are basic to almost any organization's program. The quickest way to introduce people to an organization is to hand them a brochure. Because a brochure often provides a first impression of an organization, it should contain a concise history of the organization and be visually appealing, simply written, and contain basic information. The writer should answer a reader's obvious questions: What does the organization do? Where are its facilities? What services does it offer? How do I go about participating in its activities and accessing its services? When appropriate, it may include a membership application form or a coupon to accompany a donation. Operation of a speakers bureau or showings of films provided by general headquarters of national nonprofit organizations are other ways to inform the public of an organization's mission. Organizations often design logos, or symbols, that help make their materials memorable to the public.

Newsletters. Another basic piece of printed material is a news bulletin, usually monthly or quarterly, mailed to members, the news media, and a carefully composed list of other interested parties. In addition to the publication and distribution of brochures explaining an organization's objectives, periodic newsletters distributed to opinion leaders are a quiet but effective way to tell an organization's story.

Fund-Raising

Finding ways to pay the bills is a critical problem for virtually all nonprofit organizations, even those that receive government grants to finance part of their work. Fundraising methods are now highly developed, particularly for nonprofit organizations.

Although the largest, most publicized donations are made by corporations and foundations, individual contributions far exceed combined corporate and foundation giving. In fact, individual contributions amount to about 77 percent, of annual U.S. philanthropic donations or about $199 billion (see the Insights box on page 409 for a breakdown of annual donations).

Depending on their needs, voluntary organizations may try to catch minnows— hundreds of small contributions—or angle for the huge marlin, a large corporate gift. Some national organizations raise massive sums. In 2004, for example, the YMCA raised $483 million, followed by Catholic Charities ($318 million), the Salvation Army ($310 million), and the Red Cross ($306 million). In the aftermath of Hurricane Katrina in 2005, the Red Cross received a whopping $2.4 billion in donations to help victims.

Public relations professionals may participate directly in fund-raising by organizing and conducting solicitation programs or they may serve as consultants to specialized development departments in their organizations. Organizations often employ professional firms to conduct their fund-raising campaigns on a fee basis. In those cases, the organizations' public relations professionals usually serve a liaison function.

Motivations for Giving. An understanding of what motivates individuals and companies to give money or volunteer their time is important to anyone involved in fund-raising. An intrinsic desire to share a portion of one's resources, however small, with others—an inherent generosity possessed in some degree by almost everyone—is a primary factor. Another urge, also very human, if less laudable, is ego satisfaction. Hence, the donor who makes a large contribution gets a building named for his or her family, and individuals get their names published in a list of contributors. Peer pressure—open or subtle—is a third factor. Saying "no" to a direct request from a friend, neighbor, or coworker is difficult, and the cliché about "keeping up with the Joneses" applies here, as well.

Independent Sector commissioned the Gallup Organization to do a survey on volunteerism and giving. The survey found that 53 percent of those responding cited "assisting those who are less fortunate" as their personal motive for volunteering and giving. The second most frequently cited reason was gaining a feeling of personal satisfaction; religion was third. Only 6 percent cited tax considerations as a major reason for giving.

The Competitive Factor. Organizations should regularly analyze the competition they face from other fund-raising efforts. The competitive factor is important. The public becomes resentful and uncooperative if approached too frequently for contributions. This is why the United Way of America exists: to consolidate solicitations of numerous important local service agencies into a single unified annual campaign. The voluntary United Way management in a community, with professional guidance, announces a campaign goal. The money collected in the drive is distributed among participating agencies according to a percentage formula determined by the United Way budget committee.

The Risks of Fund-Raising. Fund-raising involves risks as well as benefits. Adherence to high ethical standards when soliciting contributions and close control of fund-raising costs, so that expenses constitute a reasonable percentage of the funds collected, are essential if an organization is to maintain public credibility. Numerous groups have had their reputations severely damaged by disclosures that only a small portion of the money they raised was applied to the causes they advocate, with the rest consumed by solicitation expenses and administrative overhead.

There are different types of campaigns that public relations professionals can implement for fund-raising efforts targeting corporations or individuals.

Corporate and Foundation Donations. Organizations seeking donations from major corporations normally should do so through the local corporate offices or sales outlets. Some corporations give local offices a free hand in making donations, up to a certain amount, to local groups. Even when the decisions are made at corporate headquarters, local recommendations are important. Requests to foundations generally should be made to the main office, which will send application forms.

Increasingly, corporations undertake programs that match employee donations. The matching most commonly is done on a dollar-for-dollar basis: If an employee gives $1 to a philanthropic cause, the employer does the same. Some corporations match at a two-to-one rate, or even higher. Corporations make contributions to charities in less direct ways, too, some of them quite self-serving. When applying for a charitable donation, an applicant should submit a "case for support" letter that covers the following elements: background of the organization, current status of organization's services, need for organization's services, sources of current funding, administration of the organization, community support, current needs of organization, and the benefits to the community of the donation.

Structured Capital Campaigns.

The effort to raise major amounts of money for a new wing of a hospital, for an engineering building on a campus, or even for the reconstruction and renovation of San Francisco's famed cable car system is often called a *capital campaign*. In a capital campaign, emphasis is placed on substantial gifts from corporations and individuals. One key concept of a capital campaign, is that 90 percent of the total amount raised will come from only 10 percent of the contributors. In a $10 million campaign to add a wing to an art museum, for example, it is not unusual that the lead gift will be $1 or $2 million.

Capital campaigns require considerable expertise and, for this reason, many organizations retain professional fund-raising counsel. A number of U.S. firms offer these services; the most reputable ones belong to the Giving Institute, formerly the American Association of Fund-Raising Counsel.

Donors often are recognized by the size of their gifts, and terms such as *patron* or *founder* are used. Major donors may be given the opportunity to have rooms or public areas in the building named after them. Hospitals prepare "memorial" brochures that show floor plans and the cost of endowing certain facilities.

Direct Mail.

Although direct mail can be an expensive form of solicitation because of the costs of developing or renting mailing lists, preparing the printed materials, and mailing them, it is increasingly competitive with advertising costs directed at similarly targeted audiences. An organization can reduce costs by conducting an effective local, limited direct mail campaign on its own, if it develops an up-to-date mailing list of "good" names known to be potential donors and can provide enough volunteers to stuff and address the solicitation envelopes. Regional and national organizations, and some large local ones, either employ direct mail specialists or rent carefully chosen mailing lists from list brokers.

Attractive, informative mailing pieces that motivate recipients to donate are keys to successful solicitation. The classic direct mail format consists of a mailing envelope, letter, brochure, and response device, often with a postage-paid return envelope.

Recently, however, the *Chronicle of Philanthropy* has reported a sharp decline in direct mail contributions to several large national organizations, such as the Disabled American Veterans and Easter Seals. The publication asserts, "Americans have become increasingly fed up with direct-mail appeals from charities."

Sponsorship of Events.

The range of events a philanthropic organization can sponsor to raise funds is limited only by the imagination of its members. Participation contests are a popular method. Walkathons and jogathons appeal to the current American emphasis on exercise. Nationally, the March of Dimes holds an annual 32-kilometer WalkAmerica in 1,100 cities on the same day, but see the Insights box on page 424 about potential walkathon overload on the part of the public.

Staging parties, charity balls, concerts, exhibitions, and similar events in which tickets are sold is another widely used fund-raising approach. Often, however, big parties create more publicity than profit, with 25 to 50 percent of the money raised going to expenses. Other methods include sponsorship of a motion picture premiere, a

ON THE JOB >>

Competing Charities Cause Walkathon Overload

Insights

A popular way to raise funds for everything from cancer research to AIDS prevention is for a charity to sponsor a walkathon, a bikeathon, or a 5K race, or a marathon. Indeed, it is estimated that the number of such charity events has doubled in the past 10 years and competing groups are virtually running into each other. In one day, for example, nonprofits in the Miami area held three competing runs.

The glut of charity events has created problems for the organizers as well as cities where they are held. According to the *Wall Street Journal,* "Charity groups now find themselves not only competing for donor dollars, but also for participants and popular dates on which to hold their events." One result is a degree of cooperation among similar groups. Emily Callahan, spokesperson for the Susan G. Komen Breast Cancer Foundation, told the

newspaper that her group and the Avon Foundation do check race schedules "to make sure they are not cannibalizing each other." Unfortunately, such cooperation is the exception rather than the rule as rival groups compete for funds.

At the same time, many cities are beginning to limit the number of such events because of crowd congestion, traffic jams, street closings, and increased cost of city services. Boston, for example, now limits road races to about 60 annually, and New York is limiting the number of runs held in Central Park. Some cities, such as San Francisco, are charging charities more for permits to cover the cost of police overtime and cleanup crews. The Leukemia and

Lymphoma Society, which organized the San Diego Rock 'n' Roll Marathon, for example, had to pay the city $125,000 for permits and services.

Despite the competition of events, and major cities imposing new restrictions on various runs, USA Track & Field reports that $656 million was raised in 2005 by what *Wall Street Journal* reporter Sally Beatty calls, "legions of sneaker-clad Samaritans."

Source: Beatty, Sally. "Walkathon Overload." *Wall Street Journal,* June 6, 2006, W1, W8.

theater night, or a sporting event. Barbecues flourish as money-raisers in western U.S. cities. Seeking to attract donors from the under-30 age group, some organizations use the fun approach by raffling off pop culture items, as when one group raffled Madonna's sequined brassiere (for $2,500) and a T-shirt by artist Felix Gonzalez-Torres with the message "Nobody Owns Me" (for $50).

Solicitation of Funds over Television. In this method, a television station sets aside a block of airtime for the telethon sponsored by a philanthropic organization. Best known of the national telethons is the one conducted annually by comedian Jerry Lewis to raise funds to combat muscular dystrophy. Another high-profile event was the celebrity telethon to aid victims of Hurricane Katrina in September 2005.

Telephone Solicitations. Solicitation of donations by telephone is a relatively inexpensive way to seek funds but is of uncertain effectiveness. Many groups hold down their costs for solicitation by using a WATS (Wide Area Telephone Service) line that provides unlimited calls for a flat fee, without individual toll charges. However, some people resent receiving telephone solicitations. If the recipient of the call is unfamiliar with the cause, it must be explained clearly and concisely—which is not always easy for a volunteer solicitor to do. In addition, there is now a national Do Not Call Registry that prevents fundraisers from randomly calling people, though legitimate charities are exempt from the regulation. Converting verbal telephone promises into confirmed written pledges also is problematic. The normal method is for the sponsoring organization to send a filled-in pledge form to the donor for signature.

Use of 800 or 900 Telephone Numbers. Toll-free 800 telephone numbers that permit callers to phone an organization without incurring long-distance costs have been in use for years. A 900 code, on the other mind, charges callers for each call placed, with the phone company taking a service charge from this fee, and the remainder going to the party being called.

Commercial Enterprises. Rather than depending entirely on contributions, some nonprofit organizations go into business on their own or make tie-ins with commercial firms from which they earn a profit. Use of this approach is growing, but entails risks that must be carefully assessed. Three types of commercial money-raising are the most common: (1) licensing use of an organization's name to endorse a product and receiving payment for each item sold, such as American Heart Association's commission for its endorsementof Healthy Choice frozen dinners; (2) sharing profits with a corporation from sales of a special product, such as Newman's Own salad dressing, and (3) operating a business that generates revenue for the organization, such as the Metropolitan Museum of Art's gift shop.

Health Organizations

There are two types of organizations in the health sector. One is hospitals, some of which are nonprofit and some of which are for-profit. Because hospitals sell a product (improved health), parallels exist between their public relations objectives and those of other corporations. They focus on diverse audiences, both external and internal; involve themselves in public affairs and legislation because they operate under a maze of government regulations; and stress consumer relations, which involves keeping patients and their families satisfied, as well as seeking new clients. Hospitals produce publications and publicity for external and internal audiences. They have an additional function that other corporate public relations practitioners don't need to handle—the development and nurturing of volunteer networks.

The other type of organization is private and government health agencies, which serve the public interest by providing health care, funding for health initiatives, and oversight. The most familiar health agencies are adminstered at the federal and state levels. Private organizations, such as Planned Parenthood and the Medical Foundation for AIDS and Sexual Health, frequently offer medical and wellness assistance targeted to specific issues or populations. Both governmental and nonprofit health agencies offer numerous opportunities for public relations professionals.

Public relations professionals who specialize in health communication have an impact on all Americans who are concerned about personal health risks as well as threats to financial security from burdensome medical costs. Essentially, health communicators strive to convey health information, prevention measures, and emergency response information as a means of reducing health risks. Because personal health and the related costs are so important to us, health issues and related policies often are leading stories in the news. Medical breakthroughs, high-profile drugs such as Viagra, the graying of 76 million baby boomers, and the ongoing controversies over health costs, medical malpractice reform and claims of excessive profits for doctors and health care companies guarantee robust opportunities to practice sophisticated public relations.

Public relations work for hospitals and health agencies is a large and expanding field. The role of health organizations has taken on new dimensions with emerging diseases, natural disasters, and the threat of terrorism as well as growing concern of health and quality of life. In addition to caring for ill and injured patients, hospitals and health agencies conduct both preventive and responsive health programs and provide other health-related social services that go well beyond the traditional institutional concept. Public relations specializations in issues management or risk and crisis communications naturally fit this growing field.

Hospitals

Hospital public relations programs have four basic audiences: patients, medical and administrative staffs, news media, and the community as a whole. The four audiences overlap, but each needs a special focus. Careful scrutiny can identify significant subaudiences within these four, for example, the elderly; pregnant women; victims of heart disease, cancer, and stroke who need support groups after hospitalization; potential financial donors to the hospital; and community opinion leaders whose goodwill helps to build the institution's reputation. Each group can be cultivated by public relations techniques discussed in Chapter 10.

The public relations staff of a hospital has two primary roles: (1) to strengthen and maintain the public's perception of the institution as a place where medical skill, compassion, and efficiency are paramount, and (2) to help market the hospital's array of services. Many hospitals have sought to redefine themselves as community health centers. Basically, hospitals, like hotels, must have high room-occupancy rates to succeed financially. They augment this fundamental source of income by creating and marketing supplementary services, an area that offers opportunities and challenges for public relations people.

The reputations of some hospitals have been damaged by the public's perception of them as cold institutions that don't care enough about individual patients. Complaints by patients about poor food and brusque nurses add to the problem. Sponsorship of community health fairs, offering free screenings to detect symptoms of certain diseases, and low-cost comprehensive blood tests are examples of methods hospitals use to create a postive image.

On the other hand, the tension between health care providers and those who pay for services is an ongoing source of conflict and the impetus for risk communication to reduce expenses through the prevention of illness. Federally financed Medicaid, which assists low-income patients, has been under recurring political attack. Older Americans sometimes struggle to obtain eligibility for Medicare, a form of government-operated insurance they help finance from their Social Security benefits. Health maintenance organizations (HMOs), in which individuals and families can buy memberships, seek to hold down medical costs by limiting their members' choice of doctors and reserving the right to refuse payment for certain procedures. Conflicting interests create the undertow that pulls politicians, officials, patients, and doctors into the ever-present conflict over access and quality of care.

Health Agencies

Many health agencies combat a specific diseases through education, research, and treatment, whereas others deliver generalized health services in communities. Federal and state governments are the largest health agencies, though many foundations and charities provide health services. Nonprofit health agencies range from national organizations such as the American Heart Association, the American Cancer Society, and the National Multiple Sclerosis Society to smaller groups such as the Conservation, Food & Health Foundation in Boston.

The Department of Health and Human Services (HHS) is the federal government's leading health agency. Its budget (nearly $700 billion proposed in 2007) amounts to nearly one-quarter of all federal spending. HHS provides more than 300 programs, including emergency preparedness, Head Start for preschoolers, maternity and infant programs, disease prevention and immunizations, and insurance programs such as Medicaid and Medicare. Divisions include major initiatives such as the Food and Drug Adminstration, Centers for Disease Control and Prevention (CDC), and the National Institutes for Health (NIH), as well as smaller services such as the Adminstration on Aging and the Agency for Healthcare Research and Quality. (See the Insights box on page 428 for more information on a CDC campaign.) The NIH is the largest branch with an annual budget of $28 billion and more than 17,000 employees. Established in 1887, the NIH annually supports about 35,000 research and other grant projects.

In addition to federal health initiatives, each state has a statewide health agency. Within the states, many regions, counties, and cities provide taxpayer-supported health services as well. HHS provides funds and guidance to state and local health agencies. With the assistance of private nonprofit foundations, they provide a coordinated network of free or low-cost health services.

Public relations professionals should build working relationships with these agencies not only to secure funding but also to build coalitions for health campaigns or programs. Public relations professionals working for these agencies deal with an enormous amount of public information, and need to be prepared to handle crisis situations. For example, they must understand both the technical apects of a public health risk such as a chemical spill or disease outbreak and the needs of the community in order to facilitate effective diaglogue between emergency responders, affected members of the public, and the media.

Health Campaigns

Health campaigns to prevent and respond to diseases, and to promote health and quality of life, began applying social marketing practices in the late 1980s. A number of public relations strategies and techniques have been implemented for these initiatives mainly by federal and state governments and private health agencies.

Breast cancer awareness, the importance of diet and exercise, and encouraging screenings for colon cancer are examples of recent health campaigns sponsored by government and nonprofit health organizations. The American College of Emergency Physicians (ACEP), for instance, sponsors a Risky Drinking Campaign, an alcohol awareness program; Failure Is Not an Option, a project to alert the public to the

— ON THE JOB >> —

The Centers for Disease Control and Prevention National Immunization Program

Insights

The Centers for Disease Control and Prevention (CDC), located in Atlanta, Georgia, operate the National Immunization Program (NIP). The program mission is to provide "consultation, training, promotional, educational, epidemiological, and technical services to assist health departments in planning, developing, and implementing immunization programs." The NIP supports the establishment of vaccine supply contracts, assists with immunization programs, and tracks possible outbreaks of disease through strategic communication efforts.

The CDC's public awareness and educational programs focus on alerting the public about possible threats. NIP's programs are publicized through PSAs, news releases, radio and television programs, pamphlets, and posters. Information about immunization is directly distributed through local health departments, hospitals, and doctors' offices. The NIP's Web site is particularly effective. A section entitled "In the Spotlight . . . for the Public" offers daily updates about disease outbreaks, potential threats, and immunization schedules. Other links on the home page provide information aimed at different target population including parents of young children, adolescents, and the aging. Additional links direct visitors to sections devoted to frequently asked questions, statistics, and surveys, and offer fact-driven and hands-on public information. A section entitled "Media" provides links to press releases, media resources, and academic research, and a section for health care providers offers vaccine guidelines, information kits, and software tools for both health professional and patient training guides.

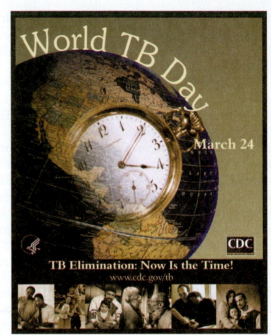

The CDC uses a variety of public relations strategies to reach the public, such as posters distributed to public health agencies. "World TB Day," Poster, CDC, 2005.

symptoms of heart failure; and the Partnership for Anthrax Vaccine Education, a partnership with George Washington University to provide the latest information about vaccination initiatives. In addition to having altruistic motives, the ACEP sponsors these campaigns as a public relations tool to build goodwill and a positive public image.

The Healthy People Initiative is among the most ambitious and comprehensive health campaigns. Initiated in 1979 by the Department of Health and Human Services, Healthy People was designed to assess the health status of the nation. Healthy People 2010, the latest iteration of the program, focuses on setting health goals and providing clinically based disease prevention services. According to the

Healthy People Web site (http://www.healthypeople.gov), the campaign represents and unprecedented partnership between more than 350 private and nonprofit organizations and 270 state agencies.

Publicity and educational materials available on the Healthy People Web site are targeted to consumers as well as health care professionals. A section entitled "Be a Healthy Person" provides links to information about making informed health decisions, as well as contact information and toll-free numbers for organizations that provide health care advice. A fundamental question about all of these public relations efforts is how best to measure use this information and health outcomes to create more effective campaigns. Public relations professionals particularly need well-developed research skills in this area.

Another example is a recent health campaign launched by the food industry that arose from a serious health scare. The issue was bacterial contamination of precut vegetables. Television news producers often aired "buyer beware" segments on the dangers of precut salad ingredients, citing lists of common, harmless bacteria normally found on the vegetables and suggesting that their presence could mean that dangerous bacteria might appear.

Having identified the emerging issue, the food industry hired the Londre Group and Fineman Associates to undertake communication efforts for the salad suppliers. Risk communication tactics included publicity that featured university food scientists debunking stories about the innocuous bacteria, video news releases to set forth the scientific facts, trade media briefings, face-to-face meetings with food editors, national opinion surveys, and an array of additional actions. (See the PR Casebook on page 430 about the food industry's response to another area of health concern—"junk food.")

The new frontier for health communication is tailored messaging, delivering messages to targeted individuals based on their specific interests, concerns, and health conditions through appropriate channels. Professor Matthew Kreuter at Saint Louis University employs a tailoring engine developed by his programming group in the Health Communication Research Laboratory to make tailoring feasible and efficient for large audiences.

Indicative of the growing sophistication of health care public relations is the targeting of women for consumer information; 60 percent of doctor visits and 59 percent of prescription drug purchases are made by women, according to Kym White, managing director of Ogilvy Public Relations Worldwide's Health & Medical Practice. Audience targeting also was the thrust of a study entitled *Femstat 3 Report: American Women and Self-Care*. The study found that 50 percent of women get information mainly from their primary care doctors, 24 percent from magazines and newspapers, 7 percent from television and radio, and 5 percent from self-help books. Much of the health information that women receive is from public relations sources targeting this population.

Health information and advice on the Internet has grown exponentially over the past several years. The National Cancer Institute has a single database with over 650 articles on cancer risk. According to *O'Dwyer's PR Services Report*, 55 percent of the adult population has online access, and 86 percent of them use the Internet to find health-related information. Some experts estimate that nearly 25 percent of all Web searching is health related. Public relations companies now produce video and audio programming on the Web for their health care clients, providing doctors, medical reporters, investors, and patients with medical and pharmaceutical information.

PRCASEBOOK

Food Industry Battles Ban on Junk Food Sales in Public Schools

There are many contingent factors that influence public relations efforts, for example, government regulation, activist groups' claims, and public perception. Such factors often compete and are in conflict. Public relations professionals should attempt to reach a satisfactory or at least partially beneficial resolution for groups whose interest they represent.

Concern over the obesity rate of American children has pitted concerned parents, health officials, and some school districts against fast-food and soft drink companies. According to the Centers for Disease Control and Prevention, nearly 1 out of 3 children are now obese. Health professionals generally cite a high-fat diet associated with increased soft drink and fast-food consumption as a leading cause of childhood obesity. As a result, many school districts have banned vending machines sales during school hours. For example, the Los Angeles County Unified School district voted to gradually eliminate the sale of soda and other sugary drinks, and New York City schools have restricted what can be sold in vending machines.

Coca-Cola and other soft drink companies have tried to reach a compromise and pledged to offer healthy alternatives in school vending machines. However, the food industry's main strategy is to reject the causal link between sugar and high-fat food and obesity, claiming that a sedentary lifestyle is the culprit. Groups with seemingly credible names such as the American Council of Fitness and Nutrition (ACFN), the Nutrition Advisory Council (NAC) and the Center for Consumer Freedom (CCF) have expressed their opposition to proposed bans. Because they are actually funded by the food industry, observers have labeled such organizations as "astroturf," the artificial grass used on football fields, because they masquerade as grassroots campaigns. According to an article in the *San Francisco Chronicle* published August 10, 2003, the ACFN, NAC, and CCF are underwritten by restaurant and snack food interests.

The Department of Agriculture has denied requests to measure compliance from groups such as Commercial Alert

Students in Chicago snack on soda and chips bought from school vending machines. Tim Boyle/Getty Images, Newsweek, April 18, 2006 (www.msnbc.msn.com/id/12359367).

despite federal regulations stipulating reduction in junk food and soda sales in schools. The White House too has been slow to act. According to a news release issued by the Grocery Manufacturers Association (GMA), Tommy Thompson, former Health and Human Services secretary, advised GMA members to "'go on the offensive' against critics blaming the food industry for obesity."

Nevertheless, the public overwhelmingly supports restrictions on soft drink and junk food sales in schools, according to a poll taken by the *Wall Street Journal* in February 2005. They found that 83 percent of adults agree that "public schools need to do a better job of limiting children's access to unhealthy foods like snack foods, sugary soft drinks and fast food."

Source: Gary Ruskin and Juliet Schor. "Junk Food Nation." *The Nation*, August 12, 2005.

Educational Organizations

Educational institutions include programs that provide child care, instruction for primary and secondary students, colleges, universities, trade schools, and special needs schools. These organizations are often licensed or regulated by state and federal agencies, as in the case of primary and secondary schools, or by private accreditation bodies such as the Southern Association of Colleges and Schools. Most educational institutions have nonprofit status insofar as they do not have shareholders who receive proceeds or profits from their operation and they are formed specifically for charitable, scientific, or educational purposes. Educational institutions take on a staggering array of organizational structures and functions. Like other nonprofit organizations, educational institutions are often supported to a greater or lesser degree by government agencies, but also usually depend on donations from alumni or other donors for supplemental support.

Colleges and Universities

Higher education is big business in the United States. California, the most populous state, with 35 million residents, spends $17 billion annually on four-year public colleges and universities. Another $6 billion is spent on two-year community colleges.

It's also a business that has millions of customers—students. In the United States, almost 16 million students are enrolled at more than 4,000 college and universities. Almost every one of these institutions has personnel working in such activities as public relations, marketing communications, and fund-raising.

In large universities, the vice president for development and university relations (that person may have some other title) supervises the office of development, which includes a division for alumni relations, and also an office of public relations; these functions are often combined in smaller institutions. Development and alumni personnel seek to enhance the prestige and financial support of the institution. Among other activities, they conduct meetings and seminars, publish newsletters and magazines, and arrange tours. Their primary responsibilities are to build alumni loyalty and generate funding from private sources.

The public relations director, generally aided by one or more chief assistants, supervises the information news service, publications, and special events. Depending on the size of the institution, perhaps a dozen or more employees will carry out these functions, including writing, photography, graphic design, broadcasting, and computer networking.

The most visible aspect of a university public relations program is its news bureau. Among other activities, an active bureau produces hundreds of news releases, photographs, and special columns and articles for the print media. It prepares programs of news and features about students' acheivements, faculty activities, and campus personalities for stations. It provides assistance and information for reporters, editors, and broadcasters affiliated with the state, regional, and national media. The staff responds to hundreds of telephone calls from members of the news media and the public seeking information.

Serving Their Publics

To carry out their complex functions, top development and public relations specialists must be a part of the management team of the college or university. At some institutions this is not so, and the public relations program suffers. Ideally, public relations staff should attend all top-level meetings involving the president and other administrators, learning the whys and wherefores of decisions made and lending counsel. Only then can they satisfactorily develop action programs and respond to questions from the publics those programs concern. They are indeed the voice of the administration. The following are brief descriptions of the key publics for colleges and universities:

Faculty and Staff. Every sound public relations program begins with the internal constituency. Able college presidents involve their faculty and staff in decision making to the fullest extent possible, given the complexities of running a major institution. It is a maxim that the employees of a company or institution serve as its major public relations representatives because they come into contact with so many people. Good morale, a necessity, is achieved in large measure through communication.

Students. Because of their large numbers and the many families that they represent, students make up the largest public relations arm—for good or bad—that a university has. The quality of the teaching they receive and their overall experience are the greatest determinants of their allegiance to the institution. However, a sound administrative attitude toward students, involving them as much as possible in decisions that affect their campus lives, is extremely important. So are other forms of communication, including student publications and broadcast stations, among others. When, upon graduation, they are asked to join the university's alumni association, chances are good that, if they are pleased with their collegiate experience, many will support the university in the future.

Alumni and Other Donors. The loyalty and financial support of alumni are crucial to the ongoing operations of a college or university. Alumni are considered the major foundation of any fund-raising effort because of their immediate association with the institution. Donors who are not alumni also are cultivated for major gifts based on their interest in particular fields or disciplines. Colleges and universities raise money for a variety of purposes. This may include such projects as recruiting new faculty, buying equipment, building student residence halls, providing scholarships, remodeling classrooms, and upgrading campus computer networks.

Indeed, fund-raising has increased dramatically at most public and private universities in recent years as costs have risen and allocations from state legislatures and federal agencies have dramatically declined. Total nongovernmental financial support for education was $38.6 billion in 2005, according to Giving USA, a unit of the Giving Institute, which publishes an annual tally of charitable contributions. This amount represents 14.8 percent of the total charitable giving in the United States, which was $260 billion in 2005. In addition to annual operating fund campaigns, universities are increasingly conducting long-range capital campaigns for large amounts of money. In 2006, at least 25 American universities were in the process of raising $1 billion or more. For example, John Hopkins University had a goal of $2 billion by 2007, but had already raised more than that amount by mid-2006.

Government. State and federal governments often hold the key to whether universities receive sufficient monies to maintain facilities, faculty, and programs. Most large institutions have someone who regularly monitors the state legislature on appropriations and issues ranging from laboratory experiments on animals to standardized tests and taxes. Their work includes (1) competing with other state institutions for money, (2) defending proposed increases in higher education budgets and arguing against cuts, (3) establishing an institution's identity in the minds of legislators, and (4) responding to lawmakers' requests for information. According to Robert Dickens, coordinator of government relations for the University of Nevada at Reno: "When I say I'm a lobbyist, some people look at me as if I need a shower. It's a new business with the universities, and some people think it's a dirty business. But nothing's dirtier than not having resources."

The Community. A college or university must maintain a good relationship with the members of the community in which it is situated. The greatest supporters that an institution may have are the people within its immediate geographic area, many of whom mingle with its faculty, staff members, and students. Tax dollars also are an immense benefit, although the fact that university property is tax exempt may impose a strain unless the institution voluntarily agrees to some form of compensation for services such as fire and police protection.

In order to bridge the town–gown gap, faculty and staff members are encouraged to achieve community visibility through work with civic and other organizations. Business groups often take the lead. The Chamber of Commerce in Lawrence, Kansas, for example, for many years sponsored an annual barbecue to give faculty and towns-people an opportunity to get to know each other better.

Prospective Students. Suffering from declining revenues, increased operation costs, and a dwindling pool of prospective students occasioned by lower birthrates, many colleges have turned to highly competitive recruiting methods. Some, in the "hard-sell" classification, use extensive advertising in print and broadcast media and on billboards. Other colleges and universities have replaced their catalogs and brochures with slick four-color materials that use bright graphics and catchy headlines to lure students. Most, if not all, now use the Web.

Various other recruiting devices are used. Vanderbilt University sent personalized videotapes to about 40 highly coveted high school seniors. The College of the Atlantic took prospective students on a sailing party aboard a 90-foot yacht. Stanford University was host to 750 high school students who stayed overnight in dormitory rooms, visited classes, attended a musical program, and participated in a campus scavenger hunt. Brown University each spring sponsors a party for up to 250 prospects on an Amtrak train traveling between Washington, D.C. and Providence, Rhode Island.

Government Organizations

Government organizations share some characteristics of nonprofit organizations. Ideally, the mission of government is public service; no one makes private profit directly from the operation of government, and governments are noncommercial. In practice, there is widespread perception that administrations fall far short to these ideals, but the shortcomings of some government officials and employees should not blind us to the tangible benefits of the democratic system. In order for federal, state, and local governments to function efficiently, each branch must communicate effectively with their respective constituents. From election campaigns to military recruitment to floating a bond issue, the circulation of information—the core function of public relations—is an essential aspect of government administration. Skilled public relations professionals are required at every level to ensure that information is

PRCASEBOOK

Duke University Defends Reputation in Lacrosse Scandal

Scandal and controversy seem to gravitate to powerful and visible institutions. Despite public relations efforts to maintain a long-standing reputation, it may be tarnished in an instant by a single incident. Restoring an institution's image requires tenacity, delicacy, and grace.

In April 2006, two Duke University Lacrosse players were indicted for allegedly raping an African-American exotic dancer that they had hired for a party. The ensuing scandal seriously tarnished the North Carolina school's reputation. Salacious details about the players' alleged behavior, the school's tolerance of rowdy conduct, and the public's perception of the university as a bastion of elitism presented challenges to the school's public relations division. As a result, some some called for the university to end NCAA Division I athletics on the campus.

The scandal led to intense media scrutiny and a barrage telephone calls, letters, and e-mails from both detractors and defenders. According to David Jarmul, Duke vice president for news and communications, the school wants to "make it clear to the news media that we're not going to engage in the daily ins and outs of the legal case." Nevertheless, they maintained close communication with local television and print media. Jarmul and John Burness, senior vice president for public affairs and government relations, noted that the university was pleased with the "nuanced" media coverage. A link to news articles, both positive and negative, appeared on Duke's home page.

In April 2006, the university hired Burson-Marsteller to coach administrators, faculty, staff, and students on how to speak to the media. Later in the year, the university retained Edelman Worldwide for ongoing counseling work. According to *New York Times* writer Duff Wilson, a group of Duke supporters also hired Robert Bennett, a former lawyer for Bill Clinton, to "help mount a public-relations campaign counteracting the negative attention on the university." Alumni and trustees with legal, journalistic, and public relations backgrounds also pitched in.

Demonstrators listen to Duke president Richard Brodhead, right, at a news conference about the men's lacrosse team on March 28, 2006; AP Photo by Sara D. Davis.

Nevertheless, Duke was criticized for taking a seemingly distant attitude. Mike Paul, president of MGP & Associates PR, a sports management firm, offered this advice:

> The president needs to send a message to the victim of the situation saying, "We're still not sure who did this to you, but I have seen the photos of your face beaten up. We want to make clear [that] if anyone associated with this university was responsible for this, they will be held accountable."

Despite the damage to Duke's reputation as an elite university, a record number of more than 19,000 high school seniors vied for 3,800 spots.

On April 11, 2007, all charges were dropped against the Lacrosse players by the attorney general of North Carolina after finding that the local district attorney acted unethically in the case. Whether the intense media coverage of the alleged rape will have long term effects on the university remains an open question.

disseminated clearly, efficiently, and to the widest number of people. "A nation of well-informed men who have been taught to know and prize the rights which God has given them cannot be enslaved," wrote Benjamin Franklin. "It is in the region of ignorance that tyranny begins."

Federal Government

The U.S. government is said to be the world's premier collector of information. It also is maintained, without much disagreement, that the government is one of the world's greatest disseminators of information.

Advertising is another governmental activity. Federal agencies spend several hundred million dollars a year on public service advertising, primarily to promote military recruitment, government health services, and the U.S. Postal Service. The following sections discuss the public affairs efforts of federal agencies, Congress, and the White House.

Government Agencies. Public affairs officers (PAOs) and public information specialists engage in tasks common to the public relations department of corporation. They typically answer press and public inquiries, write news releases, work on newsletters, prepare speeches for top officials, oversee the production of brochures, and plan special events. Senior-level public affairs specialists also try to counsel top management about communications strategies and how the agency should respond to crisis situations.

One of the largest public affairs operations in the federal government is conducted by the U.S. Department of Defense (DOD), which is the cabinet-level agency that oversees the armed forces. Its operations vary from the mundane to the exotic. One of the longest-running public relations efforts has been the preparation and distribution of "hometown" releases by the military. The Fleet Hometown News Center, established during World War II, sends approximately 1 million news releases annually about the promotions and transfers of U.S. Navy, Marine Corps, and Coast Guard personnel to their hometown media.

A more exotic assignment for a military public affairs officer is to give background briefings and escort journalists who want to cover battlefield military operations. A large number of PAOs were assigned as escorts when the military initiated the policy of "embedding" journalists within military units during the 2003 invasion and occupation of Iraq. See the Ethics box on page 436 about the controversy over paying journalists for favorable stories.

The Pentagon (a common name for the Department of Defense derived from the agency's headquarters) also engages in recruitment drives. In the spring of 2006, concerned about not meeting recruitment goals, the DOD paid United Airlines $36,000 to run a 13-minute video news release entitled "Today's Military" as part of the in-flight entertainment package. The campaign, which features exciting military jobs such as an Air Force language instructor and animal care specialist based in Hawaii, is designed to appeal to parents or other adult role models who in turn may recommend the military to children or relatives. Another major operation of the Pentagon is assisting Hollywood with the production of movies. More than 20 public information specialists are assigned as liaisons with the film and television industries. They review scripts and proposals, advise producers on military procedures, and decide how much assistance, if any, a film or TV show portraying the military should receive. Movies portraying the military in a positive light, such as *Pearl Harbor* (2001) or *Saving Private Ryan* (1998), are more likely to receive assistance from the military than those with less flattering or ambiguous messages, such as *Broken Arrow* (1996) or *Jarhead* (2005). The military denied requests for assistance from Oliver Stone for *Platoon* (1986) and *Born on the Fourth of July* (1989), presumably because his films often raise questions about government actions and motives.

Other federal agencies also conduct campaigns to inform citizens. In many cases, a public relations firm is selected through a bidding process to execute the campaign. Between mid-2003 and early 2006, the Bush administration spent over $1.6 billion on

— ON THE JOB >> —

Pay for Play: U.S. Government Plants Favorable Stories in the Iraqi Press

Ethics

It is a classic dilemma: what constitutes public information versus propaganda? Does the nature of the War on Terrorism justify using questionable means or should public relations efforts, no matter what the situation, be guided by ironclad ethical standards? Such situations are not necessarily as cut and dry as they may appear. Fighting an enemy that does not adhere to the traditional rules of engagement may require different public relations approaches.

In November 2005, the *Los Angeles Times* reported that the Pentagon and the U.S. military had contracted with the Lincoln Group to plant more than 1,000 "good-news" stories in several Iraqi and Arab papers. The contract specified that the public relations firm, which is based in Washington, D.C., was to inform the Iraqi people of American goals and the progress being made in order to gain public support. Lincoln paid reporters stipends of a few hundred dollars per month to write positive stories and paid the editors of papers such as *Azzaman* and *al Sabah* between $40 to $2,000 to publish articles prepared by Lincoln staffers, soldiers at "Camp Victory," and military public relations officers.

According to *New York Times* reporters Jeff Gerth and Scott Shane, the contract further stipulated that the Lincoln group would compensate "temporary spokespersons" and disseminate "alternative or diverting messages which divert media and public attention" to "deal instantly with the bad news of the day." In most cases, the source of the articles and opinion pieces was not revealed, nor was it made clear that the spokespersons represented the views of the U.S. government and the "Coalition of the Willing."

For the most part, the military and U.S. government defended their actions. Lt Col. Steven A. Boylan argued that such "pay for play" was necessary because Iraqi papers "normally don't have access to those kinds of stories." Michael Rubin, formerly of the Coalition Provisional Authority, stressed the need for "an even playing field" because the insurgents use deceptive messages. Gen. Peter Pace, however, expressed concern that planting stories without attribution may "be detrimental to the proper growth of democracy." According to the *New York Times,* national security advisor Stephen J. Hadley reported that President Bush is also "very troubled" by the disclosure. Nevertheless, a 2006 Pentagon review of the secret program found it to be "appropriate," though it recommended establishing guidelines regarding the attribution of authorship.

Journalists have widely denounced the practice of pay for play. "Ethically, it's indefensible," said Patrick Butler, vice president of the International Center of Journalists in Washington. Likewise, the Public Relations Society of America has issued a condemnation of the practice. Pamela Keaton, director of public affairs for the congressionally funded Institute for Peace, worried about the long-term effects of what she sees as a propaganda campaign: "I think there are places where we need to draw the line—and one of them is using the news media for psyops purposes. It will get to the point where the news media won't trust anybody, and the people won't trust what's being quoted in news articles."

Source: Jeff Gerth and Scott Shane, "U.S. Is Said to Pay to Plant Articles," *New York Times,* December 1, 2005.

hundreds of contracts with advertising and public relations firms to promote its position on issues such as energy policies, the Medicare prescription plan, and No Child Left Behind. The DOD spent another $1.1 billion on advertising and media contracts. Opposition leaders, such as Nancy Pelosi (D-California) and Henry A. Waxman (D-California), have criticized the expenditures as "covert propaganda," a viewpoint supported by the revelation that conservative columnist Amstrong Williams had been contracted for $240,000 to promote the No Child Left Behind Act in his columns and radio appearances (see the Ethics box on page 437). "On a smaller scale,

— ON THE JOB >> —

Promoting No Child Left Behind

Ethics

Does the government have the right to promote its programs with taxpayer money, even when partisan issues are involved? Should they take extraordinary steps to acknowledge their role in public relations campaigns? The public relations efforts of federal government for the No Child Left Behind (NCLB) Act suggest ethical questions that will face politicians and public relations professionals working for them in the coming years.

Signed into law by President Bush in 2001, NCLB requires that every school provide adequate educational opportunities for all students. The law stipulates that teachers be held accountable for performance in the classroom, that progress be documented by test scores, that schools have community support, and that teaching and administrative staff be highly qualified.

From the onset, the Bush administration has used public relations strategies to gain support for NCLB from communities and families. For example, the Department of Education paid the public relations firm Ketchum $1 million to produce and distribute video news releases that promoted the programs. Ketchum also evaluates newspaper articles, radio shows, and television programs for favorable coverage. A government Web site entitled "No Child Left Behind Is Working" keeps citizens informed about positive developments with topics such as "NCLB Benefits Children, Empowers Parents, Supports, Teachers and Strengthens Schools" and "Multiple studies and reports show that

"The No Child Left Behind Act provides new training opportunities for teachers to develop their professional skills and their knowledge," said President George W. Bush during an education rally at the Daughters of the American Revolution (DAR) Constitution Hall in Washington, D.C., January 9, 2002. White House photo by Tina Hager.

student achievement is rising across America."

Occasionally, the administration's public relations efforts have gone awry. In 2004, investigative journalists discovered that part of the contract with Ketchum included paying conservative commentator Armstrong Williams $240,000 to promote NCLB in television and radio appearances. Representative George Miller of California was among the many members of Congress who questioned using taxpayer money for what he considered illegal promotion of the administration's initiative.

Particularly at issue is the use of VNRs, which are often run by TV stations without attribution, a practice that is often done in broadcasting. A federal law prohibits the government from engaging in what is in effect covert propaganda in support of partisan issues. The Government Accounting Office ruled in September 2005 that federal money should not be used to produce VNRs or other news releases, without openly acknowledging the government's role in their production. In other words, critics say Ketchum's public relations campaign may have skirter the law because it was not always made clear that the government paid for the production of video news releases.

the Brylski Company, a public relations firm operated almost entirely by women, has several contracts with the state of Louisiana to publicize educational issues.

The information campaigns just described are fairly common in most federal agencies. At times, however, public affairs staffs can find themselves on the front lines of a crisis or a controversy that involves handling hundreds of press calls in a single day.

The Department of Homeland Security, which was formed by merging 22 different agencies, experienced a variety of growing pains. One problem was cohesion; it took time to get public affairs staffs from so many agencies to operate as a unit. There were also problems in message formulation. Dennis Murphy, director of public affairs for border and transportation security, told *PRWeek*, "We want to get the word out quickly . . . but operations folks want to make sure we're not saying too much." The color coding system for security alerts initially caused some confusion and even panic among the public, resulting in minor modifications and a public relations campaign to explain its meaning and implications.

Congressional Efforts.

The House of Representatives and the Senate are also major disseminators of information. Members regularly produce a barrage of news releases, newsletters, recordings, brochures, taped radio interviews, and videotapes— all designed to inform voters back home about Congress and keep them in the minds of voters.

Critics complain that most materials are self-promotional and have little value. The franking privilege (free postage) is singled out for the most criticism. The late Senator John Heinz, a Republican from Pennsylvania, once distributed 15 million pieces of mail, financed by taxpayers, during one election year. Obviously, the franking privilege is a real advantage for an incumbent.

All members of Congress also employ a press secretary. According to Edward Downes of Boston University, "Capitol Hill's press secretaries play a significant role in the shaping of America's messages and consequent public policies. In their role as proxy for individual members, the press secretaries act as gatekeepers, determining what information to share with, and hold from, the media; thus, they have command over news shared with the citizenry."

White House Efforts.

At the apex of government public relations efforts is the White House. The president receives more media attention than all the federal agencies and Congress combined. It is duly reported when the president visits a neighborhood school, tours a housing development, meets a head of state, or even chokes on a pretzel while watching a football game.

All presidents have taken advantage of the intense media interest to implement public relations strategies that would improve their popularity, generate support for programs, and explain embarrassing policy decisions. And each president has had his own communication style.

Ronald Reagan, by most accounts, was considered a master communicator. He was extremely effective on television and could make his remarks seem spontaneous even when he was reading a teleprompter. He understood the importance of using symbolism and giving simple, down-to-earth speeches with memorable, personal appeal. Reagan's approach was the effective use of carefully packaged sound bites and staged events. Terrance Hunt, an Associated Press reporter who covered the Reagan years, says the former president's funeral in 2004 recalled the high style and stagecraft of his presidency. "Presidential appearances were arranged like movie scenes with Reagan in the starring role. There was a heavy emphasis on staging and lighting," says Hunt.

George H. W. Bush (senior) was no Ronald Reagan as a public speaker, but he did project enthusiasm for his job and had a friendly, but formal, working relationship with the White House press corps. Bill Clinton, on the other hand, was more populist in his communication style. He was at home with today's information technology, experts say, and made effective use of television talk shows. Clinton was most effective when he talked one-on-one with an interviewer or a member of the audience.

President George W. Bush also has adopted Reagan's approach to stagecraft and symbolism. A team of television and video experts makes sure every Bush appearance is well choreographed for maximum visual effect. The Bush administration's concept of stagecraft has also manifested itself in tight control over information and limited media access. Bush, for example, gave substantially fewer press conferences, interviews, and other media events than either Bill Clinton or his father in their first two years in office. According to Ken Auletta, a respected chronicler of the communications industry, the younger Bush was wary of the press and thought journalists as a whole were too liberal to do a decent job of objectively covering the White House. Auletta's article January 2004 in the *New Yorker* was titled, "Fortress Bush: How the White House Keeps the Press Under Control." No doubt because of the criticism, however, Bush recently has made a point of holding more press conferences and granting greater access to the media. His administration still favors press outlets sympathetic to his viewpoint such as Fox News.

The most visible person, on a daily basis, is the president's press secretary, who has the high-pressure duty of briefing reporters on a daily basis. In 2006, Tony Snow succeeded Scott McClellan as President Bush's press secretary. It came as little surprise to pundits that Bush selected Snow, a conservative op-ed journalist and commentator Fox News.

State Governments

Every state provides public information services. In California, the most populous state, there are about 175 public information officers (PIOs) in about 70 state agencies. On a daily basis, PIOs provide routine information to the public and the press on the policies, programs, and activities of the various state agencies.

State agencies conduct a variety of public information and education campaigns, often with the assistance of public relations firms that have been selected through a bidding process. A state agency, for example, will issue a request for proposal (RFP) and award a contract on the basis of presentations from competing firms.

One primary program area is health and safety. Most states, in recent years, have spent considerable money convincing people not to smoke. The funds, from the national tobacco settlement and state-imposed cigarette taxes, have provided somewhat of a windfall in available funds. California, for example, generates about $120 million annually from tobacco taxes, and about 10 percent of that is devoted to anti-smoking advertising and public relations. It's somewhat ironic, however, that as smoking decreases, the amount of taxes collected also decreases, and there is less money for such campaigns.

The California Department of Health Services (DHS) runs campaigns on a variety of health issues, such as encouraging immunization for children, screening for breast cancer, and preventing teen pregnancy. The California Highway Patrol (CHP) also conducts safety campaigns. One recent campaign was an effort to increase seat belt use and decrease drunk driving accidents among African Americans. Statistical data indicated that this audience was less likely to use seat belts and more likely to die in an alcohol-rated crash than other demographic groups.

States also promote tourism through advertising and public relations campaigns. Tourism and conventions are the second largest industry in Wisconsin, so the Department of Tourism concentrates on branding Wisconsin as a destination for cheese lovers (350 types of cheese are produced here) and beer drinkers ("Beer Capital of the U.S."). The Illinois Department of Commerce and Economic Opportunity recently awarded a $6.5 million contract to Edelman Worldwide to develop a tourism campaign. Pennsylvania spends between $8 million and $12 million annually promoting tourism.

Another area is economic development. Delaware, a small state with less than 800,000 people, hired a public relations firm to conduct a $600,000 campaign to attract business investment. The public relations firm used the slogan "It's good being first," referring to Delaware being the first state to ratify the U.S. Constitution. The public relations firm admitted it was a difficult assignment. The firm's president told *PRWeek*, "As opposed to having a bad image, Delaware simply has no image at all."

Local Governments

Cities employ information specialists to disseminate news and information from numerous municipal departments. Such agencies may include the airport, transit district, redevelopment office, parks and recreation, convention and visitors bureau, police and fire, city council, and the mayor's office.

The information flow occurs in many ways, but all have the objectives of informing citizens and helping them take full advantage of government services. The city council holds neighborhood meetings; an airport commission sets up an exhibit showing the growth needs of the airport; the recreation department promotes summer swimming lessons; and the city's human rights commission sponsors a festival promoting multiculturalism.

Cities promote themselves to attract new business. *PRWeek* reported "The competition for cities and wider regions to attract businesses is as intense as ever, experts say, with an estimated 12,000 economic development organizations vying for the roughly 500 annual corporate moves/expansions that involve 250 or more jobs each." Consequently, many cities pump millions of dollars into attracting new business through a variety of communication tools that include elaborate brochures, placement of favorable "success" stories in the nation's press, direct mail, telemarketing, trade fairs, special events, and meetings with business executives.

Cities also promote themselves in an effort to increase tourism. An example of city information efforts is the campaign by the Panama City (Florida) Convention and Visitors Bureau to position itself as a prime destination for college students during spring break. According to *PRWeek*, the bureau spent about $300,000 promoting the city through posters, news releases, brochures, advertising, and special events to let students know that they were welcome. Indeed, the "spring breakers," as they are called, pump about $135 million into the local economy.

Public Affairs in Government

Since the ancient Egyptians established the first unified state more than 5,000 years ago, governments have engaged in what is known in the 21st century as public information and public affairs. It is not an exaggeration to say that human history is, to a large degree, rooted in the history of public relations.

There has always been a need for government communications, if for no other reason than to inform citizens of the services available and the manner in which they may be used. In a democracy, public information is crucial if citizens are to make intelligent judgments about the policies and activities of their elected representatives. Through information it is hoped that citizens will have the necessary background to participate fully in the formation of government policies.

The objectives of government information efforts have been summarized by William Ragan, former director of public affairs for the U.S. Civil Service Commission:

> Inform the public about the public's business. In other words, communicate the work of government agencies.

> Improve the effectiveness of agency operations through appropriate public information techniques. In other words, explain agency programs so that citizens understand and can take actions necessary to benefit from them.

> Provide feedback to government administrators so that programs and policies can be modified, amended, or continued.

> Advise management on how best to communicate a decision or a program to the widest number of citizens.

> Serve as an ombudsman. Represent the public and listen to its representatives. Make sure that individual problems of the taxpayer are satisfactorily solved.

> Educate administrators and bureaucrats about the role of the mass media and how to work with media representatives.

People, including journalists, often criticize public information activities as reams of useless news releases promoting individual legislators or justifying questionable policies. Such abuse, coupled with snide news stories about the cost of maintaining government "public relations" experts, rankle dedicated public information officers (PIOs) at the various state and federal agencies who work very hard to keep the public informed with a daily diet of announcements and news stories. One PIO for a California agency said, "I'd like to see the press find out what's going on in state government without us."

Indeed, a major source of media hostility seems to stem from the fact that reporters are heavily dependent on news subsidies. In one study, almost 90 percent of a state government's news releases were used by daily and weekly newspapers. The textbook *Media: An Introductory Analysis of American Mass Communications* by Peter Sandman, David Rubin, and David Sachsman puts it succinctly: "If a newspaper were to quit relying on news releases, but continued covering the news it now covers, it would need at least two or three times more reporters."

Public information efforts are justified in terms of cost-efficiency. The U.S. Department of Agriculture public affairs office, for example, receives thousands of inquiries a year. Two-thirds of the requests can be answered with a simple pamphlet, brochure, or a link on its Web site.

There is also the argument about how much the public saves through preventive public relations. The taxpayers of California spend about $7 billion annually to deal with the associated costs of teenage pregnancy, so $5.7 million spent on a successful education campaign could save the state considerably more in reduced welfare costs. Michigan's $100,000 expenditure to educate citizens about recycling aerosol cans does much to reduce the costs of opening more landfills.

An Associated Press reporter acknowledged in a story that government information does have value. He wrote:

> While some of the money and manpower goes for self-promotion, by far the greater amount is committed to an indispensable function of a democratic government—informing the people. What good would it serve for the Consumer Product Safety Commission to recall a faulty kerosene heater and not go to the expense of alerting the public to its action? An informed citizenry needs the government to distribute its economic statistics, announce its antitrust suits, tell about the health of the president, give crop forecasts.

Government Relations by Corporations

A specialized component of corporate communications, closely related to lobbying, is government relations. This activity is so important that many companies, particularly in highly regulated industries, have separate departments of government relations. The reason is simple: The actions of governmental bodies at the local, state, and federal levels have a major impact on how a business operates. Government relations specialists, often called public affairs specialists, have a number of functions: They gather information, disseminate management's views, cooperate with government on projects of mutual benefit, and motivate employees to participate in the political process.

As the eyes and ears of a business or industry, public relations practitioners spend much time gathering and processing information. They monitor the activities of many legislative bodies and regulatory agencies to keep track of issues coming up for debate and possible vote. Such intelligence gathering enables a corporation or an industry to plan ahead and, if necessary, adjust policies or provide information that may influence the nature of government decision making.

Monitoring government takes many forms. Probably the most active presence in Washington, D.C., and many state capitals are the trade associations that represent various industries. A Boston University survey showed that 67 percent of the responding companies monitored government activity in Washington through their trade associations. Second on the list were frequent trips to Washington by senior public affairs officers and corporate executives; 58 percent of the respondents said they engaged in this activity. Almost 45 percent of the responding firms reported that they also had a company office in the nation's capital.

Government relations specialists also spend a great amount of time disseminating information about the company's position to a variety of key publics. Tactics include informal office visits to government officials or testimony at public hearings. In addition, public affairs people are often called on to give speeches or write speeches for senior executives. Tactics also include writing letters and op-ed articles, preparing position papers, producing newsletters, and placing advocacy advertising.

Although legislators are a primary audience, the Foundation for Public Affairs reports that 9 out of 10 companies also communicate with employees on public policy issues. Another 40 percent communicate with retirees, customers, and other publics such as taxpayers and government employees.

Lobbying

The term *lobbyist* originally was used to describe the men who sought favors from President Abraham Lincoln, who conducted affairs of state in the lobby in the Willard Hotel near the White House during an assassination threat in 1861, and President Ulysses S. Grant, who sought refuge for a cigar and brandy in the hotel's lobby.

Today, lobbying is more formal and closely aligned with governmental relations or public affairs, and the distinction between the two often blurs. This is because most campaigns to influence impending legislation have multiple levels. One level is informing and convincing the public about the correctness of an organization's viewpoint, which the public affairs specialist does. A lobbyist directs his or her energies to the defeat, passage, or amendment of legislation and regulatory agency policies.

Lobbyists can be found at the local, state, and federal levels of government. California, for example, has about 900 registered lobbyists who represent more than 1,600 special-interest groups. The interests represented in Sacramento include large corporations, business and trade groups, unions, environmental groups, local governments, nonprofit groups, school districts, and members of various professional groups.

The number and variety of special interests multiply at the federal level. One directory of Washington lobbyists lists 20,000 individuals and organizations. The interests represented include virtually the entire spectrum of U.S. business, educational, religious, local, national, and international pursuits. Lobbying is also conducted on behalf of foreign governments as illustrated by the Global box on page 444.

The diversity of those groups can be illustrated with the debate about managed health care and patient rights. For example, opposing new regulations are (1) insurance companies, (2) HMO trade groups, (3) the United States Chamber of Commerce, (4) the National Federation of Independent Business, and (5) the American Association of Health Plans. Groups supporting patient rights include (1) a broad coalition of consumer groups, (2) the American Medical Association, and (3) the Trial Lawyers of America. The groups opposed to patient rights legislation are concerned about higher costs to employers, increased government control of health care delivery systems, and more litigation and lawsuits. As a result, miscellaneous health interests spent $53 million on lobbying between 1998 and 2004 to present their views for or against proposed legislation.

Competing lobbying efforts often cancel each other out. All this leaves legislators and regulatory personnel with the responsibility to weigh the pros and cons of an issue before voting. Indeed, *Time* magazine notes that competition among lobbyists representing different sides of an issue "do serve a useful purpose by showing busy legislators the virtues and pitfalls of complex legislation." A classic conflict is the debate between saving jobs and improving the environment. A coalition of environmental groups constantly lobbies Congress for tougher legislation to clean up industrial pollution or protect endangered species. Simultaneously, local communities and unions often argue that the proposed legislation would mean the loss of jobs and economic chaos.

Environmental groups argue in the "public interest"; so do opposing groups. Is it in the "public interest," they ask, to throw thousands of people out of work or to legislate so many restrictions on the manufacture of a product that it becomes more expensive to the average consumer? Or, should the community risk possible long-term and irreversible damage to the environment? The answer, quite often, depends on whether the person is a steelworker, a logger, a consumer, or a member of the World Wildlife Federation.

Pitfalls of Lobbying. Although a case can be made for lobbying as a legitimate activity, deep public suspicion exists about former legislators and officials who capitalize on their connections and charge large fees for doing what is commonly described as "influence peddling." Indeed, the roster of registered lobbyists in Washington includes a virtual who's who of former legislators and government officials from both the Democratic and Republican Parties. According to the watchdog group Center for Public Integrity, more than 12 percent of current lobbyists are former executives and

— ON THE JOB >> —

The Risks of Polishing an Unpopular Nation's Image

Global

In recent years, it has become increasingly common for countries to hire lobbying groups to represent their interests in Washington, D.C. In 2003, Venezuela hired Patton Boggs to help improve relations with the U.S. government, entering into a contract worth $1.2 million annually. The nation faces some enormous public relations challenges, as the American public's perception of Venezuela was less than favorable. Liberals in the United States were disturbed by the uneven distribution of wealth. Many conservatives, including members of the Bush administration, perceived Venezuela's populist president, Hugo Chavez, as a threat. Evangelical leader Pat Robertson went so far as to call for Chavez's assassination on August 22, 2005, blasting Venezuela as "a launching pad for communist infiltration and Muslim extremism all over the continent" on a *700 Club* broadcast.

After a series of brainstorming session, Patton Boggs decided on a two-pronged public relations approach. On one hand, they sought to persuade the U.S. government and citizens to not interfere in the internal politics of Venezuela. On the other, Patton Boggs concentrated on getting across the message that the country's oil wealth was now being spent to improve the lives of all Venezuelans. They recommended that Lumina Strategies and Underground Advertising be hired to handle media relations and advertising to disseminate the strategic messages. Print ads, placed in *The New Yorker*, the *New York Times*, the *Economist*, the

President Hugo Chavez of Venezuela.

International Herald Tribune, and *Roll Call* (a U.S. Congressional publication) heralded the country's progress.

The campaign was not without critics, however. The *New York Times* reported that Venezuela is "pitching itself as an egalitarian nirvana where petro-dollars are funneled straight to the poor." An opposition group composed of Venezuelan exiles displaced when Chavez took power in 2002 has countered the Venezuelan government's message, arguing that Chavez's regime threatens the region's stability and that the claim of egalitarianism is a myth. They have lobbied Congress aggressively to place economic sanctions on the country.

Chavez's subsequent actions, however, have turned U.S. public opinion against Venezuela. In June 2006, the Patton Boggs newsletter featured an article on Chavez's interruption of oil shipments to the United States, calling it a "blatant political risk." Although offering little explanation, their Web site no longer lists Venezuela among current foreign clients.

The case raises some pertinent ethical questions for public relations agencies serving foreign clients. Is it possible that Patton Boggs and the other public relations agencies may face sanctions, litigation, or loss of reputation because of their work on behalf of a country that opposes U.S. policy? Or, like lawyers, do PR firms have a responsibility to their represent clients to the best of their ability, no matter who they are?

legislative branch employees. This includes more than 200 former members of Congress (175 from the House, 34 from the Senate), and 42 former agency heads.

The Ethics in Government Act forbids government officials from actively lobbying their former agencies for one year after leaving office. Critics say that it has had little or no impact. A good case study is the U.S. Department of Homeland Security. Tom Ridge was head of the agency when it was established in 2002, but he has now left to become a lobbyist with a long list of clients from the security industry that seek contracts with Homeland Security, which has a budget of more than $40 billion to spend. Ridge is not alone. A *New York Times* article in mid-2006 reported that at least 90 officials at the Department of Homeland Security or the White House Homeland Security office—two-thirds of the most senior executives—have become lobbyists in the past several years.

Unlike federal agency personnel, members of Congress can become lobbyists immediately after leaving office. A good example is former Representative J. C. Watts (R-Oklahoma) who announced the formation of a group of lobbying and public affairs firms exactly one day after leaving office. High-ranking members of Watts' congressional staff moved with him to his new offices to begin their careers as lobbyists of their former colleagues.

Such connections, and "cashing in" on them, give the press and public the uneasy feeling that influence peddling is alive and well in the nation's capitol. It also gives credence to the cliché, "It's not what you know, but who you know." The recent scandal involving lobbyist Jack Abramoff reveals how closely tied legislators are to lobbyists. Abramoff's financial mismanagement and willingness to dispense illegal perks to legislators resulted in a lengthy prison sentence. Republican House Majority Leader Tom Delay (R-Texas) had to resign his leadership post and Ohio Congressman Bob Ney pleaded guilty to two counts of conspiracy and making false statements in the Abramoff scandal. About half a dozen other legislators and dozens of congressional aides and other government officials remain under scrutiny.

Grassroots Lobbying. Politicians of both parties have regularly decried the influence of lobbyists, but reform has taken a half-century. At least 10 times since the first loophole-riddled lobbying regulations were passed in 1946, efforts to update the law failed to get past the legislative obstacles. In 1995, however, Congress did pass a measure designed to reform lobbying, and President Clinton signed it. Part of the impetus, no doubt, was the impact of polls indicating that the public believed lobbyists had runaway influence in Washington.

One key provision was an expanded definition of who is considered to be a "lobbyist." The new law defines a lobbyist as "someone hired to influence lawmakers, government officials or their aides, and who spends at least 20 percent of his or her time representing any client in a six-month period." Another key provision requires lobbyists to register with Congress and disclose their clients, the issue areas in which lobbying is being done, and roughly how much is being paid for it. Violators face civil fines of up to $50,000.

One area exempted from the lobby reform bill was financial disclosures for so-called grassroots lobbying. In many respects, it is the fastest growing area in the political persuasion business.

Grassroots lobbying is now an $800 million industry, according to *Campaigns and Elections*, a bimonthly magazine for "political professionals." What makes it so attractive to various groups is that there are virtually no rules or regulations. The tools of such lobbying are advocacy advertising, toll-free phone lines, bulk faxing, Web sites, and computerized direct mail aimed at generating phone calls and letters from the public to Congress, the White House, and governmental regulatory agencies.

One major firm, Bonner & Associates, has a highly sophisticated communications system that includes banks of telephones and computers that can call or send letters to thousands of citizens within hours. For example, the American Bankers Association hired Bonner to kill a congressional bill that would lower credit card interest rates. The firm orchestrated 10,000 phone calls from citizens and community leaders to 10 members of the House Banking Committee. The bill died in committee.

Grassroots lobbying also involves coalition building. The basic idea is to get individuals and groups with no financial interest in an issue to speak on the sponsor's behalf. The premise is that letters and phone calls from private citizens are more influential than arguments from vested interests.

Such "grassroots" campaigns make public interest groups wonder if they really shouldn't be called "astroturf" campaigns, since the "grass" is artificial. Michael Pertschuk, codirector of the Advocacy Institute in Washington, D.C., told *O'Dwyer's PR Services Report*, "Astroturf groups are usually founded with corporate seed money that is funneled through PR firms." An example is the group National Smokers Alliance, organized by Burson-Marsteller with seed money from Philip Morris.

Election Campaigns

Public affairs activities and lobbying, either in the halls of Congress or at the grassroots level, are year-round activities. During election years, either congressional or presidential, an army of fund-raisers, political strategists, speechwriters, and communications consultants are mobilized to help candidates win elections.

The high cost of running for office in the United States has made fund-raising virtually a full-time, year-round job for every incumbent and aspirant to office. In fact, American-style campaigning is the most expensive in the world. According to the *Economist*, a colossal $4 billion was spent on the 2004 congressional and presidential races, a third more than was spent in the 2000 election. Of that amount, paid advertising by the two major presidential candidates topped $600 million. This was despite the advent of the McCain-Feingold Campaign Finance Act that was passed in 2002, which is discussed shortly.

Candidates retain professionals to organize fund-raising activities. A standard activity in Washington, D.C., and other major cities across the country is the luncheon, reception, or dinner on behalf of a candidate. The *Wall Street Journal*, for example, reported in 2004 that 14 such events were held on a single day in October, raising $650,000 for congressional incumbents. Attending such events are individual donors and lobbyists for various organizations. Although a chicken dinner or a cheese platter with crackers and champagne are not exactly worth $2,000 a person in literal terms, the idea is to show support of the candidate and to have contact with him or her. No business is actually discussed, but the occasion gives both individuals and lobbyists for special interests an opportunity to show the "flag" and perhaps influence legislation or personnel appointments at a later date after the election, if the candidate wins.

Professional fund-raisers recruit lobbyists to hawk tickets, decide whom to invite, design and mail invitations, employ people to make follow-up calls, rent the room, hire the caterer, make name tags, tell the candidate who came and who didn't, and hound attendees to make good on their pledges.

Some consultants specialize in direct mail and telemarketing. They are assisted by firms that specialize in computer databases and mailing lists. Aristotle Publishers, for example, claims to have records on 128 million registered voters. A candidate can get a tailored list of prospects using any number of demographic variables, including party affiliation, voting record, contribution record, age, geographic location, and opinions on various issues.

Other firms handle mass mailings on behalf of candidates. Kiplinger Computer and Mailing Services, for example, is capable of running envelopes at 10,000 per hour and printing personalized letters at 120 pages per minute.

The latest tool for fund-raising and reaching supporters is the Internet. One use of the Internet is for research. The *Wall Street Journal*, for example, reported that a Kerry support organization in Concord, New Hampshire, was able to track down Democratic women voters, aged 18 to 30, who were interested in abortion rights. Within seconds, the computer was able to generate the names of 812 local women and also provide a street map marking their addresses. Members of Planned Parenthood and other Kerry supporters followed up with a door-to-door visits on behalf of the presidential candidate.

Although the Internet was first used for fund-raising and building grassroots support during the 2000 presidential election, its effectiveness wasn't proven until the 2004 election. Former Vermont governor Howard Dean, an early leader in the Democratic primaries, used the Internet to build a grassroots network and raise money. Douglas Quenqua, a reporter for *PRWeek*, did a good job of describing the Dean campaign: "Dean established and motivated a huge network of supporters, not to mention raised an unprecedented amount of money in small increments, through interactive, Web-based messaging, blogs, constant e-mail communications, and prodigious use of Meetup.com, the Web site that allows people to find one another based first on common interest, then geography."

Experts say that the Internet's major value is in organizing people and getting them in contact with each other in a very cost-efficient way. Ultimately, however, winning elections still requires a great amount of one-on-one contact. Mark Macarato, co-chair in Nashville for Dean, told *PRWeek*, "When you don't have money for mailings and fund-raisers and you're outside the Democratic power structure, the Net is just a wonderful tool to get things rolling. The Internet is a very efficient way to connect people, replacing the inefficient tool of a phone call. What is changed is the ability to organize quickly and efficiently." Macarato continued, "But you need old-fashioned shoe-leather campaigning to take it from there."

Other groups of consultants and technicians also are employed by candidates in election campaigns. They are writers of position papers, speechwriters, graphic artists, computer experts, Webmasters, media strategists, advertising experts, radio and television producers, public affairs experts, pollsters, and public relations specialists. A highly visible and critical job is done by advance people who spend many hours organizing events, arranging every detail, and making sure there's a cheering crowd, with signs, when the candidate arrives. On a single day, for example, a presidential candidate may give five to seven talks at rallies in multiple states.

Summary

Public Relations of Nonprofit Organizations

Nonprofit organizations have been given tax-exempt status because their primary goal is to enhance the well-being of their members or the human condition. Fund-raising is a major public relations task in these groups. Although there is a broad range of nonprofit organizations, they all create communications campaigns and programs, require a staff (including volunteers) to handle their work, and are involved in fund-raising.

Competition, Conflict and Cooperation of Nonprofit Oranizations

For many nonprofit organizations, partnerships among members are necessary for their common interest. Competition among nonprofit agencies for their share of donations is intense. Many nonprofit groups advocating differing postions, particularly activists groups, frequently come into conflict with one another.

Membership Organizations

A membership organization is made up of people with a common interest, either business or social. Such groups include trade associations, labor unions, professional associations, and chambers of commerce.

Advocacy Groups

Advocacy groups work for social causes such as the environment, civil rights, gun ownership, or the pro-choice movement. Their efforts include lobbying, litigation, mass demonstrations, boycotts, reconciliation, and public education. As with other nonprofits, fund-raising is an ongoing issue with these groups. Advocacy groups seek to (1) develop public awareness of their purpose and activities, (2) induce individuals to use their services (3) recruit and train volunteer workers, and (4) obtain operating funds. They achieve these goals through lobbying, litigation, boycotts, mass demonstrations, and reconciliation.

Social Service Organizations

Service groups and philanthropic, cultural, and religious organizations all fall into the category of social service organizations. Their public relations goals include developing public awareness, getting individuals to use their services, creating educational materials, recruiting volunteers, and fund-raising.

Fund-Raising and Recruiting Volunteer Workers

Fund-raising is a critical issue for nonprofit oganizations. Depending on their mission and strategy, nonprofits seek donations from large corporations or foundations and small contributions from individuals. Recruiting volunteer labor is often crucial to make up for lack of operating funds and involve the community to reach the nonprofit's goals.

Health Organizations

Hospitals and health agencies are the two major organizations serving the public's health needs. Public relations professionals help communicate information about medical advances, the availability of health services, and potential health risks. Public relations for a hospital focuses on enhancing the public's perception of the institution and marketing its services. Successful health campaigns rely on effective public relations work to reach and maintain a wide audience.

Health Campaigns

Health campaigns to prevent and respond to diseases, and to promote health and quality of life, started to apply social marketing practices in the late 1980s. A number of public relations strategies and techniques have been implemented for those initiatives mainly by federal and state governments, and other private health agencies.

Colleges and Universities

Public relations at colleges and universities involves both development, or fund-raising, and enhancing the prestige of the institution. The office of development and public relations may conduct meetings, publish newsletters, and arrange tours. The audiences for communications include alumni, students, prospective students, faculty and staff, government, and the general public.

Other Educational Initiatives

Foundations, nontraditional schools, communities, and membership organizations frequently support existing educational institutions or initiate their own programs. Like colleges and schools, these initiatives often depend on public relations professionals for their success.

Federal Government Information Services

The federal government is the largest disseminator of information in the country. The apex of all government information and public relations efforts is the White House; the president's every move and action is chronicled by the mass media. Presidents throughout history have used this media attention to lead the nation, convince the public to support administration policies, and get reelected.

State Government Information Services

Various states employ public information officers to tell the public about the activities and policies of various agencies. In addition, agencies conduct a number of campaigns to inform the public about health and safety issues. Another initiative is to promote the state as a tourist destination.

Local Government Information Services

All major cities employ public information specialists to tell citizens about city services and promote economic development.

Public Affairs in Government

Governments have always engaged in campaigns to inform, motivate, and even persuade the public. In the United States, Congress forbids federal agencies from "persuading" the public, so the emphasis is on "public information" efforts. All agencies of the federal government employ public affairs officers and public information specialists. Members of Congress also engage in extensive information efforts to reach their constituents.

Government Relations

A major component of corporate communications is public affairs, which primarily deals with governmental relations at the local, state, national, and even international levels. Public affairs specialists build relationships with civil servants and elected officials and also monitor governmental actions that may affect the employer or client. Trade groups, primarily based in state capitals or Washington, D.C., have public affairs specialists representing various professions and industries.

Lobbying

A public affairs specialist primarily provides information about an organization's viewpoint to the public and gov-

ernment entities. A lobbyist has a more specialized function to directly work for the defeat, passage, or amendment of legislation and regulatory agency policies. In recent years, there has been public concern about "influence peddling" in terms of former legislators and other officials becoming lobbyists and "cashing in" on their knowledge and connections. To curb abuse, several laws have been passed to regulate lobbyists.

Election Campaigns

The cost of running for office in the United States is the highest in the world. An army of specialists, including public relations experts, are retained by major candidates to organize and raise money for election campaigns. In recent years, the Internet has played an important role in raising money, generating high visibility for candidates, and increasing the number of registered voters.

CASE ACTIVITY >>
What Would You Do?

Southern University has a potential public relations problem. The campus is midway through a 10-year contract with Coca-Cola to be the exclusive soft drink franchise for beverages in vending machines, at the student union, and in the residence halls. The contract is worth $1.4 million annually, and the university uses the revenue to pay for a variety of academic and campus life programs.

Coca-Cola, however, has been under attack by activist student groups at other universities for labor and human rights abuses at its bottling plants abroad. Activists charge that Coke has used paramilitary units in Columbia to murder union leaders and intimidate union members. In addition, the global giant is accused of damaging the environment in India by exploiting and polluting scarce water resources around its bottling plants. Student activists on other campus, using signs and chants such as "Kick Coke Off Campus" and "Diet, cherry, or vanilla. Coca-Cola is a killer," have asked campus administrators to cancel contracts and kick Coke off campus. Some campuses, such as the Rutgers University and New York University, have done just that.

A group of Southern University students have taken up the cause and have started to hold rallies on campus in

front of the student union. Also, some Coke vending machines in the residence halls have been vandalized. With the aid of national protest leaders, the students have prepared a petition asking the president of the university to immediately suspend the Coke contract. The president is in a bind; she has often spoken about social justice and the creation of a campus climate that fosters concern for the poor and disadvantaged in society. She, of course, is also concerned about losing the $1.4 million in revenue that pays for many important programs.

If you were the vice president of public relations for the university, what would you recommend? Should the university cancel the contract to satisfy the activist students? How would a decision, either way, affect the image of the president and the university? What about the effect of less money for student programs? Would agreeing with the activist students, in some way, be unfair to the majority of students who are not protesting? Is there a win-win solution for all concerned in this conflict? You might want to visit the Coke Web site, www.cokefacts.org to get the company's viewpoint. The national anti-Coke Web site is at www.killercoke.org.

Questions for Review and Discussion

1. Name some categories of social service agencies.
2. What are the differences and similarities among trade associations, labor unions, professional associations, and chambers of commerce?
3. What motivates people to serve as volunteer workers?
4. Describe commonly used types of fund-raising.
5. Identify public relations strategies and tactics that advocacy groups use to further their causes.
6. Who is the chief public relations officer on a college or university campus? Why?
7. A college news bureau is involved in a vast array of day-to-day public relations operations. Name five or six of these functions.
8. With what primary public does a sound university public relations program begin? List eight other constituencies that must be addressed in such a program.
9. What is the difference between someone working in corporate public affairs (government relations) and a lobbyist?
10. Many lobbyists are former legislators and government officials. Do you think they exercise undue influence in the shaping of legislation? Why or why not?
11. Fund-raisers play a crucial role in elections. Would you like to be a political fund-raiser? Why or why not?
12. Why do government agencies engage in "public information" efforts instead of "public relations" activities? Are there any laws involved? If so, what are they?
13. Federal agencies engage in any number of public information campaigns. What is your opinion on this? Are these campaigns just a waste of taxpayer dollars, or are they legitimate and necessary?

Suggested Readings

Arenson, Karen. "Duke Grappling with Impact of Scandal on Its Reputation." *New York Times*, April 7, 2006, A14.

Barstow, David, and Robin Stein. "Under Bush, a New Age of Prepackaged TV News." *New York Times*, March 13, 2005, www.nytimes.com/2005/03/13politics.

Giuliano, C. Peter. "Promoting the Presidential Message: The Candidates as Communicators." *The Strategist*, Winter 2005, 20–23.

Hand, Mark. "Nonprofit Sharing: PR Pros in the Nonprofit Area Often Have to Do More with Less." *PRWeek*, January 9, 2006, 19.

Herskovits, Beth. "Healthy Competition: Hospitals Are Branding Themselves in a Bid to Attract Patients." *PRWeek*, December 5, 2005, 17.

Kang, Seok, and Hanna E. Norton. "Nonprofit Organizations' Use of the World Wide Web: Are They Sufficiently Fulfilling Organizational Goals?" *Public Relations Review* 30, no. 3(2004): 279–284.

Lee, Mordecai. "The Rise and Fall of the Institute for Government Public Information Research, 1978–1981." *Public Relations Review* 32, no. 2(2006): 118–124.

Richardson, Karen. "Warren Buffett Gives $30 Billion to Gates Foundation." *Wall Street Journal*, June 26, 2006, B1–2.

Shin, Jae-Hwa, I-Huei Cheng, Yan Jin, and Glen T. Cameron. "Going Head to Head: Content Analysis of High Profile Conflicts as Played Out in the Press." *Public Relations Review* 31, no. 3(2005): 399–406.

Solberg, Rorie Spill, and Eric N. Waltenburg. "Why Do Interest Groups Engage the Judiciary? Policy Wishes and Structural Needs." *Social Science Quarterly* 87, no. 3(2006): 558–572.

Walters, Anne K. "Soft Drinks, Hard Feelings: Widespread Student Protests About Alleged Practices of Coca-Cola Overseas Prompt Some Colleges to Rethink Deals." *Chronicle of Higher Education*, April 14, 2006, A30–32.

Wang, Jian. "Managing National Reputation and International Relations in the Global Era: Public Diplomacy Revisited." *Public Relations Review* 32, no. 2(2006): 91–96.

Zhang, Juyan "Public Diplomacy as Symbolic Interactions: A Case Study of Asian Tsunami Relief Campaigns. *Public Relations Review* 32, no. 1(2006): 26–32.

Credits

p. 391: © 2004 NBAE (Photo by Jennifer Pottheiser/NBAE via Getty Images);

p. 396: John MacDougall/AFP/Getty Images;

p. 399: AP Images/Diane Bondareff;

Chapter 13

p. 406: © 2008 Alex Wong/Getty Images News/Getty Images;

p. 418: Reuters/Adeel Halim/Landov;

p. 420: Kevin Sims and Berni Georges for *All the World* magazine;

p. 424: AP Images/Michael Dwyer;

p. 428: Centers for Disease Control and Prevention;

p. 430: Tim Boyle/Getty Images;

p. 434: AP Images/Sara D. Davis;

p. 437: Reuters/Jason Reed/Landov;

p. 444: Chico Sanchez/epa/Corbis.

Index